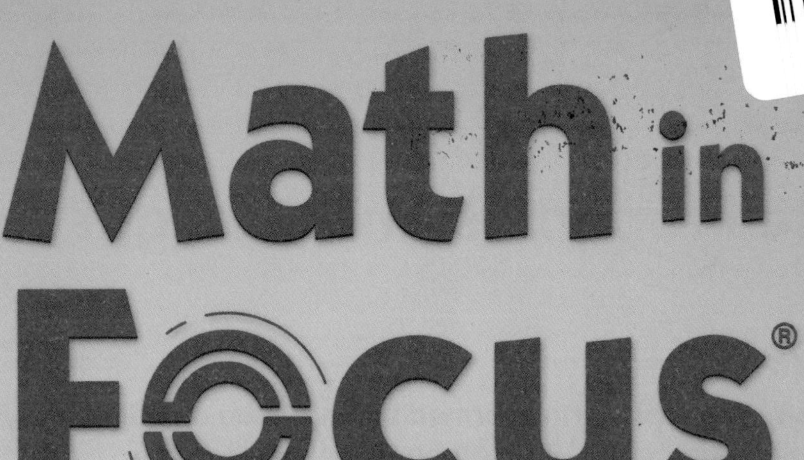

Singapore Math®
by Marshall Cavendish

Student Edition

Program Consultant
Dr. Fong Ho Kheong

Authors
Dr. Lai Chee Chong
Low Wai Cheng
Leong May Kuen

U.S. Distributor

Houghton Mifflin Harcourt.
The Learning Company™

Contents

Chapter

Angle Properties and Straight Lines

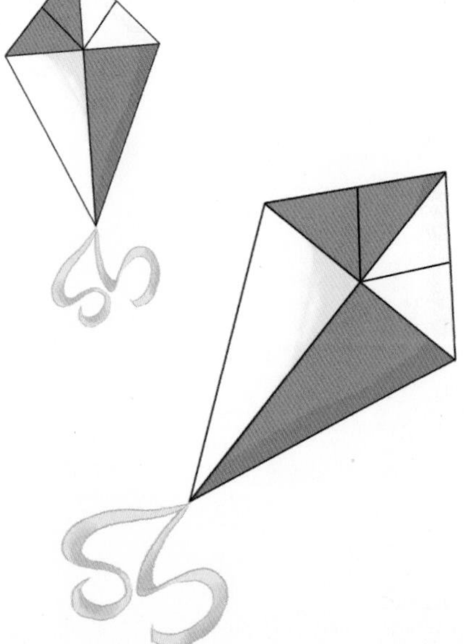

Chapter

6 Geometric Construction

▶ Activity

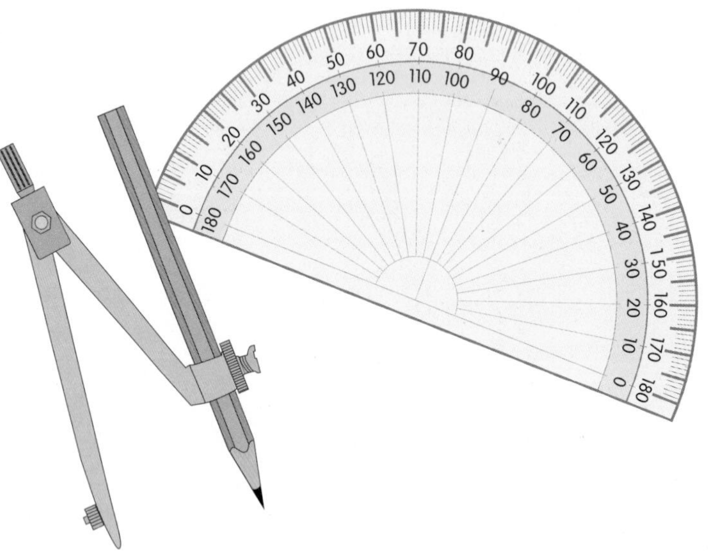

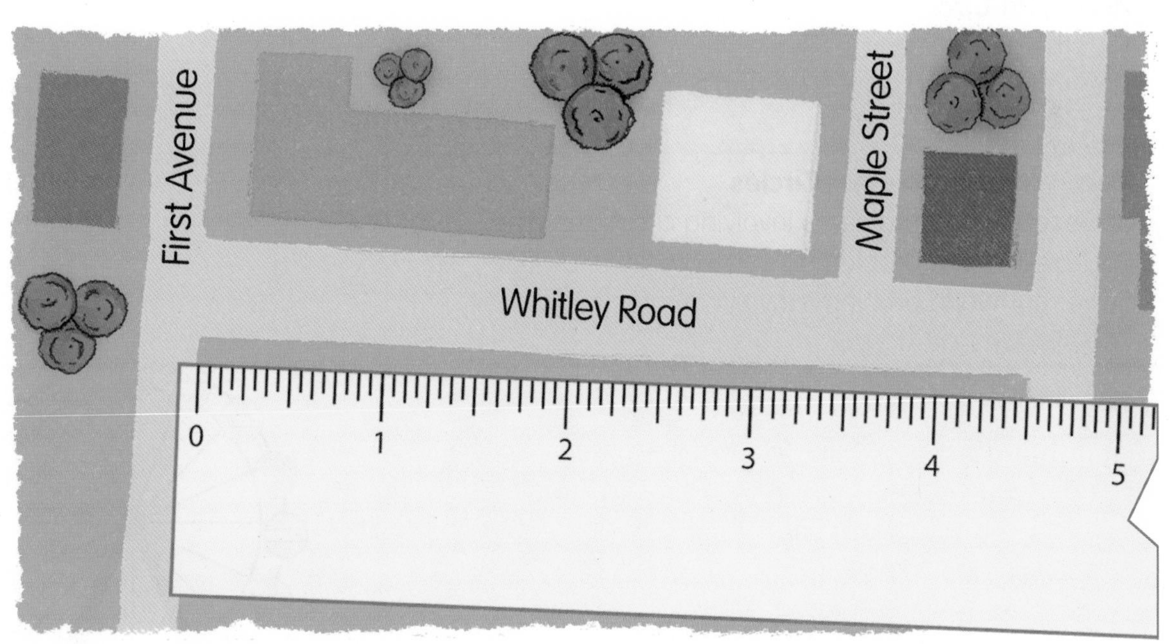
First Avenue
Maple Street
Whitley Road
0
1
2
3
4
5

Chapter

Circumference, Area, Volume, and Surface Area

Activity

Chapter

Statistics and Probability

Chapter

Probability of Compound Events

Activity

0 400 km
0 400 mi

N

0 200 km
0 200 mi

0 750 km
0 750 mi

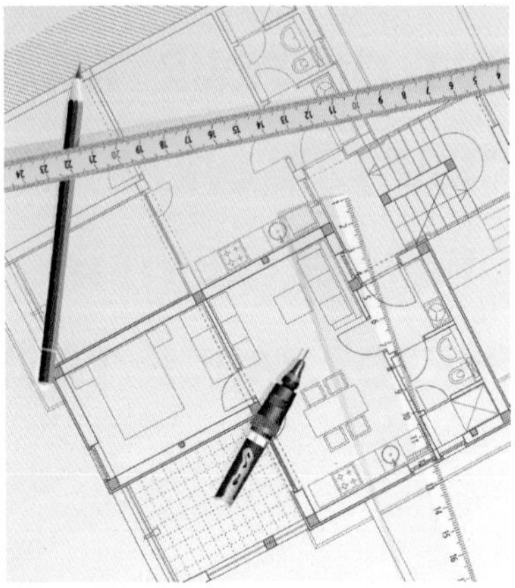

Manipulative List

Geoboards

Geometric Sets

Protractors

Transparent Counters

Preface

Math in Focus® is a program that puts you at the center of an exciting learning experience! This experience is all about equipping you with critical thinking skills and mathematical strategies, explaining your thinking to deepen your understanding, and helping you to become a skilled and confident problem solver.

Each chapter in this book begins with a real-world situation of the math topic you are about to learn.

In each chapter, you will encounter the following features:

THINK introduces a problem for the whole section, to stimulate creative and critical thinking and help you hone your problem-solving skills. You may not be able to answer the problem right away but you can revisit it a few times as you build your knowledge through the section.

ENGAGE consists of tasks that link what you already know with what you will be learning next. The tasks allow you to explore and discuss mathematical concepts with your classmates.

LEARN introduces new mathematical concepts through a Concrete-Pictorial-Abstract (C-P-A) approach, using activities and examples.

Activity comprises learning experiences that promote collaboration with your classmates. These activities allow you to reinforce your learning or uncover new mathematical concepts.

TRY supports and reinforces your learning through guided practice.

INDEPENDENT PRACTICE allows you to work on a variety of problems and apply the concepts and skills you have learned to solve these problems on your own.

Additional features include:

RECALL PRIOR KNOWLEDGE	Math Talk	MATH SHARING	Caution and Math Note
Helps you recall related concepts you learned before, accompanied by practice questions	Invites you to explain your reasoning and communicate your ideas to your classmates and teachers	Encourages you to create strategies, discover methods, and share them with your classmates and teachers using mathematical language	Highlights common errors and misconceptions, as well as provides you with useful hints and reminders
LET'S EXPLORE	**MATH JOURNAL**	**PUT ON YOUR THINKING CAP!**	**CHAPTER WRAP-UP**
Extends your learning through investigative activities	Allows you to reflect on your learning when you write down your thoughts about the mathematical concepts learned	Challenges you to apply the mathematical concepts to solve problems, and also hones your critical thinking skills	Summarizes your learning in a flow chart and helps you to make connections within the chapter
CHAPTER REVIEW	**Assessment Prep**	**PERFORMANCE TASK**	**STEAM**
Provides you with ample practice in the concepts learned	Prepares you for state tests with assessment-type problems	Assesses your learning through problems that allow you to demonstrate your understanding and knowledge	Promotes collaboration with your classmates through interesting projects that allow you to use math in creative ways

Are you ready to experience math the Singapore way? Let's go!

Chapter 5

Angle Properties and Straight Lines

Can you make that basket?

In basketball, the "launch angle" has a big effect on a player's chance of scoring. The launch angle is the acute angle the ball makes with the floor when the ball leaves the player's hands. The "release point," or the distance the player's hands are from the floor when the ball is released also affects the chances of scoring. Studies have shown that successful scorers tend to have a relatively high launch angle and release point. In this chapter, you will learn about various angle relationships.

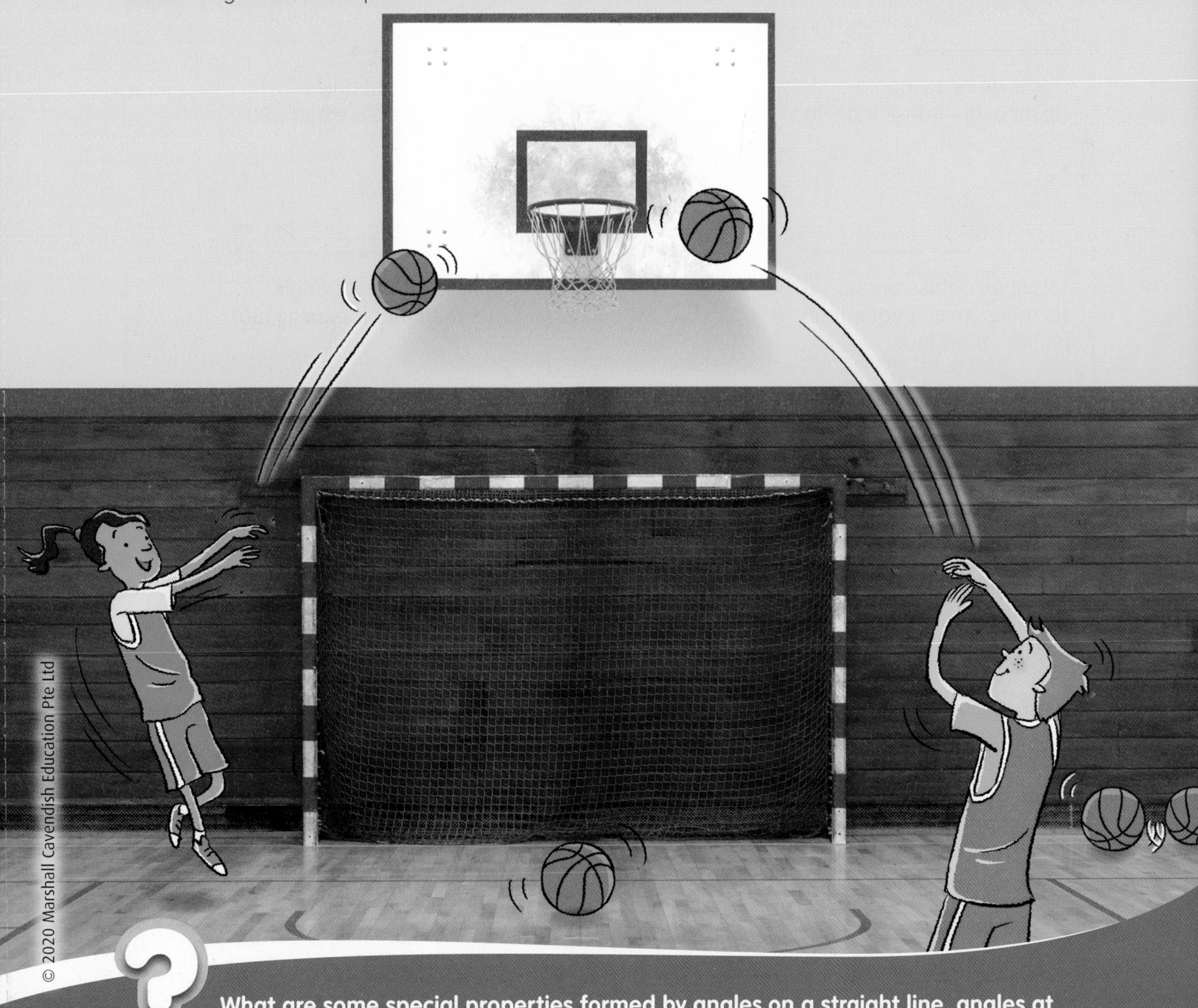

What are some special properties formed by angles on a straight line, angles at a point, and parallel lines and a transversal?

Name: ______________________ Date: ____________

Classifying angles

An angle is formed by two rays that share a common endpoint called a vertex. Angles can be named by letters or numbers. You can name this angle $\angle Q$, $\angle PQR$, or $\angle RQP$.

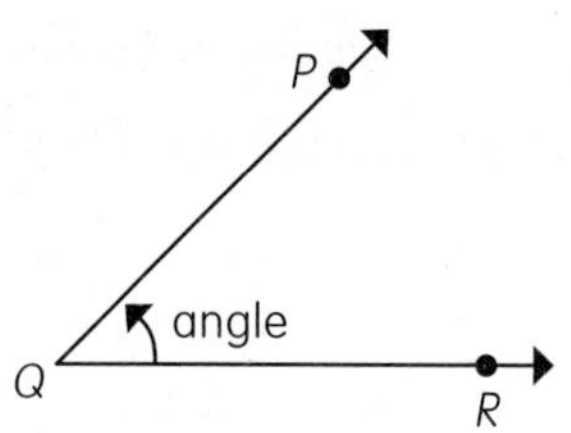

Angles are measured in degrees. The symbol for degrees is °. The statement $m\angle PQR = 45°$ means "the measure of angle *PQR* equals 45°."

You can classify angles according to their measures.

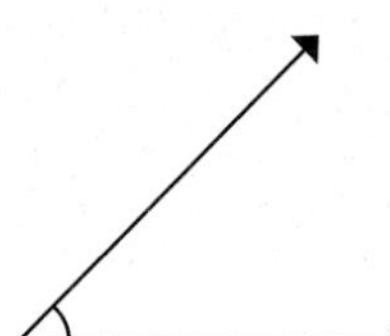

This is an acute angle.
Its measure is less than 90°.

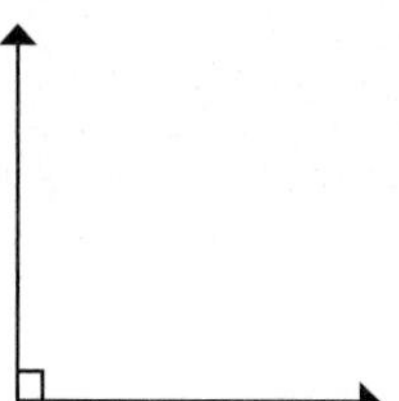

This is a right angle.
Its measure is exactly 90°.

This is an obtuse angle.
Its measure is greater than 90° but less than 180°.

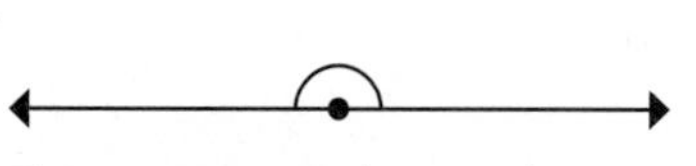

This is a straight angle.
Its measure is exactly 180°.

▶ Quick Check

State whether each angle is an acute, right, obtuse, or straight angle.

1. right angle

2. acute angle

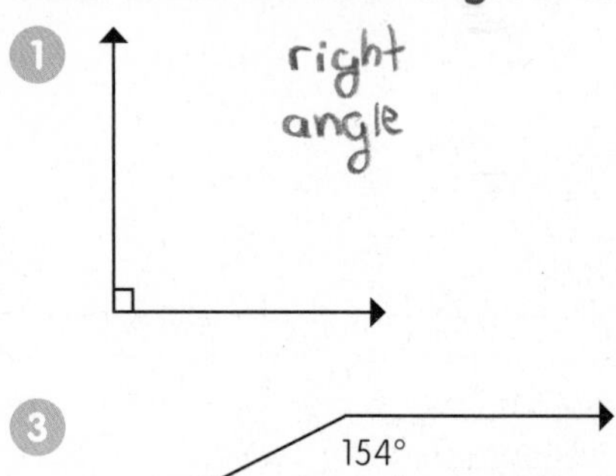

3. obtuse angle

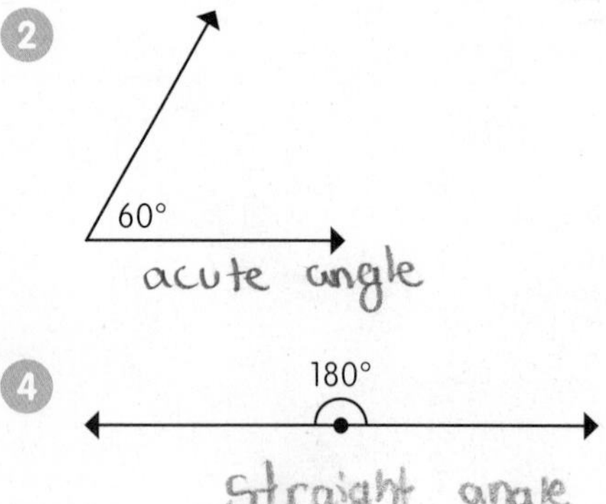

4. Straight angle

5. $m\angle w = 86°$
acute angle

6. $m\angle y = 90°$
right angle

Identifying parallel lines and perpendicular lines

When two lines in the same plane do not intersect, they are parallel to each other. They are always the same distance apart. In the figure below, $\overleftrightarrow{AB}$ is parallel to $\overleftrightarrow{CD}$. You can write $\overleftrightarrow{AB} \parallel \overleftrightarrow{CD}$.

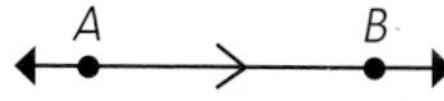

When two lines intersect to form a 90° angle, they are perpendicular to each other. In the figure below, $\overleftrightarrow{PQ}$ is perpendicular to $\overleftrightarrow{RS}$. So, you can write $\overleftrightarrow{PQ} \perp \overleftrightarrow{RS}$.

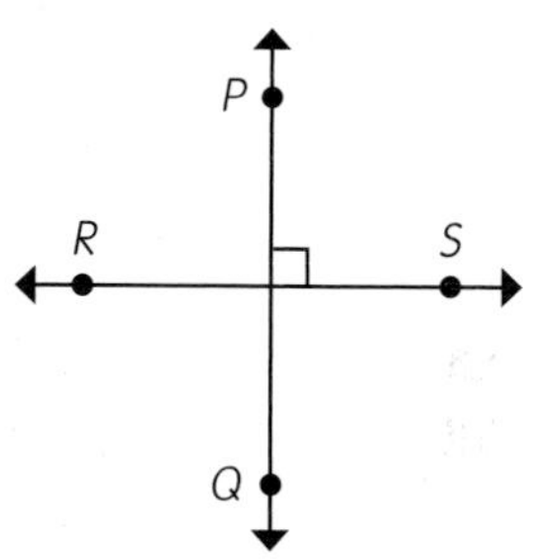

▶ Quick Check

Identify each pair of parallel line segments.

7

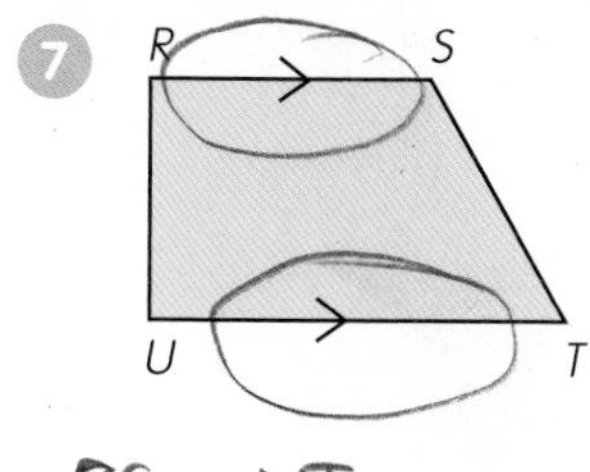

RS, UT

8

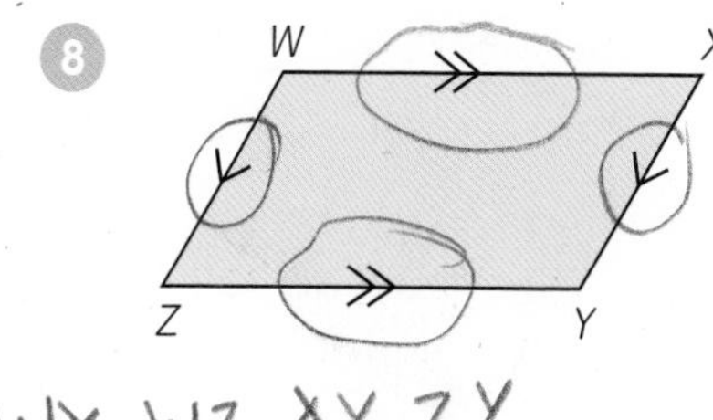

WX, WZ, XY, ZY

Identify each pair of perpendicular line segments.

9 *ABCD* is a rectangle.

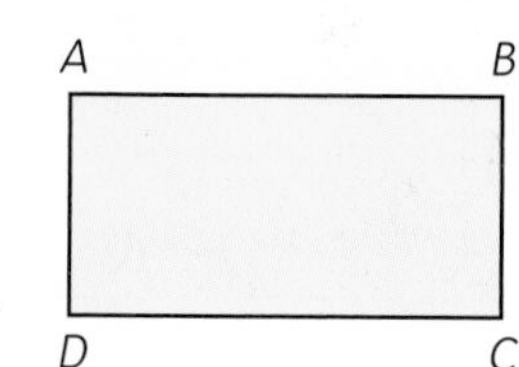

AB+DA, DC+BC

10

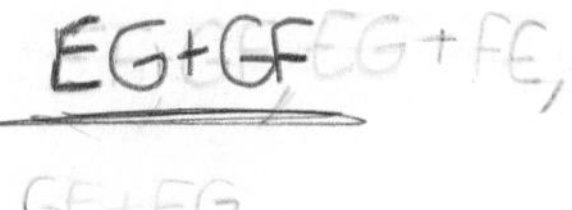

EG+GF

11

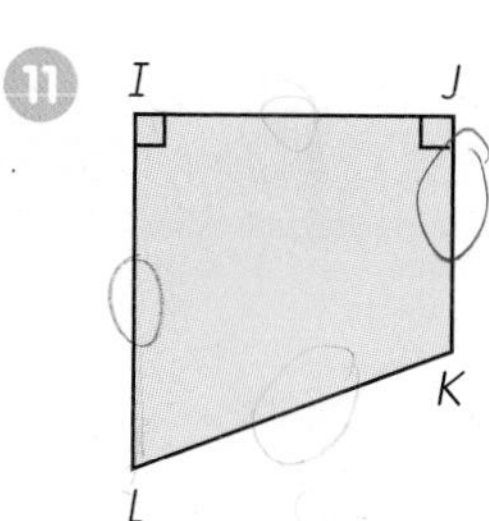

LI+JI, KJ+JI

RECALL PRIOR KNOWLEDGE

Identifying right, isosceles, and equilateral triangles

You can classify triangles according to their lengths of sides or angle measures.

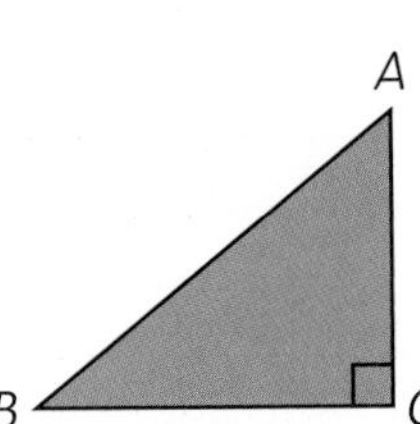

A right triangle has one right angle.

Triangle *ABC* is a right triangle. One of its angles is 90°.

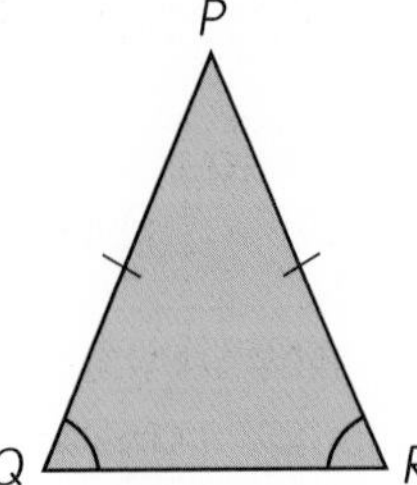

In an isosceles triangle, the angles opposite the equal sides are equal.

In triangle *PQR*, *PQ* = *PR*. So, ∠*PQR* = ∠*PRQ*.

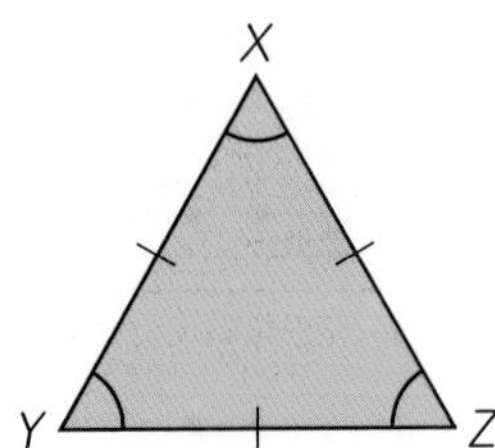

An equilateral triangle has three equal sides and three equal angles.

In triangle *XYZ*, *XY* = *YZ* = *XZ*. So, ∠*XYZ* = ∠*YZX* = ∠*ZXY*.

▶ Quick Check

Classify the triangles. Then, fill in the table.

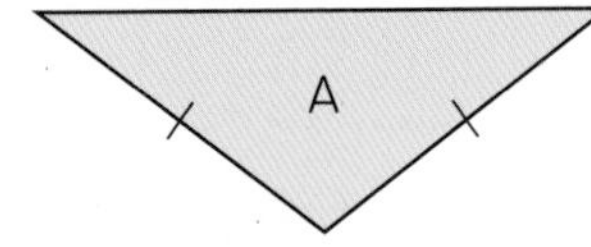

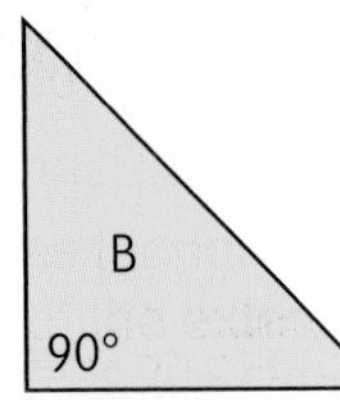

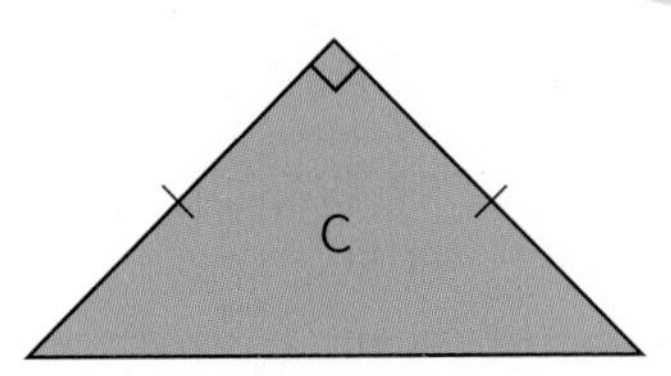

2 in.
D
2 in.
2 in.

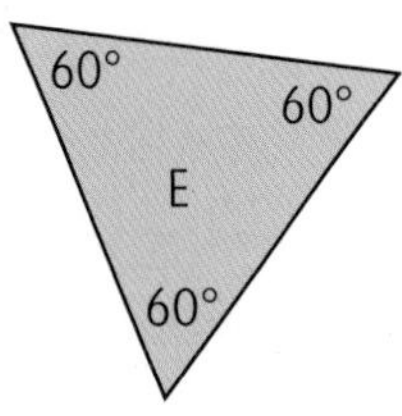

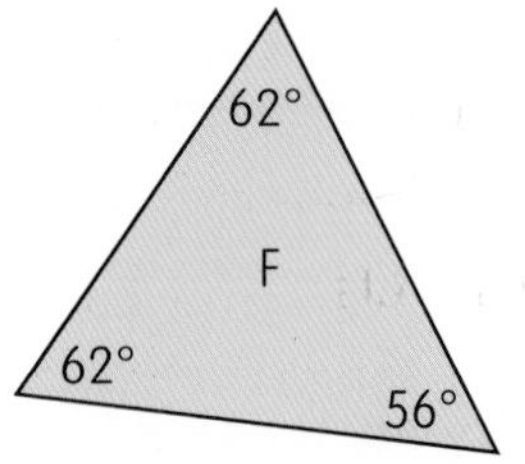

Right triangles	Isosceles triangles	Equilateral triangles
B, C	F, A	E, D

Name: ____________________ Date: ____________

1 Complementary, Supplementary, and Adjacent Angles

Learning Objectives:

- Explore the properties of complementary angles and supplementary angles.
- Explore the properties of adjacent angles.

New Vocabulary
complementary angles
supplementary angles
adjacent angles

In the diagram, $\overleftrightarrow{AB}$ is a straight line. $\angle AOC$ and $\angle DOE$ are complementary angles. $m\angle COD = (3x + 10)°$ and $m\angle EOB = (x + 20)°$. Write an equation to find the measures of $\angle COD$ and $\angle EOB$.

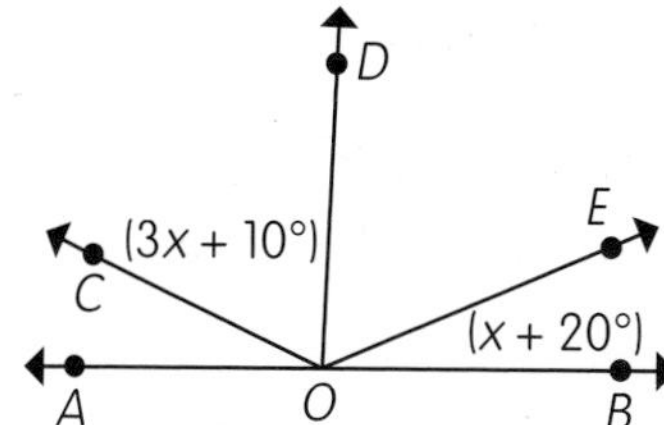

ENGAGE

Make a right angle with a piece of paper. If you draw a line to cut the right angle into two parts, what angle measures will you get? Name three possible pairs of angle measures. What pattern do you observe?

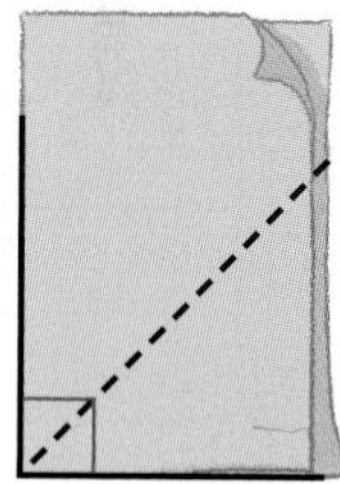

LEARN Identify complementary angles

Activity Exploring the relationship of two angles that make a right angle

Work in pairs.

① Use a geometry software to construct a line segment, $\overline{AB}$. Then, construct a second line segment, $\overline{BC}$, that is perpendicular to $\overline{AB}$. Finally, construct a line segment, $\overline{BD}$, that meets at the point B.

Example:

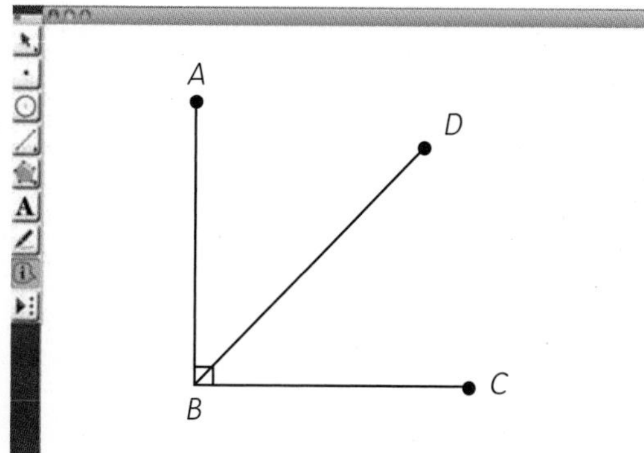

(2) Select $\angle ABC$ and find its measure.

(3) Select $\angle ABD$ and find its measure. Then, select $\angle DBC$ and find its measure.

(4) Find the sum of the measures of $\angle ABD$ and $\angle DBC$. What do you notice about the sum of their measures?

(5) Select the point *D* and drag it so that you change the measures of $\angle ABD$ and $\angle DBC$. Record your results in the table.

$m\angle ABD$	$m\angle DBC$	$m\angle ABD + m\angle DBC$

(6) As the angle measures change, what do you notice about the sum of the angle measures?

1 In the earlier activity, you found out that the sum of the angle measures of $\angle ABD$ and $\angle DBC$ is 90°. When the sum of the measures of two angles is 90°, the angles are called complementary angles.

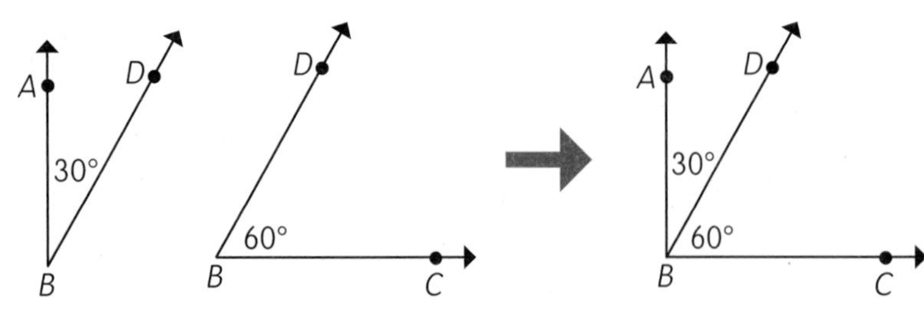

$$m\angle ABD + m\angle DBC = 30° + 60°$$
$$= 90°$$

$\angle ABD$ is the complement of $\angle DBC$, and $\angle DBC$ is the complement of $\angle ABD$.

TRY Practice identifying complementary angles and finding angle measures involving complementary angles

The diagrams may not be drawn to scale.
Name each pair of complementary angles.

1

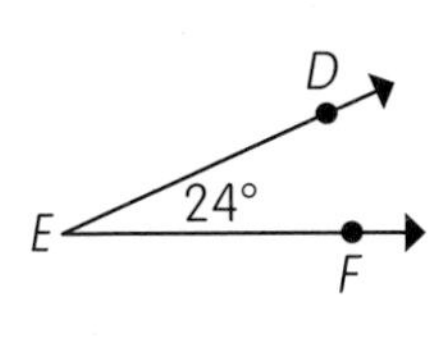

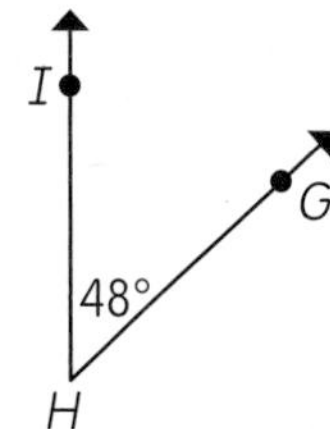

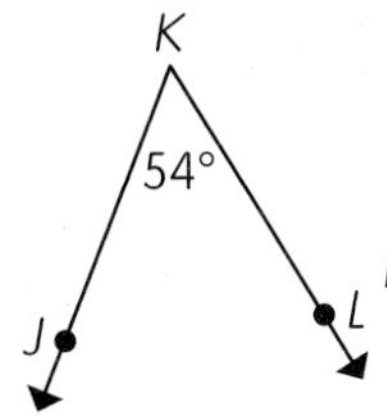

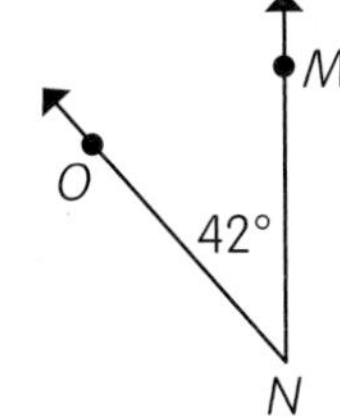

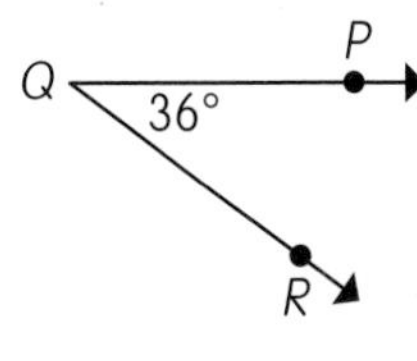

Fill in the table.

2 Angles A and B are complementary.
Find m$\angle B$ for each measure of $\angle A$.

m$\angle A$	m$\angle B$
28°	90° – 28° =
73°	
36°	
15°	

ENGAGE

Make a straight angle. If you draw a line to cut the straight angle into two parts, what angle measures will you get? Name three possible pairs of angle measures. What pattern do you observe?

LEARN Identify supplementary angles

Activity **Exploring the relationship of two angles that make a straight angle**

Work in pairs.

1. Use a geometry software to construct a line segment, $\overline{PR}$. Then, construct a second line segment, $\overline{SQ}$, that meets $\overline{PR}$ at point Q.

   Example:

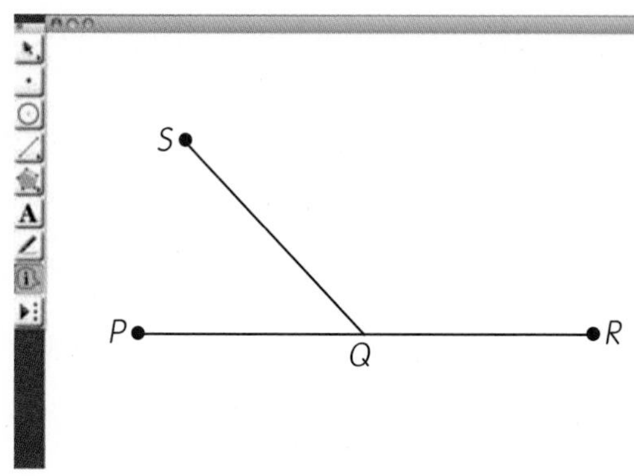

2. Select $\angle PQR$ and find its measure.

3. Select $\angle SQP$ and find its measure. Then, select $\angle SQR$ and find its measure.

4. Find the sum of the measures of $\angle SQP$ and $\angle SQR$. What do you notice about the sum of their measures?

5. Select the point S and drag it so that you change the measures of $\angle SQP$ and $\angle SQR$. Record your results in the table.

$m\angle SQP$	$m\angle SQR$	$m\angle SQP + m\angle SQR$

6. As the angle measures change, what do you notice about the sum of the angle measures?

1 In the earlier activity, you found out that the sum of the angle measures of $\angle SQP$ and $\angle SQR$ is 180°. When the sum of the measures of two angles is 180°, the angles are called supplementary angles.

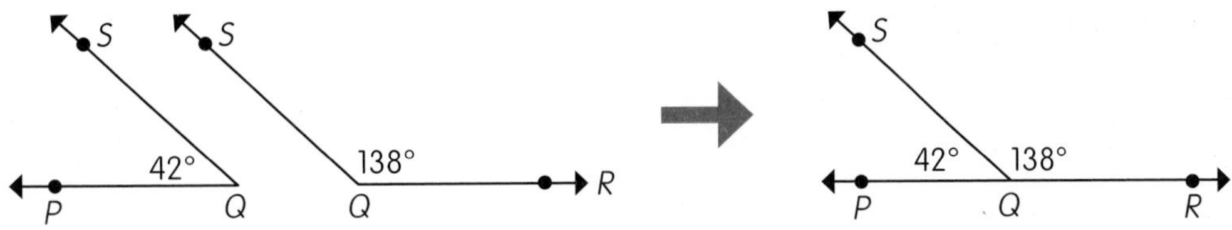

$$m\angle SQP + m\angle SQR = 42° + 138°$$
$$= 180°$$

$\angle SQP$ is the supplement of $\angle SQR$, and $\angle SQR$ is the supplement of $\angle SQP$.

TRY Practice identifying supplementary angles and finding angle measures involving supplementary angles

State whether each pair of angles is supplementary.

1 $m\angle X = 32°$ and $m\angle Y = 108°$

2 $m\angle A = 45°$ and $m\angle B = 45°$

3 $m\angle D = 12°$ and $m\angle E = 168°$

4 $m\angle V = 85°$ and $m\angle W = 95°$

Fill in the table.

5 Angles A and B are supplementary.
Find $m\angle B$ for each measure of $\angle A$.

$m\angle A$	$m\angle B$
82°	180° – 82° =
26°	
136°	
105°	

ENGAGE

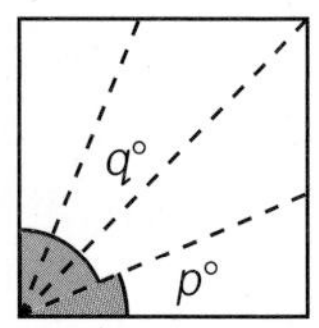

a Fold the corner of a square piece of paper into 4 equal parts. Mark one part as $p°$ and the other three parts as $q°$. How can you find the values of p and q? How is the size of each part related?

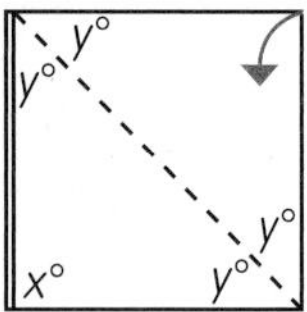

b Fold the side of a rectangular piece of paper into halves and label each part as $x°$. Now, fold the paper into half again along the diagonal. Label each new part as $y°$. What is the value of y? How are the values of x and y related?

LEARN Find angle measures involving adjacent angles

1 When two angles share a common vertex and side, but have no common interior points, they are called adjacent angles. Adjacent angles are next to and do not overlap each other.

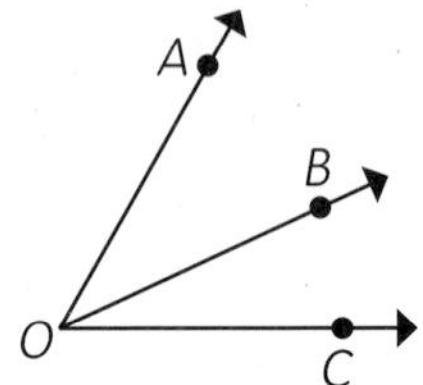

$\angle AOB$ and $\angle BOC$ are adjacent angles that share the common side $\overrightarrow{OB}$.

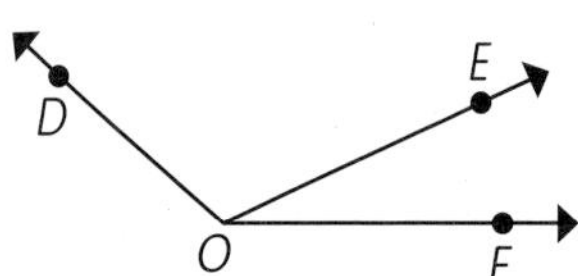

$\angle DOE$ and $\angle EOF$ are adjacent angles that share the common side $\overrightarrow{OE}$.

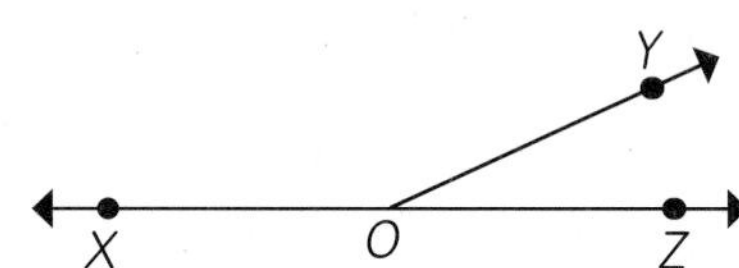

$\angle XOY$ and $\angle YOZ$ are adjacent angles on a straight line, $\overleftrightarrow{XZ}$. They share the common side $\overrightarrow{OY}$.

2 In the diagram, $\angle PQS$ and $\angle SQR$ are adjacent angles. They share a common vertex, Q, and a common side, $\overrightarrow{QS}$. $\overrightarrow{QP}$ is perpendicular to $\overrightarrow{QR}$. Find the measure of $\angle SQR$.

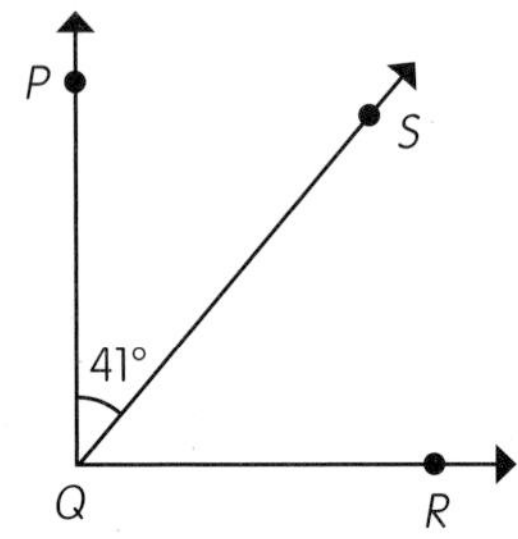

$m\angle PQS + m\angle SQR = 90°$ Comp. $\angle$s

$41° + m\angle SQR = 90°$ Substitute.

$41° + m\angle SQR - \mathbf{41°} = 90° - \mathbf{41°}$ Subtract 41° from both sides.

$m\angle SQR = 49°$ Simplify.

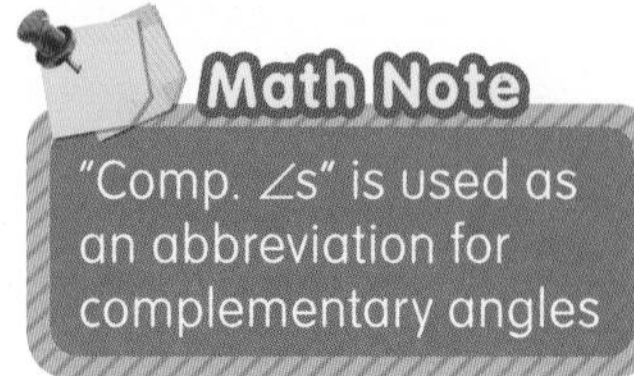

$\angle PQR$ and $\angle SQR$ share the common side $\overrightarrow{QR}$. Explain why they are not adjacent angles.

3 In the diagram, $\angle POR$, $\angle ROS$, and $\angle SOQ$ are adjacent angles. They are also angles on a straight line, $\overleftrightarrow{PQ}$. $m\angle POR + m\angle ROS + m\angle SOQ = 180°$. Find the measure of $\angle ROS$.

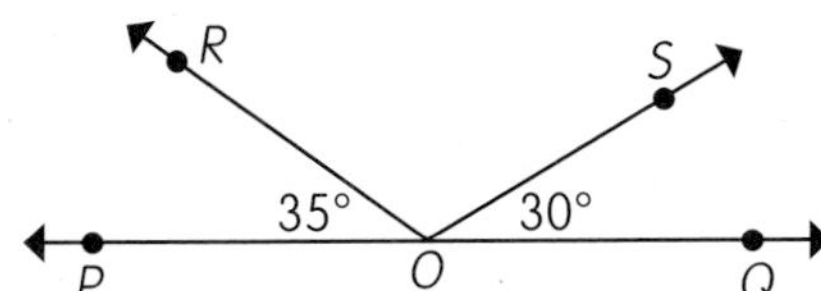

$m\angle POR + m\angle ROS + m\angle SOQ = 180°$	Adj. ∠s on a st. line
$35° + m\angle ROS + 30° = 180°$	Substitute.
$m\angle ROS + 65° = 180°$	
$m\angle ROS + 65° - \mathbf{65°} = 180° - \mathbf{65°}$	Subtract 65° from both sides.
$m\angle ROS = 115°$	Simplify.

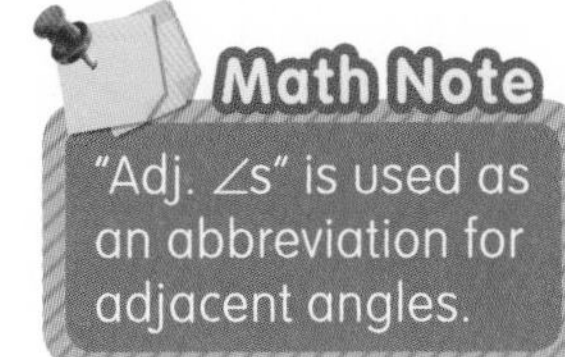

"Adj. ∠s" is used as an abbreviation for adjacent angles.

Are $\angle POR$, $\angle ROS$, and $\angle SOQ$ supplementary angles? Explain why.

4 In the diagram, $m\angle PQR = 90°$. The ratio of $a : b$ is $1 : 2$. Find the values of a and b.

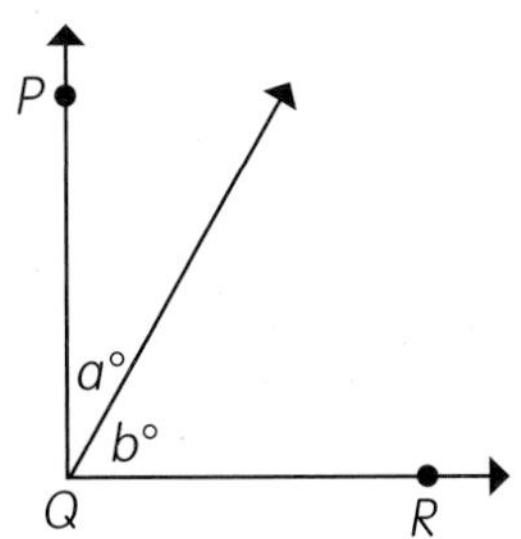

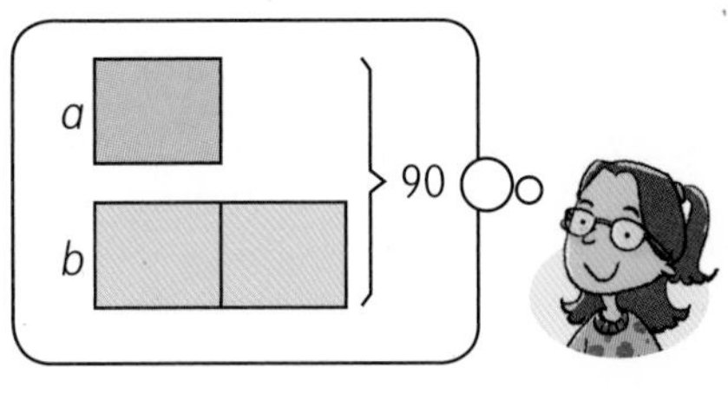

$a : b = 1 : 2$
So, $b = 2 \cdot a = 2a$.

$a° + b° = 90°$	Comp. ∠s
$a + 2a = 90$	Substitute.
$3a = 90$	Simplify.
$\frac{3a}{\mathbf{3}} = \frac{90}{\mathbf{3}}$	Divide both sides by 3.
$a = 30$	Simplify.

$b = 2 \cdot a$	
$= 2 \cdot 30$	Substitute.
$= 60$	Simplify.

TRY Practice finding angle measures involving adjacent angles

The diagrams may not be drawn to scale. Find the value of x.

1. In the diagram below, m$\angle ABC = 90°$.

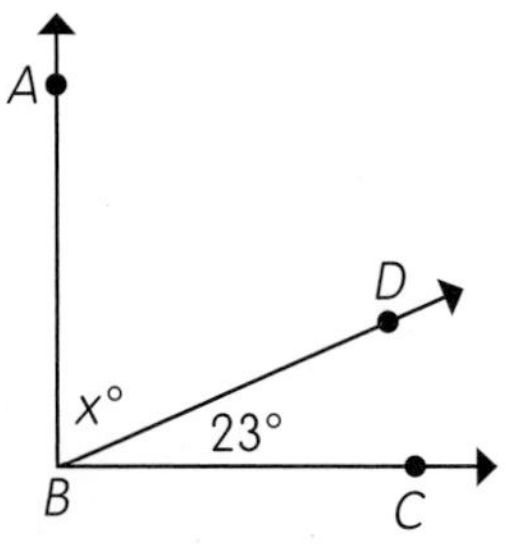

m$\angle ABD$ + m$\angle DBC$ = ______ Comp. ∠s

x + ______ = ______ Substitute.

x + ______ − ______ = ______ − ______ Subtract ______ from both sides.

x = ______ Simplify.

2. In the diagram below, $\angle AOC$, $\angle COD$, and $\angle DOB$ are adjacent angles on a straight line, $\overleftrightarrow{AB}$.

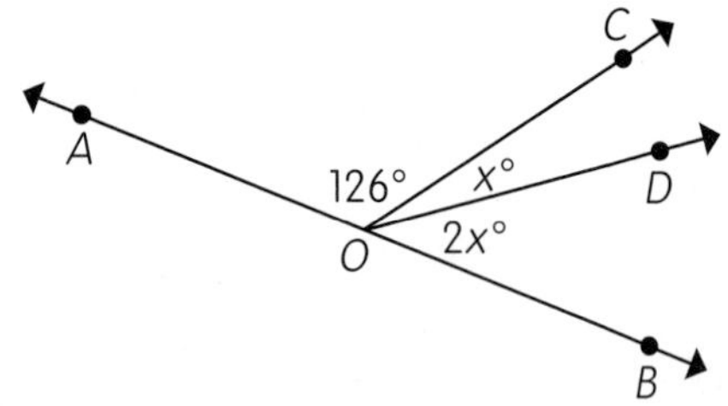

m$\angle AOC$ + m$\angle COD$ + m$\angle DOB$ = ______ Adj. ∠s on a st. line

______ + x + $2x$ = ______ Substitute.

______ + $3x$ = ______

______ + $3x$ − ______ = ______ − ______ Subtract ______ from both sides.

$3x$ = ______ Simplify.

$\frac{3x}{\quad} = \frac{\quad}{\quad}$ Divide both sides by ______.

x = ______ Simplify.

The diagrams may not be drawn to scale. In each diagram, $\overrightarrow{XW}$ is perpendicular to $\overrightarrow{XY}$. Find the value of p.

3

4

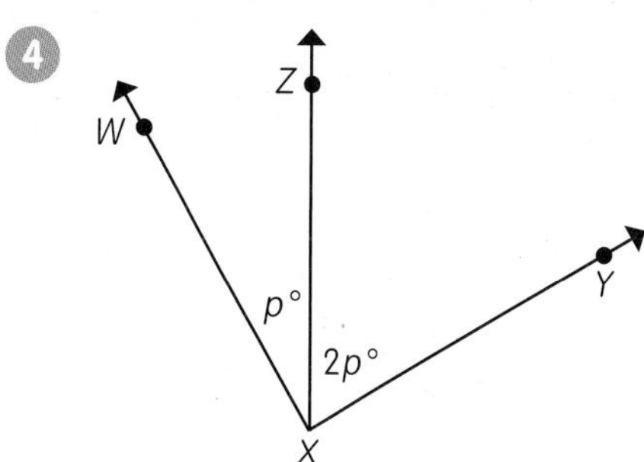

The diagrams may not be drawn to scale. In each diagram, $\overleftrightarrow{PQ}$ is a straight line. Find the value of y.

5

6

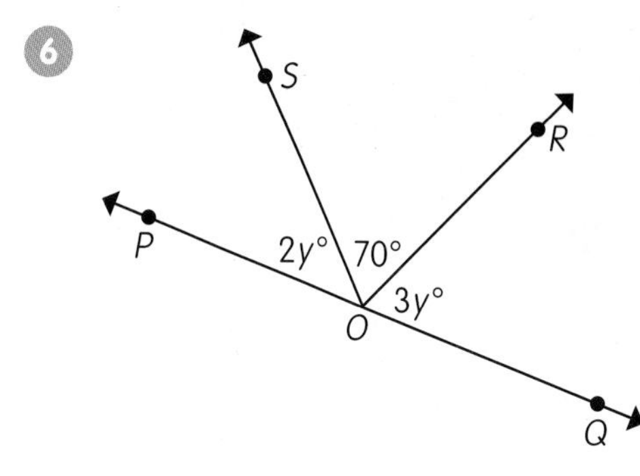

The diagram may not be drawn to scale. Find the values of x and y.

7. In the diagram below, $m\angle PQR = 90°$. The ratio of $x : y$ is $1 : 4$.

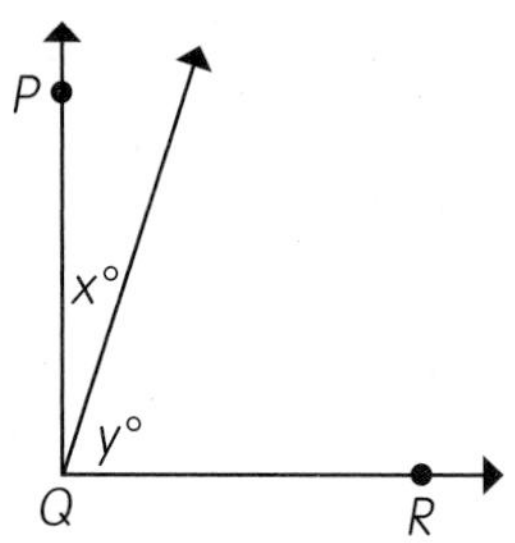

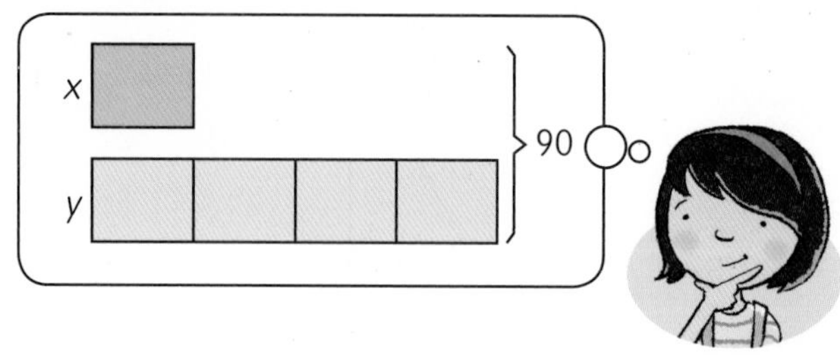

$x : y = 1 : 4$

So, $y =$ ______ $\cdot\, x =$ ______.

$x° + y° = 90°$	Comp. ∠s
$x +$ ______ $= 90$	Substitute.
______ $= 90$	Simplify.
$\dfrac{\_\_\_}{\_\_\_} = \dfrac{90}{\_\_\_}$	Divide both sides by ______.
$x =$ ______	Simplify.
$y =$ ______ $\cdot\, x$	
$=$ ______ $\cdot$ ______	Substitute $x =$ ______.
$=$ ______	Simplify.

MATH SHARING

1. **Mathematical Habit 3 Construct viable arguments**

   Carla says that a pair of complementary angles is a pair of adjacent angles but a pair of adjacent angles may not necessarily be a pair of complementary angles. Do you agree with Carla? Explain.

2. **Mathematical Habit 2 Use mathematical reasoning**

   Angles y and $3y$ are supplementary angles. What can you tell about the two angles? Discuss and explain.

Name: ________________ Date: ________________

INDEPENDENT PRACTICE

State whether each pair of angles is complementary.

1. $m\angle A = 25°$ and $m\angle B = 65°$
2. $m\angle C = 105°$ and $m\angle D = 7°$
3. $m\angle E = 112°$ and $m\angle F = 68°$
4. $m\angle G = 45°$ and $m\angle H = 45°$

State whether each pair of angles is supplementary.

5. $m\angle A = 130°$ and $m\angle B = 50°$
6. $m\angle C = 90°$ and $m\angle D = 80°$
7. $m\angle E = 120°$ and $m\angle F = 60°$
8. $m\angle G = 60°$ and $m\angle H = 30°$

Find the measure of the complement of each given angle measure.

9. 19°
10. 64°
11. 7°
12. 35°

Find the measure of the supplement of each given angle measure.

13. 78°
14. 4°
15. 153°
16. 101°

The diagrams may not be drawn to scale. $\angle ABD$ and $\angle DBC$ are complementary angles. Find the value of x.

17.

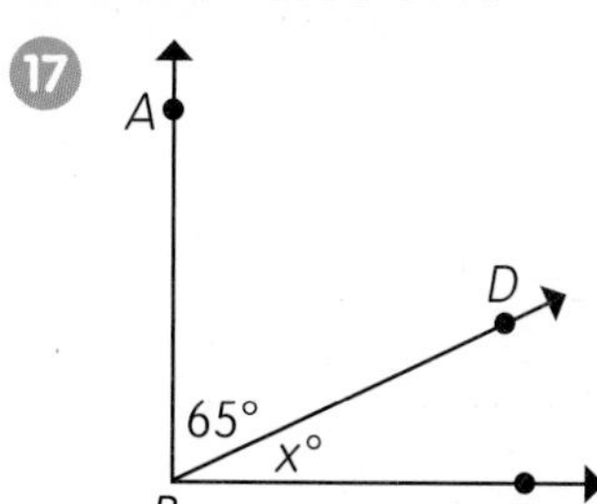

18.

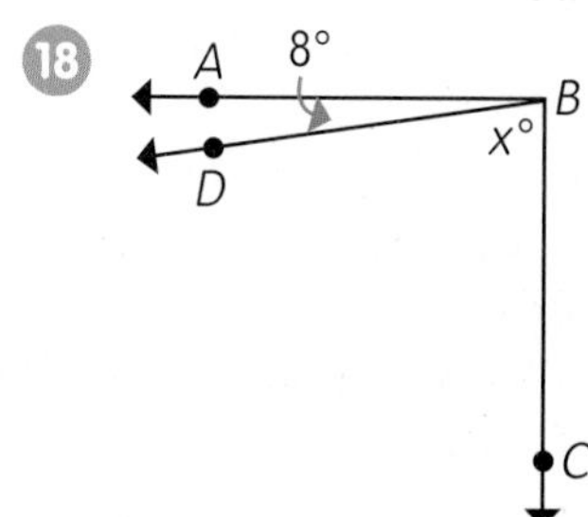

The diagrams may not be drawn to scale. $\angle PQS$ and $\angle SQR$ are supplementary angles. Find the value of m.

19
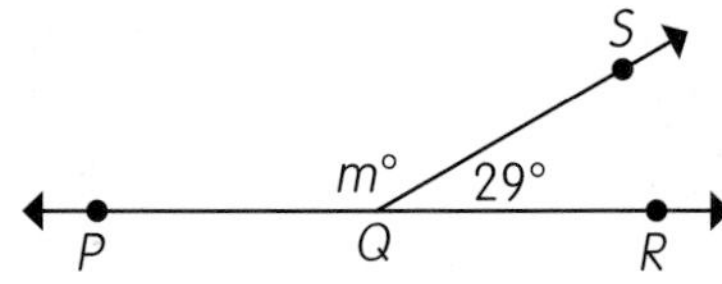

20
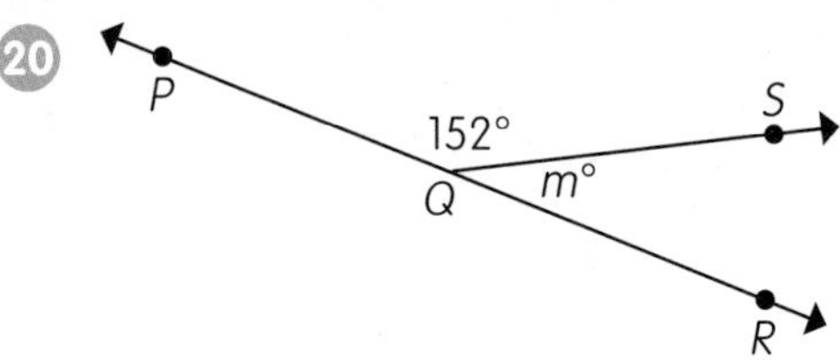

Find the measures of the complement and the supplement of each given angle measure, where possible.

21 $m\angle W = 2°$

22 $m\angle X = 40°$

23 $m\angle Y = 32°$

24 $m\angle Z = 115°$

25 **Mathematical Habit 2** **Use mathematical reasoning**
Which angle in 21 to 24 does not have both a complement and a supplement?
In general, what must be true about the measure of an angle that has both a complement and a supplement?

Identify all the angles in each diagram. State which angles are adjacent.

26
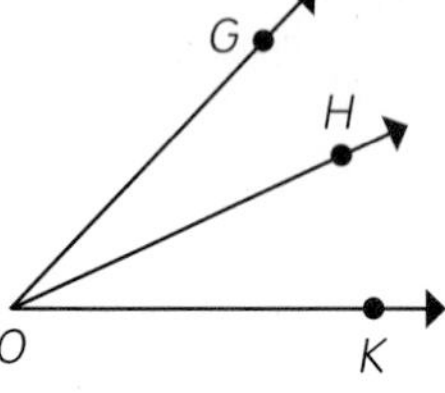

27
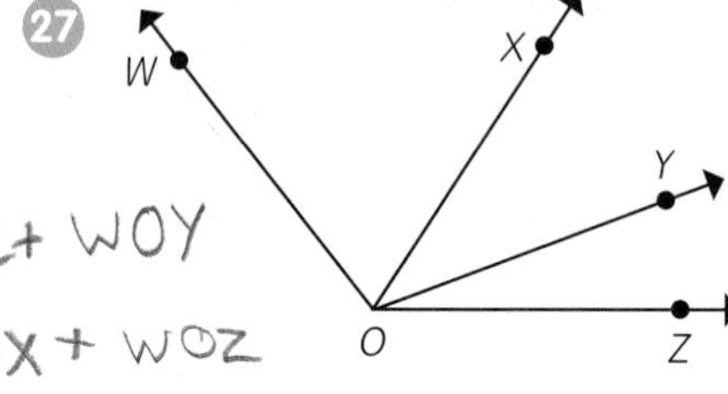

woz+ WOY
WOX + WOZ
WOX + WOY

The diagrams may not be drawn to scale. The measure of $\angle ABC = 90°$. Find the value of x.

28
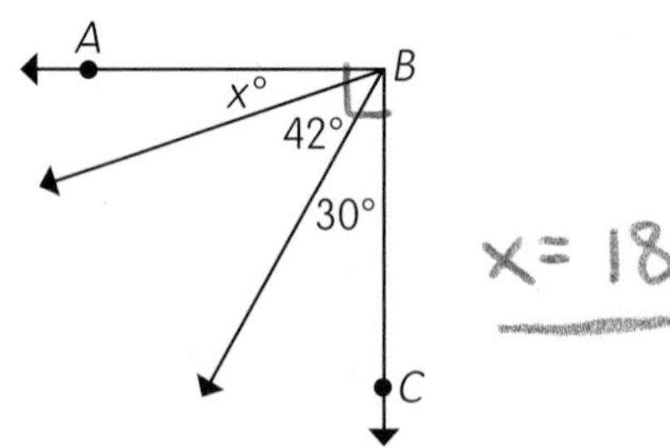

x= 18

30+42=72 → 90-72=18

29
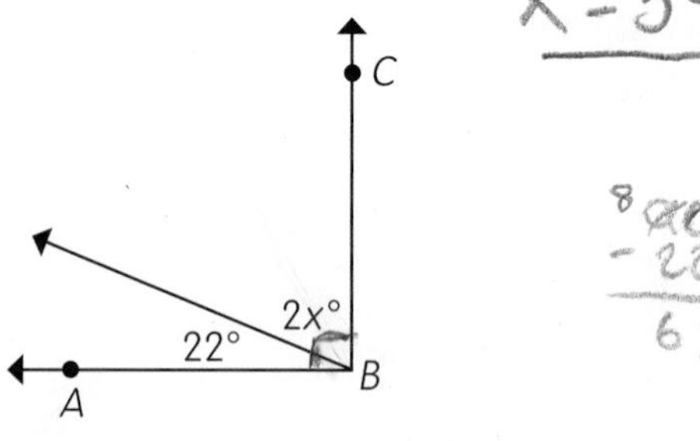

X=34

2x+22=90
- 22 -22
0 68÷2=34

30

31

The diagrams may not be drawn to scale. $\overleftrightarrow{PR}$ is a straight line.
Find the value of m.

32

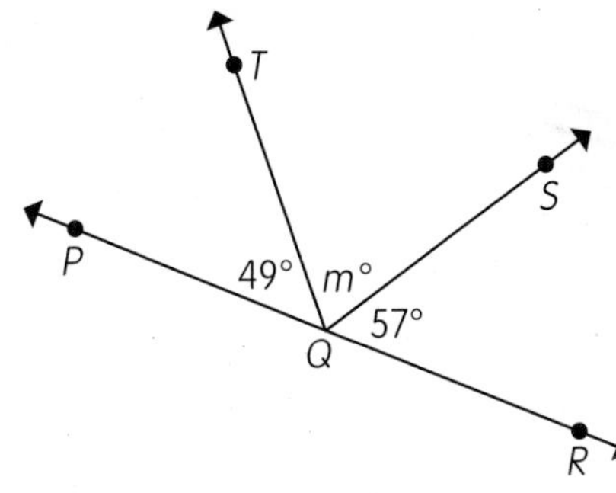

33

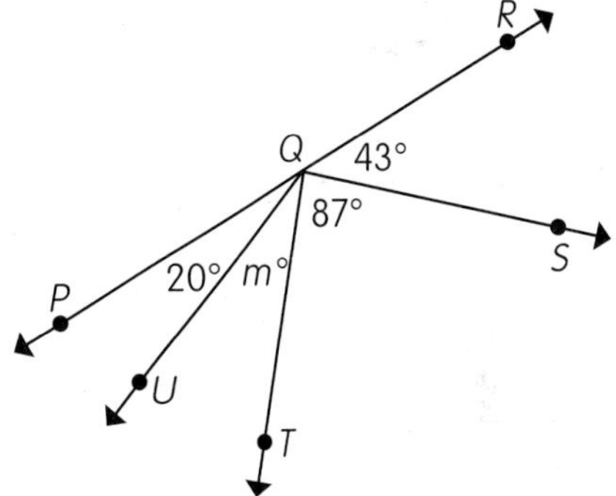

The diagrams may not be drawn to scale. The ratio $a : b = 2 : 3$.
Find the values of a and b.

34 The measure of $\angle PQR = 90°$

35 $\overleftrightarrow{PR}$ is a straight line.

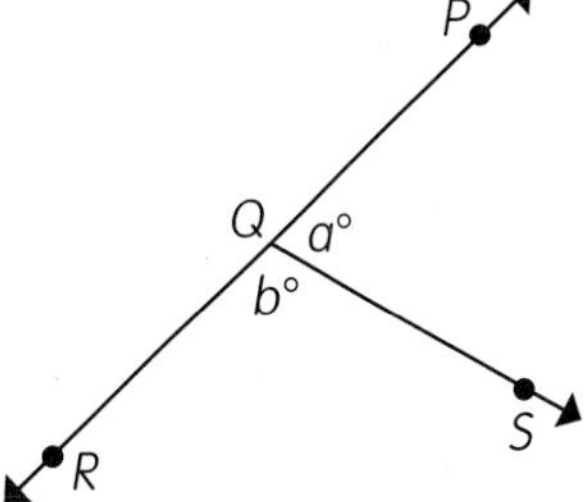

Solve.

36. The diagram shows the pattern on a stained glass window. $\overleftrightarrow{AC}$ is a straight line. $\angle EBD$ and $\angle DBA$ are complementary angles and $m\angle DBA = 30°$. Find the measures of $\angle EBD$ and $\angle CBD$.

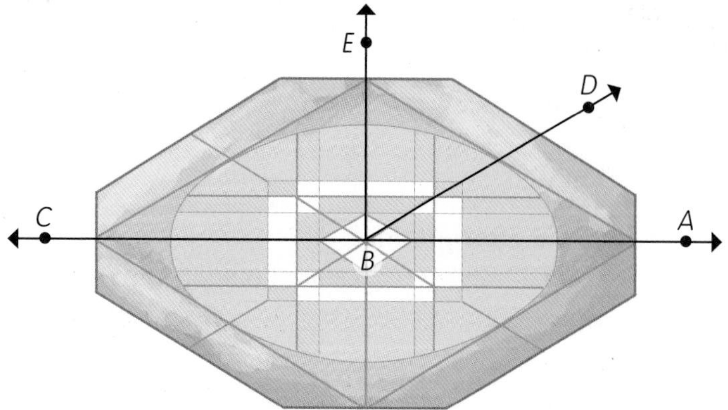

37. The diagram shows a kite. The two diagonals $\overline{MP}$ and $\overline{QT}$ are perpendicular to each other. Identify all pairs of complementary angles and all pairs of supplementary angles that are not pairs of right angles.

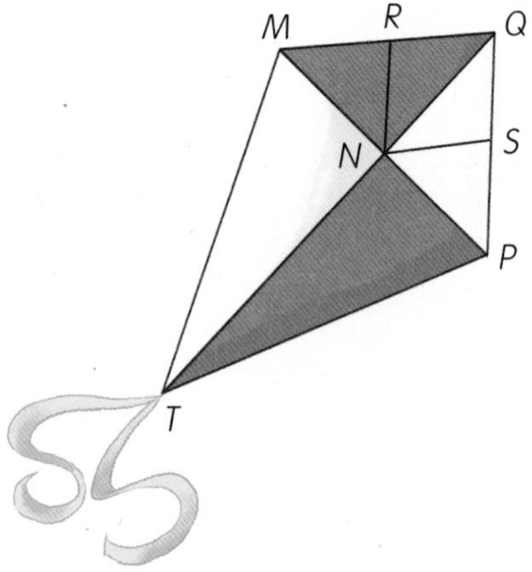

38. The measures of two supplementary angles are in the ratio of 4 : 1. Find the measures of the two angles.

Name: ______________________________ Date: ______________

Angles That Share a Vertex

Learning Objectives:

- Explore and apply the properties of angles at a point.
- Explore and apply the properties of vertical angles.

New Vocabulary
vertical angles
congruent angles

In the diagram below, $\overleftrightarrow{AB}$ and $\overleftrightarrow{CD}$ are straight lines.
The measures of $\angle EOD$ and $\angle DOF$ are in the ratio 2 : 3.
Find the measures of $\angle AOC$ and $\angle DOB$.

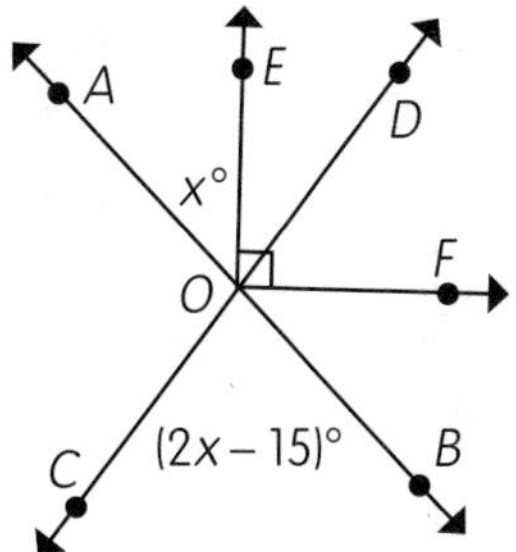

ENGAGE

Cut a circle into three parts from its center. Use a protractor to find the angle measure of each part. Then, find the sum of the three angles. Repeat the process, this time cutting a circle into five parts. What do you notice about the sum of the angles? Share your observations.

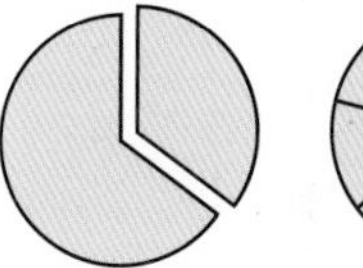

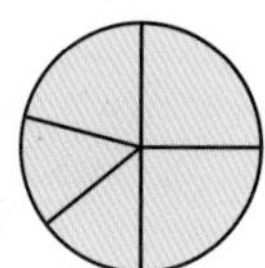

LEARN Solve problems involving angles at a point

1. In the diagram below, angles A, B, C, and D share a common vertex, O. These angles are called angles at a point. The sum of the measures of angles at a point is 360°.

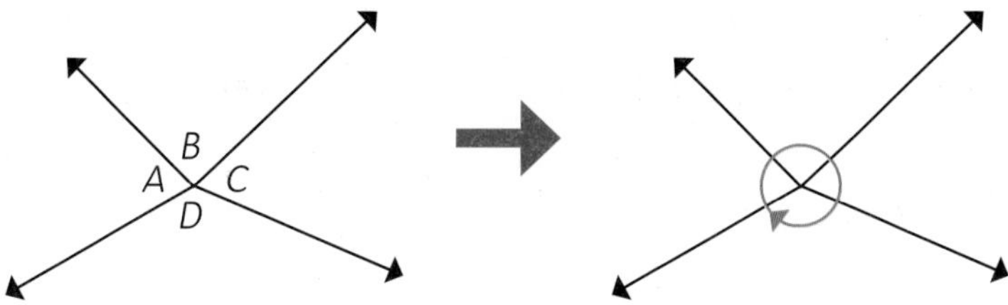

A full turn around a point is equal to 360°.

2 The diagram may not be drawn to scale.
Find the value of x.

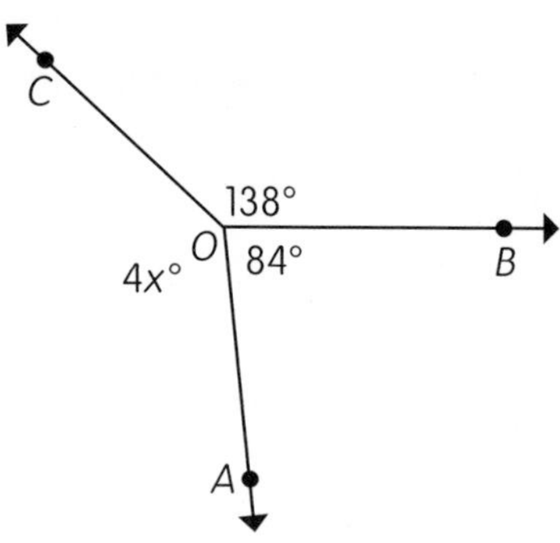

$$\begin{aligned} m\angle AOC + m\angle AOB + m\angle BOC &= 360^\circ && \angle\text{s at a point} \\ 4x + 84 + 138 &= 360 && \text{Substitute.} \\ 4x + 222 &= 360 && \text{Simplify.} \\ 4x + 222 - \mathbf{222} &= 360 - \mathbf{222} && \text{Subtract 222 from both sides.} \\ 4x &= 138 && \text{Simplify.} \\ \frac{4x}{\mathbf{4}} &= \frac{138}{\mathbf{4}} && \text{Divide both sides by 4.} \\ x &= 34.5 && \text{Simplify.} \end{aligned}$$

Math Note
"∠s at a point" is used as an abbreviation for angles at a point.

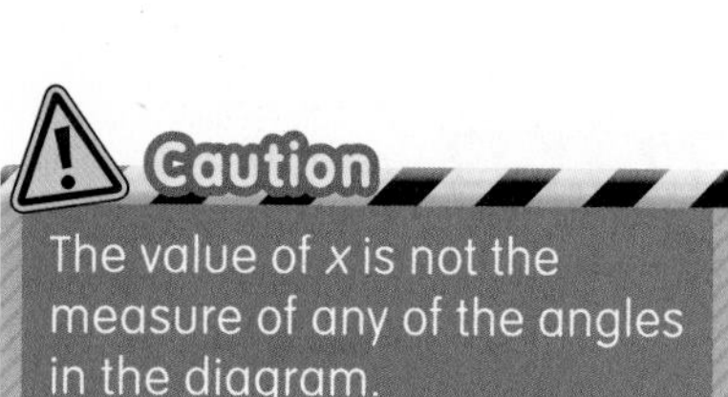

3 The diagram may not be drawn to scale. In the diagram, the ratio of $a : b : c$ is $1 : 2 : 2$.
Find the values of a, b, and c.

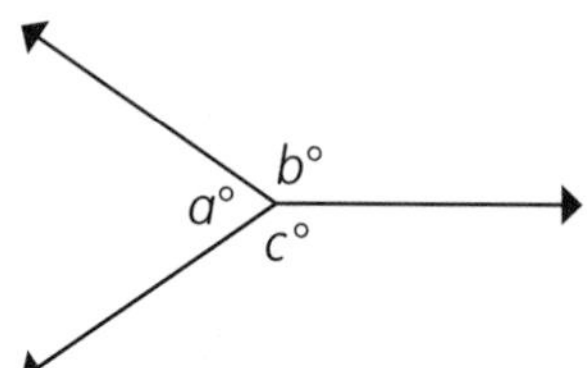

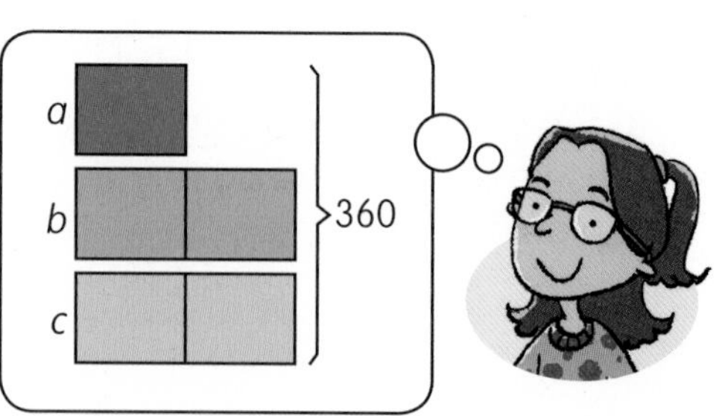

So, $b = c$
$= 2 \cdot a$
$= 2a$

$a° + b° + c° = 360°$	∠s at a point
$a + 2a + 2a = 360$	Substitute.
$5a = 360$	Simplify.
$\frac{5a}{\mathbf{5}} = \frac{360}{\mathbf{5}}$	Divide both sides by 5.
$a = 72$	Simplify.

$b = 2 \cdot a$
$= 2 \cdot 72$ Substitute $a = 72$.
$= 144$ Simplify.

$c = b$
$= 144$ Substitute $b = 144$.

TRY Practice solving problems involving angles at a point

The diagrams may not be drawn to scale. Solve.

1. Find the value of p.

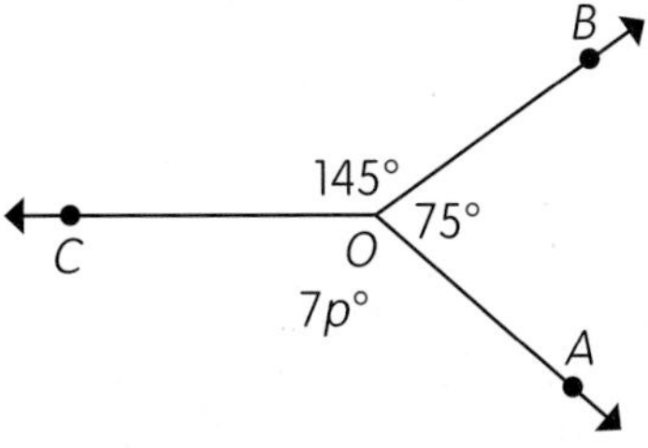

m∠AOC + m∠AOB + m∠BOC = ______	∠s at a point
______ + ______ + ______ = ______	Substitute.
______ + ______ = ______	Simplify.
______ + ______ − ______ = ______ − ______	Subtract ______ from both sides.
______ = ______	Simplify.
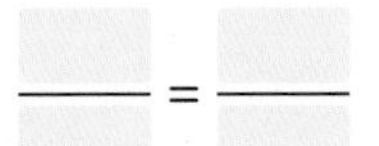	Divide both sides by ______.
p = ______	Simplify.

2 Find the value of x.

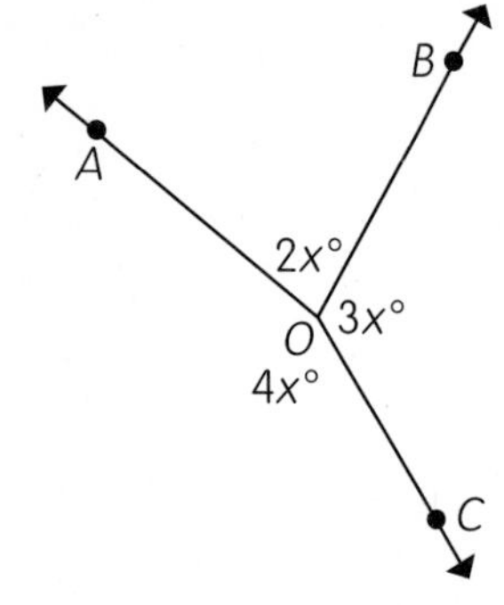

$m\angle AOC + m\angle AOB + m\angle BOC =$ ______

______ + ______ + ______ = ______

______ = ______

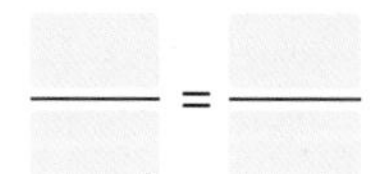

$x =$ ______

3 In the diagram, the ratio $a : b : c$ is $1 : 2 : 5$.
Find the values of a, b, and c.

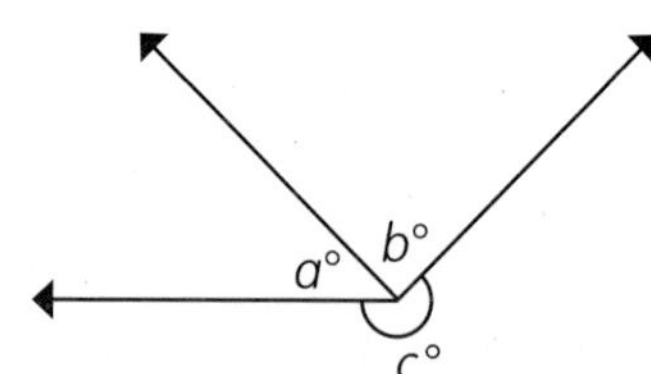

$a : b : c = 1 :$ ______ : ______

So, $b =$ ______ $\cdot\ a =$ ______, and

$c =$ ______ $\cdot\ a =$ ______.

$a° + b° + c° =$ ______

$a +$ ______ + ______ = ______

______ = ______

$a =$ ______

$b =$ ______ $\cdot\ a$

= ______ $\cdot$ ______

= ______

$c =$ ______ $\cdot\ a$

= ______ $\cdot$ ______

= ______

ENGAGE

Cut a circle and fold it into halves. Draw three lines from any point along the folded line to the circle. Label each angle formed at the point 1, 2, 3, and 4. What is the sum of all angles formed along the folded line? What do you notice? Explain your answer.

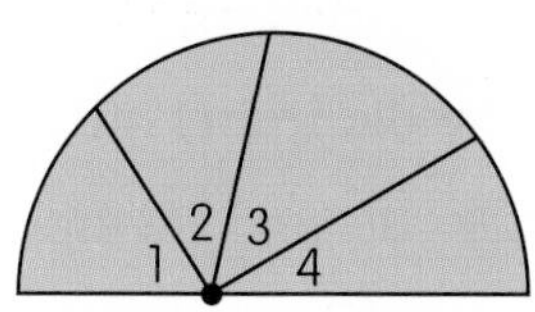

LEARN Solve problems involving angles on a straight line

1. The diagram may not be drawn to scale. $\overleftrightarrow{AB}$ is a straight line. Find the value of each variable.

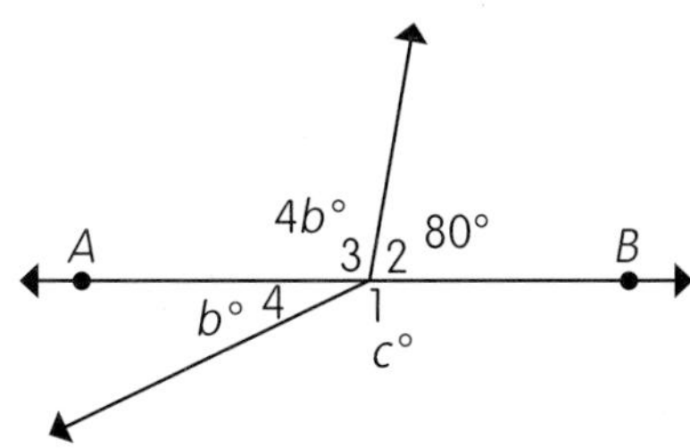

$m\angle 2 + m\angle 3 = 180°$	Adj. ∠s on a st. line
$4b + 80 = 180$	Substitute.
$4b + 80 - \mathbf{80} = 180 - \mathbf{80}$	Subtract 80 from both sides.
$4b = 100$	Simplify.
$\frac{4b}{\mathbf{4}} = \frac{100}{\mathbf{4}}$	Divide both sides by 4.
$b = 25$	Simplify.

$m\angle 1 + m\angle 4 = 180°$	Adj. ∠s on a st. line
$c + b = 180$	Substitute.
$c + 25 = 180$	Substitute $b = 25$.
$c + 25 - \mathbf{25} = 180 - \mathbf{25}$	Subtract 25 from both sides.
$c = 155$	Simplify.

TRY Practice solving problems involving angles on a straight line

The diagrams may not be drawn to scale. Solve.

1. $\overleftrightarrow{BE}$ and $\overleftrightarrow{CA}$ are straight lines. Find the values of r and q.

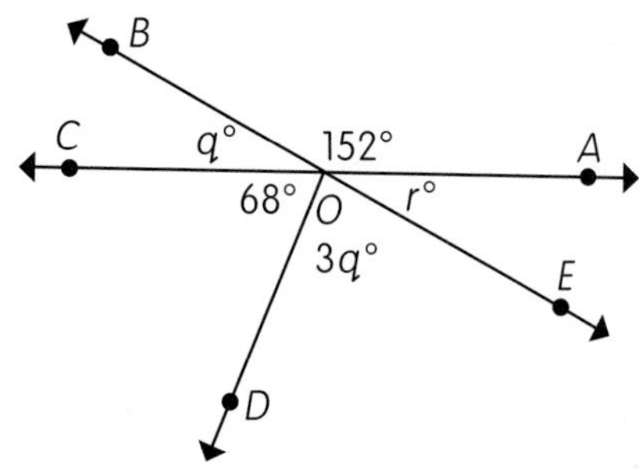

$m\angle AOB + m\angle AOE =$ ______	Adj. ∠s on a st. line
______ + ______ = ______	Substitute.
______ + ______ − ______ = ______ − ______	Subtract ______ from both sides.
______ = ______	Simplify.
$m\angle BOC + m\angle COD + m\angle DOE =$ ______	Adj. ∠s on a st. line
______ + ______ + ______ = ______	Substitute.
______ + ______ = ______	Simplify.
______ + ______ − ______ = ______ − ______	Subtract ______ from both sides.
______ = ______	Simplify.
$\frac{\text{\_\_\_}}{\text{\_\_\_}} = \frac{\text{\_\_\_}}{\text{\_\_\_}}$	Divide both sides by ______.
$q =$ ______	Simplify.

2 $\overleftrightarrow{PQ}$ is a straight line. Find the values of m and n.

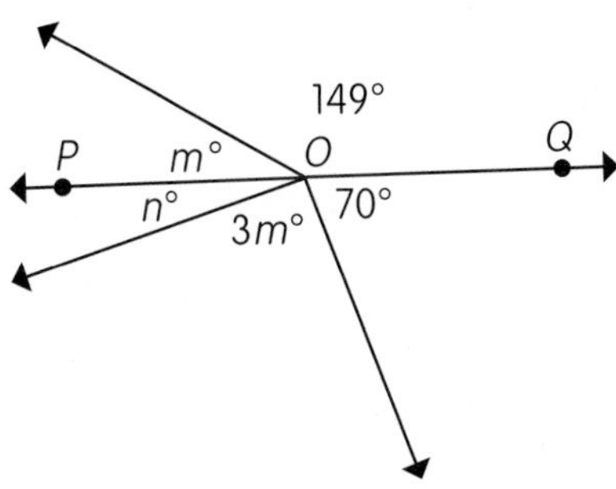

ENGAGE

Draw two straight lines that intersect each other and label the angles formed as m∠A, m∠B, m∠C, and m∠D. Use a protractor to find the measures of the four angles formed at the intersection point. What do you notice about the angles that are nonadjacent? Share your observations.

LEARN Solve problems involving vertical angles

Activity **Exploring the relationship of vertical angles**

Work in pairs.

1. Use a geometry software to construct two intersecting line segments, $\overline{AB}$ and $\overline{CD}$.

Example:

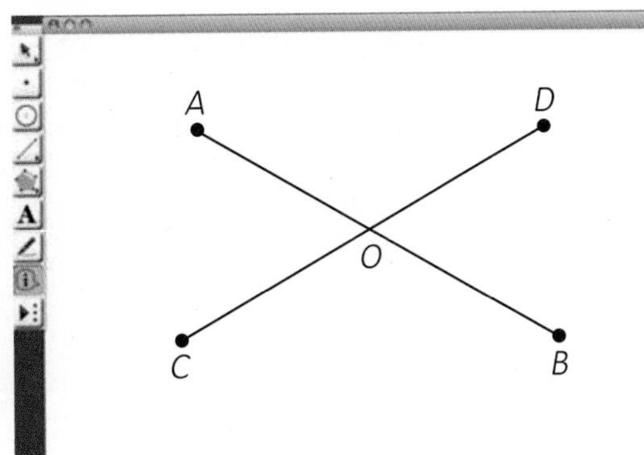

2. Select ∠*AOD* and find its measure. Then, select ∠*COB* and find its measure.

3 Select $\angle AOC$ and find its measure. Then, select $\angle DOB$ and find its measure.

4 Select the point D and drag it so that you change the measures of $\angle AOD$, $\angle COB$, $\angle AOC$, and $\angle DOB$. Record your results in two tables.

m∠AOD	m∠COB

m∠AOC	m∠DOB

5 As the measure of $\angle AOD$ changes, what do you notice about the measure of $\angle COB$?
As the measure of $\angle AOC$ changes, what do you notice about the measure of $\angle DOB$?

1 When two lines intersect each other at a point, they form four angles.
The nonadjacent angles are called vertical angles.
$\angle AOD$ and $\angle COB$ are vertical angles, so are $\angle AOC$ and $\angle DOB$.

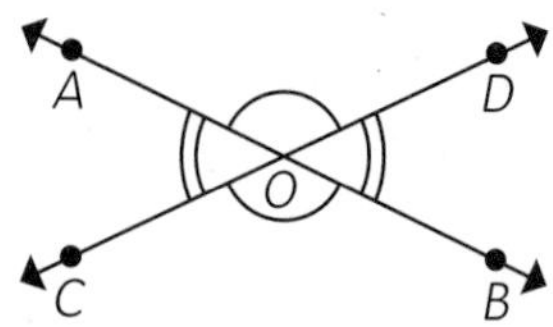

Caution

Vertical angles are formed by intersecting straight lines. Note that the nonadjacent angles in the diagram below are not vertical angles.

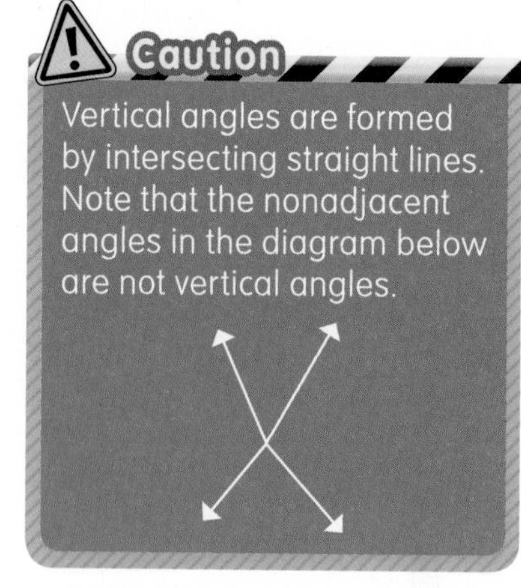

Since $\angle AOD$ and $\angle DOB$ are adjacent angles that form a straight line, they are supplementary.
$\angle AOC$ and $\angle AOD$ are also adjacent angles that form a straight line. So, they are also supplementary.

We deduce that
$m\angle AOD + m\angle DOB = 180°$ and
$m\angle DOB + m\angle BOC = 180°$.

From the equations, you can see that $\angle AOD$ and $\angle BOC$ are equal in measure.
When two angles have the same angle measure, they are called **congruent angles**.
So, vertical angles are congruent.

2 The diagram may not be drawn to scale. $\overleftrightarrow{AB}$ and $\overleftrightarrow{CD}$ are straight lines. Find the value of x.

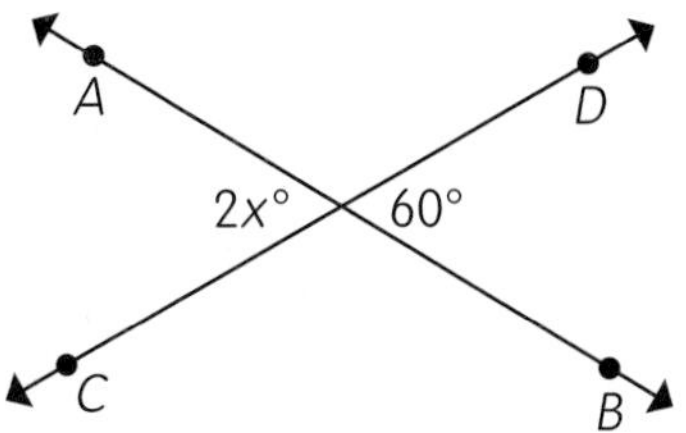

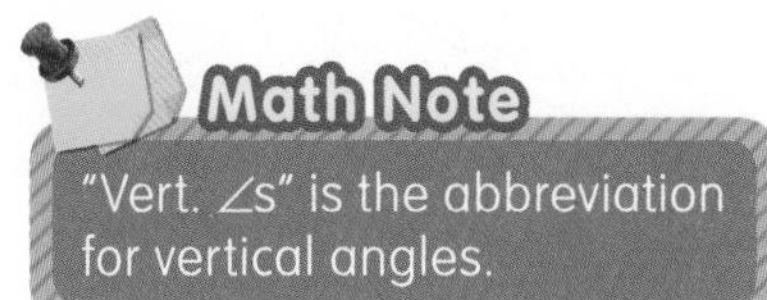

$2x° = 60°$	Vert. ∠s
$\frac{2x}{\mathbf{2}} = \frac{60}{\mathbf{2}}$	Divide both sides by 2.
$x = 30$	Simplify.

3 The diagram may not be drawn to scale. In the diagram, two straight lines intersect to form angles 1, 2, 3, and 4. Find the value of each variable if m∠1 = 76°.

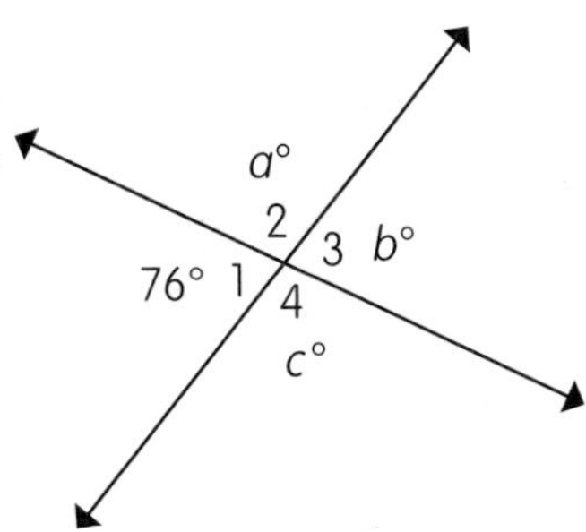

$m\angle 1 + m\angle 2 = 180°$	Supp. ∠s
$76 + a = 180$	Substitute.
$76 + a - \mathbf{76} = 180 - \mathbf{76}$	Subtract 76 from both sides.
$a = 104$	Simplify.

$m\angle 3 = m\angle 1$	Vert. ∠s
$b = 76$	Substitute.

$m\angle 4 = m\angle 2$	Vert. ∠s
$c = 104$	Substitute.

TRY Practice solving problems involving vertical angles

The diagrams may not be drawn to scale. Solve.

1. $\overleftrightarrow{AB}$ and $\overleftrightarrow{CD}$ are straight lines. Find the value of y.

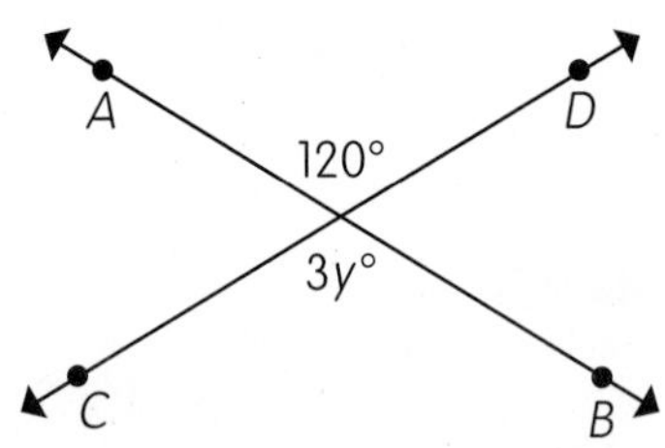

$3y° =$ ______ Vert. ∠s

$\frac{3y}{\square} = \frac{\square}{\square}$ Divide both sides by ______.

$y =$ ______ Simplify.

2. In the diagram, two straight lines intersect to form angles 1, 2, 3, and 4.
Find the value of each variable if m∠1 = 114°.

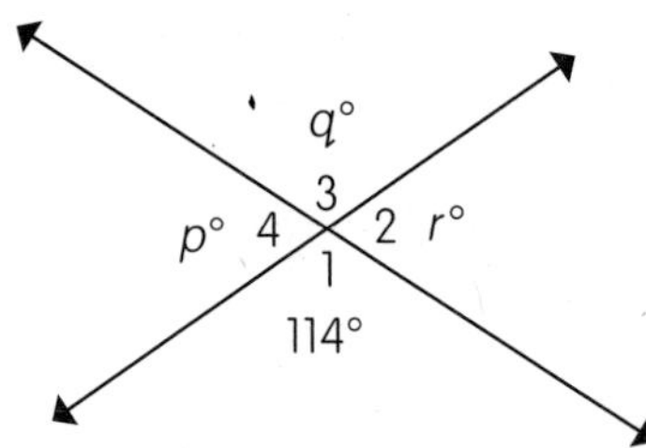

m∠1 + m∠2 = ______ Supp. ∠s

______ + ______ = ______ Substitute.

______ + ______ − ______ = ______ − ______ Subtract ______ from both sides.

______ = ______ Simplify.

m∠3 = m∠1 Vert. ∠s

$q =$ ______ Substitute.

m∠4 = m∠2 Vert. ∠s

$p =$ ______ Substitute.

Name: ______________________ Date: ____________

INDEPENDENT PRACTICE

The diagrams may not be drawn to scale. Find the value of each variable.

1

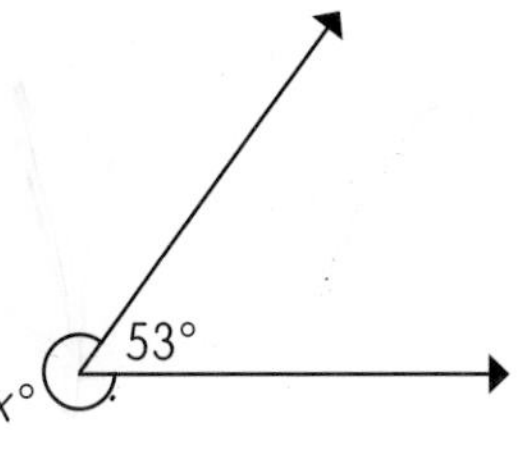

2

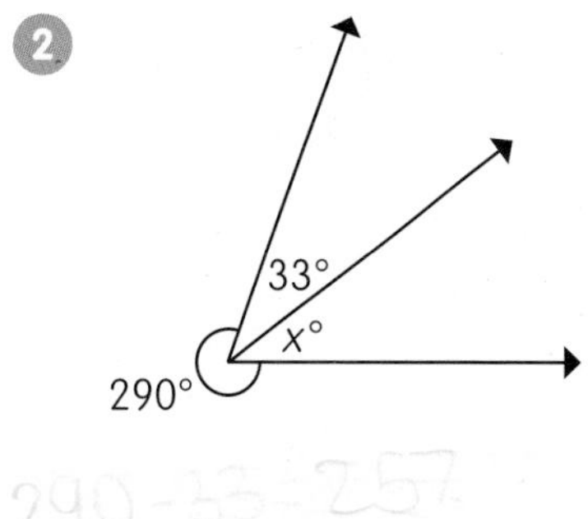

3

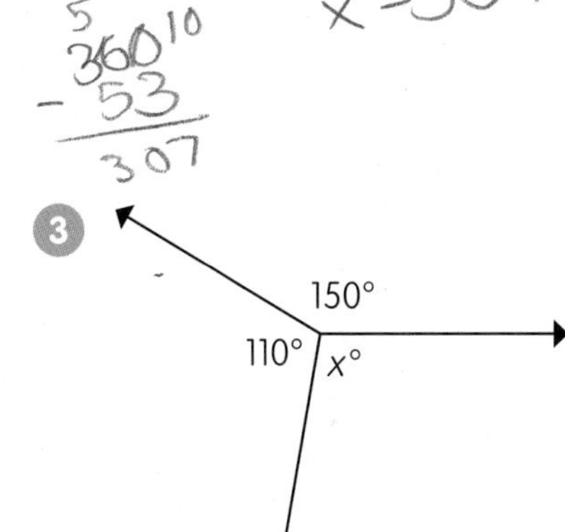

4

60°
x°
110°
95°

5 $\overleftrightarrow{AB}$ and $\overleftrightarrow{CD}$ are straight lines.

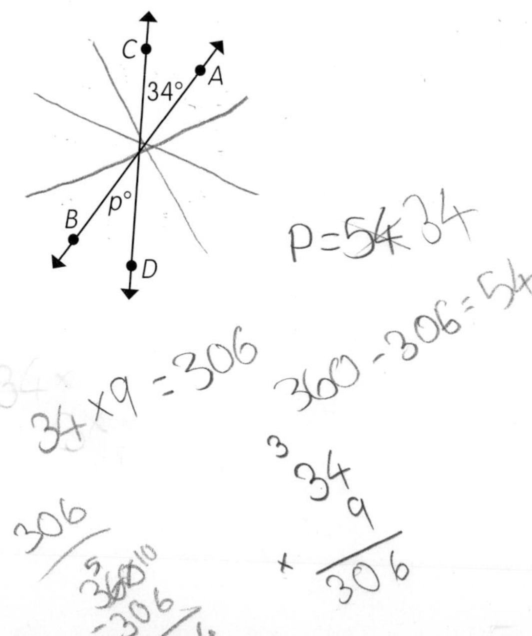

6 $\overleftrightarrow{AB}$ and $\overleftrightarrow{CD}$ are straight lines.

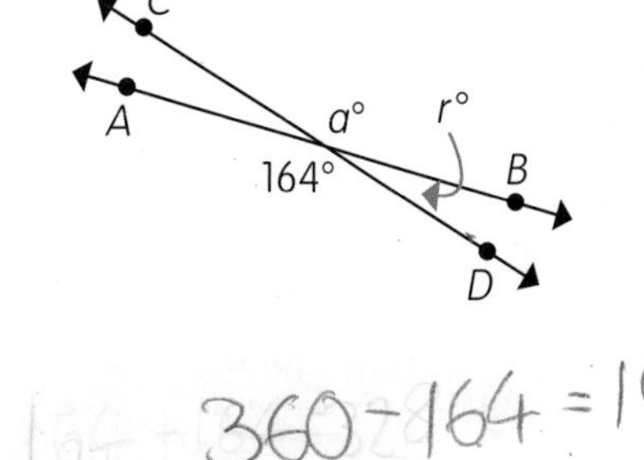

7 $\overleftrightarrow{AB}$, $\overleftrightarrow{CD}$, and $\overleftrightarrow{EF}$ are straight lines.

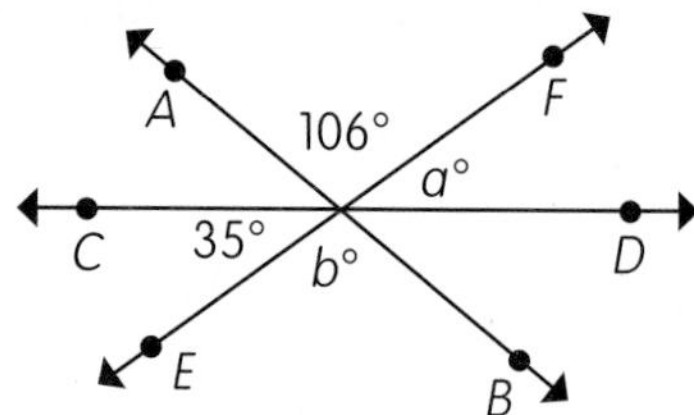

8 $\overleftrightarrow{AB}$, $\overleftrightarrow{CD}$, and $\overleftrightarrow{EF}$ are straight lines.

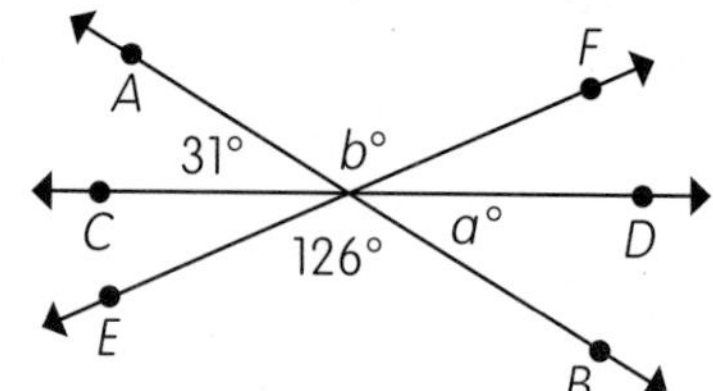

9 $\overleftrightarrow{AB}$, $\overleftrightarrow{CD}$, and $\overleftrightarrow{EF}$ are straight lines.

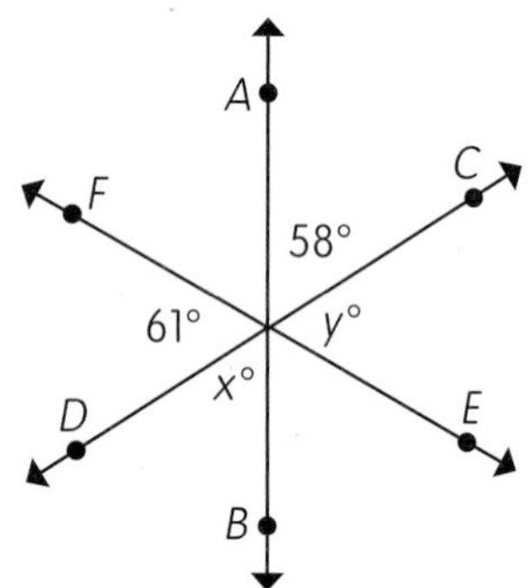

10 $\overleftrightarrow{AB}$ and $\overleftrightarrow{CD}$ are straight lines.

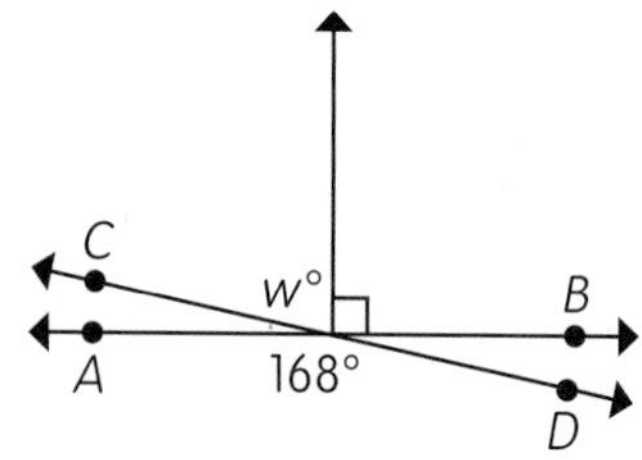

The diagrams may not be drawn to scale. Find the value of *k*.

11 $\angle h : \angle j : \angle k : \angle m = 3 : 2 : 1 : 3$

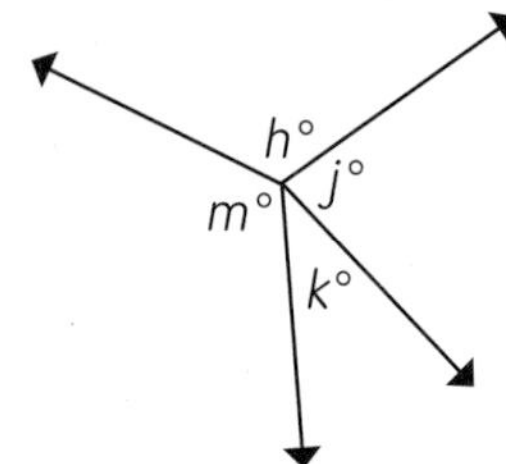

12

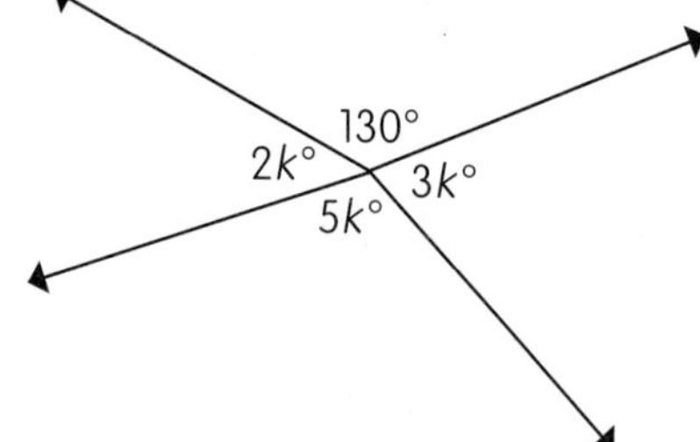

13 $\overleftrightarrow{AB}$ and $\overleftrightarrow{CD}$ are straight lines.

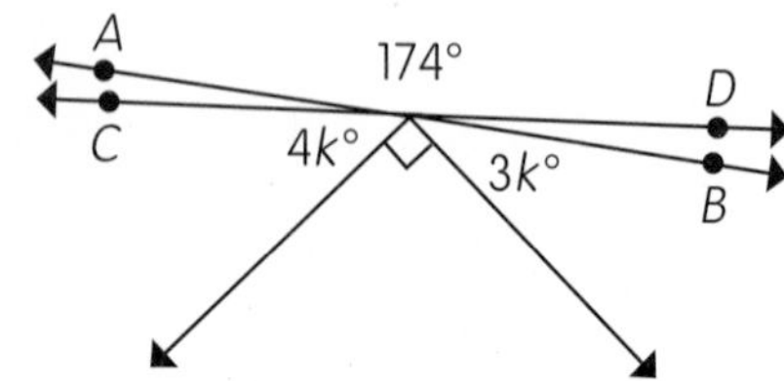

Name the pairs of vertical angles.

14. $\overline{AE}$ and $\overline{BD}$ are straight lines.

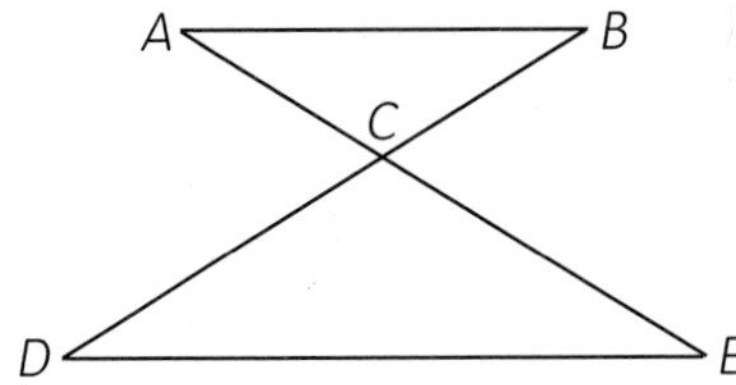

15. $\overleftrightarrow{MN}$ is a straight line and FGH is a triangle.

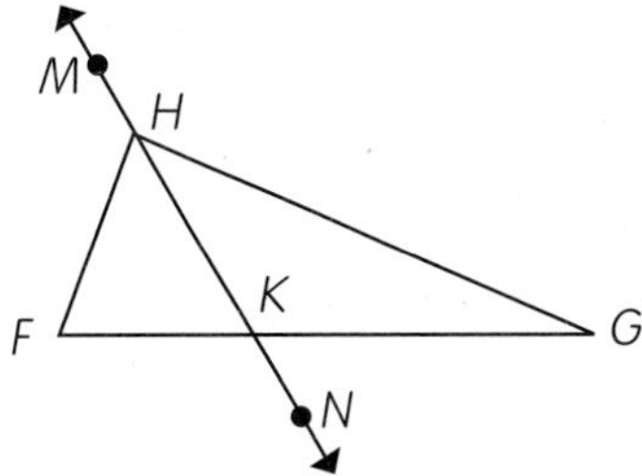

16. $\overleftrightarrow{PS}$ and $\overleftrightarrow{NR}$ are straight lines.

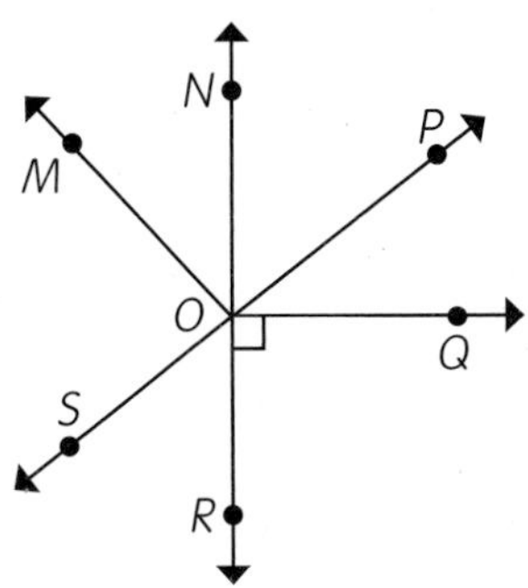

The diagrams may not be drawn to scale. Find the value of each variable.

17.

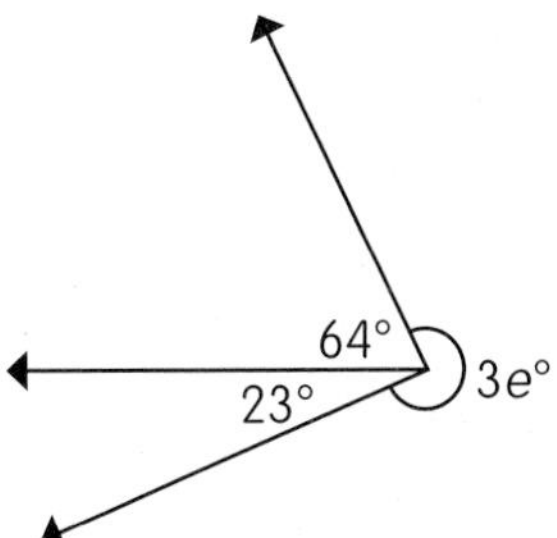

18. $\overleftrightarrow{AB}$ and $\overleftrightarrow{CD}$ are straight lines.

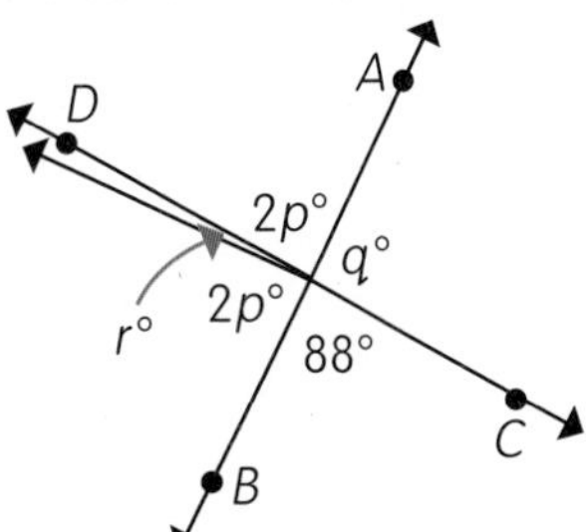

19. $\overleftrightarrow{AB}$, $\overleftrightarrow{CD}$, and $\overleftrightarrow{EF}$ are straight lines. The ratio $a : b : c = 1 : 2 : 2$.

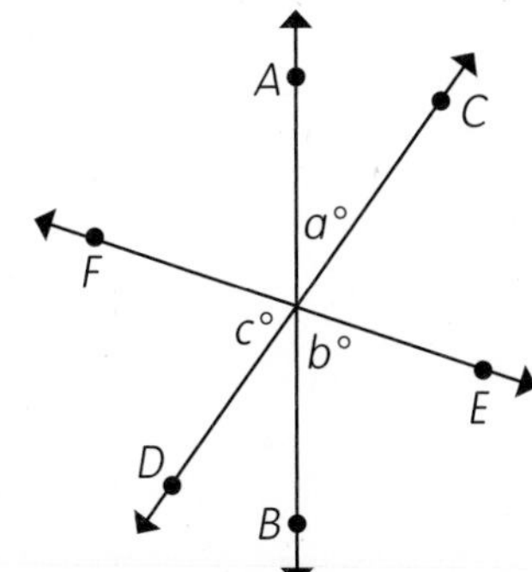

20 $\overleftrightarrow{AB}$ and $\overleftrightarrow{CD}$ are straight lines.

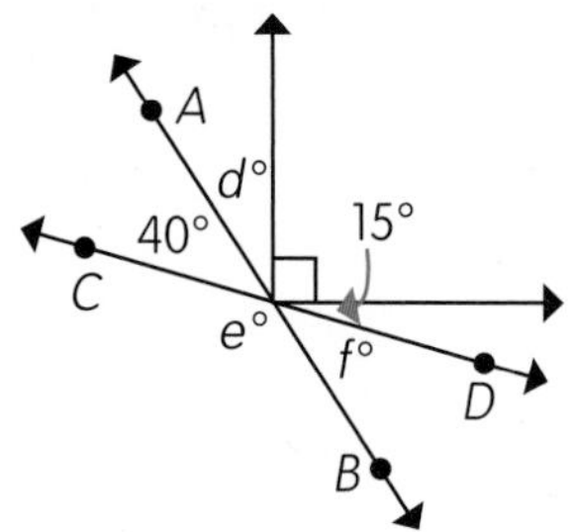

21 In the diagram, the ratio $p : q : r = 1 : 2 : 3$.

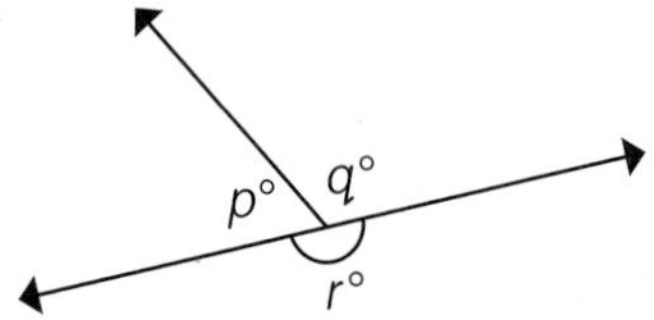

Solve.

22 If $\angle P$ and $\angle N$ are angles at a point and $m\angle P = 149°$, what is $m\angle N$?

23 If 67°, 102°, 15°, and $x°$ are angles at a point, what is the value of x?

24 The diagram may not be drawn to scale. In the diagram, $\overleftrightarrow{MP}$ and $\overleftrightarrow{QR}$ are straight lines.

a Name the angle that is vertical to $\angle MNR$.

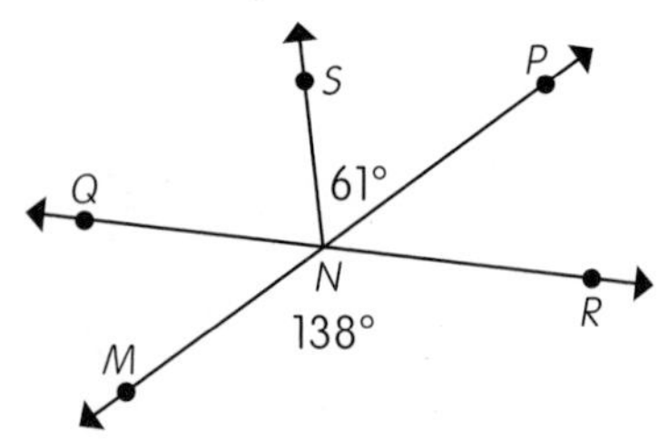

b What kind of angles are $\angle RNP$ and $\angle PNS$?

c Find the measure of $\angle QNS$.

d Find the measure of $\angle PNR$.

The diagrams may not be drawn to scale. Find the value of each variable.

25 $\overleftrightarrow{AB}$ is a straight line.

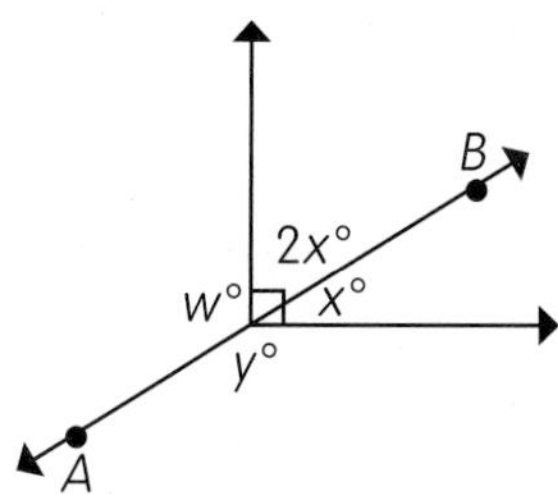

26 $\overleftrightarrow{AB}$ and $\overleftrightarrow{CD}$ are straight lines.

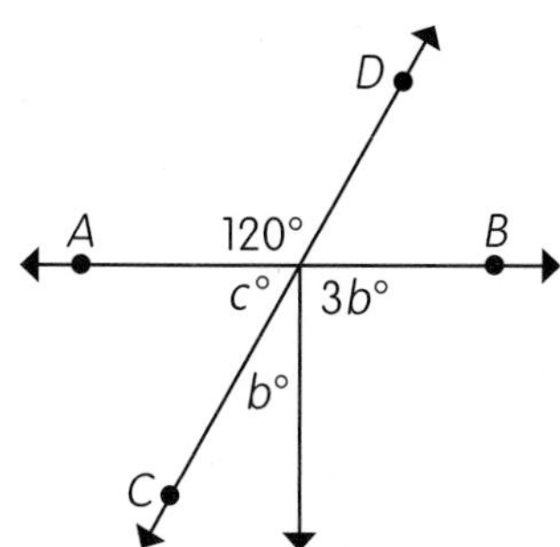

The diagrams may not be drawn to scale. $\overleftrightarrow{AB}$ and $\overleftrightarrow{CD}$ are intersecting straight lines. Find the values of p and q.

27 $\angle s : \angle r = 3 : 1$

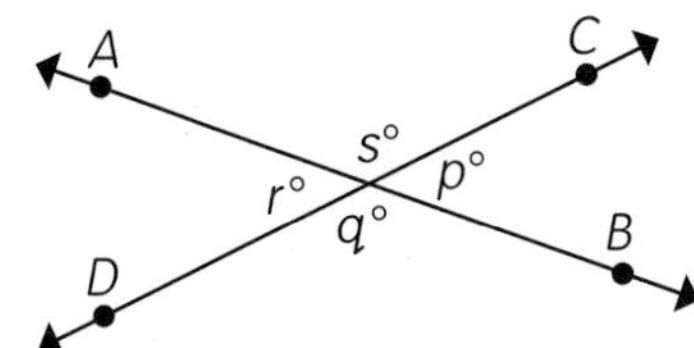

28

C
A
$2p°$
$q°$
$(p + 50)°$
B
D

Solve.

29 The diagram below shows the flag of the Philippines. m$\angle ADB$ = 60° and m$\angle ADC$ = m$\angle BDC$. Find the measures of $\angle ADC$ and $\angle BDC$.

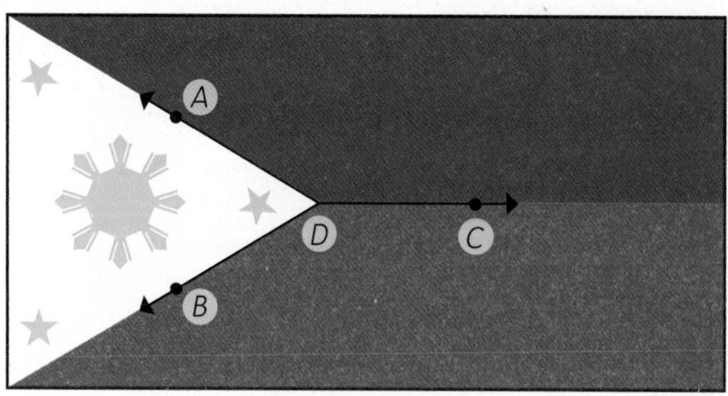

30 **Mathematical Habit 2 Use mathematical reasoning**

The diagram shows a pattern on a carpet.

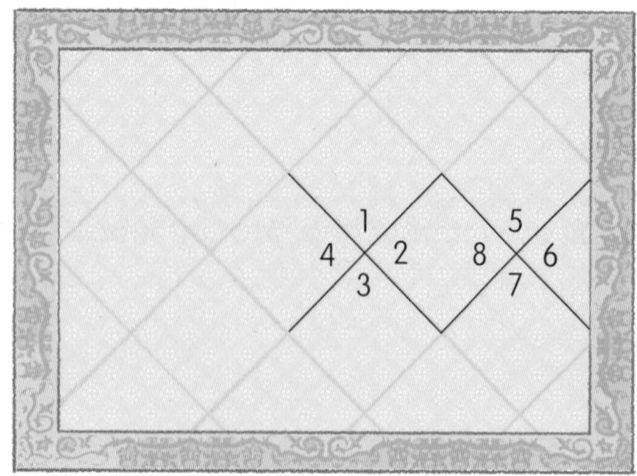

a Are $\angle 4$ and $\angle 6$ vertical angles? Explain your answer.

b Given that m$\angle 4$ = m$\angle 6$, are $\angle 4$ and $\angle 5$ supplementary angles? Explain your answer.

Name: ______________________ Date: ______________

3 Alternate Interior, Alternate Exterior, and Corresponding Angles

Learning Objectives:

- Identify the type of angles formed by parallel lines and a transversal.
- Write and solve equations to find unknown angle measures.

New Vocabulary
transversal
alternate interior angles
alternate exterior angles
corresponding angles

$\overrightarrow{BA}$ is parallel to $\overrightarrow{DC}$.
Without measuring, find the value of x.

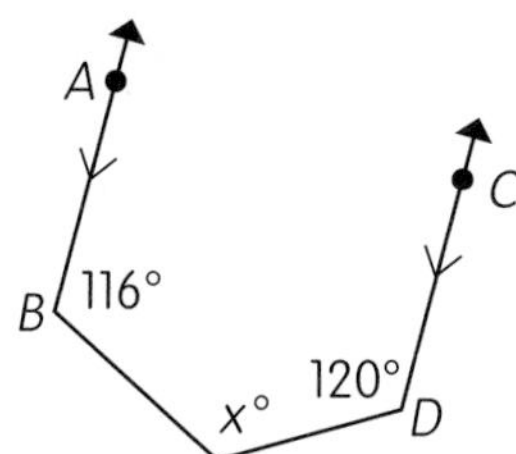

ENGAGE

Draw a pair of parallel lines, and then draw a line that intersects the pair of lines. Measure each angle formed. What do you notice about the angles? What relationship can you see?

LEARN Identify the type of angles formed by parallel lines and a transversal

Activity Exploring the angles formed by lines cut by a transversal

Work in pairs.

① Use a geometry software to construct two line segments, $\overline{AB}$ and $\overline{CD}$. Then, construct a third line segment, $\overline{PQ}$, that intersects $\overline{AB}$ and $\overline{CD}$.

Example:

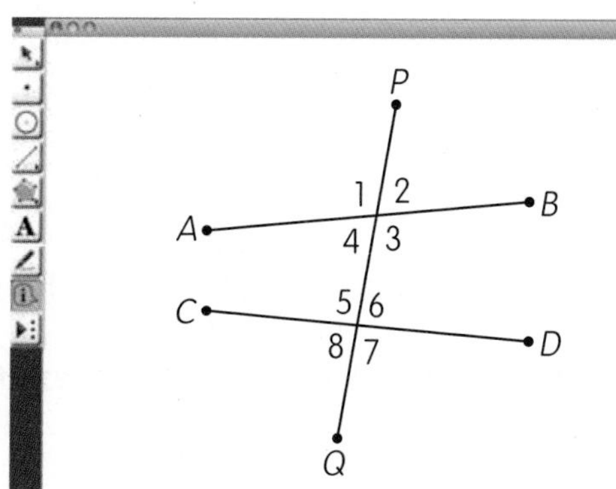

② There are eight angles formed when $\overline{PQ}$ intersects $\overline{AB}$ and $\overline{CD}$. Select each of the angles and find their measures. Record your results in the table.

m∠1	m∠2	m∠3	m∠4	m∠5	m∠6	m∠7	m∠8

③ Select the points B and D and drag them so that you change the measures of all the angles. Record the angle measures in the table.

④ Now, adjust one of the points so that $\overline{AB}$ and $\overline{CD}$ become parallel lines. What do you notice about the angle measures now? Which pairs of angles are the same?

1 The symbol || is used to denote parallel lines. In the diagram below, line AB is parallel to line CD. So, you can write $\overleftrightarrow{AB} \parallel \overleftrightarrow{CD}$.

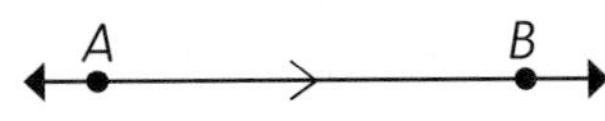

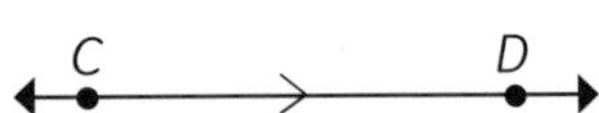

In the diagram below, $\overleftrightarrow{PQ}$ intersects $\overleftrightarrow{AB}$ and $\overleftrightarrow{CD}$. A line that crosses two or more lines is called a transversal. So, $\overleftrightarrow{PQ}$ is a transversal of $\overleftrightarrow{AB}$ and $\overleftrightarrow{CD}$.

A line that crosses two or more nonparallel lines is also called a transversal.

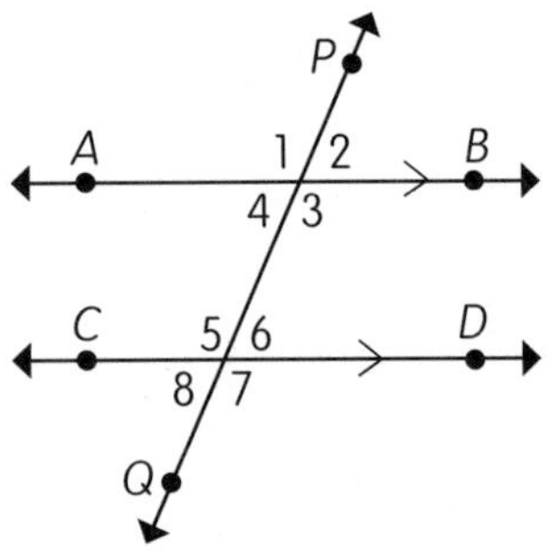

Eight angles are formed when $\overleftrightarrow{PQ}$ intersects $\overleftrightarrow{AB}$ and $\overleftrightarrow{CD}$.

A transversal forms angle pairs with special names.
$\angle 3$, $\angle 4$, $\angle 5$, and $\angle 6$ are between the parallel lines. They are called interior angles.
$\angle 1$, $\angle 2$, $\angle 7$, and $\angle 8$ are outside the parallel lines. They are called exterior angles.

2 Alternate interior angles are a pair of angles that lie inside the pair of parallel lines, and are on the opposite sides of the transversal.
$\angle 3$ and $\angle 5$ are alternate interior angles. $\angle 4$ and $\angle 6$ are also alternate interior angles.

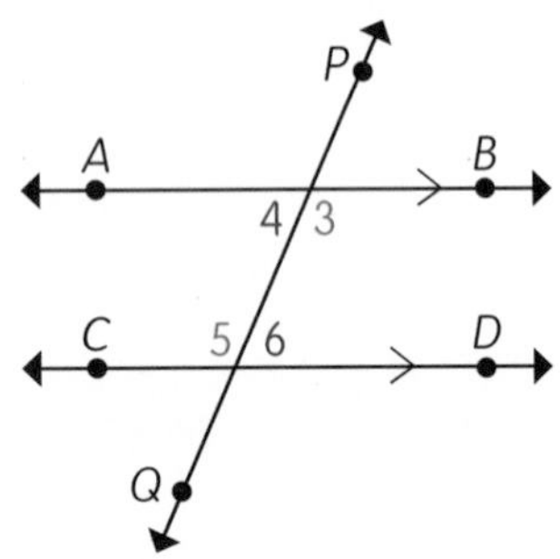

3 Alternate exterior angles are a pair of angles that lie outside the pair of parallel lines, and are on the opposite sides of the transversal.
∠1 and ∠7 are alternate exterior angles. ∠2 and ∠8 are also alternate exterior angles.

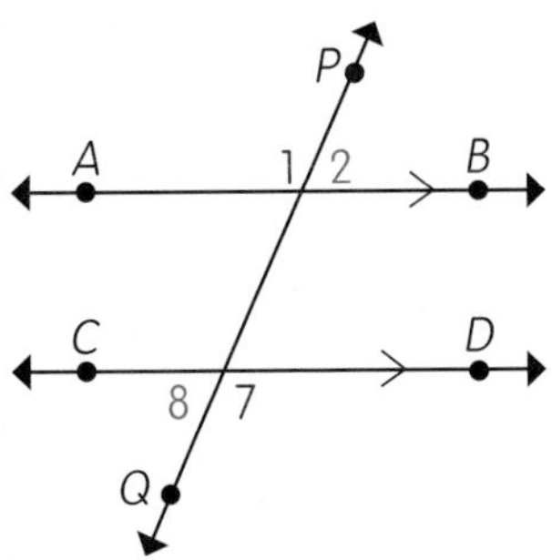

4 ∠1 and ∠5 are corresponding angles. ∠4 and ∠8 are also corresponding angles.
There are four pairs of corresponding angles in the diagram. What are the other two pairs?

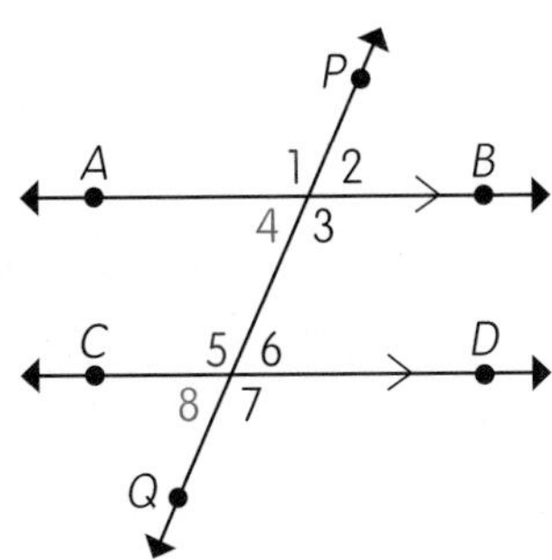

What do you notice about the measures of these angle pairs:
Alternate interior angles, alternate exterior angles, and corresponding angles?
Make a conjecture about the angle measures for each pair.

When two parallel lines are cut by a transversal,

- the alternate interior angles are always congruent (alt. int. ∠s, || lines).
- the alternate exterior angles are always congruent (alt. ext. ∠s, || lines).
- the corresponding angles are always congruent (corr. ∠s, || lines).

TRY Practice identifying the type of angles formed by parallel lines and a transversal

Use the diagram on the right to answer each question.

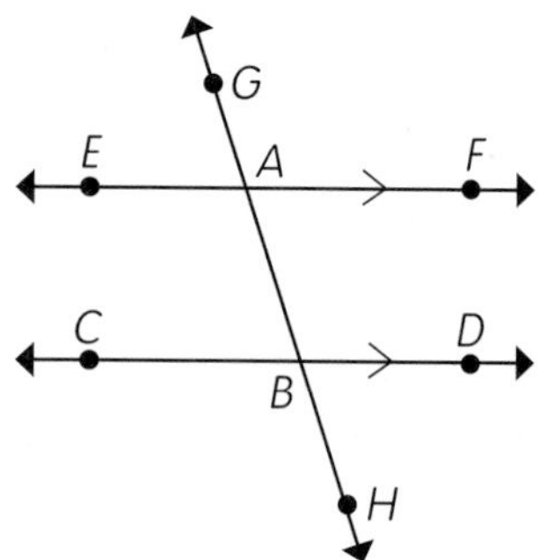

1. $\overleftrightarrow{EF}$, $\overleftrightarrow{CD}$, and $\overleftrightarrow{GH}$ are straight lines. $\overleftrightarrow{EF} \parallel \overleftrightarrow{CD}$.
   a Identify two pairs of alternate interior angles.

   b Identify two pairs of alternate exterior angles.

   c Identify two pairs of corresponding angles.

Use the diagram on the right to answer each question.

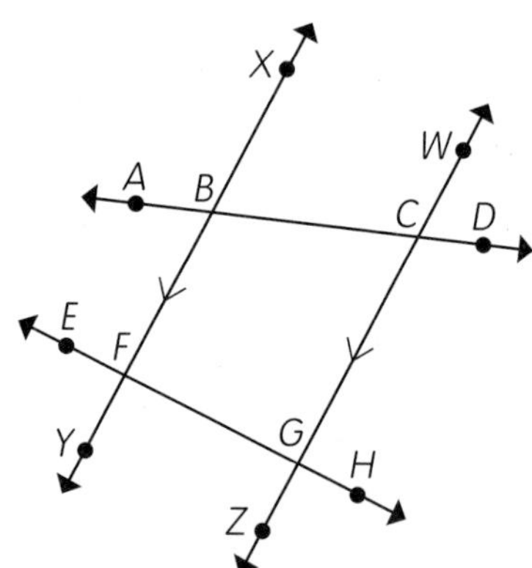

2. $\overleftrightarrow{AD}$, $\overleftrightarrow{EH}$, $\overleftrightarrow{XY}$, and $\overleftrightarrow{WZ}$ are straight lines. $\overleftrightarrow{XY} \parallel \overleftrightarrow{WZ}$.
   Identify all the pairs of angles formed by the intersection of $\overleftrightarrow{AD}$ with $\overleftrightarrow{XY}$ and $\overleftrightarrow{WZ}$.

   a Corresponding angles

   b Alternate interior angles

   c Alternate exterior angles

3. Name another transversal of the parallel lines in the diagram.

4. Identify all the pairs of angles formed by the intersection of the transversal you have identified in 3 with $\overleftrightarrow{XY}$ and $\overleftrightarrow{WZ}$.

   a Corresponding angles

   b Alternate interior angles

   c Alternate exterior angles

ENGAGE

Consider the diagram shown. Measure angle 4. Can you determine the measure of the remaining angles by using only the one measurement? Explain your thinking.

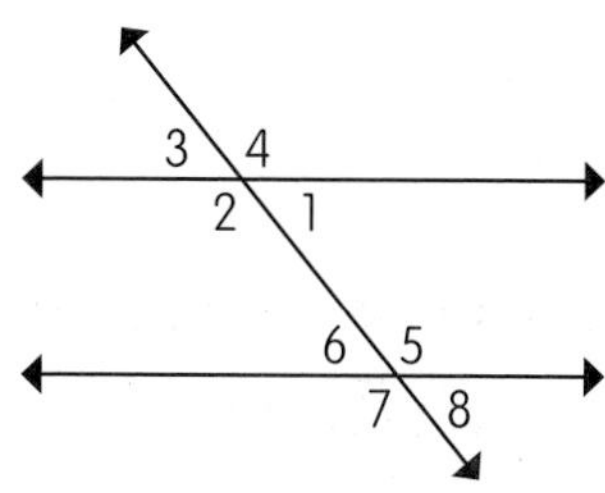

LEARN Solve problems involving parallel lines and transversals

1 The diagram may not be drawn to scale. In the diagram, $\overleftrightarrow{MN}$ is parallel to $\overleftrightarrow{PQ}$. $\overleftrightarrow{ST}$ is a straight line. m∠6 = 123°. Find each of the following angle measures.

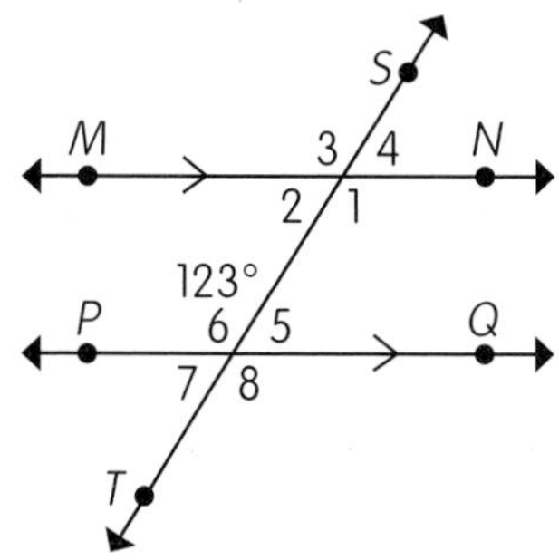

a m∠3

$\overleftrightarrow{MN}$ is parallel to $\overleftrightarrow{PQ}$ and $\overleftrightarrow{ST}$ is the transversal.

m∠3 = m∠6 = 123° Corr. ∠s

b m∠1

m∠1 = m∠6 = 123° Alt. int. ∠s

c m∠2

∠2 and ∠3 are supplementary angles.

m∠2 + m∠3 = 180°	Supp. ∠s
m∠2 + 123° = 180°	Substitute.
m∠2 + 123° **− 123°** = 180° **− 123°**	Subtract 123° from both sides.
m∠2 = 57°	Simplify.

How do you find the rest of the angle measures? Explain.

TRY Practice solving problems involving parallel lines and transversals

The diagrams may not be drawn to scale. Solve.

1. In the diagram, $\overleftrightarrow{MN}$ is parallel to $\overleftrightarrow{PQ}$. $\overleftrightarrow{ST}$ is a straight line. Find the measures of $\angle 1$, $\angle 2$, and $\angle 3$.

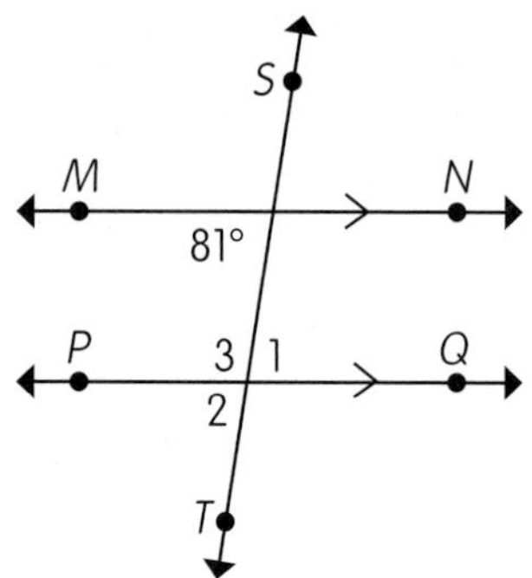

$m\angle 1 =$ ______	Alt. int. $\angle$s
$m\angle 2 =$ ______	Corr. $\angle$s
$m\angle 3 +$ ______ $= 180°$	Supp. $\angle$s
$m\angle 3 +$ ______ $= 180°$	Substitute $m\angle 2 =$ ______.
$m\angle 3 +$ ______ $-$ ______ $= 180° -$ ______	Subtract ______ from both sides.
$m\angle 3 =$ ______	Simplify.

2. In the diagram, $\overleftrightarrow{HJ}$ is parallel to $\overleftrightarrow{KM}$. $\overleftrightarrow{NP}$ is a straight line. Find the values of a and b.

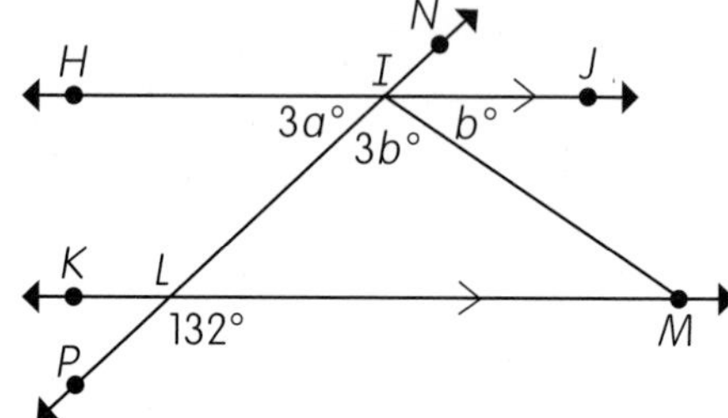

Name: ______________________ Date: ______________

INDEPENDENT PRACTICE

$\overleftrightarrow{MN}$ is parallel to $\overleftrightarrow{PQ}$. $\overleftrightarrow{ST}$ is a straight line. Identify each pair of angles as corresponding, alternate interior, alternate exterior angles, or none of the above.

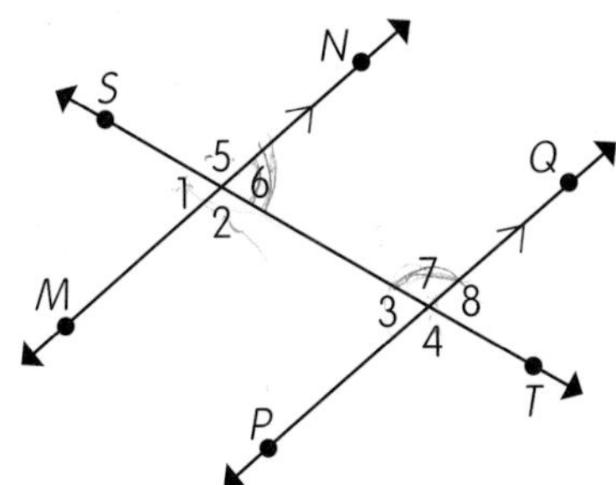

1. ∠3, ∠6 alternate interior
2. ∠5, ∠7 corresponding
3. ∠1, ∠2 none
4. ∠1, ∠8 corresponding ✗ alt exterior
5. ∠6, ∠8 corresponding
6. ∠4, ∠7 none (vertical angles)
7. ∠2, ∠7 alternate interior
8. ∠6, ∠7 corresponding ✗ none

$\overleftrightarrow{AB}$ is parallel to $\overleftrightarrow{CD}$. $\overleftrightarrow{EF}$ is a straight line. Use the diagram to answer each question.

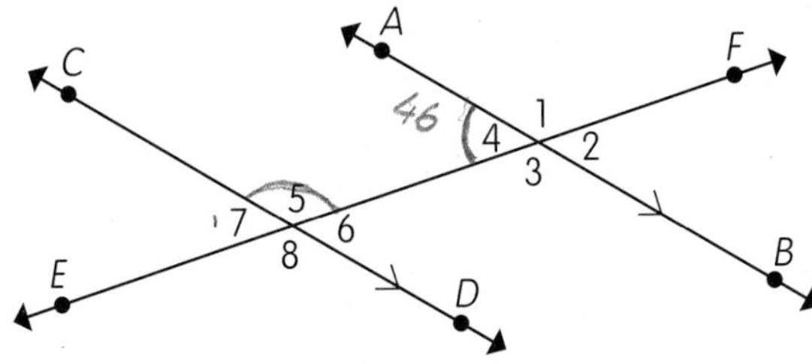

9. Name two angles that have the same measure as ∠2. 4, 6, 7
10. Name an angle that is supplementary to ∠6. 5, 8
11. If m∠4 = 46°, find m∠5. 134   180 − 46 = 134
12. If m∠1 = 131°, find m∠7.

The diagrams may not be drawn to scale. Find the measure of each numbered angle.

13. $\overleftrightarrow{MN}$ is parallel to $\overleftrightarrow{PQ}$.
$\overleftrightarrow{ST}$ is a straight line.

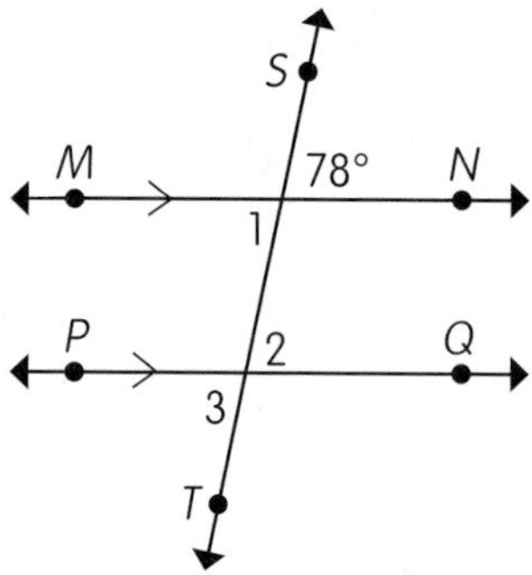

14. $\overleftrightarrow{MN}$ is parallel to $\overleftrightarrow{PQ}$.
$\overleftrightarrow{ST}$ is a straight line.

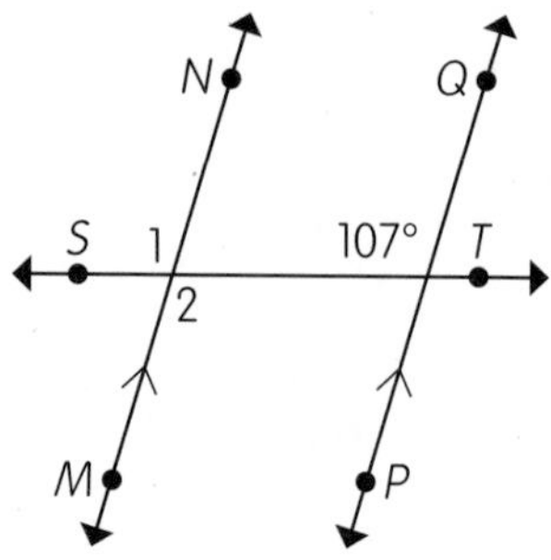

15. $\overrightarrow{PQ}$ is parallel to $\overrightarrow{RS}$.
$\overrightarrow{PT}$ is a straight line.

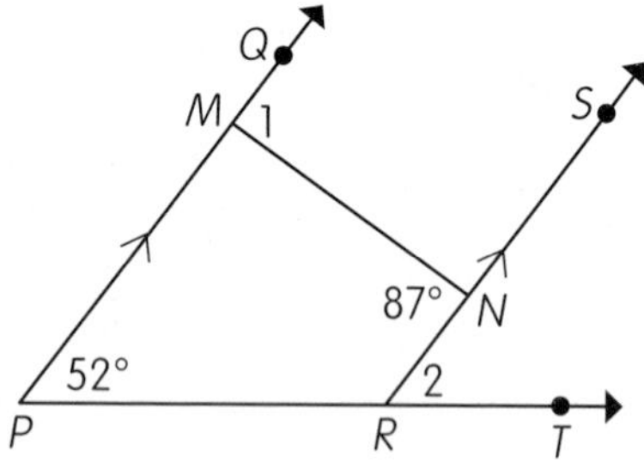

16. $\overleftrightarrow{PQ}$ is parallel to $\overleftrightarrow{RS}$.
$\overleftrightarrow{AB}$ is a straight line.

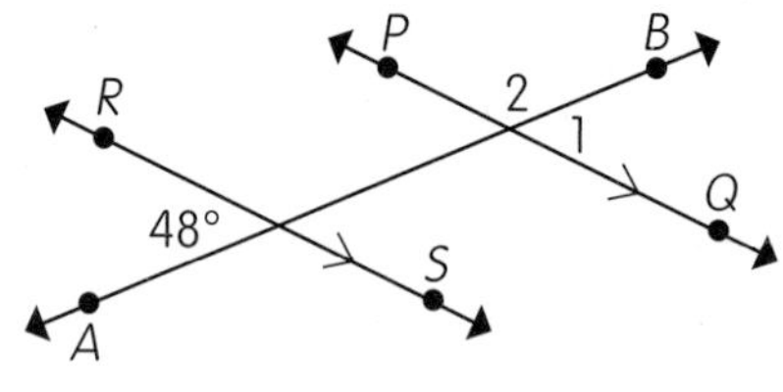

17. $\overleftrightarrow{AB}$ is parallel to $\overleftrightarrow{CD}$ and
$\overleftrightarrow{MN}$ is parallel to $\overleftrightarrow{PQ}$.

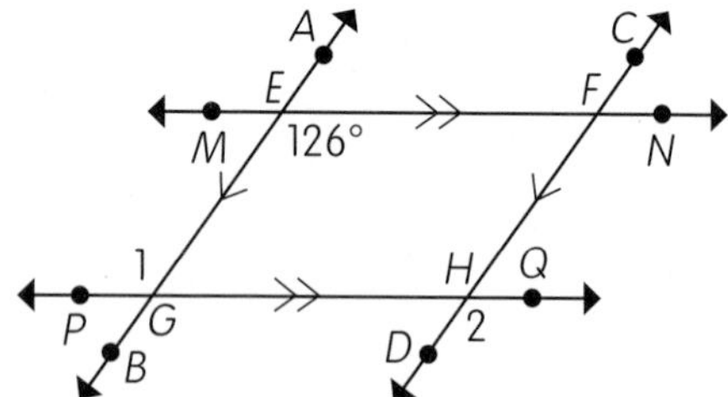

18. $\overleftrightarrow{AB}$ is parallel to $\overleftrightarrow{CD}$ and
$\overleftrightarrow{MN}$ is parallel to $\overleftrightarrow{PQ}$.

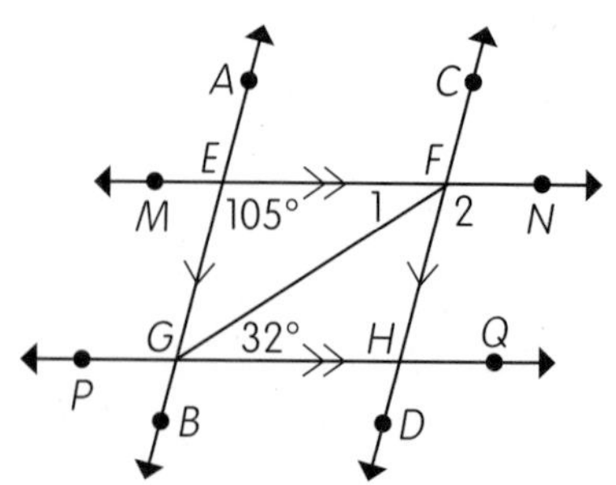

The diagrams may not be drawn to scale. Find the value of each variable.

19. $\overleftrightarrow{PQ}$ is parallel to $\overleftrightarrow{RS}$.
$\overleftrightarrow{TU}$ is a straight line.

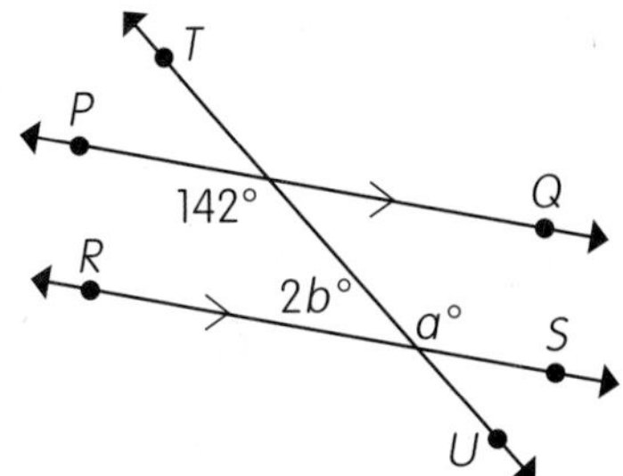

20. $\overleftrightarrow{PQ}$ is parallel to $\overleftrightarrow{RS}$.
$\overleftrightarrow{TU}$ is a straight line.

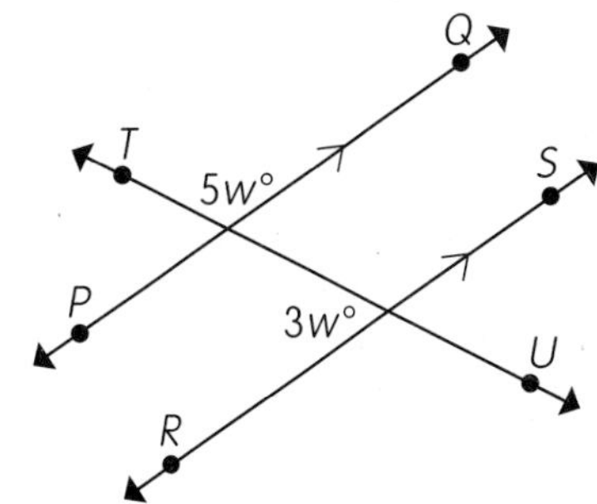

Mathematical Habit 2 Use mathematical reasoning

The diagrams may not be drawn to scale. Given that $\overleftrightarrow{RS}$ is a straight line, determine whether $\overleftrightarrow{AB}$ is parallel to $\overleftrightarrow{CD}$.
Explain your answer.

21.

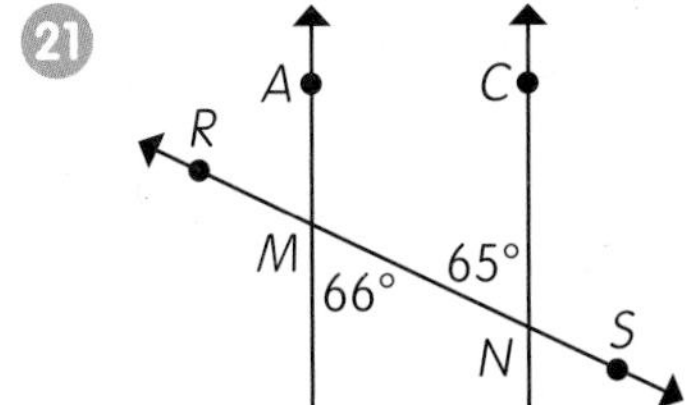

Two lines are parallel if a pair of corresponding angles formed by a transversal are congruent.

22.

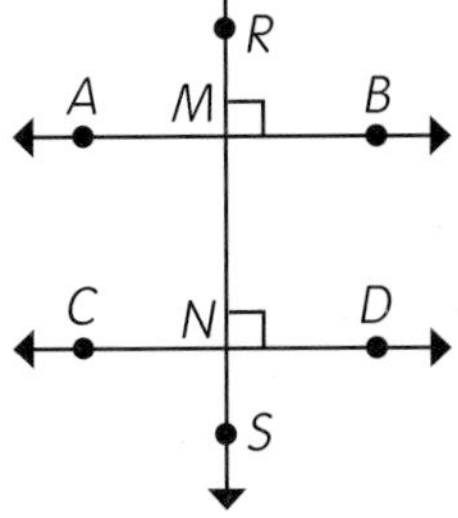

23.

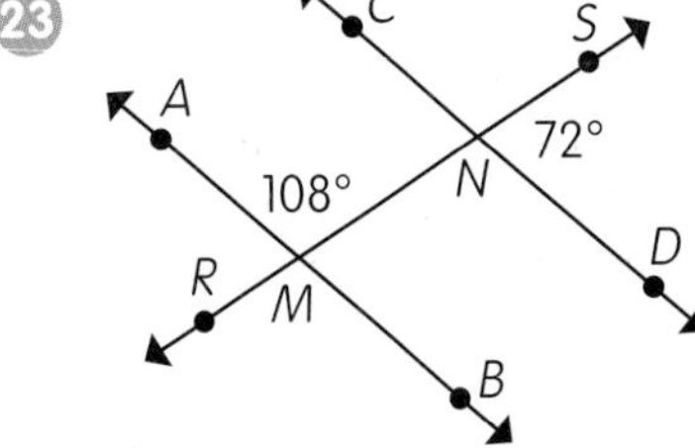

The diagrams may not be drawn to scale. $\overline{MN}$ is parallel to $\overline{PQ}$.
Find the measure of each numbered angle.

24. $\overleftrightarrow{RS}$ is a straight line.

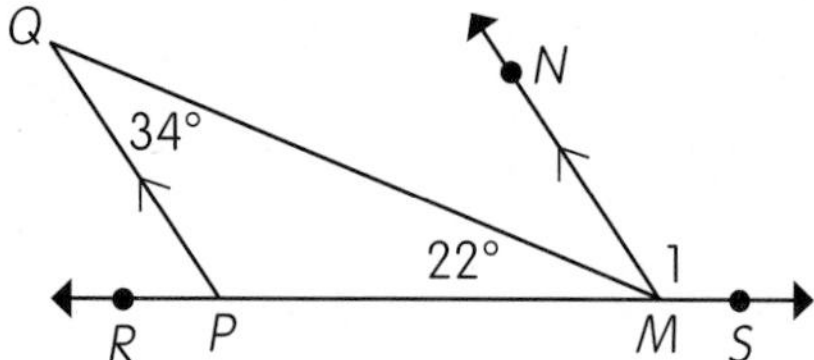

25. $\overrightarrow{MS}$ is a straight line.

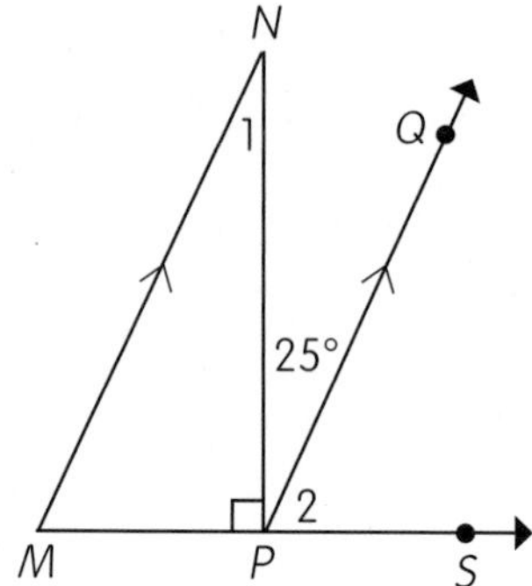

26. $\overleftrightarrow{ST}$ is a straight line.

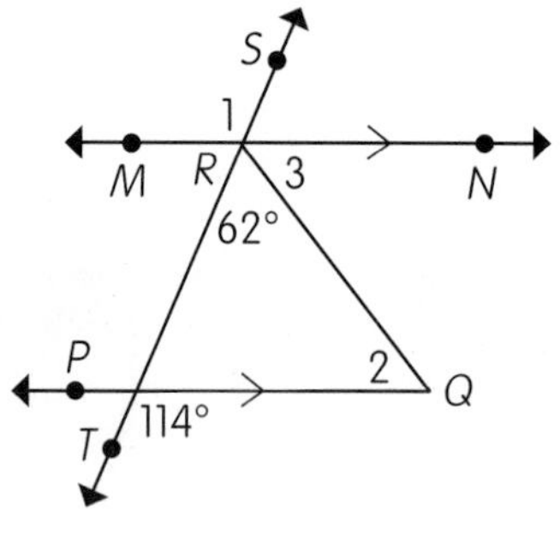

27. $\overrightarrow{PR}$ is a straight line.

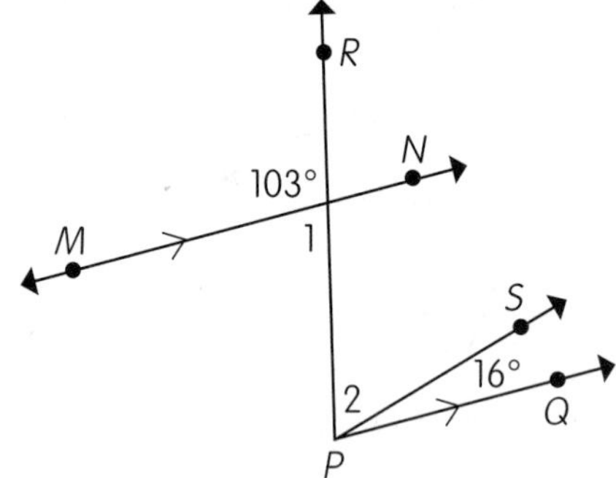

28. $\overleftrightarrow{AD}$ and $\overleftrightarrow{EH}$ are straight lines.

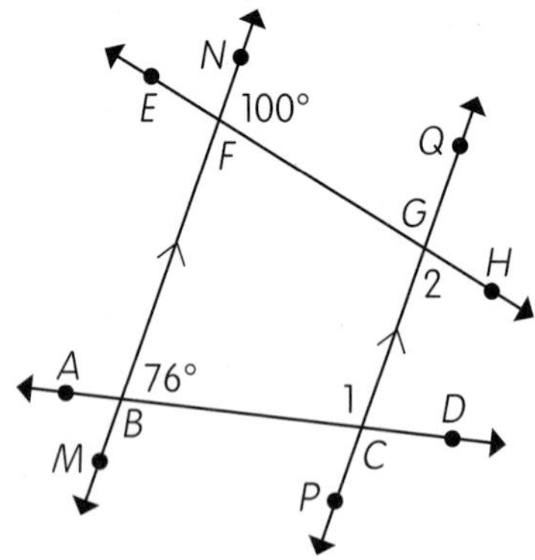

29. $\overrightarrow{MS}$ is a straight line.

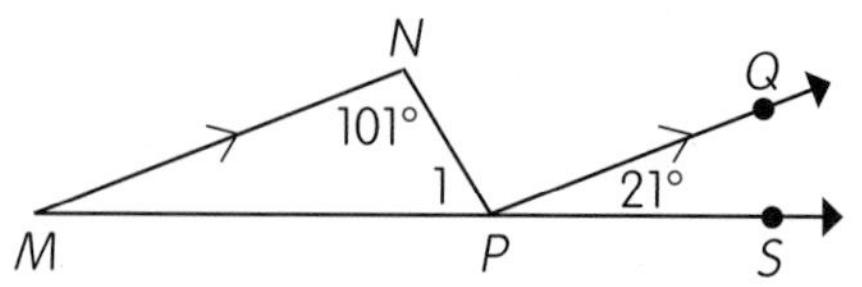

The diagrams may not be drawn to scale. $\overline{AB}$ is parallel to $\overline{CD}$. Find the value of x.

30 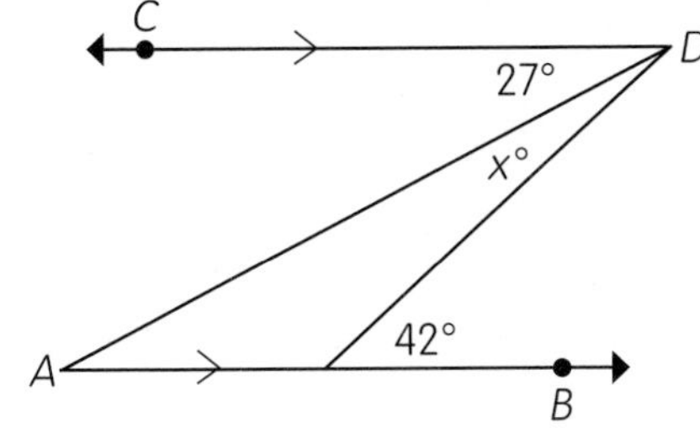

31 
$\overrightarrow{BP}$ is a straight line.

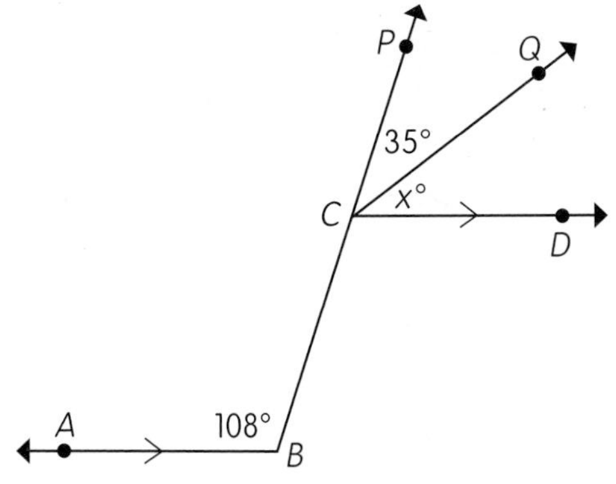

32 $\overrightarrow{BQ}$ and $\overrightarrow{DP}$ are straight lines.

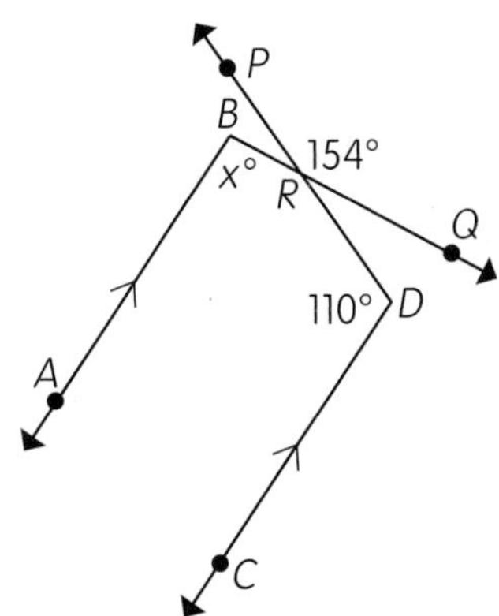

33 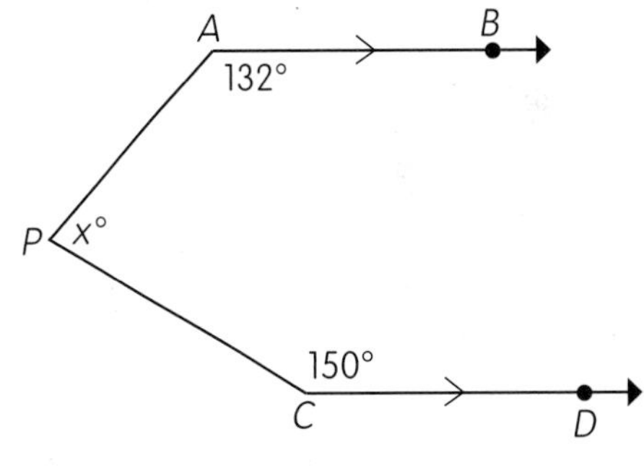

Solve.

34 In the diagram, $\overleftrightarrow{MN}$ is parallel to $\overleftrightarrow{PQ}$. $\overleftrightarrow{NP}$ is a straight line. $m\angle 1 = (x + 28)°$ and $m\angle 2 = (3x + 14)°$. Write and solve an equation to find the measures of $\angle 1$ and $\angle 2$.

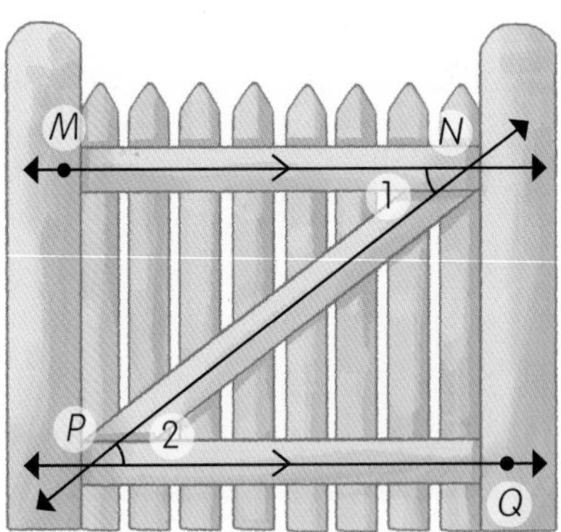

35 **Mathematical Habit 2 Use mathematical reasoning**
In a plane, if a line is perpendicular to one of two parallel lines, is it also perpendicular to the other? Explain your reasoning.

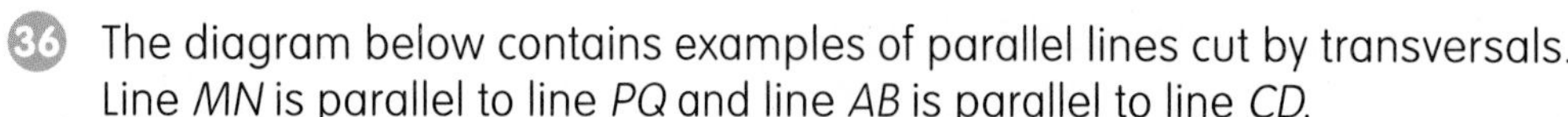

36 The diagram below contains examples of parallel lines cut by transversals. Line MN is parallel to line PQ and line AB is parallel to line CD.

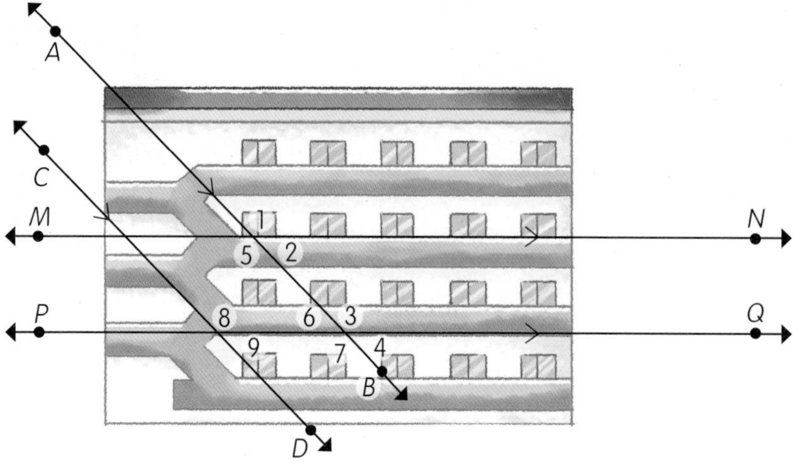

a Name two pairs of corresponding angles.

b Name all the angles that have the same measure as $\angle 1$.

37 The two mirrors used in a periscope are parallel to each other as shown. $m\angle 1 = 3x°$, $m\angle 2 = (60 - x)°$, and $m\angle 3 = 90°$. Write and solve an equation to find the value of x. Then, find the measure of $\angle 4$.

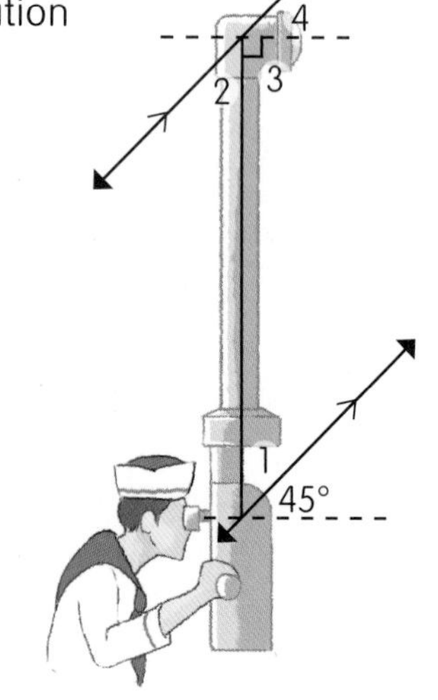

38 **Mathematical Habit 4 Use mathematical models**

Use a diagram to illustrate each of the following: transversal, corresponding angles, alternate exterior angles, and alternate interior angles. Label your diagram and explain which angles are congruent.

Name: ______________________ Date: ______________

Interior and Exterior Angles

Learning Objectives:
- Explore and apply the properties of the interior angles of a triangle.
- Explore and apply the properties of the exterior angles of a triangle.

New Vocabulary
interior angles
exterior angles

In the diagram, $\overleftrightarrow{AC}$ is parallel $\overleftrightarrow{DF}$ and $\overleftrightarrow{CG}$ is a straight line. *AEC* and *DBF* are identical isosceles triangles. Find the measures of $\angle DBF$ and $\angle AHD$.

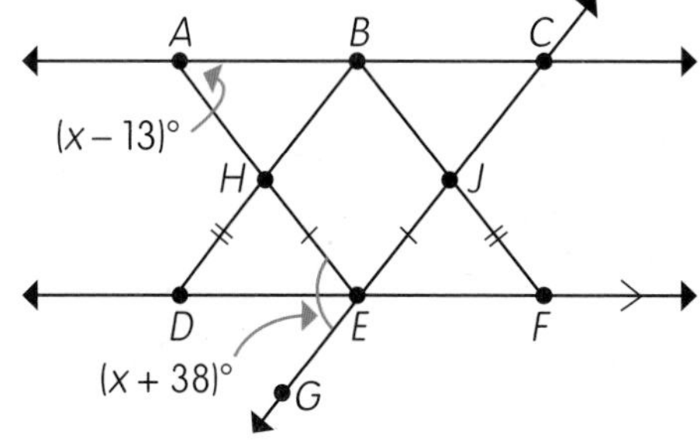

ENGAGE

a Is it possible to draw a triangle with angle measures of 80°, 90°, and 50°? Use a protractor to show why or why not.

b Based on your drawing and deduction, find three angles that can be used to draw a triangle.

LEARN Use the angle sum of a triangle to find unknown angle measures

Activity Exploring the angle sum of a triangle

Work in pairs.

① Draw and cut out a triangle. Label the three interior angles of the triangle as 1, 2, and 3.

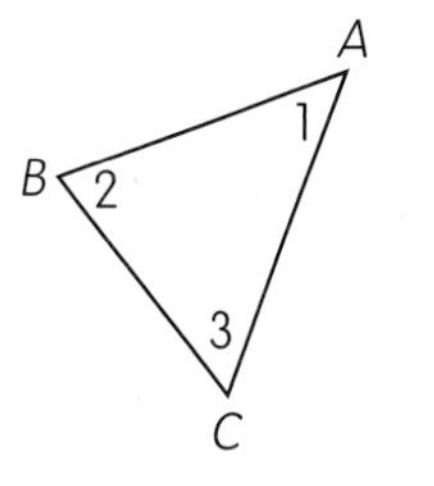

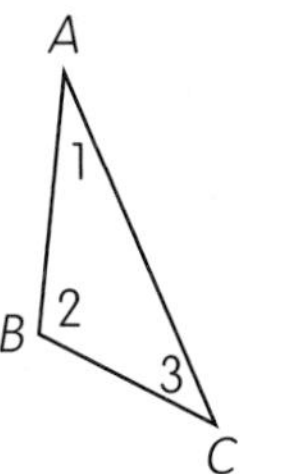

② Cut out the three angles. Then, arrange them on a straight line.

What do you notice about the sum of the measures of the three interior angles?

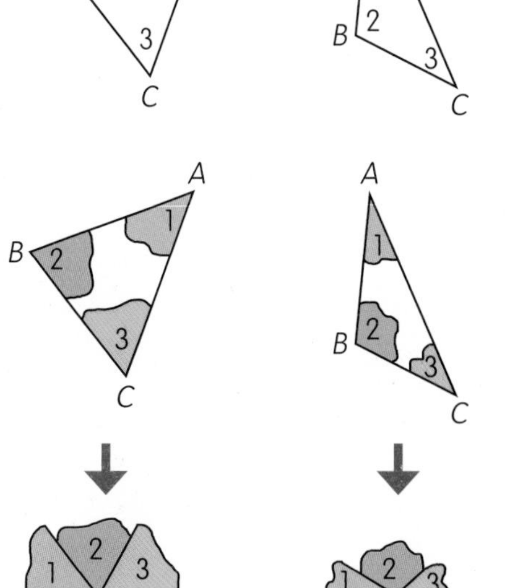

The sum of the measures of the interior angles of any triangle is 180°. This relationship is also called the angle sum of a triangle.

1. The diagram may not be drawn to scale. In triangle PQR, m$\angle QRP = 48°$ and m$\angle PQR = 31°$. Find the value of x.

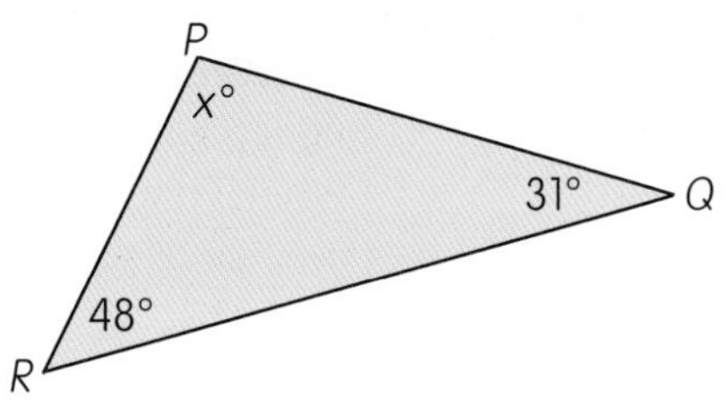

m$\angle RPQ$ + m$\angle QRP$ + m$\angle RQP = 180°$	$\angle$ sum of triangle
$x + 48 + 31 = 180$	Substitute.
$x + 79 = 180$	Simplify.
$x + 79 - \mathbf{79} = 180 - \mathbf{79}$	Subtract 79 from both sides.
$x = 101$	Simplify.

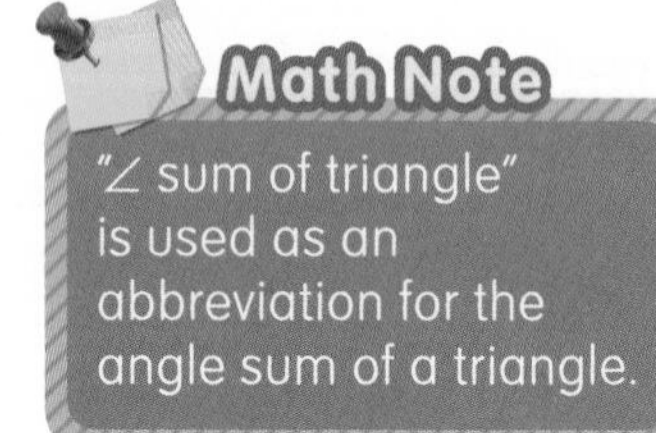

"$\angle$ sum of triangle" is used as an abbreviation for the angle sum of a triangle.

2. The diagram may not be drawn to scale. Triangle PQR is an isosceles triangle where m$\angle QPR = 40°$. Find the value of x.

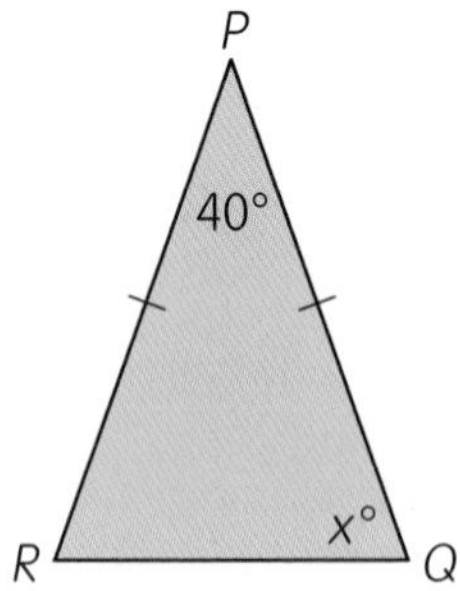

In an isosceles triangle, the angles opposite the congruent sides are congruent.

m$\angle PRQ$ = m$\angle PQR = x°$	Isosceles triangle
m$\angle QPR$ + m$\angle PQR$ + m$\angle PRQ = 180°$	$\angle$ sum of triangle
$40 + x + x = 180$	Substitute.
$40 + 2x = 180$	Simplify.
$40 + 2x - \mathbf{40} = 180 - \mathbf{40}$	Subtract 40 from both sides.
$2x = 140$	Simplify.
$\frac{2x}{\mathbf{2}} = \frac{140}{\mathbf{2}}$	Divide both sides by 2.
$x = 70$	Simplify.

TRY Practice using the angle sum of a triangle to find unknown angle measures

The diagrams may not be drawn to scale. Solve.

1. Find the value of p.

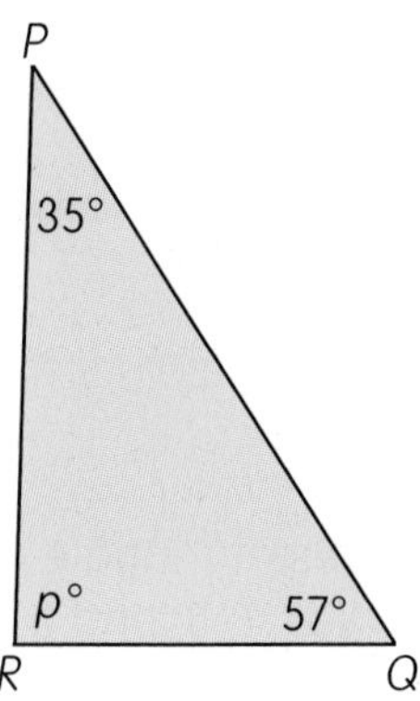

m∠RPQ + m∠QRP + m∠PQR = ______ ∠sum of triangle

______ + ______ + ______ = ______ Substitute.

______ + ______ = ______ Simplify.

______ + ______ − ______ = ______ − ______ Subtract ______ from both sides.

______ = ______ Simplify.

2. Triangle XYZ is an isosceles triangle and m∠XYZ = 55°.
Find the value of x.

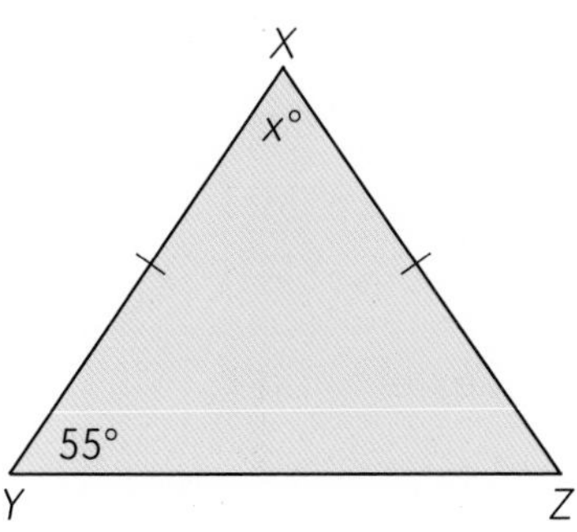

m∠XZY + m∠XYZ + m∠ZXY = ______ ∠sum of triangle

______ + ______ + ______ = ______ Substitute.

______ + ______ = ______ Simplify.

______ + ______ − ______ = ______ − ______ Subtract ______ from both sides.

______ = ______ Simplify.

ENGAGE

Use a ruler to draw a triangle. Then, extend the sides of the triangle as shown. How many angles can you identify that are related to the triangle? Use a protractor to measure one of the interior angles. With the angle measure you have found, how do you find all the other angle measures without measuring them? Share your method.

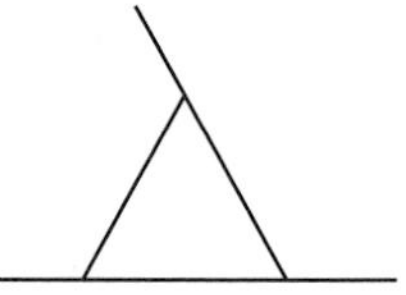

LEARN Use exterior angle relationships to find unknown angle measures

Activity Exploring the exterior angles of a triangle

Work in pairs.

1. Draw triangle *ABC*. Label the three interior angles of the triangle as 1, 2, and 3.

   Example:

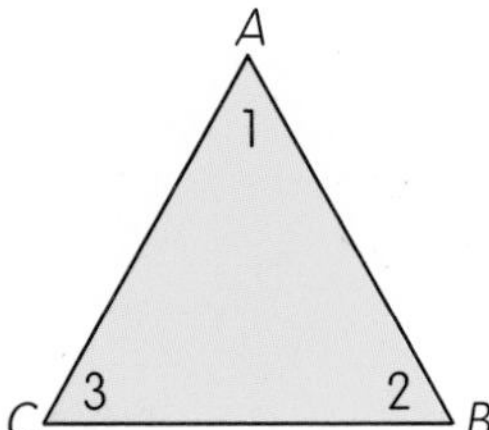

2. Then, extend the sides of triangle *ABC* to form exterior angles 4, 5, and 6.

   Example:

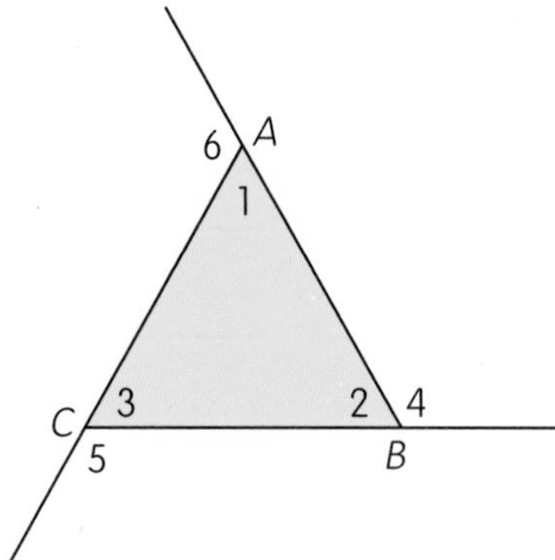

3. What is the sum of the measures of interior angles 1, 2, and 3?

4. What do you notice about the measures of each pair of adjacent exterior and interior angles at the vertices of triangle *ABC*?

   Example: $m\angle 1 + m\angle 6 = 180°$

5. What is the relationship between the exterior angle at each vertex, the adjacent interior angle, and the other two interior angles of the triangle?

⑥ Extend the sides of triangle ABC in another way to form exterior angles 7, 8, and 9.

Example:

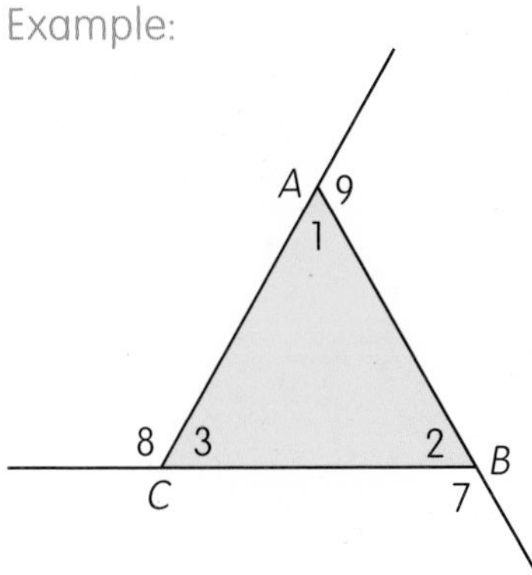

⑦ Similarly, write some equations to demonstrate the properties you observed between the exterior and interior angles of the triangle.

1. The interior angle 1 and the exterior angle 6 are adjacent angles on a straight line. The sum of adjacent angles on a straight line is 180°.
So, $m\angle 1 + m\angle 6 = 180°$.

The sum of the measures of the interior angles of a triangle is 180°.
So, $m\angle 1 + m\angle 2 + m\angle 3 = 180°$.

You can use these two equations to demonstrate a property about the exterior angles of a triangle.

$$m\angle 1 + \mathbf{m\angle 6} = 180°$$
$$m\angle 1 + \mathbf{m\angle 2} + \mathbf{m\angle 3} = 180°$$

So, $\mathbf{m\angle 2 + m\angle 3 = m\angle 6}$.

Similarly,
$$m\angle 1 + \mathbf{m\angle 2} + \mathbf{m\angle 3} = 180°$$
$$m\angle 1 + \mathbf{m\angle 9} = 180°$$

So, $\mathbf{m\angle 2 + m\angle 3 = m\angle 9}$.

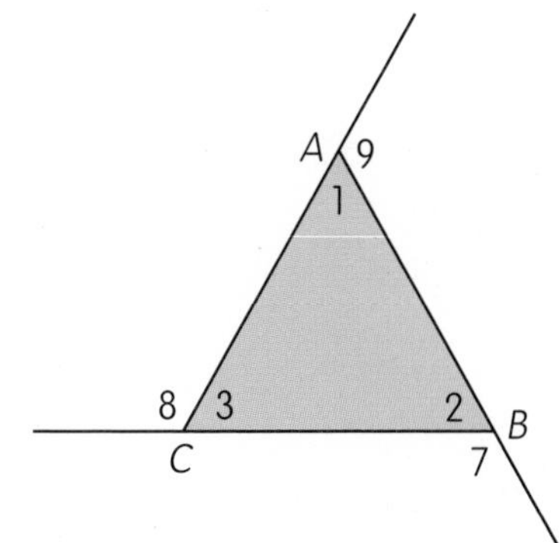

$$m\angle 3 + \mathbf{m\angle 1} + \mathbf{m\angle 2} = 180°$$
$$m\angle 3 + \mathbf{m\angle 8} = 180°$$

So, $\mathbf{m\angle 1 + m\angle 2 = m\angle 8}$.

The exterior angle of a triangle is always supplementary to the interior angle it is adjacent to, and is always equal to the sum of the other two interior angles of the triangle.

So, $m\angle 1 + m\angle 2 = m\angle 5$ or $m\angle 8$
$m\angle 1 + m\angle 3 = m\angle 4$ or $m\angle 7$
$m\angle 2 + m\angle 3 = m\angle 6$ or $m\angle 9$

2 In the diagram, $\overrightarrow{SU}$ is a straight line.
Find the value of x.

$x° = 50° + 60°$ Ext. ∠ of triangle
$x = 110$

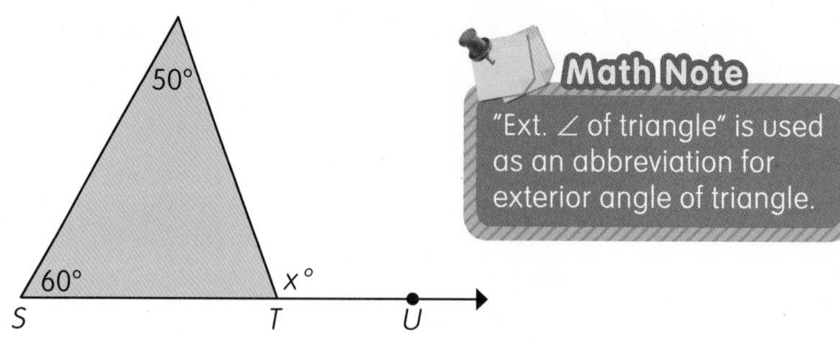

3 Triangle PQR is an isosceles triangle. $\overrightarrow{RS}$ is a straight line.
Find the measures of ∠1 and ∠2.

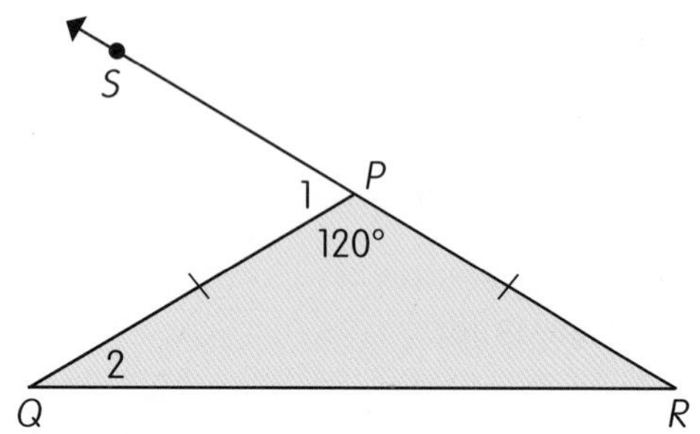

In an isosceles triangle, the angles opposite the congruent sides are congruent.

Method 1

First, use the properties of isosceles triangles and the angle sum of a triangle to find m∠2. Then, use the property of the exterior angles of a triangle to find m∠1.

$PQ = PR$
$m\angle PRQ = m\angle PQR = m\angle 2$ Isosceles triangle

$m\angle 2 + m\angle PRQ + 120° = 180°$ ∠ sum of triangle
$m\angle 2 + m\angle 2 + 120° = 180°$ Substitute $m\angle PRQ = m\angle 2$.
$2 \cdot m\angle 2 + 120° = 180°$ Simplify.
$2 \cdot m\angle 2 + 120° - \mathbf{120°} = 180° - \mathbf{120°}$ Subtract 120° from both sides.
$2m\angle 2 = 60°$ Simplify.
$\frac{2m\angle 2}{\mathbf{2}} = \frac{60°}{\mathbf{2}}$ Divide both sides by 2.
$m\angle 2 = 30°$ Simplify.

$m\angle 1 = m\angle 2 + m\angle PRQ$ Ext. ∠ of triangle
$= m\angle 2 + m\angle 2$ Substitute $m\angle PRQ = m\angle 2$.
$= 30° + 30°$ Substitute $m\angle 2 = 30°$.
$= 60°$ Simplify.

Method 2

First, use the property of adjacent angles on a straight line to find $m\angle 1$.
Then, use the property of the exterior angles of a triangle to find $m\angle 2$.

$m\angle 1 + 120° = 180°$	Adj. ∠s on a st. line
$m\angle 1 + 120° - \mathbf{120°} = 180° - \mathbf{120°}$	Subtract 120° from both sides.
$m\angle 1 = 60°$	Simplify.

$m\angle 2 + m\angle PRQ = m\angle 1$	Ext. ∠ of triangle
$m\angle 2 + m\angle 2 = m\angle 1$	Substitute $m\angle PRQ = m\angle 2$.
$2m\angle 2 = 60°$	Simplify and substitute $m\angle 1 = 60°$.
$\frac{2m\angle 2}{\mathbf{2}} = \frac{60°}{\mathbf{2}}$	Divide both sides by 2.
$m\angle 2 = 30°$	Simplify.

TRY Practice using exterior angle relationships to find unknown angle measures

The diagrams may not be drawn to scale. Solve.

1. In the diagram, $\overrightarrow{CA}$ is a straight line. Find the value of x.

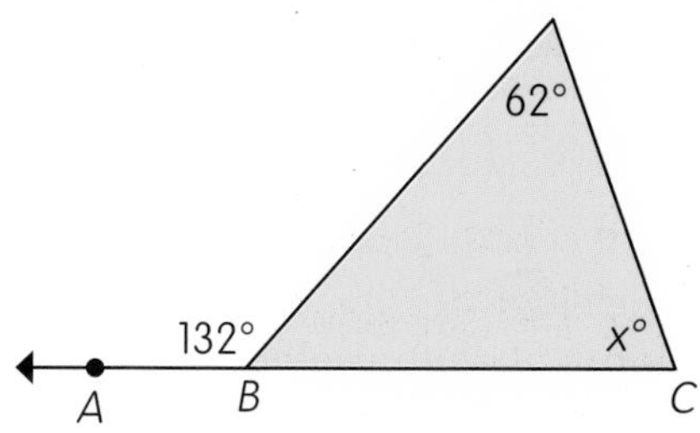

$x° +$ ______ = ______	Ext. ∠ of triangle
$x +$ ______ − ______ = ______ − ______	Subtract ______ from both sides.
$x =$ ______	Simplify.

2 In the diagram, $\overrightarrow{ZX}$ is a straight line. Find the value of y.

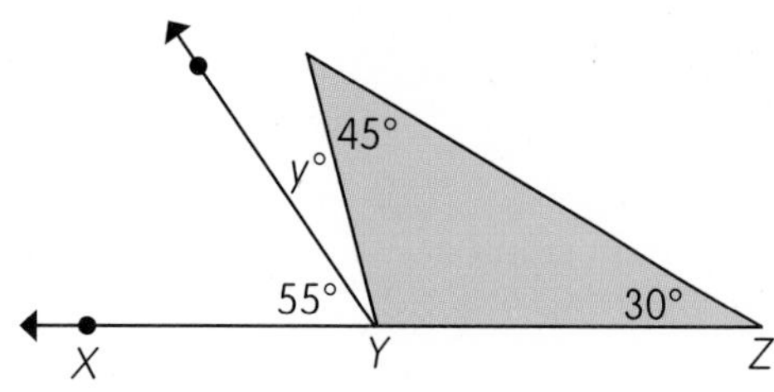

______ + $y°$ = ______ + ______	Ext. ∠ of triangle
______ + y = ______	Simplify.
______ + y − ______ = ______ − ______	Subtract ______ from both sides.
y = ______	Simplify.

3 Triangle EFG is an isosceles triangle. $\overline{EF}$ is parallel to $\overleftrightarrow{HI}$. $\overrightarrow{EJ}$ is a straight line. Find the value of x.

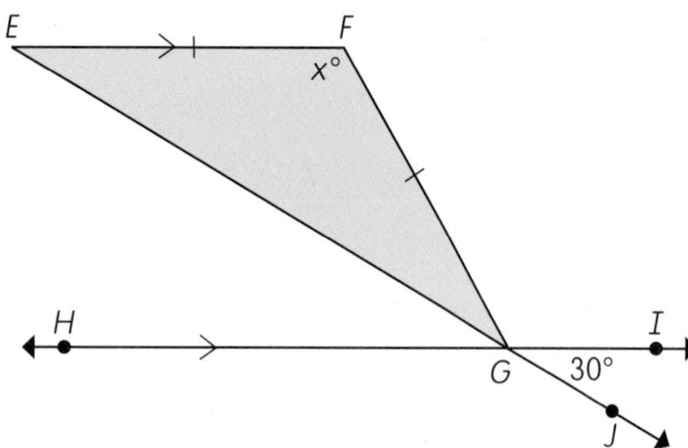

m∠FEG = m∠IGJ = ______	Corr. ∠s
m∠FGE = m∠FEG = ______	Isosceles triangle
$x°$ + ______ + ______ = ______	∠ sum of triangle
x + ______ = ______	Simplify.
x + ______ − ______ = ______ − ______	Subtract ______ from both sides.
x = ______	Simplify.

Name: ______________________ Date: ______________

INDEPENDENT PRACTICE

The diagrams may not be drawn to scale. Find the value of *y*.
In the diagrams for 4 to 6, $\overrightarrow{AC}$ is a straight line.

1
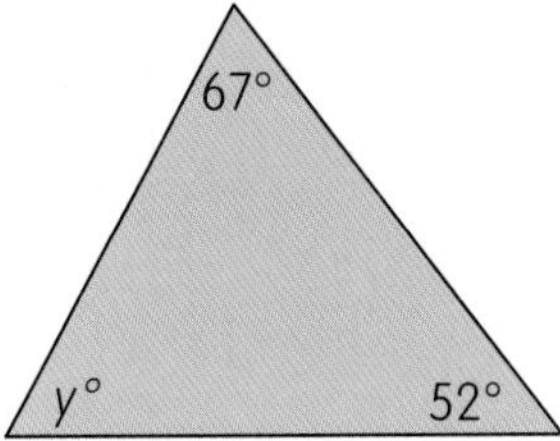

2
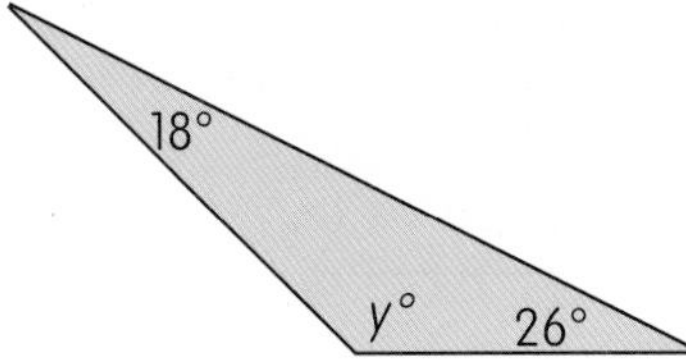

3 *EFG* is a triangle.
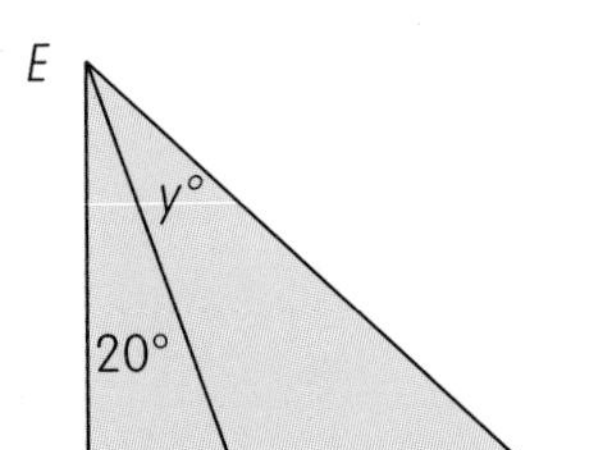

4
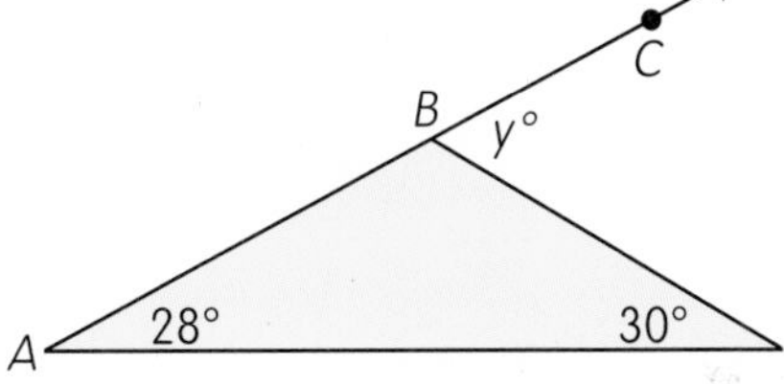

5
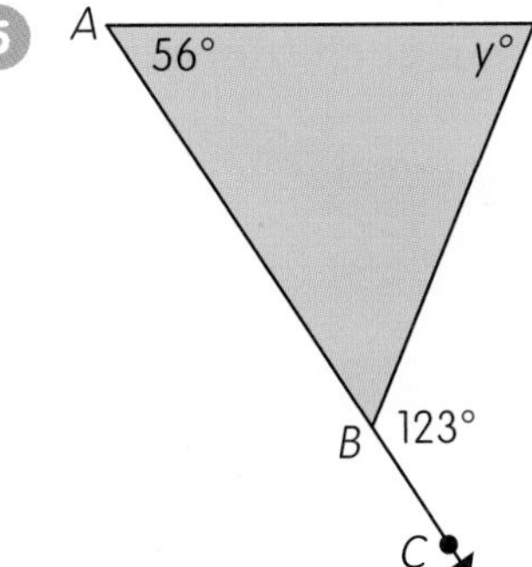

6
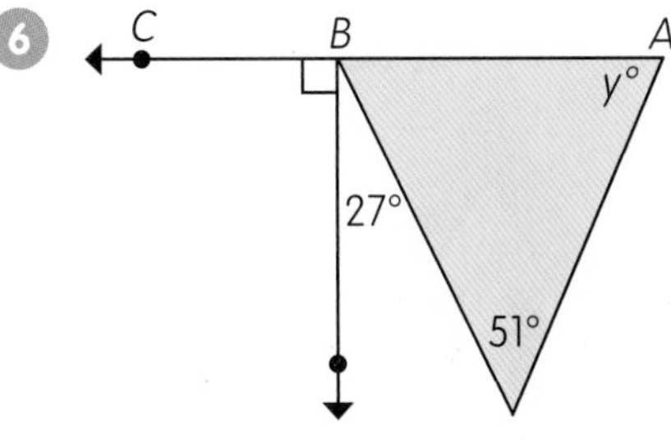

The diagrams may not be drawn to scale. Find m∠1 and m∠2.

7 *XYZ* is a triangle.
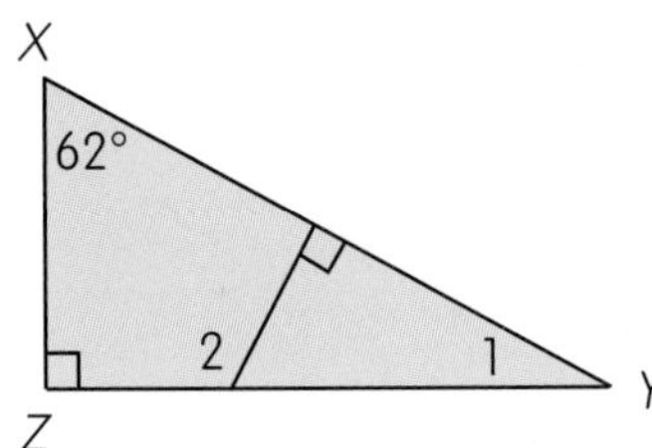

8 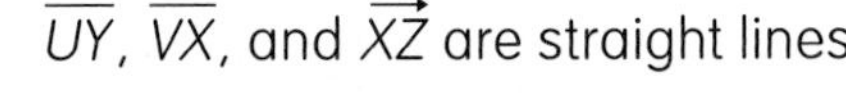
$\overline{UY}$, $\overline{VX}$, and $\overrightarrow{XZ}$ are straight lines.
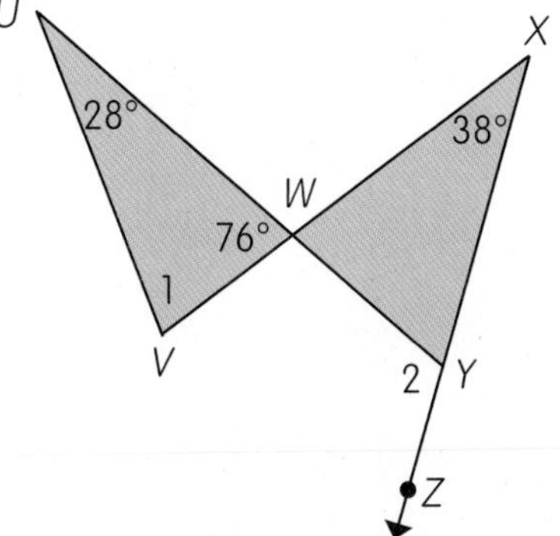

9. WXY is a triangle and $\overrightarrow{XZ}$ is a straight line.

W
70°
1
50°
2
X
Y
Z

10.

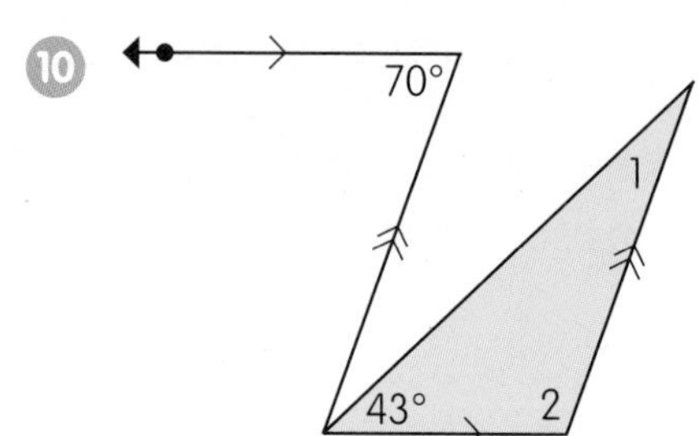

The diagrams may not be drawn to scale. Find the value of *y*.

11. $\overrightarrow{AC}$ is a straight line.

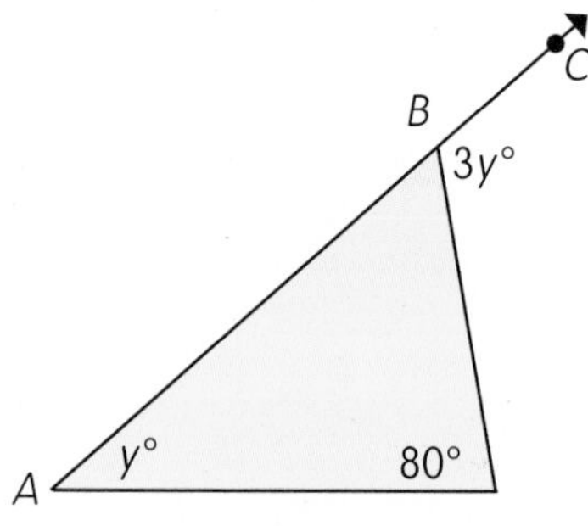

12. $\overleftrightarrow{AC}$ is a straight line.

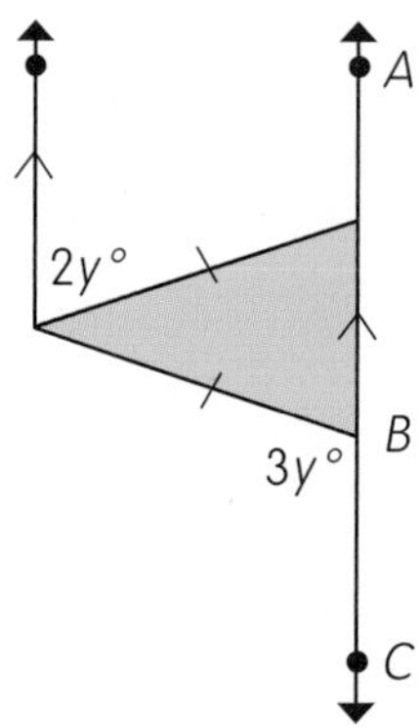

The diagrams may not be drawn to scale. Find the value of *x* and name each triangle.

13.

14.

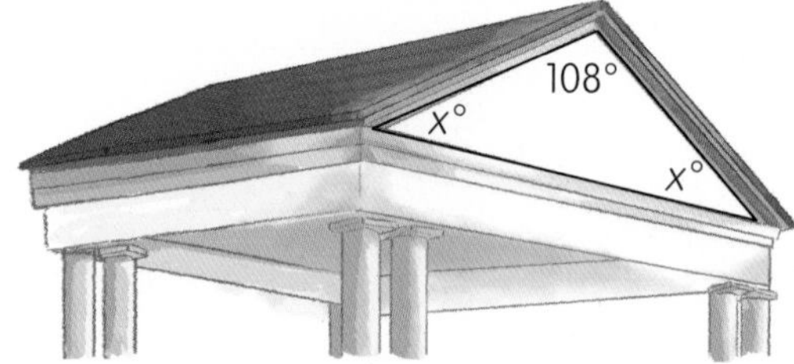

15.

The diagrams may not be drawn to scale. Find the measure of each numbered angle.

16. $\overrightarrow{AC}$, $\overline{AD}$ and $\overrightarrow{EB}$ are straight lines.

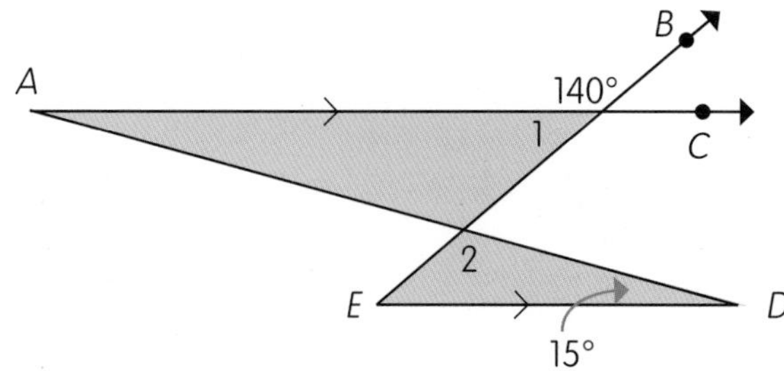

17. $\overleftrightarrow{JK}$, $\overrightarrow{ZN}$, and $\overleftrightarrow{LM}$ are straight lines. XYZ is a triangle.

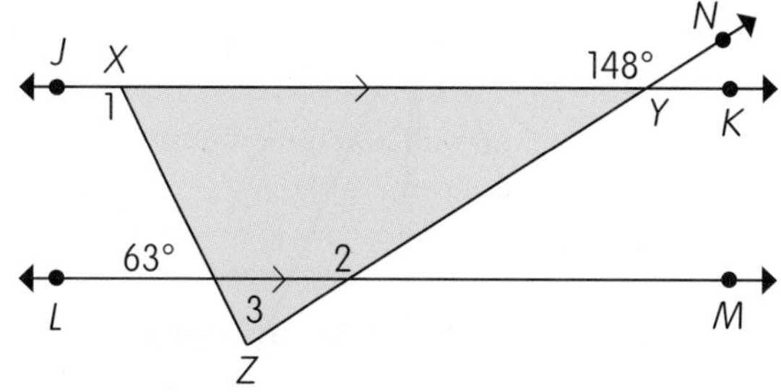

18. $\overleftrightarrow{AC}$ and $\overrightarrow{DB}$ are straight lines.

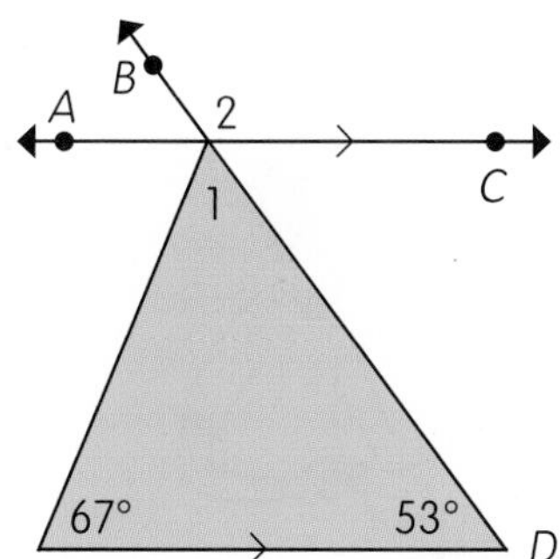

19. ACE and BDF are two triangles.

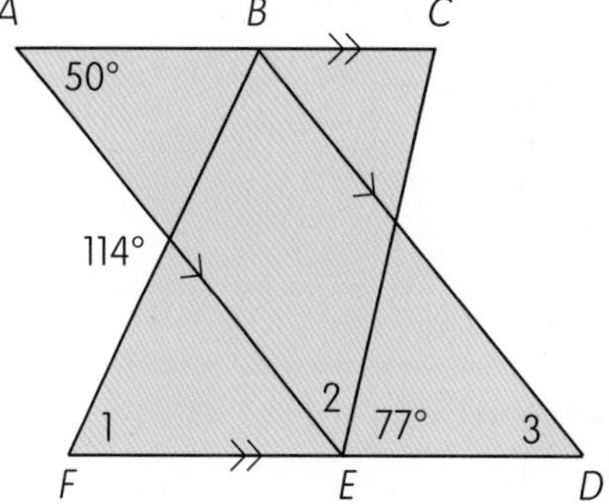

20. $\overleftrightarrow{BE}$ is parallel to $\overleftrightarrow{FH}$. $\overline{AG}$ is a straight line. Find the measure of $\angle CAD$ in terms of $\angle 1$ and $\angle 2$.

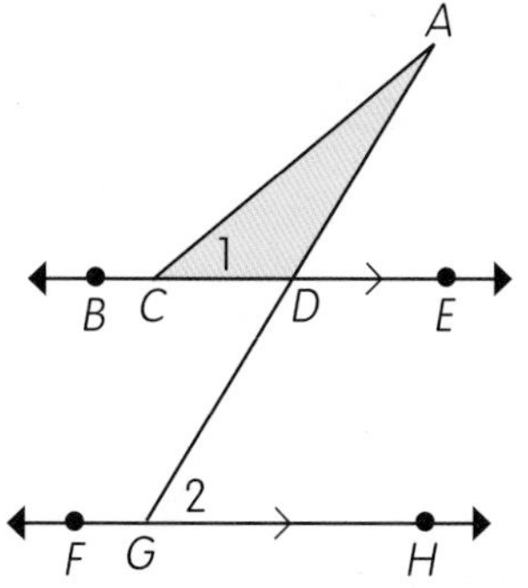

21. **Mathematical Habit 2 Use mathematical reasoning**

Explain why each of the following statements is true.

a A triangle cannot have two right angles.

b The interior angle measures of an isosceles triangle cannot be 96°, 43°, and 43°.

The diagrams may not be drawn to scale. Solve.

22 $m\angle 1 = 2x°$, $m\angle 2 = (x - 5)°$, and $m\angle 3 = 100°$. Use an equation to find the value of x. Then, find the measures of $\angle 1$ and $\angle 2$.

The diagrams may not be drawn to scale. Find the value of x.

23

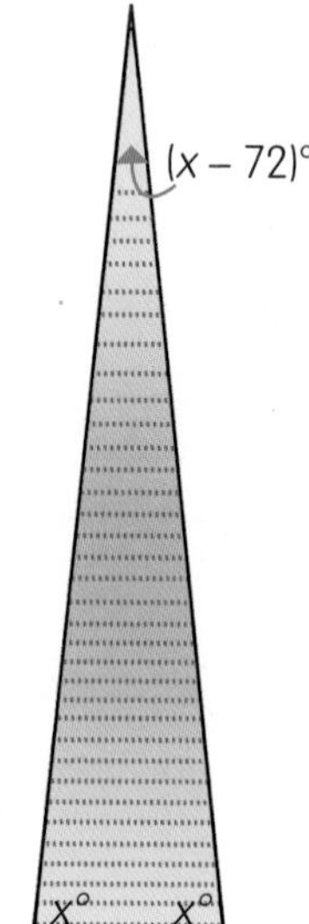

24

25

26

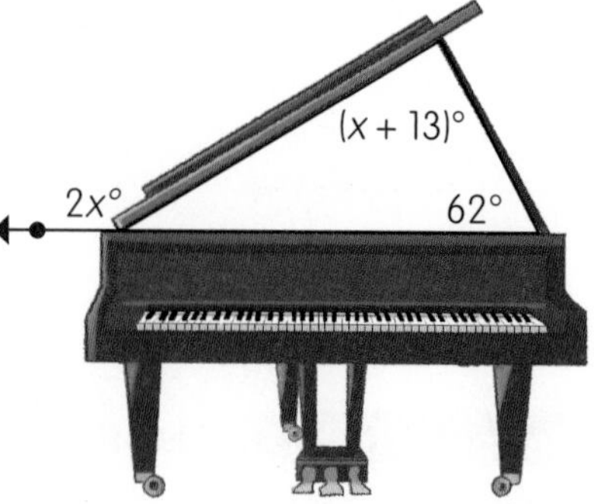

Name: ______________________ Date: ____________

Mathematical Habit 6 **Use precise mathematical language**

Leah answered the following question incorrectly. Identify Leah's mistake and write the correct solution. Explain your reasoning.

Question:

The diagram on the right may not be drawn to scale.
$\overline{PU}$, $\overline{RQ}$, $\overline{RS}$, and $\overline{TU}$ are straight lines.
Find the measures of

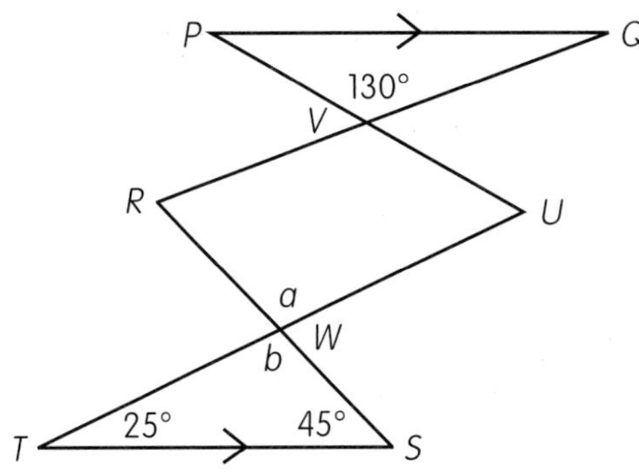

a $\angle a$ and $\angle b$.

b the supplement of $\angle a$.

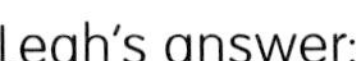

Leah's answer:

a $m\angle b = 180° - 25° - 45°$
$= 110°$ ($\angle$ sum of triangle)
$m\angle a = 130°$ (corr. $\angle$s)

b Supplement of $\angle a = 130° - 90°$
$= 40°$

Leah's mistake:

Correct solution:

PUT ON YOUR THINKING CAP!

Problem Solving with Heuristics

1 **Mathematical Habit 1 Persevere in solving problems**

The diagram may not be drawn to scale.
ABCD is a rhombus and the measure of $\angle BCD$ is 68°. *BDE* is a triangle where the measure of $\angle BED$ is 36° and the measure of $\angle BDE$ is 73°. Find m$\angle EBC$.

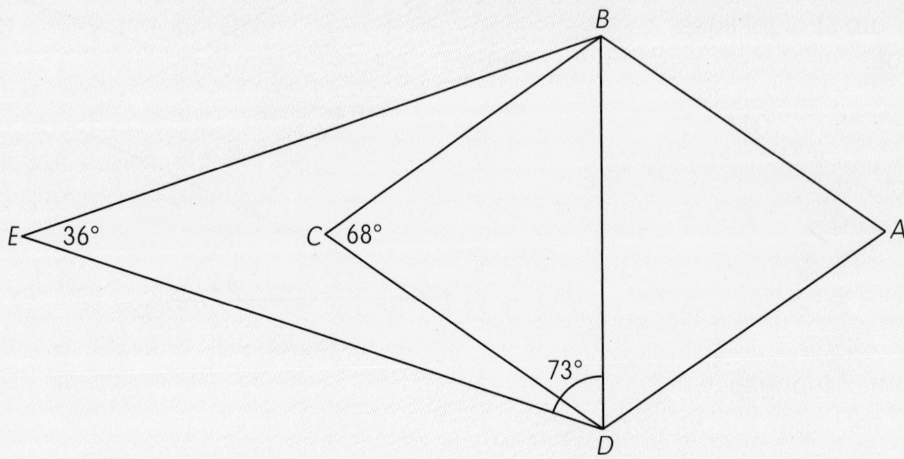

PUT ON YOUR THINKING CAP!

2 **Mathematical Habit 3** **Construct viable arguments**

Find out which of the following triangles can be constructed.

a A triangle where two of its three angles are supplementary.

b An isosceles triangle with a pair of complementary angles.

c An obtuse triangle with a pair of complementary angles.

CHAPTER WRAP-UP

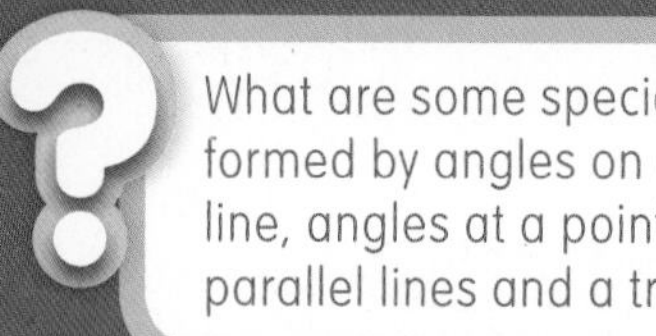

What are some special properties formed by angles on a straight line, angles at a point, and parallel lines and a transversal?

KEY CONCEPTS

- Two angles with measures that add up to 90° are called complementary angles.

  $m\angle 1 + m\angle 2 = 90°$

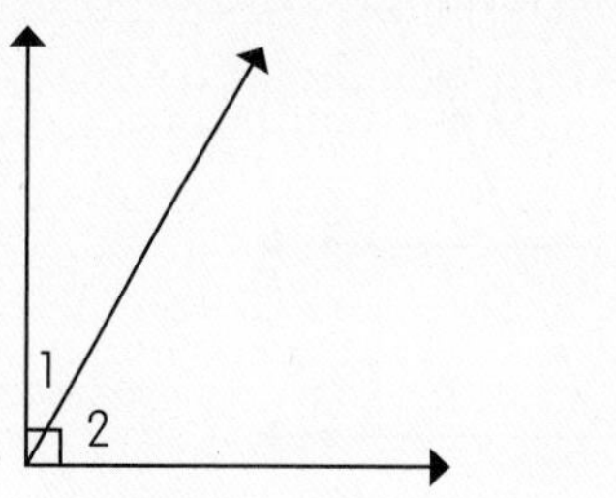

- Two angles with measures that add up to 180° are called supplementary angles.

  $m\angle 1 + m\angle 2 = 180°$

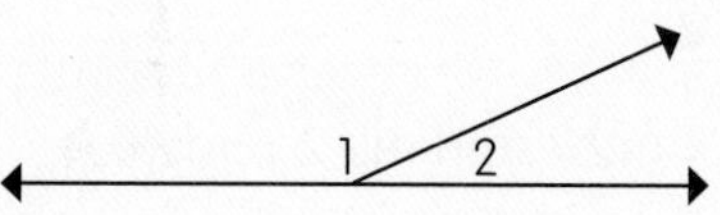

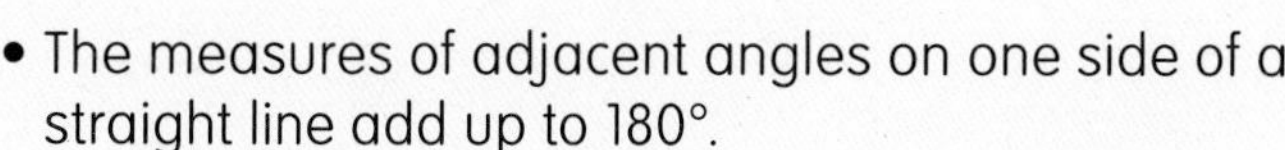

- The measures of adjacent angles on one side of a straight line add up to 180°.

  $m\angle 1 + m\angle 2 + m\angle 3 = 180°$

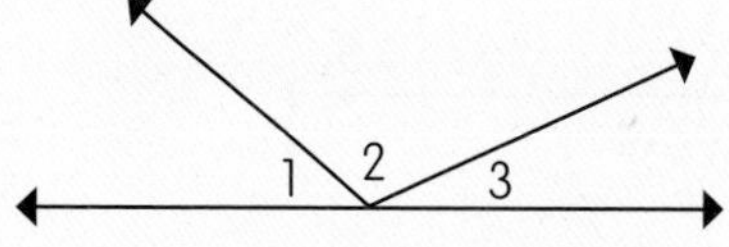

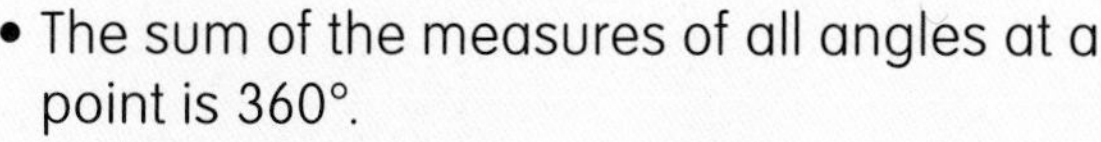

- The sum of the measures of all angles at a point is 360°.

  $m\angle 1 + m\angle 2 + m\angle 3 = 360°$

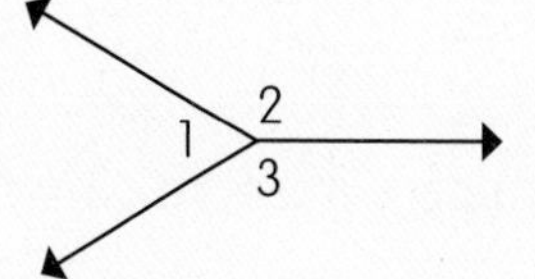

- Vertical angles are congruent.

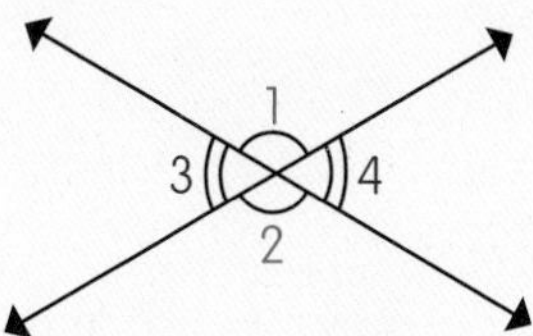

$m\angle 1 = m\angle 2$ and $m\angle 3 = m\angle 4$

- Alternate interior angles are congruent.

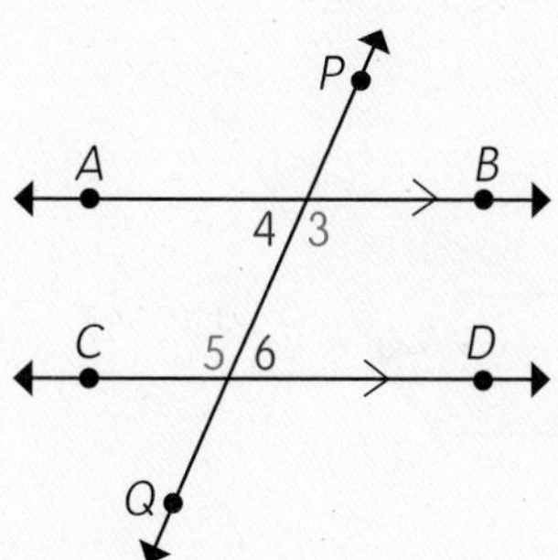

$m\angle 4 = m\angle 6$ and $m\angle 3 = m\angle 5$

- Alternate exterior angles are congruent.

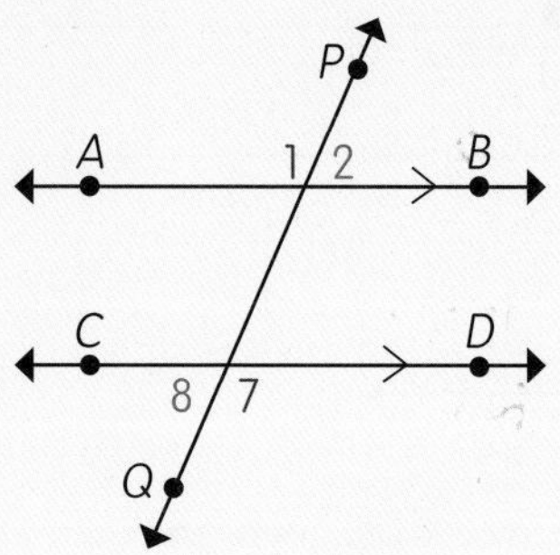

$m\angle 1 = m\angle 7$ and $m\angle 2 = m\angle 8$

- Corresponding angles are congruent.

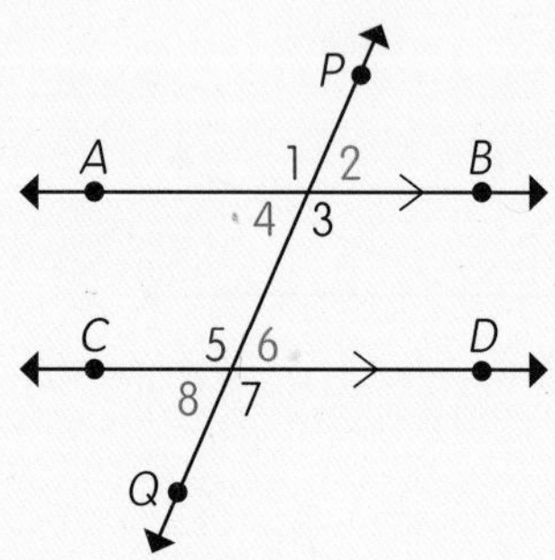

$m\angle 1 = m\angle 5$, $m\angle 2 = m\angle 6$, $m\angle 3 = m\angle 7$, and $m\angle 4 = m\angle 8$

- The sum of the measures of the interior angles of a triangle is always 180°.

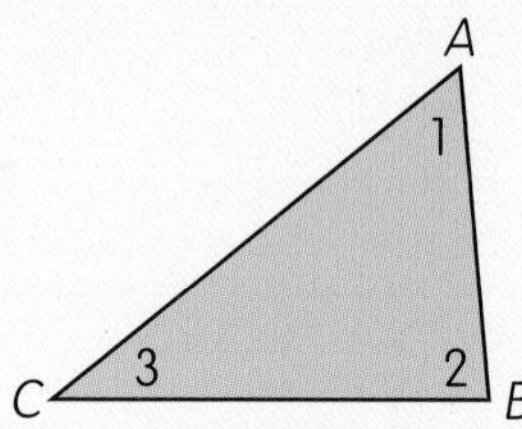

$m\angle 1 + m\angle 2 + m\angle 3 = 180°$

- The measure of an exterior angle of a triangle is equal to the sum of the measures of the interior angles that are not adjacent to the exterior angle.

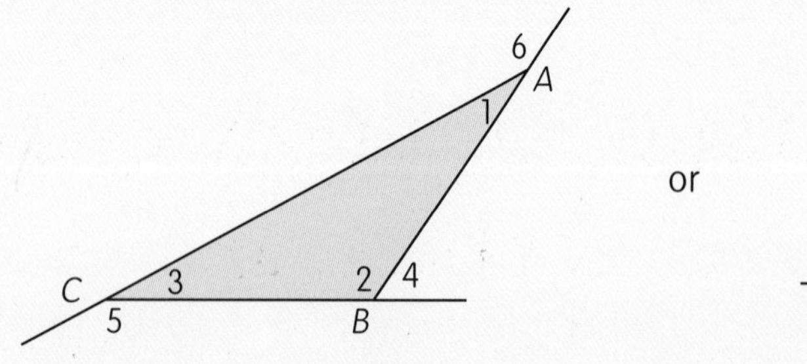

or

$m\angle 1 + m\angle 2 = m\angle 5$, $m\angle 1 + m\angle 3 = m\angle 4$, and $m\angle 2 + m\angle 3 = m\angle 6$

Name: ______________________ Date: ____________

State whether each pair of angles are supplementary, complementary, or neither.

1. m∠1 = 23° and m∠2 = 157°

   Supplementary ✓

2. m∠3 = 65° and m∠4 = 25°

   complementary ✓

3. m∠5 = 43° and m∠6 = 57°

   neither ✓

4. m∠7 = 82° and m∠8 = 8°

   complementary ✓

5. m∠9 = 110° and m∠10 = 80°

   neither ✓

6. m∠11 = 18° and m∠12 = 62°

   neither ✓

Identify the pairs of complementary or supplementary angles.

m∠*A* = 67°	m∠*B* = 80°	m∠*C* = 131°	m∠*D* = 21°
m∠*E* = 51°	m∠*F* = 46°	m∠*G* = 10°	m∠*H* = 120°
m∠*J* = 69°	m∠*K* = 60°	m∠*P* = 49°	m∠*Q* = 113°
m∠*R* = 44°	m∠*S* = 41°		

7. Name two pairs of complementary angles.

   m<B = 80° + m<G = 10° ✓
   m<P = 49° + m<S = 41° ✓

8. Name two pairs of supplementary angles.

   m<C = 131° + m<P = 49° ✓
   m<P = 49° + m<S = 41° ✓ (A + Q)

Fill in the table.

9. $\overleftrightarrow{AC}$ is a straight line. Name two pairs of angles for each type of angle pair.

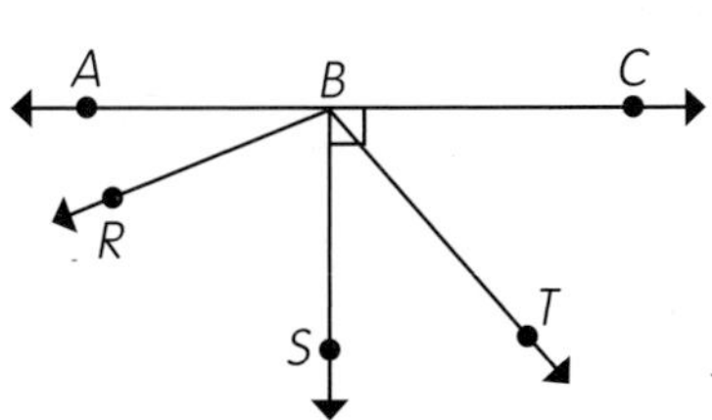

Type of Angles	First Pair	Second Pair
Complementary angles	BST + TCB	BAR + RSB
Supplementary angles	ABS + SBC ✓	ABT + TBC ✓

The diagrams may not be drawn to scale. Find the measure of each numbered angle.

10. $\overleftrightarrow{AB}$ is a straight line.

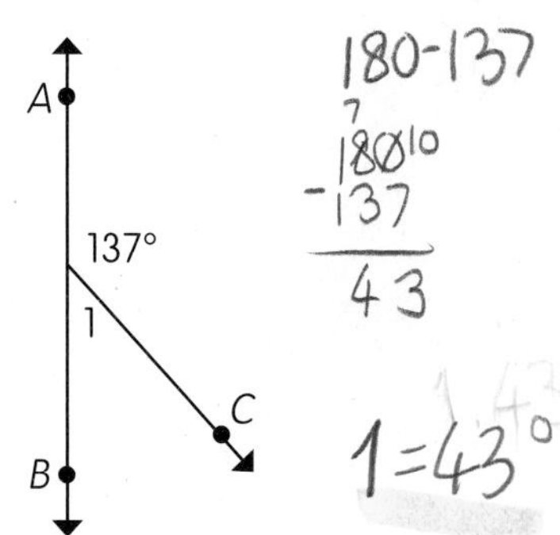

11. $\overleftrightarrow{AB}$ is a straight line.

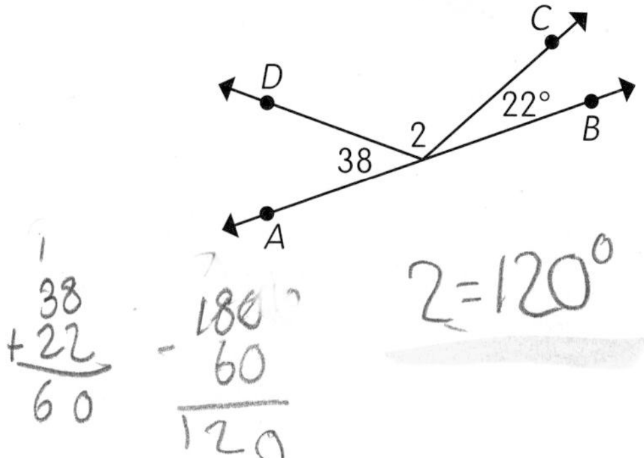

12.

A
120°
B
3
45°
C

13. $\overleftrightarrow{AB}$ is a straight line.

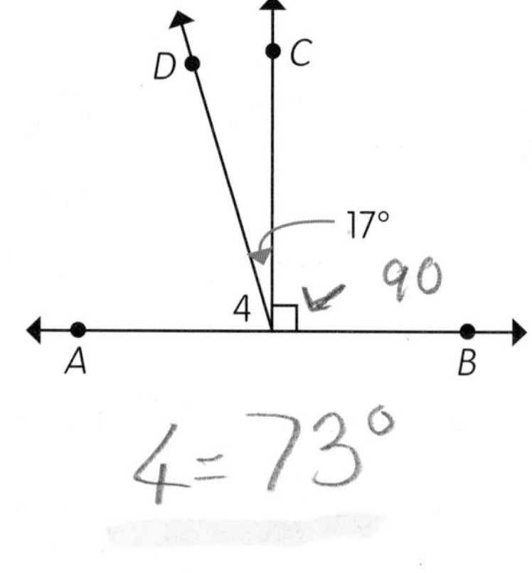

The diagrams may not be drawn to scale. Find the value of each variable.

14. $\overleftrightarrow{AB}$ is a straight line.

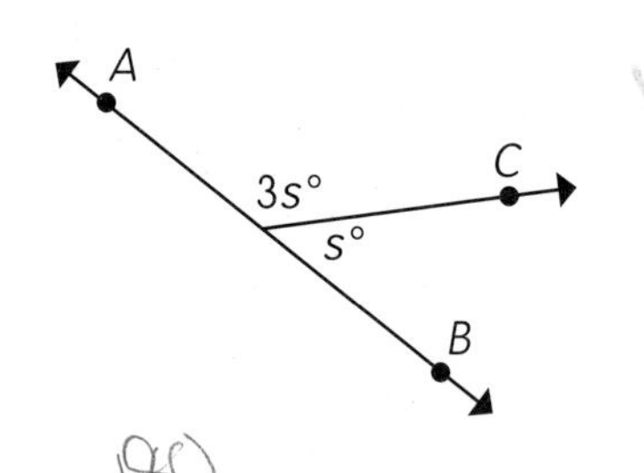

15. $\overleftrightarrow{AB}$ is a straight line.

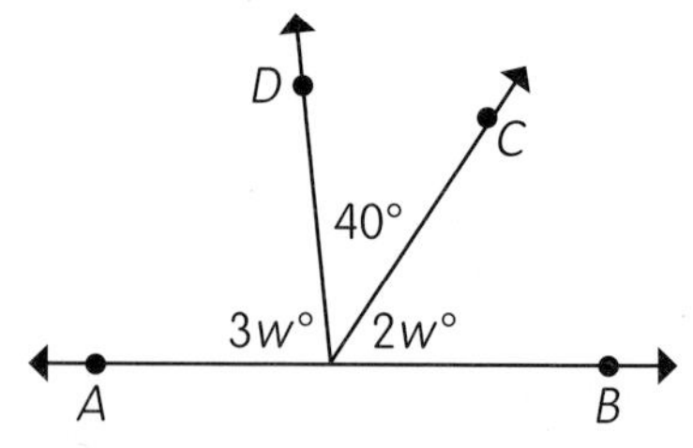

16 $\overleftrightarrow{AB}$ is a straight line.

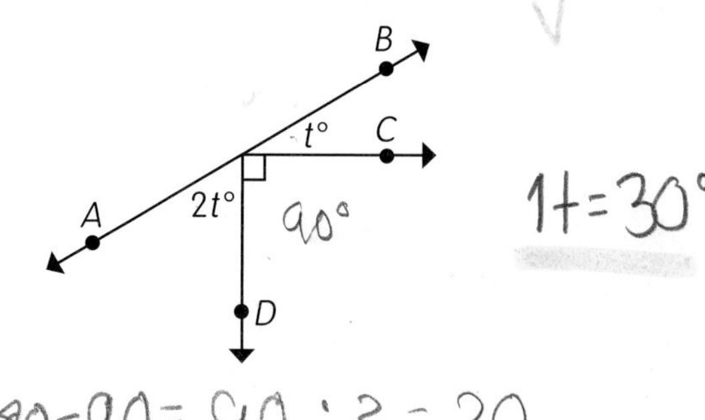

17

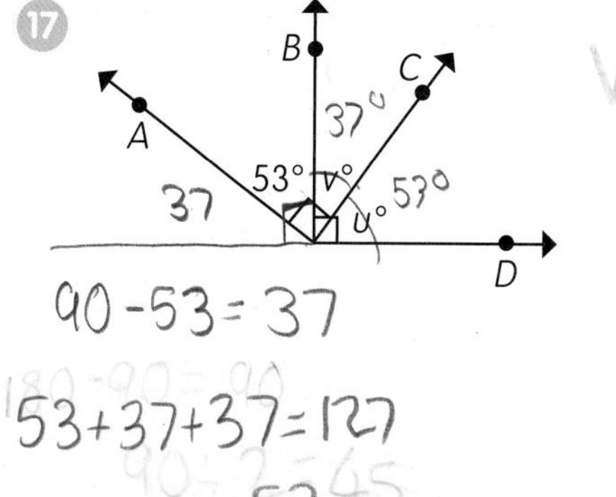

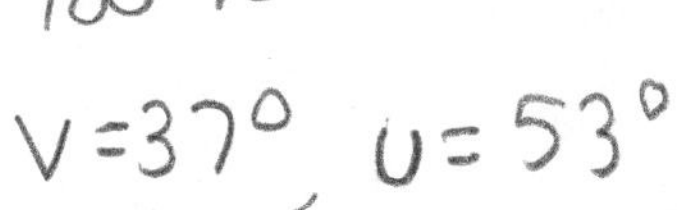

18

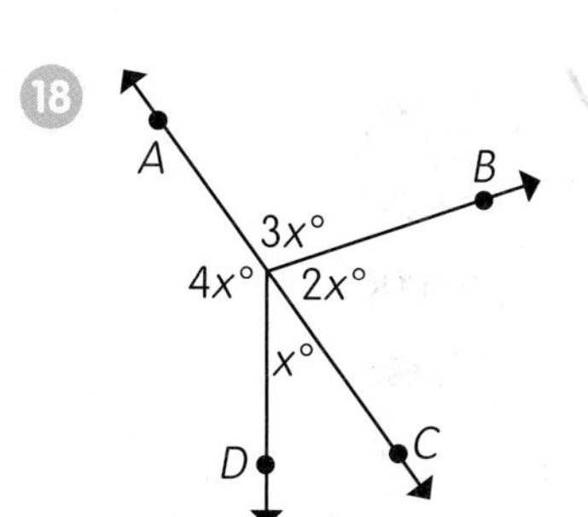

19 $\overleftrightarrow{AB}$, $\overleftrightarrow{CD}$, and $\overleftrightarrow{EF}$ are straight lines.

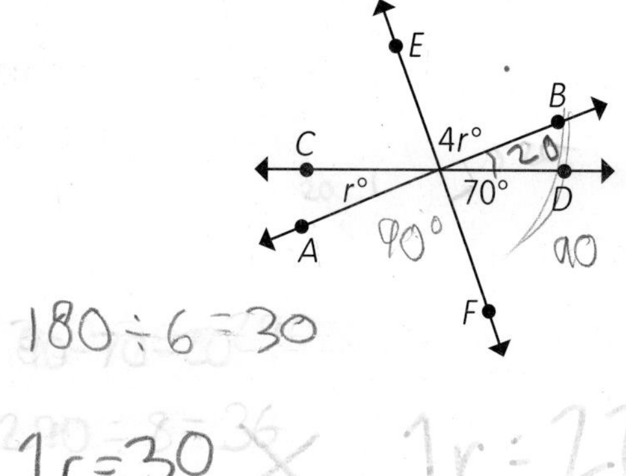

The diagrams may not be drawn to scale. Find the measure of each numbered angle.

20 $\overline{MN}$ is parallel to $\overrightarrow{PQ}$.

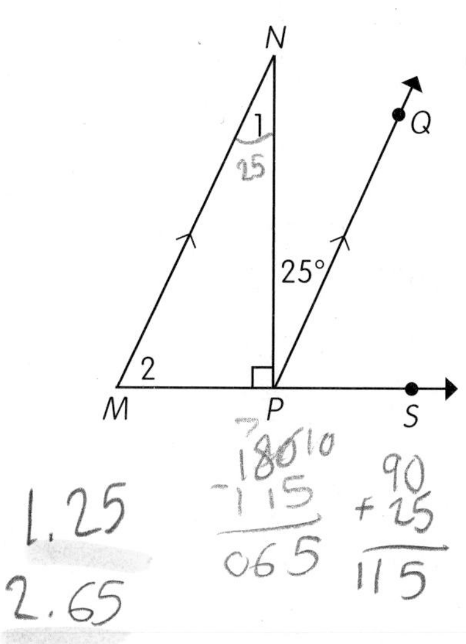

21 $\overrightarrow{ST}$ is a straight line. $\overleftrightarrow{MN}$ is parallel to $\overleftrightarrow{QP}$.

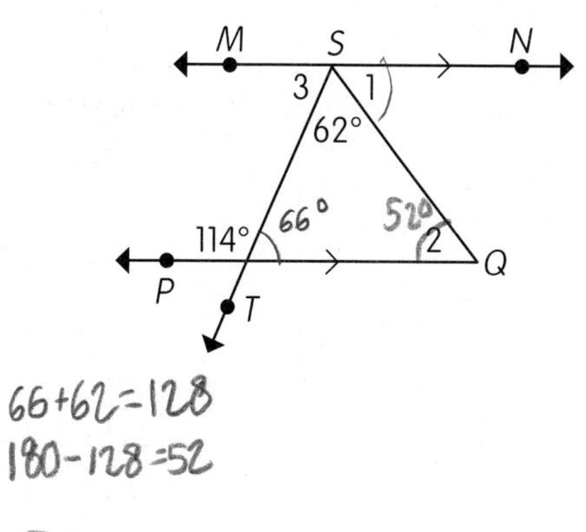

The diagrams may not be drawn to scale. Solve.

22 Find the value of x.

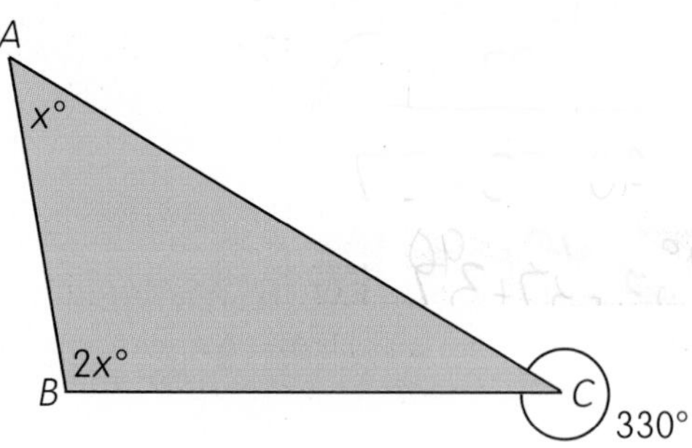

23 $ABCD$ is a rhombus. Find the measures of $\angle 1$ and $\angle 2$.

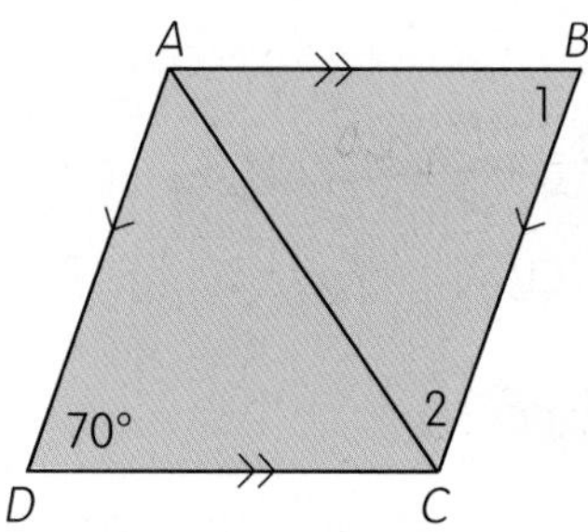

24 $ABCD$ is a rectangle. $\overline{AE}$ and $\overline{CE}$ are straight lines. $\angle FBG$ is a right angle, $m\angle ABF = 74°$, and $m\angle BEG = 42°$. Find the measures of $\angle EBG$ and $\angle BGC$.

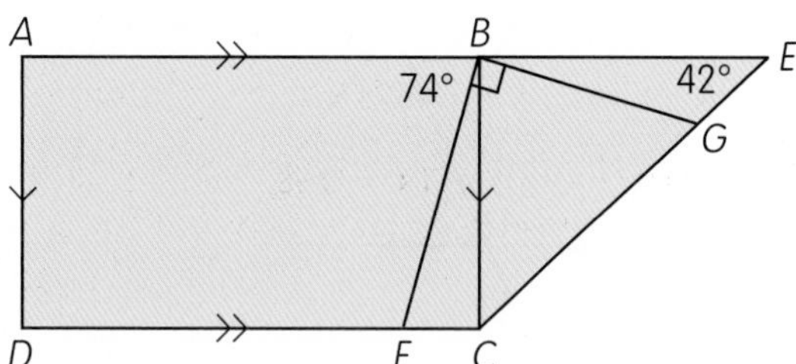

25 The diagram shows the flag of the United Kingdom. $\angle MNR = 90°$. Name two pairs of complementary and supplementary angles.

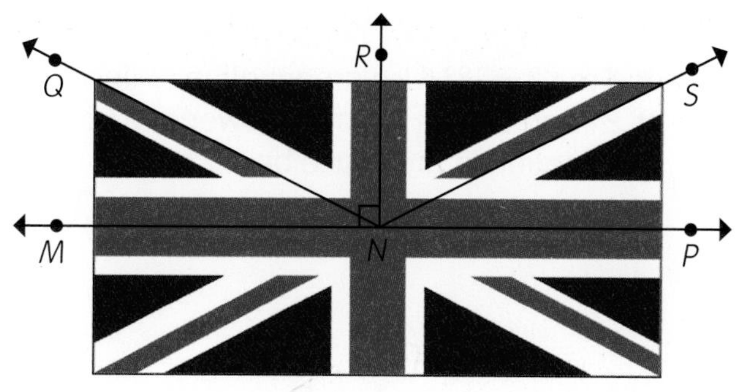

26 In the diagram, $m\angle 1 = (x - 19)°$, $m\angle 2 = (3x - 29)°$, and $m\angle 3 = x°$. $\overleftrightarrow{AB}$ is a straight line. Use an equation to find the measures of $\angle 1$, $\angle 2$, and $\angle 3$.

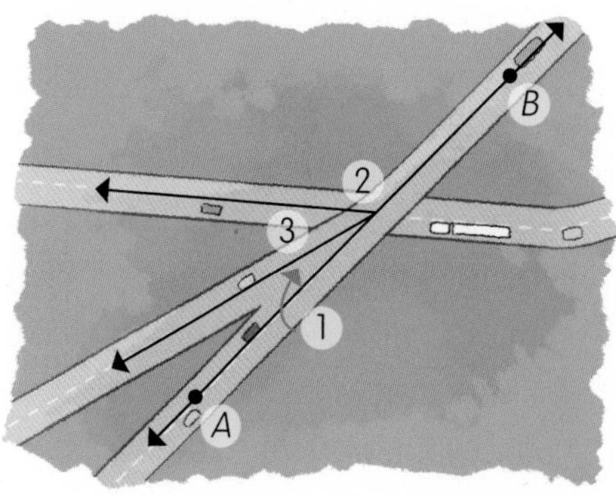

Assessment Prep

Answer each question.

27 A triangle has angles p, q, and r. Given that the triangle is an isosceles triangle, and the exterior angle measure of $\angle p$ is 30°, which of the following gives the correct dimensions of the triangle?

(A) $p = 30°$, $q = 75°$, $r = 75°$

(B) $p = 150°$, $q = 15°$, $r = 15°$

(C) $p = 30°$, $q = 30°$, $r = 120°$

(D) $p = 50°$, $q = 50°$, $r = 30°$

28 In the diagram, m∠1 = $(5x - 20)$°, m∠2 = $(2x + 14)$°, and m∠3 = 18°. Use an equation to find the measures of ∠1 and ∠2. Write your answer and your work or explanation in the space below.

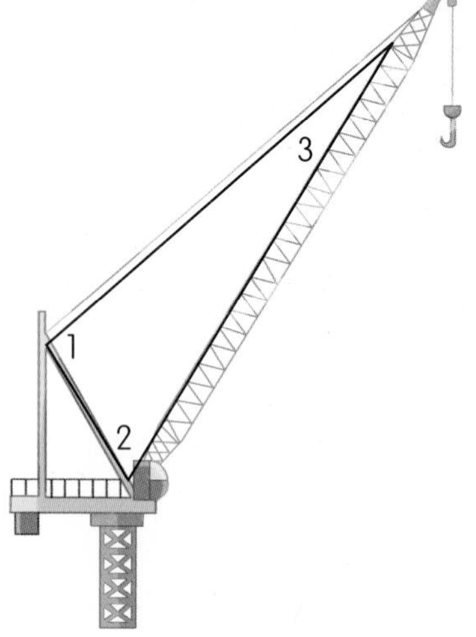

29 The diagram shows ∠1 and ∠2, which are formed by $\overleftrightarrow{MN}$ intersecting $\overleftrightarrow{PQ}$ and $\overleftrightarrow{RS}$. m∠1 = $(12x + 7)$°, m∠2 = $(10x + 15)$°, and $x = 4$. Explain how you know that $\overleftrightarrow{PQ}$ is parallel to $\overleftrightarrow{RS}$. Write your answer and your work or explanation in the space below.

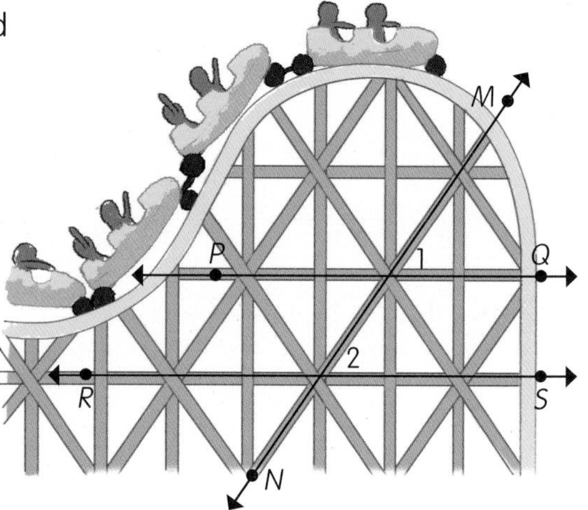

Name: ______________________ Date: ______________

Position in a Basketball Game

A drawing of Ken's position in a basketball game is shown on the right. He launches a free throw at position J. The basketball hoop is at point G.

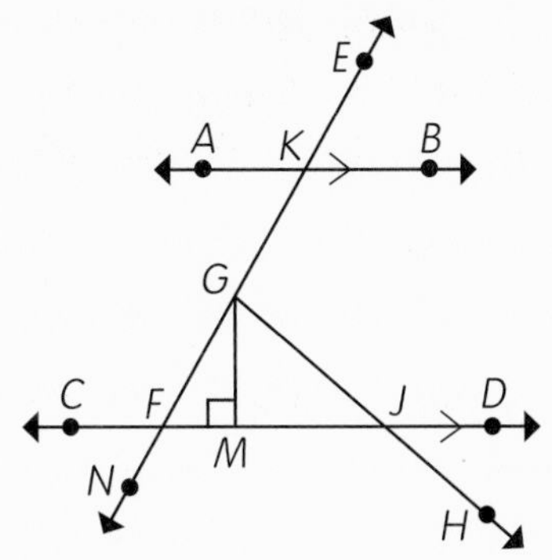

$\overleftrightarrow{GH}$ and $\overleftrightarrow{EN}$ are straight lines. $\overline{GM}$ is a line segment. $\overleftrightarrow{AB}$ is parallel to $\overleftrightarrow{CD}$, and $\overline{GM}$ is perpendicular to $\overleftrightarrow{CD}$. The ratio of the three angle measures m$\angle FGM$, m$\angle MGJ$, and m$\angle EGJ$ is 3 : 5 : 10.

1. Find the measures of the three angles, $\angle FGM$, $\angle MGJ$, and $\angle EGJ$. Use bar models or equations to solve.

2. Find the measure of $\angle DJH$. Use precise mathematical language to justify your answer.

3 Ken thinks that $\angle DJH$ and $\angle EKA$ are congruent because they are alternate exterior angles. Do you agree or disagree? Explain why.

4 A line parallel to $\overleftrightarrow{CD}$ is drawn through G so that it cuts $\angle EGJ$ into two angles. What are the measures of these angles? Use precise mathematical language to explain your answer.

Rubric

Point(s)	Level	My Performance
7–8	4	• Most of my answers are correct. • I showed complete understanding of the concepts. • I used effective and efficient strategies to solve the problems. • I explained my answers and mathematical thinking clearly and completely.
5–6.5	3	• Some of my answers are correct. • I showed adequate understanding of the concepts. • I used effective strategies to solve the problems. • I explained my answers and mathematical thinking clearly.
3–4.5	2	• A few of my answers are correct. • I showed some understanding of the concepts. • I used some effective strategies to solve the problems. • I explained some of my answers and mathematical thinking clearly.
0–2.5	1	• A few of my answers are correct. • I showed little understanding of the concepts. • I used limited effective strategies to solve the problems. • I did not explain my answers and mathematical thinking clearly.

Teacher's Comments

STEAM

Art Deco

The Empire State Building may be one of the most famous buildings in the world. The structure has appeared in hundreds of movies since 1933, when King Kong climbed 102 stories to grab the movie's heroine and horrify moviegoers.

The Chrysler Building is another famous New York landmark. Like the Empire State Building, the building is a popular movie location. Both buildings represent an architectural style called Art Deco. The style, which began in the 1920s, used sleek geometry to reflect the machine age.

Task

Work in small groups to create a visual model.

1. Art Deco architecture inspired builders across the country. Search library or online resources to find examples of Art Deco buildings in your city or state.

2. Select one of the buildings you discovered in your search or use the Chrysler Building to create a visual model. Identify and label the building's geometric features. Pay special attention to the building's variety of angles. Look for and label examples of angles you examined in this chapter.

3. Share your work. As a class, use the models you created to define Art Deco architecture.

Geometric Construction

Have you ever seen a garden maze?

A landscape architect designs outdoor spaces such as gardens and parks. In some of the more interesting gardens, you will find mazes built out of stonewalls or hedging plants. To be able to design a garden maze, a landscape architect needs to understand how geometric shapes fit together, and how their lines and angles are related to each other. A landscape architect often uses a scale drawing to visualize and design the layout of a garden before it is built. In this chapter, you will learn about geometric constructions and scale drawings.

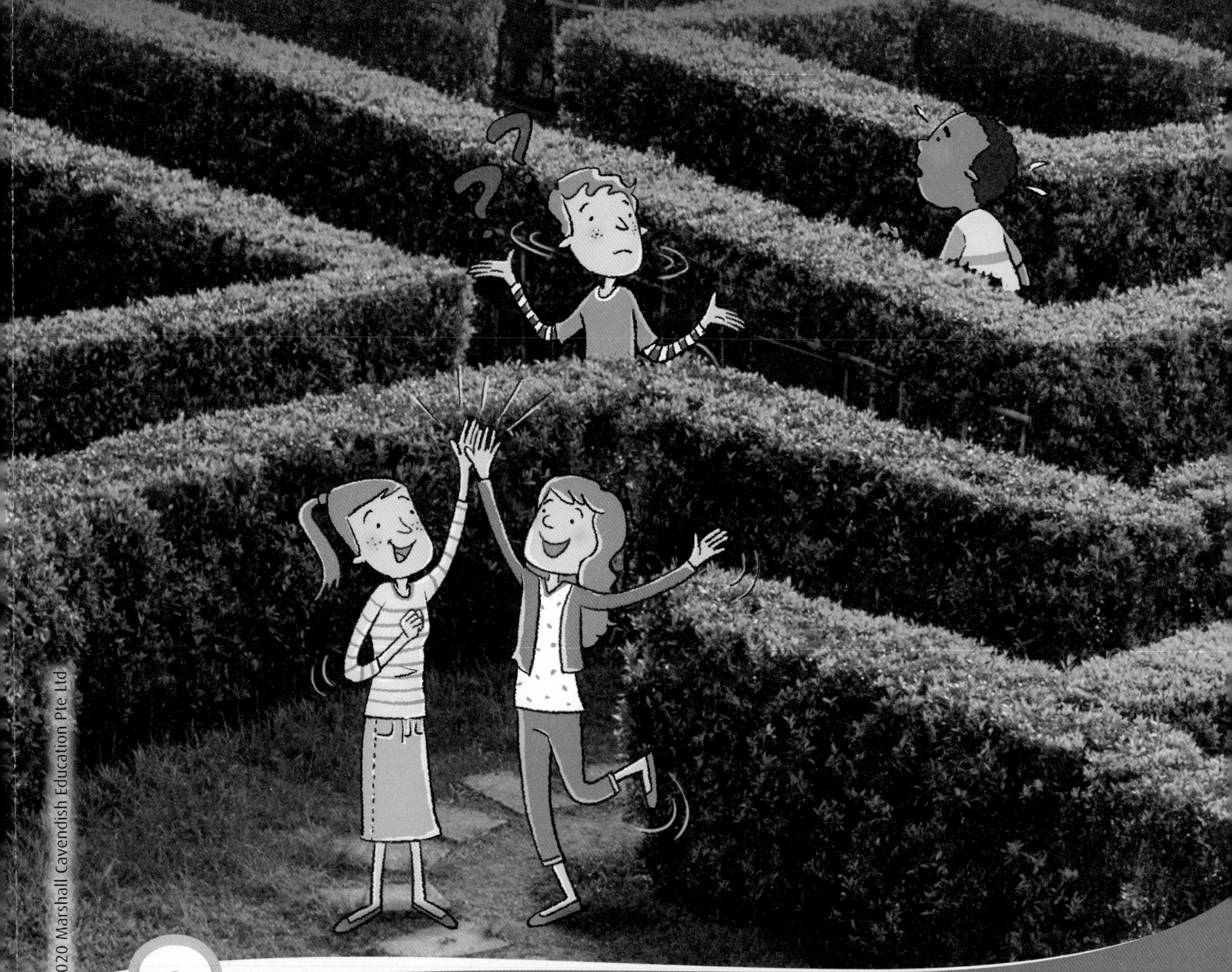

How can you use geometric constructions and scale drawings to solve real-world problems?

Name: ______________________ Date: ____________

Using a protractor to measure an angle in degrees

A ray starts from one endpoint and extends infinitely in one direction. It is specified by a point and a direction. A ray has one endpoint that marks the position from where it begins.

A ray starting from point *A* and passing through *B* is called $\overrightarrow{AB}$, which is read as "ray *AB*." The endpoint is written and read first.

Use the following steps to find the measure of an angle with a protractor.

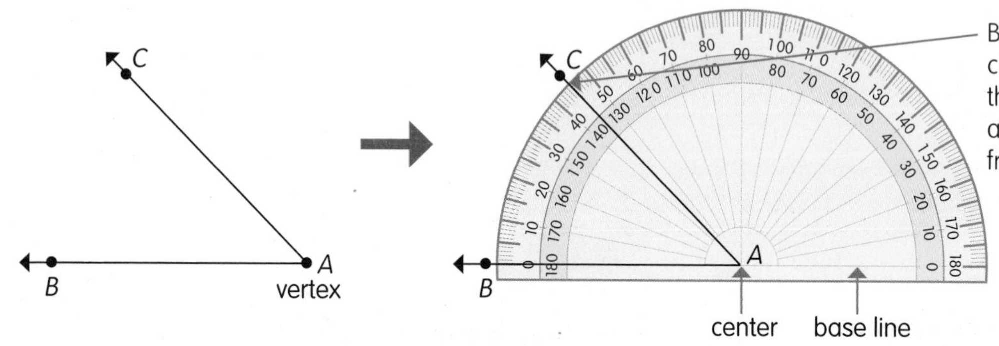

STEP 1 Place the base line of the protractor on ray $\overrightarrow{AB}$.

STEP 2 Place the center of the base line of the protractor at the vertex of the angle.

STEP 3 Read the outer scale. Ray $\overrightarrow{AC}$ passes through the 45° mark. So, the measure of the angle is 45°.

▶ Quick Check

Use a protractor to find the measure of ∠*ABC*.

1. 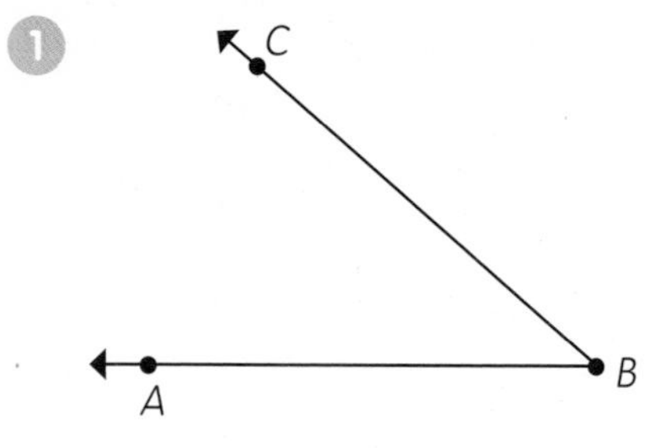

2. 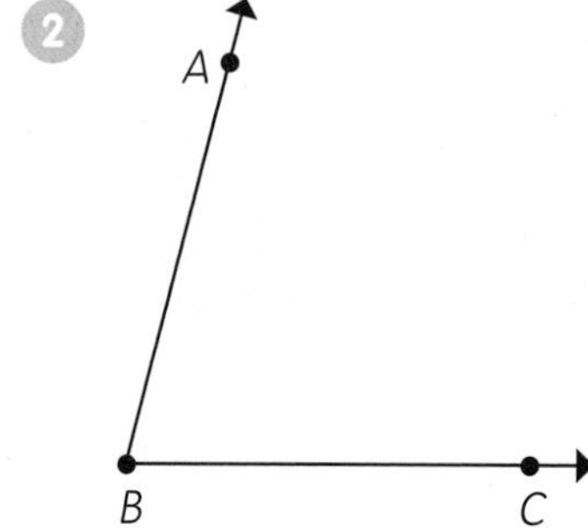

3. 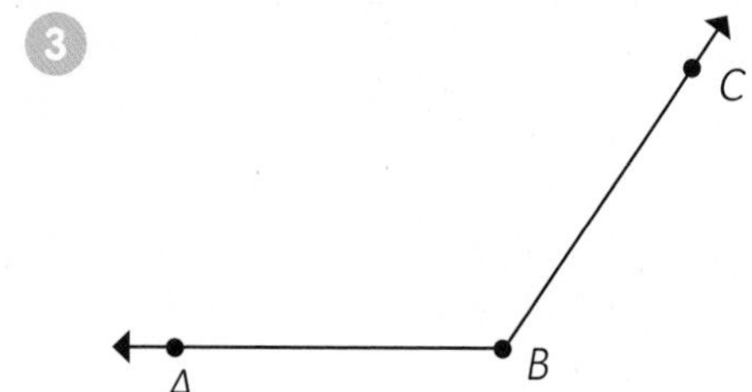

4. 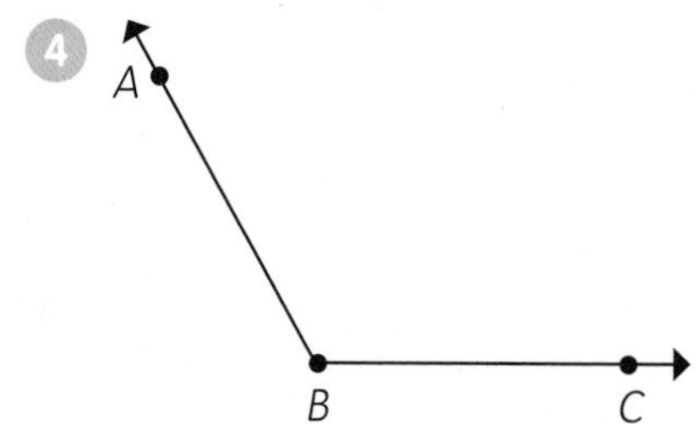

Using a protractor to draw angles

STEP 1 Draw a line and mark a point on the line. This point is the vertex.

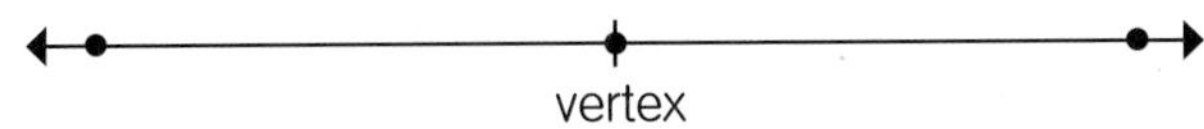

STEP 2 Place the base line of the protractor on the line and the center of the base line on the vertex.

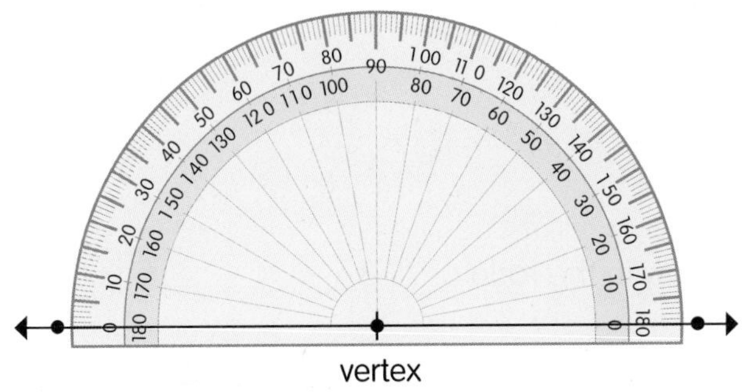

STEP 3 Use the inner scale or the outer scale to find the correct measure. For example, to draw an angle of 50°, find the 50° mark and draw a dot at that mark. Then, draw a ray from the vertex through the dot.

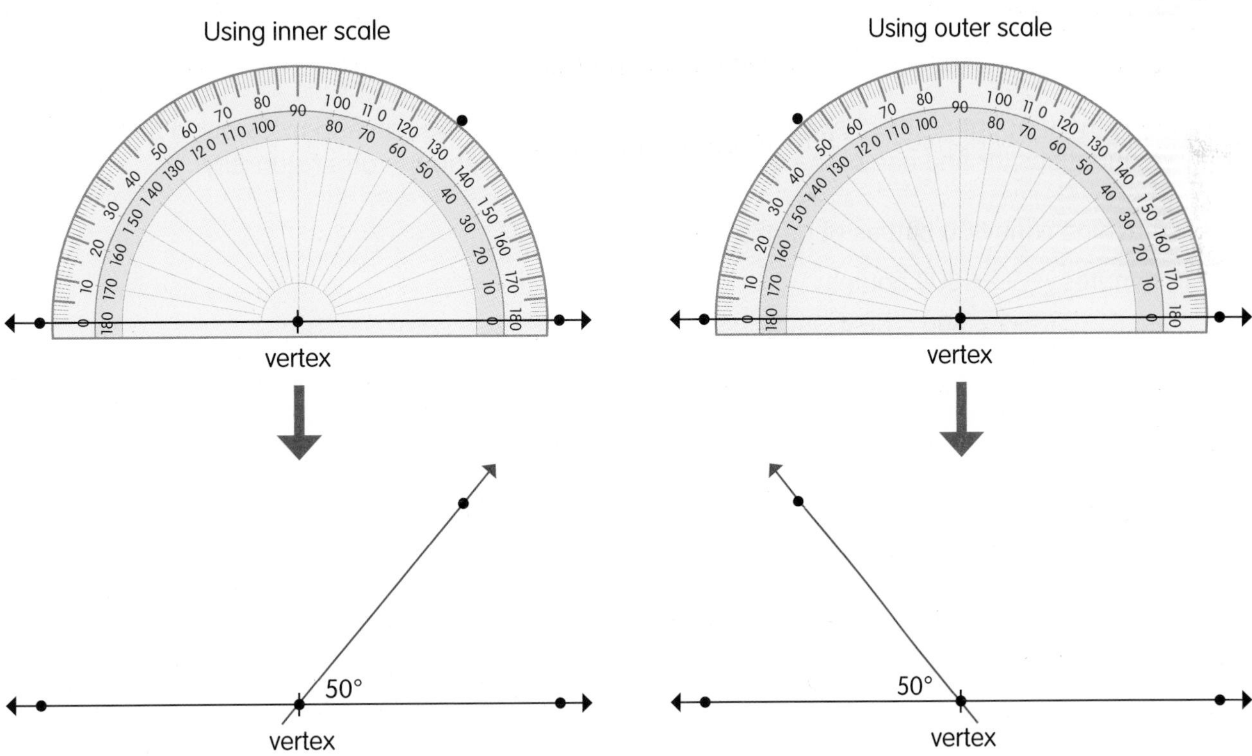

Quick Check

Use a protractor to draw each angle in two ways.

5  m∠DEF = 39°

6  m∠PQR = 146°

RECALL PRIOR KNOWLEDGE

Relating ratio and fraction

You can write a ratio as a fraction.

There are 2 apples and 5 pears on a plate.
The ratio of the number of apples to the number of pears is 2 : 5.
The same ratio can be expressed as a fraction:

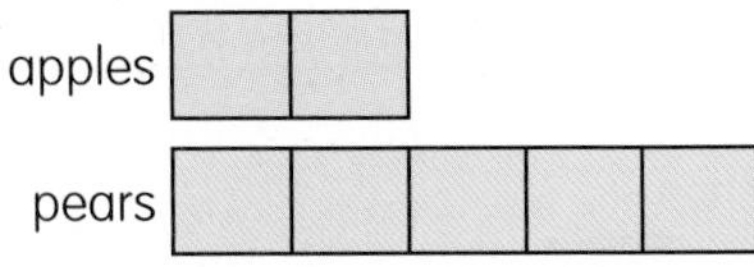

$\frac{\text{Number of apples}}{\text{Number of pears}} = \frac{2}{5}$

The number of apples is $\frac{2}{5}$ the number of pears.

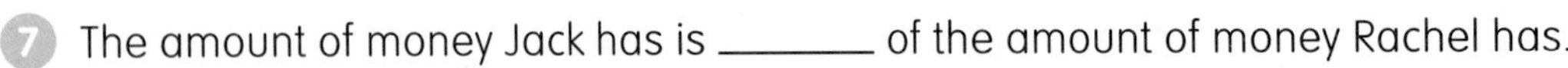

▶ Quick Check

Write each fraction.

Rachel and Jack shared an amount of money in the ratio of 7 : 3.

7. The amount of money Jack has is ________ of the amount of money Rachel has.
8. The amount of money Rachel has is ________ of the amount of money Jack has.
9. The amount of money Rachel has is ________ of the total amount of money.

Finding rate

Rate is the amount of quantity per unit of another quantity. You can find rates given the two quantities, or find one of the quantities given the rate and the other quantity.

A machine cans 800 bottles of drinks in 10 minutes.

10 minutes ⟶ 800 bottles

1 minute ⟶ $\frac{800}{10}$ = 80 bottles

The machine cans bottles of drinks at a rate of 80 bottles per minute.

▶ Quick Check

Answer each question.

10. The cost of gas is $2.71 per gallon in a city. At this rate, what is the price of
    a 10 gallons of gas?
    b 45 gallons of gas?

Name: _______________ Date: _______________

Constructing Triangles

Learning Objectives:

- Construct a triangle with given measures.
- Determine whether a unique triangle, more than one triangle, or no triangle can be drawn from given measures.

New Vocabulary
included side
included angle

Using a ruler, a compass, and a protractor, construct triangle *XYZ* with the given measures in two different ways: m∠*ZXY* = 35°, *XY* = 6.5 cm, and *ZY* = 5 cm. Then, find the two measures of ∠*ZYX*. What do you notice about the two triangles?

ENGAGE

Construct a triangle of sides 2 centimeters, 6 centimeter, and 7 centimeters. How did you construct your triangle? Share your methods and instruments used.

LEARN Construct a triangle given the lengths of all three sides

1. You will learn to construct triangles using a ruler, a compass, and a protractor. One way to construct a unique triangle involves knowing the lengths of its three sides.

2. Use a ruler and a compass to construct triangle *ABC*, where *AB* = 7 cm, *BC* = 2 cm, and *AC* = 6 cm.

Sketch the triangle.

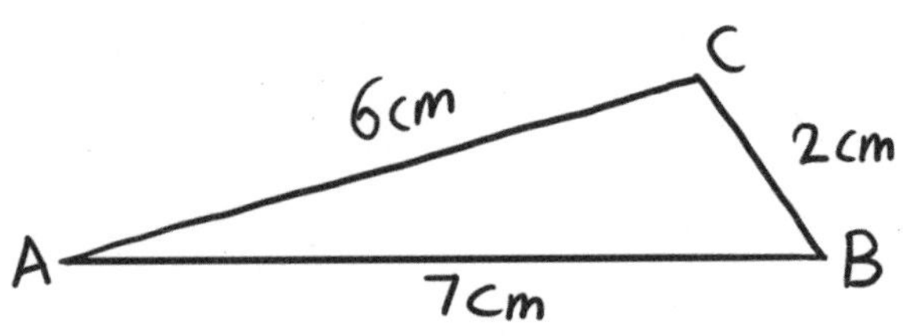

Construct a triangle given the lengths of all three sides

Use a ruler to draw a line segment that is 7 centimeters long. Label the endpoints A and B to form $\overline{AB}$.

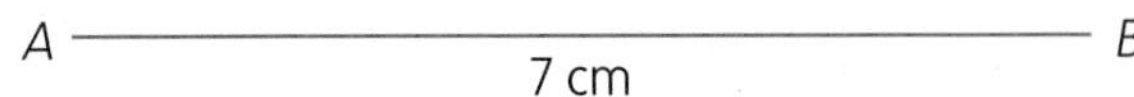

Given that $AC = 6$ cm, use the ruler to measure 6 centimeters on a compass. Then, place the spike of the compass at A and draw an arc above $\overline{AB}$.

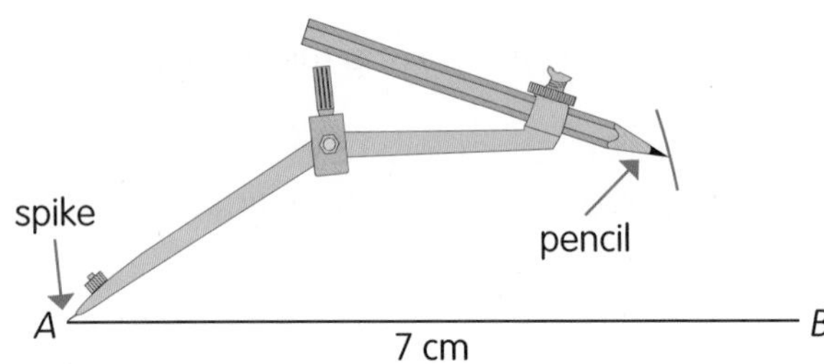

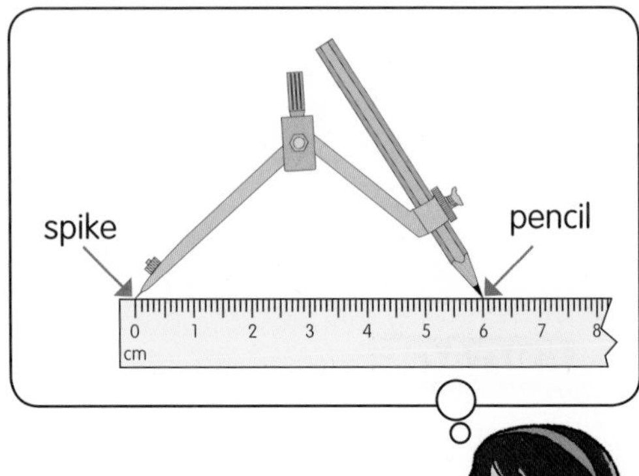

Given that $BC = 2$ cm, use the ruler to measure 2 centimeters on a compass. Then, place the spike of the compass at B and draw an arc that intersects the first arc. Label the point of intersection as C.

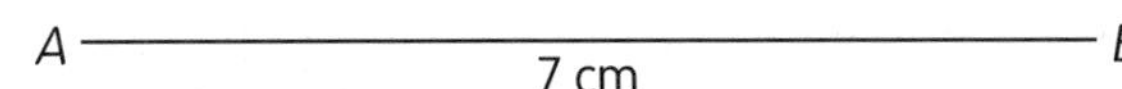

Use the ruler to draw $\overline{AC}$ and $\overline{BC}$.

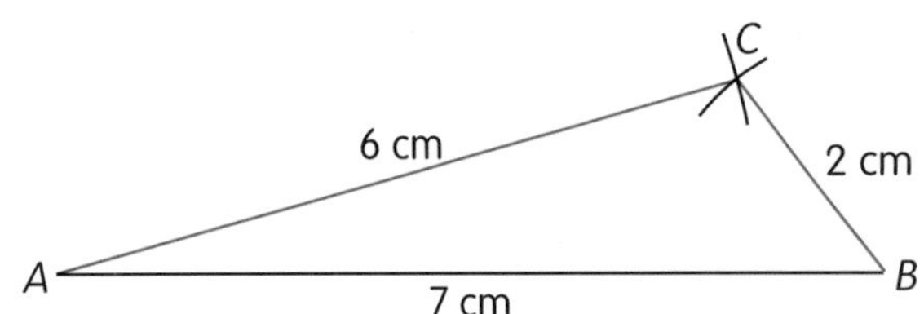

The intersection of the two arcs is 6 centimeters from A and 2 centimeters from B. So, $AC = 6$ cm and $BC = 2$ cm.

TRY Practice constructing a triangle given the lengths of all three sides

Use a ruler and a compass to construct the triangle.

1. Triangle PQR, where $PQ = 5.6$ cm, $QR = 4.5$ cm, and $PR = 8.2$ cm.

ENGAGE

Use a protractor, compass, and ruler to construct a triangle with one angle measuring 80° and a second angle measuring 30°. Measure the sides of your triangle. What observations can you make?

LEARN Construct a triangle given the measures of two angles and an included side

1. Another way to construct a unique triangle involves knowing the measures of two angles and an included side.

Example:

80° 30°

4.3 cm

The side measuring 4.3 centimeters is common to the two angles measuring 80° and 30°.

Math Note

An "included side" in a triangle is the side that is common to two angles in the triangle.

2. Use a ruler and a protractor to construct triangle *XYZ*, where m∠*XYZ* = 40°, m∠*XZY* = 35°, and *YZ* = 8 cm.

STEP 1 Sketch the triangle.

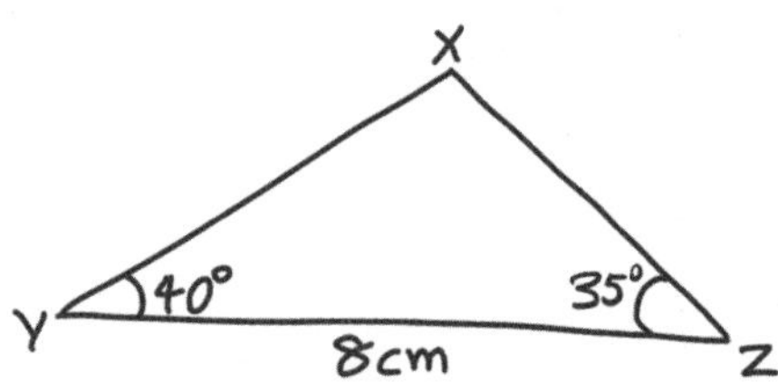

Math Note

$\overline{YZ}$ is the included side between ∠*Y* and ∠*Z*.

STEP 2 Use a ruler to draw $\overline{YZ}$ with a length of 8 centimeters.

Y *Z*

8 cm

STEP 3 Using a protractor, draw ∠*Y* with a measure of 40°.

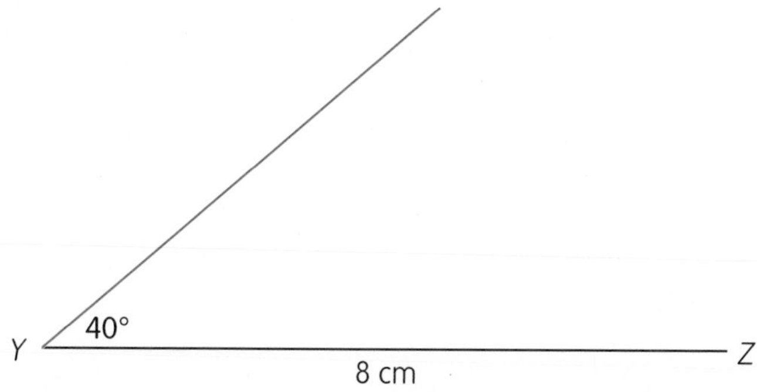

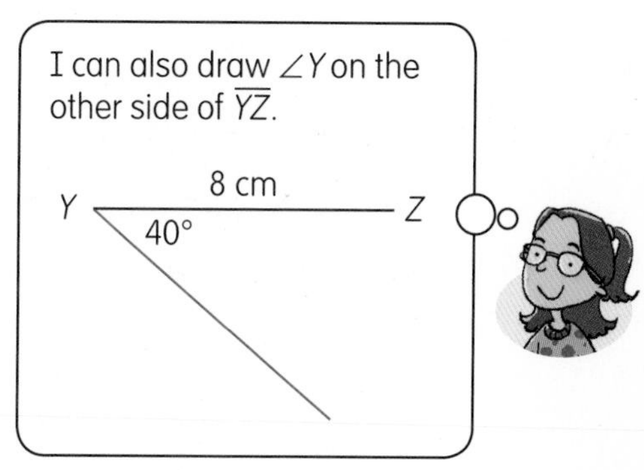

STEP 4 Using a protractor, draw $\angle Z$ with a measure of 35°. Label the point where the two rays intersect as X.

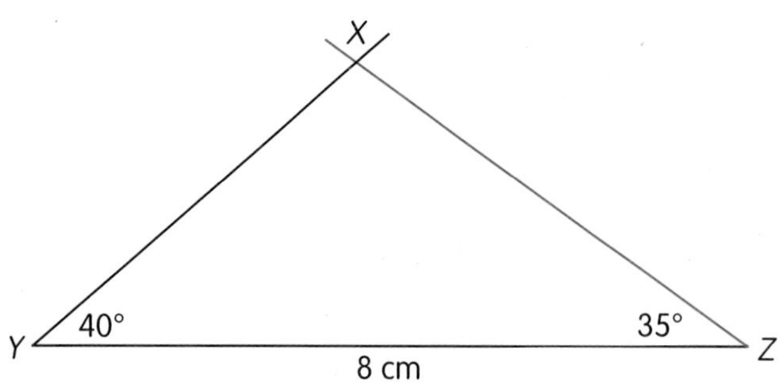

TRY Practice constructing a triangle given the measures of two angles and an included side

Use a ruler, a compass, and a protractor to construct the triangle.

1. Triangle ABC, where $BC = 4$ cm, $m\angle ABC = 25°$, and $m\angle ACB = 120°$.

ENGAGE

Mark wants to buy triangular tiles for his bathroom. He is looking for a triangular tile that measures 3 inches on one side and 4 inches on another and has a 60° angle between the sides. Is it possible? Use a compass, ruler, and protractor to justify your answer.

LEARN Construct a triangle given the measures of two sides and an included angle

1. Another way to construct a unique triangle involves knowing the measures of two sides and an included angle.

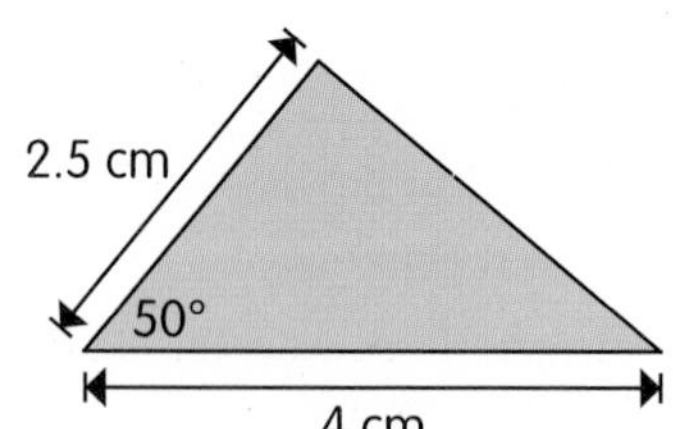

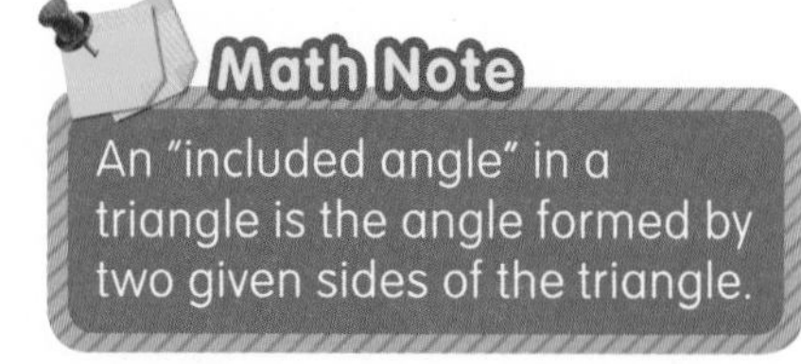

2 Use a ruler, a compass, and a protractor to construct triangle XYZ, where $XY = 5$ cm, $XZ = 3.5$ cm, and $m\angle YXZ = 50°$.

 STEP 1 Sketch the triangle.

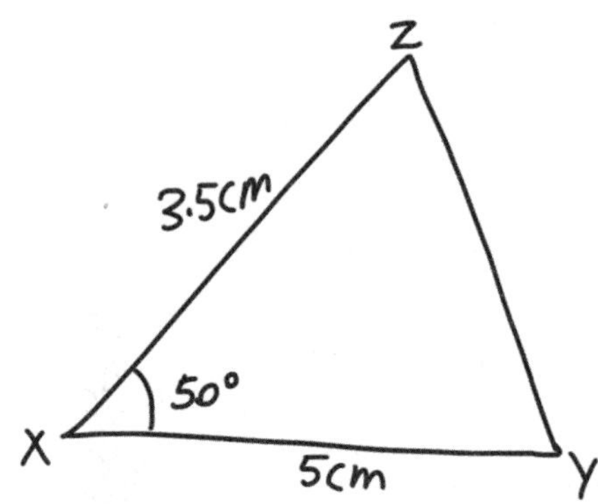

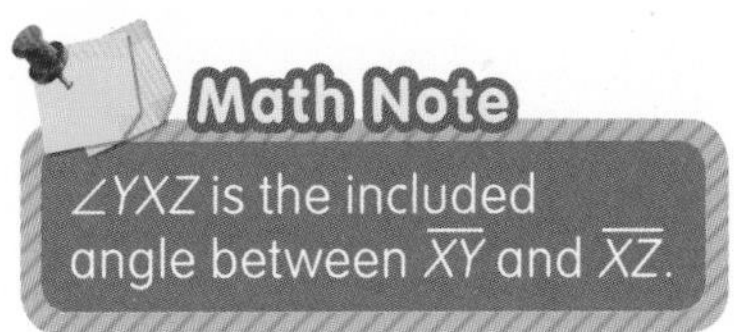

$\angle YXZ$ is the included angle between $\overline{XY}$ and $\overline{XZ}$.

 STEP 2 Use a ruler to draw $\overline{XY}$ with a length of 5 centimeters.

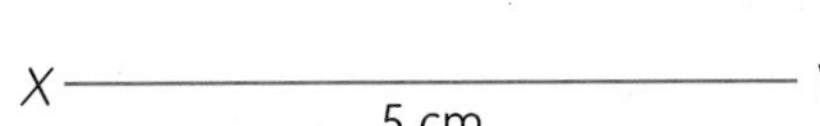

STEP 3 Using a protractor, draw $\angle X$ with a measure of 50°.

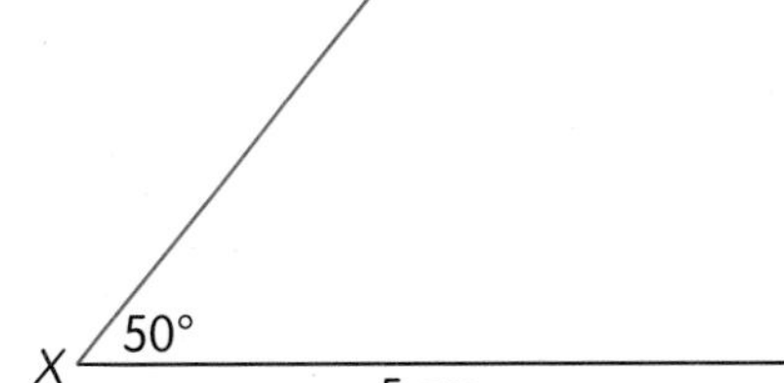

 STEP 4 Given that $XZ = 3.5$ cm, use a ruler to measure 3.5 centimeters on a compass. Then, place the spike of the compass at X and draw an arc intersecting the ray drawn in Step 3. Label this point of intersection as Z.

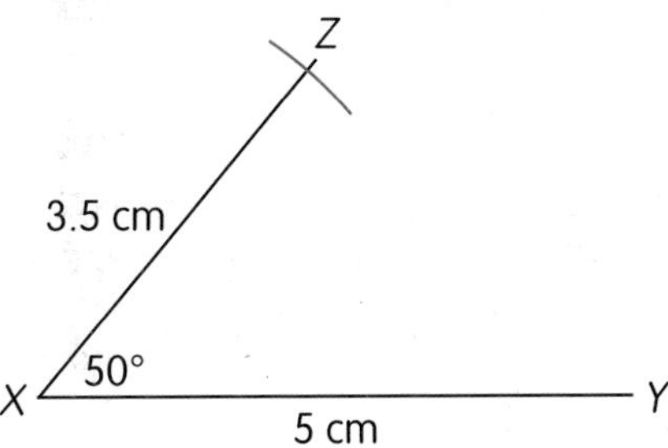

 STEP 5 Draw $\overline{YZ}$.

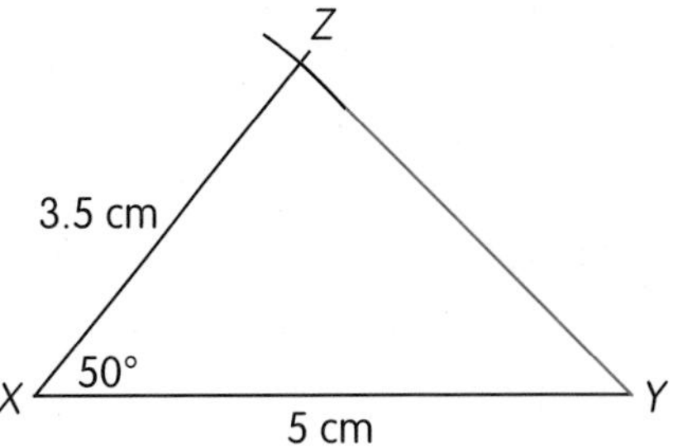

Math Talk

Could you have started with the 3.5-centimeter side?
How would this change the steps used to draw the triangle?
How would it affect the resulting triangle?

TRY Practice constructing a triangle given the measures of two sides and an included angle

Use a ruler, a compass, and a protractor to construct the triangle.

1. Triangle KLM, where $KL = 8.2$ cm, $KM = 6.9$ cm, and $m\angle LKM = 75°$.

ENGAGE

a What are the steps you will take to construct an obtuse triangle?

b In an obtuse triangle, if the measure of one angle is 35° and the perimeter of the triangle is 30 centimeters, what are possible side lengths of the triangle?

LEARN Construct a triangle given the measures of two sides and a nonincluded angle

1. It is possible to construct a triangle given the measures of two sides and a nonincluded angle.

2. Use a ruler, a compass, and a protractor to construct obtuse triangle WXY, where $WY = 4.5$ cm, $WX = 2.5$ cm, and $m\angle XYW = 25°$.

STEP 1 Sketch the triangle.

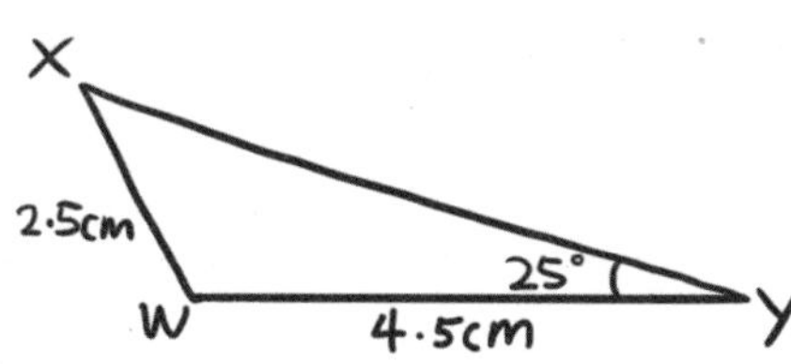

To make this sketch, look for a line segment that forms a side of the given angle. Use $\overline{WY}$ for the base of the triangle.

STEP 2 Use a ruler to draw $\overline{WY}$ with a length of 4.5 centimeters.

W —— Y
4.5 cm

STEP 3 Using a protractor, draw $\angle Y$ with a measure of 25°.

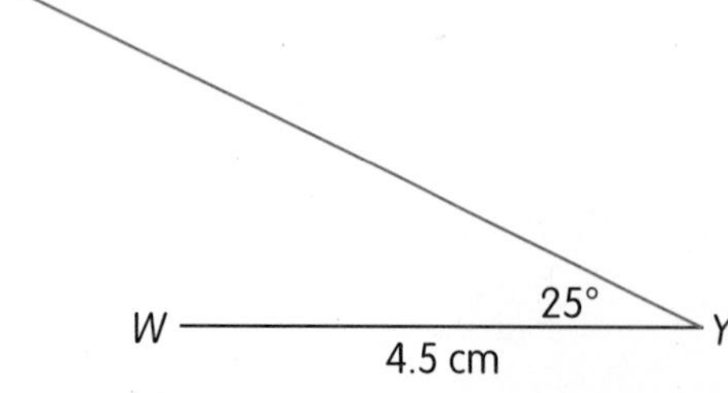

Given that $WX = 2.5$ cm, use a ruler to measure 2.5 centimeters on a compass. Then, place the spike of the compass at W and draw an arc intersecting the ray drawn in Step 3. Label this point of intersection as X.

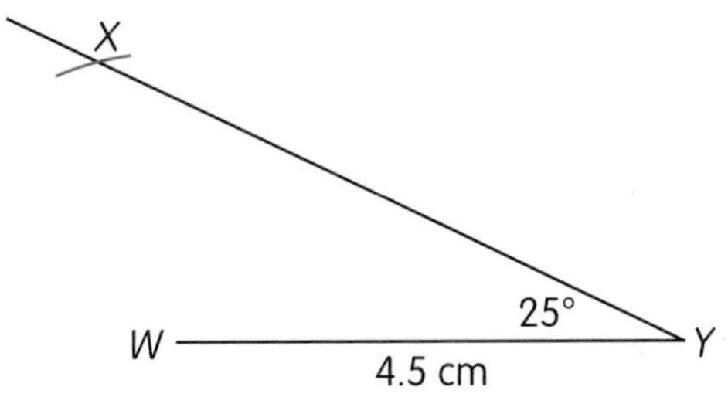

Draw $\overline{WX}$.

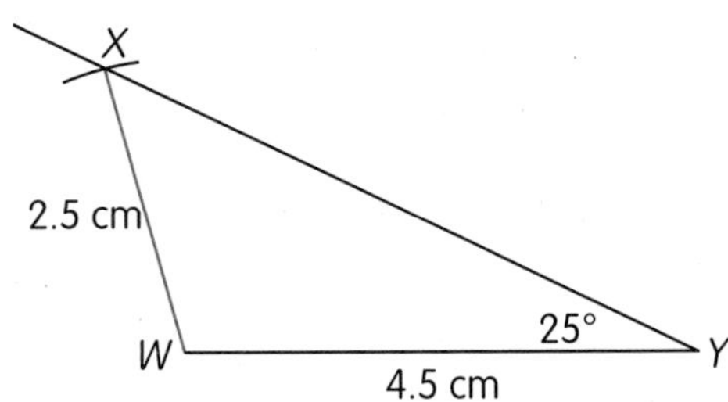

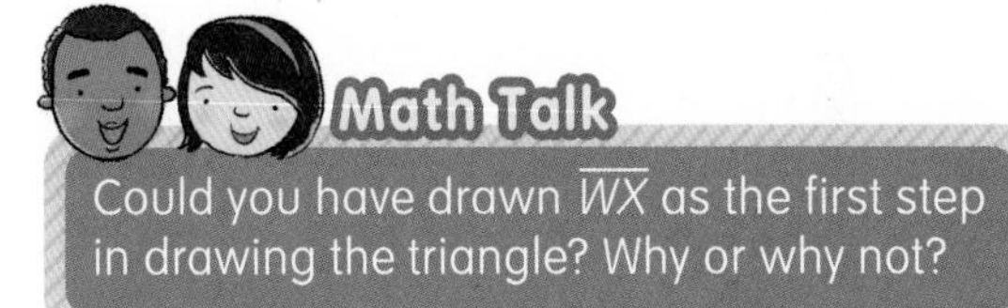

TRY Practice constructing a triangle given the measures of two sides and a nonincluded angle

Use a ruler, a compass, and a protractor to construct the triangle.

1. Triangle XYZ, where $XY = 7$ cm, $XZ = 9$ cm, and $m\angle XYZ = 125°$.

ENGAGE

Construct triangle STU, where $ST = 5$ cm, $TU = 3$ cm, and $m\angle UST = 25°$, in two different ways. What do you notice about the triangles? Share your observations.

LEARN Identify the conditions that determine a unique triangle

Activity Deciding whether given measures can be used to construct triangles

Activity 1

1. Use a geometry software to construct each of the following triangles with the given lengths, if possible.

Triangle	Length of sides (cm)		
A	2	3	7
B	4	4	8
C	3	4	6

(2) **Mathematical Habit 2 Use mathematical reasoning**
Were there any triangles you could not construct? Why do you think it is not possible to construct the triangle(s)? Explain.

(3) Measure each of the three angles of the triangle(s) you drew in (1).

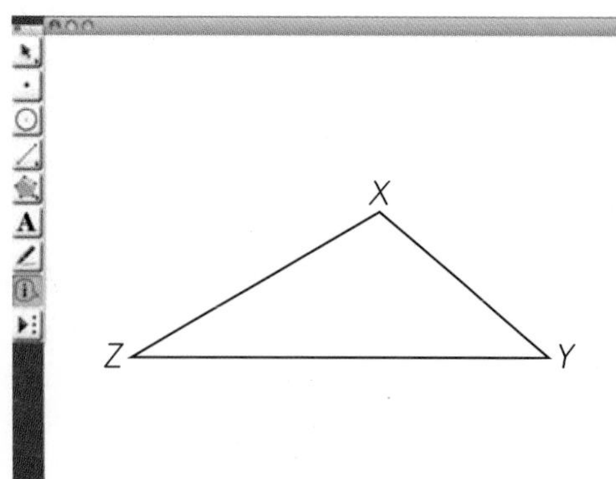

$ZY = ?$ $m\angle ZXY = ?$
$ZX = ?$ $m\angle XYZ = ?$
$XY = ?$ $m\angle YZX = ?$

What do you notice about the size of each angle and the length of its opposite side?

(4) Draw another triangle with different lengths. Is your observation correct?

> The sum of the two shorter sides of any triangle is greater than its longest side. The side opposite the largest angle is the longest. Similarly, the side opposite the smallest angle is the shortest.

Activity 2

(1) Use a ruler, a compass, and a protractor to construct each of the following triangles, if possible.

a Triangle ABC, where $AB = 7$ cm, $BC = 8$ cm, and $AC = 11$ cm.
b Triangle DEF, where $DE = 4.6$ cm, $EF = 6$ cm, and $DF = 12$ cm.
c Triangle GHI, where $GH = 6$ cm, $HI = 5$ cm, and $m\angle GHI = 50°$.
d Triangle JKL, where $JK = 6$ cm, $JL = 4.7$ cm, and $m\angle JKL = 50°$.
e Triangle MNP, where $MN = 7$ cm, $m\angle MNP = 60°$, and $m\angle PMN = 40°$.

(2) **Mathematical Habit 2 Use mathematical reasoning**
Were there any triangles you could not construct? Were there any triangles that you could construct in more than one way? Explain.

Math Talk

Is it always possible to construct a unique triangle given information about some of its measures? Justify your answer.
a Given three side lengths
b Given two side lengths and an angle measure

1. Suppose you are given these measures for triangle XYZ, $m\angle YXZ = 40°$, $XY = 7.4$ cm, and $YZ = 3$ cm. When you try to draw the triangle, you will notice that $\overline{YZ}$ is not long enough to intersect the third side of the triangle.

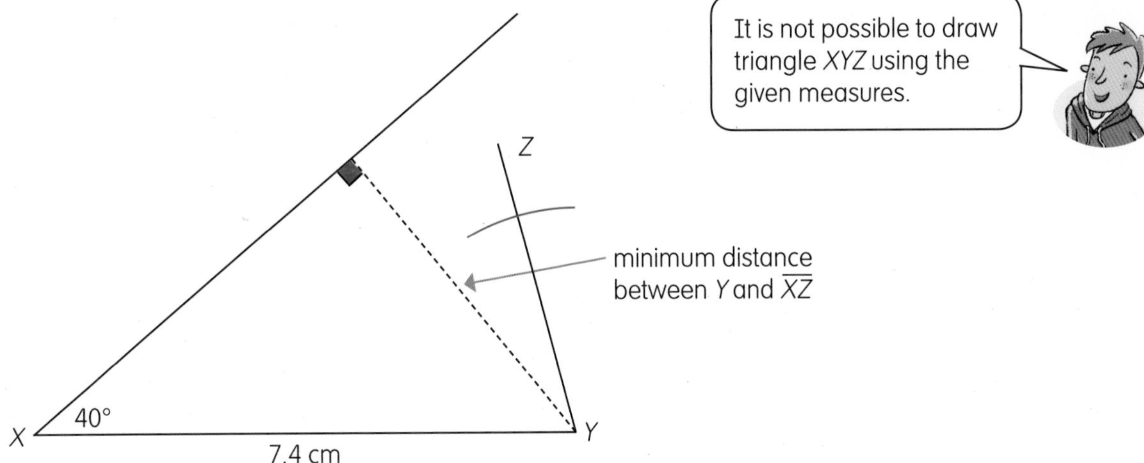

2. Suppose you are given these measures for triangle XYZ, $m\angle YXZ = 40°$, $XY = 7.4$ cm, and $YZ = 5.2$ cm. After drawing $\overline{XY}$ and $\angle X$, you will discover that you can draw two different triangles.

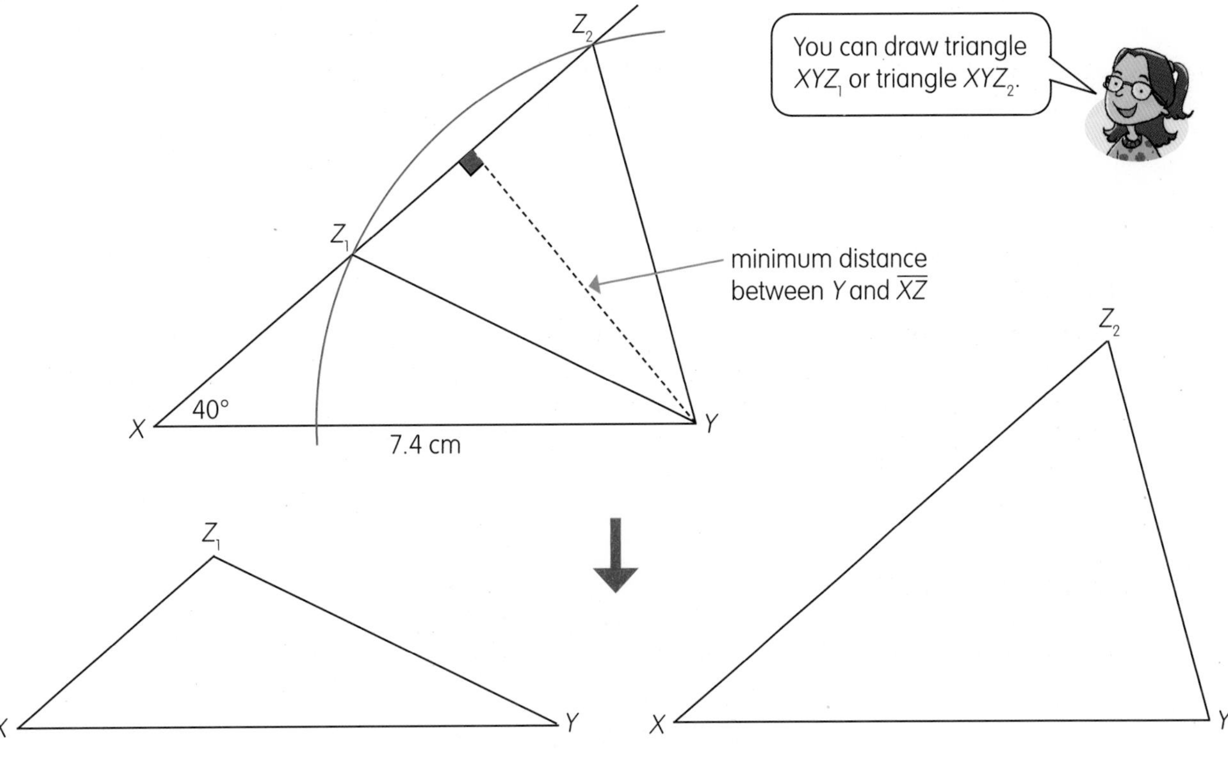

You can construct one, more than one, or no triangle, depending on the given measures.

TRY Practice identifying the conditions that determine a unique triangle.

Use a ruler, a compass, and a protractor to construct each triangle, if possible. Then, determine the number of triangles that can be constructed.

1. Triangle ABC, where $AB = 8$ cm, $BC = 6.5$ cm, and $AC = 3.8$ cm.

2. Triangle XYZ, where $XY = 7$ cm, $YZ = 5.5$ cm, and $m\angle YXZ = 50°$.

3. Triangle DEF, where $DE = 8$ cm, $DF = 5$ cm, and $m\angle DEF = 50°$.

4. Triangle PQR, where $PQ = 4.8$ cm, $QR = 5.4$ cm, and $m\angle PQR = 100°$.

5. Triangle ABC, where $AB = 6.2$ cm, $BC = 4.8$ cm, and $m\angle BAC = 75°$.

6. Triangle STU, where $ST = 7.7$ cm, $SU = 5.2$ cm, and $m\angle STU = 40°$.

Name: ____________________ Date: ____________

INDEPENDENT PRACTICE

Use the given information to construct each triangle.

1. In triangle CDE, $CD = 7$ cm, $DE = 4$ cm, and $CE = 6.5$ cm.

2. In triangle ABC, $BC = 6$ cm, $m\angle ABC = 30°$, and $m\angle ACB = 60°$. Find $m\angle BAC$ and $\overline{AC}$.

3. In an equilateral triangle, each side length is 6.5 centimeters long.

4. In triangle ABC, $AB = 4$ cm, $AC = 5$ cm, and $m\angle ABC = 40°$.

5. In triangle ABC, $AB = 6$ cm, $BC = 8$ cm, and $AC = 10$ cm. What kind of triangle is triangle ABC? Classify it by both sides and angles.

6. In triangle XYZ, $XY = XZ = 4$ cm, $YZ = 5$ cm. Find $m\angle XZY$.

Solve.

7. Triangle PQR has the dimensions shown in the diagram.
   a Construct triangle PQR.

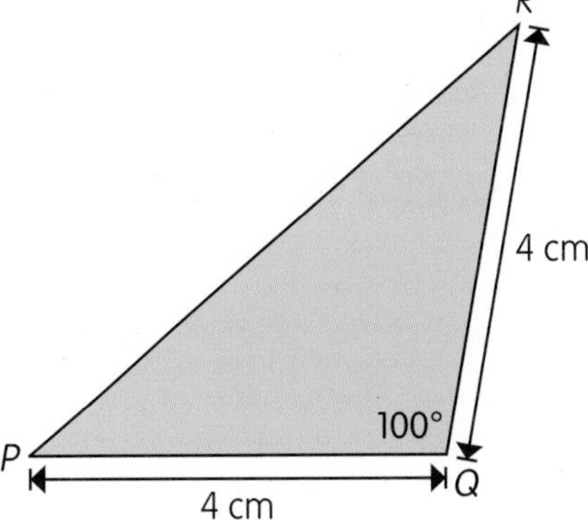

   b From your construction, measure the length of $\overline{PR}$ using a ruler.

   c Find the measures of $\angle P$ and $\angle R$ without using a protractor. Justify your answer.

8 **Mathematical Habit 2 Use mathematical reasoning**
Is it possible to construct a triangle *PQR* in which *PQ* = 12 cm, *PR* = 5 cm, and *QR* = 4 cm? Explain.

9 Three triangles have angle measures of 50° and 60°. In one triangle, the side included between these angles is 2 centimeters. In the second triangle, the included side length is 3 centimeters, and in the third triangle, the included side length is 4 centimeters.

a Construct the three triangles.

b In each triangle, what is the measure of the third angle?

c Using the triangles constructed to help you, what can you deduce about the number of triangles that can be constructed if you are given three angle measures of a triangle but not the measure of any side length?

10 **Mathematical Habit 2 Use mathematical reasoning**
Suppose you are given three angle measures with a sum of 180°. Can you construct a triangle given this information? Can you construct other different triangles? Explain.

Name: ______________________ Date: __________

2 Scale Drawings and Lengths

Learning Objectives:

- Identify the scale factor.
- Calculate lengths and distances from scale drawings.
- Solve length problems involving scale drawings.

New Vocabulary
scale
scale factor

THINK

The scale of a map is 1 inch : 25 miles. If the actual distance between two towns is 125 miles, how far apart are the two towns on the map?

ENGAGE

Measure the length of your desk. Now, take a photo of the top view of your desk. Measure the length of the desk in the photo. How many times smaller is the desk in the photo than your actual desk? Discuss.

LEARN Identify scale and scale factor

1. Geometric constructions and scale drawings are closely related to each other in real life. For example, engineers and designers use geometric principles and constructions to make actual-sized drawings of objects, such as machine components or pieces for do-it-yourself assembly kits.

   However, it is not always possible to draw an object at its actual size. You may need to use a scale drawing that shows the object at a larger or a smaller size. Floor plans and maps are examples of scale drawings.

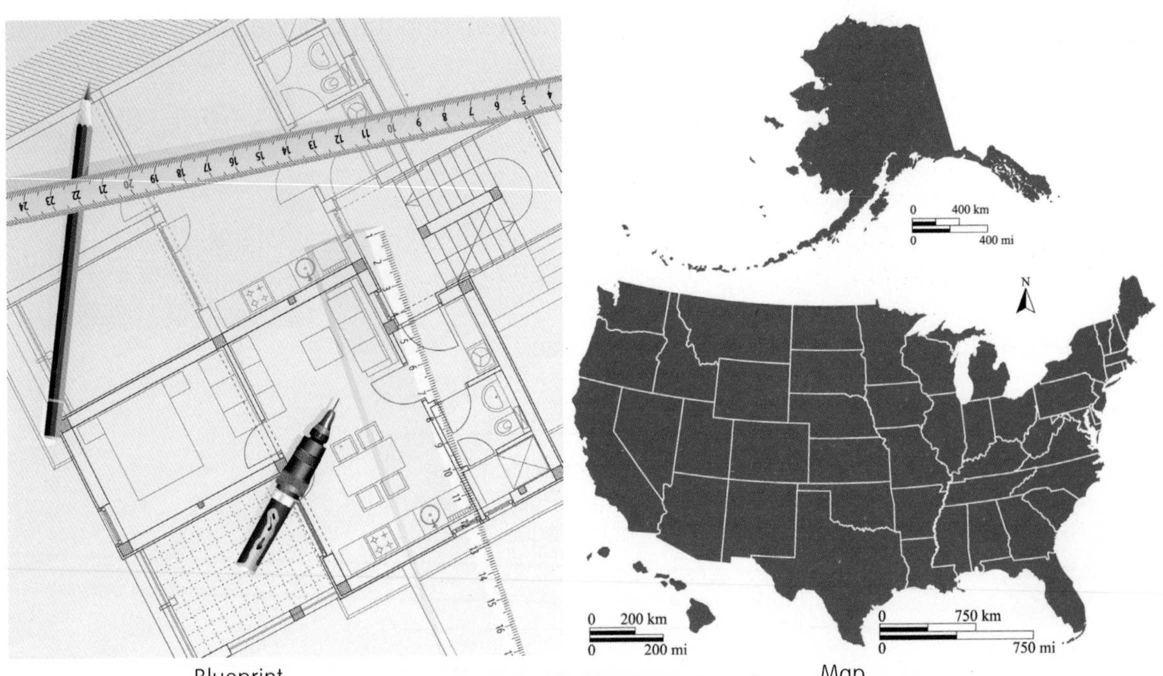

Blueprint

Map

2 The scale of a scale drawing is a comparison of a length in the drawing to the corresponding length in the actual object. In the floor plan on the right, 1 inch on the drawing represents 10 feet in the actual room. You can write the scale as 1 inch to 10 feet or 1 inch : 10 feet.

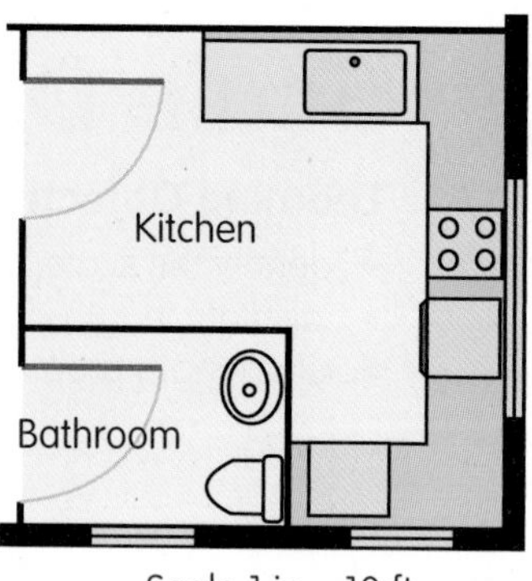

Scale 1 in. : 10 ft

The scale factor of a scale drawing is the ratio of a length in the drawing to the corresponding length in the actual object, expressed in the same units. You can find the scale factor for the drawing by remembering that 1 foot = 12 inches, and then rewriting 10 feet as 120 inches.

Scale factor $= \frac{1}{120}$

The scale factor is sometimes called the constant of proportionality.

3 Using a photocopier, you want to reduce this poster to the smaller size shown. What percent reduction should you choose?

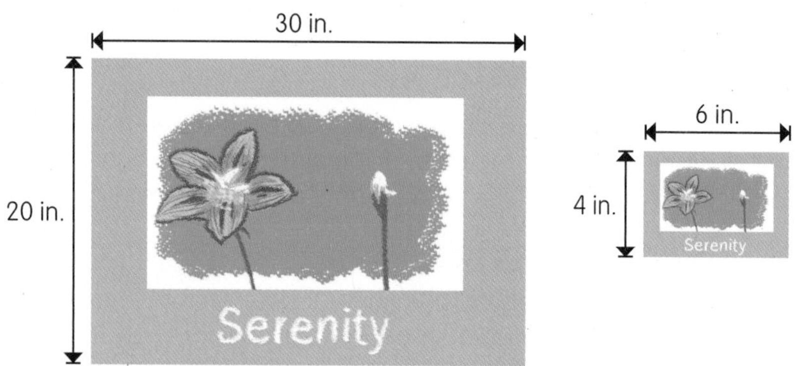

The 30-inch length of the poster is to be 6 inches in the reduction.
The 20-inch height is to be 4 inches in the reduction. Find the scale factor of the reduction. Then, write the scale factor as a percent.

Scale factor $= \frac{6 \text{ in.}}{30 \text{ in.}}$ → Reduced length / Actual length

$= \frac{1}{5}$

$= 20\%$

You need to reduce it to 20% of its original size.

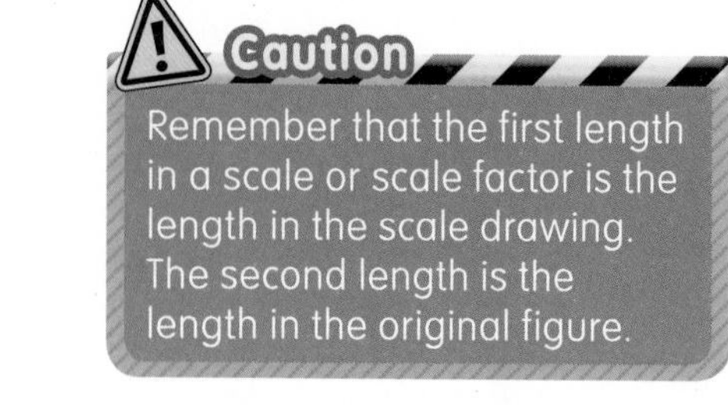

You can check your answer by multiplying the scale factor by the height of the original poster. You should get the height of the reduced copy.

$20 \cdot \frac{1}{5} = 4$ in.

Activity Drawing a scale figure and calculating the scale factor

Work in pairs.

1. The figure below is formed by nine squares and a triangle enclosed in a polygon. Produce scale drawings of the figure using two square grids of different grid sizes.

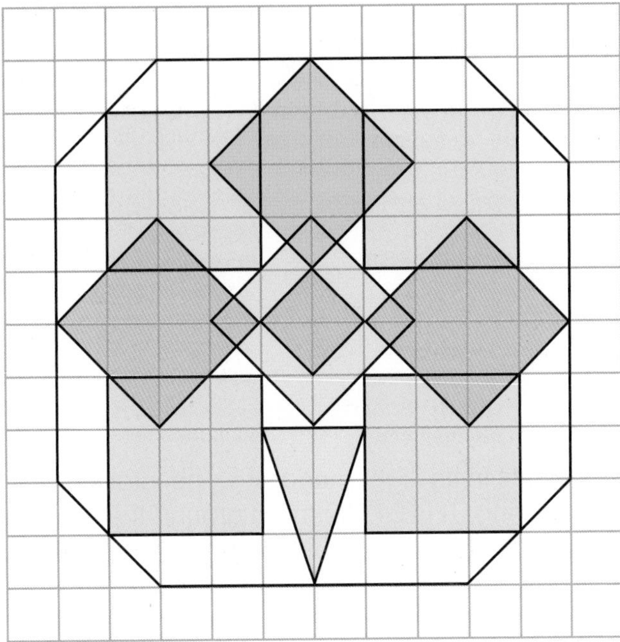

2. Use your ruler to measure a length in the original drawing. Then, measure the corresponding length in each of your scale drawings.

3. Find the scale factor for each drawing using:

$$\frac{\text{Length in reduced or enlarged drawing}}{\text{Length in original drawing}}$$

4. Compare and check your answers with your classmates'.

TRY Practice calculating a scale factor

The diagrams are not drawn to scale. Calculate the scale factor.

1. Trapezoid A has been enlarged to produce trapezoid B. Find the scale factor.

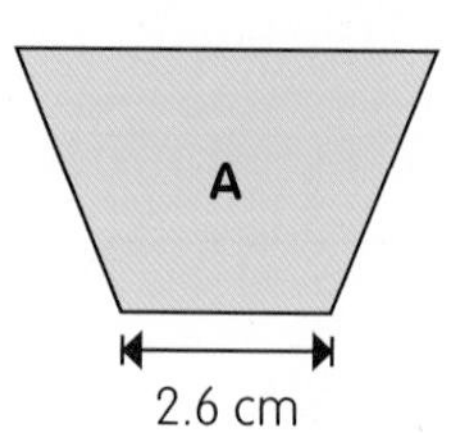

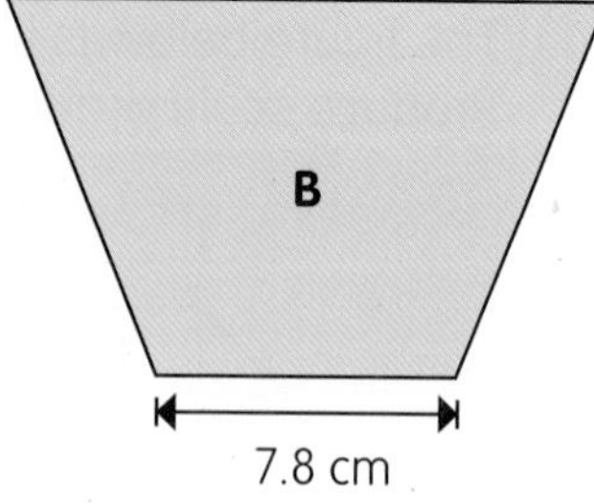

Scale factor $= \dfrac{\text{Scaled length}}{\text{Original length}}$

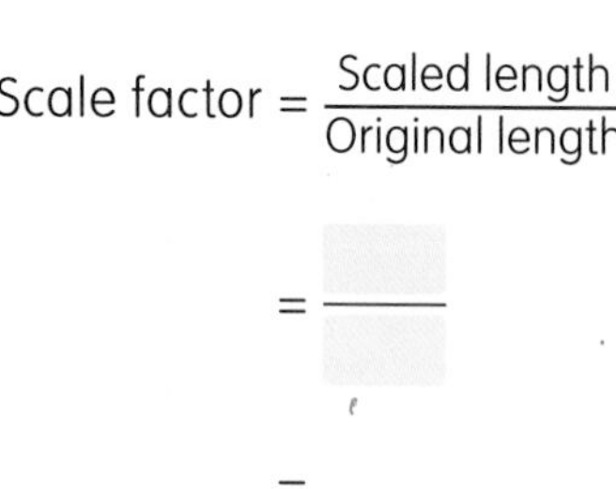

$= \dfrac{\quad}{\quad}$

$=$ ______

ENGAGE

An airline wants to use a map to show its flight routes in its flight magazine. The total length available on the page in the magazine is 14 inches long. It is 24,902 miles around the equator. Approximately, what would the scale have to be for the airline to show the entire world map? Explain your thinking.

LEARN Calculate lengths and distances from scale drawings

1. The scale on a map compares a distance on the map to an actual distance. Often the scale is shown using different units, such as 1 inch : 24 meters. Sometimes a map scale is written without units, such as 1 : 20,000. This scale factor means that 1 centimeter on a map represents an actual distance of 20,000 centimeters or 200 meters.

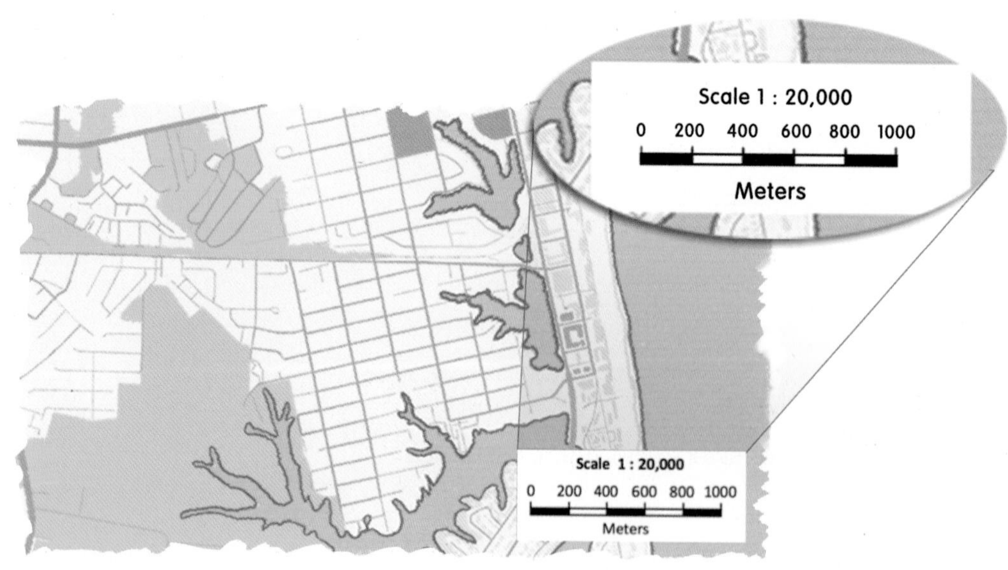

2 The scale of a map is 1 inch : 25 miles. If the length of Whitley Road on the map is 4.5 inches, find the actual length of Whitley Road, in miles.

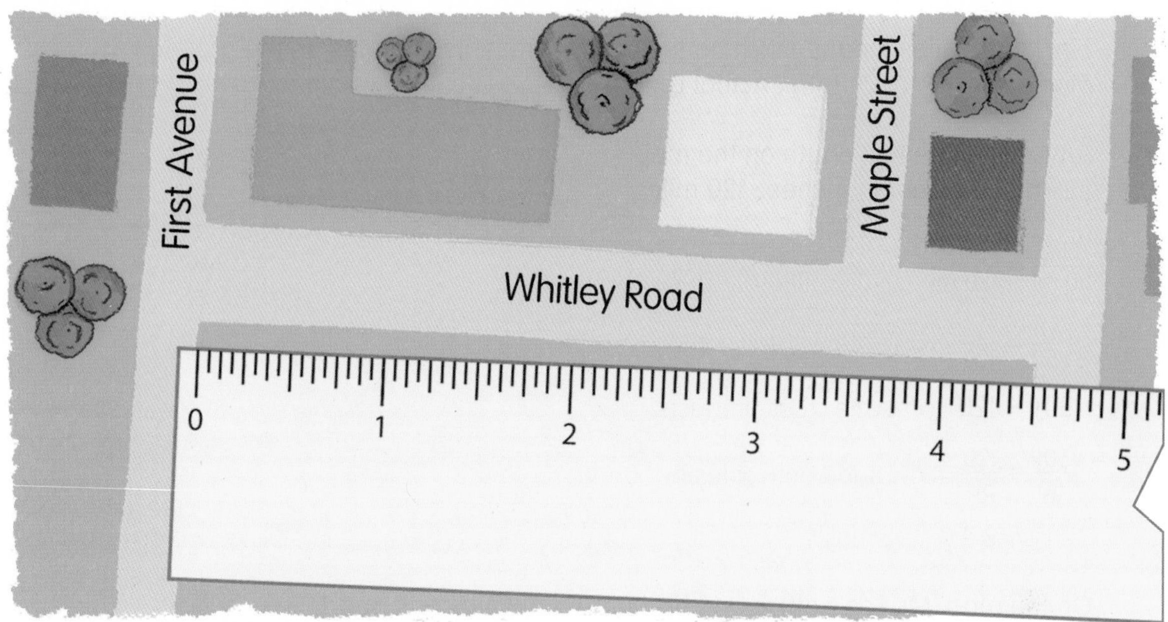

1 inch : 25 miles means 1 inch on the map represents 25 miles on the ground.
Map scale = Map length : Actual length

Let x miles be the actual length of Whitley Road.
1 inch : 25 miles = 4.5 inches : x miles

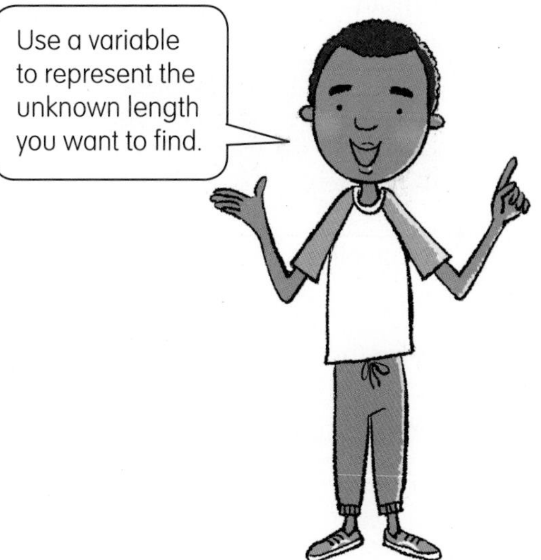

$\frac{1 \text{ in.}}{25 \text{ mi}} = \frac{4.5 \text{ in.}}{x \text{ mi}}$ Write ratios in fraction form.

$\frac{1}{25} = \frac{4.5}{x}$ Write without units.

$1 \cdot x = 4.5 \cdot 25$ Write cross products.

$x = 112.5$ Simplify.

The actual length of Whitley Road is 112.5 miles.

Math Talk

The actual length of First Avenue is 150 miles.
How do you find the length of First Avenue on the map? Explain.

3 The actual distance between Mr. Lee's office and his home is 120 miles. A map that shows his office and his home uses a scale of 1 inch : 50 miles. How far apart on the map are Mr. Lee's office and his home?

1 inch : 50 miles means 1 inch on the map represents 50 miles on the ground.
Map scale = Map length : Actual Length

Let y inches be the length on the map.
1 inch : 50 miles = y inches : 120 miles

$\frac{1 \text{ in.}}{50 \text{ mi}} = \frac{y \text{ in.}}{120 \text{ mi}}$ Write ratios in fraction form.

$\frac{1}{50} = \frac{y}{120}$ Write without units.

$50y = 120$ Write cross products.

$\frac{50y}{50} = \frac{120}{50}$ Divide both sides by 50.

$y = 2.4$ Simplify.

On the map, Mr. Lee's office and his home are 2.4 inches apart.

4 A train model is built on a scale of 1 : 64. The length of the locomotive of the train model is 8 inches, while the length of the coal tender is 5 inches. Find the actual lengths of the locomotive and the coal tender in feet. Round your answers to the nearest tenth.

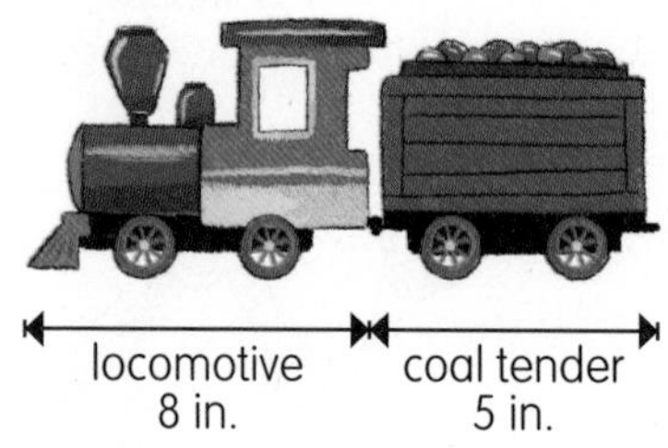

Let x be the actual length of the locomotive, and y be the actual length of the coal tender.

1 : 64 = Scaled length of the locomotive : Actual length of the locomotive.

$1 : 64 = 8 : x$ Substitute values.

$\frac{1}{64} = \frac{8}{x}$ Write ratios in fraction form.

$x = 8 \cdot 64$ Write cross products.

$x = 512$ Simplify.

12 in. = 1 ft

$512 \text{ in.} = \frac{1}{12} \cdot 512$

$\approx 42.7 \text{ ft}$

The actual length of the locomotive is about 42.7 feet.

1 : 64 = Scaled length of coal tender : Actual length of coal tender

$1 : 64 = 5 : y$ Substitute values.

$\frac{1}{64} = \frac{5}{y}$ Write ratios in fraction form.

$y = 5 \cdot 64$ Write cross products.

$y = 320$ Simplify.

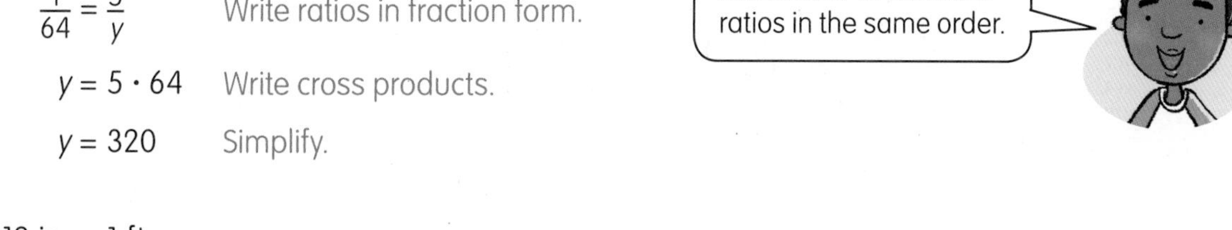

12 in. = 1 ft

$320 \text{ in.} = \frac{1}{12} \cdot 320$

$\approx 26.7 \text{ ft}$

The actual length of the coal tender is about 26.7 feet.

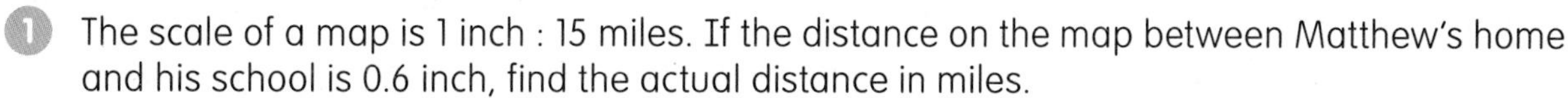

TRY Practice calculating lengths and distances from scale drawings

Solve.

1. The scale of a map is 1 inch : 15 miles. If the distance on the map between Matthew's home and his school is 0.6 inch, find the actual distance in miles.

   1 inch : 15 miles means ______ inch on the map represents ______ miles on the ground.

   Let x miles be the actual distance.
   1 inch : 15 miles = 0.6 inch : x miles

   $\frac{1 \text{ in.}}{15 \text{ mi}} = \frac{0.6 \text{ in.}}{x \text{ mi}}$ Write ratios in fraction form.

   $\frac{1}{15} = \frac{0.6}{x}$ Write without units.

   $1 \cdot x =$ ______ $\cdot$ ______ Write cross products.

   $x =$ ______ Simplify.

   The actual distance is ______ miles.

2 The actual distance between Boston and New York is about 220 miles. A map uses a scale of 1 inch : 85 miles. About how far apart on the map are the two cities? Round your answer to the nearest tenth.

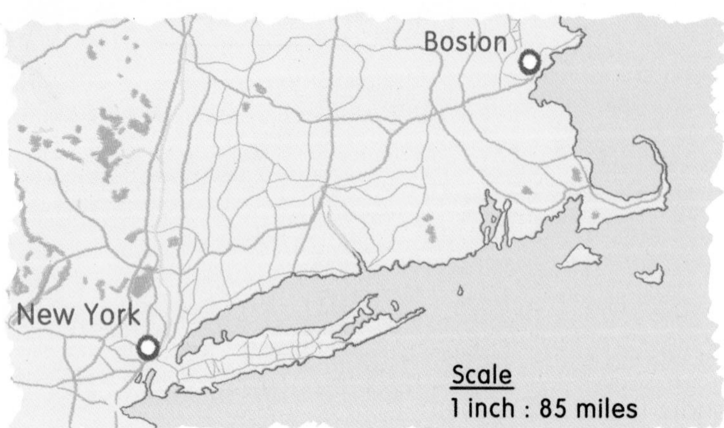

1 inch : 85 miles means ______ inch on the map represents ______ miles on the ground.

Let x inches be the length on the map.
1 inch : 85 miles = x inches : 220 miles

$$\frac{1 \text{ in.}}{85 \text{ mi}} = \frac{x \text{ in.}}{220 \text{ mi}}$$ Write ratios in fraction form.

$$\frac{1}{85} = \frac{x}{220}$$ Write without units.

______ $\cdot x =$ ______ $\cdot$ ______ Write cross products.

$\frac{\_\_\_}{\_\_\_}x = \frac{\_\_\_}{\_\_\_}$ Divide both sides by ______.

$x \approx$ ______ Simplify.

On the map, the two cities are about ______ inches apart.

3 A car model is built using a scale of 1 : 18.
The length of the car model is 12 inches.
Find the actual length of the car in feet.

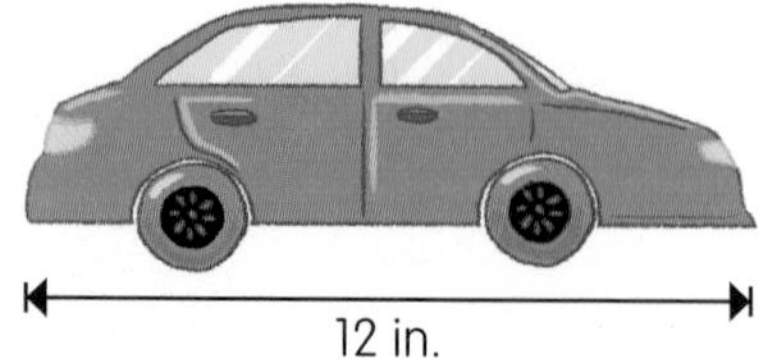

Name: ________________ Date: ________

INDEPENDENT PRACTICE

Solve.

1. A model of a ship is 6 inches long. The actual ship is 550 feet (6,600 inches). Find the scale factor used for the model.

2. On a blueprint, the length of a wall is 5 inches. The actual length of the wall is 85 feet. What scale is used for the blueprint?

3. An artist made a painting of a water pitcher. Then, the artist reduced the size of the painting. Find the scale factor of the reduction.

4. In a scale drawing, a sofa is 3 inches long. If the actual length of the sofa is 5 feet long, find the scale factor.

5. The height of a building in a drawing is 15 inches. If the actual height of the building is 165 feet, find the scale factor of the drawing.

6. Daniel is making a scale drawing of his classroom for a project. The length of his classroom is 30 feet long. In his drawing, the length of the classroom is 6 inches. Find the scale factor of Daniel's drawing.

7. Two cities are 7 inches apart on a map. If the scale of the map is 0.5 inch : 3 miles, what is the actual distance between the two cities?

8. A road map of a city uses a scale of 1 inch : 3 miles. If a street in the city is 1.3 inches long on the map, what is the actual length of the street?

9. The scale of a map is 1 inch : 85 miles.

   a On the map, a river is 14 inches long. Find the actual length of the river in miles.

   b The actual distance between two towns is 765 miles. Find the distance on the map between these towns.

10. Goodhope River is 48 miles long. What is the length of the river on a map with a scale of 1 inch : 15 miles?

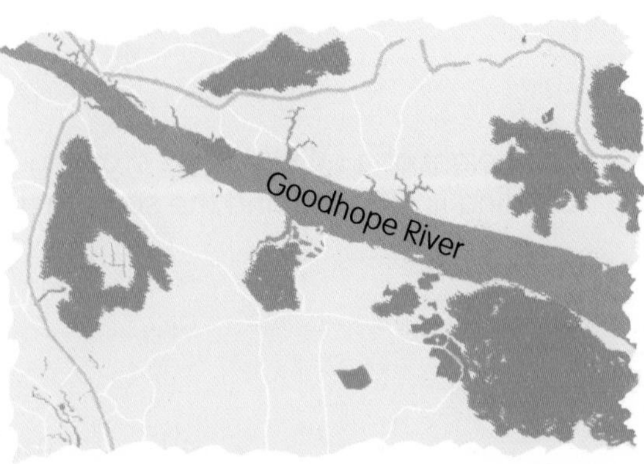

11. A map is drawn using a scale of 1 inch : 165 miles. The length of a road on the map is 12 inches. Find the actual length of the road.

12. On a map, 2 inches represents an actual distance of 64 miles. Towns A and B are 608 miles apart. Find the distance between the two towns, in inches, on the map.

13. The map shows two roads labeled A and B.

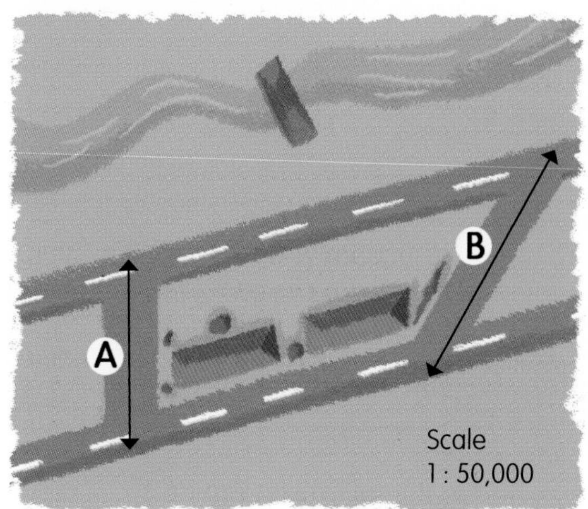

a Using a ruler, measure, in centimeters, the lengths of roads A and B.

b Using the scale given, find, in kilometers, the actual lengths of roads A and B.

14. The map shows seven cities in Florida. Using the scale on the map, use a ruler to measure the distance between the following pairs of cities. Then, find the actual distance between them in miles.

a Orlando and West Palm Beach

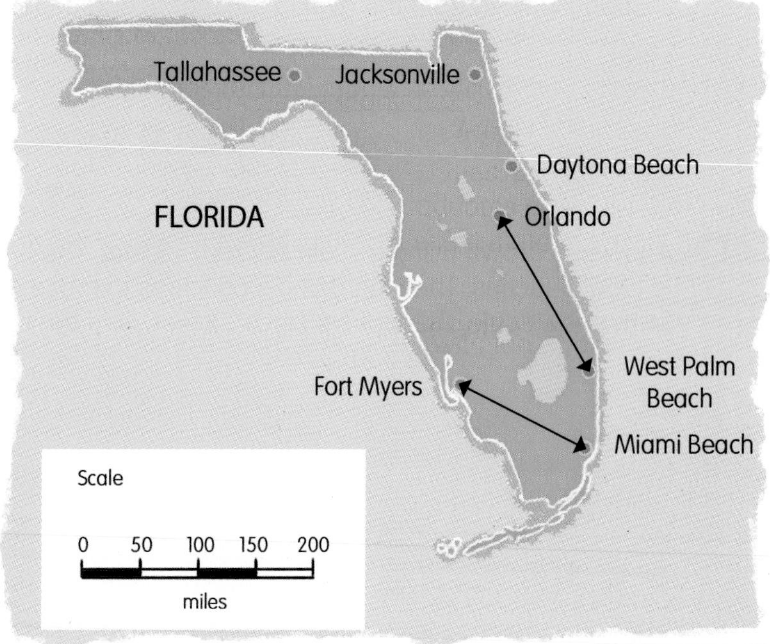

b Fort Myers and Miami Beach

15 Each student walked in a straight line from one point to another. Use a centimeter ruler to measure distances on the map shown. Use the scale on the map to find the distance each student walked in meters.

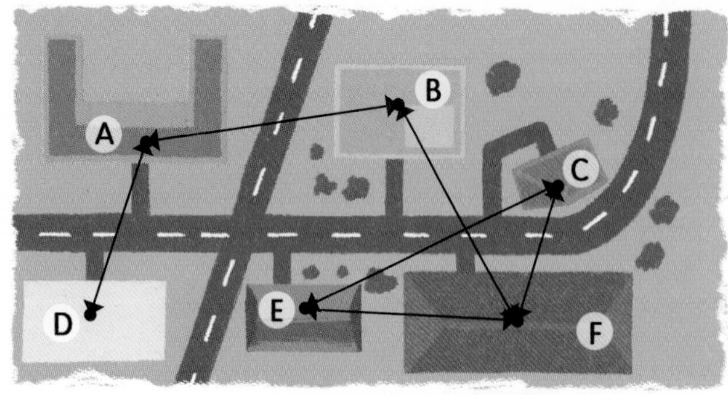

Scale
1 : 12,500

Legend	
A: School	B: Gym
C: Restaurant	D: Library
E: Movie theater	F: Motel

a Aaron walked from the library to the school, and then to the gym.

b José walked from the motel to the restaurant, and then to the movie theater.

c Shanti walked from the gym to the motel, and then to the movie theater.

16 A tower is drawn using a scale of 1 inch : 3 feet. The height of the tower in the drawing is 1 foot 5 inches. Then, an architect decides to make a new scale drawing of the tower. In the new scale, the scale is 1 inch : 5 feet. Find the height of the tower in the new drawing.

Name: ______________________ Date: ______________

3 Scale Drawings and Areas

Learning Objectives:

- Identify the relationship between scale factor and area.
- Solve area problems involving scale drawings.

The scale of a city map is 1 : 15,000. If the area of a park in the city is 5 square inches on the map, what is the actual area of the park?

ENGAGE

Use a graph paper or geoboard to enlarge a unit square by a scale factor of 2, 3, and 4. How do you find the side length and the area of each enlarged square? What do you observe?

LEARN Calculate areas from scale drawings

Activity Exploring the relationship between scale factor and corresponding area

A square of side 1 centimeter has an area of 1 square centimeter. In this activity, you will explore how enlarging such a square by a scale factor affects its area.

1. Suppose you enlarge the square by a scale factor of 2. Find the side length and the area of the resulting square.

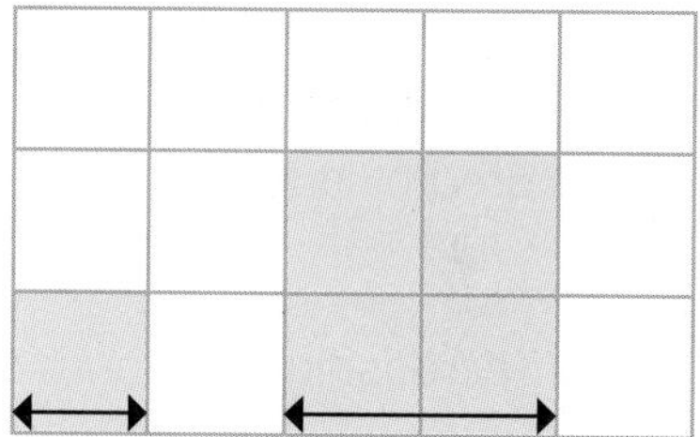

2. Suppose you enlarge the square by a scale factor of 3. Find the side length and the area of the resulting square.

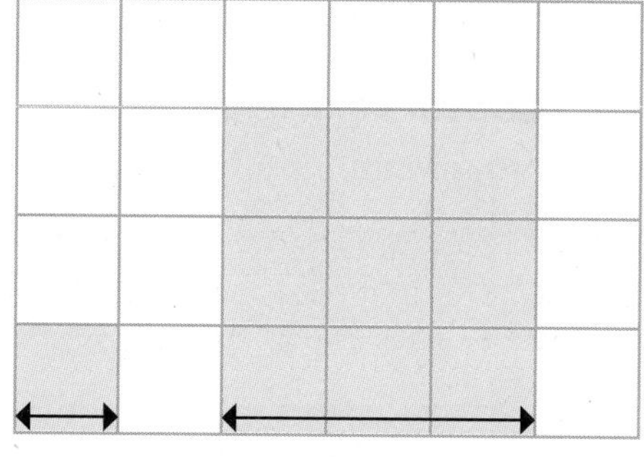

③ Suppose you enlarge the square by a scale factor of 4. Find the side length and the area of the resulting square.

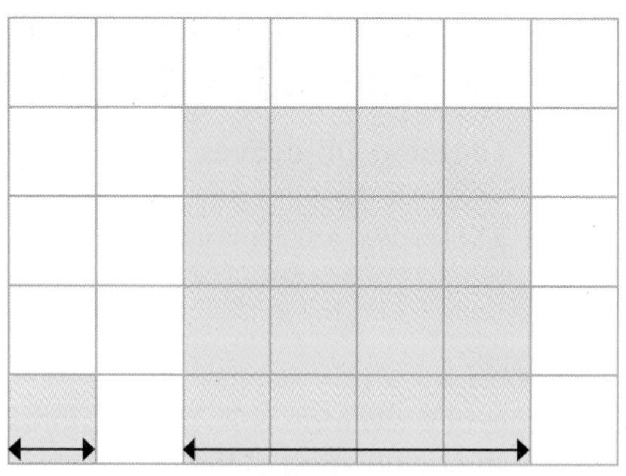

④ Fill in the table.

Scale Factor	Length	Area
1	1 cm	$1 \cdot 1 = 1 \text{ cm}^2$
2	2 cm	$2 \cdot 2 = 2 \text{ cm}^2 = 4 \text{ cm}^2$
3	3 cm	
4		
5		
k		

a Increasing the length of a square by a factor of 5 increases the area by a factor of ______.

b Increasing the length of a square by a factor of k increases the area by a factor of ______.

⑤ **Mathematical Habit 8 Look for patterns**
Compare the side lengths and the areas for the various scale factors. What pattern do you observe? What relationship between scale factor and area can you deduce?

1 You learned that a scale of 1 : 10 means that a length of 1 centimeter on the map corresponds to an actual length of 10 centimeters. On such a map, an area of 1 square centimeter corresponds to an actual area of $10 \cdot 10 = 100$ square centimeters.

A scale of 1 inch : 9 feet on a map means that 1 inch on the map corresponds to an actual length of 9 feet. On such a map, an area of 1 square inch corresponds to an actual area of $9 \cdot 9 = 81$ square feet.

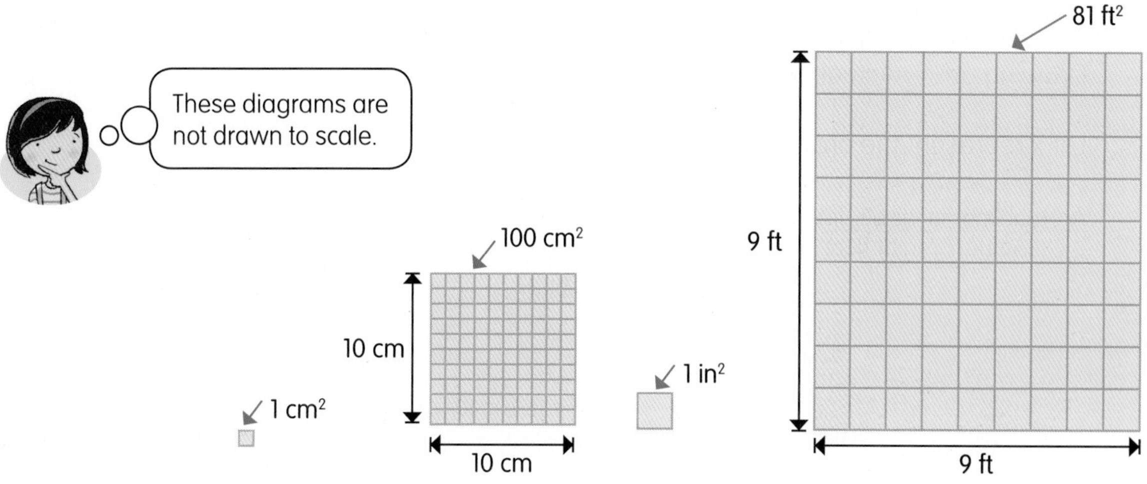

2 The scale on a map is 1 inch : 4 feet. The map shows a garden, and on the map the area of the garden is 8 square inches. Find the actual area of the garden.

Map length : Actual length = 1 in. : 4 ft
Map area : Actual area = 1^2 in^2 : 4^2 ft^2

Let x represent the actual area of the garden in square feet.

$\frac{\text{Area of garden on map}}{\text{Actual area of garden}} = \frac{1}{16}$ Write a proportion.

$\frac{8}{x} = \frac{1}{16}$ Substitute.

$x = 8 \cdot 16$ Write the cross products.

$x = 128$ Simplify.

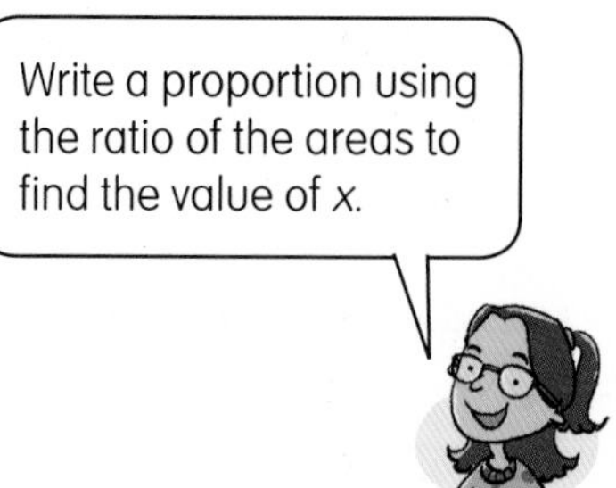

The actual area of the garden is 128 square feet.

3 The actual floor area of an auditorium is 4,500 square feet. Tyler needs to make a scale drawing of the auditorium to calculate the cost of carpeting the floor. He uses a scale of 1 inch : 25 feet. Find the area of the floor in Tyler's scale drawing.

Drawing length : Actual length = 1 in. : 25 ft
Drawing area : Actual area = 1^2 in^2 : 25^2 ft^2

Let x represent the area of the floor in the scale drawing in square inches.

$\frac{\text{Area of floor on scale drawing}}{\text{Actual area of floor}} = \frac{1}{625}$	Write a proportion.
$\frac{x}{4{,}500} = \frac{1}{625}$	Substitute.
$625 \cdot x = 4{,}500$	Write cross products.
$\frac{625x}{625} = \frac{4{,}500}{625}$	Divide both sides by 625.
$x = 7.2$	Simplify.

The floor area in the scale drawing is 7.2 square inches.

Activity **Interpreting the scale on scale drawings**

Work in groups.

Activity 1

1. The diagram is a floor plan of a small apartment. The scale of the floor plan is 1 centimeter : 1 meter.

Kitchen and dining room
Closet
Bathroom
Bedroom
Living room

2. Find the actual dimensions and floor area of the bedroom.

3. Can another bed measuring 2 meters by 1 meter fit into the bedroom? How do you know?

Activity Making a scale drawing

Work in groups.

Activity 2

① Discuss with your group members what your ideal classroom would be like, and then make a sketch of that classroom.

② Measure the actual dimensions of your classroom, as well as the doors, windows, and furniture in the classroom. Record the measurements in a table.

Example:

	Length	Width
Classroom		
Door		
Window		
Desk		
Bookcase		

③ Based on the actual dimensions above, draw a floor plan of your ideal classroom, and explain the choice of the scale used. Share your drawing with your classmates.

TRY Practice calculating areas from scale drawings

Solve.

1. Sofia makes a scale drawing of her yard. On the drawing, 1 inch represents 8 feet, and the area of a patch of grass is 12 square inches. Find the actual area of the patch of grass.

Map length : Actual length = ______ : ______

Map area : Actual area = ______ : ______

Let y represent the actual area of the patch of grass in square feet.

$\frac{\text{Area of patch of grass on map}}{\text{Actual area of patch of grass}} = \frac{\square}{\square}$ Write a proportion.

$\frac{\square}{y} = \frac{\square}{\square}$ Substitute.

______ · y = ______ · ______ Write cross products.

y = ______ Simplify.

The actual area of the grass patch is ______ square feet.

2 An architect is making a blueprint for a conference room that will have a floor area of 196 square feet. Given that the scale on the blueprint is 1 inch : 7 feet, find the floor area of the conference room on the blueprint.

Blueprint length : Actual length = _______ : _______

Blueprint area : Actual area = _______ : _______

Let *y* represent the area of the conference room on the blueprint in square inches.

$\frac{\text{Area of room on blueprint}}{\text{Actual area of room}} = \frac{\square}{\square}$ Write a proportion.

$\frac{y}{\square} = \frac{\square}{\square}$ Substitute.

_______ $\cdot\ y =$ _______ $\cdot$ _______ Write cross products.

$\frac{\square}{\square}y = \frac{\square}{\square}$ Divide both sides by _______.

$y =$ _______ Simplify.

The floor area of the conference room on the blueprint is _______ square inches.

LET'S EXPLORE

1 Figure A has been enlarged or reduced to produce figure B. Measure the lengths of each figure and calculate the scale factor for each pair of figures.

Figure A	Figure B	Enlargement or reduction	Scale factor

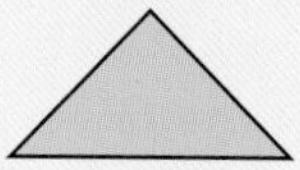	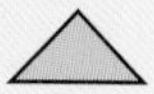		
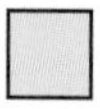			
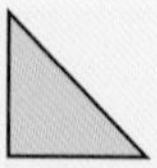			

2 What can you say about the scale factor when there is an enlargement?

3 What can you say about the scale factor when there is a reduction?

Name: ______________________ Date: ______________

INDEPENDENT PRACTICE

Solve.

1. On a map, 1 inch represents an actual distance of 2.5 miles. The actual area of a lake is 12 square miles. Find the area of the lake on the map.

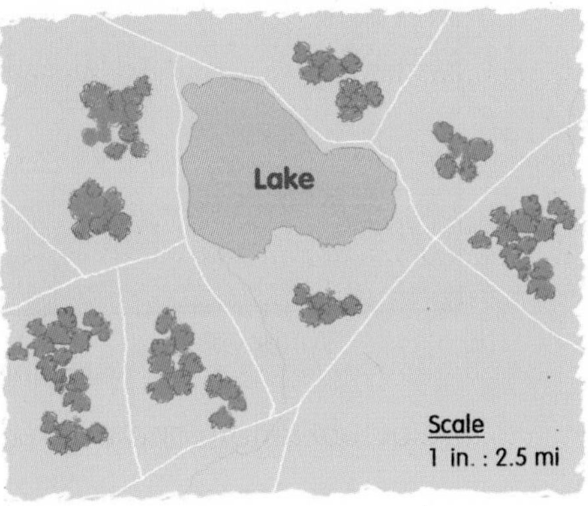

2. On a map, the area of a nature reserve is 54.2 square inches. The scale of the map is 1 inch : 8 miles. Find the actual area of the nature reserve.

3. The scale of a map is 1 : 1,500. Given that each side of a square piece of land measures 4 inches on the map, find the actual area of this piece of land to the nearest tenth of an acre. (1 ft = 12 in.; 1 acre = 43,560 ft^2)

4 The diagram shows the floor plan of a house. Use the scale on the floor plan to find each of the following.

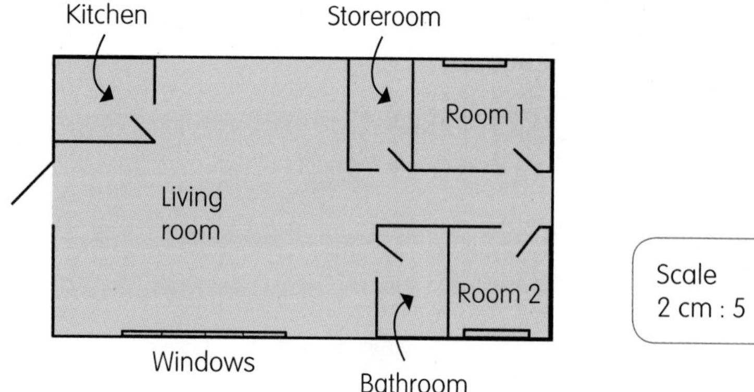

Scale
2 cm : 5 m

a The actual length and width of room 1.

b The width of the windows in the living room on the floor plan given that the actual width is 2.2 meters.

c The actual area of the floor of the house to the nearest square meter.

Mathematical Habit 6 Use precise mathematical language

Alex answered the question below incorrectly. Identify Alex's mistake and write the correct solution. Explain your reasoning.

Triangle *ABC* has been reduced to triangle *A'B'C'* as shown below. Find the scale factor and the value of *x*.

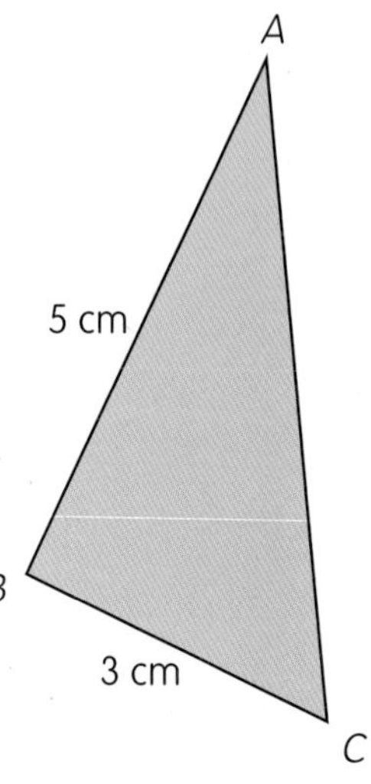

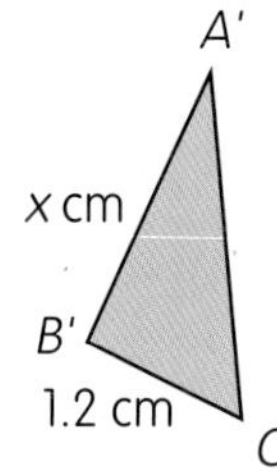

Alex's answer:

Scale factor = $\frac{3}{1.2} = 2.5$

Value of $x = 5 \cdot 2.5 = 12.5$ cm

Correct solution:

PUT ON YOUR THINKING CAP!

Problem Solving with Heuristics

1 **Mathematical Habit 5 Use tools strategically**
Construct triangle *ABC*, where $AB = AC$, $BC = 8$ cm, and $m\angle ABC = 37°$. Triangle *ABC* is enlarged to produce triangle *DEF* by a scale factor of 2.5. Find the area of triangle *DEF*.

2 **Mathematical Habit 1 Persevere in solving problems**
Map A is reduced to map B by 25%. The area of a lake on map A is 16 square centimeters. Given that 1 centimeter on map B represents 2 kilometers, find the actual area of the lake.

CHAPTER WRAP-UP

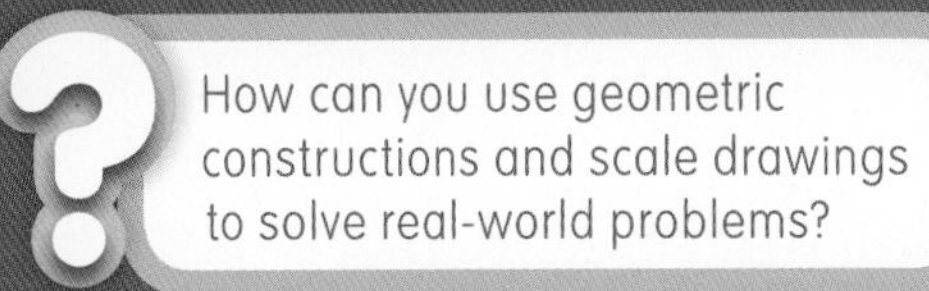

Lines

Angles

Circles

Arcs

to draw

to measure

to draw

Straightedges

Protractors

Compasses

use

Geometric Constructions

Scale Drawings

are reduced or enlarged representations of

2-dimensional figures and 3-dimensional objects

can be used to draw

use

Triangles

A scale

written as the ratio of

Length in drawing : Actual length

$\left(\text{Length in drawing}\right)^2 : \left(\text{Actual Length}\right)^2$

can be used to find

can be used to find

Lengths or distances

Areas

KEY CONCEPTS

- You can draw a triangle given the lengths of three sides or certain combinations of side lengths and angle measures.
- You can draw a unique triangle if you are given any of the following:
  - lengths of the three sides
  - lengths of two sides and the measure of the included angle
  - two angle measures and the length of the included side
- Sometimes you can draw more than one triangle using the given information about a triangle. If you are given two side lengths and the measure of an angle not included between those sides, you may be able to draw two triangles.

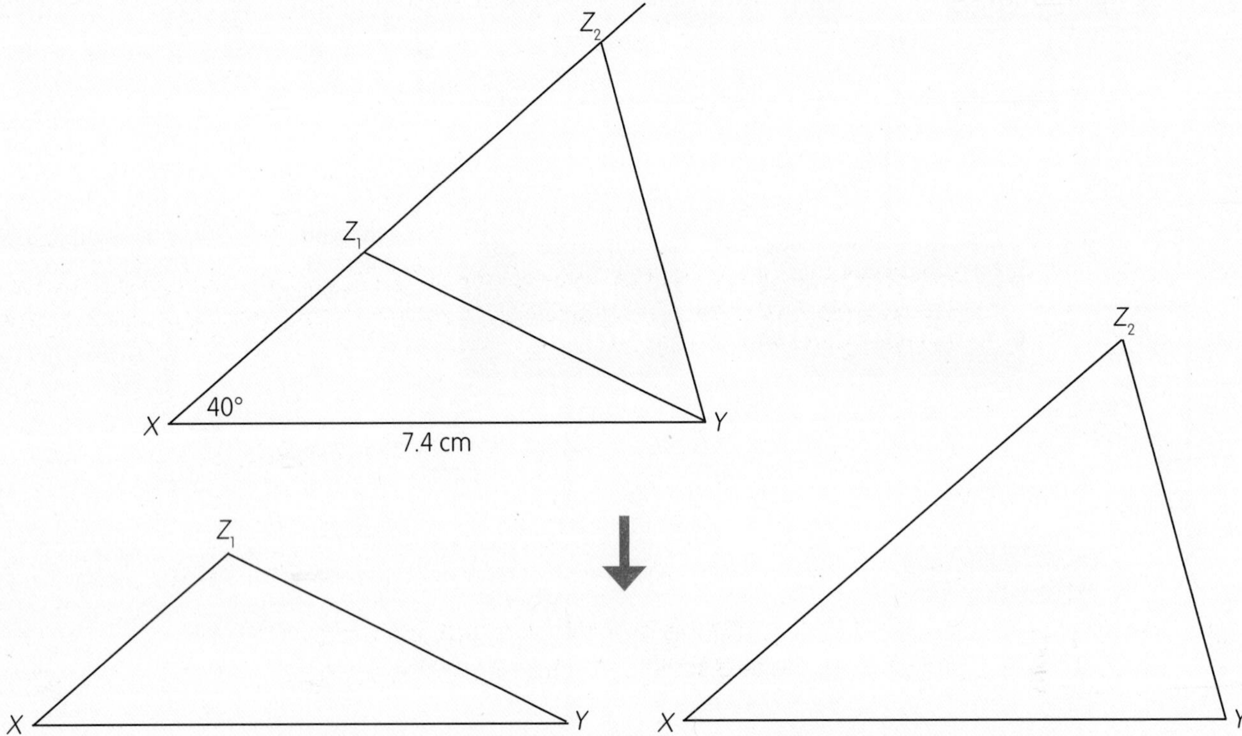

- Sometimes you cannot draw a triangle given a set of three side lengths. You can only draw a triangle if the sum of the lengths of any two sides is greater than the length of the third side.
- Scale drawings are used to represent reductions or enlargements of two-dimensional figures or three-dimensional objects.
- The scale of a scale drawing compares a length in the drawing to the corresponding length in the object.
  Scale = Length in drawing : Actual length
- In a scale drawing, if a length in an object decreases or increases by a factor of k, then the area of the object decreases or increases by a factor of k^2.

Name: ______________________________ Date: ______________

Use the given information to find the number of triangles that can be constructed. Try constructing the triangles to make your decision.

1 Triangle WXY, where $WX = 4.5$ cm, $m\angle XWY = 60°$, and $m\angle WXY = 40°$.

2 Triangle ABC, where $AB = 5$ cm, $AC = 4.5$ cm, and $m\angle CAB = 60°$.

3 Triangle DEF, where $DE = 3$ cm, $EF = 4$ cm, and $DF = 8$ cm.

Solve.

4 A rectangular garden is 15 meters long and 9 meters wide. Use a scale of 1 centimeter to 3 meters to make a scale drawing of the garden.

5 The scale of the floor plan of a room is 1 inch : 6.5 feet. On the floor plan, the room is 8 inches long and 6 inches wide. What are the actual dimensions of the room?

6. A model of a car is made using a scale of 1 : 25. The actual length of the car is 4.8 meters. Calculate the length of the car model in centimeters.

7. The scale on a map is 1 inch : 120 miles. On the map, a highway is 5 inches long. Find the actual length of the highway in miles.

8. Construct an isosceles triangle WXY such that $WX = WY = 5$ cm and $XY = 4$ cm. Construct another isosceles triangle ABC such that $AB = AC = 10$ cm and $BC = 8$ cm. Is triangle ABC an enlargement or a reduction of triangle WXY? Explain your answer and give the scale factor. Justify your answer.

9 The scale of a map is 1 inch to 5 feet. Find the area of a rectangular region on the map given that the area of the actual region is 95 square feet.

10 The floor plan of a building has a scale of $\frac{1}{4}$ inch to 1 foot. A room has an area of 40 square inches on the floor plan. What is the actual room area in square feet?

11 The scale of a map is 1 : 2,400. Given that a rectangular piece of property measures 2 inches by 3 inches on the map, what is the actual area of this piece of property to the nearest tenth of an acre? (1 acre = 43,560 ft^2)

12 Chris wants to make kites for a family picnic. Before making the kites, he makes a kite model using a scale of 1 centimeter : 4 inches to find the lengths and angles of each kite. The diagram shows the measurements of the actual kite. He knows that $\overline{AC}$ is perpendicular to $\overline{BD}$, $BN = ND$, and $AN = 6$ in. Construct the model he will use and find the measures of $\angle ABC$, and the lengths $\overline{AB}$ and $\overline{BC}$ in the actual kite.

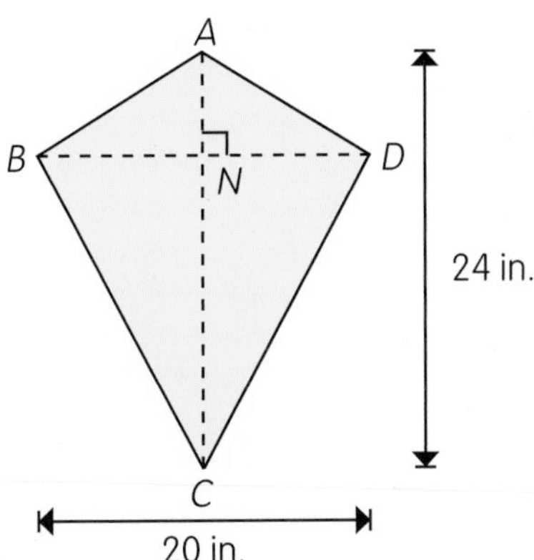

Assessment Prep

Answer each question.

13 Which of the following options will allow you to draw one unique triangle? Choose all that apply.

(A) Three given angles

(B) Two given angles and one given side length

(C) Three given side lengths

(D) One given angle and two given side lengths

(E) Two given side lengths and one given included angle

14 Emma builds an airplane model that is 80 centimeters long. Given that the actual airplane is 40 meters long, what is the scale factor of her model?

(A) $\frac{1}{50}$

(B) $\frac{1}{2}$

(C) 2

(D) 50

15 The scale of a map is 1 : 200. Given that each side of a square piece of land measures 6 inches on the map, find the actual area of this piece of land in square feet. Write your answer and your work or explanation in the space below. (1 ft = 12 in.)

Name: ____________________ Date: ____________

A trip to a garden maze

The scale of a map of a garden maze is 1 inch : 86 feet.
A rectangle, *ABCD*, where *AB* = 5 inches and *BC* = 2.25 inches, is drawn over the map of the garden maze.

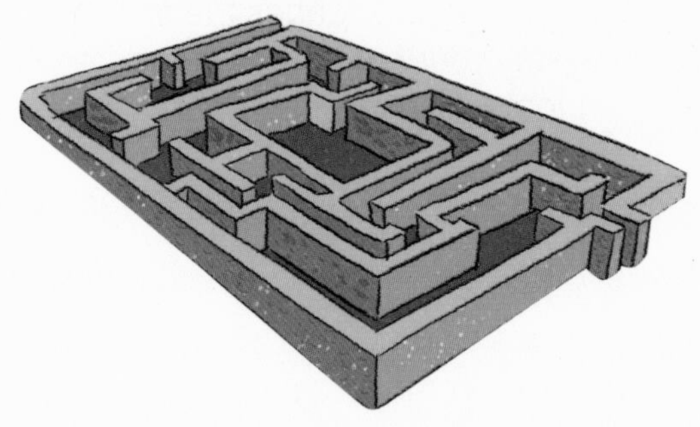

1. Find the actual perimeter of the garden maze in feet.

2. Find the actual area of the garden maze in square feet.

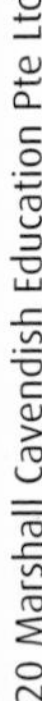

3 Dylan says that since inch is a smaller unit than foot, the map of the garden maze will be smaller if he changes the scale from 1 inch : 86 feet to 1 inch : 86 inch. Do you agree? Justify your reasoning. Illustrate with an example using the answers you found in 1 or 2. (1 foot = 12 inches)

Rubric

Point(s)	Level	My Performance
7–8	4	• Most of my answers are correct. • I showed complete understanding of the concepts. • I used effective and efficient strategies to solve the problems. • I explained my answers and mathematical thinking clearly and completely.
5–6	3	• Some of my answers are correct. • I showed adequate understanding of the concepts. • I used effective strategies to solve the problems. • I explained my answers and mathematical thinking clearly.
3–4	2	• A few of my answers are correct. • I showed some understanding of the concepts. • I used some effective strategies to solve the problems. • I explained some of my answers and mathematical thinking clearly.
0–2	1	• A few of my answers are correct. • I showed little understanding of the concepts. • I used limited effective strategies to solve the problems. • I did not explain my answers and mathematical thinking clearly.

Teacher's Comments

Chapter 7

Circumference, Area, Volume, and Surface Area

How are crop circles made?

Crop circles are large geometric patterns of flattened crops, said to have first appeared in the countryside of the United Kingdom in the 1970s. The number of crop circle sightings peaked in the 1980s and 1990s, when increasingly elaborate circular patterns were discovered, including some that illustrated complex mathematical equations.

There are many theories as to how crop circles were created. One common belief is that they are messages from intelligent extraterrestrial life! However, many have proved to be the work of clever pranksters. In this chapter, you will learn to solve problems involving two- and three-dimensional figures such as circles and prisms, including many that you see in everyday life.

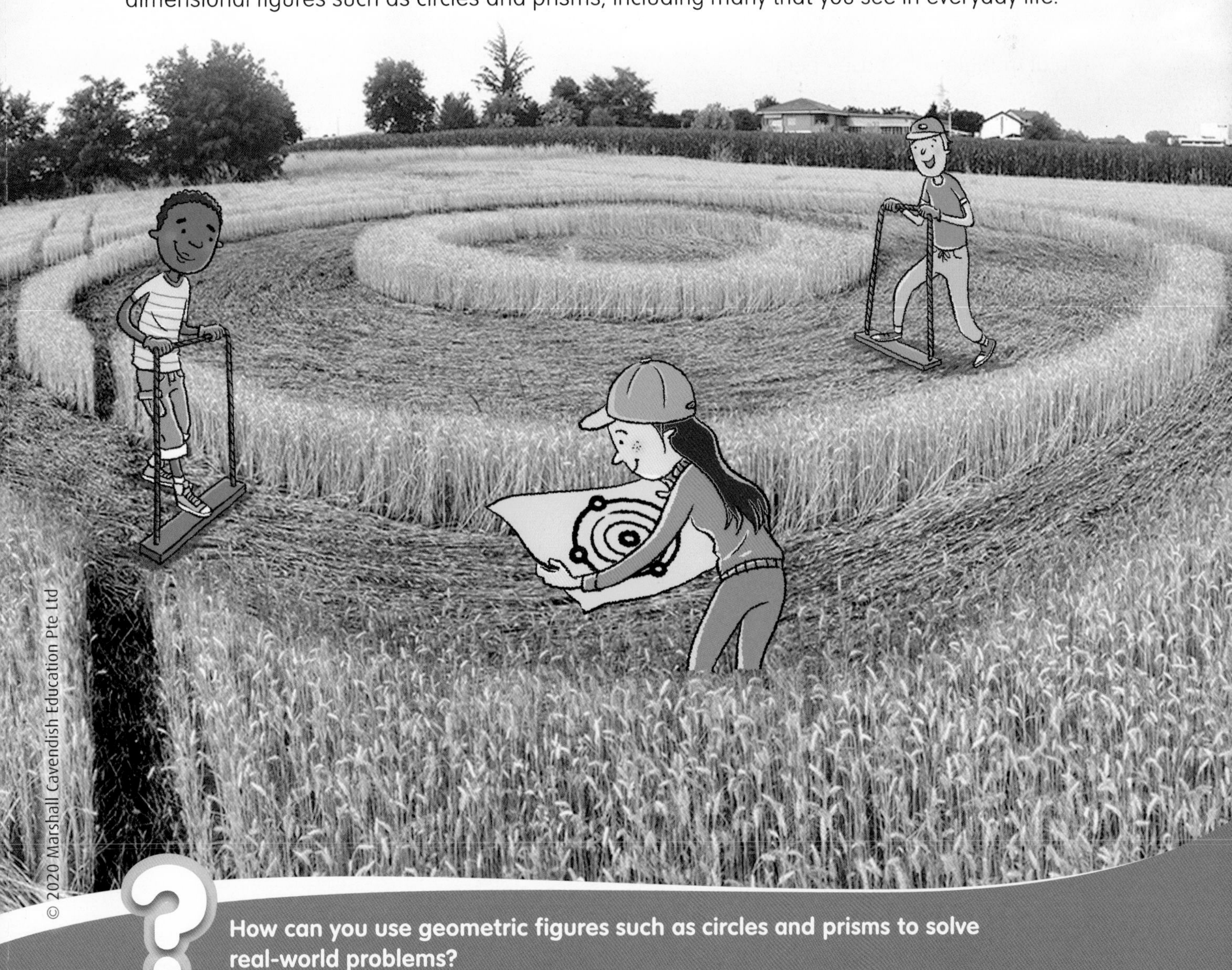

How can you use geometric figures such as circles and prisms to solve real-world problems?

Name: ______________________ Date: ____________

Finding the area of a triangle

Any side of a triangle can be its base. The perpendicular distance from the opposite vertex to the base is the height of the triangle.

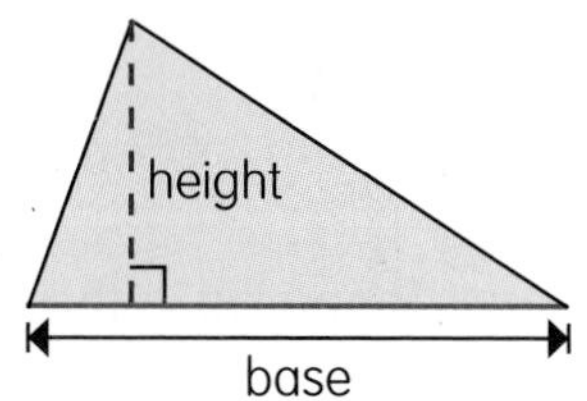

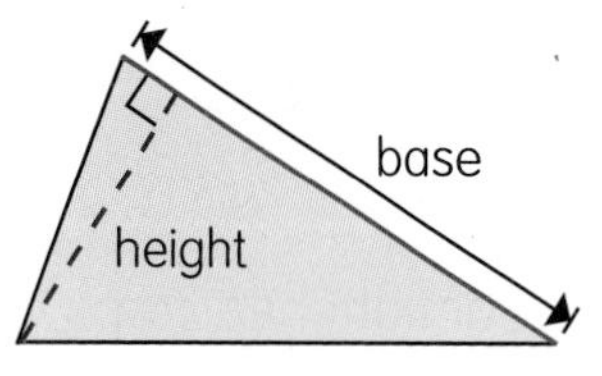

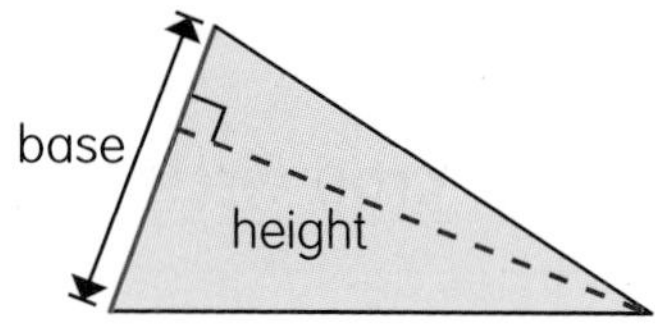

The height of a triangle may lie outside the triangle.

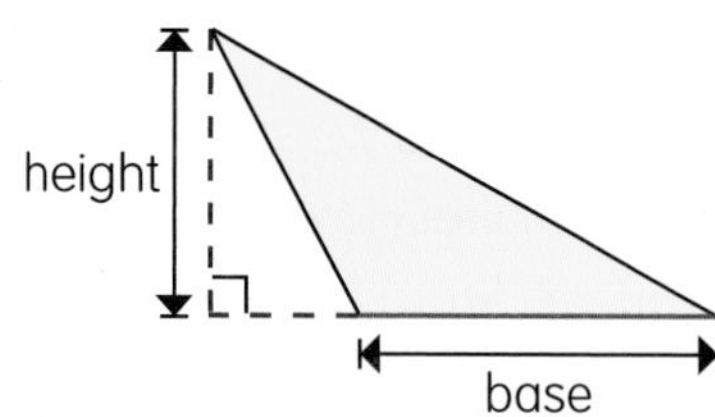

$$\text{Area of triangle} = \frac{1}{2} \cdot \text{base} \cdot \text{height}$$
$$= \frac{1}{2}bh$$

▶ Quick Check

Find the area of each shaded triangle.

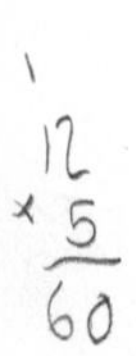

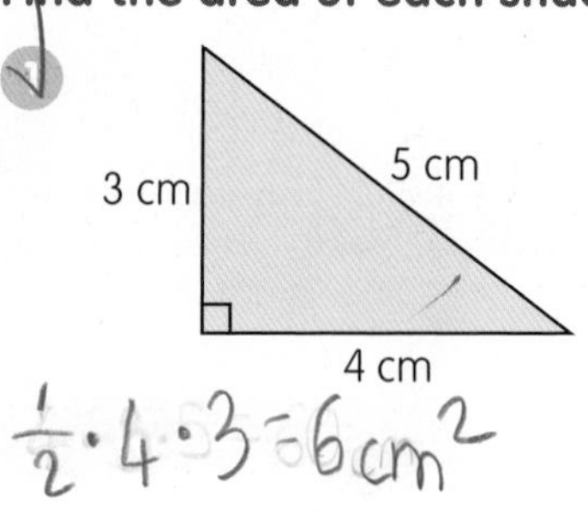

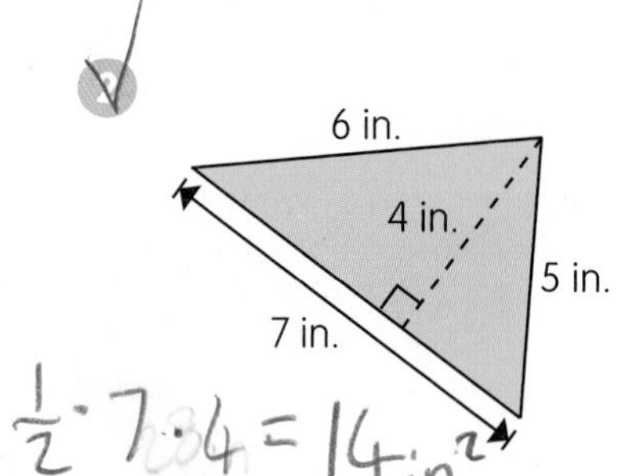

3

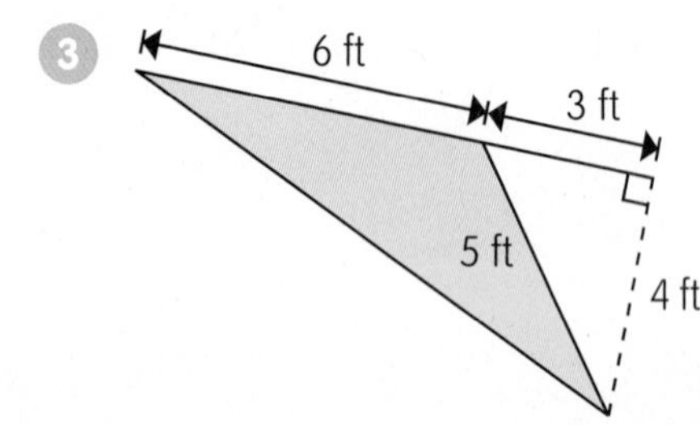

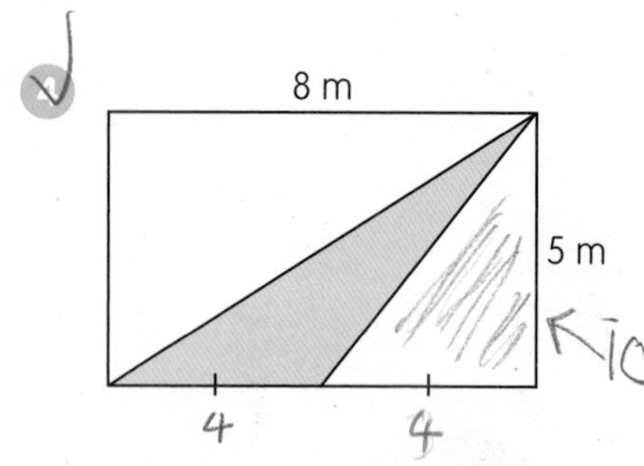

Finding the area of a parallelogram and a trapezoid

a In the parallelogram, b is the base and h is the height.

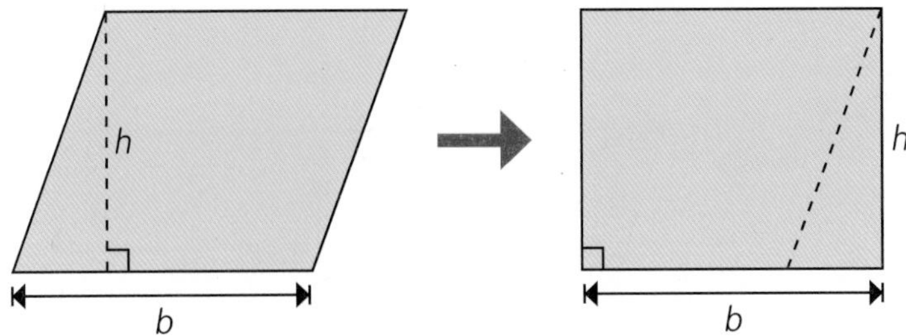

Area of parallelogram = bh

b In the trapezoid, b_1 and b_2 are the bases and h is the height.

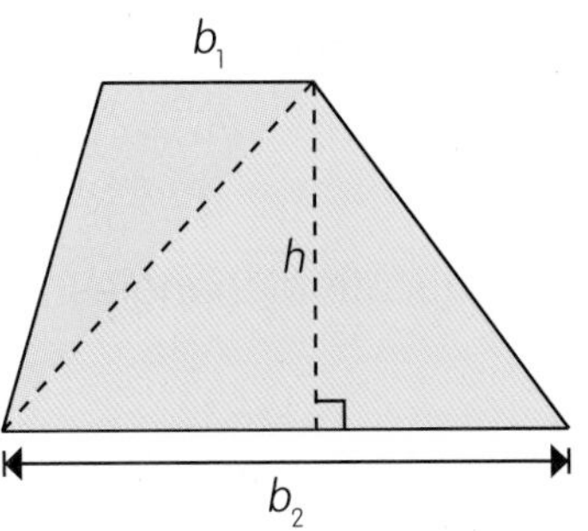

Area of trapezoid = $\frac{1}{2}h(b_1 + b_2)$

▶ Quick Check

Find the area of each parallelogram or trapezoid.

5

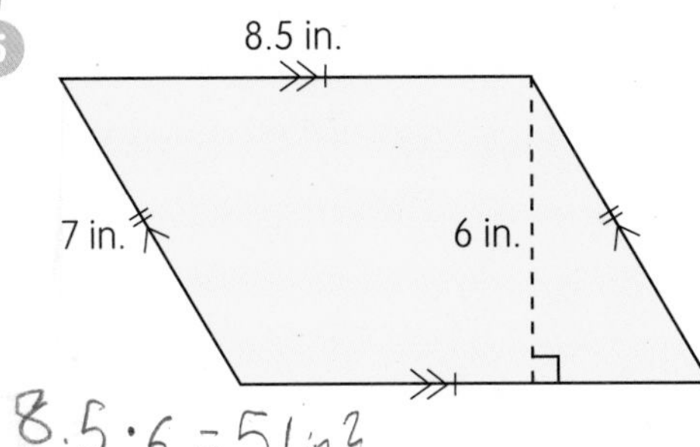

8.5 · 6 = 51 in²

6

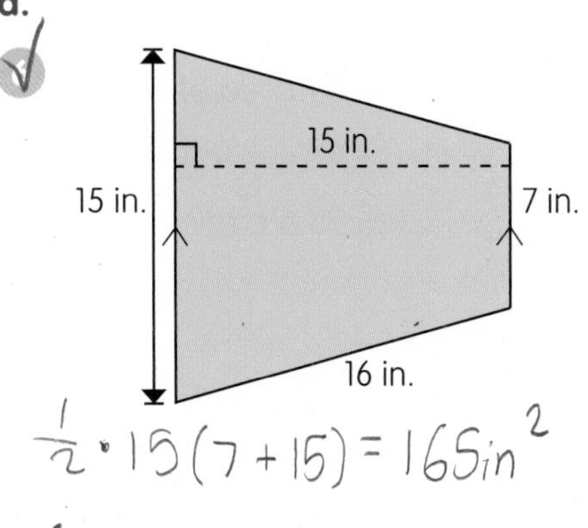

$\frac{1}{2}$ · 15(7 + 15) = 165 in²

7

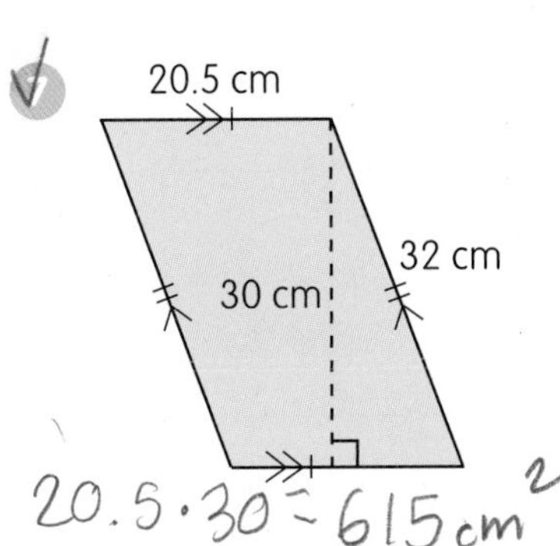

20.5 · 30 = 615 cm²

8

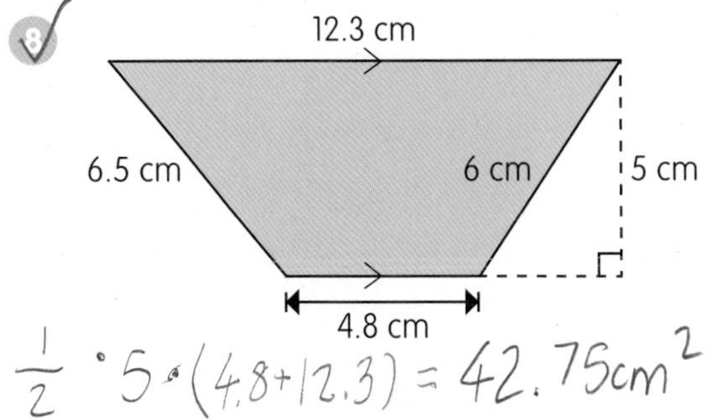

$\frac{1}{2}$ · 5 · (4.8 + 12.3) = 42.75 cm²

Finding the area of other polygons

a The area of a regular pentagon is the sum of the areas of 5 identical isosceles triangles.

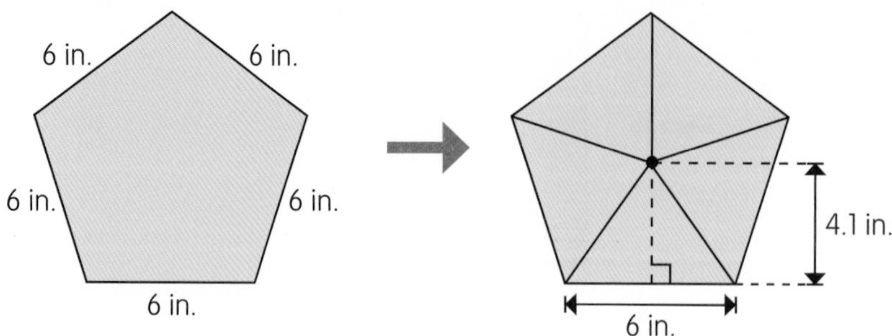

$$\begin{aligned}\text{Area of pentagon} &= 5 \cdot \text{area of triangle}\\ &= 5 \cdot \frac{1}{2}bh\\ &= 5 \cdot \frac{1}{2} \cdot 6 \cdot 4.1\\ &= 61.5 \text{ in}^2\end{aligned}$$

b The area of a regular hexagon is the sum of the areas of 6 identical equilateral triangles.

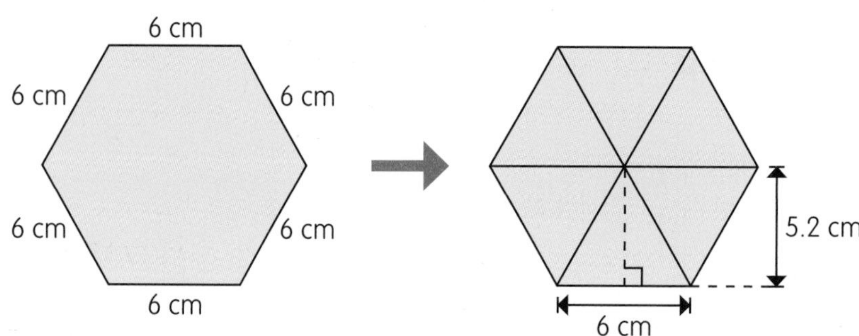

$$\begin{aligned}\text{Area of hexagon} &= 6 \cdot \text{area of triangle}\\ &= 6 \cdot \frac{1}{2} \cdot 6 \cdot 5.2\\ &= 93.6 \text{ cm}^2\end{aligned}$$

▶ Quick Check

Find the area of each regular pentagon or hexagon.

1

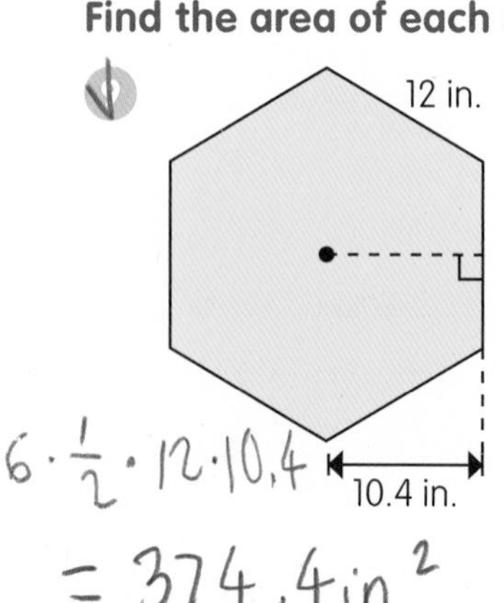

$6 \cdot \frac{1}{2} \cdot 12 \cdot 10.4$

$= 374.4 \text{ in}^2$

2

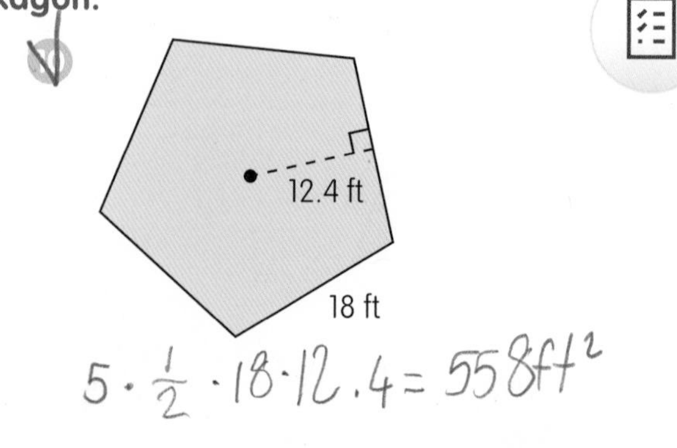

$5 \cdot \frac{1}{2} \cdot 18 \cdot 12.4 = 558 \text{ ft}^2$

Finding the volume of cubes, rectangular prisms, and composite solids

a Volume of a cube = edge · edge · edge
= 2 · 2 · 2
= 8 in^3

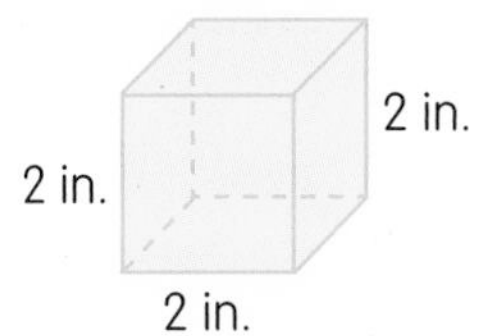

b Volume of a rectangular prism = length · width · height
= 5 · 4 · 2
= 40 in^3

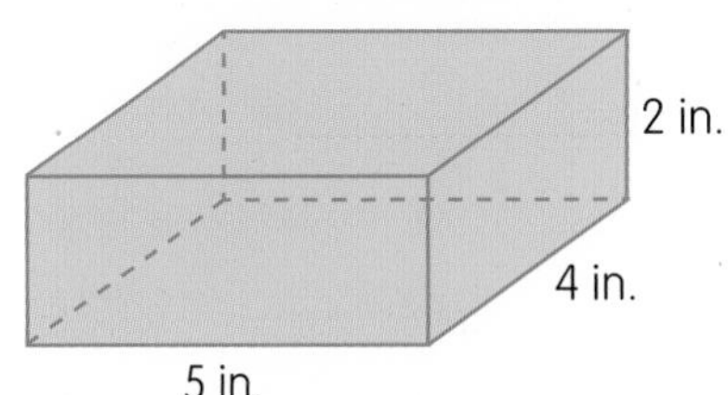

c Volume of a composite solid
= volume of cube + volume of rectangular prism
= 8 + 40
= 48 in^3

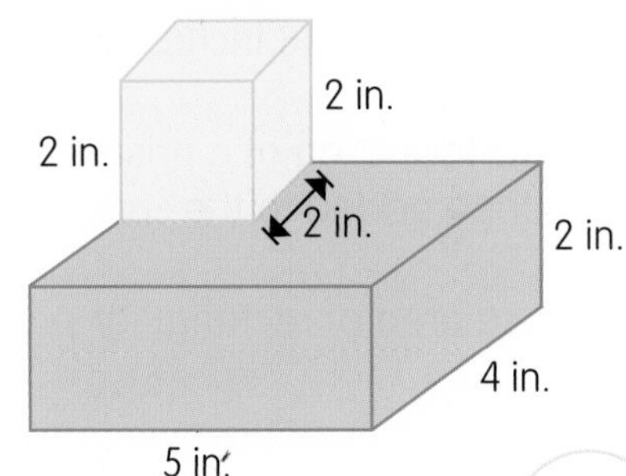

▶ Quick Check

Find the volume of each cube or rectangular prism.

11

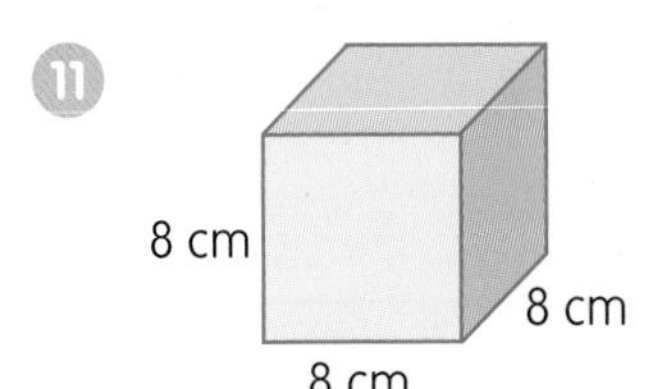

12

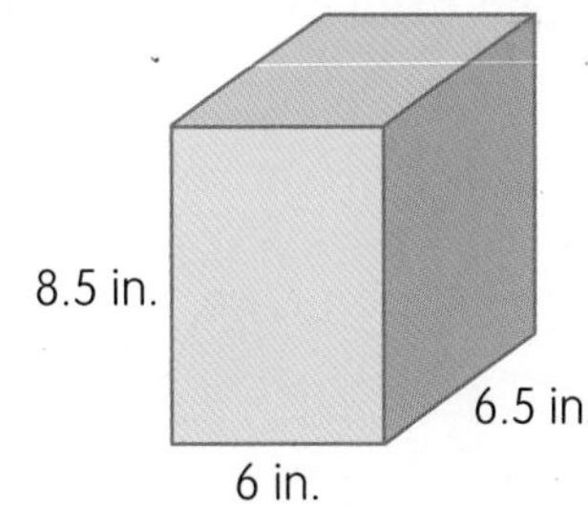

Find the volume of each composite solid.

13

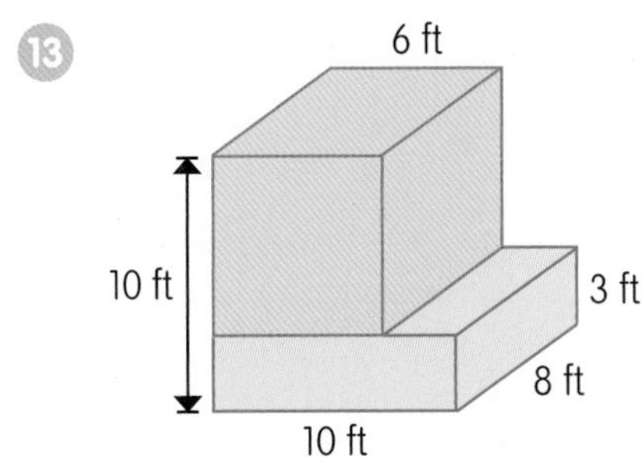

14

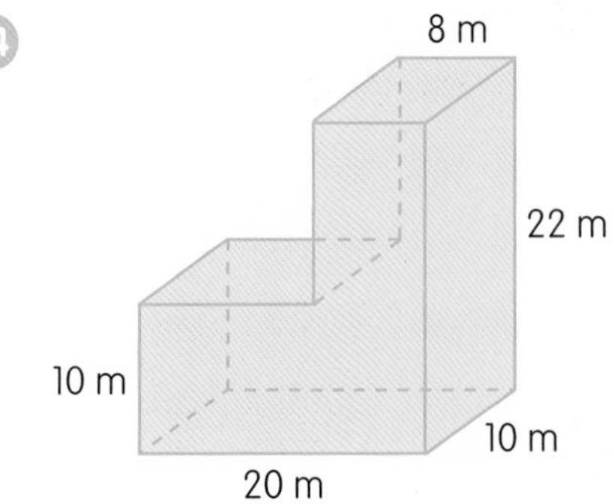

Finding the surface area of a solid

The surface area of a solid is the area of its net.

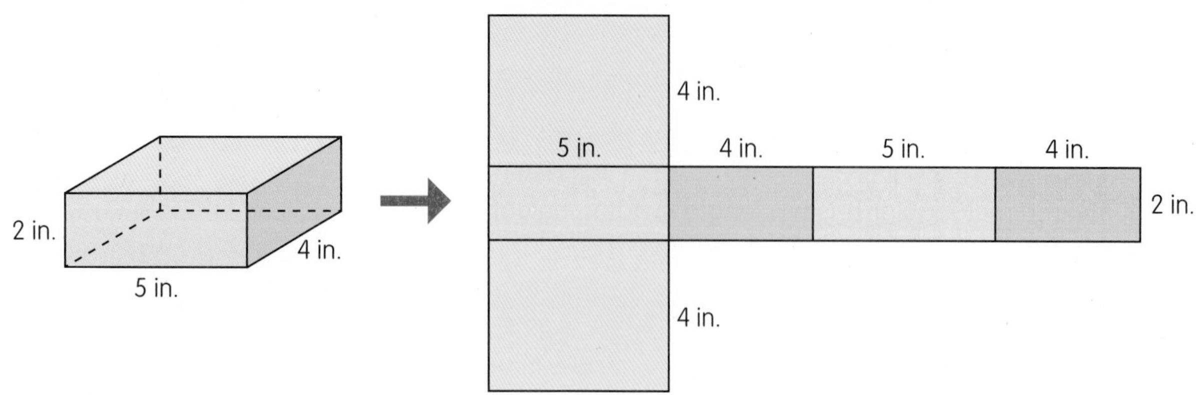

The total area of the blue and green faces is equal to the area of the rectangle of length $5 + 4 + 5 + 4 = 18$ inches and width 2 inches.

The surface area of a prism is equal to the perimeter of the base multiplied by the height, and then added to the sum of the areas of the two bases.

$$\begin{aligned}\text{Surface area of rectangular prism} &= 2 \cdot (5 + 4 + 5 + 4) + 2 \cdot (5 \cdot 4)\\ &= 36 + 40\\ &= 76 \text{ in}^2\end{aligned}$$

▶ Quick Check

Find the surface area of the triangular prism.

15

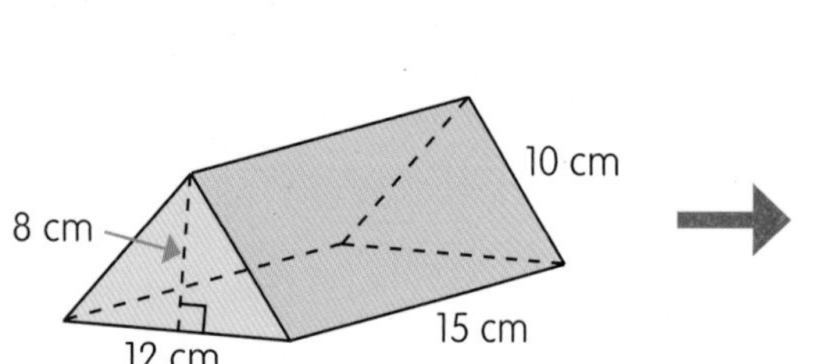

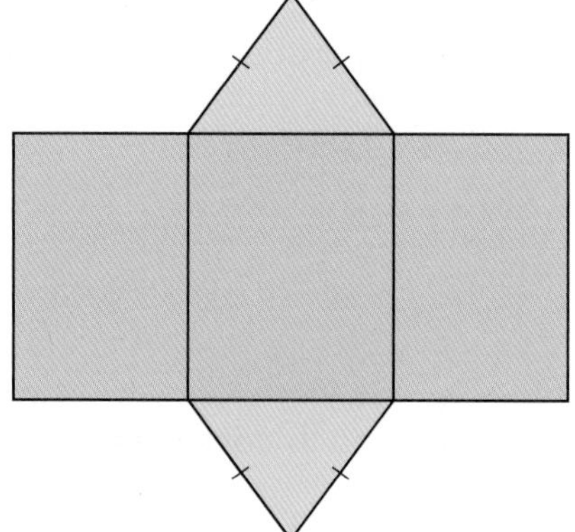

Name: ______________________ Date: ______________

Radius, Diameter, and Circumference of a Circle

Learning Objectives:

- Identify parts of a circle.
- Recognize that a circle's diameter is twice its radius.
- Use a formula to find the circumference of a circle.
- Identify semicircles and quarter circles, and find the distance around them

New Vocabulary

center
diameter
semicircle
arc
radius, radii
circumference
quadrant

The distance around a semicircle is approximately 257 inches. What is the diameter of its related circle? Use 3.14 as an approximation for π.

ENGAGE

Fold a paper circle into quarters. Unfold the circle and use a ruler and pencil to draw along the fold lines. Name these line segments *AOB* and *COD*. Without measuring, what can you say about the lengths of $\overline{OA}$, $\overline{OB}$, $\overline{OC}$, and $\overline{OD}$? What is the relationship between $\overline{OA}$, $\overline{OB}$, $\overline{AOB}$? Share your observations.

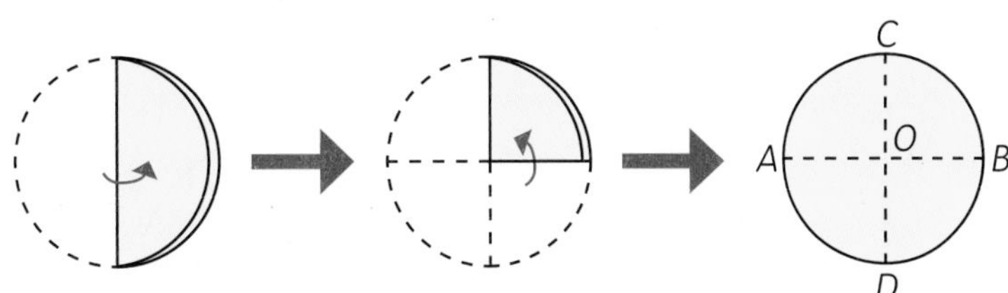

LEARN Identify the center, radius, and diameter of a circle

1

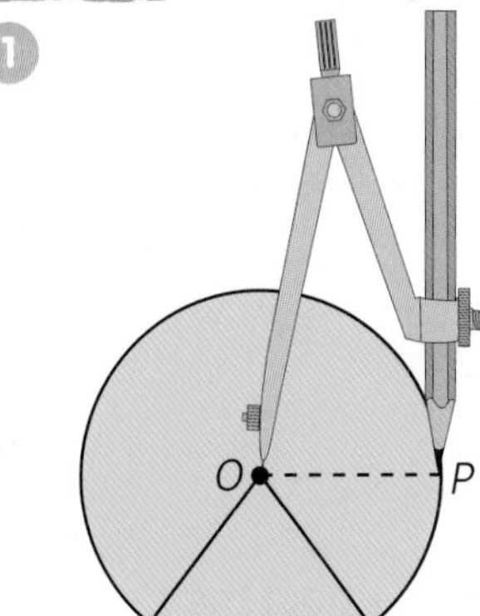

O is the center of the circle.
$\overline{OP}$ is a radius of the circle.
$\overline{OQ}$ and $\overline{OR}$ are also radii of the circle.
$OP = OQ = OR$

The plural of radius is radii. In a circle, all its radii have the same length.

A radius is a line segment connecting the center and a point on the circle.

Identify the center, radius, and diameter of a circle

2 $\overline{QP}$ and $\overline{RS}$ pass through the center of the circle, O.
$\overline{PQ}$ is a diameter of the circle.
$\overline{RS}$ is another diameter of the circle.

$\overline{TU}$ does not pass through the center of the circle. It is not a diameter of the circle.

In a circle, all its diameters have the same length.

A diameter of a circle is a line segment that connects two points on the circle and passes through the center of the circle.

Activity **Exploring the relationships between different lengths in a circle and relating the sizes of circles to their diameters**

Work in pairs.

1. Measure a length on a ruler with a compass. Then, place the spike at a point and move the pencil 360° around to draw a circle.

Example:

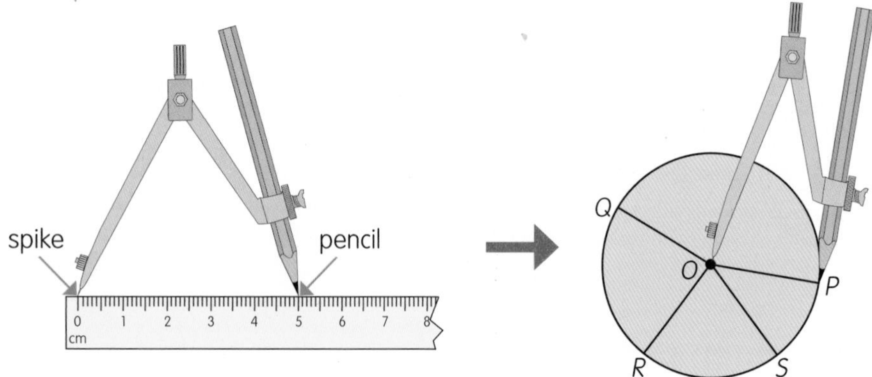

2. Mark the center as O and four points on the circle, P, Q, R, and S. Then, measure the lengths of $\overline{OP}$, $\overline{OQ}$, $\overline{OR}$, and $\overline{OS}$. What do you notice?

3. Measure the diameter of the circle and compare it with the lengths in (2).
What do you notice about the diameter of the circle and its radius?

4. Repeat (1) to (3) by drawing circles of different sizes. What do you notice about the diameter of the circle as the size of the circle changes?

TRY Practice identifying the center, radius, and diameter of a circle

Solve.

1. In the figure, O is the center of the circle with $\overline{AB}$, $\overline{CD}$, and $\overline{ED}$ as shown.

   a Name all the diameters that are drawn in the circle.

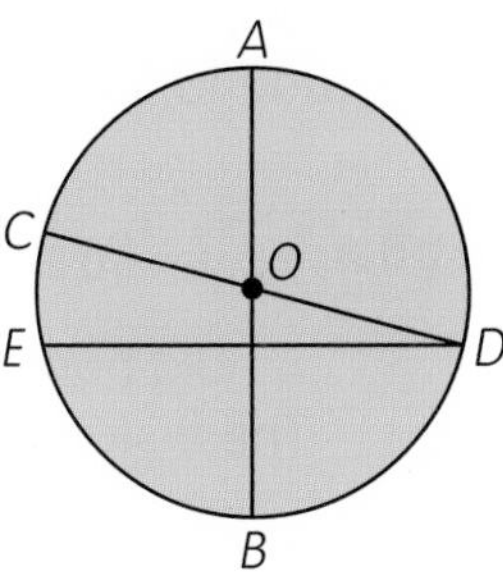

   b Which line segment that joins two points on the circle is not a diameter? Explain why it is not a diameter.

2. The radius of a circle is 6 centimeters. What is the length of its diameter?

   Diameter = 2 • radius

   = ______ • ______

   = ______ cm

   The diameter of the circle is ______ centimeters.

3. The diameter of a circle is 15 inches. What is the length of its radius?

   Radius = diameter ÷ 2

   = ______ ÷ ______

   = ______ in.

   The radius of the circle is ______ inches.

4. Diego drew a circle with a compass. The distance between the spike and the pencil on his compass is 3.5 centimeters. What is the radius of the circle he drew? What is the diameter?

ENGAGE

a Take a circular object, such as a round coin. Discuss ways to find the distance around the object.
b Now, trace the outline of a circular object on a piece of paper. How do you find the distance around the circle? Discuss.

LEARN Identify the circumference of a circle

1 A hula hoop has the shape of a circle.
The distance around the hoop is called its circumference.

The circumference of a circle is the distance around it.

2 Julia used a string to go round a circle of diameter 9 centimeters. Then, she measured the length of the piece of string to find the circumference of the circle.

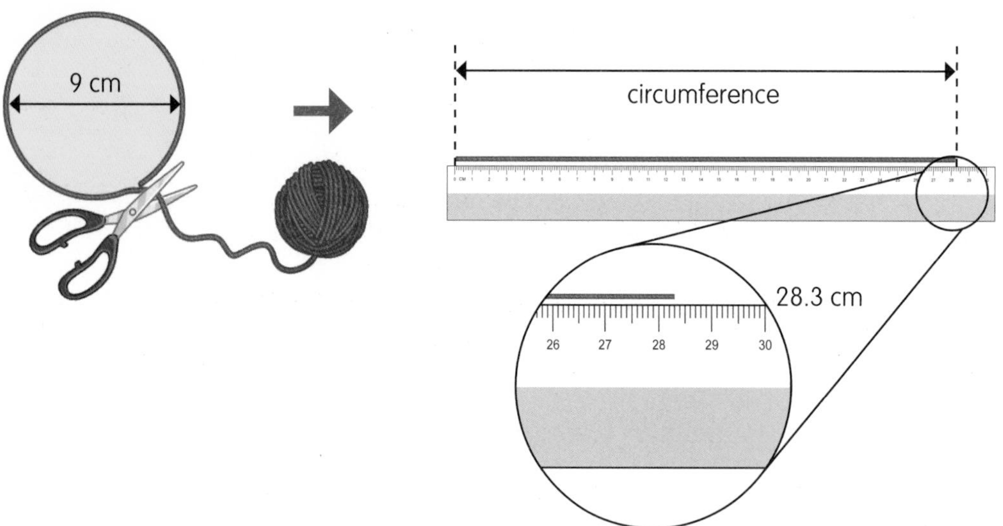

She found that the circumference of the circle is slightly more than 3 times its diameter.

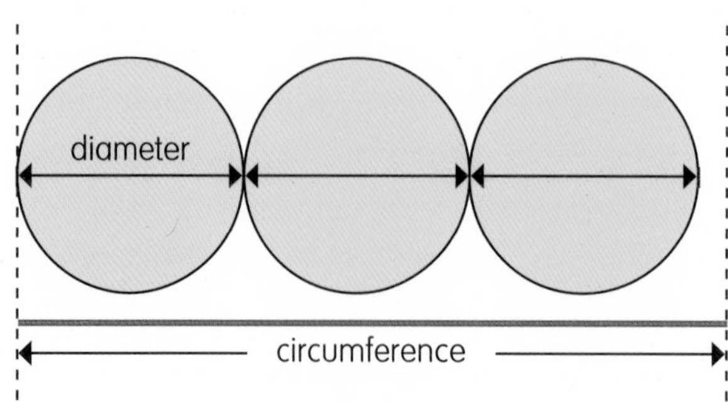

TRY Practice identifying the circumference of a circle

Answer each question.

1. O is the center of the circle on the right.
   a Draw the circumference of the circle in blue.
   b Draw a radius of the circle in red.
   c Draw a diameter of the circle in green.

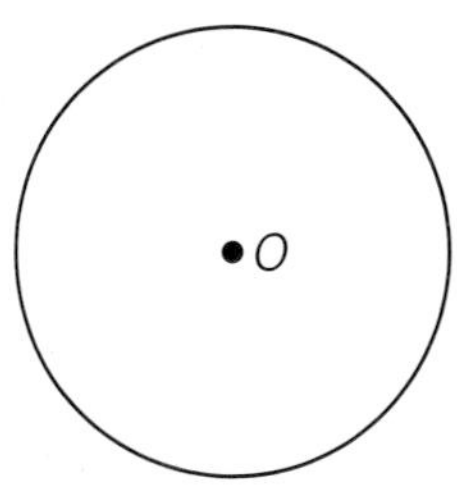

ENGAGE

Use a compass to draw three different-sized circles. What is the ratio of the circumference of each circle to its diameter? Is this true for all circles? Explain your reasoning.

LEARN Find the circumference of a circle

Activity Investigating the relationship between diameter of a circle and its circumference

Work in pairs.

Activity 1

1. Use a string to measure the circumference of each circle to the nearest tenth of a centimeter. Then, divide the circumference of each circle by its diameter. Round your answers to the nearest tenth. Record your results in the table below.

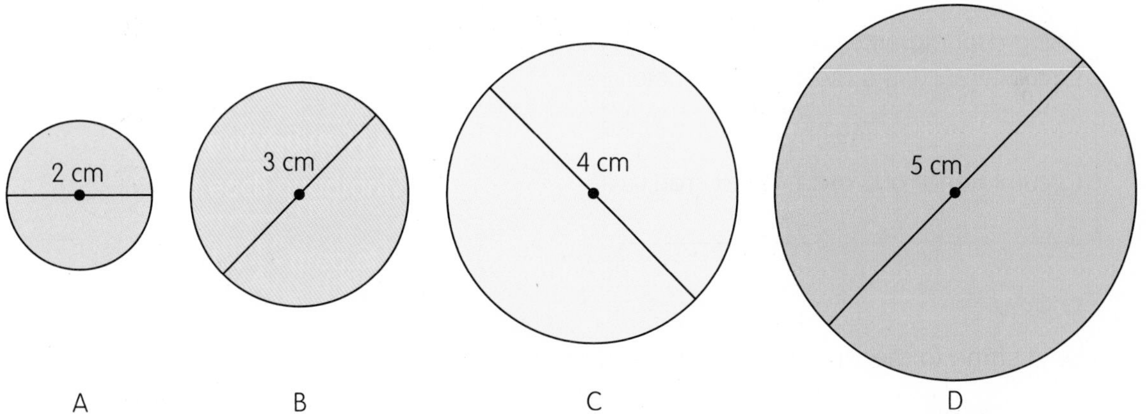

Circle	Diameter (cm)	Circumference (cm)	Circumference ÷ Diameter (round to the nearest tenth)
A	2		
B	3		
C	4		
D	5		

(2) What do you notice about the quotients when you divide the circumference by the diameter?

The circumference of any circle divided by its diameter always gives the same value. The Greek letter π is used to represent this value. π is the ratio of the circumference to the diameter of a circle.

Read π as "pie." Any value of π is an approximation.

(3) Press [π] [=] on your calculator to display the value of π. Round the value of π to

a 1 decimal place.

b 2 decimal places.

c 3 decimal places.

The value of π is often approximated as 3.14 or $\frac{22}{7}$.

(4) Since circumference ÷ diameter = π,
circumference = $\pi \cdot$ diameter

Since the diameter of a circle is 2 times its radius,
Circumference = $\pi \cdot$ diameter
= $2 \cdot \pi \cdot$ radius

Using d for diameter and r for radius,
Circumference of a circle = $\pi \cdot$ diameter
= πd

Circumference of a circle = $2 \cdot \pi \cdot$ radius
= $2\pi r$

Activity 2

(1) Use a string to measure the circumference of a circular object, such as a disc.

(2) Mark a point on the circular object. Then, roll the object along a straight line until it makes one complete turn.

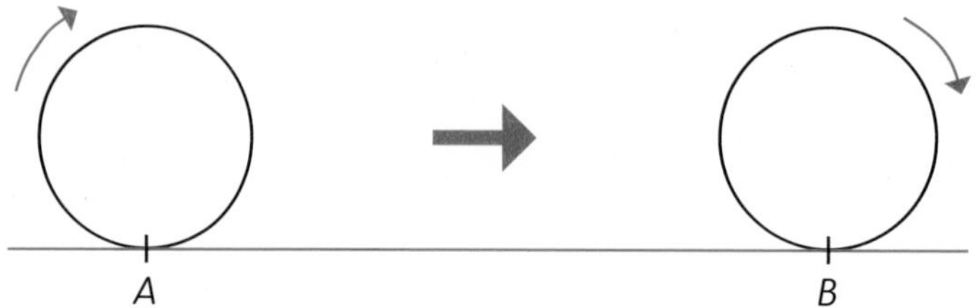

③ Measure the distance *AB*.

④ Compare the distance *AB* with the circumference of the object. What do you observe?

> The distance covered by one complete turn of a circle is equal to the circumference of the circle.

1 Find the circumference of the plate. Use $\frac{22}{7}$ as an approximation for π.

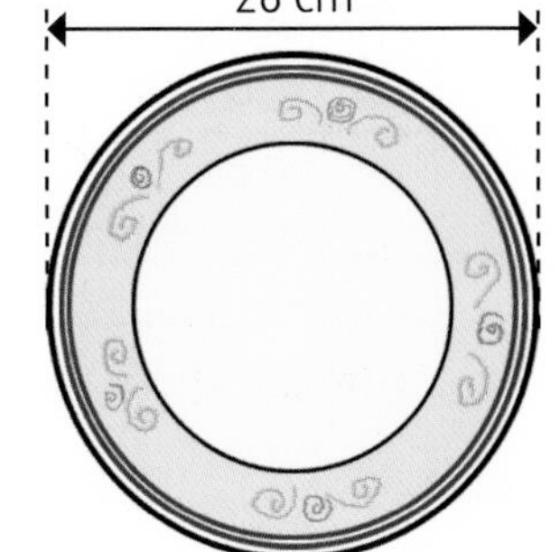

Circumference $= \pi d$	Write the formula.
$\approx \frac{22}{7} \cdot 28$	Substitute.
$= \frac{22}{\cancel{7}_1} \cdot \frac{\cancel{28}^4}{1}$	Divide by the common factor, 7.
$= 22 \cdot 4$	Simplify.
$= 88$ cm	Multiply.

The circumference of the plate is approximately 88 centimeters.

2 Mr. Turner rolls a circular disc one complete turn along the floor. The diameter of the disc is 0.7 meter. Find the distance traveled by the disc. Use $\frac{22}{7}$ as an approximation for π.

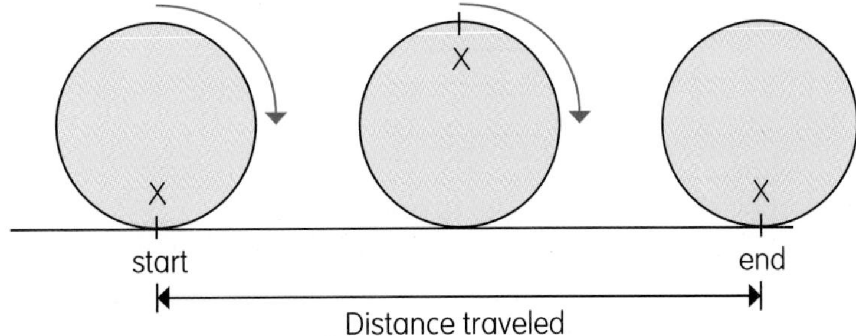

Distance traveled = circumference of disc

$\approx \frac{22}{7} \cdot 0.7$

$= 2.2$ m

The distance traveled by the disc is approximately 2.2 meters.

TRY Practice finding the circumference of a circle

Fill in the table. Use $\frac{22}{7}$ as an approximation for π.

1

Circle	Radius (in.)	Diameter (in.)	Circumference (in.)
A		14	
B	21		
C	10.5		

Fill in the table. Use 3.14 as an approximation for π.

2

Circle	Radius (cm)	Diameter (cm)	Circumference (in.)
D		25	
E	16		
F	8.25		

Solve.

3 Timothy rolled a bicycle wheel of diameter 56 centimeters through 10 complete turns. Find the distance traveled by the bicycle wheel. Use $\frac{22}{7}$ as an approximation for π.

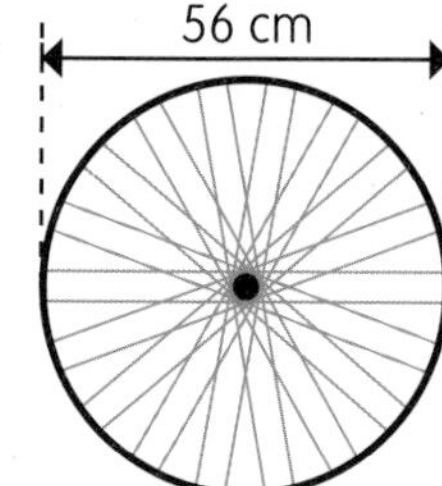

Distance traveled by bicycle wheel = ________ • circumference of bicycle wheel

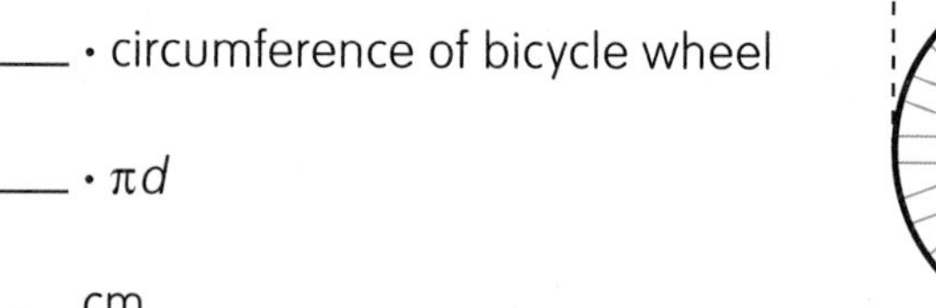

= ________ • πd

≈ ________ cm

The distance traveled by the bicycle wheel is approximately ________ centimeters.

4 A circular lid has a diameter of 7 inches. How many complete turns does it make to cover a distance of 110 inches? Use $\frac{22}{7}$ as an approximation for π.

Circumference of lid = πd

≈ ________ in.

Number of complete turns = ________ ÷ ________

= ________

The lid makes about ________ complete turns to cover 110 inches.

ENGAGE

1. Fold a paper circle into halves and then quarters. Measure the length of the curved edge of
   a the whole circle.
   b half of the whole circle.
   c a quarter of the whole circle.
   Is $\frac{1}{4}$ of the circumference of the whole circle the same as the length of the curved edge of a quarter of the whole circle? Why or why not?

2. How can you find the length of the curved edge of a quarter circle? Discuss the step you will take.

LEARN Find the distance around a semicircle and a quadrant

1. When you divide a circle into equal halves, each half circle is called a semicircle.

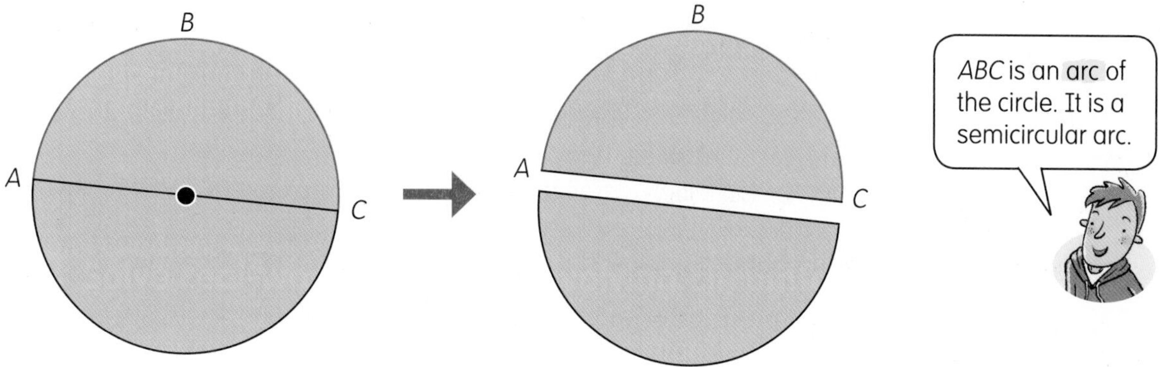

The length of the semicircular arc *ABC* is half the circumference of the circle.

2. When you divide a circle into quarters, each quarter circle is called a quadrant.

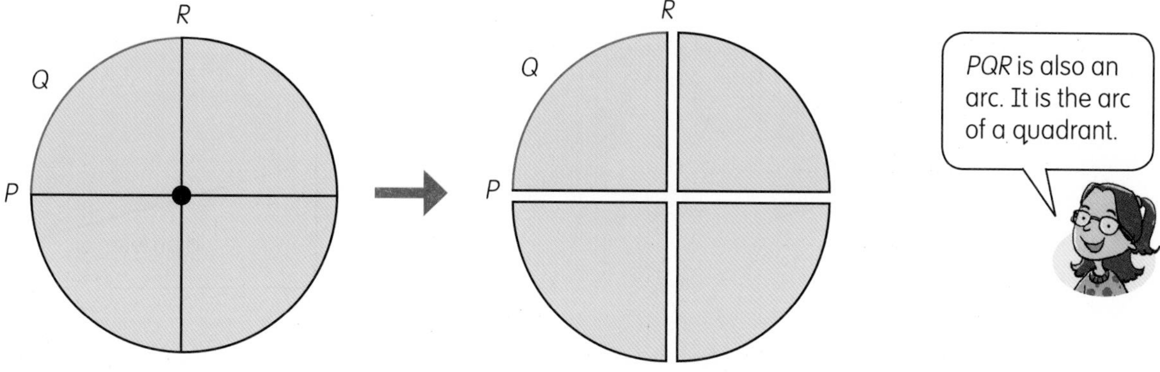

The length of arc *PQR* of the quadrant is one quarter the circumference of the circle.

3 A length of wire is bent into a semicircular arc. The length of $\overline{EF}$ is 21 centimeters. Find the length of the wire. Use $\frac{22}{7}$ as an approximation for π.

Circumference $= \pi d$ Write the formula.
$\approx \frac{22}{7} \cdot 21$ Substitute.
$= 66$ cm Multiply.

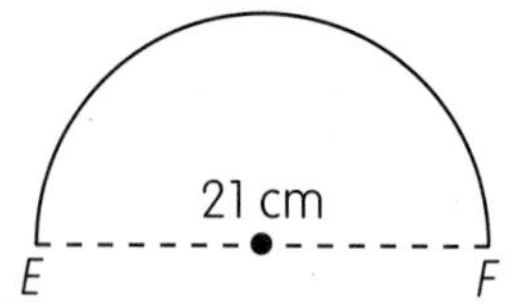

Length of semicircular arc $= \frac{1}{2} \cdot 66$
$= 33$ cm

Length of wire = length of semicircular arc
= 33 cm

The length of the wire is approximately 33 centimeters.

4 A circular ring of radius 5 inches is cut into four equal parts. Find the length of each arc of a quadrant. Use 3.14 as an approximation for π.

Circumference $= 2\pi r$ Write the formula.
$\approx 2 \cdot 3.14 \cdot 5$ Substitute.
$= 31.4$ in. Multiply.

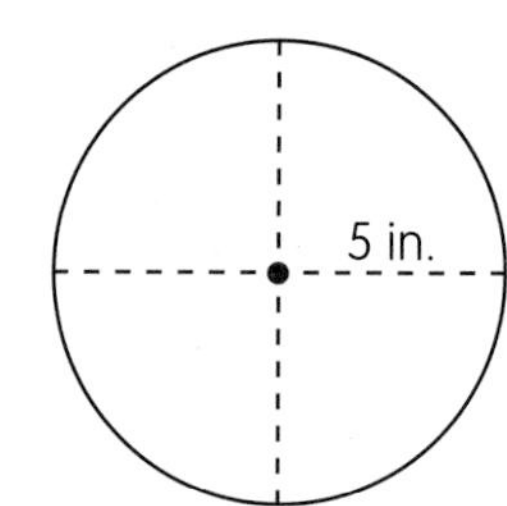

Length of each arc of the quadrant $= \frac{1}{4} \cdot 31.4$
$= 7.85$ in.

The length of each arc of a quadrant is approximately 7.85 inches.

5 A circle of diameter 14 inches is cut into halves. Find the distance around one of its semicircles. Use $\frac{22}{7}$ as an approximation for π.

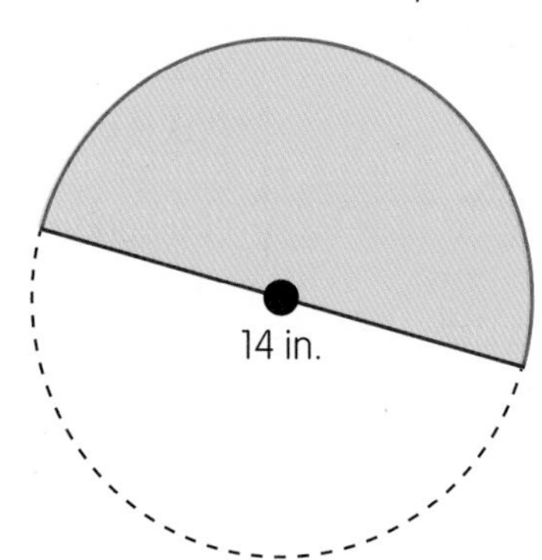

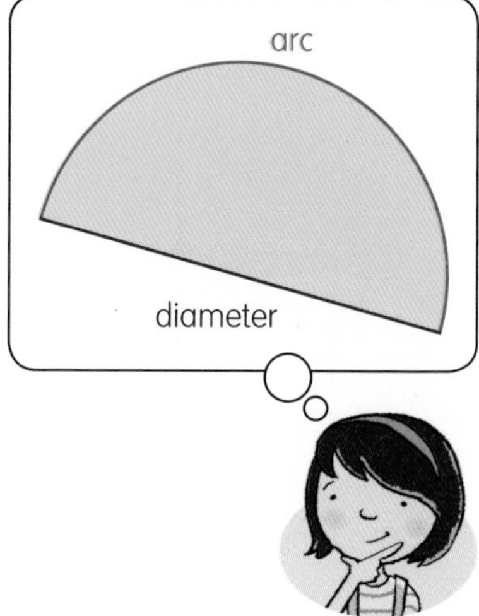

Distance around semicircle = length of arc of semicircle + diameter

$$= \left(\frac{1}{2} \cdot \pi d\right) + \text{diameter}$$

$$\approx \left(\frac{1}{2} \cdot \frac{22}{7} \cdot 14\right) + 14$$

$$= 22 + 14$$

$$= 36 \text{ in.}$$

The distance around one of its semicircles is approximately 36 inches.

6 A circle of radius 5 centimeters is cut into quarters. Find the distance around one of its quadrants. Use 3.14 as an approximation for π.

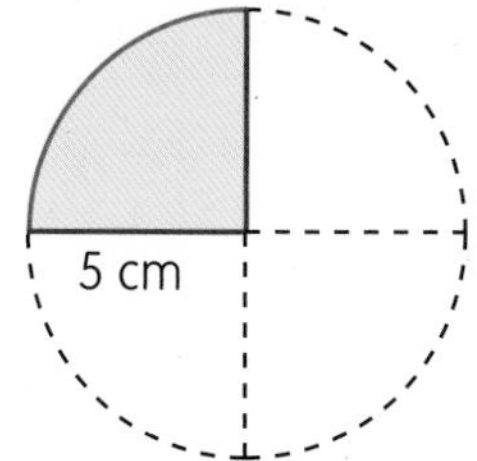

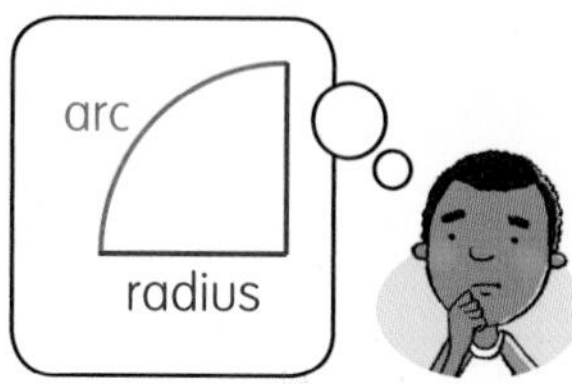

Distance around quadrant = length of arc of quadrant + 2 radii

$$= \left(\frac{1}{4} \cdot 2\pi r\right) + (2 \cdot 5)$$

$$\approx \left(\frac{1}{4} \cdot 2 \cdot 3.14 \cdot 5\right) + 10$$

$$= 7.85 + 10$$

$$= 17.85 \text{ cm}$$

The distance around one of its quadrants is approximately 17.85 centimeters.

TRY Practice finding the distance around a semicircle and a quadrant

Solve.

1. A length of wire is bent into a semicircle of diameter 21 centimeters. Find the length of the wire. Use $\frac{22}{7}$ as an approximation for π.

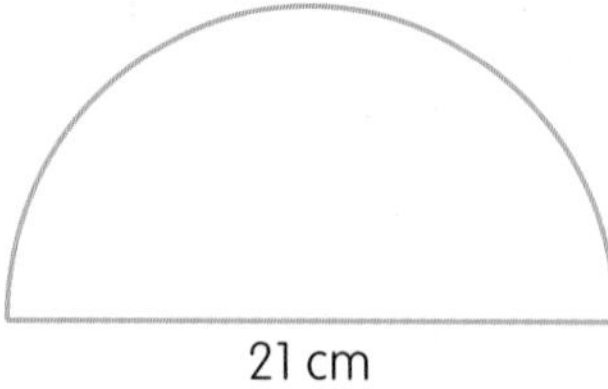

Length of wire = length of arc of semicircle + diameter

$= (\_\_\_\_\_ \cdot \pi d) + \_\_\_\_\_$

$\approx \_\_\_\_\_ + \_\_\_\_\_$

$= \_\_\_\_\_$ cm

The length of the wire is approximately _____ centimeters.

2. A quadrant is cut out from a square of side 10 inches. Find the distance around the quadrant. Use 3.14 as an approximation for π.

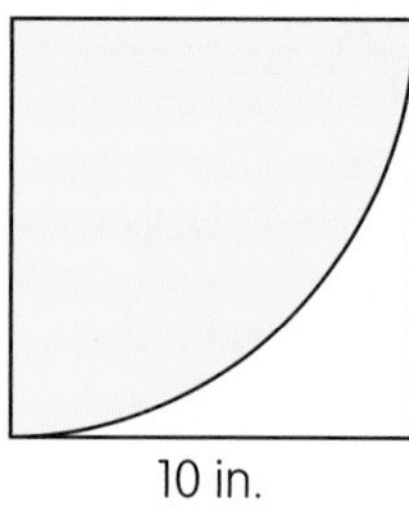

Distance around quadrant = length of arc of quadrant + 2 radii

$= (\_\_\_\_\_ \cdot 2\pi r) + (2 \cdot \_\_\_\_\_)$

$\approx \_\_\_\_\_ + \_\_\_\_\_$

$= \_\_\_\_\_$ in.

The distance around the quadrant is approximately _____ inches.

Name: ____________________ Date: __________

INDEPENDENT PRACTICE

***O* is the center of the circle and $\overline{XY}$ is a straight line. Fill in each blank.**

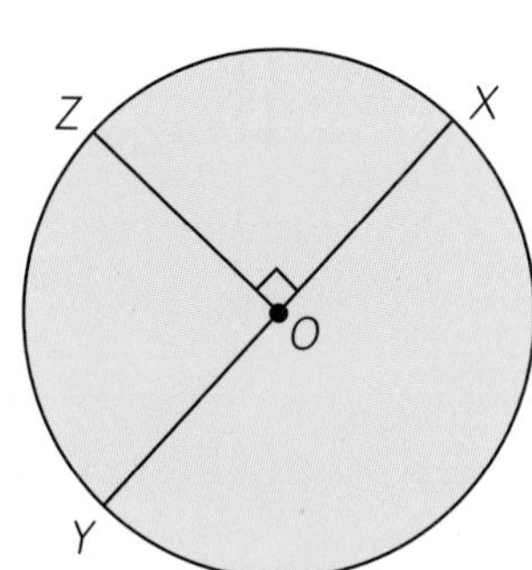

1. $\overline{OX}$, $\overline{OY}$, and $\overline{OZ}$ are ______________ of the circle.

2. $\overline{XY}$ is the ______________ of the circle.

3. OX = ________ = ________

4. XY = ________ $\cdot$ OZ

5. Circumference of the circle = π $\cdot$ ______________

Find the circumference of each circle. Use $\frac{22}{7}$ as an approximation for π.

6.

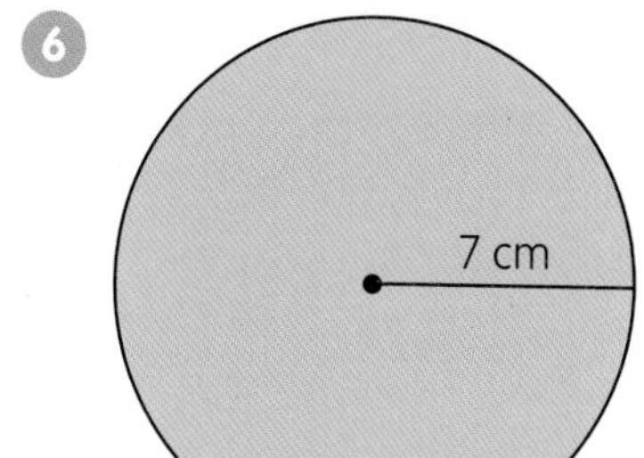

7.

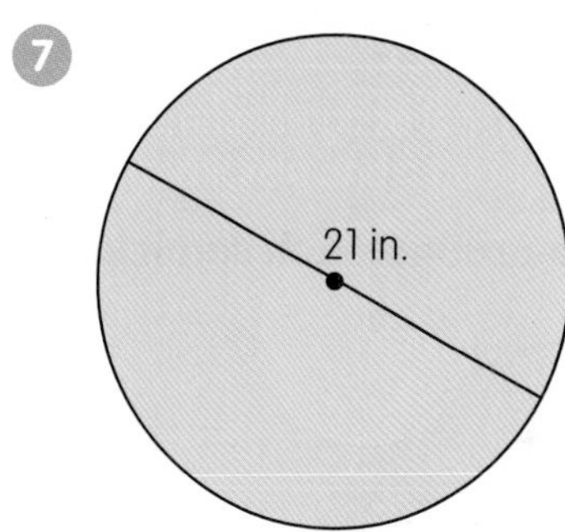

8.

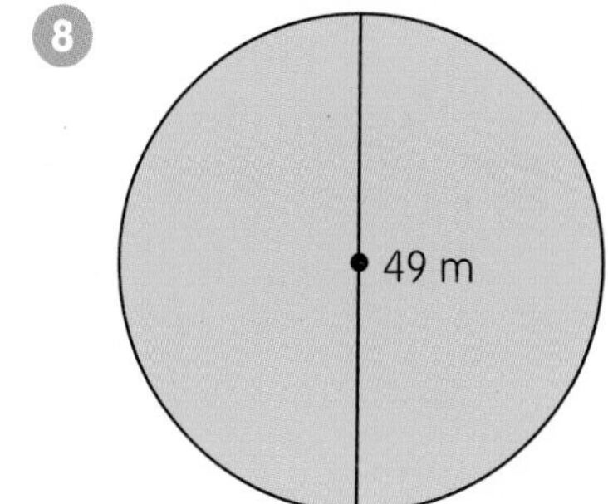

9.

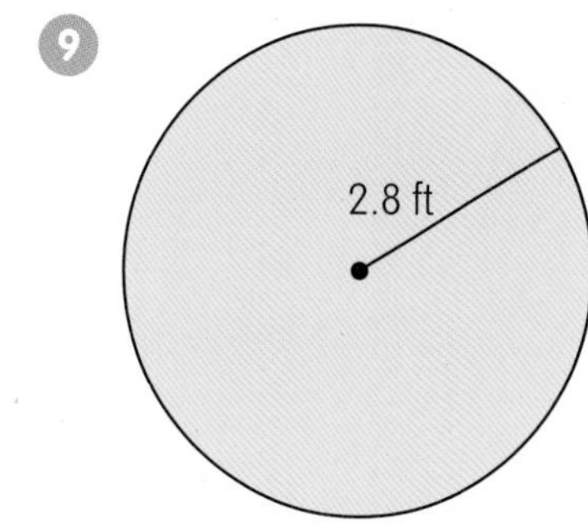

Find the length of each arc. Use $\frac{22}{7}$ as an approximation for π.

10
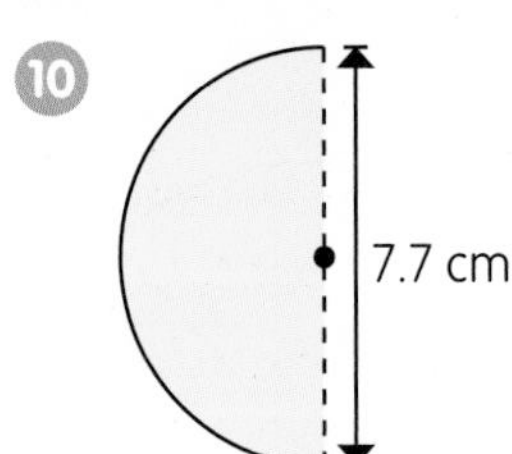

11
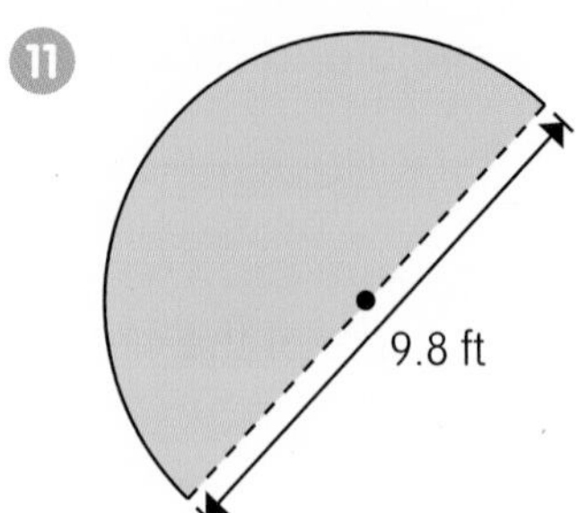

12
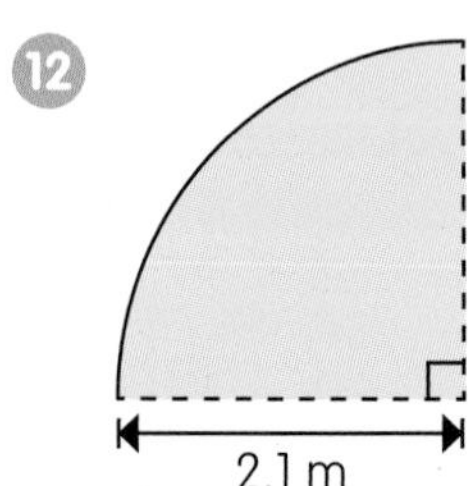

13
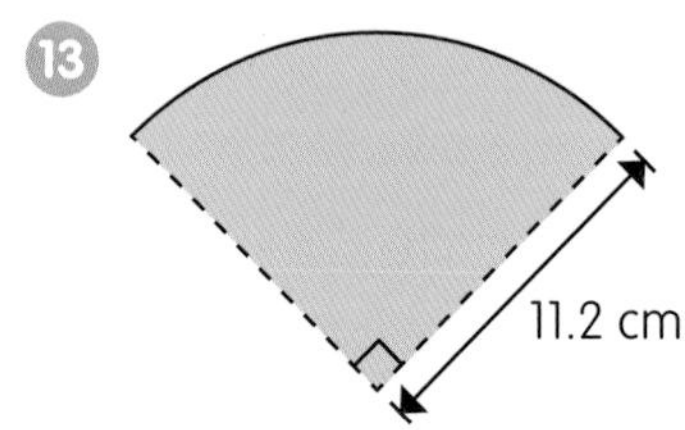

Find the distance around each semicircle. Use 3.14 as an approximation for π.

14
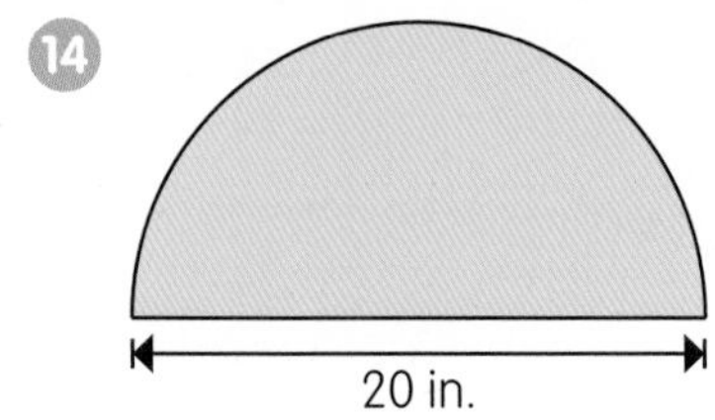

15
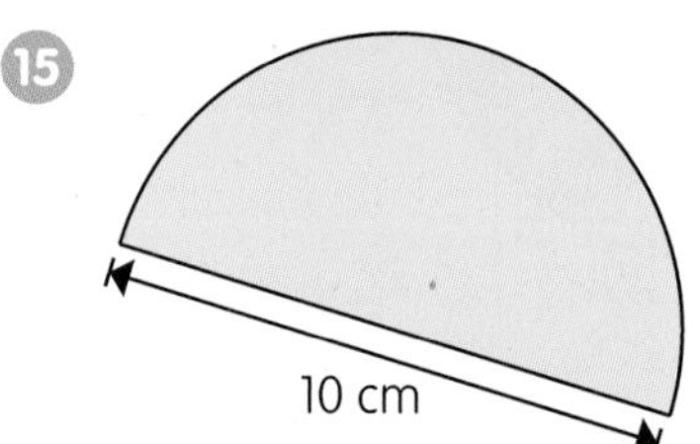

16
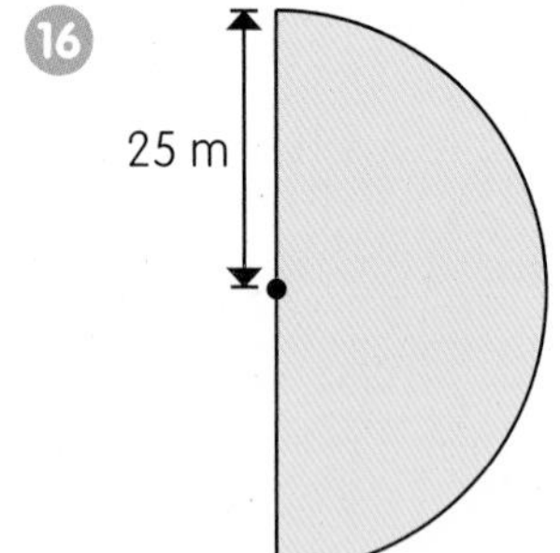

17
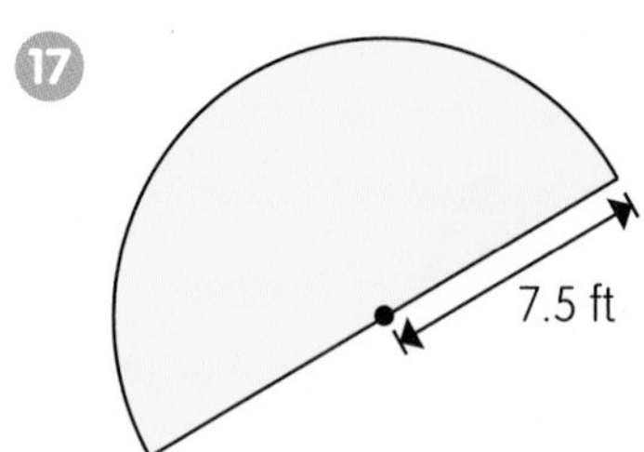

Find the distance around each quadrant. Use $\frac{22}{7}$ as an approximation for π.

18
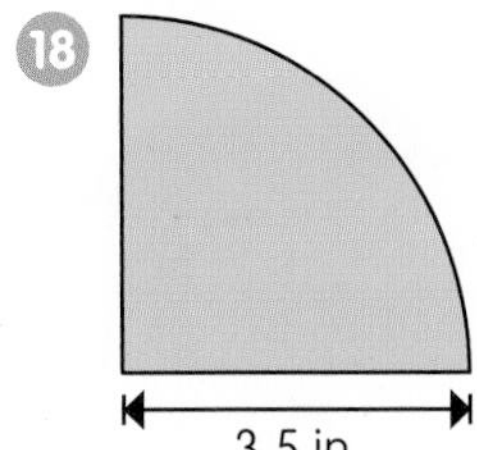

19
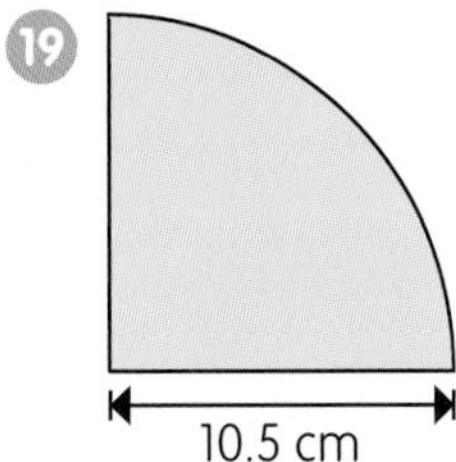

20
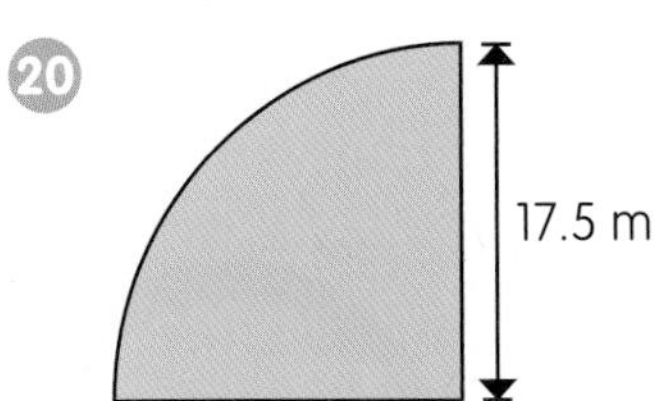

21
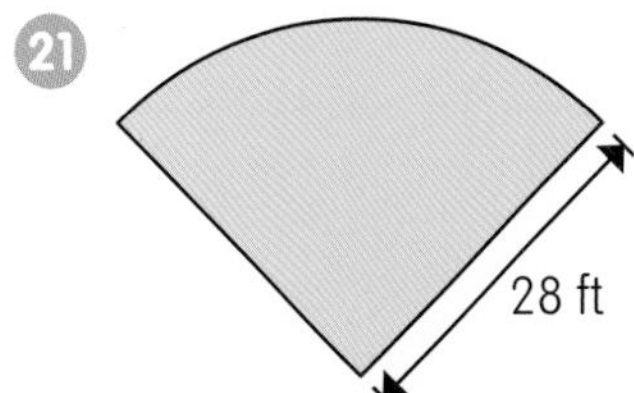

Solve. Use 3.14 as an approximation for π.

22 The diameter of a giant Ferris wheel is 135 meters. Find its circumference.

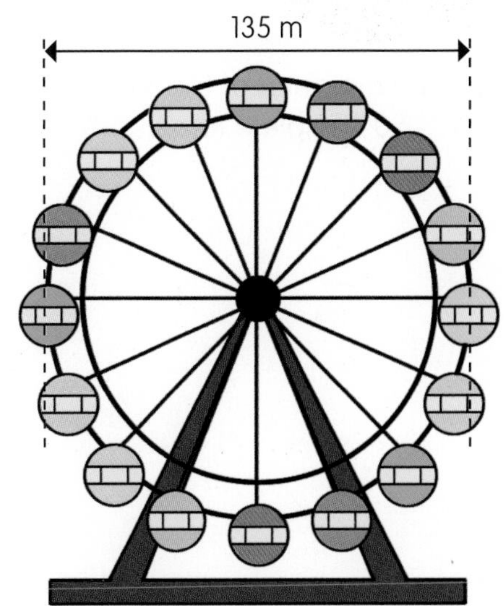

23 Ethan wants to add a fence around his semicircular backyard. What is the distance around his backyard?

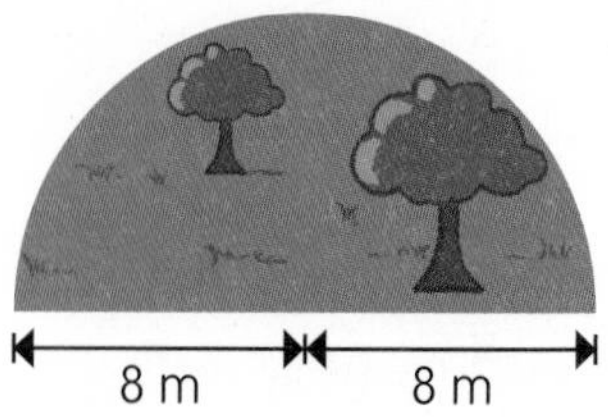

24 If the radius of a wheel is 14 inches, what is the distance traveled when the wheel turns around 100 times?

25 The diameter of the wheel of a car is 45 centimeters. Find the distance it covers in 50 complete turns.

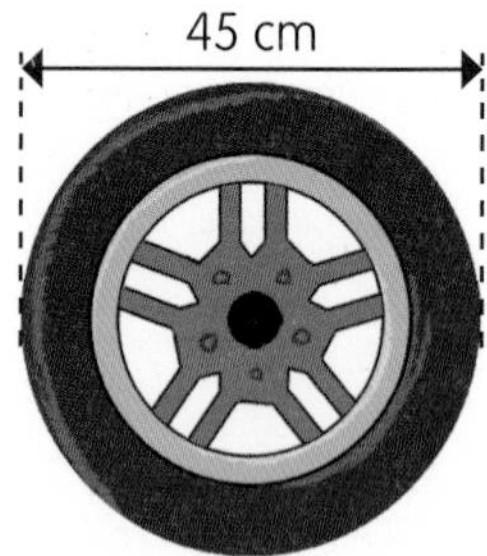

Name: ______________________ Date: ______________

2 Area of a Circle

Learning Objectives:

- Use formula to find the areas of circles, semicircles, and quadrants.

The figure on the right shows a circle inside a square.
The area of the circle is approximately 1,256 square inches.
What is the area of the square?
Use 3.14 as an approximation for π.

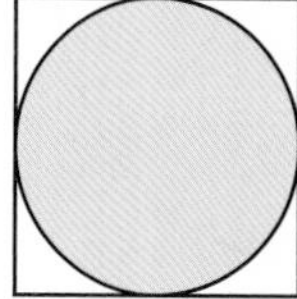

ENGAGE

On a piece of grid paper, draw a circle with a diameter of 4 centimeters and a square of sides 4 centimeters.

a How can you find the area of the circle? Discuss the steps you would take to find the area of the circle.

b What is the area of the square? What can you observe about the area of the circle and the area of the square? Discuss.

LEARN Find the area of a circle

Activity Estimating the area of a circle

Work in pairs.

Activity 1

① The figure on the right shows a circle of radius r in a square. Find the area of the square in terms of r.

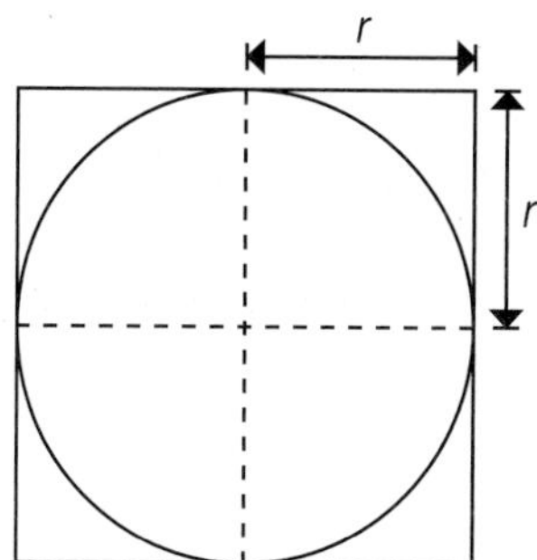

② Draw a square in the circle as shown. Then, find the area of the square in terms of r.

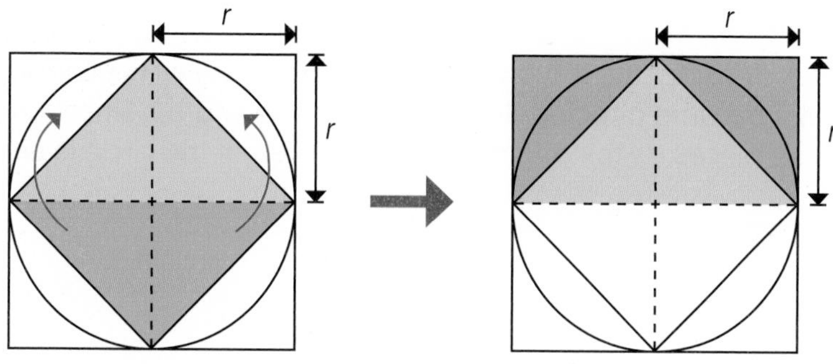

③ Estimate the area of the circle using the areas found in ① and ②.

The area of the circle is less than ________ square units but is more than ________ square units.

The area of the circle is about ________ square units.

Activity 2

① A diameter divides a circle of radius r into 2 semicircles. Find the length of the red arc in terms of π and r.

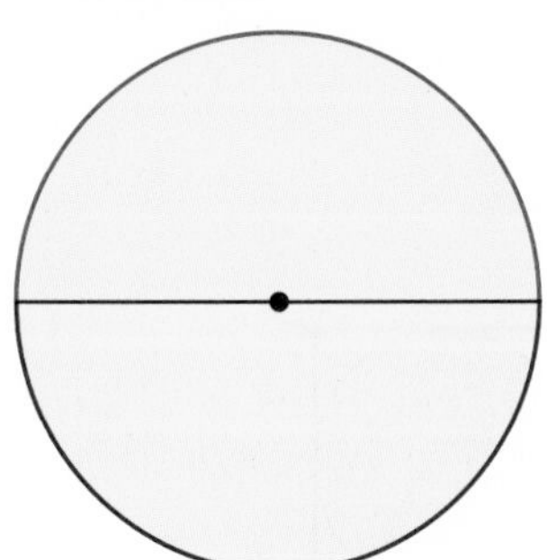

Length of red arc
= Half circumference of circle

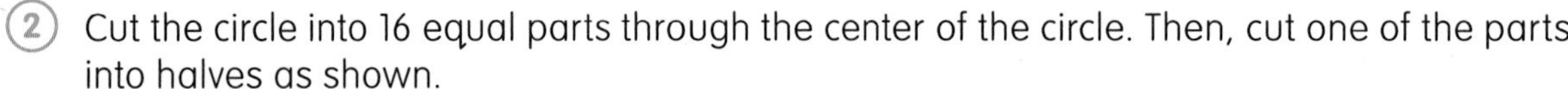

② Cut the circle into 16 equal parts through the center of the circle. Then, cut one of the parts into halves as shown.

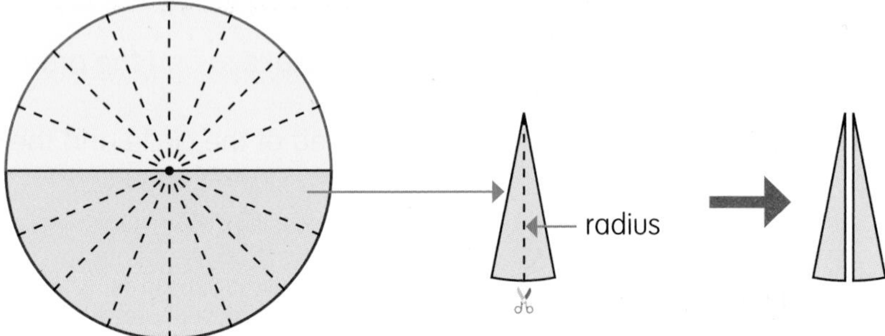

③ Arrange all the pieces to form Figure 1. Next, cut the pieces into 32 equal parts and cut one of the parts into halves to form Figure 2

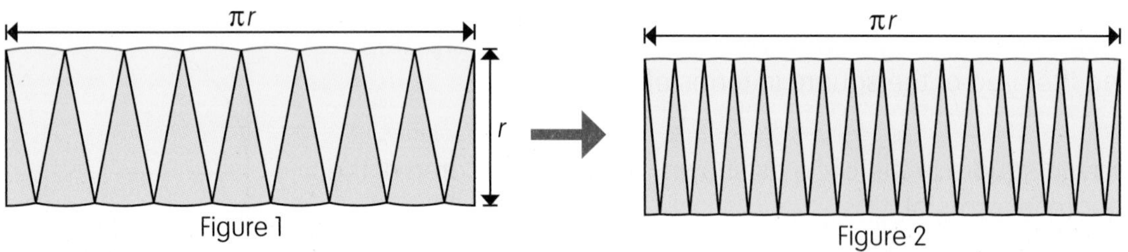

Figure 1

Figure 2

④ As the number of pieces keeps increasing, the top and bottom of the figure will become straight lines. Then, the figure will become a rectangle of length πr and width r. Since the rectangle is made up of the same pieces as the original circle, the area of the circle is equal to the area of the rectangle.

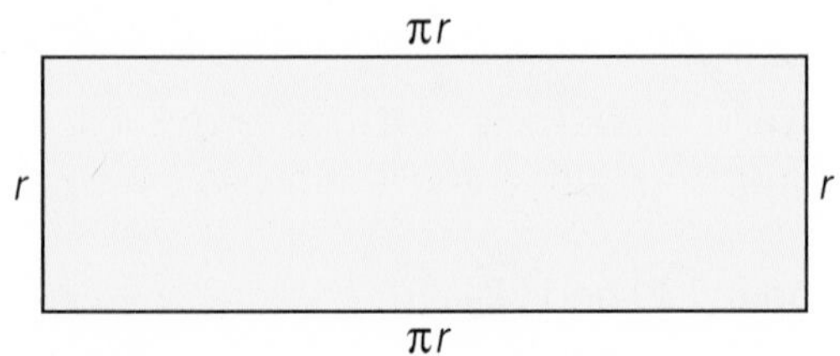

Area of a circle = area of rectangle
$= \pi r \cdot r$
$= \pi r^2$

1. The radius of a circular disc is 7 inches. Find its area. Use $\frac{22}{7}$ as an approximation for π.

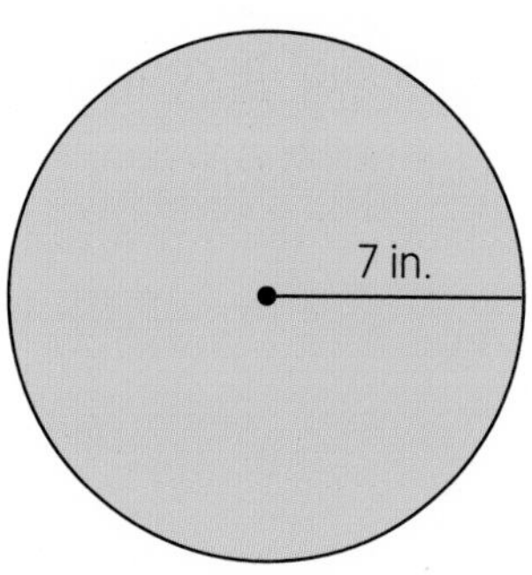

Area $= \pi r^2$	Write the formula.
$\approx \frac{22}{7} \cdot 7^2$	Substitute.
$= \frac{22}{\cancel{7}_1} \cdot 7 \cdot \cancel{7}^1$	Divide by the common factor, 7.
$= 22 \cdot 7$	Simplify.
$= 154 \text{ in}^2$	Multiply.

The area of the disc is approximately 154 square inches.

2. The diameter of a circular clock face is 24 centimeters. Find its area. Use 3.14 as an approximation for π.

Radius of circular clock face = diameter ÷ 2
$= 24 \div 2$
$= 12 \text{ cm}$

Area $= \pi r^2$	Write the formula.
$\approx 3.14 \cdot 12^2$	Substitute.
$= 3.14 \cdot 144$	Simplify.
$= 452.16 \text{ cm}^2$	Multiply.

The area of the circular clock face is approximately 452.16 square centimeters.

TRY Practice finding the area of a circle

Solve. Use 3.14 as an approximation for π.

1. Find the area of a circle that has a radius of 18 centimeters.

   Area = πr^2

   ≈ _______ • _______^{2}

   = _______ • _______

   = _______ cm^2

   The area of the circle is approximately _______ square centimeters.

2. Find the area of a circle that has a radius of 15 inches.

   Area = πr^2

   ≈ _______ • _______^{2}

   = _______ • _______

   = _______ in^2

   The area of the circle is approximately _______ square inches.

3. Find the area of a circle that has a diameter of 26 centimeters.

   Radius = diameter ÷ 2

   = _______ ÷ _______

   = _______ cm

   Area = πr^2

   ≈ _______ • _______^{2}

   = _______ • _______

   = _______ cm^2

   The area of the circle is approximately _______ square centimeters.

ENGAGE

Recall how you would find the area of a circle. How are the areas of a semicircle and a quadrant related to the area of the circle? Discuss how you can find the areas of a semicircle and a quadrant using the area of a circle.

LEARN Find the area of a semicircle and a quadrant

1 A circle of diameter 14 feet is cut into equal halves.

Find the area of each semicircle.

Use $\frac{22}{7}$ as an approximation for π.

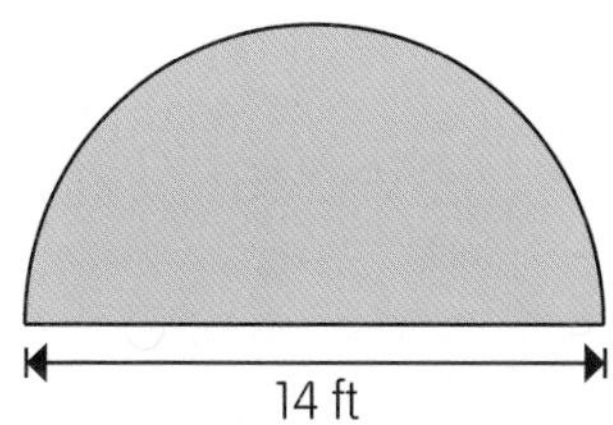

Radius of circle = diameter ÷ 2
= 14 ÷ 2
= 7 ft

Area of semicircle $= \frac{1}{2} \cdot$ area of circle

$= \frac{1}{2} \cdot \pi r^2$ Write the formula.

$\approx \frac{1}{2} \cdot \frac{22}{7} \cdot 7^2$ Substitute.

$= \frac{1}{\cancel{2}_1} \cdot \frac{\cancel{22}^{11}}{\cancel{7}_1} \cdot 7 \cdot \cancel{7}^1$ Divide by the common factors, 2 and 7.

$= 11 \cdot 7$ Multiply.

$= 77 \text{ ft}^2$ Simplify.

The area of each semicircle is approximately 77 square feet.

2 Colin cuts a circle of radius 14 centimeters into 4 quadrants.
Find the area of each quadrant. Use $\frac{22}{7}$ as an approximation for π.

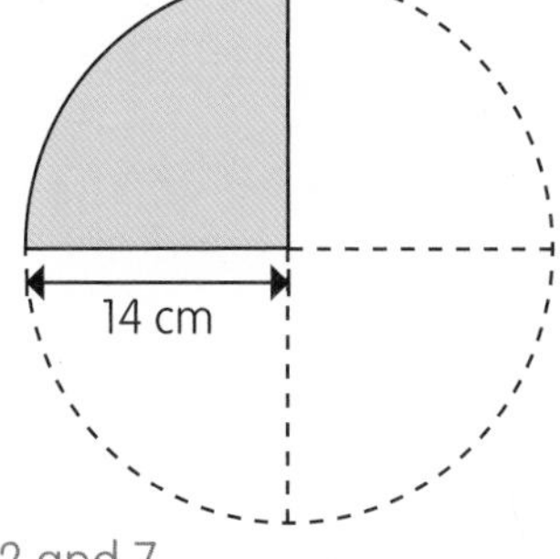

Area of quadrant $= \frac{1}{4} \cdot$ area of circle

$= \frac{1}{4} \cdot \pi r^2$ Write the formula.

$\approx \frac{1}{4} \cdot \frac{22}{7} \cdot 14^2$ Substitute.

$= \frac{1}{\cancel{4}_2} \cdot \frac{\cancel{22}^{11}}{\cancel{7}_1} \cdot 14 \cdot \cancel{14}^2$ Divide by the common factors, 2 and 7.

$= \frac{308}{2}$ Multiply.

$= 154 \text{ cm}^2$ Simplify.

The area of each quadrant is approximately 154 square centimeters.

TRY Practice finding the area of a semicircle and a quadrant

Solve.

1. Find the area of the semicircle. Use 3.14 as an approximation for π.

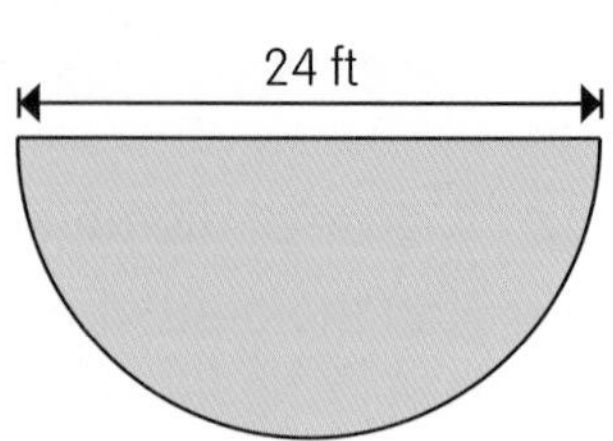

Radius of circle = diameter ÷ 2

$= \_\_\_\_\_\_ \div 2$

$= \_\_\_\_\_\_$ ft

Area of semicircle $= \frac{1}{2} \cdot$ area of circle

$= \frac{1}{2} \cdot \pi r^2$

$\approx \frac{1}{2} \cdot \_\_\_\_\_\_ \cdot \_\_\_\_\_\_^2$

$= \frac{1}{2} \cdot \_\_\_\_\_\_ \cdot \_\_\_\_\_\_$

$= \_\_\_\_\_\_$ ft^2

The area of the semicircle is approximately ______ square feet.

2. The diameter of a circle is 42 inches. Find the area of one of its quadrants. Use $\frac{22}{7}$ as an approximation for π.

42 in.

Radius of circle = diameter ÷ 2

$= \_\_\_\_\_\_ \div 2$

$= \_\_\_\_\_\_$ in.

Area of quadrant $= \frac{1}{4} \cdot$ area of circle

$= \frac{1}{4} \cdot \pi r^2$

$\approx \frac{1}{4} \cdot \_\_\_\_\_\_ \cdot \_\_\_\_\_\_^2$

$= \frac{1}{4} \cdot \_\_\_\_\_\_ \cdot \_\_\_\_\_\_$

$= \_\_\_\_\_\_$ in^2

The area of one of its quadrants is approximately ______ square inches.

Name: ______________________ Date: ______________

INDEPENDENT PRACTICE

Find the area of each circle. Use 3.14 as an approximation for π.

1. 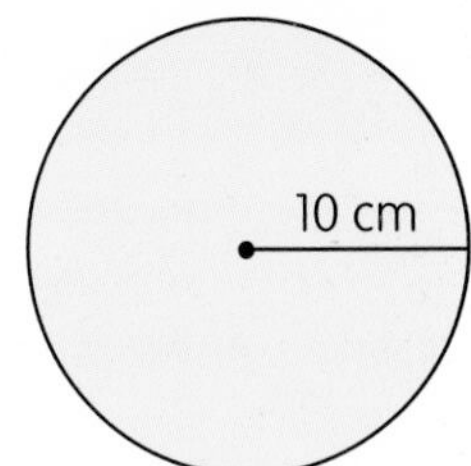

2. 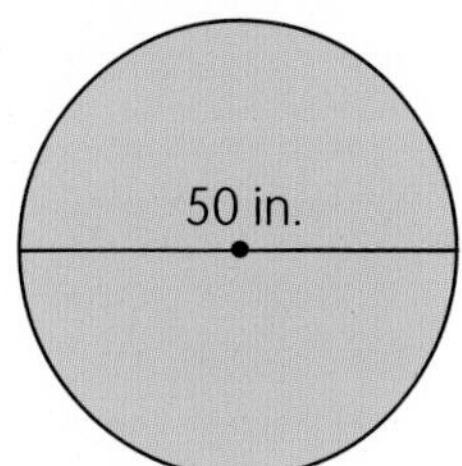

Find the area of each circle. Use $\frac{22}{7}$ as an approximation for π.

3. 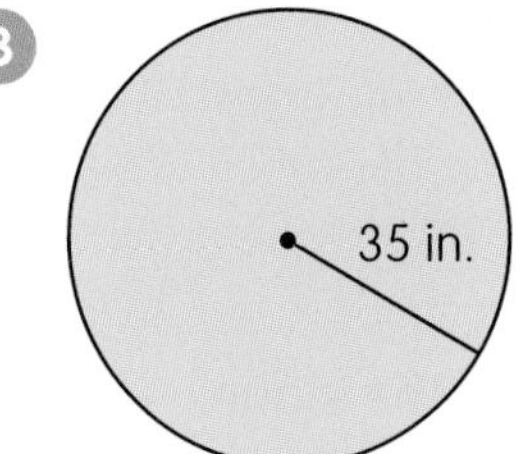

4. 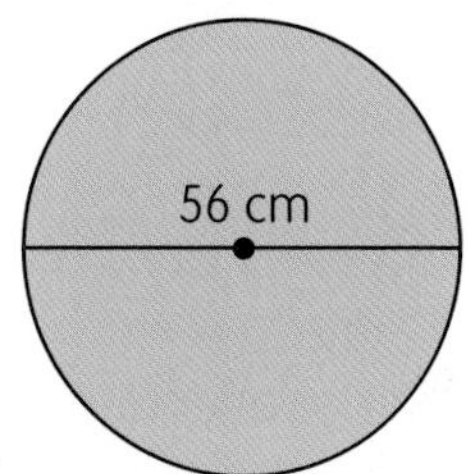

Find the area of each semicircle. Use $\frac{22}{7}$ as an approximation for π.

5. 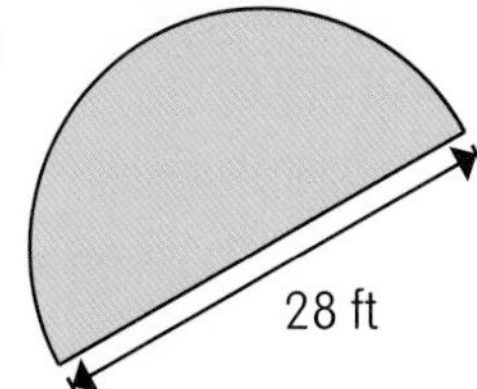

6. 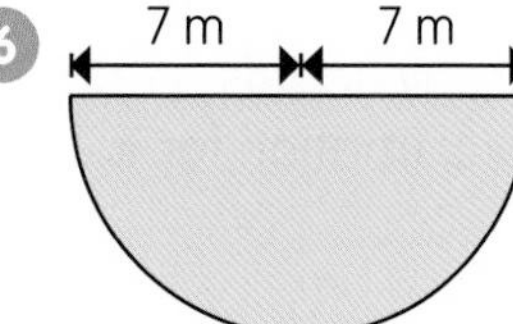

Find the area of each quadrant. Use 3.14 as an approximation for π. Round your answer to the nearest tenth.

7 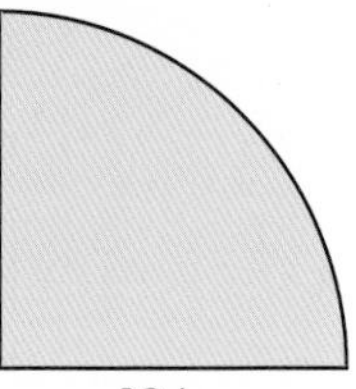

8  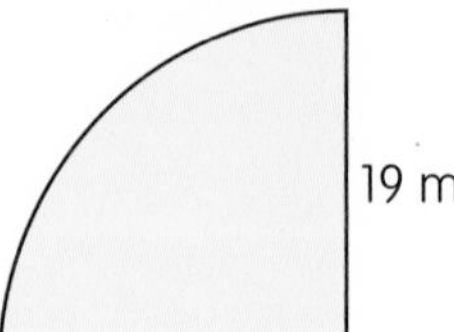

Solve.

9 A circular pendant has a diameter of 7 centimeters. Find its area. Use $\frac{22}{7}$ as an approximation for π.

10 The shape of the stage of a lecture theater is a semicircle. Find the area of the stage. Use 3.14 as an approximation for π.

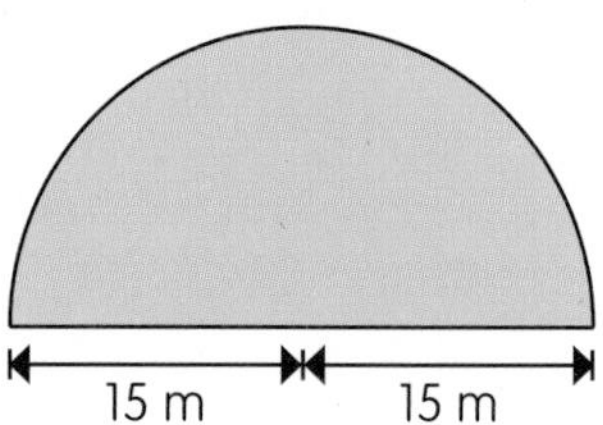

11 The shape of a balcony floor is a quadrant. Find the area of the balcony floor. Use 3.14 as an approximation for π.

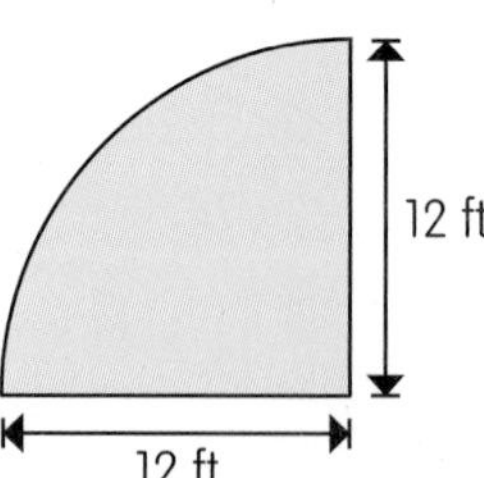

Name: _______________ Date: _______________

Real-World Problems: Circles

Learning Objectives:

- Solve real-world problems involving area and circumference of circles.
- Solve real-world problems involving semicircles, quadrants, and composite figures.

The figure is formed by three semicircular arcs.
Find the distance around the figure and its area.
How can you solve it in another way?

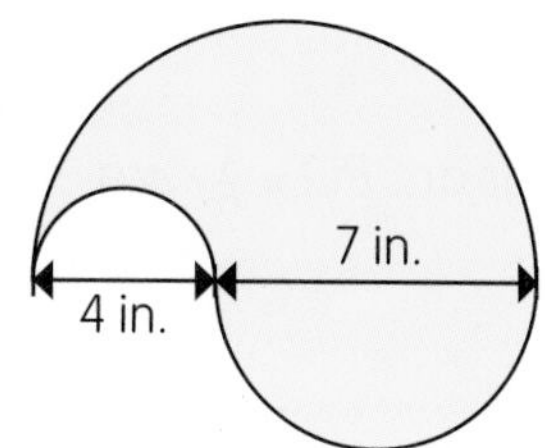

ENGAGE

Find the distance around the figure on the right.
How can you describe the distance in terms of r?

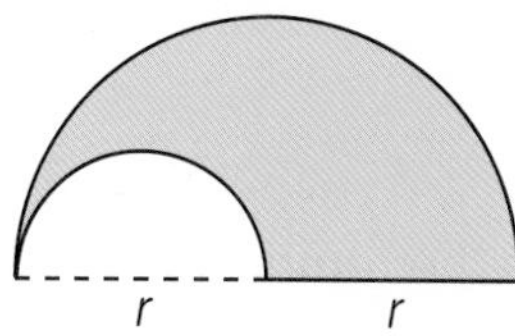

LEARN Solve real-world problems involving circumference

1 A metalworker cuts out a smaller semicircle from a larger one as shown in the figure. Find the distance around the remaining figure after the smaller semicircle is removed. Use $\frac{22}{7}$ as an approximation for π.

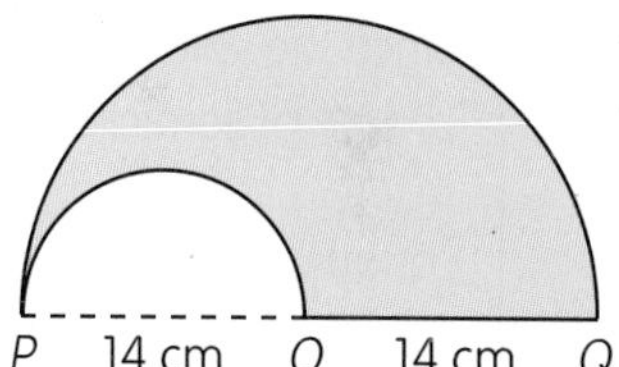

 Understand the problem.

What does the metalworker do to obtain the remaining figure?
What lengths make up the figure?
What do I need to find?

 Think of a plan.

The distance around the remaining figure is made up of the lengths of the two semicircular arcs and $\overline{OQ}$. I can use the formula for the circumference of a circle to find the lengths of the two semicircular arcs.

STEP 3 Carry out the plan.

Diameter of smaller semicircle = radius of larger semicircle
= 14 cm

Length of semicircular arc $PQ = \frac{1}{2} \cdot 2\,\pi r$

$\approx \frac{1}{{}_1\cancel{2}} \cdot \cancel{2}^{1} \cdot \frac{22}{{}_1\cancel{7}} \cdot \cancel{14}^{2}$

$= 1 \cdot 22 \cdot 2$

$= 44$ cm

Length of semicircular arc $PO = \frac{1}{2} \cdot \pi d$

$\approx \frac{1}{{}_1\cancel{2}} \cdot \frac{\cancel{22}^{11}}{{}_1\cancel{7}} \cdot \cancel{14}^{2}$

$= 1 \cdot 11 \cdot 2$

$= 22$ cm

Distance around the remaining figure = semicircular arc PQ + semicircular arc PO + OQ
= 44 + 22 + 14
= 80 cm

The distance around the remaining figure is approximately 80 centimeters.

STEP 4 Check the answer.

Since the value of π is approximately 3, I can check my answer using estimation.
Length of semicircular arc $PQ \approx \frac{1}{2} \cdot 2 \cdot 3 \cdot 14 = 42$ cm

Length of semicircular arc $PO \approx \frac{1}{2} \cdot 3 \cdot 14 = 21$ cm

The estimated lengths are close to the lengths found in Step 3. My answer is reasonable.

2. The shape of a table top is made up of a semicircle and a quadrant. Find the distance around the table top. Use 3.14 as an approximation for π.

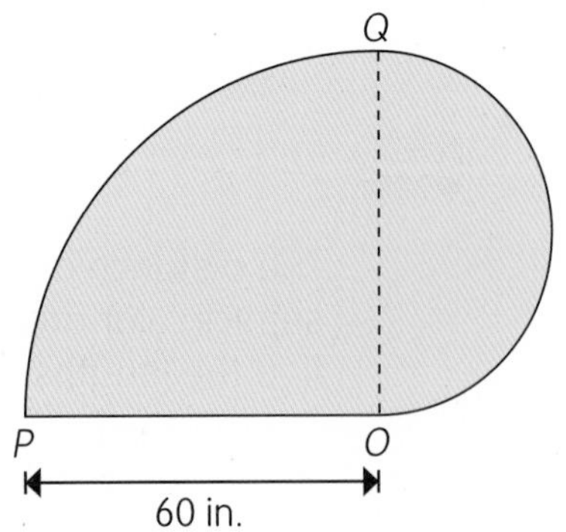

Length of semicircular arc $QO = \frac{1}{2} \cdot \pi d$

$\approx \frac{1}{2} \cdot 3.14 \cdot 60$

$= 94.2$ in.

Length of arc $PQ = \frac{1}{4} \cdot 2\pi r$

$\approx \frac{1}{{}_1\cancel{4}} \cdot 2 \cdot 3.14 \cdot \cancel{60}^{15}$

$= 1 \cdot 2 \cdot 3.14 \cdot 15$

$= 94.2$ in.

Distance around the table top
= length of semicircular arc QO + length of arc PQ + PO
= 94.2 + 94.2 + 60
= 248.4 in.

The distance around the table top is approximately 248.4 inches.

TRY Practice solving real-world problems involving circumference

Solve. Use 3.14 as an approximation for π.

1. A greeting card is made up of three semicircles. O is the center of the large semicircle. Zane wants to decorate the distance around the card with a ribbon. How much ribbon does Zane need? Round your answer to the nearest inch.

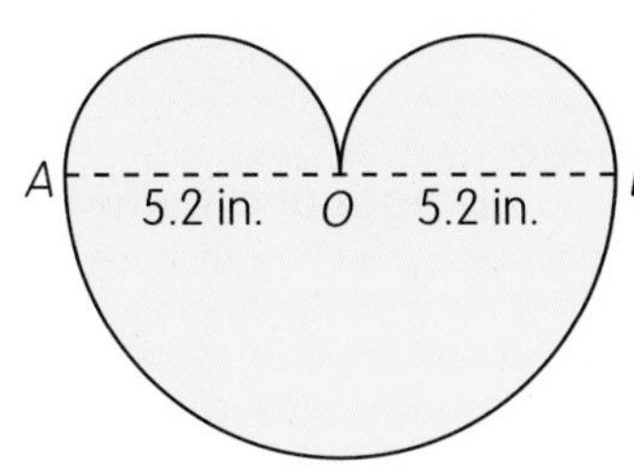

Length of semicircular arc $AB = \frac{1}{2} \cdot 2\pi r$

$\approx$ ______ $\cdot$ ______ $\cdot$ ______ $\cdot$ ______

$= 1 \cdot$ ______ $\cdot$ ______

$=$ ______ in.

Semicircular arcs AO and OB have the same length.

Total length of semicircular arcs AO and OB

$= 2 \cdot \frac{1}{2} \cdot \pi d$

$\approx$ ______ $\cdot$ ______ $\cdot$ ______ $\cdot$ ______

$= 1 \cdot$ ______ $\cdot$ ______

$=$ ______ in.

Distance around the card
= length of semicircular arc AB + total length of semicircular arcs AO and OB

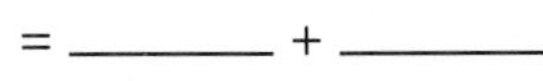

$=$ ______ + ______

$=$ ______ in.

$\approx$ ______ in.

Zane needs approximately ______ inches of ribbon.

2. As part of her artwork, Amir bends a length of wire into the figure shown. The figure is made up of a semicircle and a quadrant. Find the length of the wire.

Length of semicircular arc $PQ = \frac{1}{2} \cdot 2\pi r$

$\approx$ ______ $\cdot$ ______ $\cdot$ ______ $\cdot$ ______

$=$ ______ $\cdot$ ______ $\cdot$ ______

$=$ ______ cm

Length of arc $RO = \frac{1}{4} \cdot 2\pi r$

$\approx$ ______ $\cdot$ ______ $\cdot$ ______ $\cdot$ ______

$=$ ______ cm

Distance around the figure = length of semicircular arc PQ + length of arc RO + RP + OQ

$=$ ______ + ______ + ______ + ______

$=$ ______ cm

The length of the wire is approximately ______ centimeters.

ENGAGE

How do you find the area of a circular disc of diameter 14 centimeters, that has a circular hole of diameter 1.4 centimeters? Share the steps you would take to find the area. Does your method differ from your partner's?

LEARN Solve real-world problems involving area of a circle

1. A jewelry designer is making a pendant. The pendant will be a circular disc (center O) with a circular hole cut out of it, as shown. The radius of the disc is 35 millimeters. Find the area of the pendant. Use $\frac{22}{7}$ as an approximation for π.

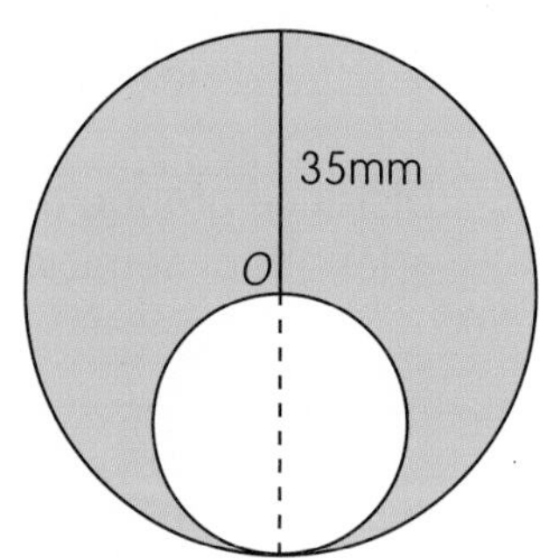

Area of disc $= \pi r^2$

$\approx \frac{22}{7} \cdot 35^2$

$= \frac{22}{\cancel{7}_1} \cdot 35 \cdot \cancel{35}^5$

$= 22 \cdot 35 \cdot 5$

$= 3{,}850 \text{ mm}^2$

Radius of circular hole = diameter ÷ 2

$= 35 \div 2$

$= 17.5$ mm

$$\text{Area of circular hole} = \pi r^2 \approx \frac{22}{7} \cdot 17.5 \cdot 17.5 = 962.5 \text{ mm}^2$$

$$\begin{aligned}\text{Area of pendant} &= \text{area of disc} - \text{area of circular hole}\\ &= 3{,}850 - 962.5\\ &= 2{,}887.5 \text{ mm}^2\end{aligned}$$

The area of the pendant is approximately 2,887.5 square millimeters.

2 Maria baked a 12-inch vegetarian pizza. She ate a quarter of the pizza for lunch. Find the area of the remaining pizza. Use 3.14 as an approximation for π.

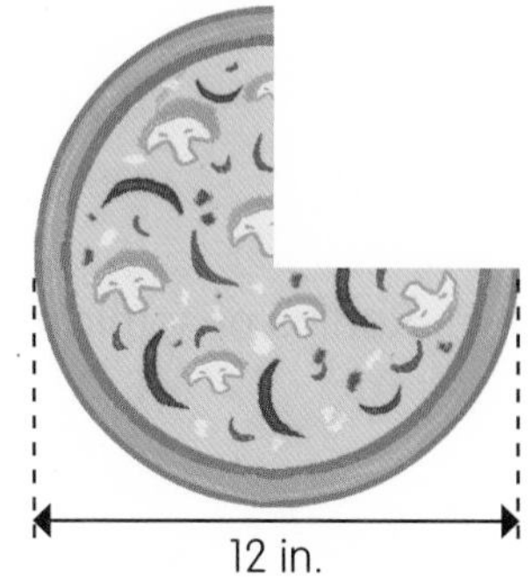

$$\begin{aligned}\text{Radius} &= \text{diameter} \div 2\\ &= 12 \div 2\\ &= 6 \text{ in.}\end{aligned}$$

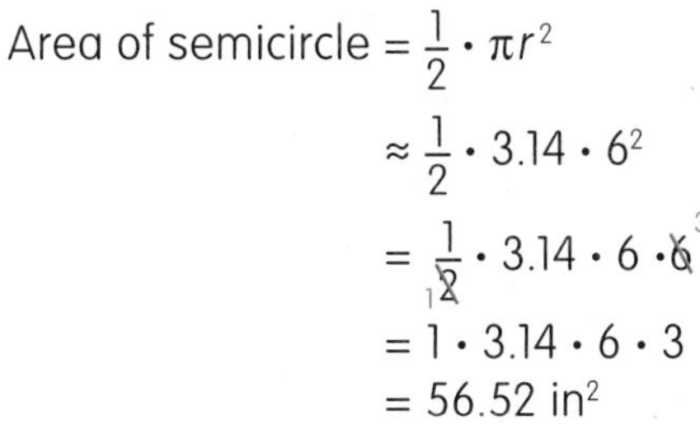

$$\begin{aligned}\text{Area of semicircle} &= \frac{1}{2} \cdot \pi r^2\\ &\approx \frac{1}{2} \cdot 3.14 \cdot 6^2\\ &= \frac{1}{\not{2}_1} \cdot 3.14 \cdot 6 \cdot \not{6}^3\\ &= 1 \cdot 3.14 \cdot 6 \cdot 3\\ &= 56.52 \text{ in}^2\end{aligned}$$

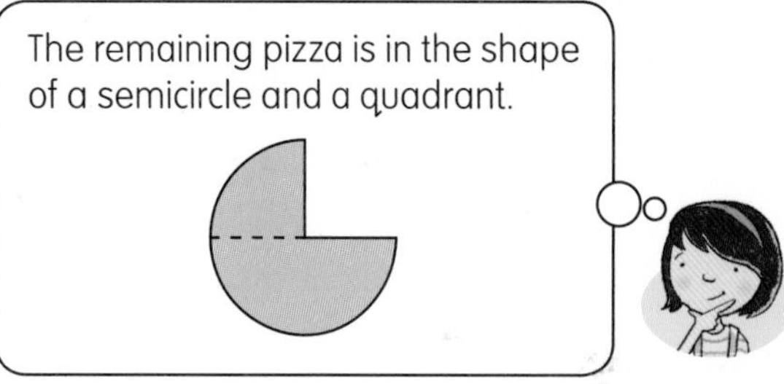

$$\begin{aligned}\text{Area of quadrant} &= \frac{1}{4} \cdot \pi r^2\\ &\approx \frac{1}{4} \cdot 3.14 \cdot 6^2\\ &= \frac{1}{\not{4}_1} \cdot 3.14 \cdot \not{6}^3 \cdot \not{6}^3\\ &= 1 \cdot 3.14 \cdot 3 \cdot 3\\ &= 28.26 \text{ in}^2\end{aligned}$$

$$\begin{aligned}\text{Area of remaining pizza} &= \text{area of semicircle} + \text{area of quadrant}\\ &= 56.52 + 28.26\\ &= 84.78 \text{ in}^2\end{aligned}$$

The area of the remaining pizza is approximately 84.78 square inches.

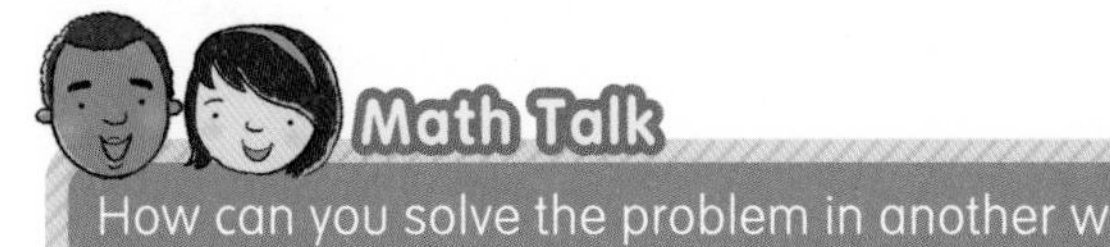

TRY Practice solving real-world problems involving area of a circle

Solve.

1. Alex recycled some old fabric to make a rug. He cut out a quadrant and two semicircles to make the rug. Find the area of the rug. Use $\frac{22}{7}$ as an approximation for π.

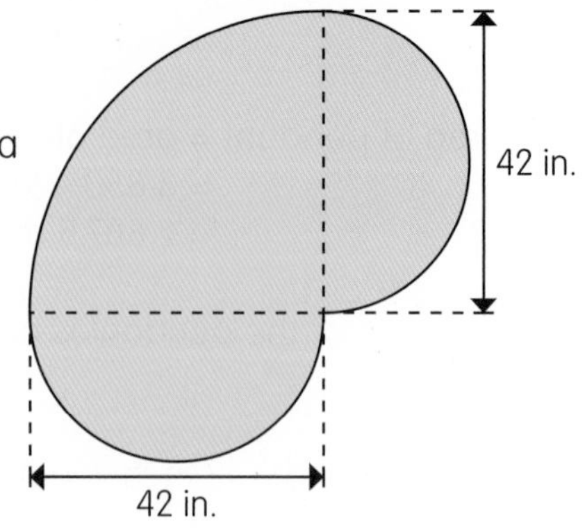

Area of quadrant $= \frac{1}{4} \cdot \pi r^2$

$\approx$ _______ $\cdot$ _______ $\cdot$ _______^{2}

$=$ _______ $\cdot$ _______ $\cdot$ _______ $\cdot$ _______

$=$ _______ in^2

Radius of semicircle = diameter $\div$ 2

$=$ _______ $\div$ _______

$=$ _______ in.

Area of two semicircles $= 2 \cdot \frac{1}{2} \cdot \pi r^2$

$\approx$ _______ $\cdot$ _______ $\cdot$ _______ $\cdot$ _______^{2}

$=$ _______ $\cdot$ _______ $\cdot$ _______ $\cdot$ _______

$=$ _______ in^2

Area of rug = area of quadrant + area of two semicircles

$=$ _______ $+$ _______

$=$ _______ in^2

The area of the rug is approximately _______ square inches.

2. A graphic designer creates a design for a company logo. The design is a green semicircle with a white quadrant, as shown. Find the area of the green part of the design. Use 3.14 as an approximation for π.

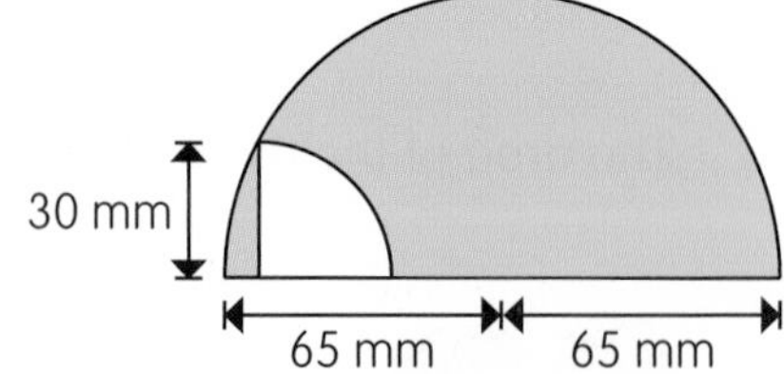

Area of semicircle $= \frac{1}{2} \cdot \pi r^2$

$\approx$ _______ $\cdot$ _______ $\cdot$ _______^{2}

$=$ _______ $\cdot$ _______ $\cdot$ _______ $\cdot$ _______

$=$ _______ mm^2

Area of quadrant $= \frac{1}{4} \cdot \pi r^2$

$\approx$ ______ $\cdot$ ______ $\cdot$ ______^{2}

$=$ ______ $\cdot$ ______ $\cdot$ ______ $\cdot$ ______

$=$ ______ mm^2

Area of green part = area of semicircle – area of quadrant

$=$ ______ $-$ ______

$=$ ______ mm^2

The area of the green part of the design is approximately ______ square millimeters.

ENGAGE

A wheel of radius 13 inches and another wheel of diameter 29 inches each made one full revolution starting from the same point. How do you find out how far apart they are now? Share your method.

LEARN Solve real-world problems involving rates and circles

1 The tire of a car has a radius of 10.5 inches. How many revolutions does the tire need to make for the car to travel 13,200 inches? Use $\frac{22}{7}$ as an approximation for π.

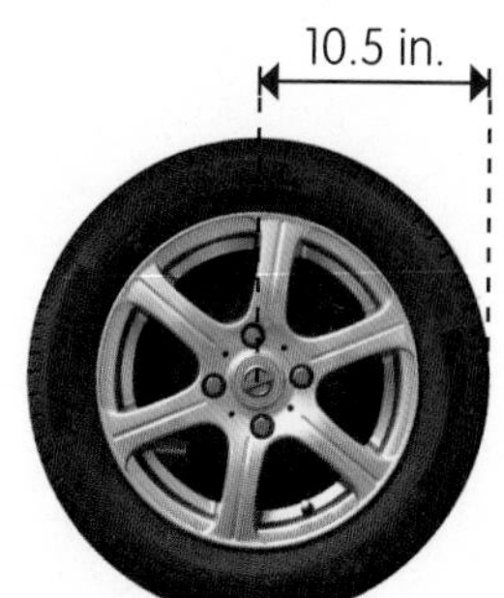

Circumference of tire $= 2\pi r$

$\approx 2 \cdot \frac{22}{7} \cdot 10.5$

$= \frac{22}{\cancel{7}_1} \cdot \cancel{21}^3$

$= 66$ in.

The car travels approximately 66 inches with one revolution of the tire.

Number of revolutions = distance ÷ circumference of tire

$= 13{,}200 \div 66$

$= 200$

The tire needs to make approximately 200 revolutions to travel 13,200 inches.

TRY Practice solving real-world problems involving rates and circles

Solve.

1. The diameter of a bicycle wheel is 60 centimeters. How far does the wheel travel when it makes 35 revolutions? Give your answer in meters. Use 3.14 as an approximation for π.

   Circumference of wheel = πd

   $\approx$ ______ • ______

   = ______ cm

   Distance traveled = circumference of wheel • number of revolutions

   = ______ • ______

   = ______ cm

   = ______ m

   The wheel travels approximately ______ meters.

2. Wheels A and B are placed side by side on a straight road. The diameter of wheel A is 56 inches. The diameter of wheel B is 35 inches. Suppose each wheel makes 15 revolutions. Find the difference in distance traveled between the wheels after they have made these 15 revolutions. Use $\frac{22}{7}$ as an approximation for π.

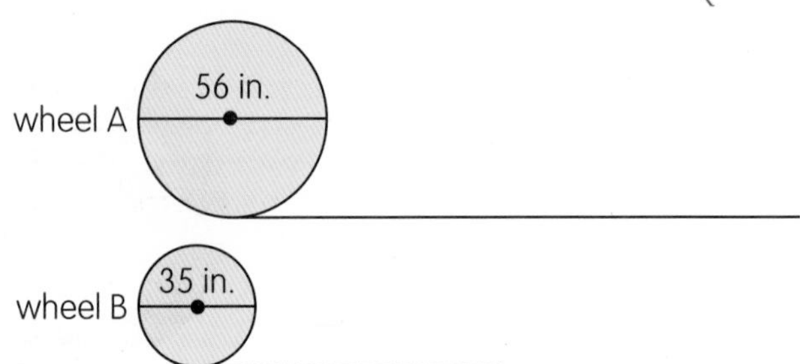

   Distance traveled by wheel A = 15 • πd

   $\approx$ ______ • ______ • ______

   = ______ in.

   Distance traveled by wheel B = 15 • πd

   $\approx$ ______ • ______ • ______

   = ______ in.

   Difference in distance traveled = Distance traveled by wheel A – Distance traveled by wheel B

   = ______ – ______

   = ______ in.

   The difference in distance traveled between the wheels is approximately ______ inches.

Name: ______________________ Date: ______________

INDEPENDENT PRACTICE

Solve.

1. The radius of a circular pond is 8 meters. Find its area and circumference.
   Use 3.14 as an approximation for π.

✓ $A = 200.96 m^2$ $3.14 \cdot 2 \cdot 8 =$ 50.24

✓ $C = 50.24 m$

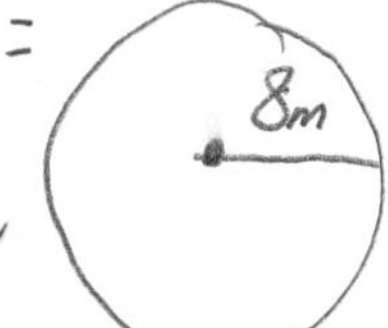

$3.14 \cdot 8^2$
$3.14 \cdot 64 = 200.96$

2. The diameter of a metal disc is 26 centimeters. Find its area and circumference.
   Use 3.14 as an approximation for π.

✓ $A = 530.66 cm^2$ $3.14 \cdot 2 \cdot 13 =$ 81.64

✓ $C = 81.64 cm$

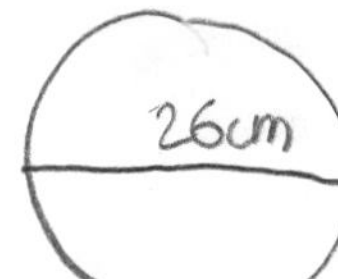

$3.14 \cdot 13^2$
$3.14 \cdot 169 = 530.66$

3. The shape of a carpet is a semicircle.
   Use $\frac{22}{7}$ as an approximation for π.

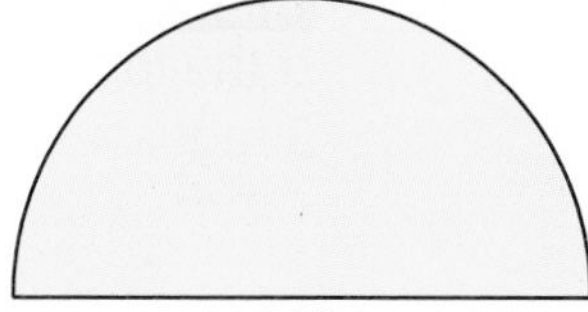

   ✓ a Find its area.

   $A = 77 ft^2$

   $\frac{22}{7} \cdot 7^2$

   $\frac{22}{7} \cdot 49 = 154 ft^2 \div 2 = 77$

   b Carla wants to put a fringed border on all sides of the carpet.
   How many feet of fringe are needed?

   $3.14 \cdot 2 \cdot 7 = 43.96 + 14 = 57.96 ft \div 2 = 35.98 ft$

4. The circumference of the rim of a wheel is 301.44 centimeters. Find the diameter of the rim.
   Use 3.14 as an approximation for π.

   301.44

   96 cm

5. A Japanese fan is made out of wood and cloth.
   The shape of the fan is made up of two overlapping quadrants.
   What is the area of the portion that is made of cloth?
   Use $\frac{22}{7}$ as an approximation for π.

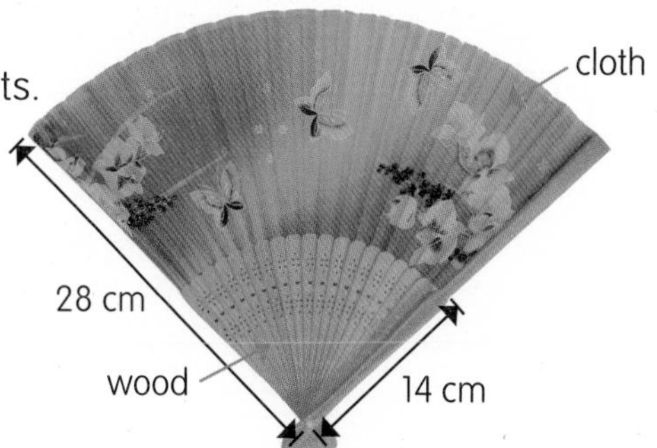

6 A pancake restaurant serves small silver-dollar pancakes and regular-size pancakes. Use 3.14 as an approximation for π.

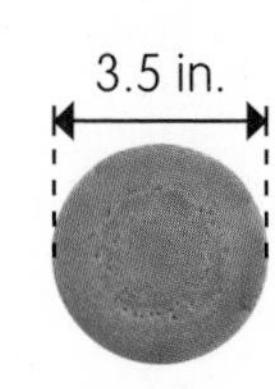

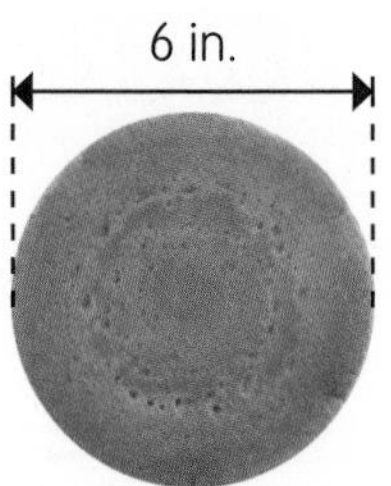

a What is the area of a small silver-dollar pancake? Round your answer to the nearest tenth of an inch.

b What is the area of a regular-size pancake? Round your answer to the nearest tenth of a square inch.

c **Mathematical Habit 3 Construct viable arguments**
If the total price of 6 small silver-dollar pancakes is the same as the total price of 3 regular-size pancakes, which is a better deal?

7 A designer drew an icon as shown. O is the center of the circle, and $\overline{AB}$ is a diameter. Two semicircles are drawn in the circle. If AB is 28 millimeters long, find the area of the shaded part. Use $\frac{22}{7}$ as an approximation for π.

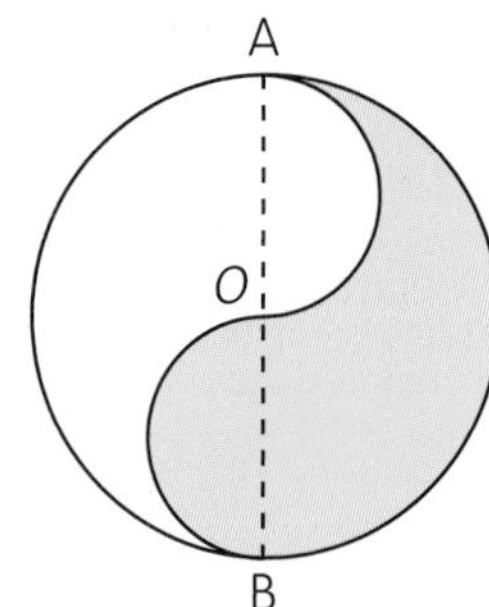

8 The diameter of a circular fountain in a city park is 28 feet. A sidewalk that is 3.5 feet wide will be built around the fountain. Use $\frac{22}{7}$ as an approximation for π.

a Find the area of the sidewalk.

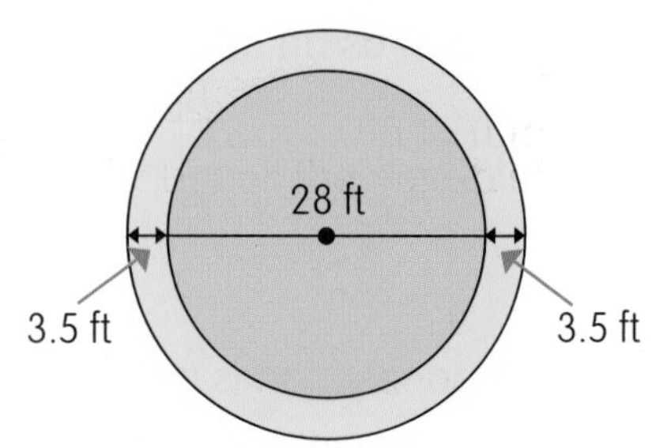

b 0.8 bag of concrete is needed for every square foot of the new sidewalk. What is the minimum number of bags needed?

Name: ______________________ Date: ______________

Area of Composite Figures

Learning Objectives:

- Find the area of figures composed of triangles, quadrilaterals, polygons, and circular regions.
- Solve real-world problems involving area of composite figures.

The figure on the right is made up of four overlapping semicircles in a square. Find the area of the shaded parts.

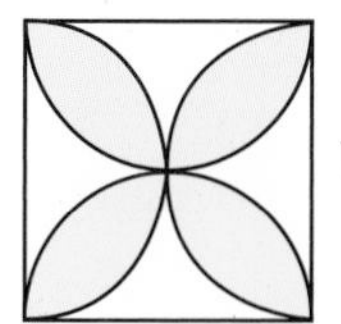

ENGAGE

1. How can you find the area of each shape?
   - **a** a square of sides 4 centimeters
   - **b** a triangle with a base of 2 centimeters and a height of 4 centimeters

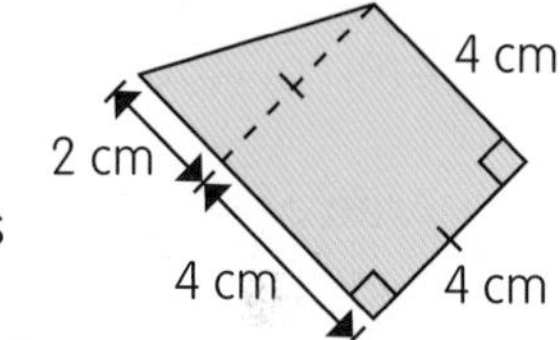

2. Look at the figure on the right. How can you find the area of the figure? Discuss.

LEARN Find the area of composite figures

1. Figure *PQRS* is made up of the triangles *PQS* and *QRS*. Find the area of figure *PQRS*.

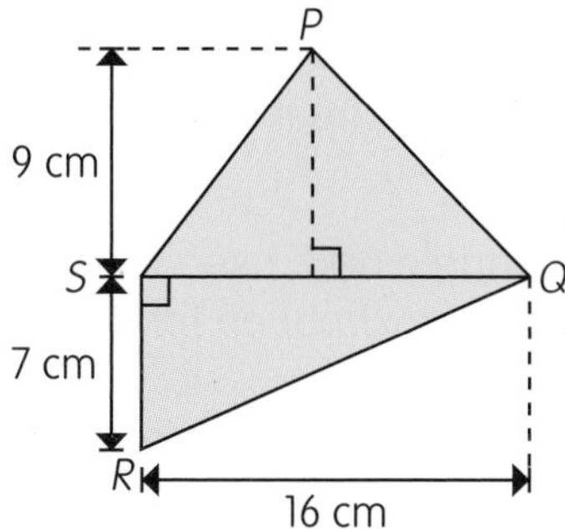

Area of *PQRS* = area of triangle *PQS* + area of triangle *QRS*

Area of triangle *PQS* $= \frac{1}{2} \cdot 16 \cdot 9$
$= 72 \text{ cm}^2$

Area of triangle *QRS* $= \frac{1}{2} \cdot 16 \cdot 7$
$= 56 \text{ cm}^2$

Area of *PQRS* $= 72 + 56$
$= 128 \text{ cm}^2$

The area of figure *PQRS* is 128 square centimeters.

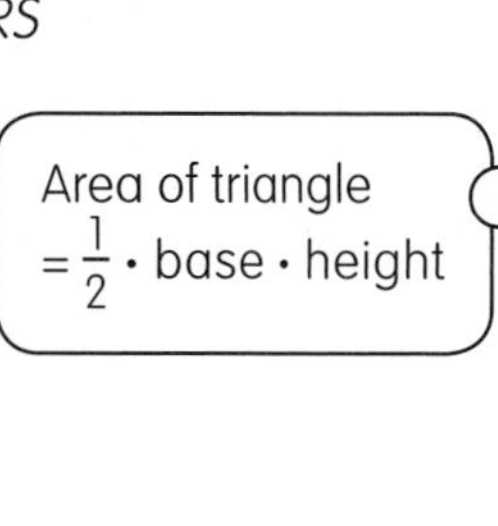

2 Figure $ABCDEF$ is made up of a square $CDEF$ and a triangle ABC. Find the area of figure $ABCDEF$.

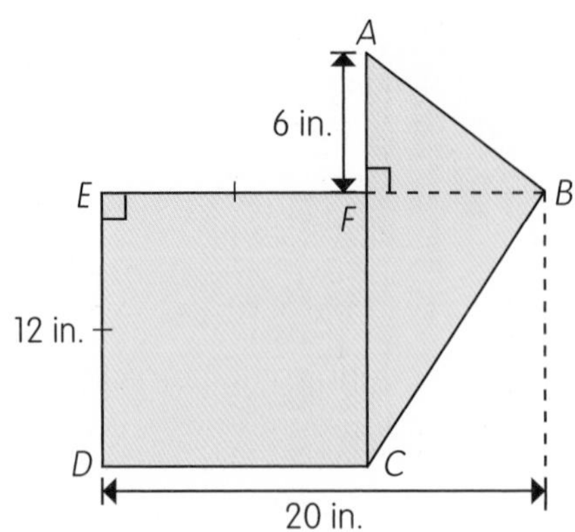

Area of $ABCDEF$ = area of square $CDEF$ + area of triangle ABC

Area of square $CDEF = 12 \cdot 12$
$= 144 \text{ in}^2$

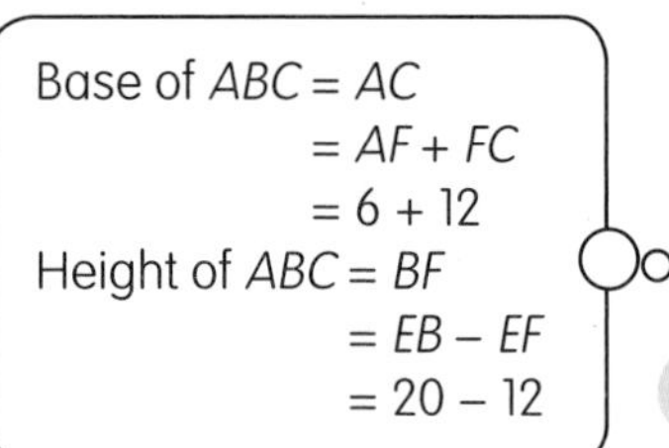

Area of triangle $ABC = \frac{1}{2} \cdot 18 \cdot 8$
$= 72 \text{ in}^2$

Area of $ABCDEF = 144 + 72$
$= 216 \text{ in}^2$

The area of the figure $ABCDEF$ is 216 square inches.

3 A flower bed is made up of a rectangle and a semicircle. Find the area of the flower bed. Use 3.14 as an approximation for π.

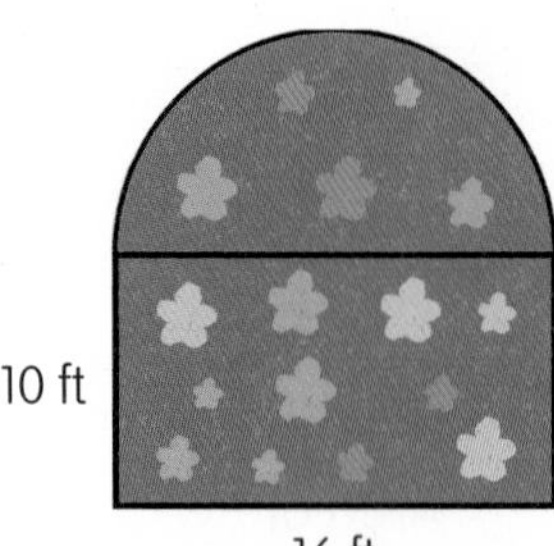

Area of flower bed = area of semicircle + area of rectangle

Area of semicircle $\approx \frac{1}{2} \cdot 3.14 \cdot 8^2$
$= 100.48 \text{ ft}^2$

Area of rectangle $= 16 \cdot 10$
$= 160 \text{ ft}^2$

Diameter = 16 ft
Radius = 16 ft ÷ 2

Area of flower bed $= 100.48 + 160$
$= 260.48 \text{ ft}^2$

The area of the flower bed is approximately 260.48 square feet.

TRY Practice finding the area of composite figures

Solve.

1. The figure is composed of a trapezoid and a semicircle. The height of the trapezoid is equal to the radius of the semicircle. Find the area of the figure. Use 3.14 as an approximation for π.

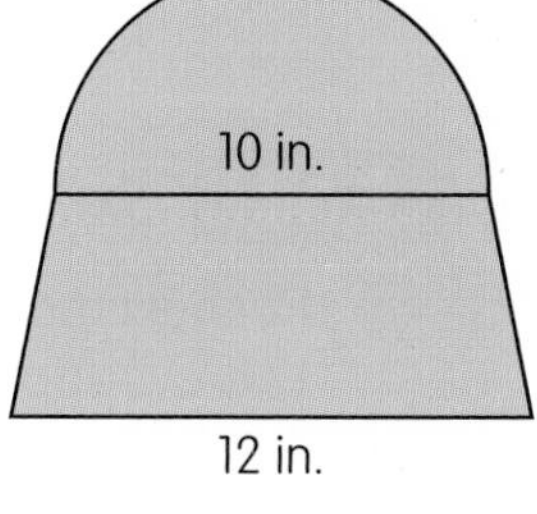

Area of figure = area of semicircle + area of trapezoid

Area of semicircle $\approx \frac{1}{2} \cdot$ ______ $\cdot$ ______ $\cdot$ ______

= ______ in^2

Area of trapezoid $= \frac{1}{2} \cdot$ ______ $\cdot$ (______ + ______)

= ______ in^2

Area of figure = ______ + ______

= ______ in^2

The area of the figure is approximately ______ square inches.

2. The figure *ABCD* is composed of triangles *ABF*, *BCD*, and *AFD*. *AEFG* is a rectangle. Find the area of *ABCD*.

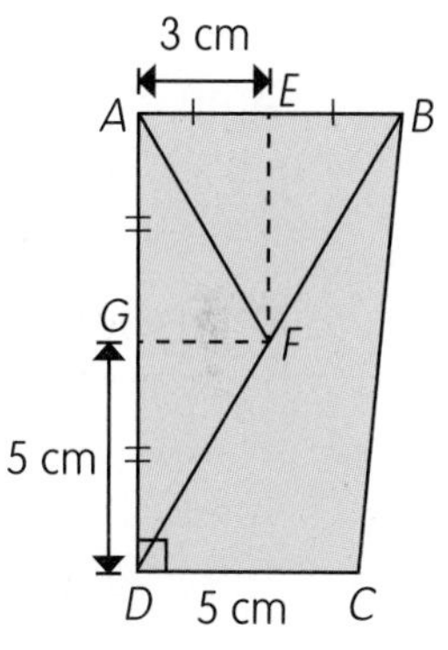

Area of figure *ABCD* = area of *ABF* + area of *BCD* + area of *AFD*

Area of *ABF* $= \frac{1}{2} \cdot$ ______ $\cdot$ ______

= ______ cm^2

Area of *BCD* $= \frac{1}{2} \cdot$ ______ $\cdot$ ______

= ______ cm^2

Area of *AFD* $= \frac{1}{2} \cdot$ ______ $\cdot$ ______

= ______ cm^2

Area of *ABCD* = ______ + ______ + ______

= ______ cm^2

The area of the figure *ABCD* is ______ square centimeters.

ENGAGE

Look at the figure on the right. How can you find the area of the shaded part? What are the steps you would take to find the area? Discuss.

LEARN Solve problems involving area of composite figures

1. Rachel created a petal of a paper flower by cutting along the outlines of two overlapping quadrants within a square piece of paper.

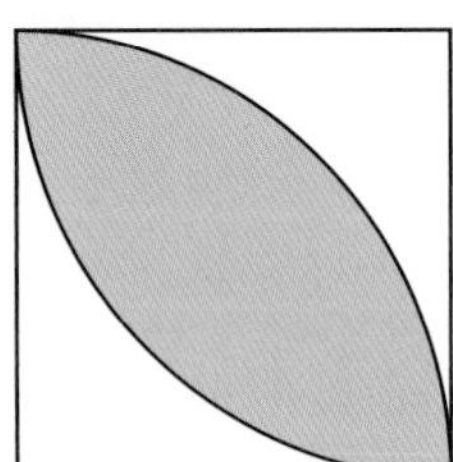

14 cm

a Find the area of the petal. Use $\frac{22}{7}$ as an approximation for π.

Area of petal = $2 \cdot$ (area of quadrant – area of triangle)

Area of quadrant $\approx \frac{1}{4} \cdot \frac{22}{7} \cdot 14 \cdot 14$

$= 154 \text{ cm}^2$

Area of triangle $= \frac{1}{2} \cdot 14 \cdot 14$

$= 98 \text{ cm}^2$

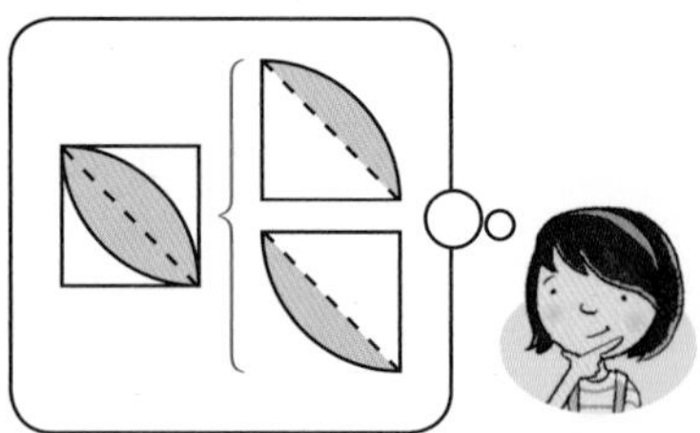

Area of petal $= 2 \cdot (154 - 98)$

$= 2 \cdot 56$

$= 112 \text{ cm}^2$

The area of the petal is approximately 112 square centimeters.

b Find the area of the remaining piece of paper.

Area of remaining piece of paper = area of square – area of petal

$= (14 \cdot 14) - 112$

$= 196 - 112$

$= 84 \text{ cm}^2$

The area of the remaining piece of paper is approximately 84 square centimeters.

2 A running track comprises two semicircles and a rectangle. It has a field within.

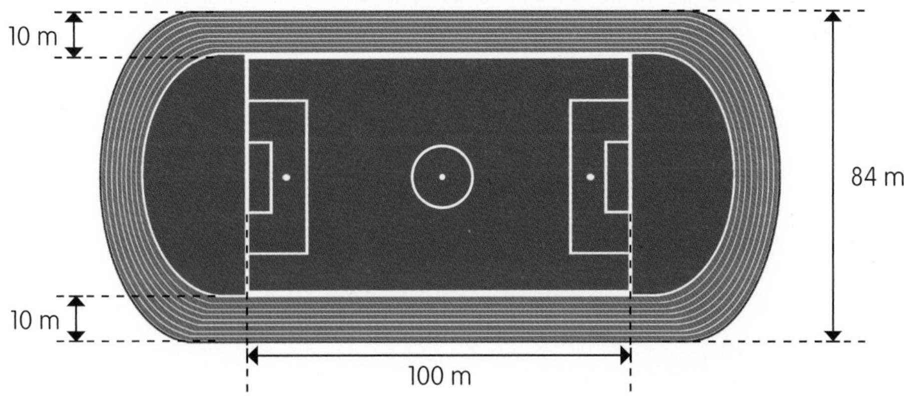

a Find the area of the field. Use 3.14 as an approximation for π.

Area of field = area of two semicircles + area of rectangle

$$\text{Area of two semicircles} = 2 \cdot \frac{1}{2} \cdot \pi r^2$$
$$\approx \cancel{2}^{1} \cdot \frac{1}{\cancel{2}_{1}} \cdot 3.14 \cdot 32 \cdot 32$$
$$= 3{,}215.36 \text{ m}^2$$

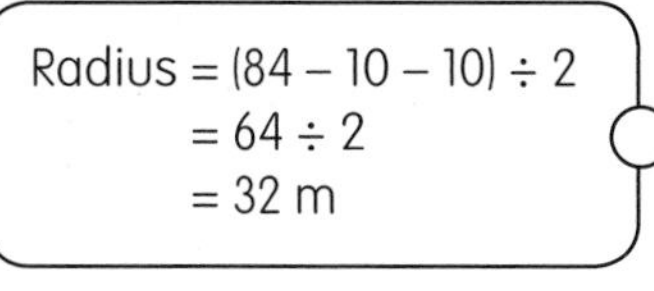

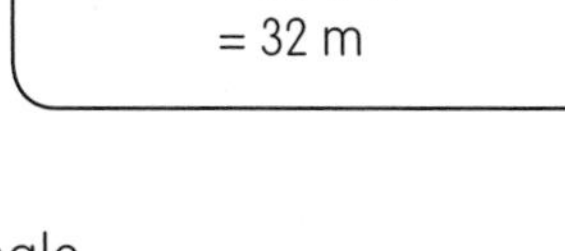

$$\text{Area of rectangle} = 100 \cdot 64$$
$$= 6{,}400 \text{ m}^2$$

$$\text{Area of field} = \text{area of two semicircles} + \text{area of rectangle}$$
$$= 3{,}215.36 + 6{,}400$$
$$= 9{,}615.36 \text{ m}^2$$

The area of the field is approximately 9,615.36 square meters.

b A gardener is hired to cut the grass in the field. She cuts the grass at an average rate of 40 square meters per minute. How many hours will she take to cut the grass of the entire field? Round your answer to the nearest hour.

$$\text{Time taken} = \text{area of field} \div \text{rate of cutting grass}$$
$$\approx 9{,}615.36 \div 40$$
$$= 240.384 \text{ min}$$
$$\approx 4 \text{ h}$$

The gardener will take approximately 4 hours to cut the grass of the entire field.

3 The figure below is made up of two trapezoids *ABEF* and *BCDE*. The area of triangle *FGE* is 26 square inches and the area of trapezoid *BCDE* is 82.5 square inches. *BG* is equal to *GE*. Find the area of triangle *BDE*.

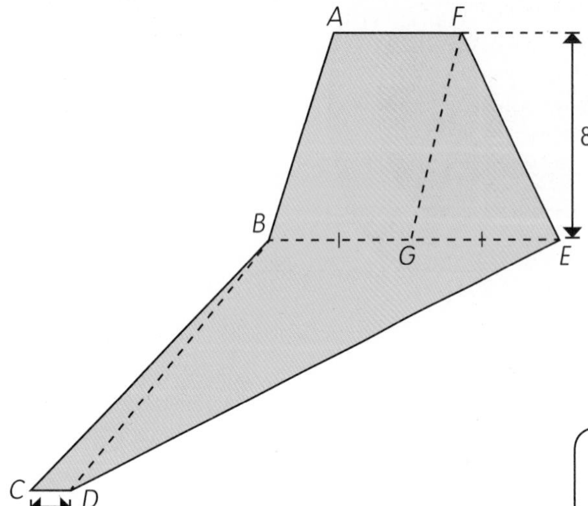

To find the area of triangle *BDE*, I have to first find its base and height.

Since area of triangle $FGE = 26$ in^2,

$$\text{Area of triangle } FGE = \frac{1}{\cancel{2}_1} \cdot GE \cdot \cancel{8}^4$$

$$4 \cdot GE = 26$$

$$4 \cdot GE \div 4 = 26 \div 4$$

$$GE = 6.5 \text{ in.}$$

Since $BG = GE$, $BE = 2 \cdot GE$

$$= 2 \cdot 6.5$$

$$= 13 \text{ in.}$$

The base of triangle *BDE* is 13 inches.

If h is the height of trapezoid *BCDE*,

$$\frac{1}{2}h(2 + 13) = 82.5$$

$$7.5h = 82.5$$

$$7.5h \div 7.5 = 82.5 \div 7.5$$

$$h = 11$$

Since the height of trapezoid *BCDE* is the same as the height of triangle *BDE*, the height of triangle *BDE* is 11 inches.

$$\text{Area of triangle } BDE = \frac{1}{2} \cdot 13 \cdot 11$$

$$= 71.5 \text{ in}^2$$

The area of triangle *BDE* is 71.5 square inches.

The area of triangle *BDE* is smaller than the area of trapezoid *BCDE*. 71.5 in^2 is less than 82.5 in^2. My answer is reasonable.

TRY Practice solving problems involving area of composite figures

Solve.

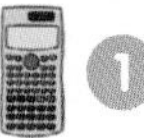

1. Alex cuts out the logo for his school's swim club from a rectangular piece of paper. The logo is made up of a quadrant and a triangle. Find the area of the remaining piece of paper. Use 3.14 as an approximation for π.

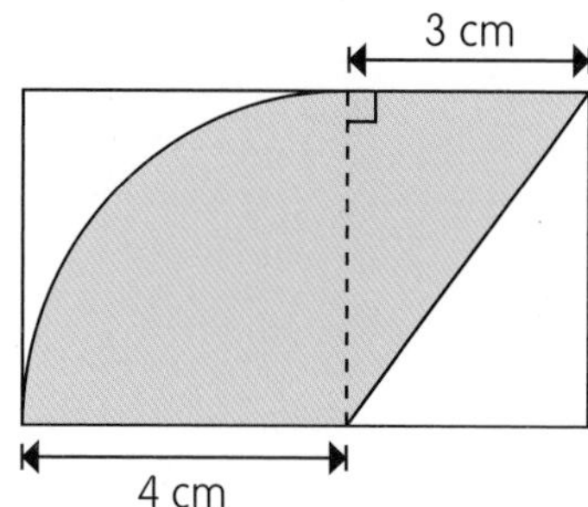

Area of remaining piece of paper
= area of rectangle – (area of quadrant + area of triangle)

Area of rectangle = ______ • ______

= ______ cm²

Area of quadrant $\approx \frac{1}{4}$ • ______ • ______ • ______

= ______ cm²

Area of triangle = $\frac{1}{2}$ • ______ • ______

= ______ cm²

Area of remaining piece of paper = ______ – (______ + ______)

= ______ – ______

= ______ cm²

The area of the remaining piece of paper is approximately ______ square centimeters.

2 A field is composed of a rectangle with two semicircles at the sides. Given that each square foot of grass costs \$0.50, how much will it cost to plant grass to cover the entire field? Use $\frac{22}{7}$ as an approximation for π.

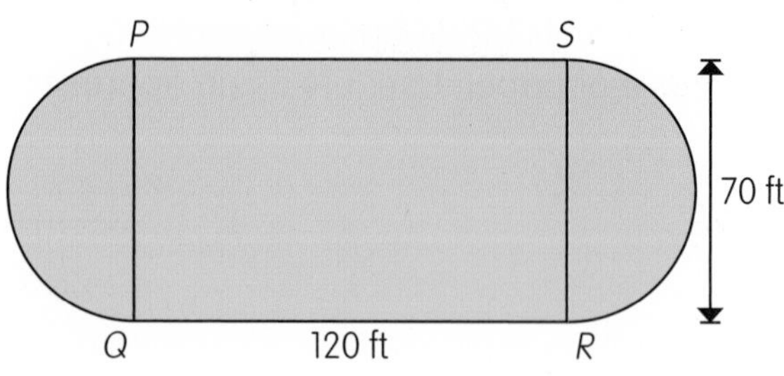

3 Figure *VWXYZ* is made up of a triangle and a trapezoid. The area of trapezoid *VXYZ* is 56 square centimeters. The ratio of the height of trapezoid *VXYZ* to $\overline{RW}$ is 2 : 1. Find the area of figure *VWXYZ*.

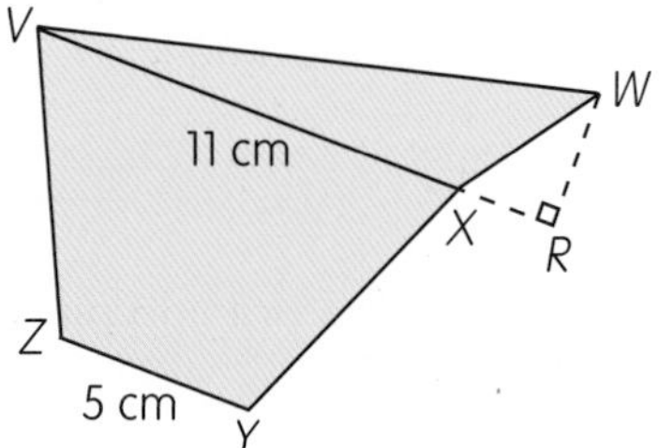

Name: ______________________ Date: ______________

INDEPENDENT PRACTICE

Find the area of each composite figure.

1

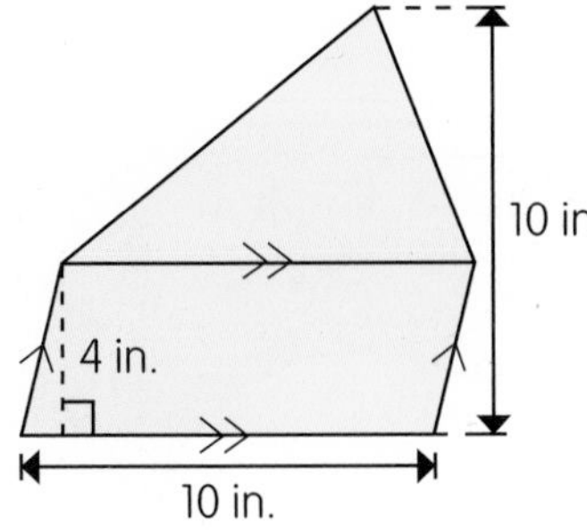

2

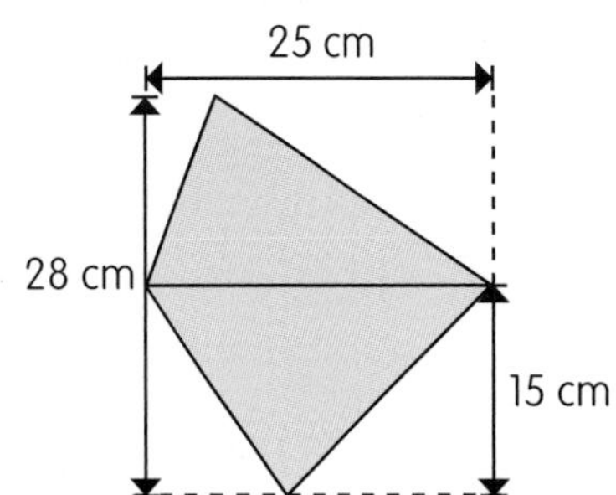

Find the area of each shaded region. Use 3.14 as an approximation for π.

3

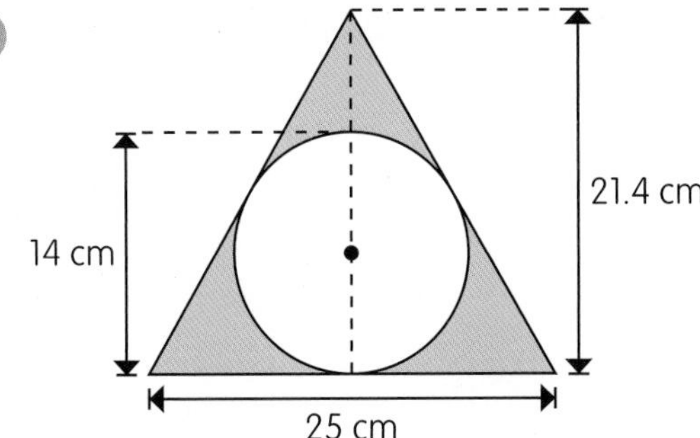

4

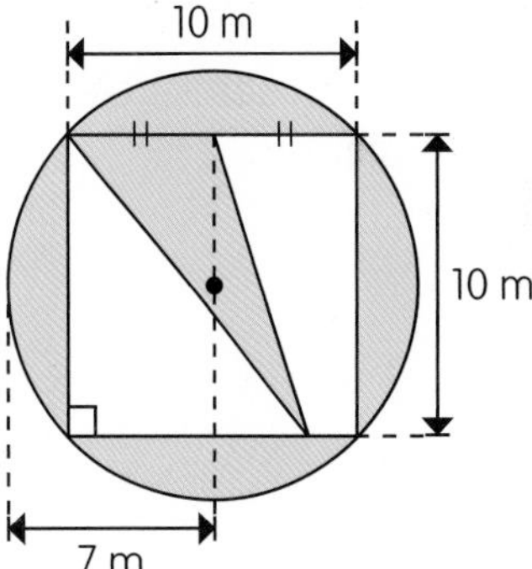

Solve.

5 A park is shaped like a rectangle with a semicircle on one end, and another semicircle cut out of one side. Find the area of the park. Use $\frac{22}{7}$ as an approximation for π.

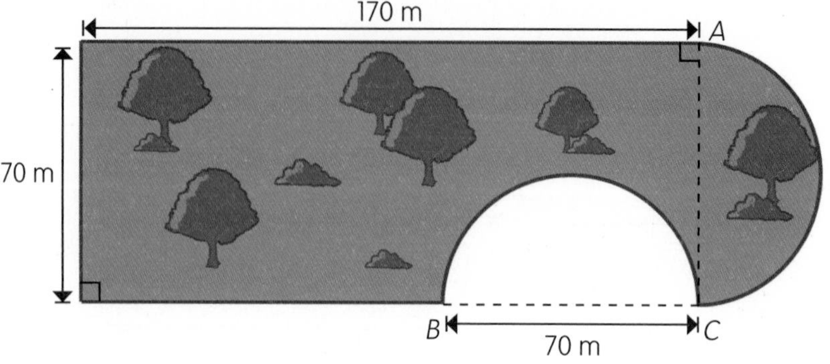

6 The diagram shows an athletic field with a track around it. The track is 4 feet wide. The field is a rectangle with semicircles at the two ends. Find the area of the track. Use 3.14 as an approximation for π.

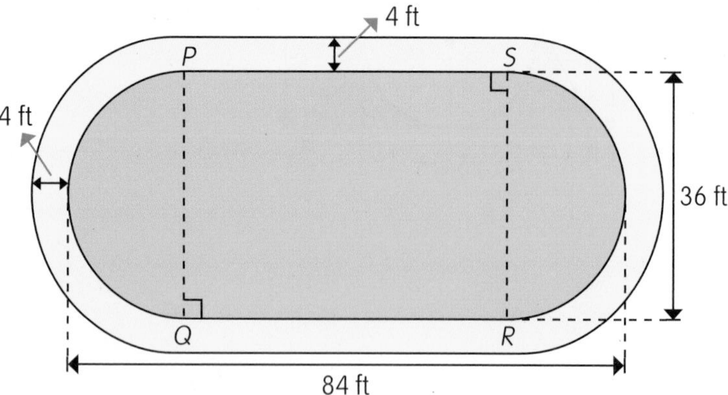

7 Four identical drinking glasses each have a radius of 5 centimeters. The glasses are arranged such that they touch each other. Find the area of the green portion. Use 3.14 as an approximation for π.

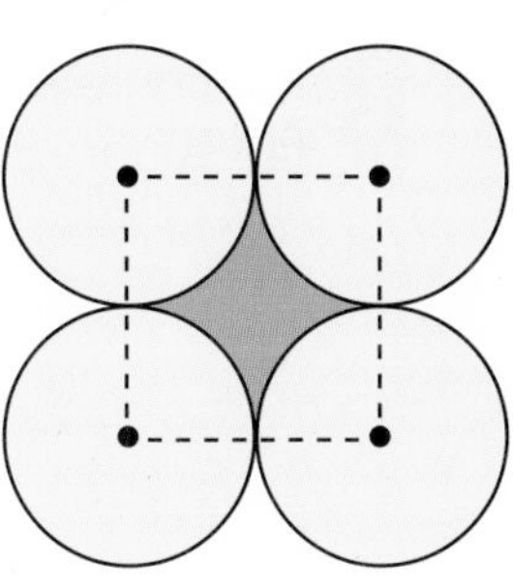

8 A wire is bent to make the shape as shown. The shape is made up of four identical circles. Each circle intersects two other circles. The four circles meet at a common point *T*, which is the center of square *PQRS*. Use $\frac{22}{7}$ as an approximation for π.

a Find the length of the wire.

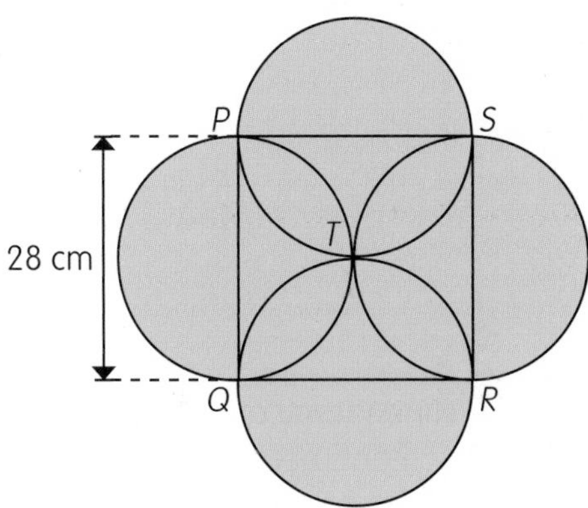

b Find the area of the whole shape.

9 The figure is made up of a trapezoid and a triangle. The area of the triangle is 144 square inches. Find the area of the figure.

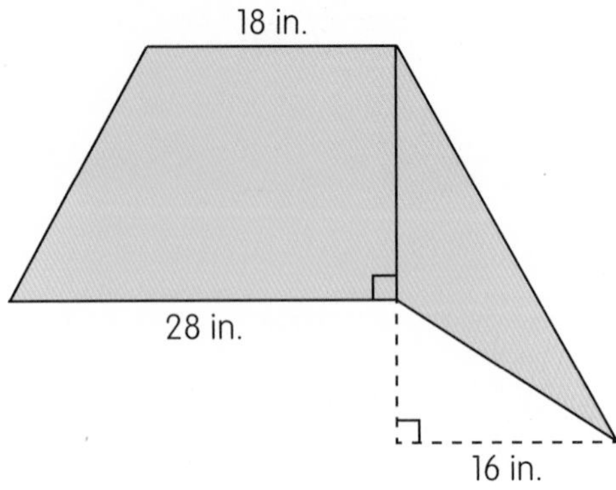

10 Nine identical circles are cut from a square sheet of paper whose sides are 36 centimeters long. If the circles are as large as possible, what is the area of the paper that is left after all the circles are cut out? Use 3.14 as an approximation for π.

Name: ______________________ Date: ______________

5 Volume of Prisms

Learning Objectives:
- Identify cross sections of solids.
- Use formula to find the volumes of prisms.

New Vocabulary
cross section
plane

THINK

The prism shown has bases that are regular pentagons. Its volume is 3,000 cubic centimeters. Find the distance around one of its pentagonal bases.

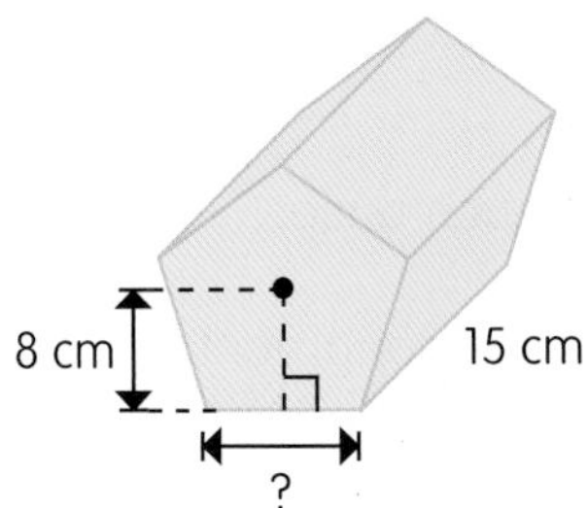

ENGAGE

How would you slice the cake shown into four pieces such that each piece has the same perimeter around the base as the original cake?

LEARN Identify cross sections of solids

1. A plane is a flat surface that extends infinitely. When a plane slices through a solid, we get a cross section, which is a two-dimensional shape. The shape of the cross section depends on how the plane slices the solid.

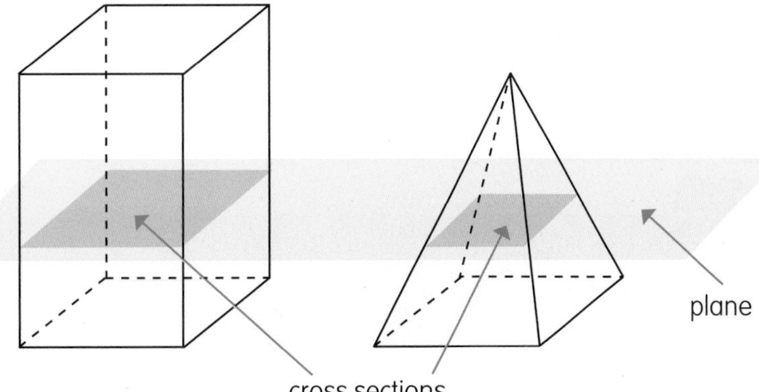

2 The rectangular prism below is sliced horizontally in two places: along segment $\overline{AB}$ parallel to the bases and along segment $\overline{CD}$ parallel to the bases.

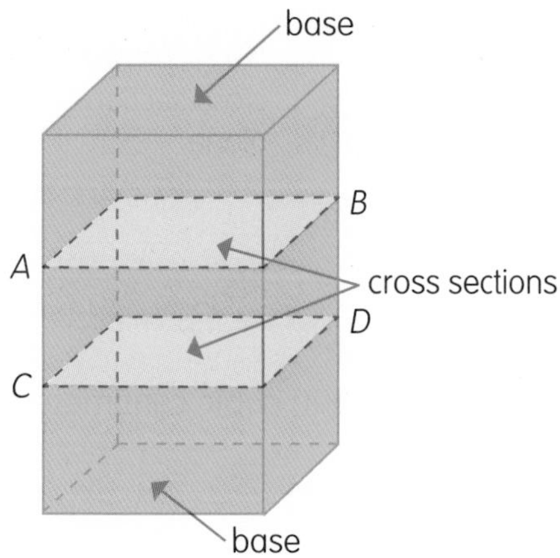

Each slice through a solid figure is called a cross section.

The cross section formed through $\overline{AB}$ is a rectangle that is congruent to each base.
The cross section through $\overline{CD}$ is also congruent to each base.
Any cross section of a rectangular prism that is parallel to the bases will be congruent to the bases. So, the prism has uniform cross sections.

3 The triangular prism below is sliced horizontally through $\overline{PQ}$ and $\overline{RS}$ parallel to the bases.
The cross sections formed are triangles that are congruent to each base.
So, a triangular prism also has uniform cross sections.

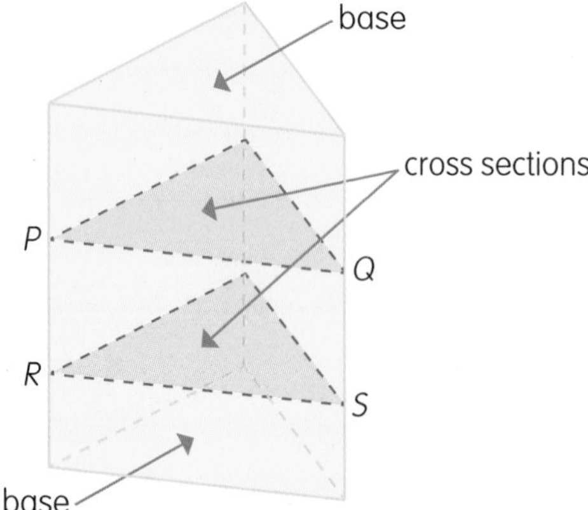

The cross sections are identical triangles that are of the same size as the base.

In general, any prism has uniform cross sections when it is sliced parallel to the bases of the prism.

What happens when you slice the rectangular prism vertically, parallel to two of its faces?
What happens when you slice the triangular prism vertically, parallel to one of its rectangular faces?
Will the cross sections be congruent? Explain.

4. The rectangular pyramid below is sliced horizontally through $\overline{WX}$ and $\overline{YZ}$ parallel to its base. The cross sections are similar rectangles that are of different sizes.

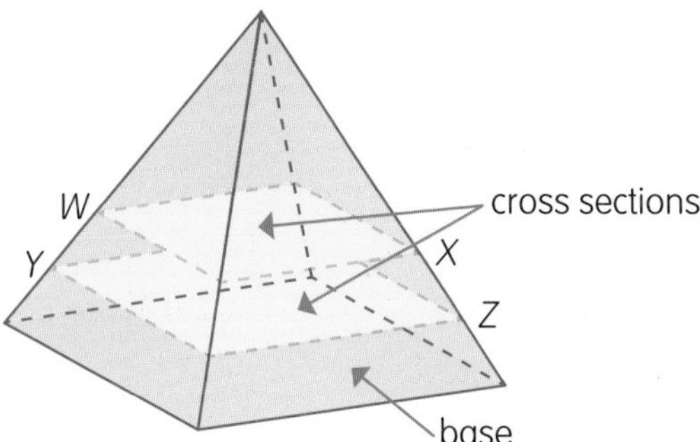

In general, when a pyramid is sliced parallel to its base, the cross sections will have the same shape as the base of the pyramid but they will be of different sizes.

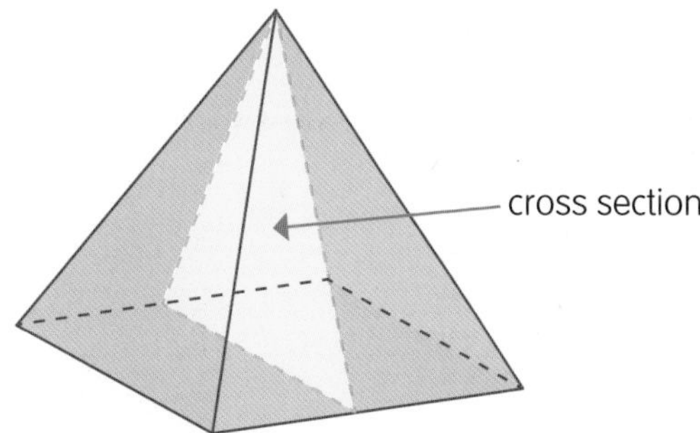

When a pyramid is sliced through its vertex such that the cross section is perpendicular to its base, the cross section will be a triangle.

What happens when you slice a sphere? What shape will the cross section be? Suppose you make another slice that is parallel to the first, will the cross sections be congruent? Explain.

TRY Practice identifying cross sections of solids

State what shape the cross section is when a solid is sliced as described.

1. A rectangular prism is sliced parallel to its base.

2. A rectangular pyramid is sliced parallel to its base.

3. A cube is sliced parallel to a face.

State whether slices parallel to each given slice will form uniform cross sections. If not, explain why not.

4 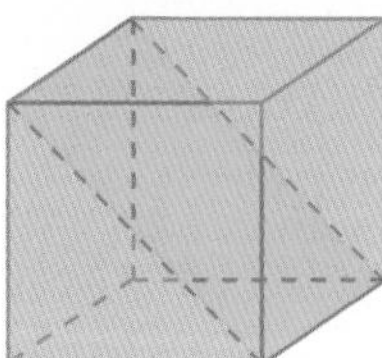

5 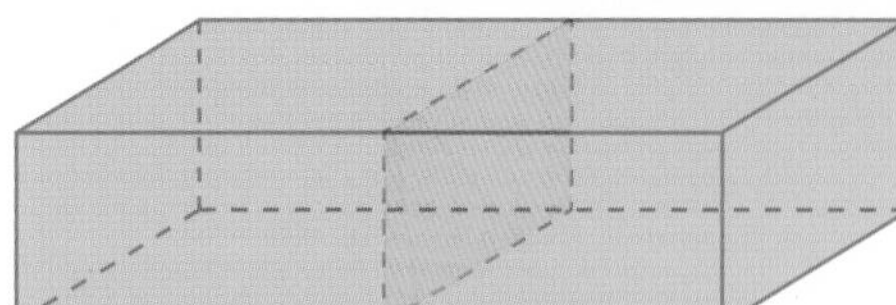

6 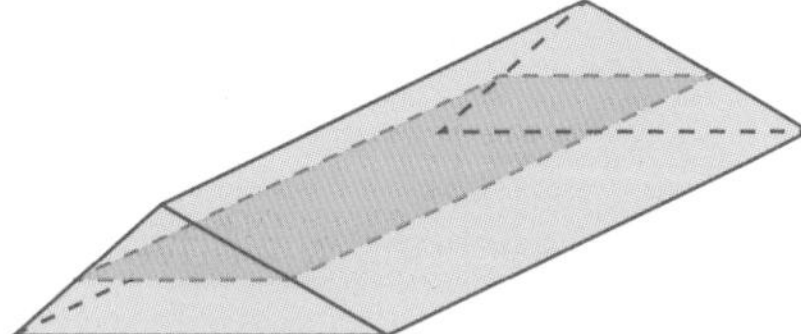

Each solid is sliced twice parallel to its base. Draw the two cross sections.

7 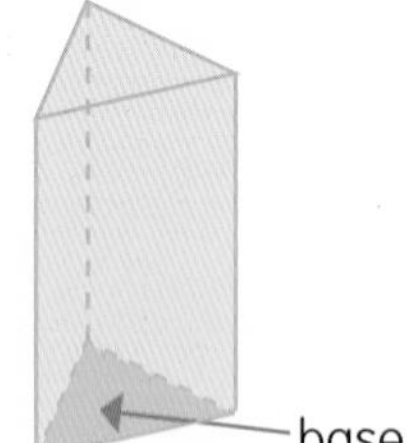

8 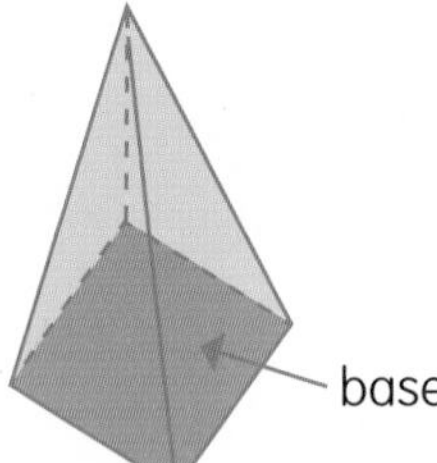

9 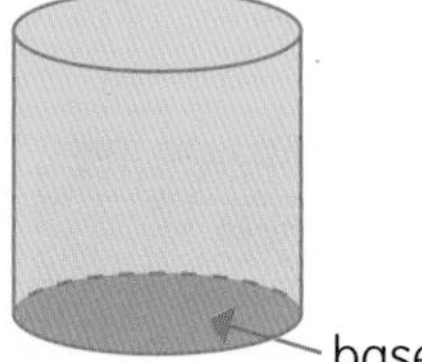

10 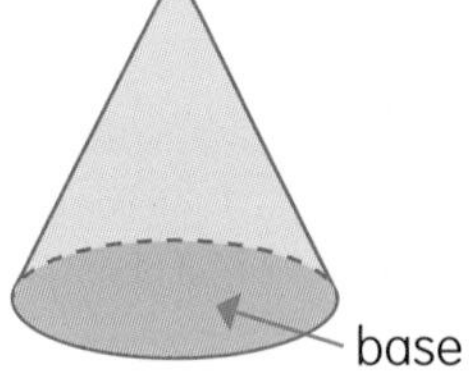

ENGAGE

Prism A is a rectangular prism. The length is 10 centimeters, the width is 5 centimeters, and the height is 8 centimeters. Given the information, how can you find the volume of prism A? How can you find the volume in another way? Prism B has bases that are parallelograms. The length is x centimeters, the width is y centimeters and the height is z centimeters. Discuss the steps you will take to find the volume of Prism B.

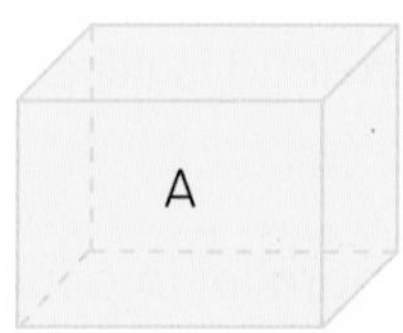

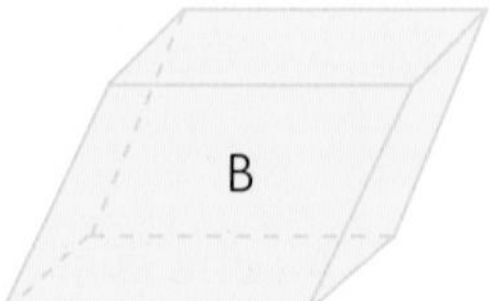

LEARN Find the volume of a prism

1. Since length · width = area of base,

Volume of a rectangular prism = length · width · height
= area of base · height

Since all prisms have a uniform cross section when sliced parallel to the base, you can use this formula to find the volume of all prisms:

Volume of prism = area of base · height

You can write the formula as $V = Bh$, where B represents the area of the base, and h represents the height of the prism.

2. Find the volume of the triangular prism as shown.

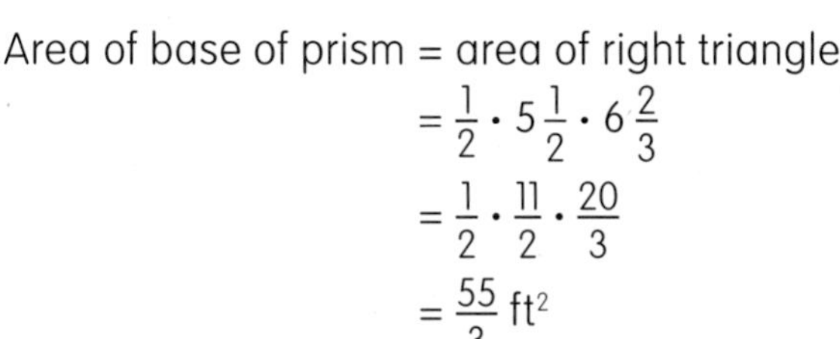

Area of base of prism = area of right triangle

$$= \frac{1}{2} \cdot 5\frac{1}{2} \cdot 6\frac{2}{3}$$

$$= \frac{1}{2} \cdot \frac{11}{2} \cdot \frac{20}{3}$$

$$= \frac{55}{3} \text{ ft}^2$$

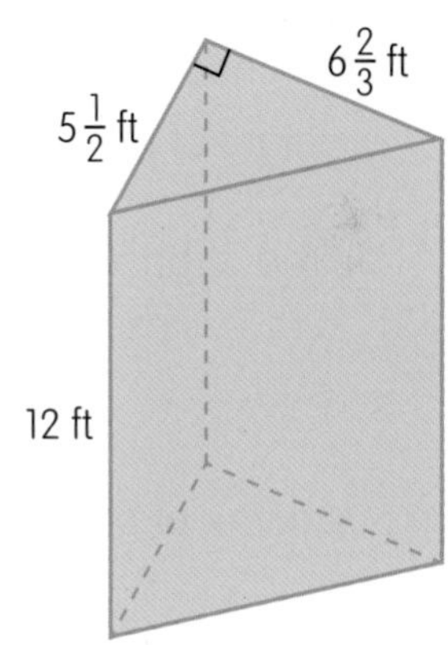

Volume of prism = area of base · height

$$= \frac{55}{3} \cdot 12$$

$$= 220 \text{ ft}^3$$

The volume of the prism is 220 cubic feet.

3. The prism shown has bases that are regular pentagons. Find the volume of the prism.

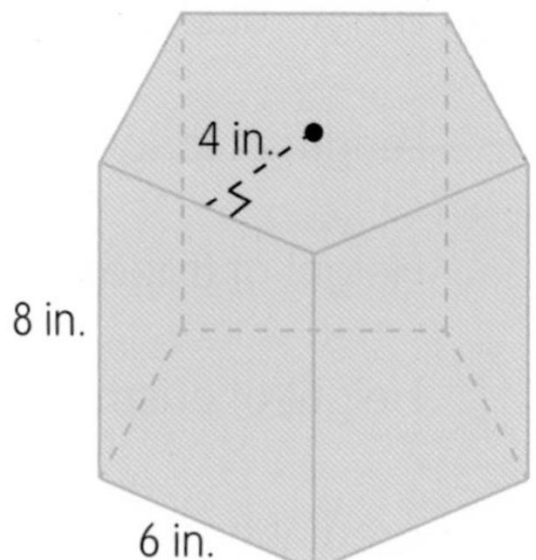

Area of base of prism = area of pentagon

$$= 5 \cdot \frac{1}{2} \cdot 6 \cdot 4$$

$$= 60 \text{ in}^2$$

$V = Bh$

$= 60 \cdot 8$

$= 480 \text{ in}^3$

The volume of the prism is 480 cubic inches.

TRY Practice finding the volume of a prism

Find the volume of each prism.

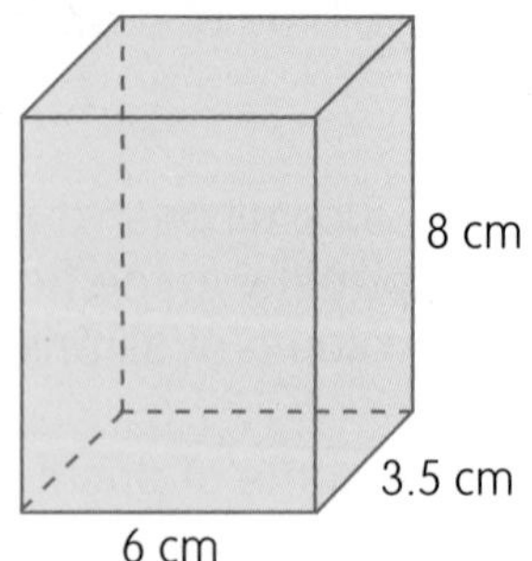

1. Area of base = ______ · ______

 = ______ cm^2

 Volume of prism = ______ · ______

 = ______ cm^3

 The volume of the prism is ______ cubic centimeters.

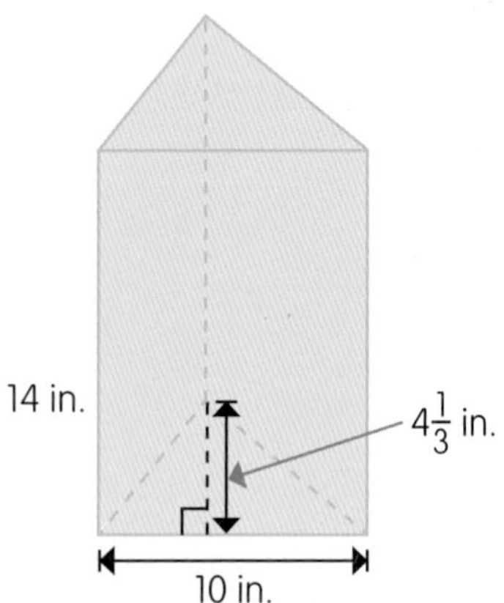

2. Base of triangle = 10 in.
 Height of triangle = $4\frac{1}{3}$ in.
 Height of prism = 14 in.

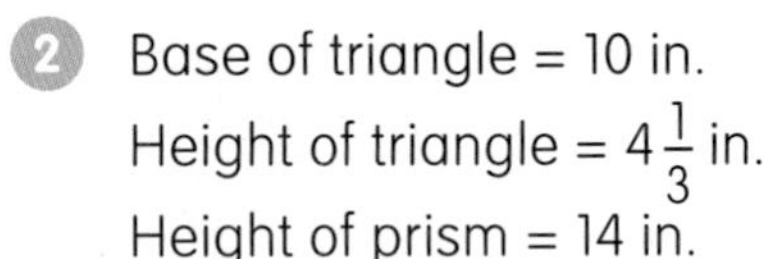

 Area of base = $\frac{1}{2}$ · ______ · ______

 = ______ in^2

 Volume of prism = ______ · ______

 = ______ in^3

 The volume of the prism is ______ cubic inches.

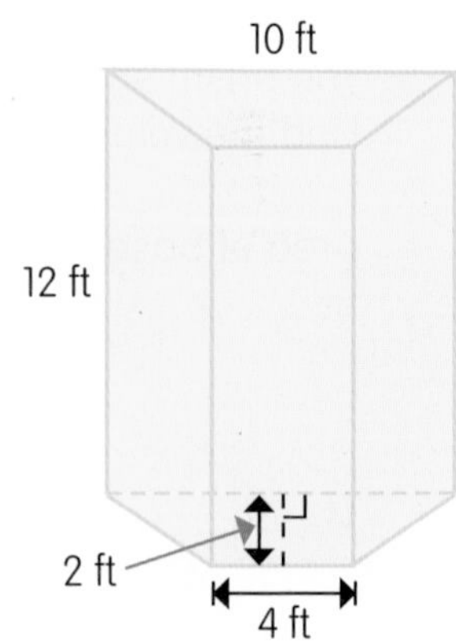

3. Length of shorter base of trapezoid = ______ ft

 Length of longer base of trapezoid = ______ft

 Height of trapezoid = ______ ft

 Height of prism = ______ ft

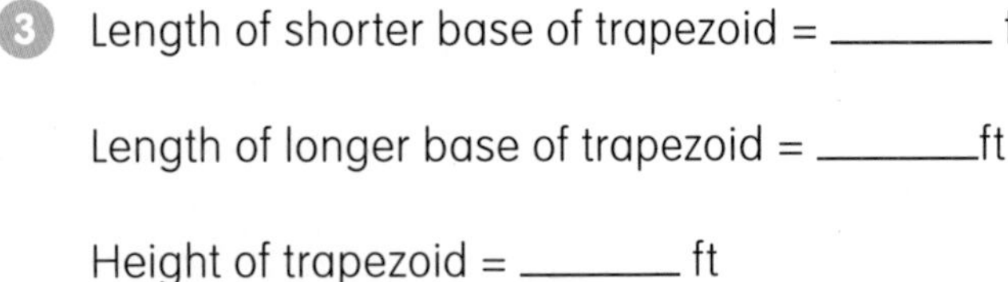

 Area of base = $\frac{1}{2}$ · ______ · (______ + ______)

 = $\frac{1}{2}$ · ______ · ______

 = ______ ft^2

 Volume of prism = ______ · ______

 = ______ ft^3

 The volume of the prism is ______ cubic feet.

Name: ______________________ Date: ______________

INDEPENDENT PRACTICE

State whether slices parallel to each given slice will form uniform cross sections. If not, explain why not.

1. 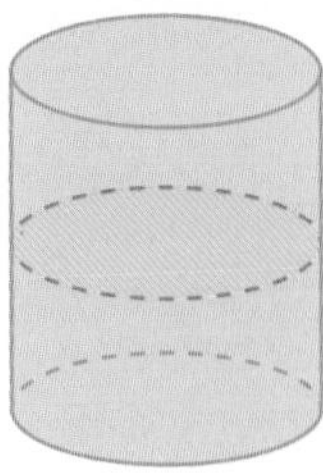

2. 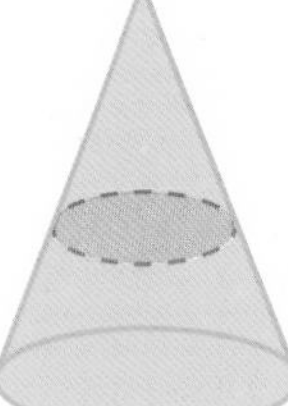

3. 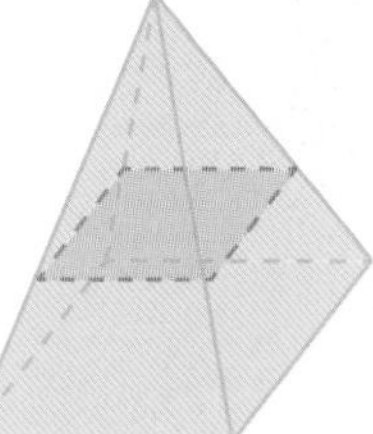

4. 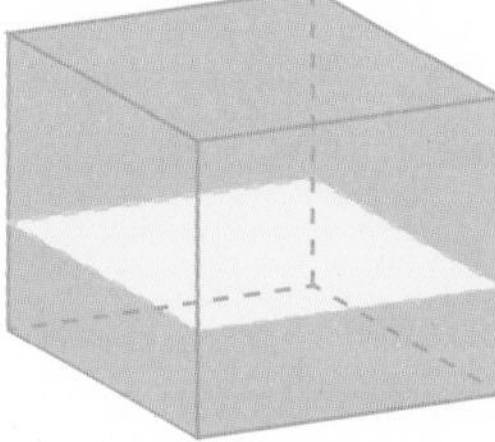

Each solid is sliced twice parallel to its base. Draw the two cross sections.

5. 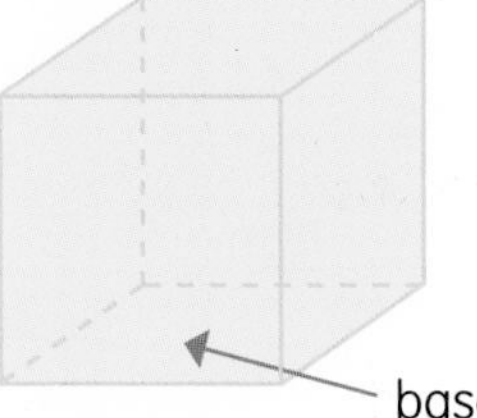

6. 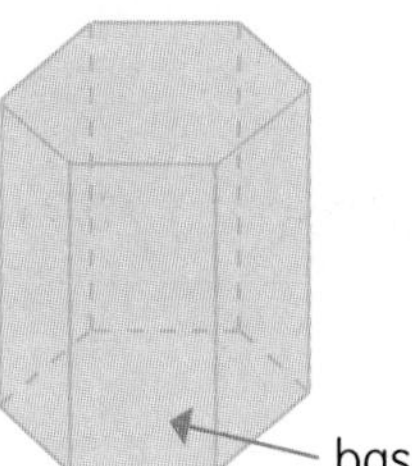

7. 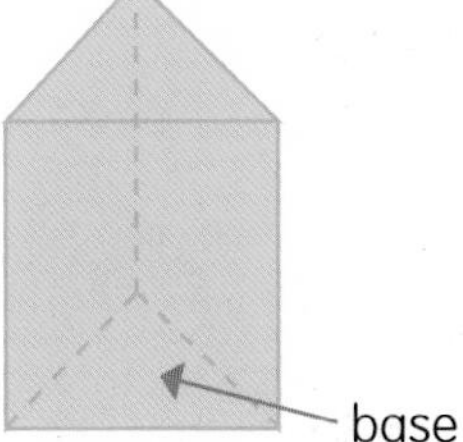

8. 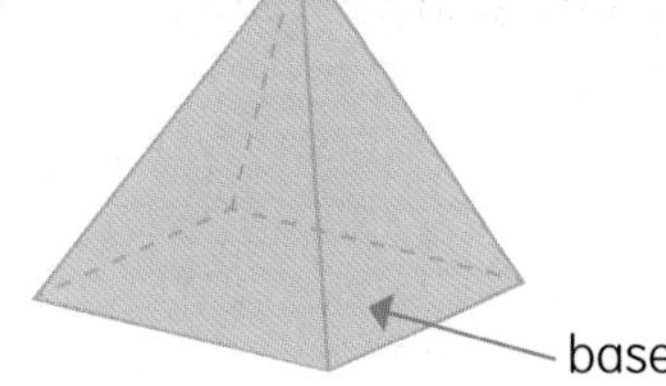

Find the volume of each triangular prism.

9

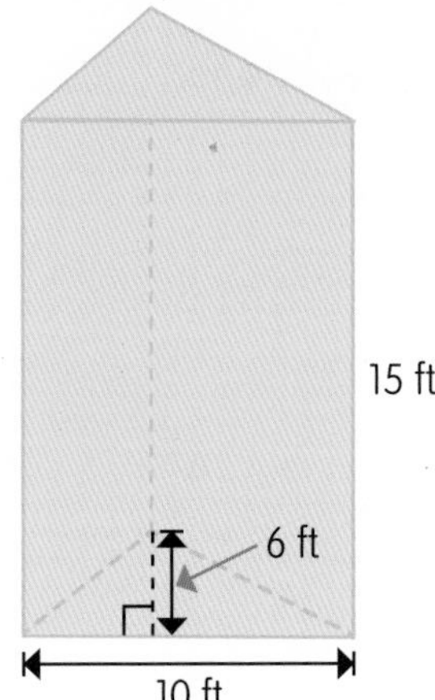

10

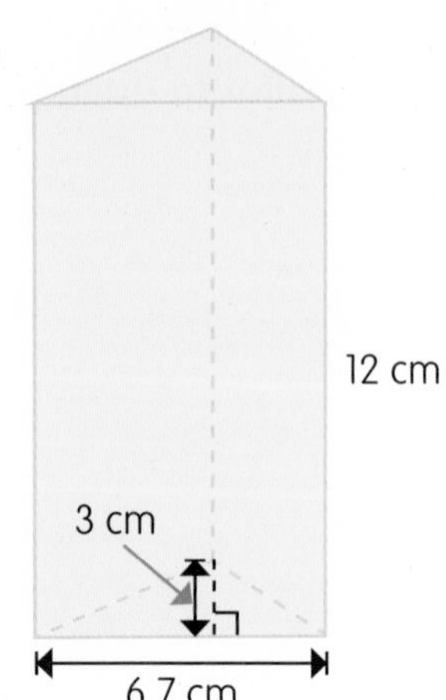

Solve.

11 The bases of the prism shown are trapezoids. Find the volume of the prism.

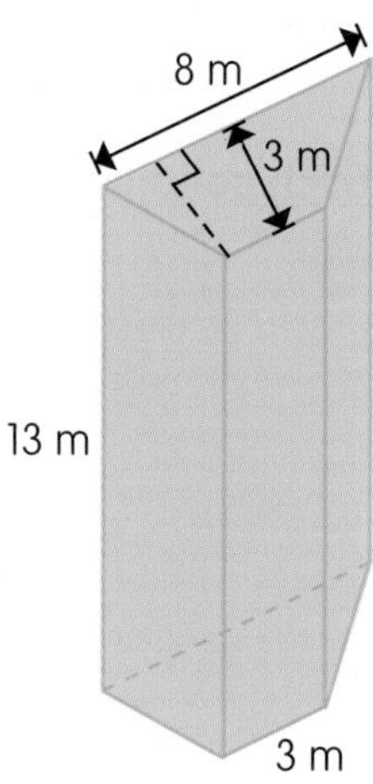

12 The volume of a triangular prism is 700 cubic centimeters. Two of its dimensions are given in the diagram. Find the height of the triangular base.

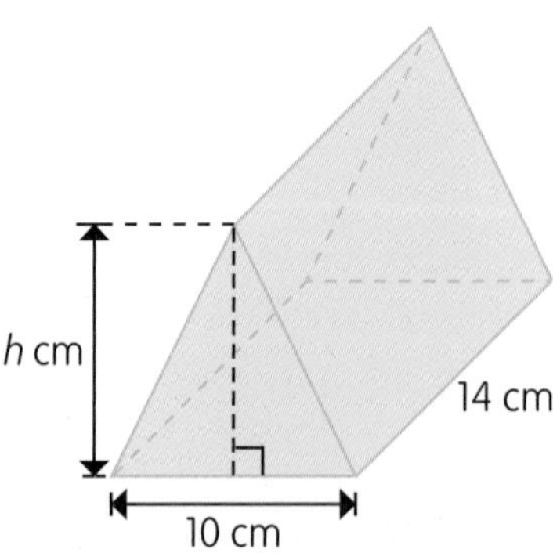

Real-World Problems: Surface Area and Volume

Learning Objective:

- Solve real-world problems involving volume and surface area. of three-dimensional objects composed of triangles, quadrilaterals, polygons, cubes, and right prisms.

THINK

The garden shed is composed of a rectangular prism and a triangular prism. The volume of the shed is 720 cubic feet. Find its surface area.

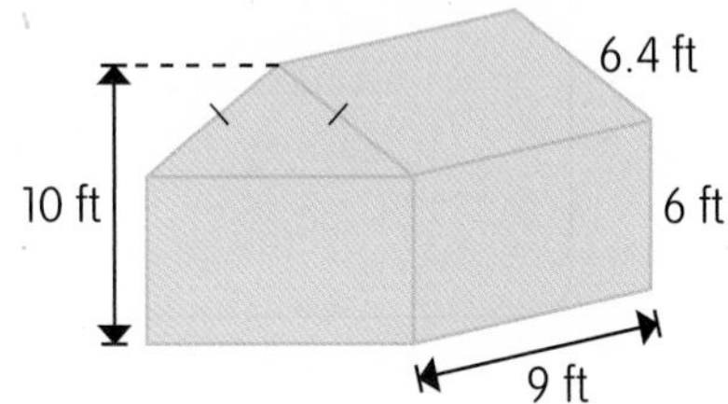

ENGAGE

Recall how you would find the volume of a rectangular prism. Mark with letters the edges of the door stopper that you need to know to find the volume and surface area. Then, write down the expressions for finding the volume and surface area of the door stopper. Compare your expressions with your partner's.

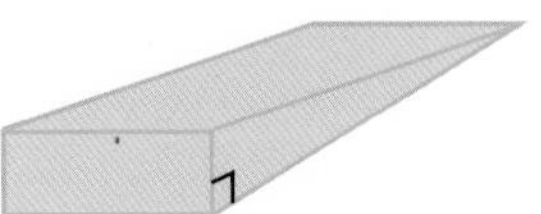

LEARN Solve real-world problems involving surface area and volume of prisms

1. Ashley cut a block of wood for her carpentry work. The block of wood is a prism with the dimensions shown.

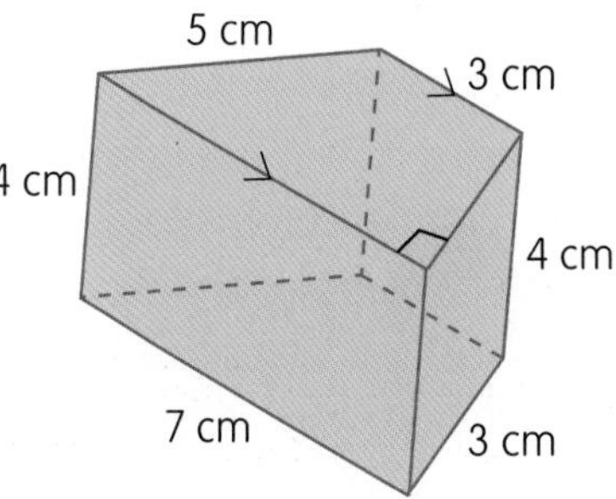

a Find the volume of the block of wood.

The base of the prism is a trapezoid.

$$\begin{aligned}\text{Area of base} &= \frac{1}{2}h(\text{sum of lengths of parallel sides})\\ &= \frac{1}{2} \cdot 3 \cdot (3 + 7)\\ &= \frac{1}{2} \cdot 3 \cdot 10\\ &= 15 \text{ cm}^2\end{aligned}$$

$$\begin{aligned}V &= Bh\\ &= 15 \cdot 4\\ &= 60 \text{ cm}^3\end{aligned}$$

The volume of the block of wood is 60 cubic centimeters.

b Ashley painted the block of wood yellow. Find the surface area of the block of wood.

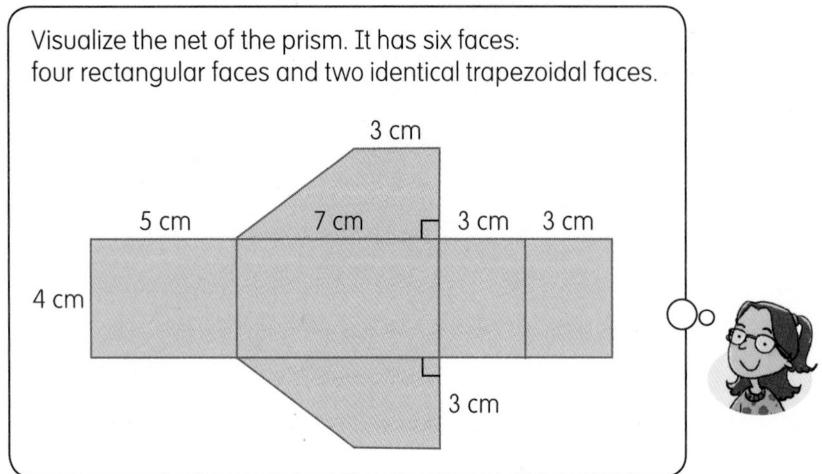

Total area of trapezoidal faces $= 2 \cdot 15$
$= 30\ \text{cm}^2$

Total area of rectangular faces $= (5 + 7 + 3 + 3) \cdot 4$
$= 18 \cdot 4$
$= 72\ \text{cm}^2$

Surface area = Area of net of prism
$= 30 + 72$
$= 102\ \text{cm}^2$

The surface area of the block of wood is 102 square centimeters.

What happens if you are given the volume of the prism instead of its height? How do you find the missing height? Explain.

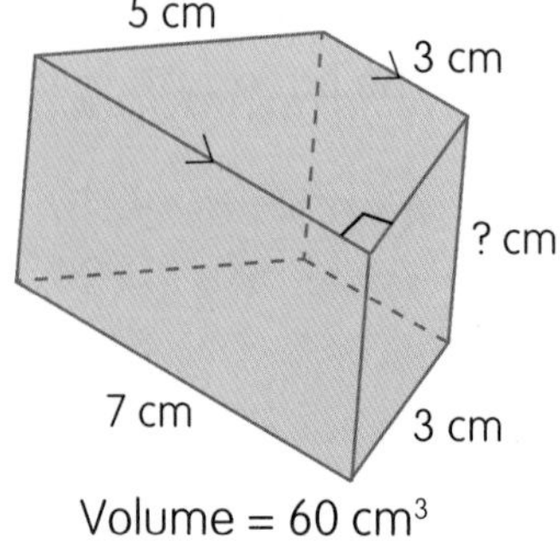

Volume = 60 cm^3

2 Alex made a wooden birdhouse. His birdhouse is a prism with two faces that are pentagons and has a circular hole as shown.

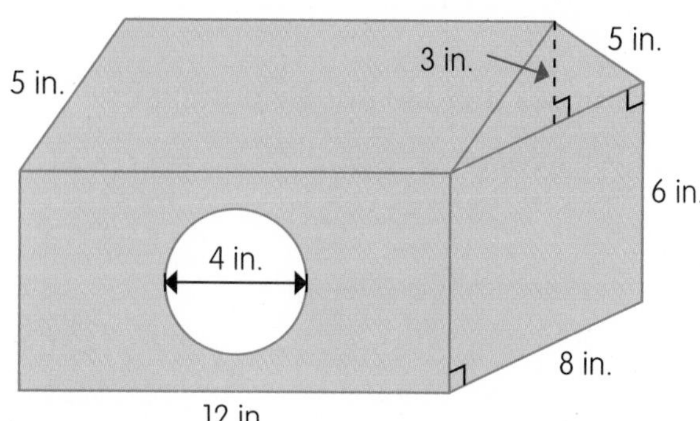

a Find the surface area of the birdhouse, including its floor. Use 3.14 as an approximation for π.

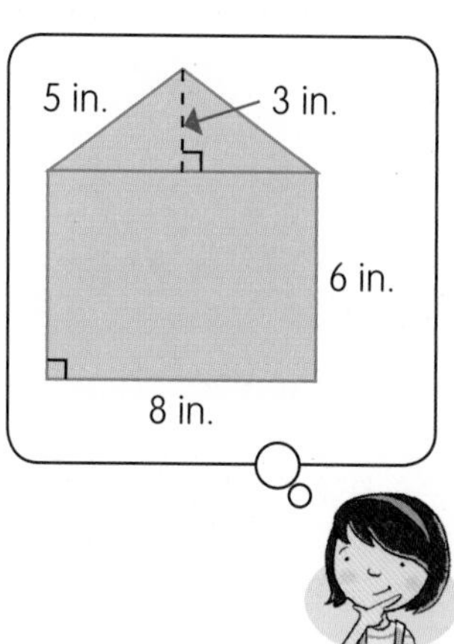

$$\begin{aligned}\text{Total area of pentagonal faces} &= 2 \cdot \left(\frac{1}{2} \cdot 8 \cdot 3 + 8 \cdot 6\right) \\ &= 2 \cdot 60 \\ &= 120 \text{ in}^2\end{aligned}$$

$$\begin{aligned}\text{Total area of rectangular faces} &= (5 + 6 + 8 + 6 + 5) \cdot 12 \\ &= 30 \cdot 12 \\ &= 360 \text{ in}^2\end{aligned}$$

$$\begin{aligned}\text{Area of circle} &\approx 3.14 \cdot 2 \cdot 2 \\ &= 12.56 \text{ in}^2\end{aligned}$$

$$\begin{aligned}\text{Surface area} &= 120 + 360 - 12.56 \\ &= 467.44 \text{ in}^2\end{aligned}$$

The surface area of the birdhouse is approximately 467.44 square inches.

b Find the volume of space within the birdhouse.

The birdhouse is made up of a triangular prism and a rectangular prism.

$$\begin{aligned}\text{Volume of triangular prism} &= Bh \\ &= \frac{1}{2} \cdot 8 \cdot 3 \cdot 12 \\ &= 144 \text{ in}^3\end{aligned}$$

$$\begin{aligned}\text{Volume of rectangular prism} &= 12 \cdot 8 \cdot 6 \\ &= 576 \text{ in}^3\end{aligned}$$

$$\begin{aligned}\text{Volume of prism} &= \text{volume of triangular prism} + \text{volume of rectangular prism} \\ &= 144 + 576 \\ &= 720 \text{ in}^3\end{aligned}$$

The volume of space within the birdhouse is 720 cubic inches.

TRY Practice solving real-world problems involving surface area and volume of prisms

Solve.

1 A metal bar is a prism with bases that are parallelograms.

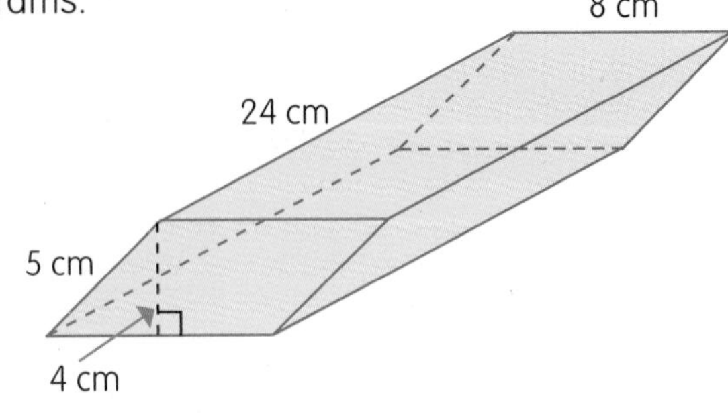

a Find the volume of the metal bar.

Area of parallelogram
= base of parallelogram • height of parallelogram

= ______ • ______

= ______ cm^2

Volume of metal bar
= base area of prism • height of prism

= ______ • ______

= ______ cm^2

The height of the prism is the edge that is perpendicular to the base.

The volume of the metal bar is ______ cubic centimeters.

b Find the surface area of the metal bar.

Total area of faces that are parallelograms = ______ • ______

= ______ cm^2

Total area of rectangular faces

= (______ + ______ + ______ + ______) • ______

= ______ • ______

= ______ cm^2

Surface area of metal bar = Total area of six faces

= ______ + ______

= ______ cm^2

The surface area of the metal bar is ______ square centimeters.

 2 A storage chest is a prism with bases that are pentagons. The diagram shows the dimensions of the storage chest. The capacity of the storage chest is 855 cubic inches.

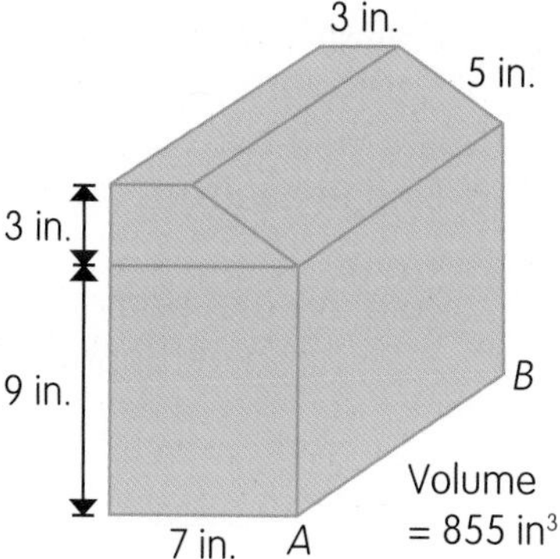

a Find the height AB of the prism. Round your answer to the nearest hundredth.

Area of pentagonal base
= area of trapezoid + area of rectangle

$= \frac{1}{2} \cdot$ ______ $\cdot$ (______ + ______) + ______ $\cdot$ ______

= ______ + ______

= ______ in^2

Volume = Bh

______ = ______ $\cdot AB$

$\frac{}{} = \frac{}{} \cdot AB$

$AB \approx$ ______ in. (to the nearest hundredth)

The height of the prism is approximately ______ inches.

b Find the surface area of the prism. Round your answer to the nearest hundredth.

Total area of pentagonal faces = ______ $\cdot$ ______

= ______ in^2

Total area of rectangular faces

= (______ + ______ + ______ + ______ + ______) $\cdot$ ______

= ______ $\cdot$ ______

= ______ in^2

Surface area of prism = Area of net of prism

= ______ + ______

= ______ in^2

The surface area of the prism is approximately ______ square inches.

3 For his art project, Carlos made a model of his house out of cardboard. The model is made up of a rectangular prism with two square faces and a triangular prism.

a Find the surface area of the model.

13 cm
10 cm
12 cm
15 cm
10 cm

Total area of pentagonal faces
= 2 • (area of triangle + area of square)

$= 2 \cdot \left(\frac{1}{2} \cdot \_\_\_\_ \cdot \_\_\_\_ + \_\_\_\_ \cdot \_\_\_\_\right)$

$= 2 \cdot (\_\_\_\_ + \_\_\_\_)$

$= 2 \cdot \_\_\_\_$

$= \_\_\_\_$ cm^2

Total area of rectangular faces

$= (\_\_\_\_ + \_\_\_\_ + \_\_\_\_ + \_\_\_\_ + \_\_\_\_) \cdot \_\_\_\_$

$= \_\_\_\_ \cdot \_\_\_\_$

$= \_\_\_\_$ cm^2

Surface area = ____ + ____

$= \_\_\_\_$ cm^2

The surface area of the model is approximately ____ square centimeters.

b Find the volume of the model.

Volume of triangular prism $= \frac{1}{2} \cdot \_\_\_\_ \cdot \_\_\_\_ \cdot \_\_\_\_$

$= \_\_\_\_$ cm^3

Volume of rectangular prism = ____ • ____ • ____

$= \_\_\_\_$ cm^3

Volume of model = volume of triangular prism + volume of rectangular prism

$= \_\_\_\_ + \_\_\_\_$

$= \_\_\_\_$ cm^3

The volume of the model is ____ cubic centimeters.

Name: ______________________ Date: ______________

INDEPENDENT PRACTICE

Solve.

1. Abigail made a gift box. The gift box is a prism with bases that are regular hexagons, and has the dimensions as shown.

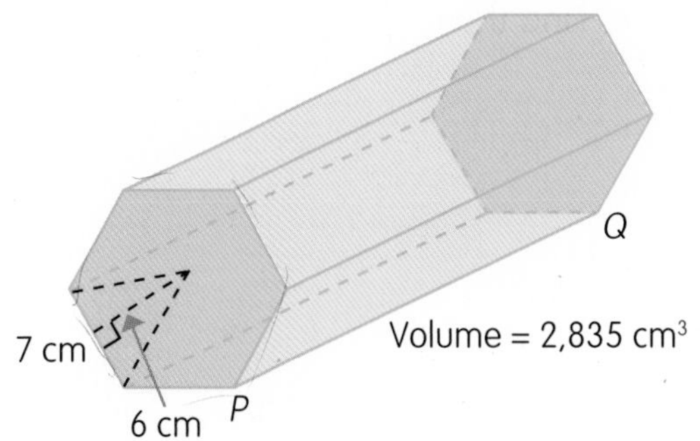

a Find the height PQ of the prism.

V = area of base · h

$7 \cdot 6 \cdot \frac{1}{2} = 21 \cdot 6 = 126$

$2{,}835 \div 126 = 22.5$ cm ✓

b Find the surface area of the prism.

$126 + 126 = 252$

$7 \cdot 22.5 = 157.5 \cdot 6 = 945 + 252 = 1197$ cm^2 ✓

2. Jack glued a cubical block of wood and another piece of wood that is in the shape of a triangular prism to make a door wedge. What is the volume and surface area of the door wedge?

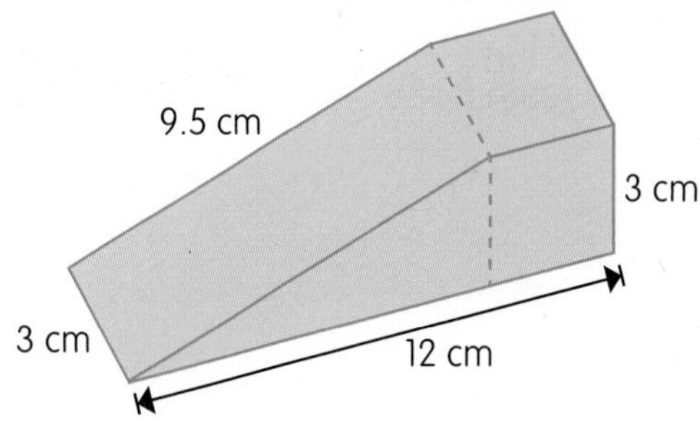

3 Mr. Turner built a shed to store his tools. The shed has a roof that is in the shape of a triangular prism.

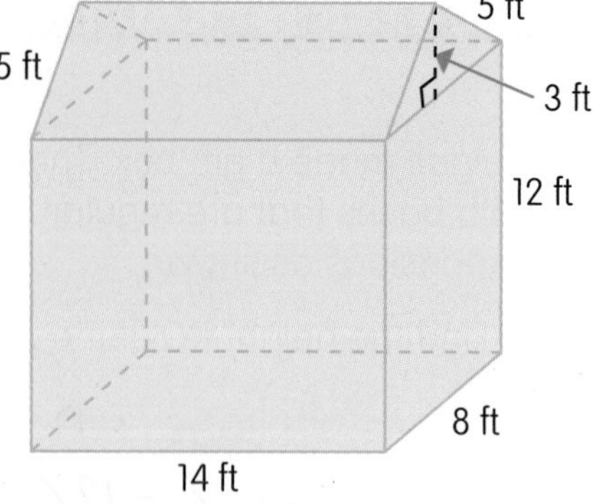

a Find the amount of space the shed occupies.

b Find the surface area of the shed, including its floor.

4 The volume of a solid triangular prism is 726 cubic centimeters. Its height is 12 centimeters and its bases are congruent right isosceles triangles. Find the lengths of the equal sides of each base.

Mathematical Habit 3 Construct viable arguments

An 8-inch vegetarian pizza costs $6. A 16-inch vegetarian pizza costs twice as much. Issac thinks that buying two 8-inch pizzas is the same as buying one 16-inch pizza. Is he correct? Explain your answer. Use 3.14 as an approximation for π.

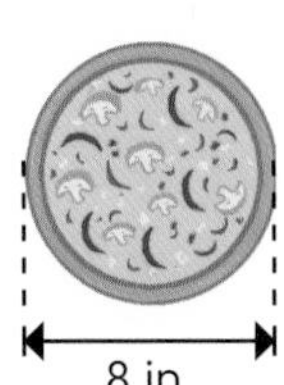

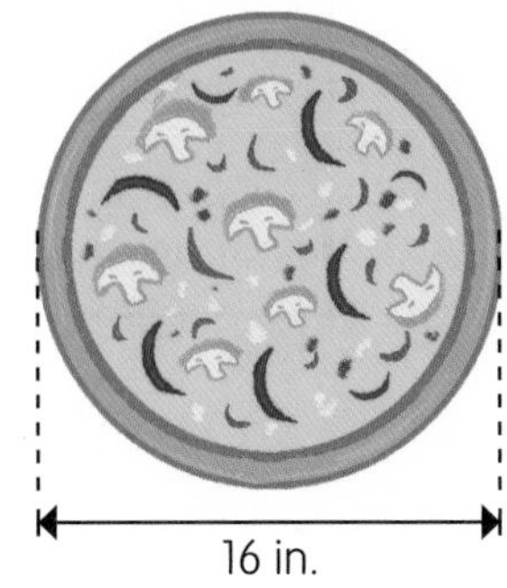

Problem Solving with Heuristics

1 **Mathematical Habit 1 Persevere in solving problems**
The figure shows two identical overlapping quadrants. Find the distance around the shaded part. Use 3.14 as an approximation for π. Round your answer to the nearest tenth of a centimeter.

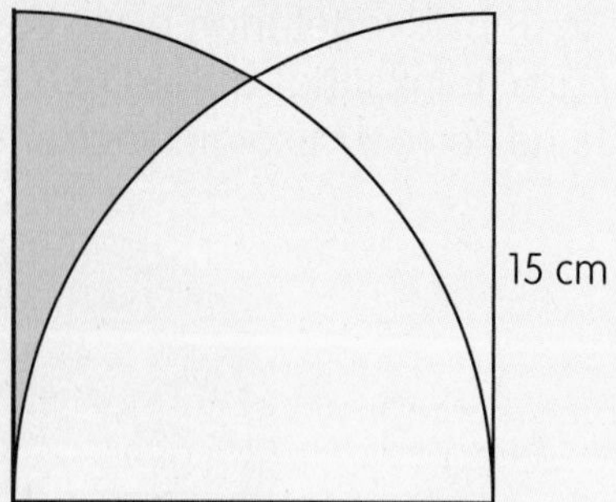

2 **Mathematical Habit 1 Persevere in solving problems**
A cushion cover design is created from a circle of radius 7 inches, and 4 quadrants. Find the total area of the shaded parts of the design. Use $\frac{22}{7}$ as an approximation for π.

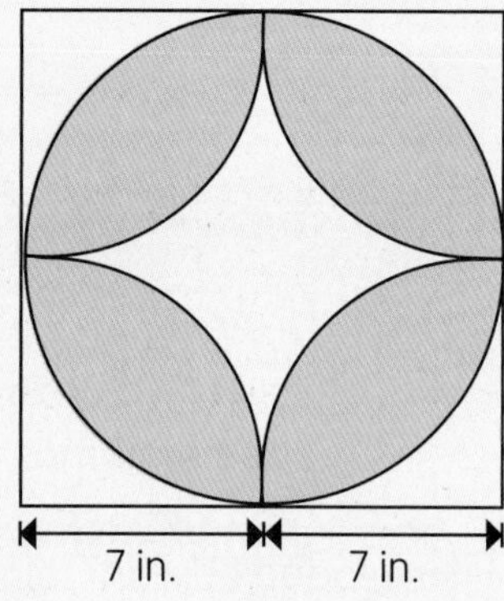

3 **Mathematical Habit 1 Persevere in solving problems**
Two identical wheels are placed along a straight path so that their centers are 9.31 meters apart. The radius of each wheel is 3.5 centimeters. They are pushed towards each other at the same time, each making one revolution per second. How long does it take for them to knock onto each other? Use $\frac{22}{7}$ as an approximation for π.

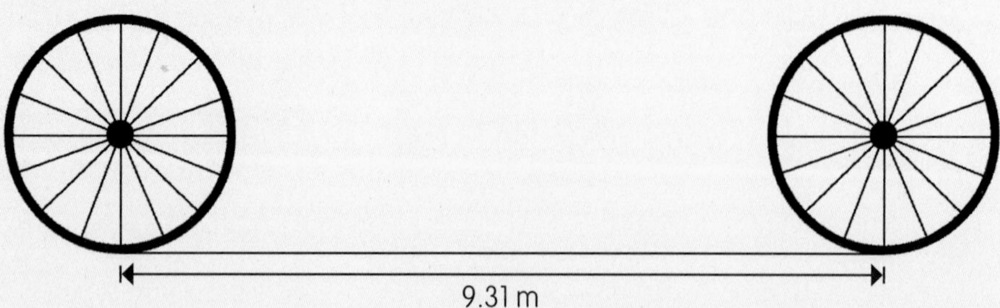

4 **Mathematical Habit 2 Construct viable arguments**

Containers A and B are in the shape of triangular prisms. Container A is filled to the brim with water and container B is empty. Timothy wants to pour some water from container A into container B so that the water level in both containers is the same. Find the new height of water in each container.

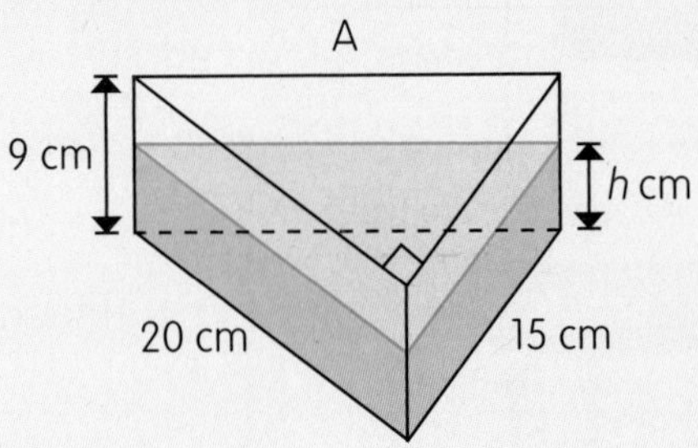

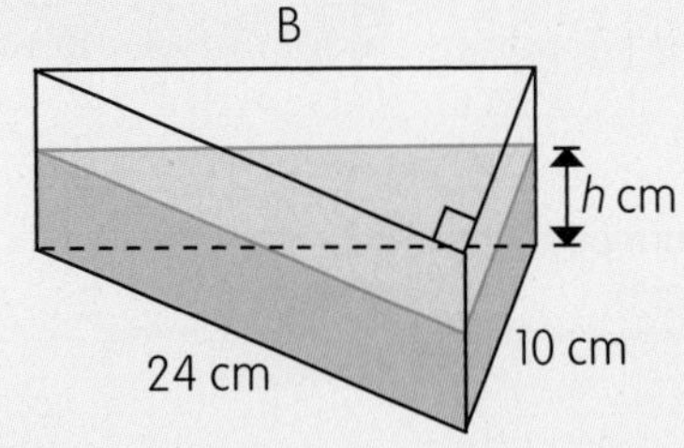

5 **Mathematical Habit 2 Construct viable arguments**

A barrel contains 600 cubic inches more water than a tank with a trapezoidal base. The lengths of the parallel sides of the trapezoid are 6 inches and 12 inches, and the perpendicular distance between them is 5 inches. When 200 cubic inches of water are poured from the tank into the barrel, the volume of water in the barrel is 11 times the volume of water left in the tank. Find the height of the water left in the tank. Round your answer to the nearest tenth of an inch.

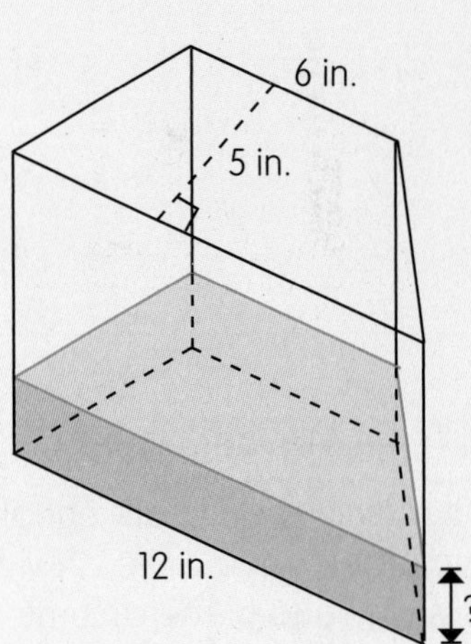

CHAPTER WRAP-UP

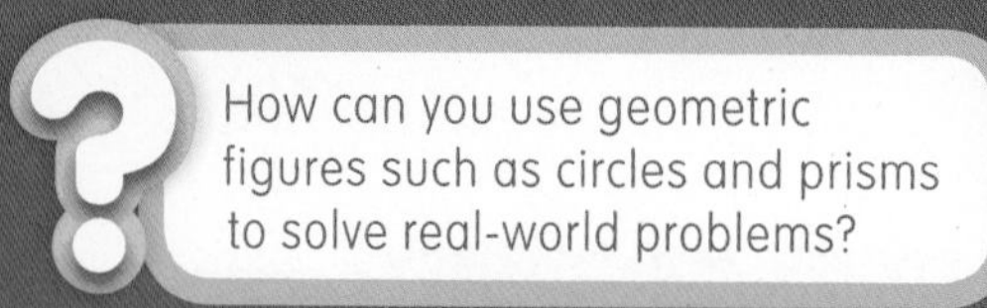

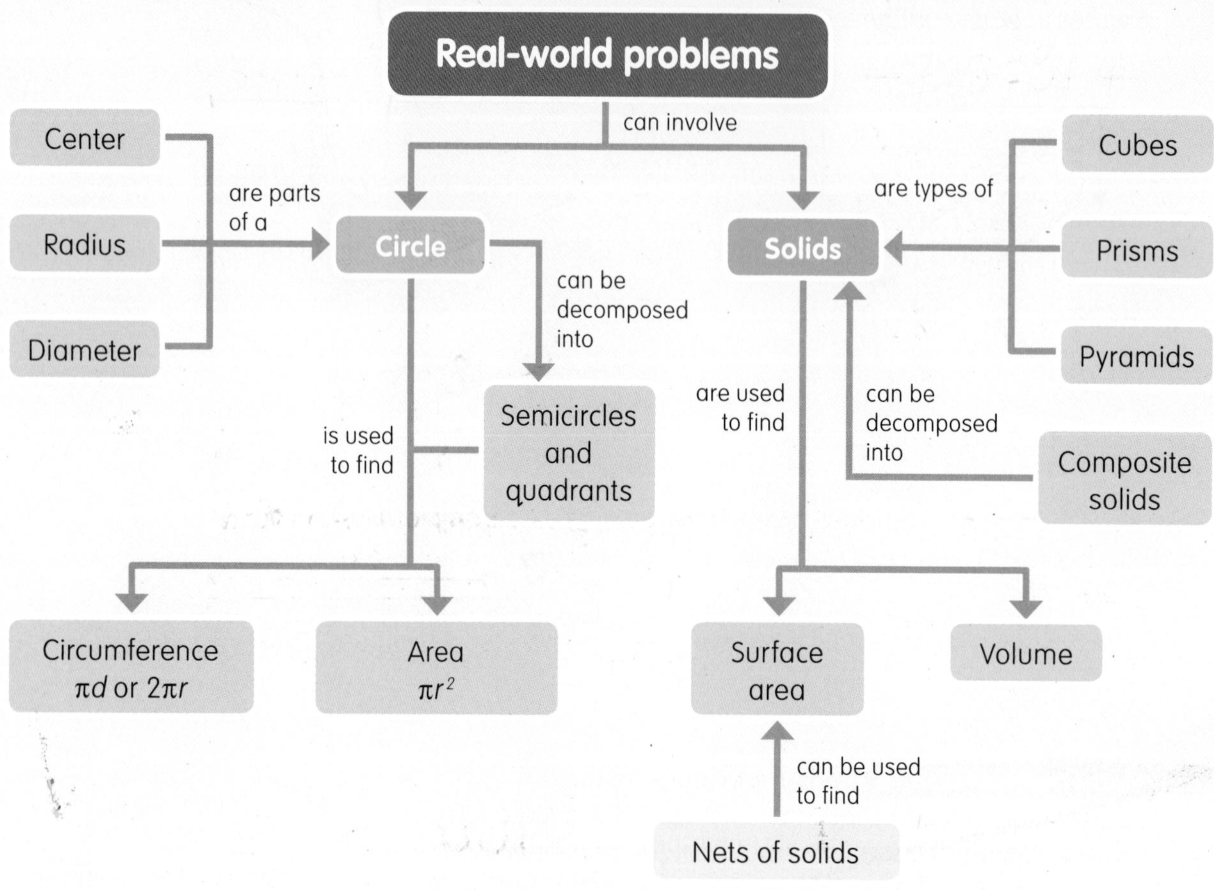

KEY CONCEPTS

- All radii of a circle are equal.
- A diameter of a circle is twice its radius.
- π is the ratio of the circumference to the diameter of a circle.
- The volume of a prism is the base area of the prism multiplied by its height.
- The surface area of a prism is the perimeter of its base multiplied by its height plus twice the area of its base.
- The volume of a composite solid can be found by decomposing it into right prisms, and then adding the volumes of the right prisms.

Name: ______________________________ Date: ______________

Find the circumference and area of each circle. Use $\frac{22}{7}$ as an approximation for π.

1

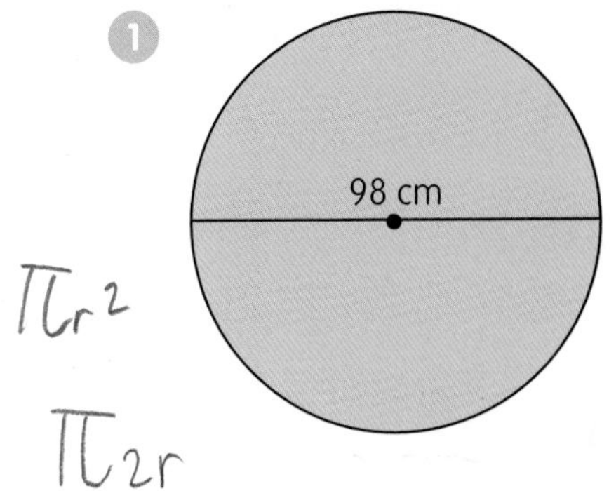

πr^2

$\pi 2r$

$\frac{22}{7} \cdot 2 \cdot 49 = 308$ cm ✓

$\frac{22}{7} \cdot 49^2 = 7{,}546$ cm^2

2

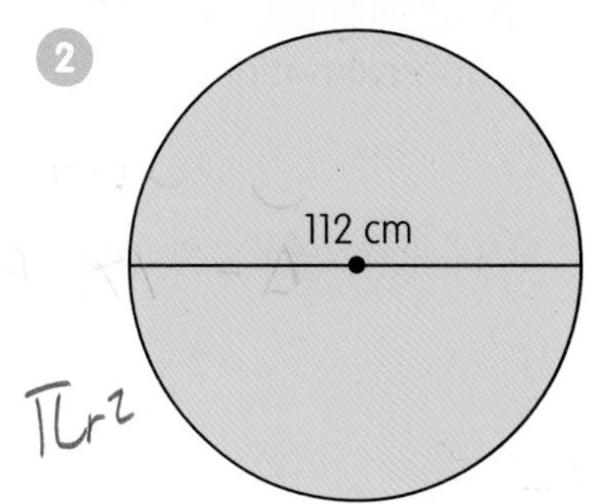

πr^2

$\pi 2r$

$\frac{22}{7} \cdot 2 \cdot 56 = 352$ cm ✓

$\frac{22}{7} \cdot 56^2 = 9{,}856$ cm^2

Find the distance around each semicircle. Use $\frac{22}{7}$ as an approximation for π.

3

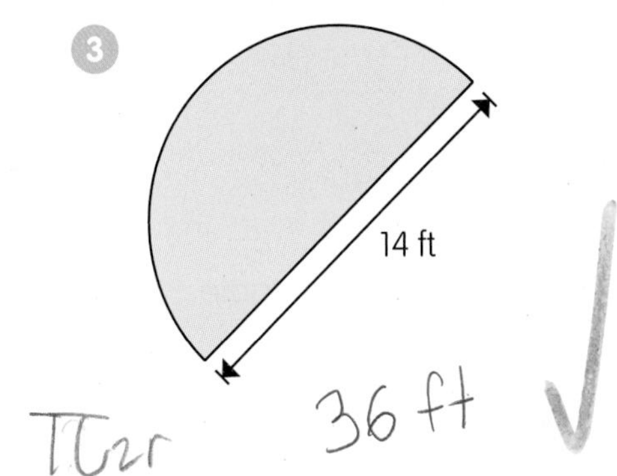

$\pi 2r$ 36 ft ✓

$\frac{22}{7} \cdot 2 \cdot 7 = 44$ ft $\div 2 = 22$ ft $+ 14 =$ 36 ft

4

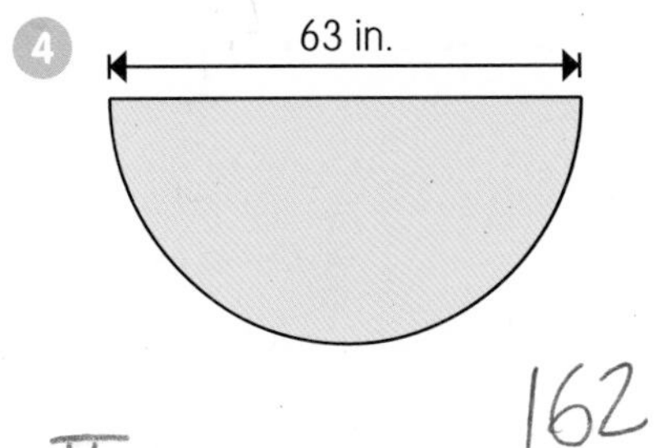

$\pi 2r$ 162 in ✓

$\frac{22}{7} \cdot 2 \cdot 31.5 = 198 \div 2 = 99$ in $+ 63 =$

Find the distance around each quadrant. Round your answer to the nearest tenth. Use 3.14 as an approximation for π.

5

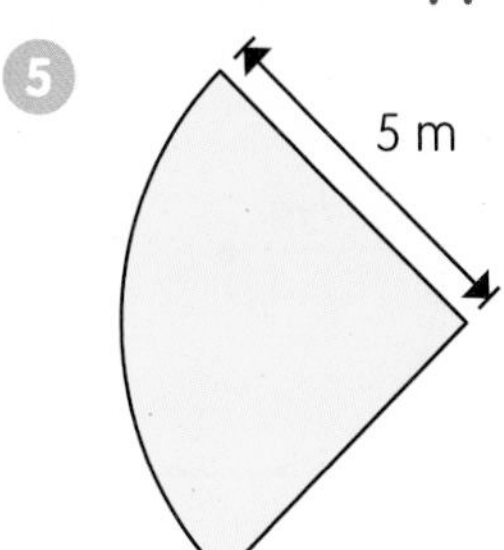

✗ = 17.85

$\pi 2r$

$3.14 \cdot 2 \cdot 5 = 31.4 \div 4 = 15.7$ m

6

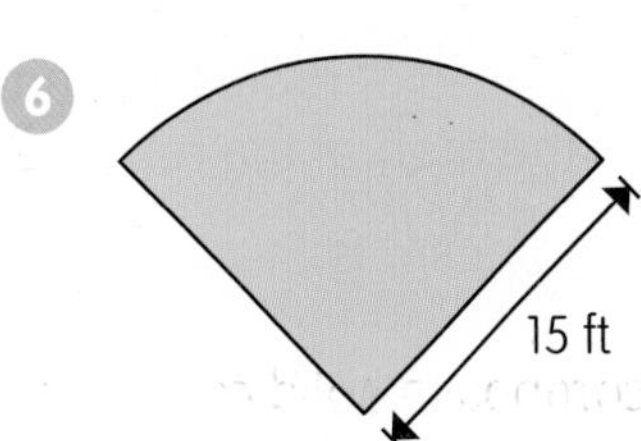

✗ = 53.55

$\pi 2r$

$3.14 \cdot 2 \cdot 15 = 94.2$ ft

Solve.

7. The diameter of a flying disc is 10 inches. Find the circumference and area of the disc. Use 3.14 as an approximation for π.

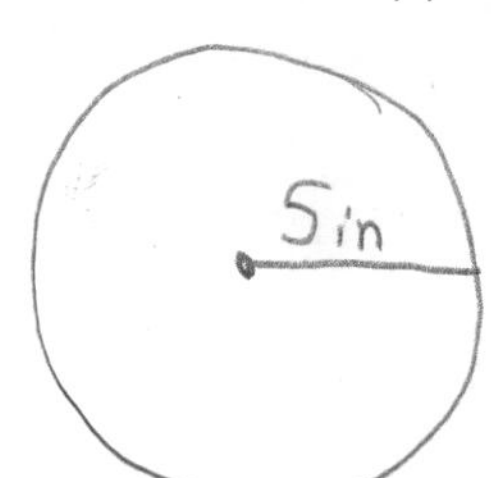

C=31.4in
A=78.5in²

πc2r
3.14·2·5=31.4
πr²
3.14·5²
3.14·25=78.5

8. The area of a compact disc is $452\frac{4}{7}$ square centimeters. What is the diameter of the compact disc? Use $\frac{22}{7}$ as an approximation for π.

452.57÷2=226.285 diameter
226.285*2= 413.1425=radius

9. The circumference of a circular table is 816.4 centimeters. Find the radius of the table. Use 3.14 as an approximation for π.

816.4÷3.14÷2=130

10. Noah cuts out a circle of radius 30 centimeters from a square piece of paper. What is the area of the remaining piece of paper? Use 3.14 as an approximation for π.

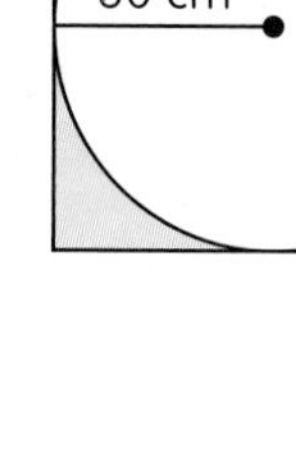

area of square = 3600−2826=774cm
area of circle=2826

3.14×30²=2826
60×60=3600

11 The wheel of a road bike has a diameter of 0.6 meter. It made 800 complete turns in 5 minutes. If the wheel turns at a constant speed, what will the distance covered by the wheel be in an hour? Use 3.14 as an approximation for π.

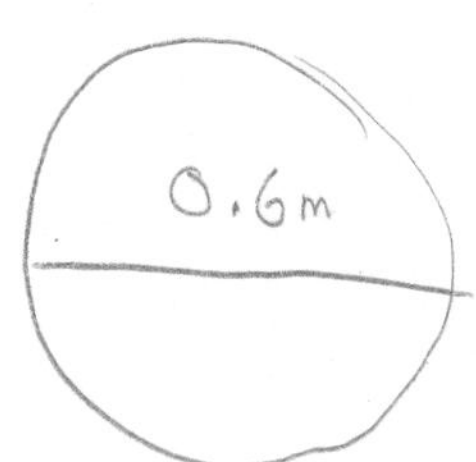

12 The figure shows four identical quadrants enclosed in a square. The length of a side of the square is 20 inches. Find the area of the blue part. Use 3.14 as an approximation for π.

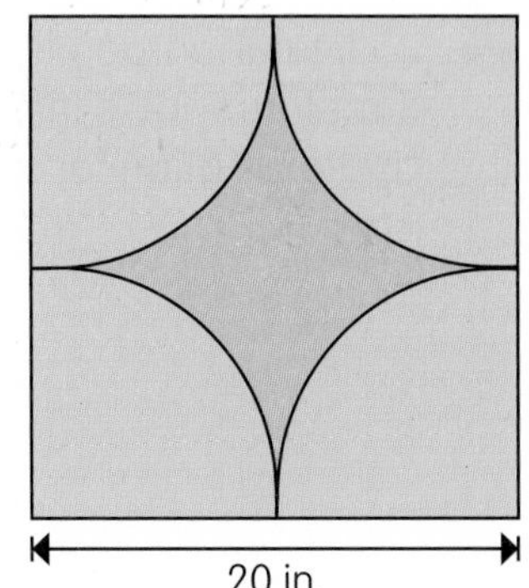

13 The figure shows 3 identical circles. X, Y, and Z are the centers of the circles, and the radius of each circle is 15 feet. $\frac{1}{6}$ of each circle is shaded. What is the total area of the shaded portion? Round your answer to the nearest tenth of a foot. Use 3.14 as an approximation for π.

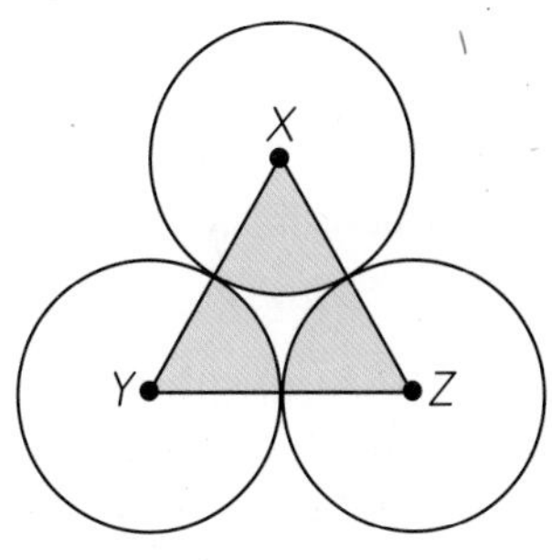

14 The figure is made up of one semicircle and two quadrants. The distance around the figure is 97.29 inches. Find the value of k. Use 3.14 as an approximation for π.

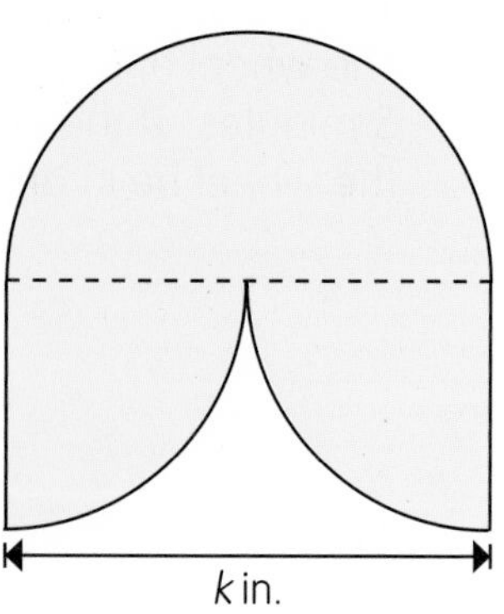

15 A circular garden is surrounded by a cement path that is 3 meters wide. Find the area of the path. Use 3.14 as an approximation for π.

πr^2

$3.14 \cdot 50^2$ = 913.74

$3.14 \cdot 2{,}500 = 7850$

$3^2 \times 3.14 = 28.26 = 7821.74$

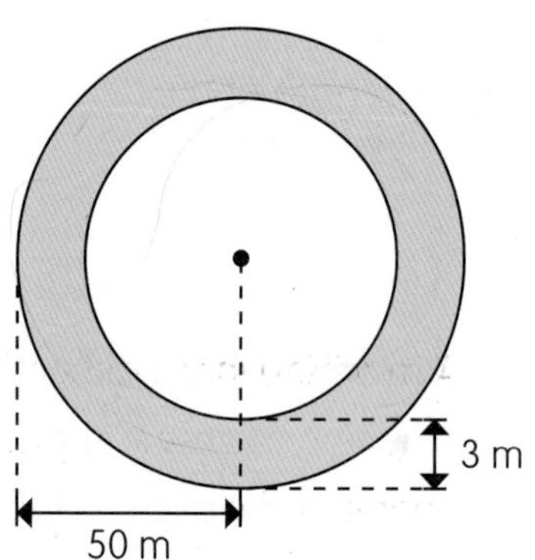

16 A water fountain shoots up a jet of water. The water falls back down onto the ground in the shape of a circle. Michelle wants the circle of water on the ground to be 0.7 meter wider on each side. She gradually increases the strength of the water jet. The area of the circle of water increases at 0.2 square meter per second. Use $\frac{22}{7}$ as an approximation for π.

a Find the area of the original circle of water.

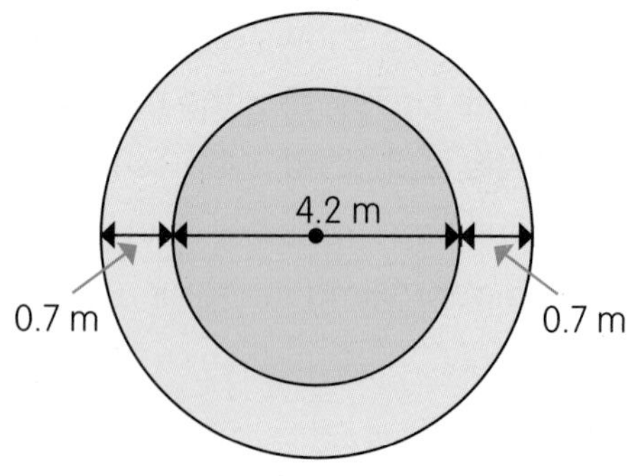

b Find the area of the larger circle of water.

c How long does it take for the original circle of water to become the larger circle of water? Round your answer to the nearest second.

17 A machine in an assembly line stamps pieces of metal. The stamping plate on the machine travels in a path shaped like the arc of a quadrant as the stamping plate opens and closes. It takes the machine 5 seconds to open and close the stamping plate one time. Use $\frac{22}{7}$ as an approximation for π.

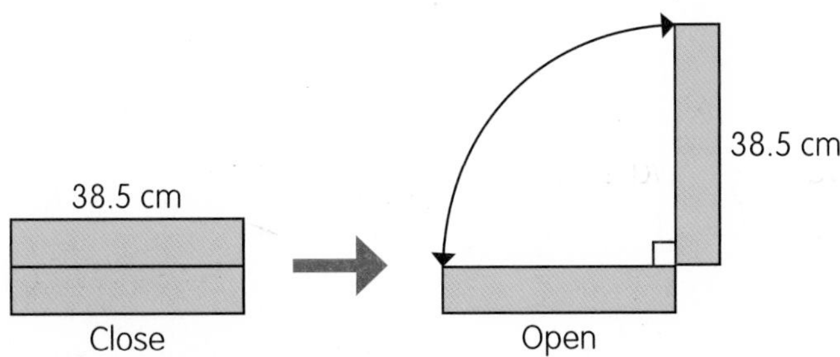

a Find the total distance the outside edge of the stamping plate travels when the machine opens and closes one time.

b Find the speed of the stamping plate's outside edge in centimeters per second.

c Assume the machine starts and ends in an open position. How many seconds will it take the machine to stamp 500 pieces of metal?

Find the volume and surface area of each prism.

18 This prism has two identical bases that are trapezoids.

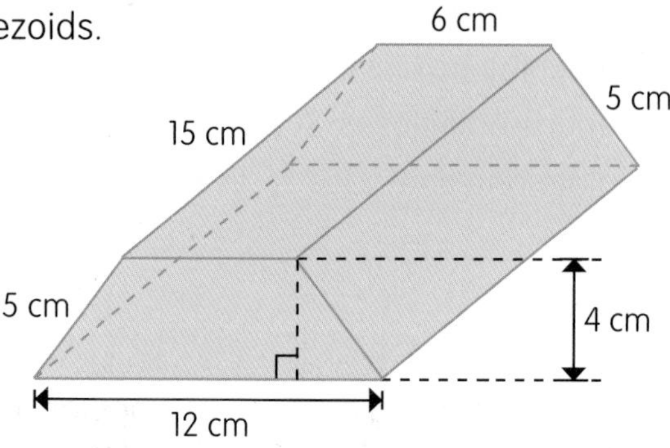

19 This prism has two identical bases that are rhombuses.

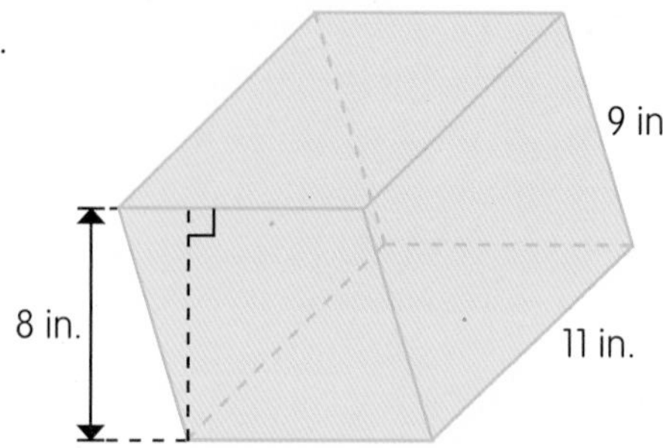

20 The volume of the triangular prism is 180 cubic meters. Find the height of the triangular prism.

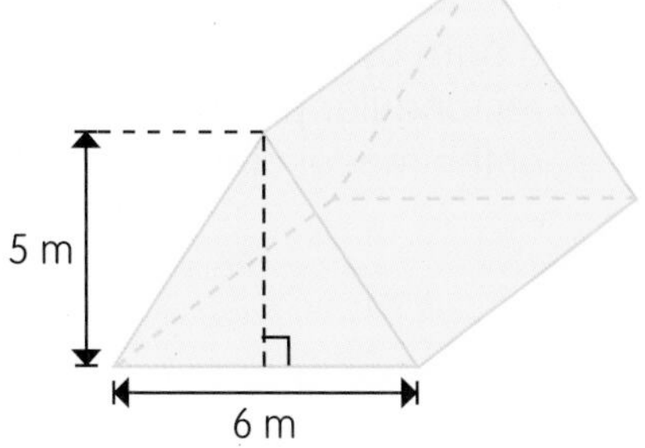

21 Find the volume and surface area of the solid.

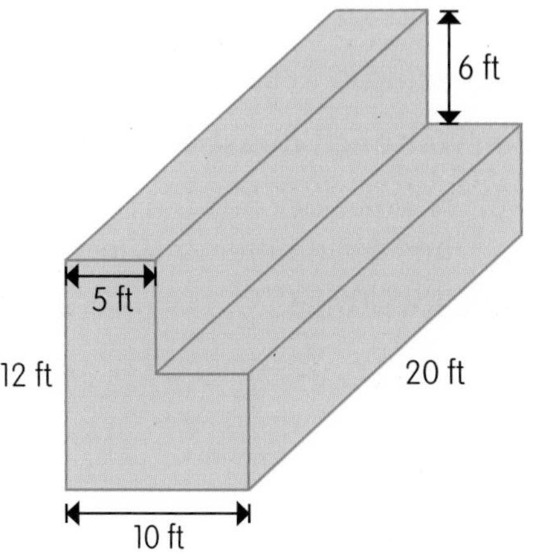

22 Hugo made a decorative piece for his bedroom door by sawing out two rectangular prisms from a block of wood to form the letter "H." He then painted it blue. Find the volume and surface area of the decorative piece.

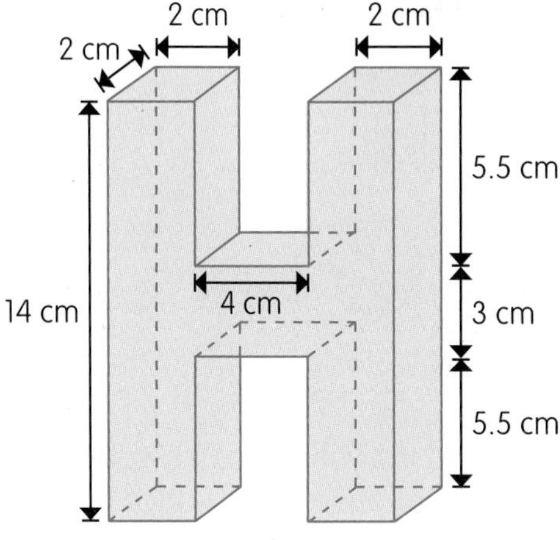

23 For her woodworking project, Laila built a model of a barn by stacking a trapezoidal prism on top of a rectangular prism. Find the volume and surface area of the model of the barn.

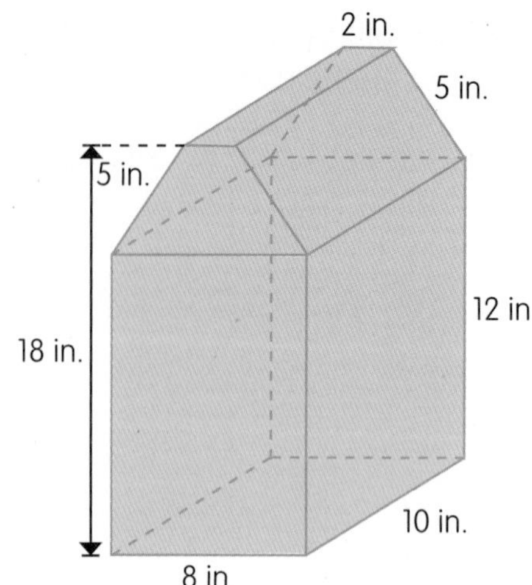

Assessment Prep

Answer each question.

24 A wall clock has a diameter of 18 inches. The circular orange clock face has a diameter of 16 inches. What is the area of the gray frame around the clock face?

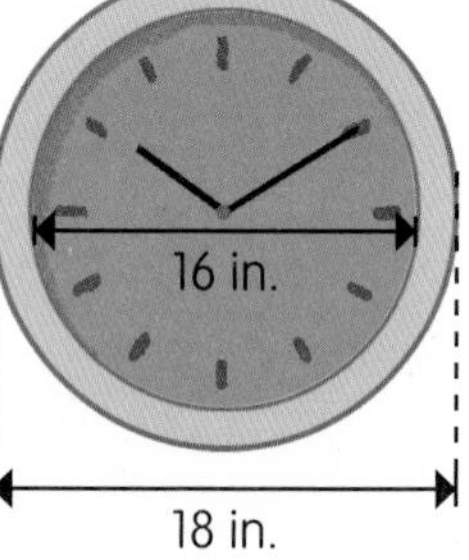

Ⓐ $(\pi \cdot 18 \cdot 18) - (\pi \cdot 16 \cdot 16)$

Ⓑ $(\pi \cdot 9 \cdot 9) - (\pi \cdot 8 \cdot 8)$

Ⓒ 16π

Ⓓ 18π

25 Solid A is sliced parallel to its bases. Which of the following shows its cross section?

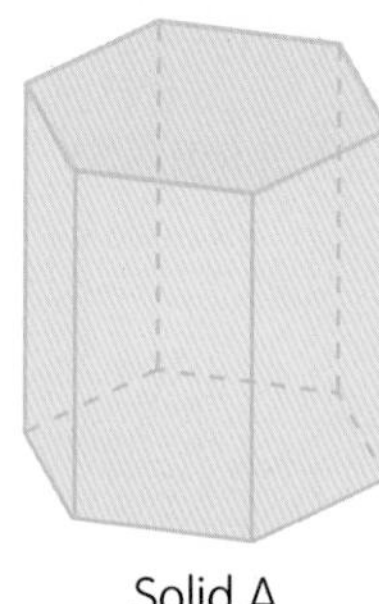
Solid A

Ⓐ 

Ⓑ 

Ⓒ

Ⓓ 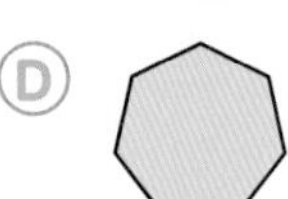

26 Find the volume of the solid. Write your answer and your work or explanation in the space below.

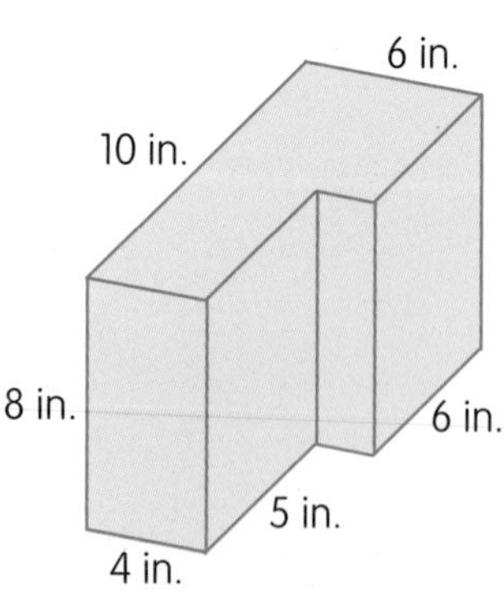

Name: ______________________ Date: ______________

Create Designs with Circles

For her art project, Clara created a few designs with circles on square pieces of paper.

1. Find the area of the colored part in each of the following designs. Use 3.14 as an approximation for π.

a

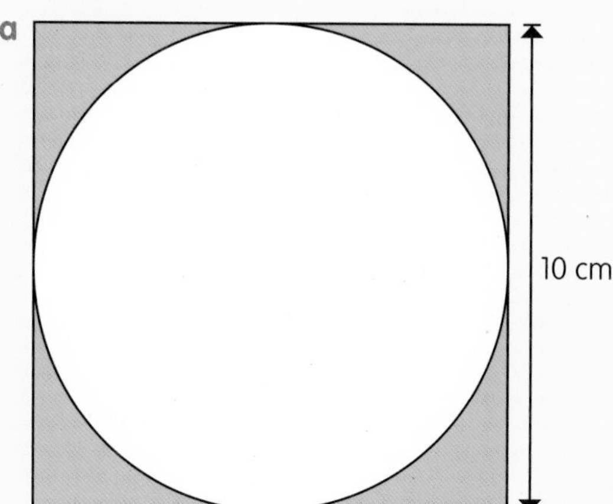

b

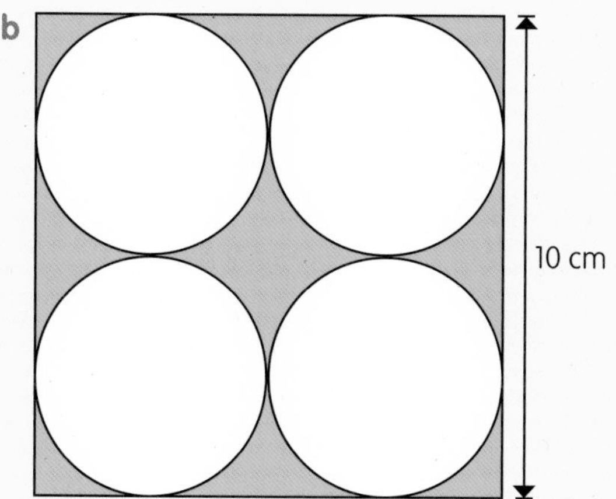

c

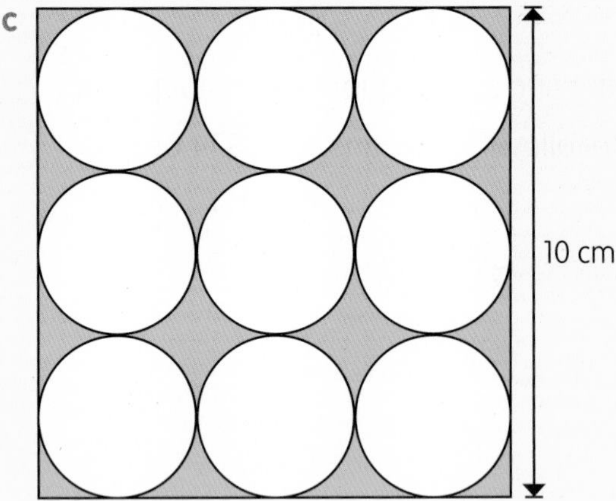

d

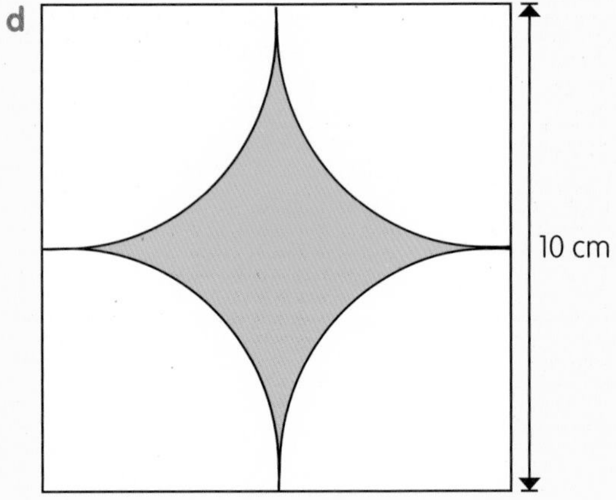

e 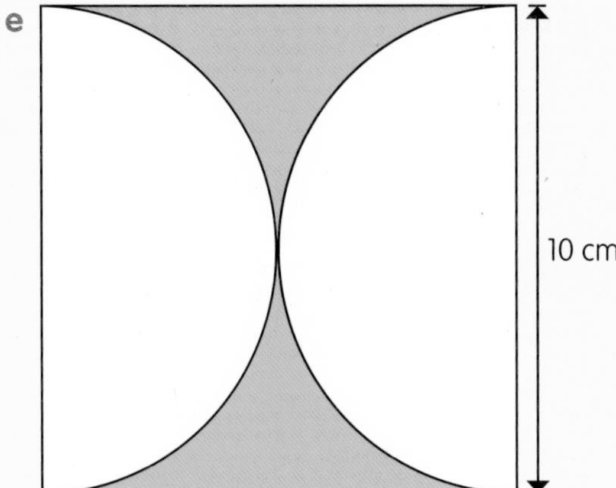

2 a What pattern do you observe about the areas of the colored part of all the designs in 1?

b What is the rule of the pattern?

c What is the area of the shaded part of this figure?

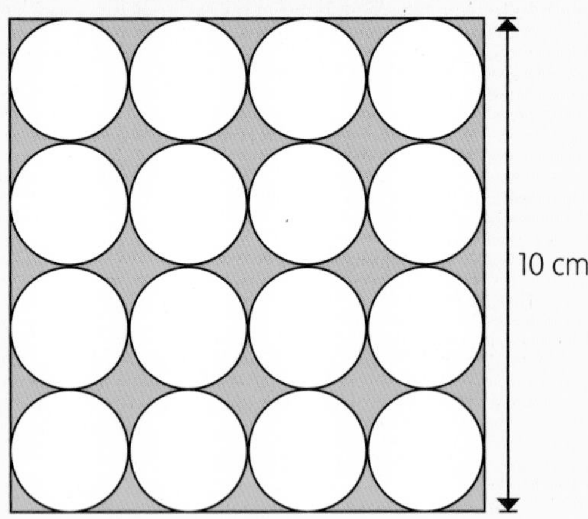

Rubric

Point(s)	Level	My Performance
7–8	4	• Most of my answers are correct. • I showed complete understanding of the concepts. • I used effective and efficient strategies to solve the problems. • I explained my answers and mathematical thinking clearly and completely.
5–6	3	• Some of my answers are correct. • I showed adequate understanding of the concepts. • I used effective strategies to solve the problems. • I explained my answers and mathematical thinking clearly.
3–4	2	• A few of my answers are correct. • I showed some understanding of the concepts. • I used some effective strategies to solve the problems. • I explained some of my answers and mathematical thinking clearly.
0–2	1	• A few of my answers are correct. • I showed little understanding of the concepts. • I used limited effective strategies to solve the problems. • I did not explain my answers and mathematical thinking clearly.

Teacher's Comments

Chapter 8 Statistics and Probability

How can you predict the future?

Will it be sunny next week? Based on data collected from current weather conditions and historical records, weather forecasters are able to predict the likelihood of a sunny day next week. Of course, weather conditions change all the time, so there might not be any sun at all.

What about seemingly random events such as predicting the outcome of a game? How can you predict the likelihood of winning a game of chance? In this chapter, you will learn to use data to make better predictions and informed decisions.

How do you collect data to gain meaningful information about a population and predict the likelihood of an event occurring?

Name: ______________________ Date: ______________

Finding the range, quartiles, and the interquartile range of a set of data

In statistics, you can measure how data values vary by finding the range, quartiles, and interquartile range of a set of data.

Consider the data set, {13, 18, 6, 1, 20, 11, 36, 45, 28, 27, 34, 7}.

To find the range, find the difference between the greatest and the least values.

Range = greatest value – least value
= 45 – 1
= 44

To find the quartiles of the data values, first arrange the values in ascending order.
Then, find the medians.

Lower half | Upper half

1 6 7 11 13 18 20 27 28 34 36 45

$$Q_2 = \frac{18 + 20}{2} = 19$$

$$Q_1 = \frac{7 + 11}{2} = 9 \qquad Q_3 = \frac{28 + 34}{2} = 31$$

The median of the lower half is called the first quartile (or lower quartile). It is written as Q_1.
The median of the set of data is called the second quartile. It is written as Q_2.
The median of the upper half is called the third quartile (or upper quartile). It is written as Q_3.

You can draw a diagram to show how the data are related to the quartiles. From the diagram, you can see that 50% of the values are between 9 and 31.

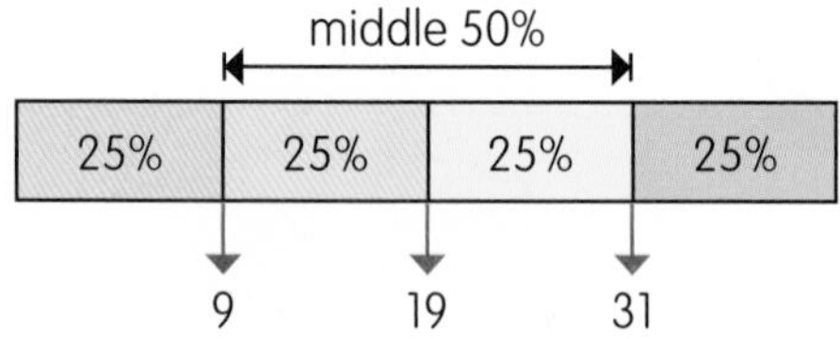

The range between the lower and the upper quartiles is called the interquartile range.

Interquartile range = upper quartile – lower quartile
= 31 – 9
= 22

▶ Quick Check

The data below are the heights of some plants in inches.
Answer each question.

8.2	3.2	4.1	2.8	9	6	5
5.4	8.4	6.6	9.5	3.7	7	2.1

1. Find the range of the heights.

2. Find the three quartiles (Q_1, Q_2, Q_3) of the heights.

3. Find the interquartile range of the heights.

Interpreting box plots

Quartiles and interquartile ranges can be represented by a box plot (or box-and-whisker plot). A box plot shows how data are clustered around the median and spread out along a number line.

You can draw a box plot using five values, collectively known as the 5-point summary.
Example:

- Least value = 2
- Lower quartile (Q_1) = 4
- Median (Q_2) = 6
- Upper quartile (Q_3) = 11
- Greatest value = 15

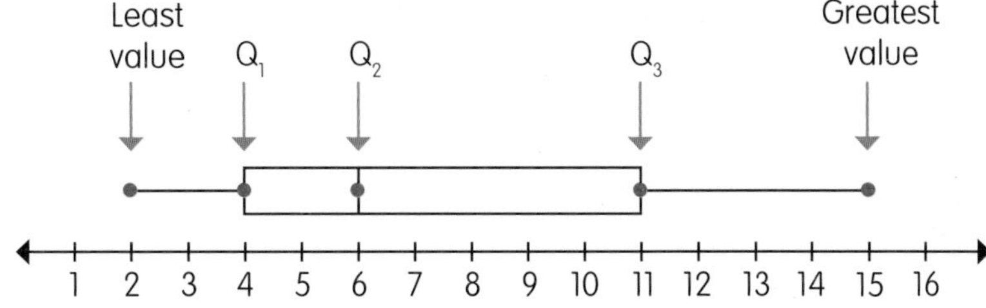

▶ Quick Check

The data below are the scores of some students for a math quiz.
Answer each question.

8	6	7	8	6	5	6	9	8	5

4. Draw a box plot of the scores and label it with the 5-point summary.

Finding and interpreting the mean absolute deviation of a set of data

The mean absolute deviation (MAD) of a set of data is the average distance of the data values from the mean of the data. It is the sum of the distances divided by the total number of data values.

Consider the data set, {1, 3, 7, 9}. The mean of the data is $\frac{(1 + 3 + 7 + 9)}{4} = 5$.

Using a number line, you can find the distance of each data value from the mean.

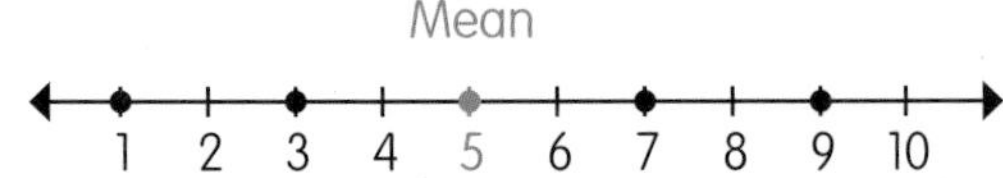

Value	Distance from the mean
1	4 units
3	2 units
7	2 units
9	4 units

$$\text{MAD} = \frac{(4 + 2 + 2 + 4)}{4}$$
$$= 3$$

Since distances are never negative, MAD is never a negative number.

Data that are clustered near the mean will have a small MAD.
Data that are spread over a wide range will have a greater MAD.

▶ Quick Check

The data below are the scores of some players for a game. Answer each question.

19	15	12	10	18
23	21	14	16	12

5 Find the mean of the scores.

6 Find the MAD of the scores.

Expressing a part of a whole as a fraction or a percent

Express 3 liters out of 12 liters as a fraction and as a percent.

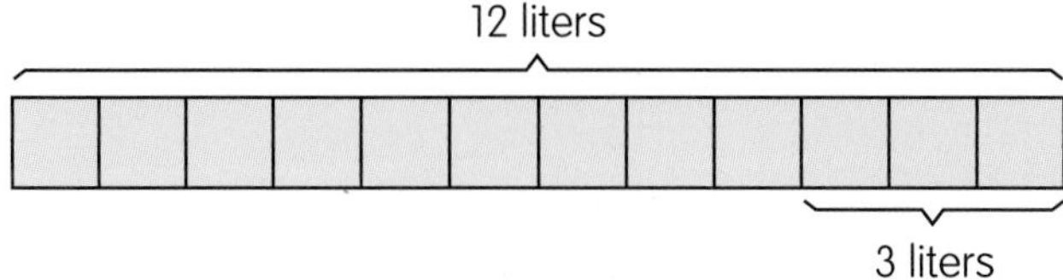

$\frac{3}{12} = \frac{1}{4}$

To find the percent, rewrite $\frac{1}{4}$ as an equivalent fraction with a denominator of 100.

$$\begin{aligned}\frac{1}{4} &= \frac{1 \cdot 25}{4 \cdot 25} \\ &= \frac{25}{100} \\ &= 25\%\end{aligned}$$

So, 3 liters out of 12 liters can be expressed as the fraction $\frac{1}{4}$ or as 25%.

Express the remaining 9 liters out of 12 liters as a percent.

100% – 25% = 75%   Subtract 25% from 100%.

So, 9 liters out of 12 liters as a percent is 75%.

▶ Quick Check

Answer each question

7. Express 10 ounces out of 25 ounces of baking flour as a fraction in simplest form.

8. 12 out of 40 pieces of fruit in a basket are lemons. What fraction of the pieces of fruit are lemons? Write your answer in simplest form.

9. If there are 36 boys in a group of 50 students, what percent of the students are girls?

Expressing a fraction or a decimal as a percent, and vice versa

a Express $\frac{7}{9}$ as a percent. Round your answer to the nearest hundredth.

$\frac{7}{9} = \frac{7}{9} \cdot 100\%$ Multiply the fraction by 100%.

$= \frac{700}{9}\%$ Write as an improper fraction.

$= 77.78\%$ Express the fraction as a decimal. Then, round.

b Express 55% as a fraction in simplest form.

$55\% = \frac{55}{100}$ Express the percent as a fraction.

$= \frac{55 \div 5}{100 \div 5}$ Divide both the numerator and denominator by the greatest common factor, 5.

$= \frac{11}{20}$

c $126\% = \frac{126}{100}$ Express the percent as a fraction.

$= 1.26$ Express the fraction as a decimal.

▶ Quick Check

Write each percent as a fraction or a mixed number in simplest form.

10 54%

11 115%

12 19.5%

13 1.4%

Write each percent as a decimal.

14 28%

15 9%

16 34.5%

17 256%

Expressing a ratio as a fraction or a percent

A ratio that compares a part to a whole can also be expressed as a fraction and as a percent.

The trees in an orchard are pear trees and apple trees. The ratio of pear trees to apple trees is 7 to 13.

a What fraction of the trees are pear trees?

b What percent of the trees are pear trees?

a

Number of pear trees = 7 units
Total number of trees = 7 + 13 = 20 units

$$\frac{\text{Number of pear trees}}{\text{Total number of trees}} = \frac{7}{20}$$

So, the fraction of pear trees to all the trees is $\frac{7}{20}$.

b $\frac{7}{20} \cdot 100\% = \frac{700}{20}\%$ Multiply the fraction by 100%.

$= 35\%$ Simplify.

So, 35% of the trees in the orchard are pear trees.

▶ Quick Check

Answer each question.

18 A bookcase holds 20 history books, 23 science fiction books, and 49 mystery books.

a What fraction of the books are science fiction books?

b What percent of the books are science fiction books?

Solving a histogram problem

The table shows the heights of 78 trees in a park rounded to the nearest foot.

Height (ft)	Number of Trees
60–69	11
70–79	20
80–89	22
90–99	15
100–109	6
110–119	4

The histogram displays the information about the heights of trees.

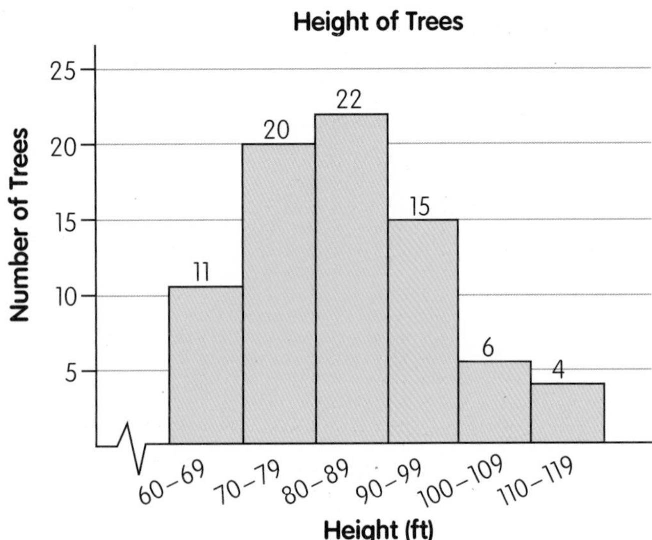

The heights of 25 trees are at least 90 feet. 42 of 78 trees have heights of 70 to 89 feet. So, about 54% of the trees are from 70 to 89 feet tall.

▶ Quick Check

Answer each question.

19 The table shows the mass of 100 steel bars rounded to the nearest kilogram.

a Draw a histogram to display this information.

b How many steel bars have a mass from 10 to 39 kilograms?

c What percent of the steel bars have a mass of at least 20 kilograms, but less than 50 kilograms?

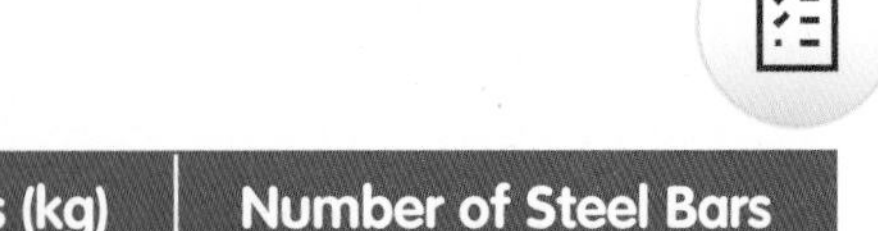

Mass (kg)	Number of Steel Bars
10–19	15
20–29	33
30–39	18
40–49	24
50–59	10

Name: ______________________ Date: ______________

1 Random Sampling Methods

Learning Objectives:

- Understand the concepts of a population and sample.
- Apply different random sampling methods.
- Simulate a random sampling process.

New Vocabulary

population
sample
sample size
random sample
unbiased sample
biased sample
simple random sampling
stratified random sampling
systematic random sampling

A grocery chain has more than 500 stores located in 17 states. To find out about their customers' opinions of service in its stores, the grocery chain decides to survey 2,550 customers, 150 in each state. Customers will be surveyed at 5 stores in each state, with the store numbers randomly chosen using a random number table. In each store, customers exiting the store will be selected at 15-minute intervals. Explain how the survey employs three methods of random sampling.

ENGAGE

Recall how you find the average speed of a car. Discuss what the difference between constant speed and average speed is. Now, make a list of information you would need to find the average speed of cars on a freeway during peak hours. Share your list.

LEARN Identify a suitable sampling method

1. In statistics, a population is the entire group of members (people, objects, or events) from which information is drawn. Information is gathered to understand characteristics of a population, for example, the average salaries of adults between ages 20 and 30 in the United States. It may be impractical to study or analyze all members of a large population. Instead, you can choose a part or a sample of the population to study and observe. The number of members in a sample is called the sample size.

   You may wonder what the average starting salary of college graduates is in the United States. In this situation, all college graduates in the United States make up the population that you want to study. The characteristic you want to know is their starting salaries. It is too time consuming and impractical to gather information from all college graduates across the country. Instead, you can select a sample of 1,000 college graduates to represent the entire population.

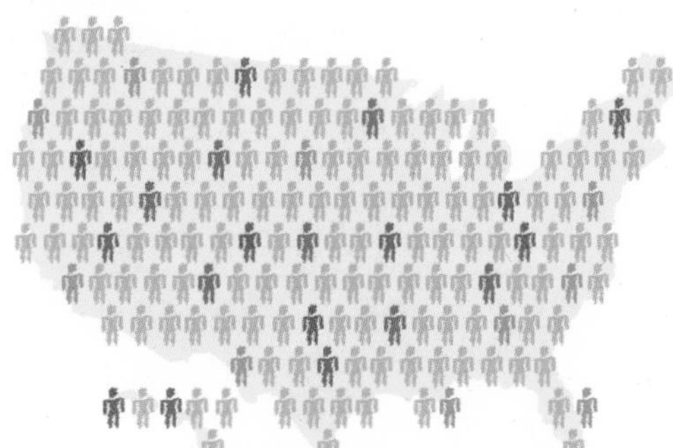

2 If you were to study a sample of 1,000 college graduates, and then use your observations to make conclusions about all college graduates in the United States, you would have to ensure that the graduates in your sample are representative of all college graduates in the United States. To ensure that your sample is representative, you can choose a random sample. A random sample is sometimes called an unbiased sample. A random sample has two characteristics:

- Every member of the population has an equal chance of being selected.
- Selection of members is independent of each other.

You cannot predict which members of a population will be chosen for a random sample because members are selected randomly. A sample in which members are not randomly selected is called a biased sample.

3 Simple random sampling is a sampling method in which every member of a population has an equal chance of being selected for the sample. In other words, you select members from a population without any pre-planned order. Some of the examples include:

a Using a sampling frame
In carrying out a household survey using telephone interviews, you may randomly flip to a page in a telephone directory and randomly choose a telephone number on the page. You repeat the process until you have gathered enough members for your sample.

b Lottery method
To generate a random sample of 50 students from a school population, you may assign a unique number to each student. Then, randomly pick numbers from a box that holds all the numbers, until you have picked 50.

c Using a random number table

Suppose you want to pick a random sample of 30 people from a town that has 500 residents. You can first assign a unique 3-digit number from 001 to 500 to each resident. Then, use a random number table like the one shown below to select the members of the sample.

	1	2	3	4	5	6	7	8	9	10	11	12	13	14	15	16	17	18	19	20
1	8	0	9	4	2	5	2	5	6	2	4	7	1	3	4	7	7	4	3	3
2	3	5	6	3	2	1	9	8	8	2	1	1	9	0	4	5	2	6	1	8
3	1	3	3	0	6	3	3	1	3	7	5	3	9	6	9	3	8	7	3	8
4	3	5	6	5	0	0	1	6	2	2	4	3	6	4	3	2	4	7	9	6
5	7	8	5	0	5	9	2	6	5	5	8	8	7	3	1	1	2	1	9	2
6	4	4	9	0	5	4	1	7	9	7	2	7	6	1	5	3	5	9	8	1
7	6	5	4	5	9	1	0	4	9	3	1	8	8	8	1	9	7	5	3	7
8	3	6	2	6	5	9	9	5	1	2	1	5	9	7	5	3	9	2	2	3
9	4	6	6	5	4	8	2	0	7	5	5	4	0	6	1	2	9	6	6	3
10	6	4	9	8	7	5	1	9	0	4	7	4	7	8	1	8	6	8	3	2
11	6	7	2	2	9	8	6	9	9	3	6	1	7	8	7	5	4	8	8	3
12	9	7	4	8	5	9	3	2	5	1	1	5	2	7	2	1	0	0	3	3
13	5	6	4	1	1	4	1	7	1	4	1	9	7	4	3	4	8	1	6	5
14	7	4	4	4	9	2	0	0	8	8	4	0	5	8	8	2	4	3	9	8
15	8	2	7	9	3	0	1	9	4	6	7	2	3	7	4	3	3	9	7	9
16	0	1	6	1	7	6	1	7	1	0	2	4	2	3	6	7	2	8	9	1
17	7	3	8	8	9	7	5	9	7	5	5	5	6	6	2	4	9	9	7	7
18	7	8	3	0	4	7	1	4	3	6	9	5	2	9	1	9	1	8	0	4
19	9	8	8	7	4	2	1	6	6	5	2	6	4	5	3	5	8	4	3	0
20	1	2	6	1	2	5	1	6	8	5	6	9	2	3	1	0	3	9	3	9

Choose any row. Then, from left to right, read off random 3-digit numbers from 001 to 500. If the number is greater than 500, disregard the number and move on to the next 3-digit number. The numbers are then matched to the members of the town.

For example, randomly pick row 20. From row 20, select numbers 126, 125, 168, 569 (discarded), 231, 039, and so on, until you get 30 numbers.

d Using a computer

Instead of using a random number table, you may also use a random number generator on a calculator or a computer to generate random numbers.

You want a sample of 50 households. Suppose you randomly flip to a page of a telephone directory and pick the first 50 telephone numbers. Is the sample unbiased? Explain.

4 In **stratified random sampling**, you first divide the population into nonoverlapping groups by their characteristics. Then, randomly select members from each group. Some of the examples include:

a Suppose you want to know the mean salary of working adults in a city. You first divide them into age groups, and then randomly select adults from each age group. The number of adults selected from each age group is not necessarily the same.

b Suppose you want to conduct a survey on whether people prefer to eat organic food. To make sure that you have an equal number of men and women in your survey, you may want to divide the people by their genders.

5 To carry out **systematic random sampling**, you select the first member randomly, and then select subsequent members at regular intervals. Some of the examples include:

a There are 300 households in a district. Suppose you want to obtain a 25-member sample, label all the households in a numeric sequence, and divide the number of households by the sample size: $\frac{300}{25} = 12$. Pick the first household at random. Then, select every twelfth household from there for subsequent members of the sample. For example, if the first household is number 5, then the numbers for subsequent members are 17, 29, 41, 53, 65, and so on.

b Suppose you want to conduct an opinion poll among tourists at a historical site and you intend to spend 4 hours to poll 30 tourists at random, divide the amount of time by the sample size: $\frac{4 \cdot 60}{30} = 8$ minutes. After polling the first tourist at random, select subsequent tourists at 8-minute intervals.

c Suppose a quality inspector intends to pick a random sample of 25 cans out of 5,000 cans of food from a production line for examination, he can divide the total number of cans by the sample size: $\frac{5{,}000}{25} = 200$. After he picks the first can of food, he will then pick every 200th can from the production line for inspection.

Activity **Exploring how a random sampling process affects data collection**

Work in groups.

Activity 1

1 Choose 40 students to participate in this activity. Ask how long it took them to get to school today.

2 Assign each of the 40 students a 2-digit number from 01 to 40.

③ Use the random number table on page 215 to pick five 2-digit numbers. Discard any 2-digit numbers greater than 40.

Example:

6545 **91<u>04</u>** **93<u>18</u>** **88<u>19</u>** **75<u>37</u>** **<u>27</u>35**

④ Ask the five students whose numbers match those you picked in ③ the following question and record the results.

About how many minutes did it take you to commute to school today?

⑤ Find the mean and the mean absolute deviation of the data you collected in ④.

⑥ Repeat ③ to ⑤ to generate new random samples, and to collect and analyze the data from each sample.

⑦ **Mathematical Habit 6 Use precise mathematical language**
Does the mean number of minutes vary greatly from sample to sample? Does the mean absolute deviation vary greatly from sample to sample? What are some problems you encountered in the random sampling process? Describe.

Activity 2

① Read up about the strengths and weaknesses of the three random sampling methods.

② Make a list of the strengths and weaknesses in a table.

Sampling method	Strengths	Weaknesses
Simple random sampling		
Stratified random sampling		
Systematic random sampling		

③ **Mathematical Habit 2 Use mathematical reasoning**
Do you find that a weakness of one method can be addressed by another method? Explain.

Every sampling method has its strengths and weaknesses. Each method is designed for specific purposes. You may find that more than one method can be used in a particular situation or it may be necessary to combine two methods to obtain the best possible random sample.

TRY Practice identifying a suitable sampling method

For each situation, describe which sampling method you will choose and how you will apply it. Justify your choice.

1. A journalist would like to find out what attendees think of the large computer fair they are attending. He decides to interview 50 people.

2. A poultry farm keeps 3,000 birds. An agricultural safety and health officer needs to check whether any of the birds might be infected with a virus and would like to take a random sample of 20 birds for inspection.

3. A local authority plans to conduct an opinion poll of people in McCree County as to whether they are in favor of putting more restaurants in a historical landmark site. The county consists of six districts. The authority intends to generate a random sample of 300 to 400 people.

4. A truckload of 3,000 oranges was delivered to a wholesale market. You are allowed to check 1% of the oranges as a random sample before deciding whether to accept the shipment.

5. A grocer would like to find out what items the store should carry to attract more customers. The grocer wants to survey 100 people in the neighborhood.

Name: ______________________ Date: ______________

INDEPENDENT PRACTICE

State which sampling method is being described.

1. A frozen yogurt store sells 5 flavors: vanilla, chocolate, strawberry, macadamia nut, and peppermint. To check the quality of the frozen yogurt, 5 tubs of each flavor were sampled.

2. A group of students conducted an online poll of Internet users by randomly selecting 500 Internet users.

3. To check the freshness of the bagels at a bakery, the baker randomly picked 5 bagels at an interval of every hour.

4. Unique numbers were assigned to the members of a country club. The club manager used a random number generator to choose 150 numbers that were matched to members of the club.

5. Out of 100 students, the teachers randomly choose the first student and every sixth student thereafter.

6. To assess pollution levels in a region, water samples are taken from 5 rivers and 2 lakes for analysis.

Refer to the situation to answer each question.

7. 2,000 runners participated in a marathon. You want to randomly choose 60 of the runners to find out how long it took each one to run the race. Describe how you would select the 60 runners if you use a

   a. simple random sampling method.

   b. systematic random sampling method.

   c. stratified random sampling method.

Refer to the situation to answer each question.

8. There are 1,650 trees growing in 5 areas within a park. The trees are numbered from 1 to 1,650. A systematic random sample of 40 trees is needed to check whether there are fungi causing root rot among the trees. Describe how you would carry out a

   a. systematic random sampling method.

   b. stratified random sampling method.

9. A poll is taken in a small town to find out which candidate voters will choose in an election. A stratified sampling method is used to generate a random sample of 500 residents. The table shows the town population and the sample size within each group.

	Men	Women
Number of Residents	5,000	8,000
Sample Size	250	250

   a. The stratified random sample has been criticized for not being representative of the population. What could possibly be the problem with the random sample?

   b. How would you improve the above stratified random sampling?

Name: ______________________ Date: ______________

2 Making Inferences About Populations

Learning Objectives:

- Make inferences about a population using statistics from a sample.
- Use an inference to estimate a population mean.
- Make comparative inferences about two populations using two sets of sample statistics.

New Vocabulary
inference

The mean test scores for class A and class B are 76 and 65, respectively. The mean absolute deviation of class A is 20.5 and that of class B is 5. Chris thinks that class A performed better. Explain if you agree or disagree with Chris.

ENGAGE

Susan has a bag of marbles. She chooses a marble and then replaces it. Of her ten trials, she picks a red marble 8 times. What is reasonable to conclude about the bag of marbles? Explain.

LEARN Use an inference to estimate a population mean

1. Statistics is used to gain information about a population by examining a sample of the population. You are able to make valid inferences about a population from a sample only if the sample is representative of the population. As such, you expect the sample to inherit characteristics you want to study from the population. To ensure that a sample is representative of the population, you have to take random samples.

   When you make inferences about a population, you draw conclusions about the population based on a sample. Inference is necessary because characteristics of a large population are often impossible to obtain. For example, it would be difficult to collect data on the number of eggs laid and eaglets hatched in every eagle's nest in a state. Instead, you can use a random sample to make inferences about the population.

   When you infer characteristics of a population based on a random sample, you are making an approximation. Suppose you collect numerical data about a sample and calculate that the mean of the data is 50, you may infer that the mean for the population is approximately 50. In reality, the mean for the population may not be exactly 50, because the population's characteristics may not be exactly the same as the sample's.

2 Suppose that a population consists of 10 test scores:

67, 80, 54, 76, 90, 48, 65, 60, 73, and 80.

Since the population is small, the population mean can be easily calculated.

$$\text{Population mean} = \frac{67 + 80 + 54 + 76 + 90 + 48 + 65 + 60 + 73 + 80}{10}$$
$$= 69.3$$

Suppose you take a random sample of four of the test scores: $S_1 = \{80, 48, 73, 80\}$.

$$\text{Sample mean of } S_1 = \frac{80 + 48 + 73 + 80}{4}$$
$$= 70.25$$

Suppose you take another random sample of four of the test scores:
$S_2 = \{67, 54, 90, 60\}$.

$$\text{Sample mean of } S_2 = \frac{67 + 54 + 90 + 60}{4}$$
$$= 67.75$$

Suppose you take yet another random sample of four of the test scores:
$S_3 = \{80, 54, 76, 90\}$.

$$\text{Sample mean of } S_3 = \frac{80 + 54 + 76 + 90}{4}$$
$$= 75$$

You can then find the average of all of the sample means:

$$\text{Average of sample means} = \frac{70.25 + 67.75 + 75}{3}$$
$$= 71$$

When you average the three sample means, you get 71. This value is also an approximation of the population mean. In general, the population mean is usually unknown.

The sample means show that none of them is equal to the population mean, all three sample means are only approximations of the population mean.

Different samples of the same sample size produce different approximations of the population mean. The mean of the sample means is also an estimate of the population mean.

Activity Using statistics from a sample to describe variability of a population

Work in pairs.

(1) Find a book with 200 to 300 pages. Determine which sampling method you intend to use to find the mean word length of the book.

The population is made up of all the words in the book.
The length of a word is defined by the number of letters in it.
The population characteristic is the mean word length.

(2) Generate five random samples. Each sample consists of 20 words.

(3) For each sample, record the length of each of the 20 words in a table. Then, calculate the mean and the mean absolute deviation for each sample.

	Word	Word Length	Distance from Mean
1			
2			
⋮			
20			
Total			
Sample mean			
Mean absolute deviation (MAD)			

(4) Calculate the mean of the sample means when you have completed (1) to (3) for all 20 samples.

(5) **Mathematical Habit 2 Use mathematical reasoning**
What is the estimate of the population mean word length? By observing the mean absolute deviations of the five samples, describe informally whether the words in the book vary greatly in length.

TRY Practice using an inference to estimate a population mean

Solve.

1. A population consists of the test scores of 60 students. A random sample of 10 scores has been collected from the population: {18, 10, 6, 9, 10, 14, 17, 10, 9, 11}.

   a Calculate the sample mean and use it to approximate the population mean.

   $$\text{Sample mean} = \frac{18 + 10 + 6 + 9 + 10 + 14 + 17 + 10 + 9 + 11}{\quad}$$

   $$= \underline{\qquad\qquad}$$

   b Calculate the mean absolute deviation (MAD) of the sample.

Data Item	Mean	Distance of Data from the Mean
18		
10		
6		
9		
10		
14		
17		
10		
9		
11		

Sum of the distances =

MAD =

c Draw a dot plot for the scores and the mean.

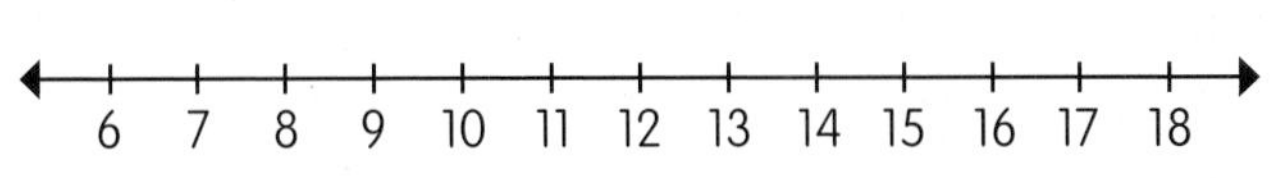

Score

Draw a horizontal number line that extends from 6 to 18.

d Using the ratio of the MAD to the mean and the dot plot, describe informally how varied the scores are.

2 A random sample of ages {15, 5, 8, 7, 18, 6, 15, 17, 6, 15} of 10 children was collected from a population of 100 children.

a Calculate the sample mean age of the children and use it to estimate the population mean age.

b Calculate the MAD of the sample.

c Calculate the MAD to mean ratio.

d Draw a dot plot for the ages and the mean age.

e Using the MAD to mean ratio and the dot plot, describe informally how varied the population ages are.

ENGAGE

The mean scores of a science test for Class A and Class B are both 75. The range of scores for Class A is 50 and that of Class B is 10. How do you know which class performed better? Explain your reasoning.

LEARN Make comparative inferences about two populations

1 The weights of the players on two football teams are summarized in the box plots.

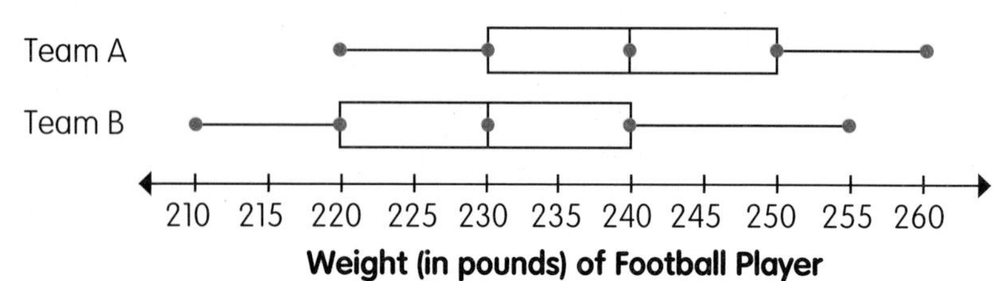

When comparing the means or medians of two populations, take into account their measures of variation.

a Show that the two teams have the same measure of variation (that is, the difference between the three quartiles) and the same interquartile range.

Team A

$Q_2 - Q_1 = 240 - 230$
$= 10$ lb

$Q_3 - Q_2 = 250 - 240$
$= 10$ lb

Interquartile range $= 250 - 230$
$= 20$ lb

Team B

$Q_2 - Q_1 = 230 - 220$
$= 10$ lb

$Q_3 - Q_2 = 240 - 230$
$= 10$ lb

Interquartile range $= 240 - 220$
$= 20$ lb

So, the difference between the quartiles and the interquartile range are the same for the two teams.

b Express the difference in median weight in terms of the interquartile range.

$$\frac{\text{Difference in median weight}}{\text{Interquartile range}} = \frac{240 - 230}{20} = \frac{10}{20} = \frac{1}{2} \text{ lb}$$

c What inference can you draw about the weight distributions of the players of the two teams?

50% of the Team A players are heavier than the upper quartile of Team B. Only 25% of the Team B players are heavier than the median of Team A. Team A players are heavier in general.

2 A class of students completed two science tests. The scores are presented in the box plots.

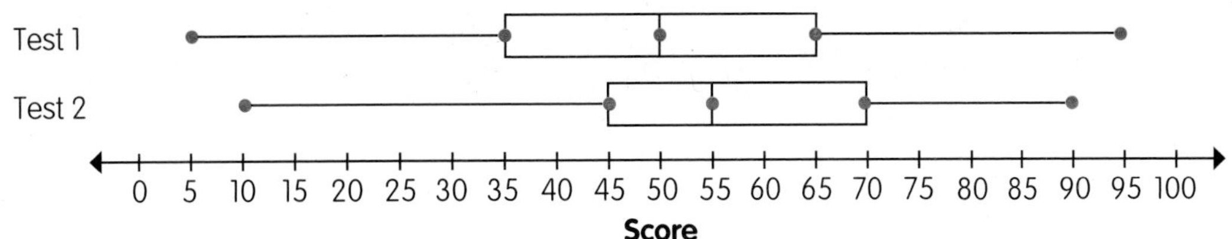

a Find the median and the range of each test.

Test 1

Median = 50
Range = 95 – 5
= 90

Test 2

Median = 55
Range = 90 – 10
= 80

b Which test has a wider spread of data?

Test 1 has a greater range than Test 2. So, Test 1 has a wider spread of data.

c On which test did the class perform better?

Test 1: 50% of the scores are between 35 and 65.

Test 2: 50% of the scores are between 45 and 70.

So, the class performed better on Test 2.

The box plot visually shows that students did better on Test 2. On 4 of the 5 statistics of the 5-point summary, the results were better on Test 2 than on Test 1.

3 The table shows the game scores of Kyle and José.

Kyle's Scores	2	3	8	5	3	4	4	6	5	4
José's Scores	9	5	1	1	2	8	9	2	1	6

a Find the mean scores for Kyle and José.

Kyle's mean score

$= \frac{2+3+8+5+3+4+4+6+5+4}{10}$

$= \frac{44}{10}$

$= 4.4$

José mean score

$= \frac{9+5+1+1+2+8+9+2+1+6}{10}$

$= \frac{44}{10}$

$= 4.4$

b Calculate the mean absolute deviation of Kyle's and José's scores.

Kyle's Scores	Kyle's Mean	Distance of Data from the Mean	José's Scores	José's Mean	Distance of Data from the Mean
2	4.4	2.4	9	4.4	4.6
3	4.4	1.4	5	4.4	0.6
8	4.4	3.6	1	4.4	3.4
5	4.4	0.6	1	4.4	3.4
3	4.4	1.4	2	4.4	2.4
4	4.4	0.4	8	4.4	3.6
4	4.4	0.4	9	4.4	4.6
6	4.4	1.6	2	4.4	2.4
5	4.4	0.6	1	4.4	3.4
4	4.4	0.4	6	4.4	1.6

Sum of the distances for Kyle
= 2.4 + 1.4 + 3.6 + 0.6 + 1.4 + 0.4 + 0.4 + 1.6 + 0.6 + 0.4
= 12.8

MAD for Kyle $= \frac{12.8}{10}$
$= 1.28$

Sum of the distances for José
= 4.6 + 0.6 + 3.4 + 3.4 + 2.4 + 3.6 + 4.6 + 2.4 + 3.4 + 1.6
= 30

MAD for José $= \frac{30}{10}$
$= 3$

c Draw separate dot plots for Kyle's scores and for José's scores.

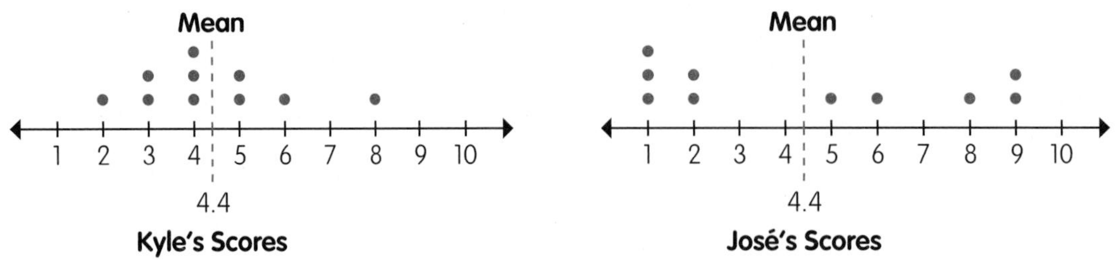

d Compare Kyle's and José's statistics. Then, compare their dot plots.

Both Kyle and José have the same mean score. José's mean absolute deviation is more than twice of Kyle's mean absolute deviation. The dots in Kyle's dot plot tend to cluster around the mean score while the dots in José's dot plot tend to be spread out from the mean score. This confirms that Kyle's mean absolute deviation is less than José's mean absolute deviation.

e What conclusion can you make about the two players' performance in the game?

Kyle's performance is more consistent since most of his scores are close to the mean. José's performance is more inconsistent since his scores vary widely between very low and very high scores.

TRY Practice making comparative inferences about two populations

Solve.

1. The ages of two groups of children are summarized in the box plots.

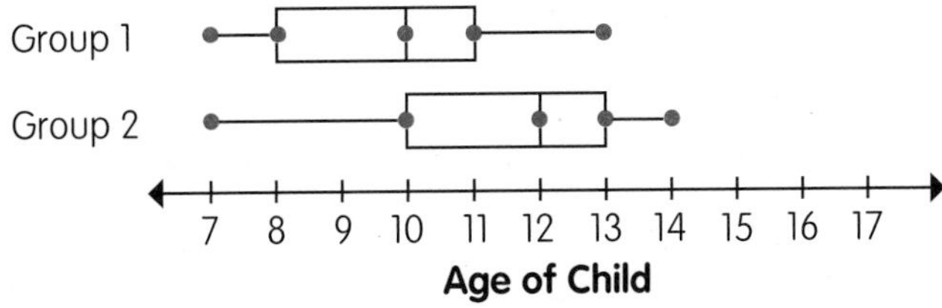

a Show that the two groups have the same measure of variation (that is, the difference between quartiles) and the same interquartile range.

b Express the difference in median age in terms of the interquartile range.

c What inference can you draw about the age distributions of the children in the two groups?

2 Two classes took a math test. The results are summarized in the box plots.

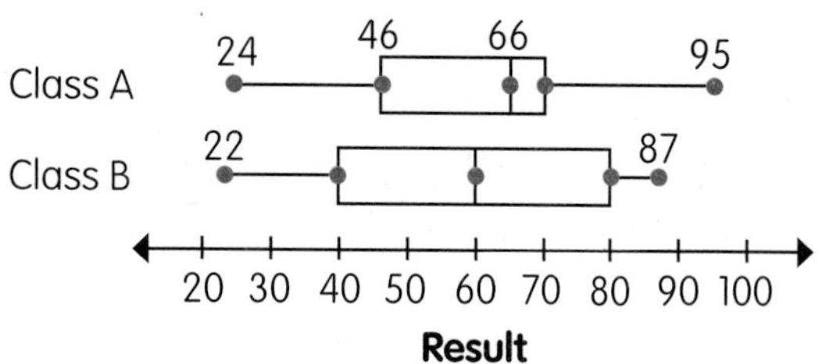

a For which class are the data more spread out? Explain.

b Comment on the performance of the two classes.

3 The numbers of questions that two groups of students answered correctly in a science test are shown in the table.

Group A	Group B
5	11
15	13
20	10
14	14
6	18
19	15
10	10
10	11
7	6
14	12

a Find the mean number of correct answers for each of the two groups.

b Calculate the mean absolute deviation of each of the two groups.

c Draw separate dot plots for the two groups.

d Interpret the above statistics and the dot plots.

e What conclusion can you make about the performance of the two groups of students on the test?

Name: ______________________ Date: ______________

INDEPENDENT PRACTICE

Solve.

1 A random sample of a certain type of ball bearing produces a mean weight of 28 grams and a mean absolute deviation of 2.1 grams. What can be inferred from the sample about the population mean weight of this type of ball bearing?

2 You interviewed a random sample of 25 marathon runners and compiled the following statistics.

Mean time to complete the race = 220 minutes
MAD = 50 minutes

What can you infer about the time to complete the race among the population of runners represented by your sample?

Use the random sample below to answer each question. Round each answer to the nearest tenth.

3 A random sample of the volume, in milliliters, of 15 servings of orange juice from a vending machine is shown on the right.

251	254	254	249	250
248	250	252	251	253
247	245	255	254	251

a Use the sample mean volume to estimate the population mean volume of a serving of orange juice.

b Calculate the MAD and the MAD to mean ratio.

c Use the MAD to informally infer whether the volume of orange juice in a serving varies greatly.

Use the box plots on the right to answer each question.

4 Two large random samples of car speeds on two highways from 4 P.M. to 6 P.M. were collected. The data were summarized in two box plots.

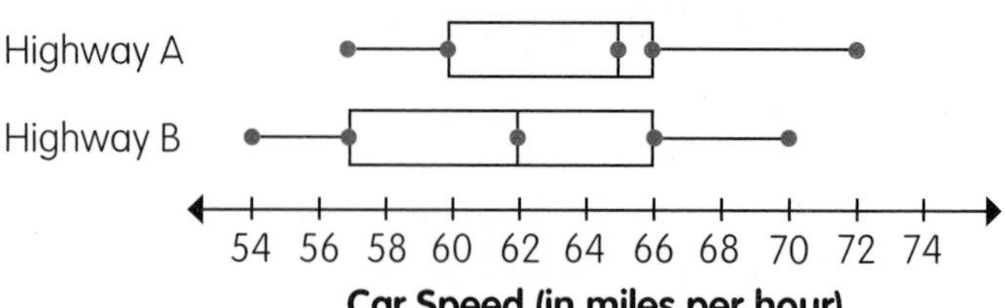

a By comparing the interquartile ranges of the two box plots, what can you infer about car speeds on the two highways for the middle 50% of the cars?

b By comparing the medians of the two plots, what inference can you make?

c Suppose the speed limit on the two highways is 65 miles per hour. What percent of the cars drove faster than the speed limit on the two highways?

d What can you infer about the overall car speeds on the two highways?

Solve.

5 Logan and Cole go jogging every morning for several weeks. The following are the mean and the MAD of the distances they jog.

	Logan	Cole
Mean	5.25 km	4.20 km
MAD	2 km	0.75 km

a What would you infer about the distances they jog if you only compare their mean distances?

b What can you conclude if you take into account both the mean and the MAD for your comparison?

Use the random samples below to answer each question.
Round each answer to the nearest tenth.

 **6** Three random samples of time taken, in seconds, to solve a crossword puzzle during a competition were collected.

S_1 = {100, 87, 95, 103, 110, 90, 84, 88}
S_2 = {75, 98, 120, 106, 70, 79, 100, 90}
S_3 = {60, 68, 110, 88, 78, 90, 104, 73}

a Calculate the mean time of each of the three samples.

b Estimate the population mean time of the competition using the mean of the three sample means.

c Combine S_1, S_2, and S_3 into one sample and use the mean in **b** to calculate the MAD of the combined sample.

d If you use the MAD found in **c** to gauge the time variation among competitors, what can you infer?

Use the random samples below to answer each question.
Round each answer to the nearest hundredth when you can.

7 Below are the history test scores of two classes of 20 students each.

Class A				
84	63	90	68	42
43	31	60	88	70
25	40	32	37	79
66	55	65	35	42

Class B				
63	66	62	66	80
55	72	77	66	58
66	68	44	60	70
66	76	75	71	74

a Find the range of scores for each class.

b Calculate the mean scores for each class.

c Calculate the MAD for each class.

d By comparing the mean scores and the MADs of the two classes, what can you infer about the performance of the two classes?

Name: ______________________ Date: ______________

3 Defining Outcomes, Events, and Sample Space

Learning Objective:
- Identify outcomes, sample space, and events.

New Vocabulary
outcome
sample space
event
experiment

A random number generator forms a 3-digit number from the digits 1, 2, 3, and 4. List the outcomes and sample space for this event. What are the favorable outcomes of getting an even number?

ENGAGE

Max is mixing red, yellow, and blue paint. What are all the different combinations he can make using two of the colors? Explain.

LEARN Identify outcomes, sample space, and events

1 When you flip a coin, it will land heads up or tails up. You can say that there are two possible outcomes of the activity: heads or tails.

The collection of all the possible outcomes of an activity is known as the sample space. Sample space is usually denoted by the letter *S*.

Head

Tail

2 An activity such as flipping a coin or rolling a number die is often called an experiment. A number die has six face values. When you roll a number die, one of these six values will appear on the top face:

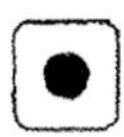
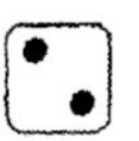

You can write the sample space of this experiment as {1, 2, 3, 4, 5, 6}.

Use braces { } to show the set of outcomes in a sample space, or to show the outcomes favorable to an event.

3 The following cards are placed face down on a table. Evelyn picks a card randomly and records the color.

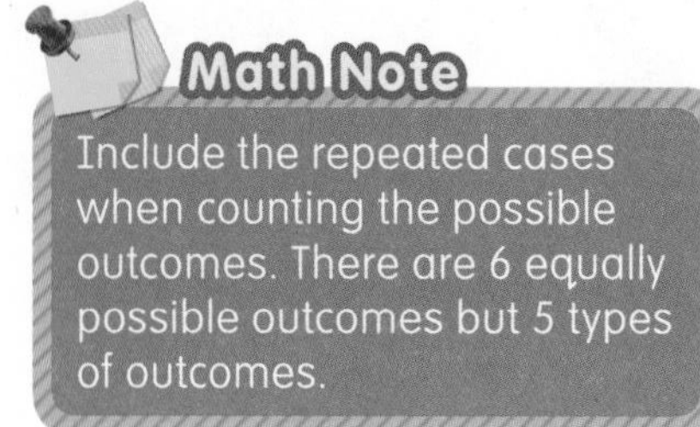

blue	green	purple	brown	green	white

There are 6 equally possible outcomes. However, there are 5 types of outcomes: blue, green, purple, brown, and white.

4 An event is a collection of outcomes from an activity. For example, when you roll a number die, the sample space is {1, 2, 3, 4, 5, 6}. The event of rolling an even number consists of the outcomes 2, 4, and 6.

Events are usually written with capital letters. If E stands for the event of getting an even number, you write E = {2, 4, 6} to show the outcomes favorable to event E.

5 There are 26 letters in the alphabet. Suppose you pick one letter randomly.

There are 26 outcomes in the sample space. The sample space is {A, B, C, D, E, F, G, H, I, J, K, L, M, N, O, P, Q, R, S, T, U, V, W, X, Y, Z}.

Let D stand for the event of picking a vowel,
E stand for the event of picking a letter that comes after the letter V in the alphabet, and
F stand for the event of picking a letter that is a consonant which comes before the letter P.

The outcomes favorable to each event are:
D = {A, E, I, O, U}
E = {W, X, Y, Z}
F = {B, C, D, F, G, H, J, K, L, M, N}

TRY Practice identifying outcomes, sample space, and events

Solve.

1. Jake spun the spinner on the right and recorded the numbers where the spinner lands.

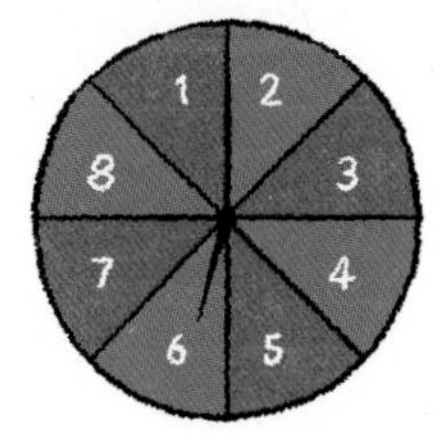

   a List all the possible outcomes.

   b State the number of outcomes in the sample space.

2. Select a letter from the list of letters: A, D, E, G, K.

   a List all the possible outcomes.

   b State the number of outcomes in the sample space.

3. Use the letter cards below to form all possible 3-letter English words.

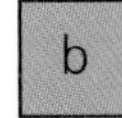

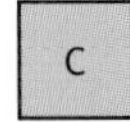

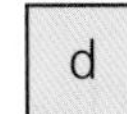

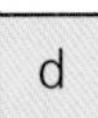

d

   a List all the possible outcomes.

   b State the number of outcomes in the sample space.

4. *Y* is the event of choosing a prime number from a list of whole numbers from 1 to 20.

   a List the outcomes favorable to event *Y*.

   The prime numbers up to 20 are _____, _____, _____, _____, _____, _____, _____, and _____.

   Y = {_____, _____, _____, _____, _____, _____, _____, _____}

   b State the number of outcomes in the sample space.

   You choose from _____ outcomes. There are _____ outcomes in the sample space.

5 You choose a shape from a bag containing these cardboard geometric shapes.

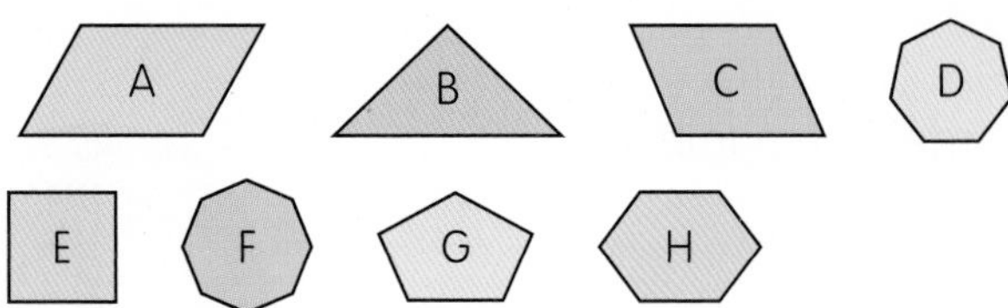

a State the number of outcomes in the sample space.

b X is the event of choosing a shape with at most 6 sides. List the outcomes favorable to event X.

X = {______, ______, ______, ______, ______, ______}

c Y is the event of choosing a shape with more than 4 angles. List the outcomes favorable to event Y.

Y = {______, ______, ______, ______}

6 X is the event of choosing a word with exactly two Es in it from the following list of words.

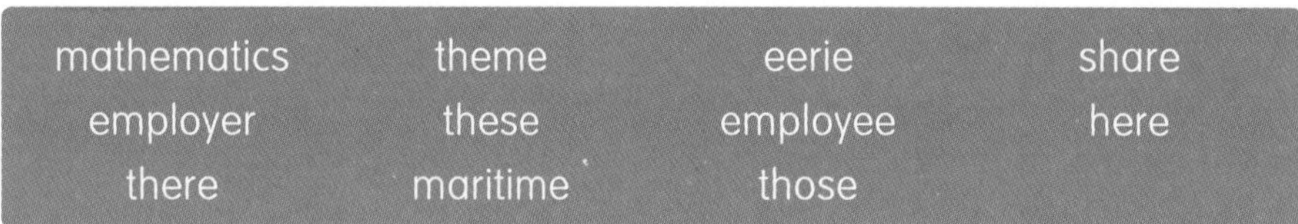

mathematics	theme	eerie	share
employer	these	employee	here
there	maritime	those	

a State the number of outcomes in the sample space.

b List all the outcomes favorable to event X.

7 Pedro flipped a coin twice and recorded the outcomes.

a List the outcomes in the sample space.

b Y is the event of having at least one coin landing heads up. State the number of outcomes favorable to event Y.

Name: ______________________ Date: ______________

INDEPENDENT PRACTICE

Solve.

1. A bag contains 2 red balls and 1 green ball. A ball is taken out from the bag. What are the types of outcomes?

2. A number die with faces numbered 1 to 6 is rolled once. What are the favorable outcomes for the event of getting a value that is evenly divisible by 3?

3. A spinner has 5 values, as shown in the diagram. You spin the spinner and record it lands.

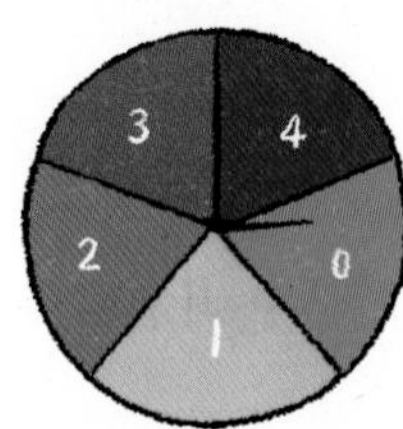

   a List all the outcomes in the sample space.

   b If event A is the event of landing on an even number, what are the outcomes favorable to event A?

4 A basketball coach has 5 forwards, 2 centers, and 5 guards. E is the event of the coach picking a forward to be the team captain. How many outcomes are favorable to event E?

5 A letter is selected from the letters in the name TYRANNOSAURUS REX. What is the number of possible outcomes?

6 A colored disk is drawn from a bag which contains the following disks.

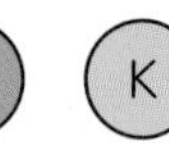

a If you record only the color of the disk, what are the types of outcomes?

b If you record only the letter on the disk, what are the types of outcomes?

c If you record both the color and the letter of the disk, what are the types of outcomes?

7. There are 10 multiple-choice questions in a test. A student gets 1 point for every correct answer and 0 points for every wrong answer. No point is awarded for a question that the student does not try to answer.

a What is the highest score a student could receive on the test?

b What is the lowest possible score a student could receive?

c What are the possible outcomes for a score on the multiple choice test?

8. A student is to be selected to play a supporting role in a drama from the list of names below.

Name	Age	Height (m)
Aki	14	1.69
Jack	15	1.58
Davi	14	1.80
Noah	16	1.55
Rachel	16	1.70
Maria	15	1.50

Name	Age	Height (m)
Diego	16	1.82
Chloe	14	1.66
Pedro	13	1.47
Eric	16	1.74
Carla	16	1.60
Ian	14	1.52

a X is the event that the selected student is 14 years old. List the outcomes favorable to event X.

b Y is the event that the selected student is at least 1.56 meters tall. List all the outcomes favorable to event Y.

c Z is the event that the selected student is at least 1.7 meters tall and at least 15 years old. How many outcomes are favorable to this event?

d W is the event that the name of the selected student has at most 4 letters. What outcomes are favorable to event W?

9 From the list of digits, 0, 5, 7, 8, you form a 3-digit number without any repeating digits. You do not include any numbers that start with 0.

a List all the outcomes of the sample space.

b List all the favorable outcomes for the event that the 3-digit number is an even number.

c List all the favorable outcomes for the event that the 3-digit number is an odd number.

10 You pick a whole number between 1 and 100. If *A* is the event that the number you picked is divisible by 3 and 7, what are the outcomes favorable to event *A*?

11 The five numeric tiles 5 6 7 8 9 are placed face down. You pick four tiles to form a 4-digit number. How many outcomes are favorable to the event of forming a number greater than 8,755?

Name: ______________________ Date: ______________

Finding Probability of Events

Learning Objectives:

- Calculate the probability of events.
- Use Venn diagrams to illustrate events and their relationships.
- Solve real-world problems involving probability.

New Vocabulary
probability
fair
biased
Venn diagram
mutually exclusive
complement
complementary events

The numbers 1 to 30 are each printed on an index card and placed in a pile. The pile of number cards are then shuffled and one card is randomly picked. Event E contains even numbers. Event T contains multiples of 3. Draw a Venn diagram to represent the sample space for this situation. Then, find the probability of picking a card that contains an even number that is also a multiple of 3.

ENGAGE

Suppose you randomly pick two of the cards on the right. Which do you think is more likely to occur, picking two cards with the same background color or two cards with the same letter? Explain your reasoning.

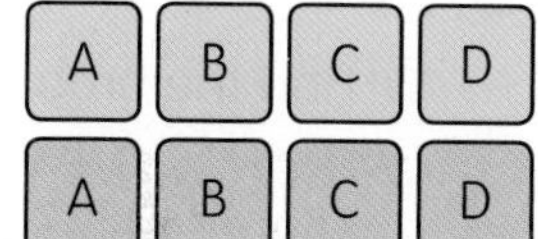

LEARN Use probability to describe the likelihood of an event

1. Suppose you pick a bead from one of the jars without looking. If you want to increase your chances of getting a black bead, you would probably choose Jar A.

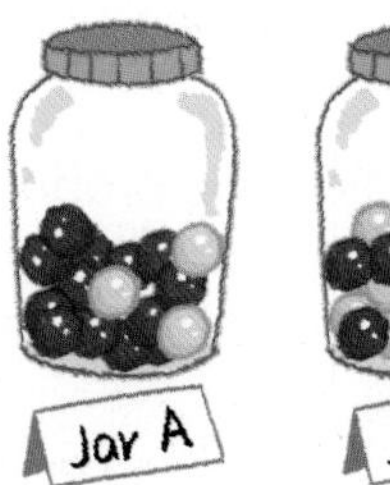

The word "chance" implies likelihood. Probability is a way to describe how good the chances are that an event will occur. A number from 0 to 1 is used to express the probability of an event.

A probability closer to 1 means that the chances of an event happening are more likely.
A probability closer to 0 means that the chances of an event happening are less likely.
A probability of 0.5 means that the event is equally likely to happen or not happen.

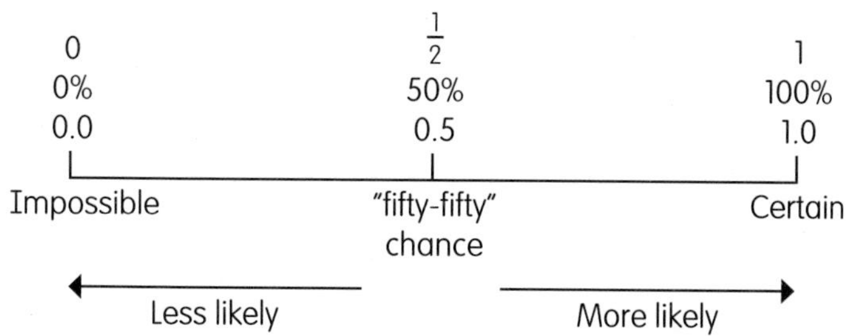

A probability can be expressed as a percent, a decimal, or a fraction between 0 and 1.

2 Suppose you flip a fair coin. The word "fair" means that the chances of the coin landing heads up or tails up are equal — the coin does not favor either outcome. A coin that favors a particular outcome is called biased.

Since the coin is equally likely to land heads up or tails up, the probability of the coin landing heads up is $\frac{1}{2}$ or 50%. The probability of the coin landing tails up is also $\frac{1}{2}$ or 50%.

It is impossible for the coin to land heads up and tails up at the same time. So, the probability of the coin landing heads up and tails up at the same time is 0.

Suppose a coin is biased such that it is more likely to land heads up than tails up. Will the probability of getting heads be greater than or less than $\frac{1}{2}$?

TRY Practice using probability to describe the likelihood of an event

Solve.

1 You roll a fair number die.

a Find the probability of getting a four.

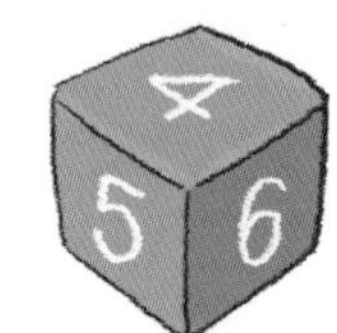

There are ______ outcomes when you roll a number die. All the outcomes are equally likely.

So, the probability of getting a four is ______.

b Find the probability of getting a seven.

It is impossible to get a seven when you roll a standard number die.

So, the probability of getting a seven is ______.

2 What is the probability that the arrow will point to a number when you spin the spinner on the right?

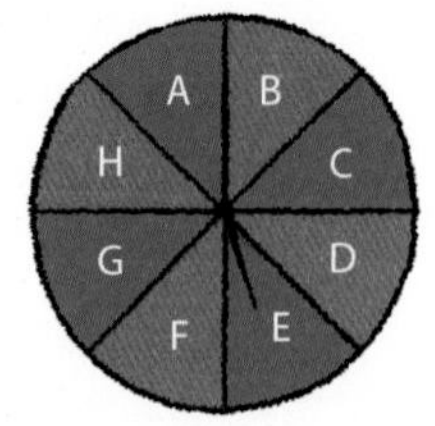

ENGAGE

Suppose you randomly pick two of the cards below. What is the probability of picking two cards with the same letter? Explain your answer.

A	B	C	D	A	B	C	D

LEARN Find the probability of an event

1 Suppose you pick a cube at random from a bag containing 6 red cubes, 9 blue cubes, and 5 green cubes. What is the probability of picking a blue cube?

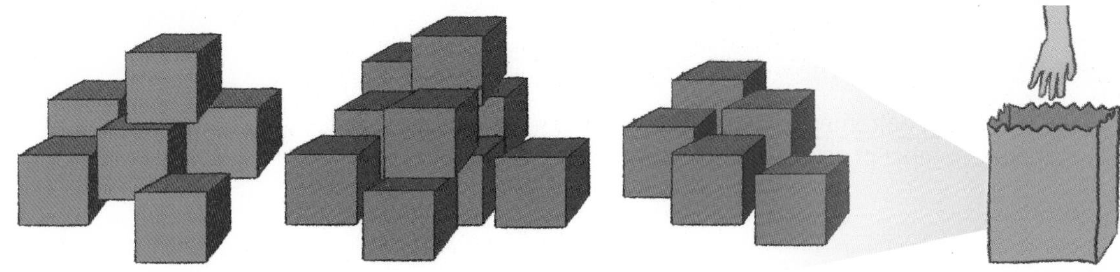

$6 + 9 + 5 = 20$

There are 20 possible outcomes of picking a cube.

Let *B* be the event of picking a blue cube.

Since there are 9 blue cubes, event *B* has 9 favorable outcomes.

There is a 9 out of 20 or $\frac{9}{20}$ chance of picking a blue cube.

$$P(B) = \frac{\text{Number of outcomes favorable to event } B}{\text{Total number of equally likely outcomes}}$$

$$= \frac{9}{20} \cdot 100\%$$

$$= 45\%$$

Write the probability of event *B* occurring as P(*B*).

There is a 45% chance of picking a blue cube.

The probability of an event *E* occurring, P(*E*), is given by:

$$P(E) = \frac{\text{Number of outcomes favorable to event } E}{\text{Total number of equally likely outcomes}} = \frac{m}{n}$$

where $0 \leq P(E) \leq 1$

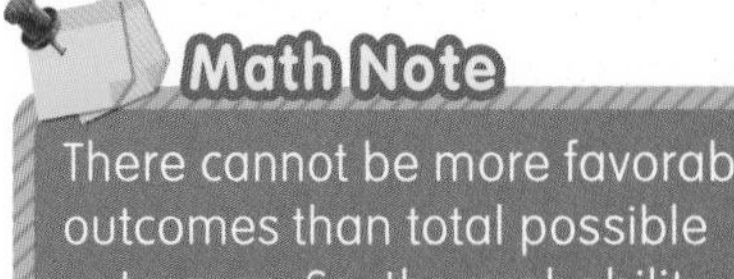

There cannot be more favorable outcomes than total possible outcomes. So, the probability of an event cannot be greater than 1.

TRY Practice finding the probability of an event

Solve.

1. Elijah has 4 short-sleeved shirts and 5 long-sleeved shirts in his closet. X is the event of Elijah randomly choosing a long-sleeved shirt. Find P(X). Express the probability as a fraction.

Event X has ______ favorable outcomes.

$$P(X) = \frac{\text{Number of outcomes favorable to event } X}{\text{Total number of equally likely outcomes}}$$

$$= \frac{\_\_\_}{\_\_\_}$$

2. A box contains 28 pink ribbons and 12 green ribbons. You randomly take a ribbon from the box without looking. Find the probability of picking a pink ribbon. Express the probability as a percent.

ENGAGE

Write the numbers from 1 to 20 on cards. Put them into two groups, A and B. The numbers in group A are even. The numbers in group B are divisible by 4. How could you organize the cards to show the relationship between group A and group B? Explain.

LEARN Use Venn diagrams to show relationships of events

1. When a coin lands heads up, it cannot also land tails up. When two events cannot happen at the same time, they are mutually exclusive events.

   You can use a Venn diagram to represent mutually exclusive events. Let H be the event that the coin lands heads up and T be the event that the coin lands tails up.

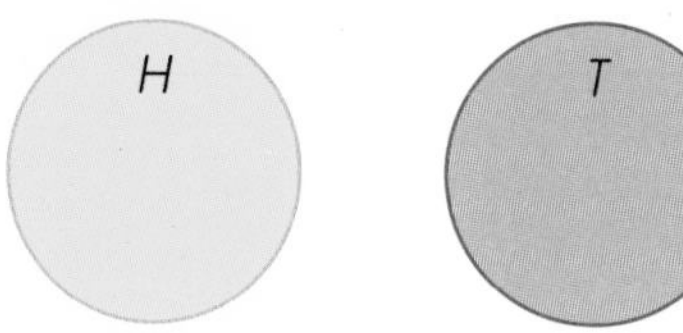

Each circle in the Venn diagram represents an event. Since event H and event T are mutually exclusive events, the circles representing the events do not overlap.

2. The events you get when you roll a number die are also mutually exclusive. Let A_1, A_2, A_3, A_4, A_5, and A_6 be the events 1, 2, 3, 4, 5, and 6. In a Venn diagram, the events are represented by nonoverlapping circles.

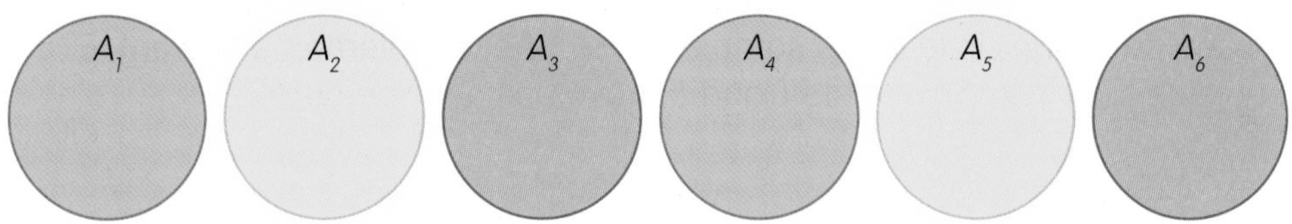

Now let E be the event of rolling an even number and let F be the event of rolling a number greater than 3.

The outcomes favorable to these events are:

$E = \{2, 4, 6\}$ and

$F = \{4, 5, 6\}$

The sample space S for rolling the number die is $\{1, 2, 3, 4, 5, 6\}$.

In the Venn diagram below, the sample space S is shown by a rectangle. The circles for events E and F overlap because the outcomes 4 and 6 are common to both events. They are not mutually exclusive events.

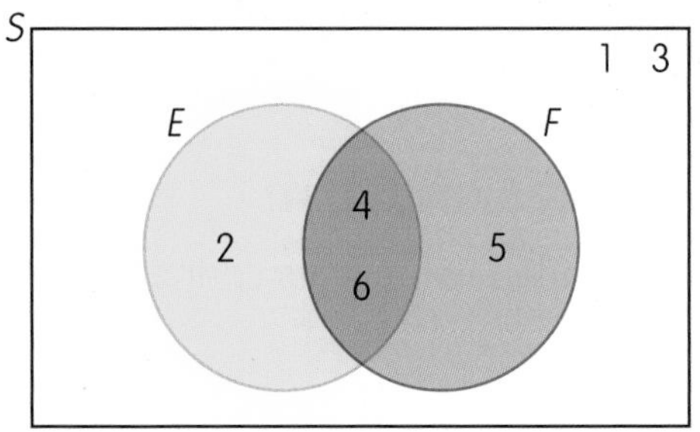

If a 4 or a 6 is rolled, both events occur at the same time. So, events E and F are not mutually exclusive.

4 is an even number and a number greater than 3.
6 is also an even number and a number greater than 3.

Math Talk

What are the probabilities of event E and event F?

3 Given an event E, the complement of event E is the event in which E does not occur. The complement of event E is written as E'. The event of getting heads is the complement of the event of getting tails from a coin toss.

The Venn diagram shows event E and its complement, E', in the sample spaces. Event E is represented by the circle in the sample space. The complementary event, E', is the region outside the circle. So, events E and E' have no common outcomes.

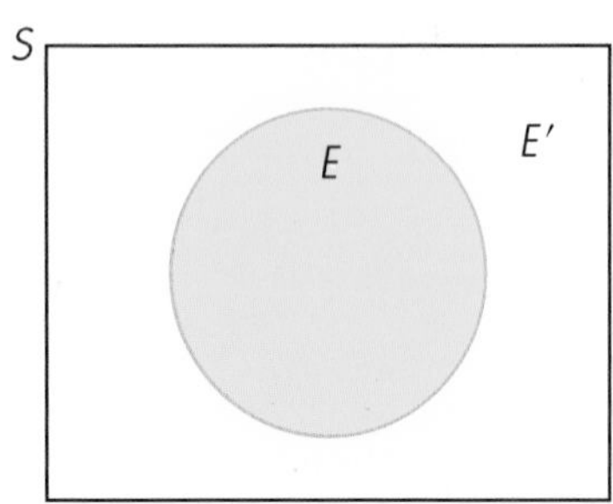

E' is read as "the complement of E."

The Venn diagram illustrates two properties of complementary events:

- events E and E' are mutually exclusive.
- $P(E) + P(E') = 1$

Math Talk

While complementary events are mutually exclusive, is it true that two mutually exclusive events are also complementary? Explain.

TRY Practice using Venn diagrams to show relationships of events

Solve.

1 Ten cards, each printed with a different whole number from 16 to 25, are shuffled and placed face down. A card is drawn at random from the ten cards.

Let A be the event of getting a number that is a multiple of 3.
Let B be the event of getting a number that is a multiple of 5.

a List all the outcomes favorable to events A and B.

A = {_____, _____, _____} List multiples of 3 from 16 to 25.

B = {_____, _____} List multiples of 5 from 16 to 25.

b Draw a Venn diagram for the sample space and the two events.
Place all possible outcomes in the Venn diagram.

The rectangle that represents the sample space includes all the whole numbers from 16 to 25. Some of these numbers are outcomes favorable to event A and some are outcomes favorable to event B.

c Are events A and B mutually exclusive? Explain.

d Find the probability of event A and the probability of event B.

2 A name is randomly chosen from a list of names: Dan, Ben, Roy, Bella, Demi, Eva, Nora, Alex, Eddy, and Sam.

Let X be the event of choosing a name with two vowels.
Let Y be the event of choosing a name made up of three letters.

a List all the outcomes favorable to events X and Y.

X = {_____, _____, _____, _____, _____} List the names with two vowels.

Y = {_____, _____, _____, _____, _____} List the names with three letters.

b Draw a Venn diagram for the sample space and the two events.
Place all possible outcomes in the Venn diagram.

The Venn diagram includes all the outcomes from the sample space. Some outcomes are favorable to event X, some are favorable to event Y, and one outcome is favorable to events X and Y. One outcome is not favorable to events X or Y.

c Are events X and Y mutually exclusive? Explain.

d Find $P(X)$ and $P(Y)$.

3. A letter is selected at random from the state name RHODE ISLAND.

Let C be the event of getting a consonant.
Let H be the event of getting a letter that comes after H in the alphabet.

a List all the outcomes favorable to events C and H.

b Draw a Venn diagram for the sample space and the two events. Place all possible outcomes in the Venn diagram.

c Are events C and H mutually exclusive? Explain.

d Find $P(C)$ and $P(H)$.

4 You randomly choose a month from the twelve months in a year.
Let A be the event of randomly choosing a month that has the letter a in its name.

a Give the meaning of event A', the complement of event A.

b List all the outcomes favorable to event A.

c List all the outcomes favorable to event A'.

d Draw a Venn diagram for the sample space and the two events.
Place all possible outcomes in the Venn diagram.

e Find $P(A)$ and $P(A')$.

ENGAGE

Randomly pick a card from 1 to 20. What is the probability of picking an odd number that is divisible by 3? Explain your reasoning.

LEARN Solve problems involving probability

1. 25% of the students in the school band play brass instruments. Among the brass players, 20% play the trombone. The band director randomly selects a band member to play a solo.

a Draw a Venn diagram to represent the information.

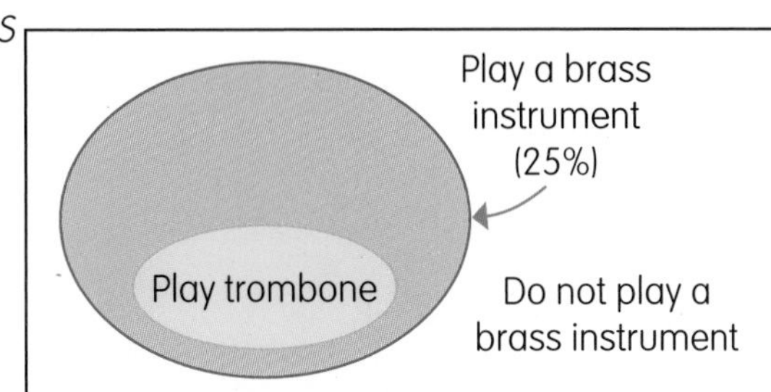

25% of the band members play brass instruments. Of these brass players, 20% play the trombone. So, 20% of 25% of the band members play the trombone.

b What is the probability of selecting a band member who does not play a brass instrument?

Since 25% of the band members play brass instruments,
100% – 25% = 75% of the band members do not play a brass instrument.

The probability of selecting a band member who does not play a brass instrument is 75%.

c What is the probability of selecting a trombone player?

20% of 25% of the band members play the trombone.

$$\begin{aligned} 20\% \text{ of } 25\% &= 0.20 \cdot 0.25 \\ &= 0.05 \\ &= 5\% \end{aligned}$$

The probability of selecting a trombone player is 5%.

2 Out of 500 students, 156 students study Spanish as a foreign language. Of those studying Spanish, 1 out of 6 students also study French. No students study French only.

a Draw a Venn diagram to represent the information.

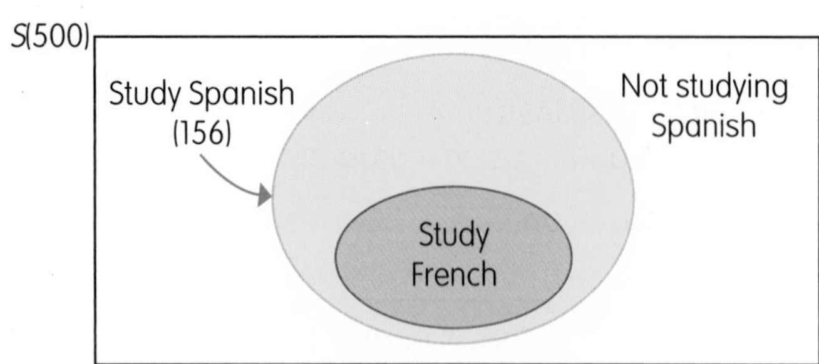

b What fraction of the students study both Spanish and French?

1 out of 6 of the 156 students studying Spanish also study French.
So, $\frac{1}{6}$ of 156 students study both Spanish and French.

$$\frac{1}{6} \text{ of } 156 = \frac{1}{6} \cdot 156$$
$$= 26$$

26 students study both Spanish and French.

$$\frac{26}{500} = \frac{13}{250}$$

$\frac{13}{250}$ of the students study both Spanish and French.

c If a student is selected at random from the 500 students, what is the probability of selecting a student who studies both Spanish and French? Give your answer as a decimal.

$$\frac{13}{250} = 0.052$$

The probability of selecting a student who studies both Spanish and French is 0.052.

TRY Practice solving problems involving probability

Solve.

1. 40% of the apples in an orchard are green and the rest of the apples are red. 5% of the red apples are rotten.

   a Fill in each blank in the Venn diagram to represent the information.

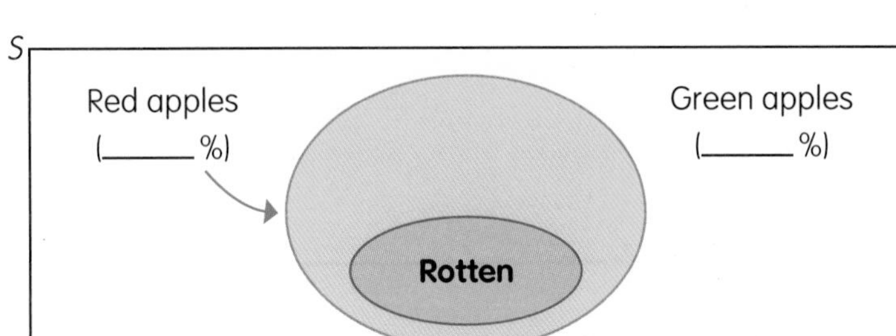

   b If you pick an apple at random in the orchard, what is the probability of picking a red apple that is not rotten? Give your answer as a decimal or a percent.

   Of all the red apples, ____% of them are not rotten.

   ____% of ____% = ____ · ____ Write percents as decimals and multiply.

   = ____ Simplify.

   = ____% Write as a percent.

   The probability of picking a red apple that is not rotten is ____.

2 Among the 200 jellybeans in a bag, 3 out of every 5 are blue jellybeans.
The blue jellybeans consist of light blue ones and dark blue ones in the ratio 2 : 1.

a Draw a Venn diagram to represent the information.

b What fraction of the jellybeans are light blue?

c If you pick a jellybean randomly from the bag, what is the probability of picking a light blue jellybean? Give your answer as a decimal.

Name: ______________________ Date: ______________

INDEPENDENT PRACTICE

Solve.

1. You rolled a fair number die with faces labeled 1 to 6.
   a What is the probability of rolling an odd number?

   b What is the probability of rolling a number less than 3?

   c What is the probability of rolling a prime number?

   d What is the probability of rolling a number greater than 1?

2. Adeline randomly chooses a disk from 6 green, 4 black, 2 red, and 2 white disks of the same size and shape.
   a What is the probability of getting a red disk?

   b What is the probability of not getting a green or white disk?

   c What is the probability of getting a black disk?

3. A letter is randomly chosen from the word MATHEMATICS. What is the probability of choosing the letter M?

4. There are 6 red marbles and 10 white marbles in a bag. What is probability of randomly choosing a white marble from the bag?

5. Numbers made up of two digits are formed using the digits 2, 3, and 4 with no repeating digits.
   a List all the possible outcomes.

   b Find the probability of randomly forming a number that is greater than 32.

   c Find the probability of randomly forming a number that is evenly divisible by 4.

6. Jack picks a letter randomly from the following list:
h, i, m, o, p, q, r, t, u, and x.
The event V occurs when Jack picks a vowel.

a Draw a Venn diagram to represent the information. Explain the meaning of the complement of event V.

b Find $P(V)$ and $P(V')$.

7. A number is randomly selected from 1 to 20. X is the event of selecting a number that is evenly divisible by 4. Y is the event of getting a prime number.

a Draw a Venn diagram to represent the information.

b Are events X and Y mutually exclusive? Explain.

c Find $P(X)$ and $P(Y)$.

8. A dodecahedron number die has 12 faces. Each face is printed with one of the numbers from 1 to 12. Suppose you roll a fair dodecahedron number die and record the value on the top face. Let A be the event of rolling a number that is a multiple of 3. Let B be the event of rolling a number that is a multiple of 4.

a Draw a Venn diagram to represent the information.

b From the Venn diagram, state whether events A and B are mutually exclusive. Explain your answer.

c Find $P(A)$ and $P(B)$.

9 This year, some students in the drama club have the same first names. Name tags for the students are shown below.

John	James	Peter	Peter	John
James	Peter	Mary	John	

One of the name tags is selected at random. Event E occurs when the name has the letter e. Event J occurs when the name tag is John.

a Draw a Venn diagram to represent the information.

b List all the types of outcomes of event E', the complement of event E.

c Are events E and J mutually exclusive? Explain your answer.

d Find P(E), P(E'), and P(J).

10 At a middle school, 39% of the students jog and 35% of the students do aerobic exercise. Of the students who do aerobic exercise, 1 out of 5 students also jogs.

a What percent of the students do both activities?

b Draw a Venn diagram to represent the information.

c What fraction of the students only jog?

d What is the probability of randomly selecting a student who does neither activity? Give your answer as a decimal.

11 A teacher chooses a student at random from a class with 20 boys and 36 girls. 25% of the students wear glasses. 15 boys in the class do not wear glasses.

a Draw a Venn diagram to represent the information.

b What fraction of the students in the class are girls who do not wear glasses?

c What is the probability that a randomly selected student is a boy who wears glasses?

12 A small town has a population of 3,200 people. 30% of the townspeople speak Italian, 20% speak French, and the rest do not speak either of these languages. 360 people speak both Italian and French.

a Draw a Venn diagram to represent the information.

b What percent of the townspeople speak only Italian?

c If you randomly pick a person in the town and speak to the person in Italian, what is the probability that the person does not understand you?

13 The 6,000 oranges harvested at an orange grove are a combination of Valencia and Navel oranges. The ratio of Valencia oranges to Navel oranges is 7 : 5. The owner of the orange grove finds that 1 in every 20 Valencia oranges and 1 in every 25 Navel oranges are rotten.

a What fraction of the oranges are not rotten?

b What is the probability that a randomly selected orange is a good orange?

c What is the probability that a randomly selected orange is a rotten Valencia?

Name: ______________________ Date: ______________

Approximating Probability and Relative Frequency

Learning Objectives:

- Find relative frequencies for data in a chance process.
- Interpret relative frequencies as probabilities and use them to make predictions.
- Compare long-run relative frequencies to related theoretical probabilities.

New Vocabulary

relative frequency
observed frequency
theoretical probability
experimental probability

THINK

A number die is rolled 100 times. The frequencies for values 1 to 6 are recorded, and the relative frequency for each value is calculated. Describe two methods for finding the relative frequency of rolling a number that is less than 6.

A bag contains a white bead and a black bead. You randomly picked a bead and replaced it and then recorded each outcome. After 12 trials, the number of times you picked a white bead is more than the number of times you picked a black bead. What are all the possible probabilities of you picking a white bead?

LEARN Solve problems involving relative frequencies

Activity Finding relative frequencies in a chance process

Work in pairs.

1. Flip a coin 20 times. Record whether the coin lands heads up or tails up after each flip in a table.

Data Value	Observed Frequency
Heads	
Tails	
Total	

The observed frequency is the number of observations of a data value. It refers to how many times a data value appears in a chance process.

2. What is the observed frequency of getting heads? What is the observed frequency of getting tails?

The relative frequency of a data value is the ratio of the observed frequency to the total number of observations in a chance process. Relative frequency can be calculated from the observed frequency.

$$\text{Relative frequency} = \frac{\text{Observed frequency of a data value}}{\text{Total number of observations}}$$

③ What is the relative frequency of getting heads? What is the relative frequency of getting tails? Write each relative frequency as a fraction or a decimal.

④ What is the sum of the relative frequencies? What do you notice?

1 The table shows the relative frequencies of men, women, and children at a park on a particular day. On that day, 600 people were in the park.

People	Relative Frequency
Men	0.54
Women	0.37
Children	0.09

Since each relative frequency represents a fraction of the total number of people, the sum of the relative frequencies is 1.
$0.54 + 0.37 + 0.09 = 1$

a How many children were at the park?

The relative frequency 0.09 means that $\frac{9}{100}$ of the 600 people at the park were children.

$0.09 \cdot 600 = 54$ Multiply the relative frequency for children by the total number of people.

There were 54 children at the park.

b How many more men than women were at the park?

$0.54 \cdot 600 = 324$ Find the number of men.

$0.37 \cdot 600 = 222$ Find the number of women.

$324 - 222 = 102$ Subtract the number of women from the number of men.

There were 102 more men than women at the park.

2 At some schools, a grade point average (GPA) is used to describe academic progress. The histogram shows data about the GPAs of 400 students at a school.

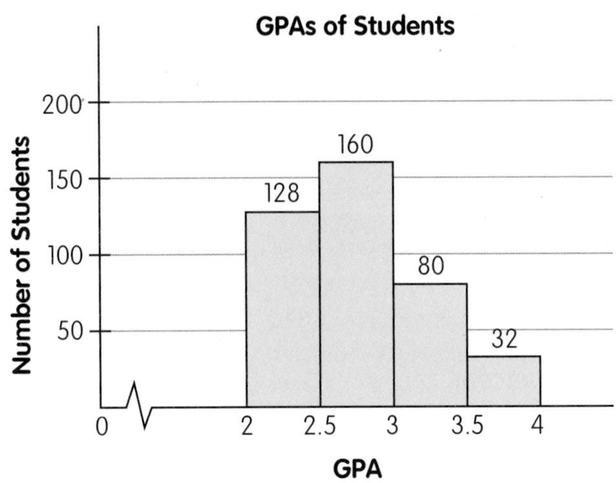

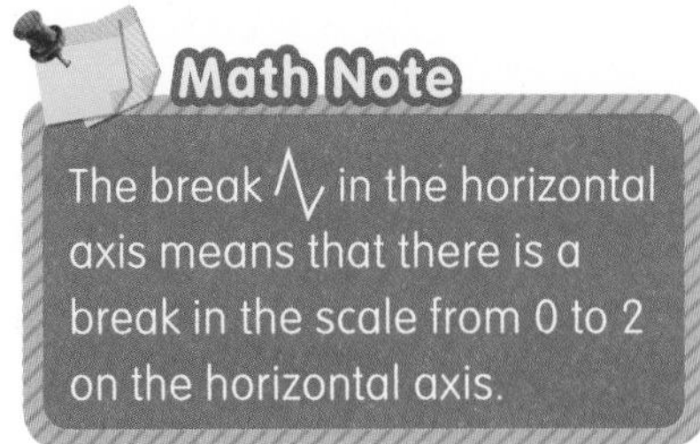

A histogram is a vertical bar graph with no spaces between the bars. Each bar represents an interval of the same size.

The lower value of each interval on the histogram shows the least possible value for the interval. The upper value shows the least possible value for the next interval. For example, the first bar shows the frequency for GPAs in the range $2 \leq \text{GPA} < 2.5$. This bar represents the number of students whose GPA is at least 2 but less than 2.5.

a What is the relative frequency of students whose GPA is at least 3? Express the answer as a fraction.

Relative frequency of students whose GPA is at least 3:

$80 + 32 = 112$ Find the number of students whose GPA is greater than or equal to 3.

$\frac{112}{400} = \frac{7}{25}$ Write 112 out of 400 students as a fraction. Simplify.

The relative frequency of students whose GPA is at least 3 is $\frac{7}{25}$.

b Find the relative frequency of students whose GPA is greater than or equal to 3, but less than 3.5. Express the answer as a percent.

80 out of 400 students have a GPA that is greater than or equal to 3 but less than 3.5.

Relative frequency for this GPA range:

$\frac{80}{400} \cdot 100\% = 20\%$

The relative frequency of the number of students whose GPA is greater than or equal to 3 but less than 3.5 is 20%.

c Draw a relative frequency histogram using percent.

128 out of 400 students have a GPA that is greater than or equal to 2 but less than 2.5.

$\frac{128}{400} \cdot 100\% = 32\%$

160 out of 400 students have a GPA that is greater than or equal to 2.5 but less than 3.

$\frac{160}{400} \cdot 100\% = 40\%$

32 out of 400 students have a GPA that is greater than or equal to 3.5 but less than 4.

$\frac{32}{400} \cdot 100\% = 8\%$

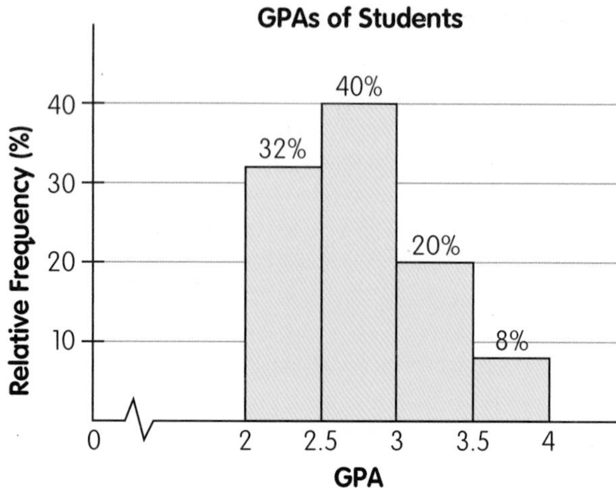

The relative frequency histogram has a horizontal axis that is the same as the frequency histogram. The scale on the vertical axis shows percents. The height of each bar is the relative frequency for the given data interval.

TRY Practice solving problems involving relative frequencies

Solve.

1. The table shows the relative frequencies for three sizes of monitors sold during a sale at a computer store. 640 monitors were sold during the sale.

Monitor	Relative Frequency
14-inch	0.15
15-inch	0.55
17-inch	0.30

Each relative frequency represents a fraction of the total number of monitors sold.
The sum of the relative frequencies is 1.

$0.15 + 0.55 + 0.30 = 1$

a How many 17-inch monitors were sold during the sale?

The relative frequency 0.30 means that $\frac{30}{100}$ of the 640 monitors sold were 17-inch monitors.

_____ · 640 = _____ Multiply the relative frequency for 17-inch monitors by the total number of monitors sold.

_____ 17-inch monitors were sold during the sale.

b How many fewer 14-inch monitors were sold than 15-inch monitors?

_____ · 640 = _____ Find the number of 14-inch monitors.

_____ · 640 = _____ Find the number of 15-inch monitors.

_____ − _____ = _____ Subtract the number of 14-inch monitors from the number of 15-inch monitors.

There were _____ fewer 14-inch monitors sold than 15-inch monitors.

2 Alex and Jose caught 40 fish over the weekend. The histogram shows the masses of the fish they caught.

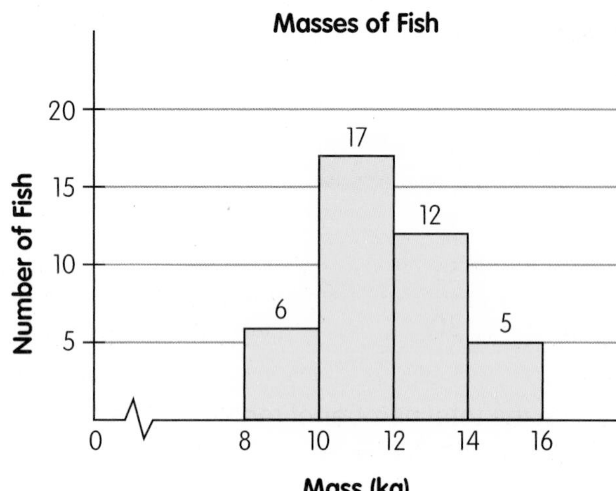

a Find the relative frequency for fish that have a mass of at least 8 kilograms but less than 10 kilograms. Give your answer as a percent.

There are _____ fish that have a mass of at least 8 kilograms but less than 10 kilograms.

$\frac{\_\_\_\_\_}{\_\_\_\_\_} = \frac{\_\_\_\_\_}{\_\_\_\_\_}$ Write _____ out of 40 fish as a fraction and simplify.

_____ · 100% = _____ Multiply by 100%.

The relative frequency for fish that have a mass of at least 8 kilograms but less than 10 kilograms is _____%.

b Draw a relative frequency histogram using percent.

_____ · 100% = _____% Find the relative frequency of fish that have a mass of at least 10 kilograms but less than 12 kilograms.

_____ · 100% = _____% Find the relative frequency of fish that have a mass of at least 12 kilograms but less than 14 kilograms.

_____ · 100% = _____% Find the relative frequency of fish that have a mass of at least 14 kilograms but less than 16 kilograms.

ENGAGE

Write the numbers from 1 to 3 on cards. You randomly picked a card and replaced it. You then recorded each outcome. After 20 trials, you made a frequency table. What is the probability of you picking the card with a 1 on it? Explain your answer.

LEARN Use relative frequencies to solve problems involving probability

1. You learned that there is a 50% chance of getting heads when you flip a fair coin. However, if you flip the coin 100 times, you may not get heads 50 times. The type of probability you learned earlier is called theoretical probability. A theoretical probability is the ratio of the number of favorable outcomes to the total number of possible outcomes. You do not have to perform an experiment to find a theoretical probability. For example, when you roll a number die, you know that the theoretical probability of rolling a 5 is $\frac{1}{6}$.

   Relative frequency is based on observations of what has happened in a chance process. It is also used as a probability measure to predict the likelihood of a future outcome. For example, suppose you roll a number die 100 times and you get a five 18 times, the experimental probability of rolling a 5 is 18 out of 100 or 0.18. An experimental probability is a probability based on data collected or observations made in an experiment.

   Most of the time, the experimental probability of an event differs from the theoretical probability. Even the same chance process carried out at different times will generate different experimental probabilities. However, the experimental probability will become closer to the theoretical probability as more experiments are carried out.

2. The types of vehicles passing through an intersection were observed one morning. The observed frequencies and relative frequencies are summarized below.

Type of Vehicles	Observed Frequency	Relative Frequency
Car	108	$\frac{108}{160} = \frac{27}{40}$
Motorcycle	12	$\frac{12}{160} = \frac{3}{40}$
Van	16	$\frac{16}{160} = \frac{1}{10}$
Truck	24	$\frac{24}{160} = \frac{3}{20}$
Total	160	1

In this experiment, 160 vehicles were observed. Among the four types of vehicles, cars had the greatest relative frequency, $\frac{27}{40}$. You may also write this relative frequency as a decimal or as a percent: $\frac{27}{40} = 0.675$ or 67.5%.

Using the relative frequencies as experimental probabilities, you can predict that there is a 67.5% chance that the next vehicle passing through the intersection will be a car.

Activity Comparing experimental and theoretical probabilities

Work in pairs.

(1) Put 10 counters (5 red, 3 blue, and 2 yellow) into a bag. Shake the bag to mix the counters. Without looking, pick a counter randomly from the bag. Record its color in a tally chart, and then put the counter back in the bag. Repeat this procedure 20 times.

(2) Combine your group's data from (1) with the data from other groups. Use the class data to make a relative frequency table like the one shown below.

Color	Observed Frequency	Relative Frequency (as a decimal)
Red		
Blue		
Yellow		

(3) Find the theoretical probability of picking each color. Then, fill in the table.

Color	Experimental probability	Theoretical probability
Red		
Blue		
Yellow		

(4) Compare the experimental and theoretical probabiltiies for each color. What do you observe?

(5) Repeat the procedure in (1) 50 times. Then, repeat (2). Compare the experimental and theoretical probabiltiies for each color now. Are the two probabilities closer than in (4)? Explain why.

TRY Practice using relative frequencies to solve problems involving probability

Solve.

1 Lauren turned the spinner 200 times and recorded the letter that the pointer landed on. The observed frequencies are summarized below.

Letter	Observed Frequency
A	36
B	44
C	28
D	52
E	40

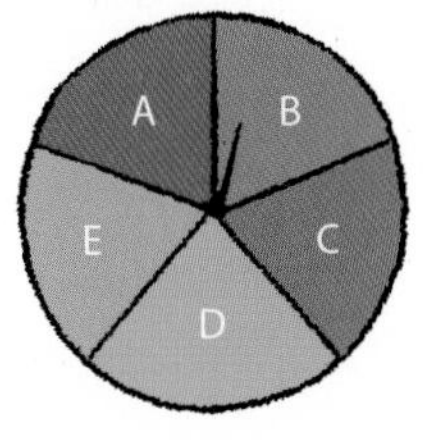

a Find the relative frequency for each of the letters. Write each relative frequency as a decimal.

Relative frequency of getting the letter A:

$\frac{36}{200} = \frac{\square}{100} = \_\_\_\_$

Relative frequency of getting the letter B:

$\frac{\square}{200} = \frac{\square}{100} = \_\_\_\_$

Relative frequency of getting the letter C:

$\frac{\square}{\square} = \frac{\square}{100} = \_\_\_\_$

Relative frequency of getting the letter D:

$\frac{\square}{\square} = \frac{\square}{100} = \_\_\_\_$

Relative frequency of getting the letter E:

$\frac{\square}{\square} = \frac{\square}{100} = \_\_\_\_$

b Predict which letter the spinner is most likely to land on if Lauren turns the spinner again. Explain your answer.

c What is the experimental probability that the spinner will not land on letter D on the next spin?

2 Luis made a dartboard as shown on the right. He threw a dart at the dartboard 100 times. He recorded the number of times the dart landed on each color. The number of times he missed hitting the dartboard was also recorded.

Outcome	Observed Frequency
Red	10
Yellow	35
Blue	48
Misses	7

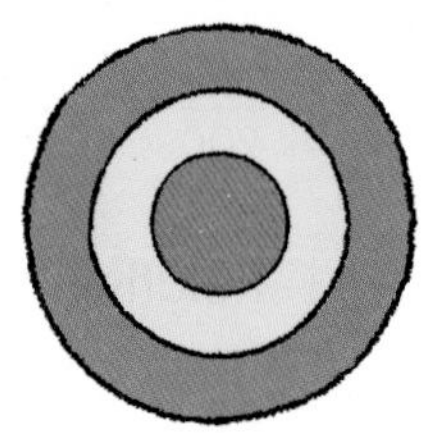

a Find the relative frequency, expressed as a decimal, for each event.

b Explain what the relative frequency of the dart landing in the red region means.

c If Luis throws the dart again, predict in which region the dart is most likely to land. Explain your answer.

Name: ______________________________ Date: ______________

INDEPENDENT PRACTICE

Solve.

1. A library conducted a survey on 2,000 library users about the types of books they usually borrow. The table shows the relative frequencies of the types of books borrowed.

Type of Books	Observed Frequency
Romance	0.28
Science fiction	0.40
Mystery	0.11
Biography	0.15
Philosophy	0.06

a What percent of the library users borrowed mystery titles?

b What percent of the library users borrowed romance or science fiction titles?

c How many library users borrowed biography titles?

2. A coin is tossed 66 times and lands heads up 36 times.

a Find the relative frequency of the coin landing heads up.

b Find the relative frequency of the coin landing tails up.

3. A number die is rolled 50 times. After each roll, the result is recorded. The table gives the observed frequency for each number on the die.

a Fill in the table. Write the relative frequency as a fraction.

Value	1	2	3	4	5	6
Observed Frequency	11	4	6	14	8	7
Relative Frequency						

b Find the relative frequency of rolling a number greater than 4. Give your answer as a fraction.

c Find the relative frequency of rolling an odd number. Give your answer as a fraction.

4. The ice hockey team Blue Thunder played 25 times during the winter season. The team had 14 wins, 8 losses, and 3 ties.

a Find the relative frequency for each of the following: wins, losses, ties. Give your answers as percents.

b Draw a relative frequency bar graph that uses percents.

c What percent of the total number of games ended in a loss or a tie?

5 You are given a deck of 52 cards showing scenes of the four seasons of the year. There are 13 cards for each season. You randomly select a card from the deck 100 times. After each selection, you record the season shown on the card and replace it in the deck for the next selection. The results are given in the table below.

Season	Spring	Summer	Fall	Winter
Observed Frequency	23	34	19	24

a Find the relative frequency of the appearance of each season.

b What is the experimental probability of selecting a card with a summer scene?

c What is the theoretical probability of selecting a card with a summer scene?

d **Mathematical Habit 6 Use precise mathematical language**
The experimental and the theoretical probabilities of selecting a card with a summer scene are not equal. Describe some factors that cause the two probabilities to be different.

e Suppose that the spring and summer cards have a red background and the fall and winter cards have a black background. What is the experimental probability of selecting a card with a black background?

f What is the theoretical probability of selecting a card with a red background?

6 A group of researchers catch and measure the length of fish before releasing them back to a river. The lengths of the 50 fish are categorized in the table below.

Length of Fish (L inches)	$L < 7$	$7 \leq L < 14$	$14 \leq L < 21$
Number of Fish	16	23	11

a Find the relative frequency of each category of fish.

b If the researchers catch and measure one more fish, what is the probability of catching a fish that is less than 7 inches long?

c What is the probability that the next fish caught will be at least 7 inches long?

d Draw a relative frequency histogram using percent.

7 A car dealership has sold 75 new cars this year. The histogram below shows frequencies for cars sold in different price ranges.

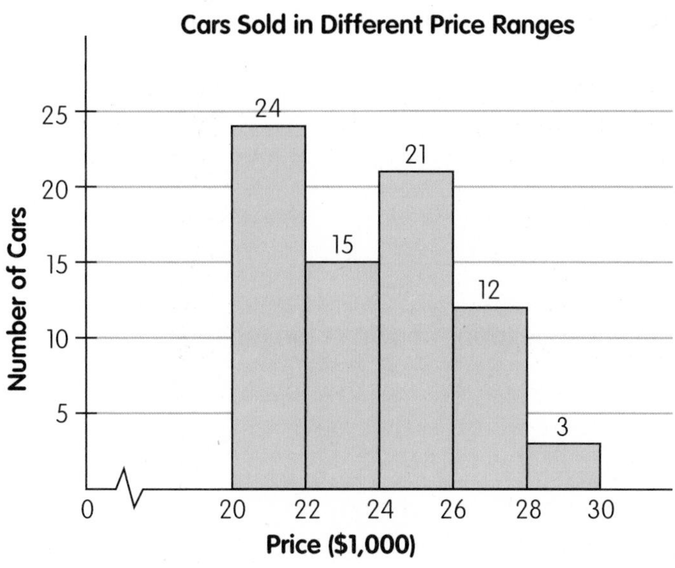

The bar for the interval 24 – 26 shows that 21 out of 75 cars were sold for prices that were greater than or equal to $24,000 but less than $26,000.

a Find the relative frequency of cars that are sold for at least $26,000 but less than $28,000. Give your answer as a percent.

b Find the relative frequency of cars that are sold for at least $20,000 but less than $24,000. Give your answer as a percent.

c What is the probability that the next car will be sold for at least $28,000 but less than $30,000?

8 A light bulb manufacturer estimates that 10% of a shipment of 600 bulbs will have a lifespan greater than or equal to 1,000 hours, but less than 2,000 hours. The manufacturer also estimates that 240 of the bulbs will have a lifespan greater than or equal to 2,000 hours, but less than 3,000 hours. The remaining light bulbs are estimated to have a lifespan greater than or equal to 3,000 hours, but less than 4,000 hours.

a Fill in the table.

Lifespan (x hours)	$1{,}000 \leq x < 2{,}000$	$2{,}000 \leq x < 3{,}000$	$3{,}000 \leq x < 4{,}000$
Number of Bulbs			

b Draw a frequency histogram for the three lifespans shown in the table.

c Find the relative frequency for the bulbs with each of the lifespans.
Then, draw a relative frequency histogram using percents.

d If you buy a light bulb from this shipment, what do you predict is the most likely lifespan of your light bulb? Explain your answer using experimental probability.

Name: ______________________ Date: ______________

Developing Probability Models

Learning Objectives:

- Apply uniform and nonuniform probability models.
- Compare experimental probability with theoretical probability.
- Use a probability model to predict outcomes of events.

New Vocabulary
probability model
probability distribution
uniform probability model
nonuniform probability model

THINK

In your own words, explain what a "uniform probability model" and a "nonuniform probability model" are. Give examples to support your explanation.

ENGAGE

The spinner is spun and the number where the spinner lands is recorded. Record in a table the possible outcomes. How can you record the probability of the spinner landing on each number on the number wheel in your table? Discuss.

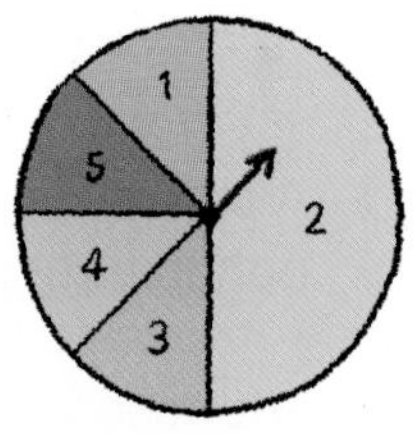

LEARN Develop probability models to find probability of events

1. Randomness is central to the concept of probability. All random phenomena have one common characteristic: they yield outcomes that are unpredictable. A probability model is a mathematical representation of a random phenomenon consisting of a sample space of outcomes, events, and the probabilities of the outcomes and events.

   All outcomes of a sample space and their probabilities can be presented in a table or a graph. Such a presentation is known as a probability distribution. You can make use of a probability model to estimate and predict the occurrence of events.

2. A probability model in which all the outcomes are equally likely to occur is called a uniform probability model. An example is the tossing of a fair coin where the probability of each outcome is the same.

   Suppose you randomly pick a counter from a group of counters below.

   The sample space consists of 5 outcomes: {yellow, red, blue, green, black}.

   Since every counter has an equal chance of being selected, the probability of selecting a counter of a particular color is $\frac{1}{5}$.

You can construct a probability model, and then use a bar graph to show the probability distribution.

Color	Yellow	Red	Blue	Green	Black
Probability	$\frac{1}{5}$	$\frac{1}{5}$	$\frac{1}{5}$	$\frac{1}{5}$	$\frac{1}{5}$

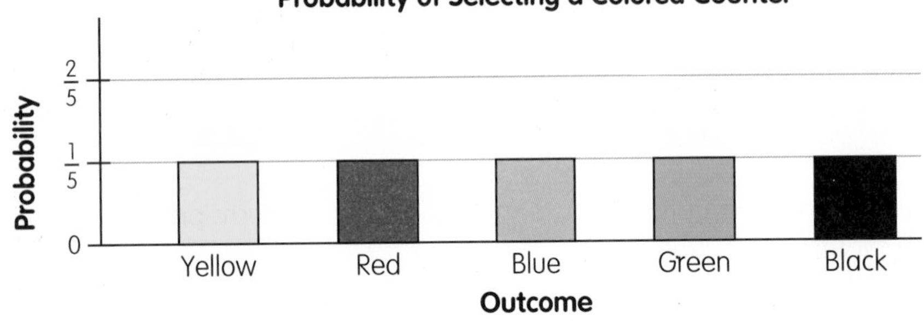

3 A probability model in which the outcomes are not equally likely to occur is called a nonuniform probability model. At least two of the outcomes will have different probabilities.

Suppose you randomly pick a colored pencil from a group of pencils below, and then record the color of each selected pencil.

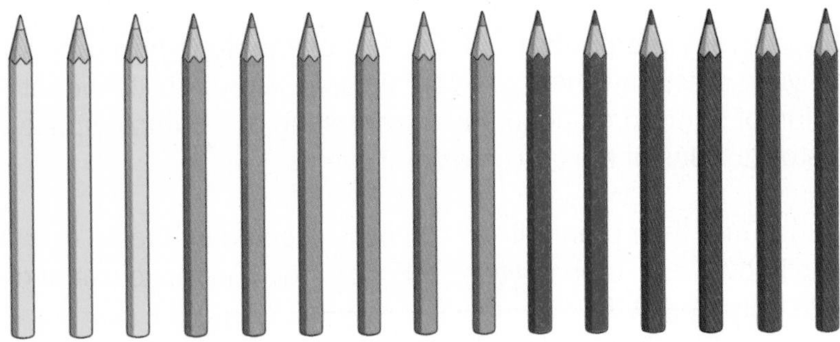

There are 15 colored pencils in total. So, the sample space has 15 outcomes. To find the probability of picking a brown pencil, let B be the event of picking a brown pencil, and use the formula:

$$P(B) = \frac{\text{Number of outcomes favorable to event } B}{\text{Total number of outcomes}}$$

$$= \frac{4}{15}$$

The probability of picking a brown pencil is $\frac{4}{15}$.

To construct a probability model, first calculate the probability of picking a pencil of each color.

The probability of picking a yellow pencil is $\frac{3}{15}$.

The probability of picking an orange pencil is $\frac{6}{15}$.

The probability of picking a green pencil is $\frac{2}{15}$.

The probability of picking a brown pencil is $\frac{4}{15}$.

Color	Yellow	Orange	Green	Brown
Probability	$\frac{3}{15}$	$\frac{6}{15}$	$\frac{2}{15}$	$\frac{4}{15}$

Then, use a bar graph to show the probability distribution.

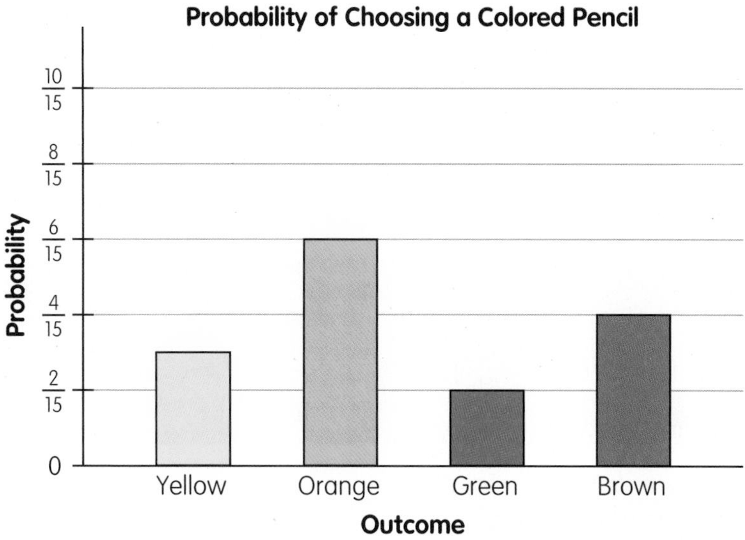

Use the table or the bar graph to compare the probabilities. The probability of getting an orange pencil is greater than the probability of getting a yellow pencil.

4 The probability of rolling the number 1 using a biased number die is $\frac{1}{4}$.
Each of the five other numbers has an equal probability of being rolled.
Find the probability of rolling the number 4.

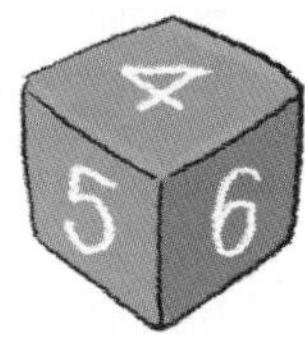

P (rolling a 1) = $\frac{1}{4}$ = 0.25

There are five other numbers and each of these numbers has an equal probability of occurring.

P (rolling a 1) + P(rolling the five other numbers) = 1
P(rolling the five other numbers) = 1 – P (rolling a 1)
= 1 – 0.25
= 0.75

The sum of the probabilities of two complementary events is equal to 1.

P (rolling a 4) = 0.75 ÷ 5
= 0.15

The probability of rolling the number 4 is 0.15.

5 The data below show the heights, in inches, of 20 players of a junior baseball team.

$63\frac{1}{4}$	70	68	59	$60\frac{1}{4}$	62	$58\frac{1}{2}$	$67\frac{5}{8}$	64	71
55	$66\frac{1}{8}$	66	57	$68\frac{1}{2}$	61	$64\frac{3}{8}$	$70\frac{1}{4}$	$55\frac{5}{8}$	60

To develop a probability model, first group the heights into four intervals:
55 to < 60, 60 to < 65, 65 to < 70, and 70 to < 75.

Interval	55 to < 60	60 to < 65	65 to < 70	70 to < 75
Frequency	5	7	5	3

The interval 55 to < 60 includes heights that are greater than or equal to 55 inches, and less than 60 inches.

Then, find the relative frequencies of the four intervals to construct the probability model.

Interval	55 to < 60	60 to < 65	65 to < 70	70 to < 75
Relative Frequency	$\frac{5}{20} = 0.25$	$\frac{7}{20} = 0.35$	$\frac{5}{20} = 0.25$	$\frac{3}{20} = 0.15$

Remember that
Relative frequency
$= \frac{\text{Observed frequency}}{\text{Total number of observations}}$

The probability model is shown below.

Interval	55 to < 60	60 to < 65	65 to < 70	70 to < 75
Probability	0.25	0.35	0.25	0.15

Finally, represent the probability distribution in a relative frequency histogram.

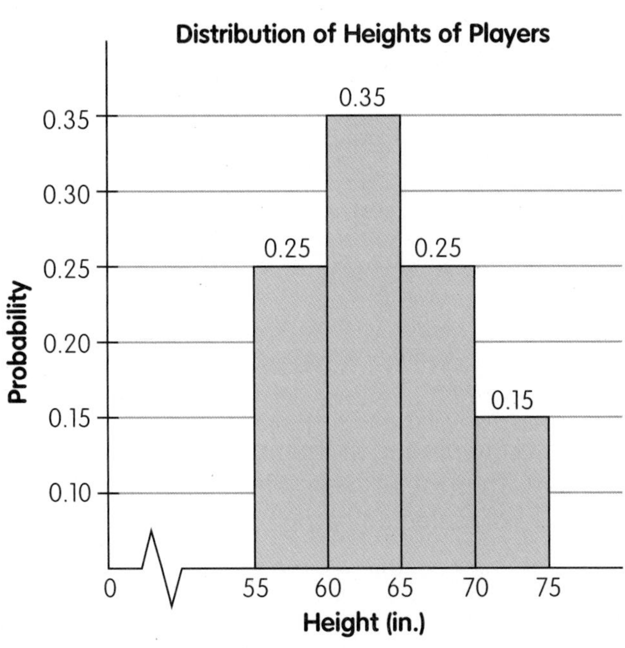

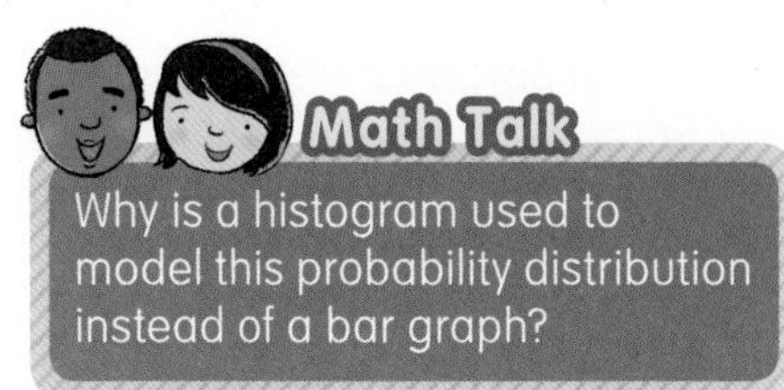

If a player is selected at random, what is the probability of selecting one who is at least 65 inches tall?

Probability of selecting a player who is at least 65 inches tall:

$0.25 + 0.15 = 0.40$ Add the probabilities for 65 to < 70 or 70 to < 75.

The probability of selecting a player who is at least 65 inches tall is 0.40.

Activity Comparing experimental and theoretical probability models

Work in pairs.

① Suppose a number is randomly selected from 0 to 9. Complete the table and bar graph to show the theoretical probability of randomly picking each number.

Number	0	1	2	3	4	5	6	7	8	9
Probability										

Theoretical Probability of Selecting a Number from 0 to 9

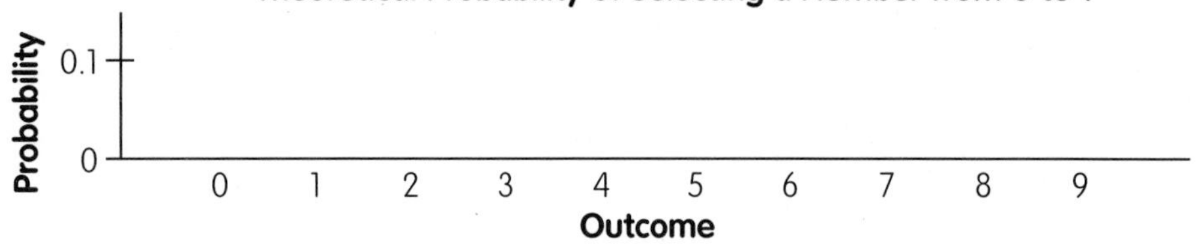

② Use a spreadsheet software to simulate the picking of random numbers from 0 to 9. Enter the formula =RANDBETWEEN(0,9) in cell A1. Then, select cells A1 to A50 and choose Fill Down from the Edit menu to model 50 randomly selected numbers.

	A	B	C	D	E	F
1	=RANDBETWEEN(0,9)					
2						
3						
4						
5						
6						
7						
8						
9						
10						

③ Present the probability distribution from ② in a table and a bar graph as in ①.

Number	0	1	2	3	4	5	6	7	8	9
Probability										

Experimental Probability of Selecting a Number from 0 to 9

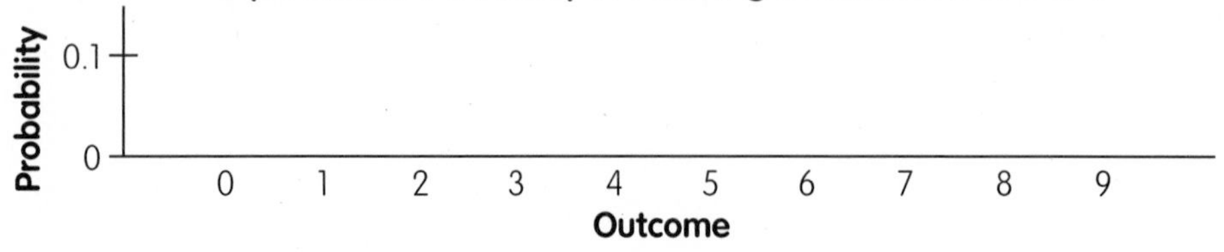

(4) Repeat the procedure in (2), this time selecting cells A1 to A100 and choose Fill Down from the Edit menu to model 100 randomly selected numbers.

(5) Present the probability distribution from (4) in a table and a bar graph.

Number	0	1	2	3	4	5	6	7	8	9
Probability										

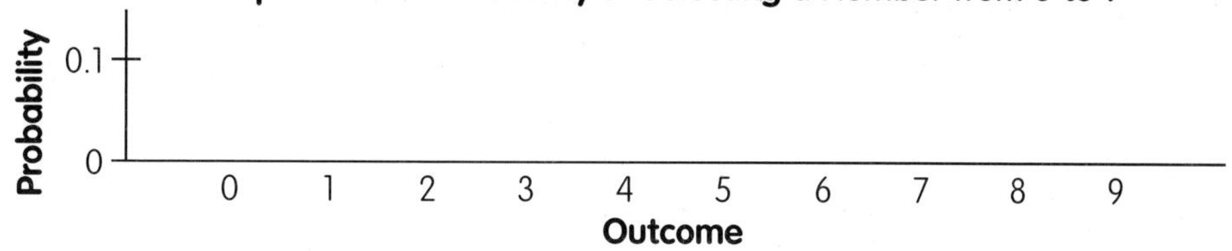

(6) **Mathematical Habit 2 Use mathematical reasoning**
Compare each of the experimental probability models you made with the theoretical probability model at the beginning of this activity. What effect does increasing the number of selected digits have on the experimental probabilities? Which experimental probability model resembles the theoretical probability model more closely? Explain.

TRY Practice developing probability models to find probability of events

Solve.

1. There are eight letter tiles in a bag. The tiles are labeled with the letters from S to Z. Rachel randomly selects a tile from the bag.

   a Define the sample space.

   b What is the probability of selecting a tile with a particular letter?

   c Construct the probability model.

d Present the probability distribution in a bar graph.

2 A number is chosen at random from the list: 1, 4, 7, 12, 21, 25, 38, 40, 45, and 48.

a Explain why a uniform probability model describes this situation.

b What is the probability of choosing 25?

c T is the event of choosing a number that is a multiple of 3. List all the outcomes that are favorable to event T.

d Find P(T).

3 There are 10 herbal tea bags of assorted flavors in a jar: 4 peppermint, 2 raspberry, 3 camomile, and 1 blackberry. Suppose you randomly pick a tea bag from the jar and note the flavor.

a Define the sample space.

b What is the probability of picking a raspberry tea bag?

c Construct the probability model of picking a tea bag.
Then, use a bar graph to represent the probability distribution.

4 Nine cards are made from each of the letters from the word "BEGINNING."
You select a card at random.

a Find the probability of getting a letter N.

b Construct the probability model.

c What is the probability of selecting a card with a consonant?

5 The data below show the heights, in centimeters, of 25 tomato plants in a greenhouse.

100	124	86	110	90
96	82	117	104	132
102	120	104	90	125
121	130	111	103	84
89	106	123	94	100

a Group the heights into six intervals: 80 to < 90, 90 to < 100, 100 to < 110, 110 to < 120, 120 to < 130, and 130 to < 140.

b Find the relative frequencies of the six intervals. Construct the probability model.

c Represent the probability distribution in a relative frequency histogram. State which type of probability distribution you have drawn.

d A plant is selected at random. What is the probability of selecting a plant whose height is greater than or equal to 100, but less than 120 centimeters tall?

Name: ______________________ Date: ____________

INDEPENDENT PRACTICE

Solve.

1. You toss a fair coin and record whether it lands heads up or tails up.

   a Define the sample space.

   b What is the probability of the coin landing heads up?

   c Construct the probability model.

   d Present the probability distribution in a bar graph.

2. A fair icosahedron number die is a 20-faced number die which has values from 1 to 20 on its faces. You roll a fair icosahedron number die and record the number on the face the number die rests on when it lands.

   a Define the sample space.

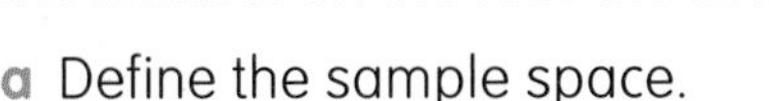

   b What is the probability of rolling a 14?

   c Construct a probability model of all possible values.

   d If A is the event of rolling a prime number, find P(A).

   e If B is the event of rolling a number divisible by 4, find P(B).

3 The spinner shown is used in a game. Before spinning the wheel, a player is given 50 points. The player then spins the wheel and adds the points indicated by the arrow to the 50 points he or she was given. The spinner has an equal chance of landing on any one of the sections.

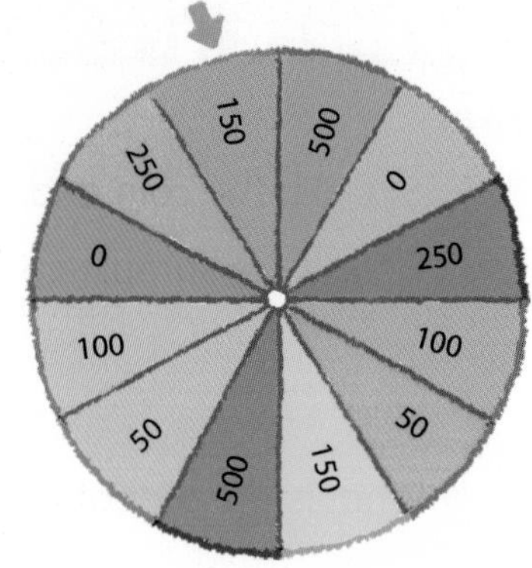

a List all the types of outcomes of the game.

b What is the probability of getting a total of 100 points?

c Construct a probability model.

d Is the probability distribution uniform? State your reason.

e If G is the event of getting a total of 300 points, find $P(G)$.

4 A rectangular wooden block is painted gold on one large face and white on the other large face. The other four faces are painted green. After tossing the block many times, Jenna finds that the block lands on the gold face one-third of the time. She also finds that the block has a 4% chance of landing on a green face.

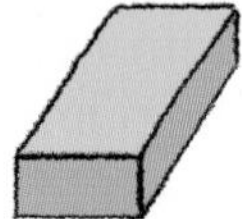

a Describe all the types of outcomes of tossing the block.

b Construct a probability model. Write the probabilities as fractions. Is the model a uniform probability model?

c What is the probability that the block lands on the white face?

5 The data show the ages of 25 people in a group.
A person is selected at random from the group.

23	27	44	34	22
30	16	48	14	31
15	33	30	43	28
40	29	21	22	15
36	19	17	27	45

a Fill in the frequency table.

Age	10 to <20	20 to <30	30 to <40	40 to <50
Number of People				

b Fill in the probability model.

Age	10 to <20	20 to <30	30 to <40	40 to <50
Probability				

c Present the probability distribution in a histogram.

d What is the probability that the selected person's age is 30 or above?

6 The table below shows 20 words taken from a novel. You randomly select a word from the 20 words.

aye	bite	cycles	don	ending
absent	band	calm	done	elm
around	bye	can	donuts	emu
ate	base	canes	drown	enough

a Fill in the frequency table.

Word Length	3-letter word	4-letter word	5-letter word	6-letter word
Number of Words				

b Fill in the probability distribution table.

Word Length	3-letter word	4-letter word	5-letter word	6-letter word
Probability				

c Present the probability distribution in a bar graph.

d What is the probability of selecting a word with at most 5 letters?

7 A quiz has three True-False questions. The correct answers, in order, are True-True-False (TTF). A student does not know any of the answers and decide to guess.

a Give the sample space of all the possible outcomes for the student guessing the three answers.

b Is this situation an example of a uniform probability model? Explain.

c Construct a probability distribution table for the model.

d What is the probability that the student gets all three answers correct?

e Let X be the event that the student gets only two correct answers. List all the possible outcomes of event X.

f Find P(X).

g Suppose you do not know that the correct answers, in order, are True-True-False. Would you be able to answer **e** and **f**? Explain.

Name: ______________________ Date: ______________

1 **Mathematical Habit 6 Use precise mathematical language**
Explain what a random sampling process is.

2 **Mathematical Habit 4 Use mathematical models**
Give an example of how a random sampling process is used in a real-world situation.

3 **Mathematical Habit 4 Use mathematical models**
Give an example of two complementary events. Draw a Venn diagram to represent the events.

Mathematical Habit 3 Construct viable arguments
Explain if you agree or disagree with each statement below.

4 If the sum of the probabilities of two mutually exclusive events is equal to 1, they must be complementary events.

5 All events having the same number of equally likely outcomes have equal probability in a uniform probability distribution.

PUT ON YOUR THINKING CAP!

Problem Solving with Heuristics

1 **Mathematical Habit 1** **Persevere in solving problems**

Alex has a pair of red socks, a pair of white socks, and a pair of black socks in his drawer. Unfortunately, the socks are not matched up with each other. Alex reaches into the drawer in the dark and pulls out two socks.

a What is the probability that the two socks are the same color?

b What is the probability that the two socks are of different colors?

2 **Mathematical Habit 2 Use mathematical reasoning**
In a game, you and your friend are asked to each select a card from a deck of ten cards with the numbers 1 to 10. Your friend selects a card from the deck. Then, you select a card from the ones remaining in the deck. You do not know your friend's number. You win if the difference between your number and your friend's number is at least 3.

a For which of your friend's numbers do you have the greatest chance of winning?

b For which of your friend's numbers do you have the least chance of winning?

c What is the probability that you will win?

CHAPTER WRAP-UP

?

How do you collect data to gain meaningful information about a population and predict the likelihood of an event occurring?

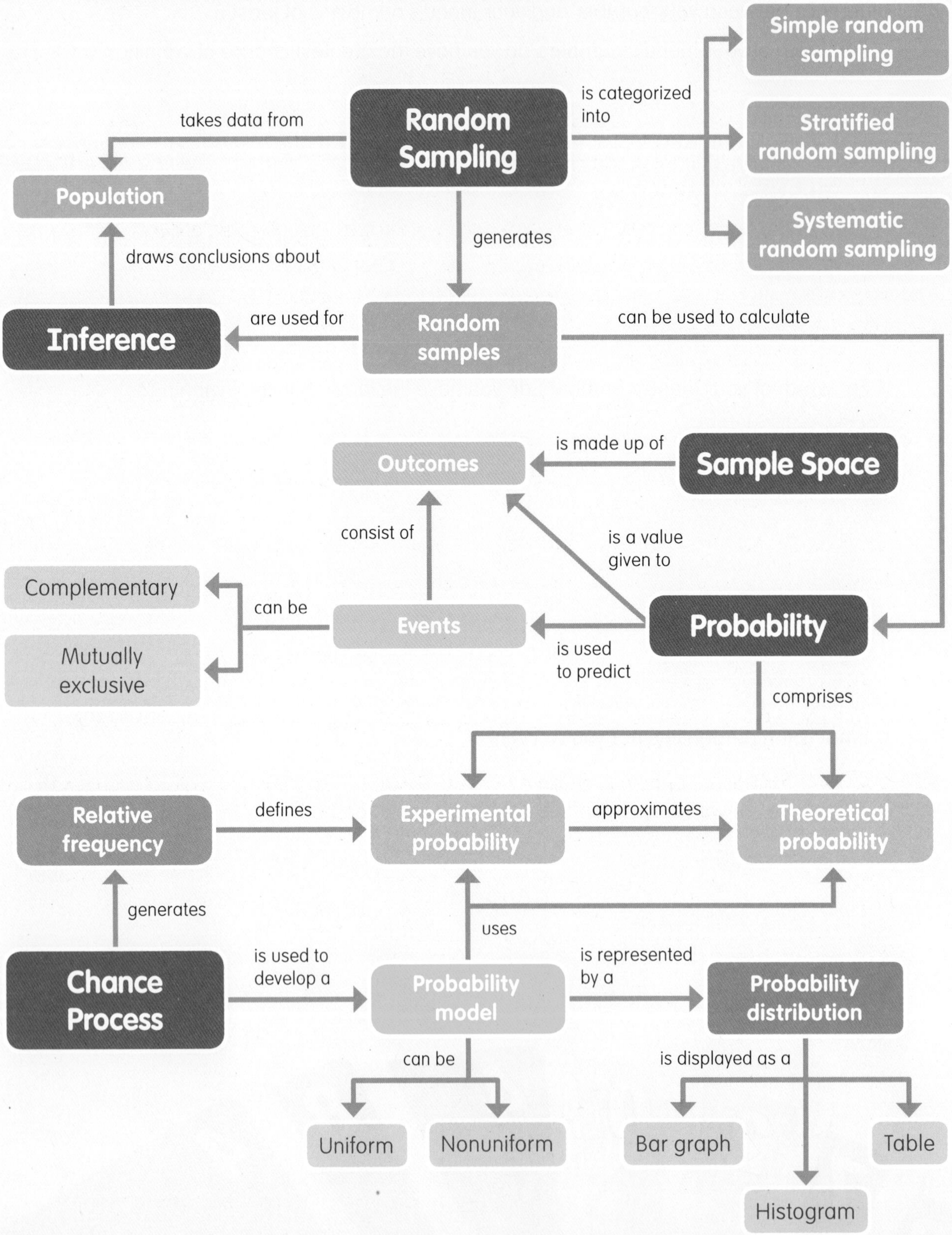

Random Sampling
takes data from
Population
is categorized into
Simple random sampling
Stratified random sampling
Systematic random sampling
generates
Random samples
are used for
Inference
draws conclusions about
can be used to calculate
Sample Space
is made up of
Outcomes
consist of
Events
can be
Complementary
Mutually exclusive
Probability
is a value given to
is used to predict
comprises
Experimental probability
approximates
Theoretical probability
Relative frequency
defines
generates
Chance Process
is used to develop a
Probability model
uses
is represented by a
Probability distribution
can be
Uniform
Nonuniform
is displayed as a
Bar graph
Table
Histogram

KEY CONCEPTS

- A sample is a set of data taken from a population. Random sampling is a process of collecting data from a population in such a way that
  - every member of the population has an equal chance of being selected, and
  - the selection of members is independent of each other.
- Three types of random sampling methods are
  - simple random sampling,
  - stratified random sampling, and
  - systematic random sampling.
- A simple random sampling method is carried out without any pre-planned order.
- A stratified random sampling method requires the population to be divided into nonoverlapping groups from which members are randomly selected.
- A systematic random sampling method is carried out by selecting the first member randomly, and subsequent members are selected at regular intervals.
- An inference in statistics is based on multiple random samples. The objectives of inference are
  - drawing conclusions about a population,
  - estimating a population characteristic, such as a population mean, and
  - drawing comparative conclusions about two populations.
- A sample space is a collection of all possible outcomes from an activity.
- An event is a collection of outcomes. Two events are mutually exclusive if they cannot happen at the same time.
- Given an event *E*, the complement of event *E* is the event that *E* does not occur. The complement of event *E* is written as E'.
- Venn diagrams can be used to illustrate mutually exclusive events, nonmutually exclusive events, complementary events, and sample spaces.
- Probability is a measure of how likely an event is to occur. It has a numeric value from 0 to 1. The number line shows what the different values mean in probability.

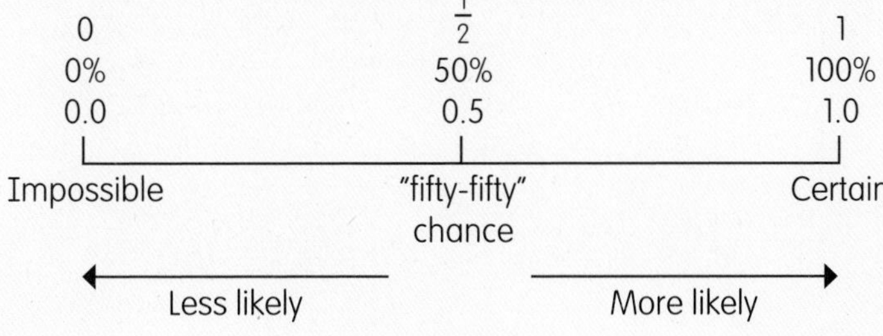

- You can use theoretical probability to predict how likely an event is to occur.
- The probability of event A, $P(A)$, is given by:
  $P(A) = \frac{\text{Number of outcomes favorable to event } A}{\text{Total number of equally likely outcomes}}$
- The theoretical probability of an event is the ratio of the number of ways the event can occur to the total number of all outcomes in the sample space.
- The experimental probability of an event is the ratio of the number of times the event has occurred to the total number of trials performed. The experimental probability approximates the theoretical probability of the event as the number of trials increases.
- A chance process is one in which data are collected as they occur by chance. You do not know the outcome before it occurs.
- Relative frequency is the ratio of the observed frequency of a data value to the total number of observations in a chance process. Relative frequency is used to compute the experimental probability.
- A probability model can be constructed using theoretical probability or experimental probability. The model is either uniform or nonuniform.
  A uniform probability model is one where all outcomes have equal probabilities.
  A nonuniform probability model is one where the outcomes do not necessarily have equal probabilities.
- A probability model can be represented by its probability distribution, which is displayed as a table, a bar graph, or a histogram.

Use the statistics given in the table to answer each question.

1. In a population of 200 students taking a science test, the following statistics for the test scores were compiled.

Mean	Median	Mode	Lower Quartile	Upper Quartile	Highest Score	Lowest Score	MAD
68.5	67.4	67	38	76	96	26	25

a By comparing the mean, the median, and the mode, what can you infer about the distribution of the test scores?

b By analyzing the statistics in the table, what can you infer about the variation of the scores?

c Estimate the number of students who scored 76 or less.

Use the data given in the table to answer each question.

2 The table summarizes the monthly sales figures, in thousands of dollars, for the women's and men's clothing departments at a store. For instance, sales in the women's department in January were $10,000.

	Jan	Feb	Mar	Apr	May	Jun	Jul	Aug	Sep	Oct	Nov	Dec
Women ($1,000)	10	15	8	12	28	34	36	18	14	16	27	40
Men ($1,000)	8	10	11	15	20	30	24	14	10	9	17	28

a Calculate the 5-point summary for each of the two departments.

b Using the same scale, draw two box plots, one for each department.

c By comparing the two box plots, describe the sales performance of the two departments.

d Calculate the mean sales figure for each of the two departments. Round each answer to the nearest dollar.

e Calculate the mean absolute deviation for each of the two departments. Round each answer to the nearest dollar.

f By comparing the means and the mean absolute deviations of the two clothing departments, what can you infer about their variability in sales?

Solve.

3. You select a card at random from 50 cards numbered from 1 to 50. What are the possible outcomes for the event of choosing a number that is a multiple of 6?

4. Three fair coins are tossed together once. List the outcomes that are favorable to the event of only two of the coins landing heads up.

5. Hayden wants to write all the two-digit numbers with no repeating digits that can be formed using the digits 5, 6, and 7.

a List all the possible outcomes.

b X is the event that the 2-digit number is divisible by 5. How many of the outcomes are favorable to event X?

6 Amy writes a computer program that will choose two letters from her own name to make a two-letter "string." The order of the letters matters. For example, AM and MA are different strings.

a List all the possible outcomes for forming a two-letter string.

b What is the probability that Amy forms a two-letter string with the letter M in it?

7 Two-digit numbers are formed using the digits 2, 3, and 4, with no repeating digits.

a List all the possible outcomes.

b What is the probability of forming a number greater than 32?

8 Victor has three videos in his playlist. One is a science fiction movie, one is an action movie, and the other is a documentary. If he shuffles the videos randomly, what is the probability that the science fiction movie is on top, the action movie is in the middle, and the documentary is on the bottom?

9 A ribbon is selected at random out of a total of 4 orange ribbons, 5 yellow ribbons, and 3 red ribbons. What is the probability of selecting an orange ribbon?

10 The spinner shown has four equal parts with numbers 1, 2, 3, and 4.

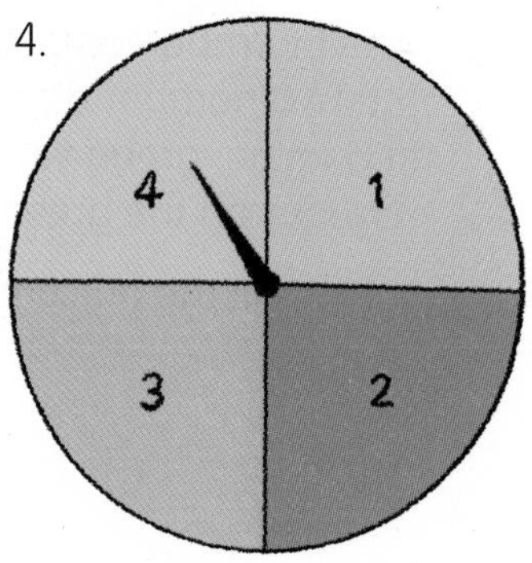

a What is the probability of landing on an even number?

b What is the probability of landing on a number less than 4?

11 Bianca and Rebecca played a game with the spinner shown. Bianca spun a 2 on 12 spins out of 50, while Rebecca spun a 2 on 19 spins out of 100.

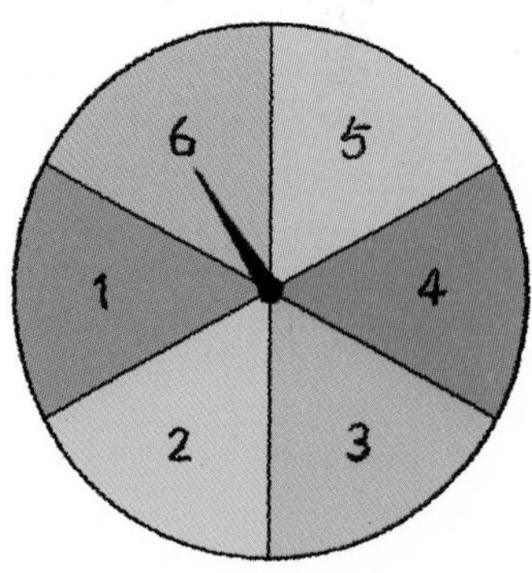

a Find each person's experimental probability of spinning a 2. Express each answer as a decimal.

b Suppose the spinner is fair, meaning that it is equally likely to land on any of the numbers, what is the theoretical probability of spinning a 2?

c Assuming the spinner is fair, what do you predict will happen to the experimental probability of getting a 2 if the spinner is spun 500 times?

12 A red number die and a green number die each have faces labeled 1 to 6. Suppose you roll the two number dice and record the values for each die as an ordered pair of numbers: (red value, green value). The event *E* is the event of getting a pair of values in which the number on the green die is greater than the number on the red die.

a Find all the outcomes favorable to event *E*.

b Find P(*E*).

13 Two fair counters are tossed together. One of the counters is white on one side and black on the other side, the other counter is white on one side, and red on the other side. They are tossed together and the face up colors of the two counters are noted. Let *E* be the event that red and black appear, and *F* be the event that at least one is white.

a Define the sample space of the experiment.

b Calculate the probability of each outcome.

c Construct the probability distribution table. Is it a uniform probability model?

d Draw a Venn diagram for events E and F. Are they mutually exclusive?

e Calculate P(E) and P(F).

14 Chloe keeps track of the number of emails she receives each day for 100 days. She then makes a table showing how many days she received 0 emails, 1 email, 2 emails, and so on, as shown in the table.

a Fill in the table below by finding each relative frequency.

Number of Emails Per Day	0	1	2	3	4	5 or more
Number of Days	5	20	15	31	27	2
Relative Frequency						

b Present the relative frequencies in a bar graph.

15 Fifty students at a school kept track of how many books they read last semester. Each student wrote the number of books he or she read in a table provided by the school librarian.

5	1	8	1	2	15	20	28	20	5
12	9	12	6	0	10	13	6	0	26
8	10	7	12	1	6	25	16	4	10
4	27	14	0	20	24	0	8	9	18
17	9	11	22	0	8	3	6	15	4

a Fill in the frequency table.

Number of Books Read	0–5	6–10	11–15	16–20	21–25	26–30
Number of Students						

b Fill in the probability distribution table.

Number of Books Read	0–5	6–10	11–15	16–20	21–25	26–30
Probability						

c Suppose the librarian selects one of the students at random. What is the probability that the student has read at least 6 books but not more than 15 books?

d What percent of the students had read 10 or fewer books?

e Present the probability distribution in a bar graph.

Assessment Prep

Answer each question.

16 A coin is flipped 10 times and the outcomes are H, H, T, H, T, T, H, H, T, H.
What is the experimental probability of the coin landing heads up on the next flip?

Ⓐ 0.4

Ⓑ 0.5

Ⓒ 0.6

Ⓓ 1

17 The spinner is spun twice and the outcomes were added. What is the probability that the sum of the outcomes is greater than 8? Write your answer and your work or explanation in the space below.

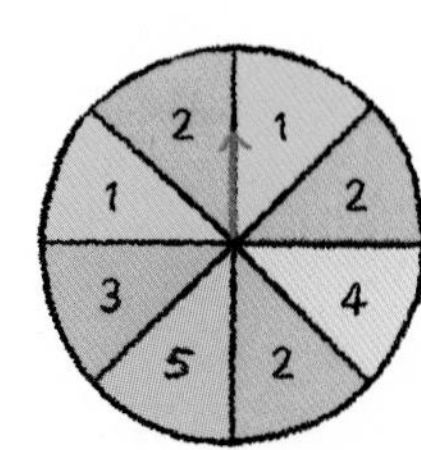

This question has two parts.

18 At a music school, 400 students were given a survey on the number of hours they practice each week. The results of this survey are shown in the relative frequency histogram.

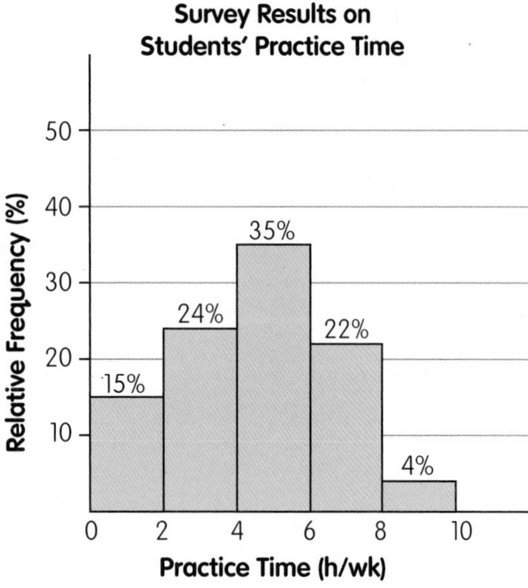

Part A

How many students practiced at least 2 hours but less than 4 hours per week?
Write your answer in the space below.

Part B

One of the students is selected at random. What is the probability that this student has practiced 6 or more hours per week?
Write your answer in the space below.

Name: ______________________ Date: ______________

The Probability Game

Eric is playing a game with his friends. The game involves obtaining two numbers from spinning the number wheel on the right and tossing a fair 6-sided number die. These are the steps of the game.

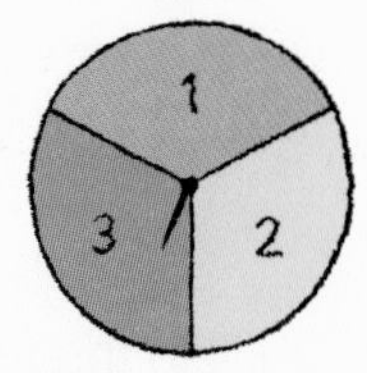

STEP 1 Guess if the sum of the two numbers obtained is odd or even.

STEP 2 Spin the number wheel.

STEP 3 Toss the number die.

STEP 4 Add up the numbers obtained from Steps 2 and 3 and check if the guess in Step 1 is correct.

1. Eric starts playing the game. He feels that the probability of getting an even sum is higher since there are more even numbers to pick from. Do you agree? Justify your reasoning.

2. What is the probability that at least one of the numbers added will be a 1 or 3? Show your work.

3. What is the probability of Eric getting a sum of 4 on his turn?

4. Eric says that the probability of getting a sum of 1 is the same as getting a sum of 10. Do you agree? Justify your reasoning.

5. a Fill in the table to show the probabilty of getting all the possible sums.

Sum	2	3	4	5	6	7	8	9
Probability								

b Find the probability that the sum is divisible by 3.

c Find the probability that the sum is not 9.

6. Eric observed 24 people playing the game. He organized their sums in the table below.

a Fill in the table to calculate the relative frequency for each sum obtained.

Sum Obtained	Observed Frequency	Relative Frequency
2	0	
3	3	
4	5	
5	3	
6	6	
7	2	
8	1	
9	4	

b Compare the experimental probability and theoretical probability obtained. What possible conclusion can Eric make from the data?

Rubric

Point(s)	Level	My Performance
7–8	4	• Most of my answers are correct. • I showed complete understanding of the concepts. • I used effective and efficient strategies to solve the problems. • I explained my answers and mathematical thinking clearly and completely.
5–6.5	3	• Some of my answers are correct. • I showed adequate understanding of the concepts. • I used effective strategies to solve the problems. • I explained my answers and mathematical thinking clearly.
3–4.5	2	• A few of my answers are correct. • I showed some understanding of the concepts. • I used some effective strategies to solve the problems. • I explained some of my answers and mathematical thinking clearly.
0–2.5	1	• A few of my answers are correct. • I showed little understanding of the concepts. • I used limited effective strategies to solve the problems. • I did not explain my answers and mathematical thinking clearly.

Teacher's Comments

PROJECT WORK

STEAM

Games at a Carnival

A carnival is a traveling funfair or circus where games are usually played. The types of carnival games are broadly categorized into games of chance and games of skills.

In a game of chance, the outcome is usually random. While in a game of skill, the outcome is largely determined on a player's mental or physical skills. In the following task, you will find out more about carnival games and design a game of chance.

Task

Work in small groups to design a game of chance.

1. With the help of the Internet, read up on some of the common types of carnival games and answer the following question: What is the winning strategy of the game?

2. Design a game of chance with your group members. You should include the following in your game design:
   a Instructions on how to play the game
   b Rules of the game
   c The theoretical probability of winning the game

3. Try out the game with your group members, and then calculate the experimental probability of winning the game.

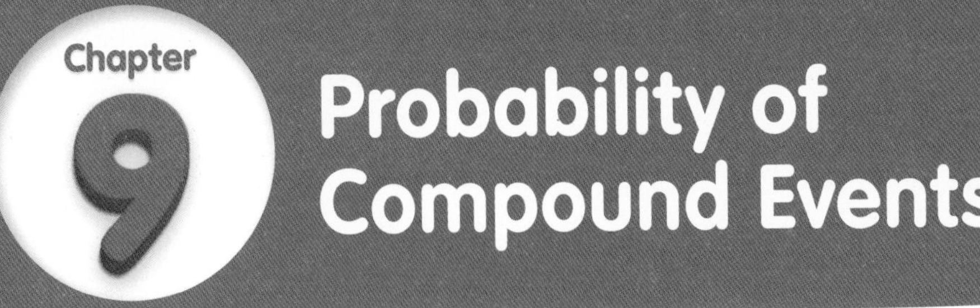

Chapter 9 Probability of Compound Events

What will be your next catch?

Suppose you are fishing in a pond stocked with largemouth bass and bluegill. You drop your line in the water and wonder which fish you will catch. If you know that there are 30 largemouth bass and 20 bluegill in the pond, you will know how to calculate the probability of catching a largemouth bass. What about the probability of catching three largemouth bass consecutively? In this chapter, you will learn how to calculate the probability of this and other compound events.

How do you find the probability of independent or dependent compound events?

Name: ______________________________ Date: ______________

Finding the probability of events

The outcomes of an event are the possible results of an activity or experiment. The collection of all possible outcomes from an activity or experiment is known as the sample space.

Suppose the number of equally likely outcomes in the sample space is n and the number of outcomes favorable to an event E is m. The probability of event E occurring, $P(E)$ is:

$$P(E) = \frac{\text{Number of outcomes favorable to event } E}{\text{Total number of equally likely outcomes}} = \frac{m}{n}$$

The probability of an event can be expressed as a percent, a decimal, or a fraction between 0 and 1.

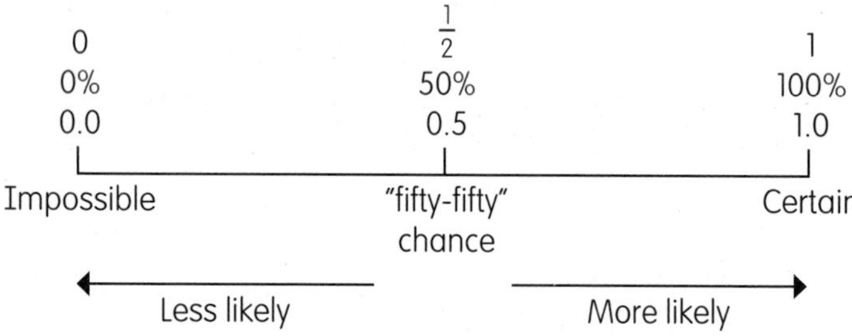

A probability closer to 1 means that the chances of an event happening are more likely.
A probability closer to 0 means that the chances of an event happening are less likely.
A probability of 0.5 means that the event is equally likely to happen or not happen.

Quick Check

Solve.

A box has 2 black balls, 7 red balls, and 3 green balls. A ball is randomly chosen from the box.

1. What is the probability of choosing a green ball?

2. What is the probability of choosing a black ball?

3. What is the probability of choosing a blue ball?

4. What is the probability of choosing a ball that is not red?

5. What is the probability of choosing a red or green ball?

Using Venn diagrams to show relationships of events

a Mutually exclusive events

Two events that cannot occur at the same time are mutually exclusive. If event A occurs, event B cannot occur; if event B occurs, event A cannot occur. For example, rolling a 1 and rolling a 6 with a toss of a number die are mutually exclusive events.

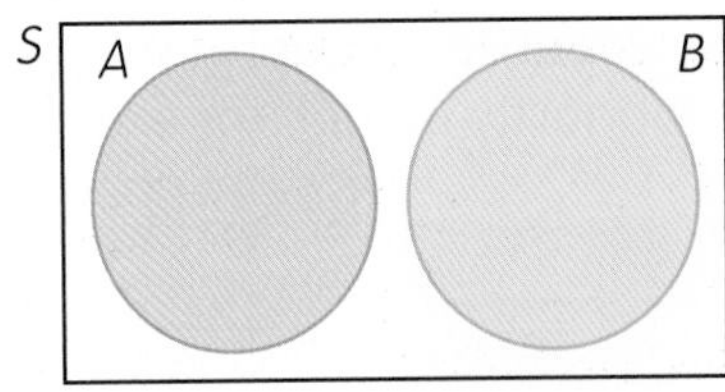

You can use a Venn diagram to represent mutually exclusive events. The circles representing events A and B do not overlap to show that the events cannot happen at the same time.

b Complementary events

Given an event E, the complement of E is the event that E does not occur. Events E and E' are mutually exclusive and their probabilities add up to 1: $P(E) + P(E') = 1$. For example, getting heads and getting tails with a flip of a coin are complementary events. However, rolling a 1 and rolling a 6 are mutually exclusive events but they are not complementary. Rolling a 1 and rolling a number other than 1 are complementary events.

S, E, E′

The Venn diagram shows event E and its complement, E', in the sample space. Event E is represented by the circle in the sample space. The complementary event, E', is the region outside the circle.

▶ Quick Check

Determine whether events *X* and *Y* are mutually exclusive or complementary.

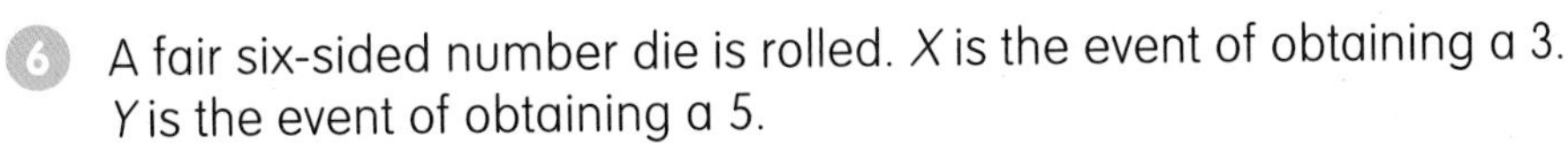

6. A fair six-sided number die is rolled. X is the event of obtaining a 3. Y is the event of obtaining a 5.

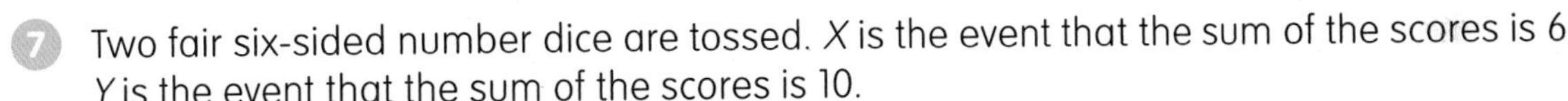

7. Two fair six-sided number dice are tossed. X is the event that the sum of the scores is 6. Y is the event that the sum of the scores is 10.

8. A number is randomly selected from 1 to 20. X is the event of choosing a number that is a factor of 24. Y is the event of choosing a number that is a multiple of 6.

9. A fair six-sided number die is tossed. X is the event of obtaining an even number. Y is the event of obtaining an odd number.

Developing probability models

A probability model consists of a sample space of outcomes, events, and the probabilities of these outcomes and events. You can represent the outcomes of a sample space and their probabilities in a table or a graph. Such a presentation is known as a probability distribution.

A probability model in which all the outcomes are equally likely to occur is called a uniform probability model. For example, rolling a fair 6-sided number die:

Value	1	2	3	4	5	6
Probability	$\frac{1}{6}$	$\frac{1}{6}$	$\frac{1}{6}$	$\frac{1}{6}$	$\frac{1}{6}$	$\frac{1}{6}$

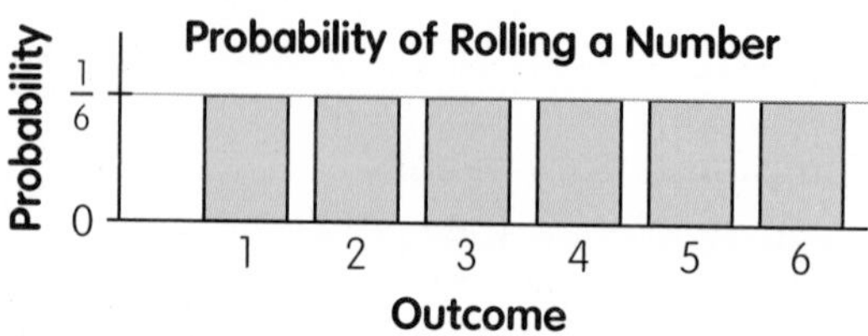

A probability model in which outcomes do not have equal probabilities is called a nonuniform probability model. For example, randomly choosing a pencil from a box of 3 yellow, 6 orange, 2 green, and 4 brown pencils:

Color	Yellow	Orange	Green	Brown
Probability	$\frac{3}{15}$	$\frac{6}{15}$	$\frac{2}{15}$	$\frac{4}{15}$

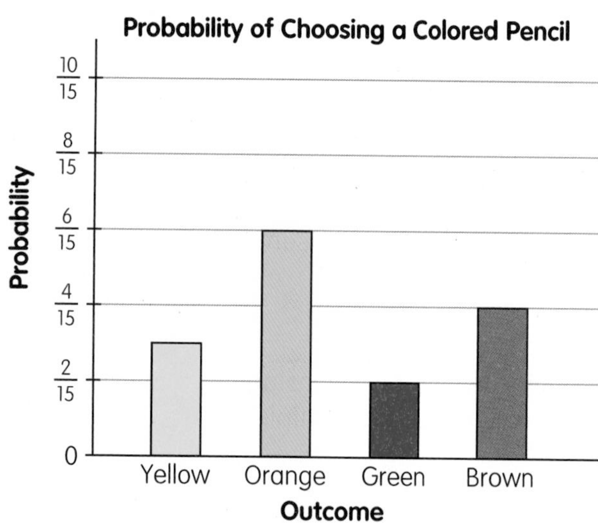

Quick Check

Solve.

There are 2 red, 5 blue, and 3 green pens in a box. Benjamin randomly selects a pen from the box.

10. Find the probability of randomly picking a blue pen.

11. Find the probability of randomly picking a pen that is not green.

12. Construct the probability model.

Name: ______________________ Date: ______________

1 Compound Events

Learning Objectives:

- Identify compound events.
- Represent compound events.

New Vocabulary
compound event
simple event
possibility diagram
tree diagram

Suppose you play a game of Rock, Paper, Scissors with your partner. What are all the possible outcomes? Record all the possible outcomes using a list of ordered pairs, a two-way grid, or a tree diagram.

ENGAGE

Suppose there is a bag with an equal number of oranges and apples. You randomly pick a piece of fruit from the bag, replace it, and then choose another piece of fruit. What is the probability of first picking an apple and then an orange? What is the probability of first picking an orange and then another orange? Discuss.

LEARN Identify compound events

1 A compound event consists of two or more simple events occurring together or one after another. For example, rolling a number die is a simple event. However, rolling a number die and tossing a coin simultaneously is a compound event.

There are six possible outcomes when you roll a number die. The sample space is {1, 2, 3, 4, 5, 6}.

There are two possible outcomes when you toss a coin. They are {*H*, *T*}, where *H* represents the outcome Heads, and *T* represents the outcome Tails.

So, the sample space of the compound event of rolling a number die and tossing a coin simultaneously is {1*H*, 1*T*, 2*H*, 2*T*, 3*H*, 3*T*, 4*H*, 4*T*, 5*H*, 5*T*, 6*H*, 6*T*}.

Braces { } are used to list the set of possible outcomes in a sample space or outcomes that are favorable to an event.

TRY Practice identifying compound events

Determine whether each event is a simple or a compound event. State the single event or identify the simple events that make up the compound event.

1. Winning a football game.

2. Getting two heads when two coins are tossed together.

3. Getting a number that is less than 2 or greater than 4 when spinning the spinner as shown once.

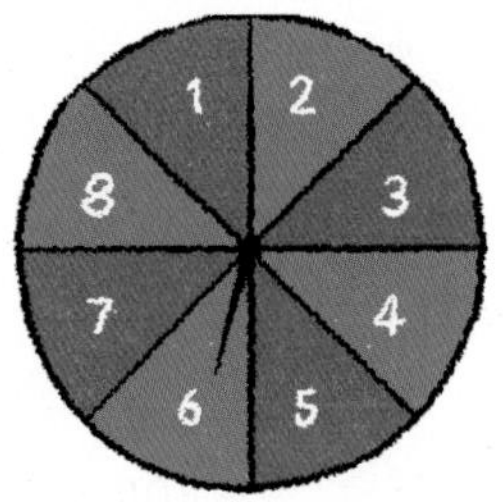

4. Getting a number that is less than 2 or greater than 4 when spinning the spinner as shown two times consecutively.

5. Getting heads when a coin is tossed and getting a 3 when a six-sided number die is rolled.

6. Rolling two fair six-sided number dice and obtaining a sum of 10 from the throws.

ENGAGE

A box contains number cards from 1 to 6. Another box contains alphabets from A to F. Make a list of all the possible outcomes in a table or a diagram. Compare your list with your partner's.

LEARN Represent the sample space for compound events

1. There are many ways to represent the sample space of a compound event. You may use an organized list to show all the possible outcomes of rolling a number die and tossing a coin simultaneously, such as the one below.

Die	1	1	2	2	3	3	4	4	5	5	6	6
Coin	H	T	H	T	H	T	H	T	H	T	H	T
Outcome	$1H$	$1T$	$2H$	$2T$	$3H$	$3T$	$4H$	$4T$	$5H$	$5T$	$6H$	$6T$

The sample space for rolling a number die and tossing a coin simultaneously is {$1H$, $1T$, $2H$, $2T$, $3H$, $3T$, $4H$, $4T$, $5H$, $5T$, $6H$, $6T$}.

2. You may also use a two-way grid to help you visualize all the possible outcomes of compound events. A two-way grid is a type of possibility diagram that represents the sample space for compound events.

To represent the outcomes on a two-way grid, list the outcomes for rolling a number die on the horizontal axis and the outcomes for tossing a coin on the vertical axis. Each intersection of grid lines represents a possible outcome for the compound event of rolling a number die and tossing a coin simultaneously.

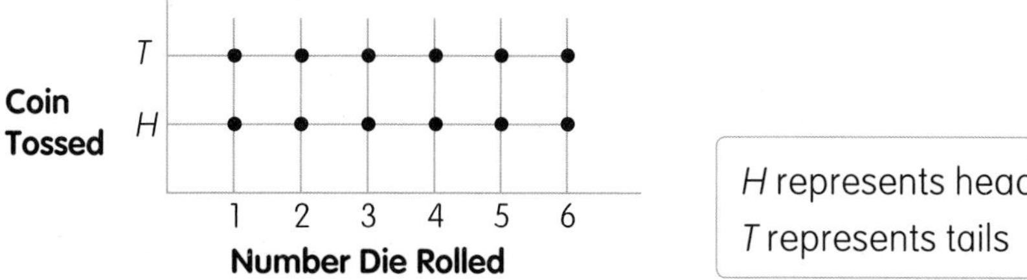

Since the two simple events occur together, the order of the events is not important. You can use a dot to indicate each possible outcome on the grid. From the diagram, you can see that there are $2 \cdot 6 = 12$ possible outcomes in the sample space for this compound event. Notice that the outcomes in the two-way grid are the same as those in the organized list for this sample space.

3 Suppose there are two spinners, each divided into three equal parts. You can show the outcomes of spinning the two spinners together using a table of ordered pairs.

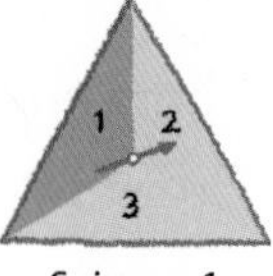

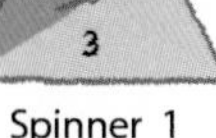

Spinner 1 Spinner 2

Spinner 2 \ Spinner 1	1	2	3
1	(1, 1)	(2, 1)	(3, 1)
2	(1, 2)	(2, 2)	(3, 2)
3	(1, 3)	(2, 3)	(3, 3)

The row and column headings of the table above list the outcomes of spinning each spinner, 1, 2, or 3. Each possible outcome of the compound event of spinning the two spinners together is written as an ordered pair: (**first event**, **second event**). You can see that there are $3 \cdot 3 = 9$ possible outcomes in the sample space.

4 A tree diagram is another type of representation of the sample space for compound events. The tree diagram below shows the outcomes of a simple event, tossing a fair coin. The branches from the node represent all the possible outcomes.

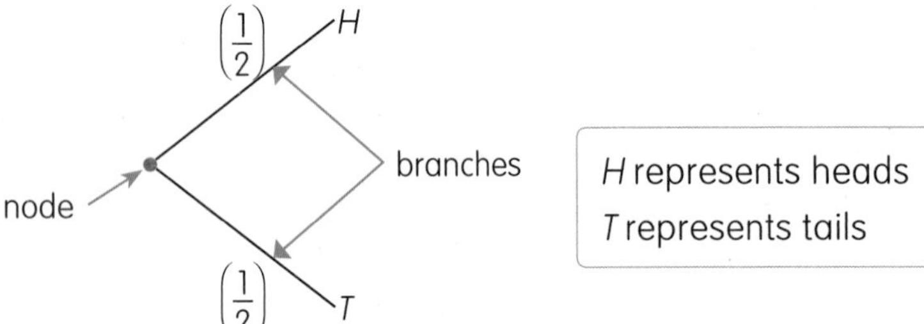

When drawing tree diagrams, take note of the following:

- Each branch starts from the same node.
- The number of branches indicates the number of outcomes the event has.
- The outcome for an event is written at the end of a branch.
- The probability of the outcome of an event is written in parentheses along the branch.
- The probabilities of the branches from each node must add up to 1.

If the coin is tossed twice consecutively, the possible outcomes are represented this way:

First Toss	Second Toss	Outcome
H	*H*	(*H*, *H*)
	T	(*H*, *T*)
T	*H*	(*T*, *H*)
	T	(*T*, *T*)

Listing the outcomes in a column is optional in a tree diagram. Determine the number of outcomes by counting the number of branches at the last event in the tree.

H represents heads
T represents tails

By counting the number of branches at the last event in the tree, you can see that there are 4 equally likely possible outcomes.

5 Suppose you turn a fair spinner and then toss a fair coin. The tree diagram below shows all the possible outcomes.

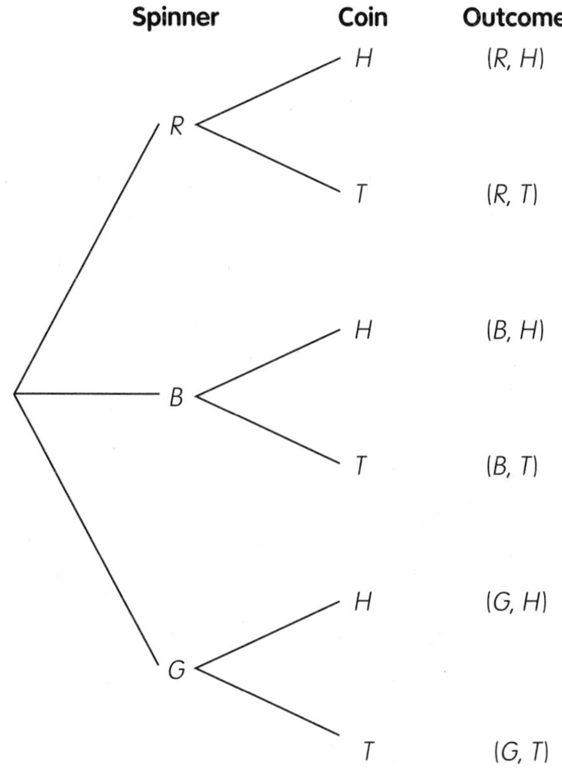

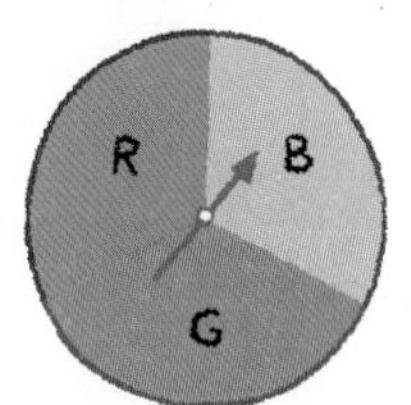

R represents red
B represents blue
G represents green
H represents heads
T represents tails

There are 6 possible outcomes for this compound event.

How would you draw the tree diagram if the order of the two simple events were reversed: toss the coin first and then turn the spinner?

TRY Practice representing the sample space for compound events

Determine the number of possible outcomes for each compound event.

1. There are four shirts in one drawer: 1 blue, 1 yellow, 1 red, and 1 gray. There are two pairs of socks in another drawer: 1 pair of gray socks and 1 pair of black socks. A shirt and a pair of socks are taken out of the drawers. How many possible outcomes are there?

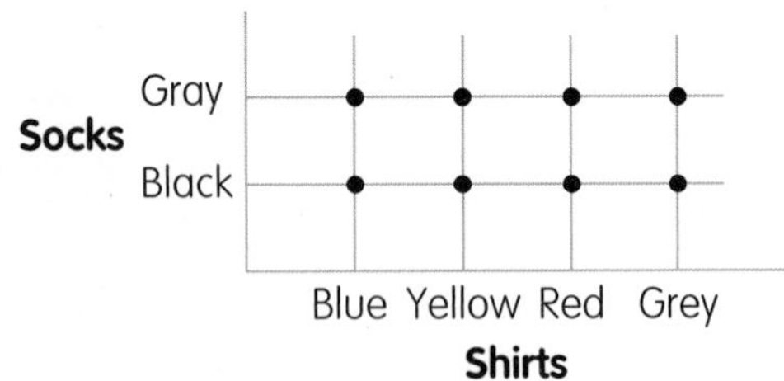

2. The results of tossing two fair six-sided number dice are added. How many possible outcomes are there?

First Toss

+	1	2	3	4	5	6
1	2	3	4	5	6	7
2	3	4	5	6	7	8
3	4	5	6	7	8	9
4	5	6	7	8	9	10
5	6	7	8	9	10	11
6	7	8	9	10	11	12

Second Toss

Write the operation of the compound event at the top left cell of the table to indicate that you are finding the sum of the outcomes of two events.

3. Colin turned the two spinners below.

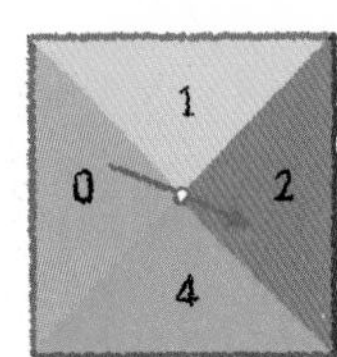

Spinner 1

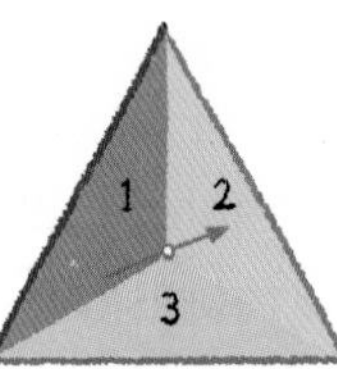

Spinner 2

Fill in the table below to make a list of all the possible outcomes. How many possible outcomes are there?

Spinner 1

Spinner 2	0	1	2	4
1	(0, 1)	(1, 1)		
2				
3				

Draw a possibility diagram and determine the number of possible outcomes for each compound event.

4. The outcomes of tossing two fair coins together.

5. The outcomes of rolling two fair six-sided number dice are multiplied.

6. The outcomes of rolling a fair six-sided number die and a fair four-sided number die with sides labeled 1 to 4. (The outcome of rolling a four-sided die is the number facing down.)

Draw a tree diagram and determine the number of possible outcomes for each compound event.

7 Orion has a yellow, a pink, and a green highlighter in his pencil case. He also has 1 red pen and 2 black pens. He randomly selects a highlighter and a pen.

8 Pedro has two bags. The first bag contains 2 blue beads and 1 green bead. The second bag contains 3 cards with the letters P, Q, and R. Pedro randomly takes an item from each bag.

9 A fair coin is tossed and then a fair four-sided color die with its faces painted yellow, green, blue, and black is rolled. (The color facing down is recorded.)

Name: ______________________ Date: ______________

INDEPENDENT PRACTICE

Determine whether each statement is True or False.

1. Selecting the letter A from the word PROBABILITY is a compound event.

2. Selecting the letter B from the word BASEBALL and then from the word ABLE is a simple event.

3. Tossing a fair six-sided number die to get either an even number or the number 5 is a compound event.

4. There are 3 red cards and 4 blue cards in a deck. Drawing two red cards in a row from the deck, without replacing the first card before drawing the second card, is a compound event.

Determine whether each event is a simple or a compound event. If it is a compound event, identify the simple events that make up the compound event.

5. Getting the number 6 when a fair six-sided number die is rolled.

6. Rolling three fair six-sided number dice and obtaining a sum of 18 from the throws.

7. Getting the number 18 when a fair twenty-sided number die is rolled.

8 Sofia has 3 red cards and 4 blue cards. She first draws a blue card. Without replacing the first card, she then draws another blue card.

Solve.

9 In the top drawer, there are two battery-operated flashlights: red and yellow. In the second drawer, there are three packages of batteries: sizes AA, C, and D. A flashlight and a package of batteries are randomly selected.

a Draw a possibility diagram to represent all possible outcomes.

b How many possible outcomes are there?

10 Two electronic spinners, A and B, are spun by pressing a button. Spinner A has four sections labeled 1 to 4, while B has three sections, labeled 1 to 3. Spinner B, due to a technical error, will never land on number 2 if Spinner A lands on a 4.

a Draw a possibility diagram to represent all possible outcomes.

b How many possible outcomes are there?

11 Matthew has two boxes. The first box contains 3 black pens and 1 red pen. The second box contains 1 green ball and 1 yellow ball. Draw a tree diagram to show all the possible outcomes for randomly drawing a pen and a ball from each box.

12 Lillian first tosses a fair six-sided number die. Then, she tosses a fair coin. Draw a tree diagram to represent all possible outcomes.

13 For a game, Jesse first rolls a fair four-sided number die labeled 1 to 4. The result recorded is the number facing fown. Then, he randomly draws a ball from a box containing two different colored balls.

a Draw a tree diagram to show all the possible outcomes.

b How many possible outcomes are there?

c **Mathematical Habit 2 Use mathematical reasoning**
If Jesse first draws a colored ball and then rolls the four-sided number die, will the number of possible outcomes be the same? Explain your reasoning.

14 Trinity first rolls a fair four-sided number die with sides labeled 1 to 4. Then, she rolls another fair four-sided number die with sides labeled 2 to 5. The results recorded are the numbers facing down.

a Draw a possibility diagram to find the number of favorable outcomes for an odd sum.

b Draw a possibility diagram to find the number of favorable outcomes for a difference greater than 2.

Name: ______________________ Date: ____________

2 Probability of Compound Events

Learning Objective:
- Calculate the probability of compound events.

A ball is randomly drawn from a bag with 3 blue balls and 1 red ball. Then, a fair n-sided die labeled 1 to n is rolled. The probability of picking a red ball and rolling the number n is $\frac{1}{48}$. Find the probability of picking a blue ball and rolling the number n.

ENGAGE

A bag contains 3 black beads and 2 white beads. You randomly pick a bead from the bag, replace it, and then choose another bead. What are all the possible outcomes? How can you find the probability of picking a white bead and then a black bead? Discuss.

LEARN Find the probability of compound events

1. From a possibility diagram, you can count the number of favorable outcomes and the total number of outcomes, then find the probability of a compound event E using:

$$P(E) = \frac{\text{Number of outcomes favorable to event } E}{\text{Total number of equally likely outcomes}}$$

Draw a tree diagram to find the probability of getting heads and then tails when a coin is tossed twice.

First Toss	Second Toss	Outcome
H	H	(H, H)
	T	**(H, T)**
T	H	(T, H)
	T	(T, T)

You want to find the probability of getting heads and then tails, so the order of outcomes is important. (H, T) is not the same as (T, H).

H represents heads
T represents tails

From the tree diagram, you can see that there are four possible outcomes: (H, H), (H, T), (T, H), and (T, T). However, there is only one favorable outcome, (H, T). So, $P(H, T) = \frac{1}{4}$.

2 Suppose that it is equally likely to rain or not rain on any given day. Draw a tree diagram and use it to find the probability that it rains exactly once on two consecutive days.

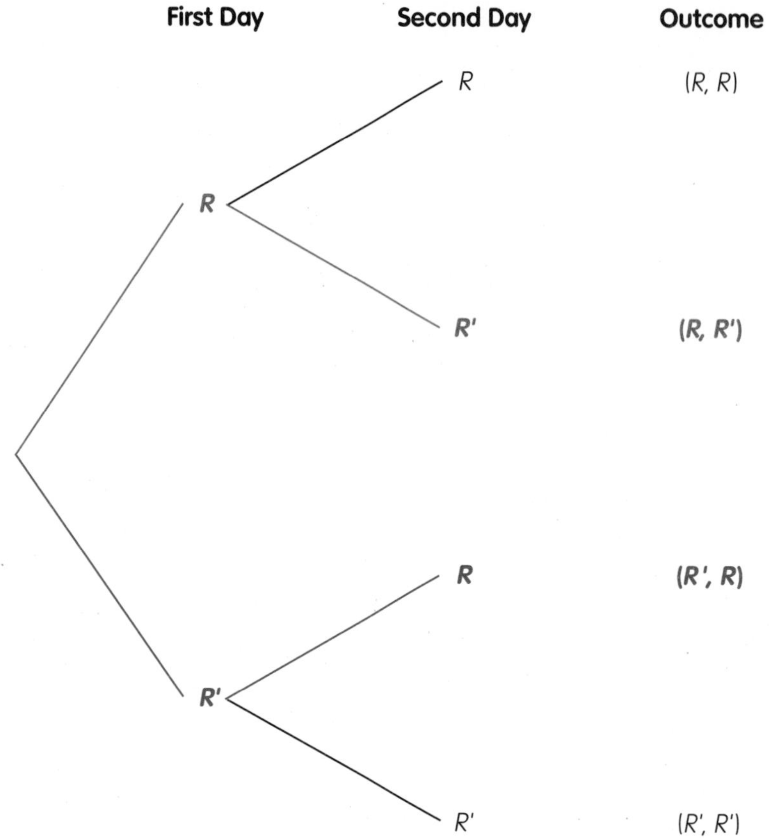

R represents raining
R' represents not raining

The favorable outcome is "rain exactly once on two consecutive days." So, you should look for the outcome that gives **(*R*, *R'*)** or **(*R'*, *R*)**, meaning either it rains on the first day or it rains on the second day.

$$P(\text{rain exactly once on two consecutive days}) = \frac{2}{4}$$
$$= \frac{1}{2}$$

3 A fair coin and a fair six-sided number die are tossed together. Find the probability of getting heads and rolling a 5.

Method 1

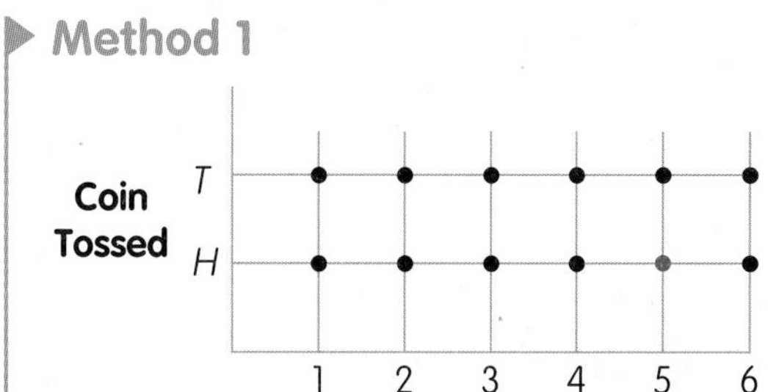

H represents heads
T represents tails

$P(H, 5) = \frac{1}{12}$

Method 2

		Number Die					
		1	2	3	4	5	6
Coin	*H*	(1, *H*)	(2, *H*)	(3, *H*)	(4, *H*)	(5, *H*)	(6, *H*)
	T	(1, *T*)	(2, *T*)	(3, *T*)	(4, *T*)	(5, *T*)	(6, *T*)

H represents heads
T represents tails

$P(H, 5) = P(5, H)$
$= \frac{1}{12}$

4 Two fair six-sided number dice are rolled. Find the probability that the sum of the two numbers rolled is a prime number.

	First Number Die						
Second Number Die +	**1**	**2**	**3**	**4**	**5**	**6**
1	**2**	**3**	4	**5**	6	**7**
2	**3**	4	**5**	6	**7**	8
3	4	**5**	6	**7**	8	9
4	**5**	6	**7**	8	9	10
5	6	**7**	8	9	10	**11**
6	**7**	8	9	10	**11**	12

Recall that a prime number is a whole number greater than 1 that has only two factors, the number itself and 1.

The prime numbers in the possibility diagram are **2**, **3**, **5**, **7**, and **11**. There are 15 prime numbers out of 36 equally likely possible outcomes.

$P(\text{sum is prime}) = \frac{15}{36}$
$= \frac{5}{12}$

5 Two fair four-sided number dice, one red (R) and one blue (B), are rolled at the same time. The number facing down on each die is recorded. The red die has faces labeled 1, 2, 4, and 7. The blue die has faces labeled 2, 5, 8, and 9. Find the probability that the number recorded from the blue die is more than 3 greater than the number recorded from the red die. That is, find $P(B - R > 3)$.

Method 1

Red Number Die

Blue Number Die	1	2	4	7
2	(1, 2)	(2, 2)	(4, 2)	(7, 2)
5	(1, 5)	(2, 5)	(4, 5)	(7, 5)
8	(1, 8)	(2, 8)	(4, 8)	(7, 8)
9	(1, 9)	(2, 9)	(4, 9)	(7, 9)

$P(B - R > 3) = \frac{7}{16}$

Method 2

Red Number Die

Blue Number Die: –	1	2	4	7
2	1	0	−2	−5
5	4	3	1	−2
8	7	6	4	1
9	8	7	5	2

$P(B - R > 3) = \frac{7}{16}$

TRY Practice finding the probability of compound events

Draw a tree diagram and find the probability.

1. Three fair coins are tossed at the same time.
   a Find the probability of getting all heads.

   b Find the probability of getting at least two tails.

Fill in the possibility diagram and find the probability.

2. Suppose you spin the two spinners on the right. Fill in the possibility diagram below. Then, find the probability that the pointers stop at 1 on Spinner 1 and blue (*B*) on Spinner 2.

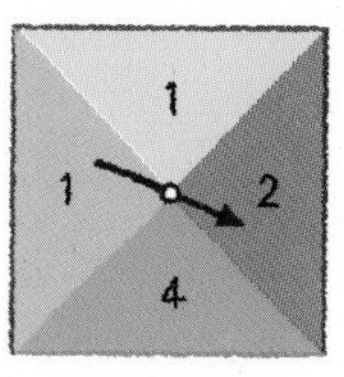

Spinner 1

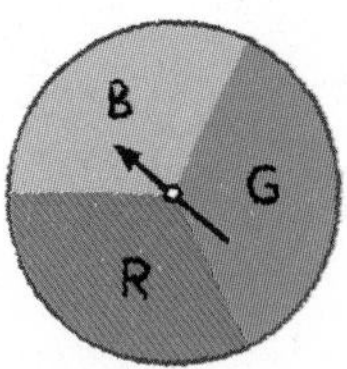

Spinner 2

Spinner 2 \ Spinner 1	1	1	2	4
B			(2, *B*)	(4, *B*)
G	(1, *G*)	(1, *G*)	(2, *G*)	(4, *G*)
R	(1, *R*)	(1, *R*)	(2, *R*)	(4, *R*)

P(1, *B*) = $\frac{\square}{\square}$ = ______

Draw a possibility diagram and find the probability.

3. Two fair four-sided number dice, each with faces labeled 1 to 4, are rolled together. The result recorded is the number facing down. Find the probability that the product of the two numbers is divisible by 2.

4. One colored disc is randomly drawn from each of two bags. Each bag has 5 colored discs: 1 red, 1 green, 1 blue, 1 yellow, and 1 white. Find the probability of drawing at least a blue or yellow disc.

5. A box has 4 marbles: 1 black, 1 green, 1 red, and 1 yellow. Another box has 3 marbles: 1 white, 1 green, and 1 red. A marble is taken at random from each box. Find the probability that a red marble is not drawn.

Name: ______________________ Date: ______________

INDEPENDENT PRACTICE

Solve.

1. A bag contains 2 blue balls and 1 red ball. Tyler randomly draws a ball from the bag and replaces it before he draws a second ball. Use a possibility diagram to find the probability that the balls drawn are of different colors.

2. A letter is randomly chosen from the word FOOD, followed by randomly choosing a letter from the word DOT. Use a tree diagram to find the probability that both letters chosen are the same.

3. There are three balls in a bag: 1 blue, 1 green, and 1 yellow. A ball is randomly picked from the bag. Then, a fair four-sided number die labeled 1 to 4 is rolled. The result recorded is the number facing down. Use a possibility diagram to find the probability of picking a yellow ball and rolling a 4.

4. Mason rolled two number dice: a fair six-sided die and a fair four-sided die labeled 1 to 4. Use a possibility diagram to find the probability of rolling the number 3 on both dice.

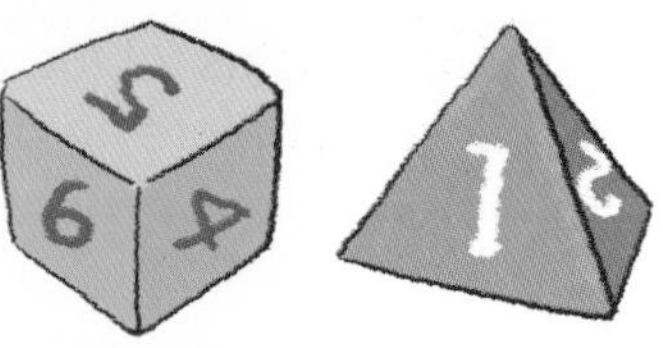

5. A bike shop has 3 bikes with 20-speed gears and 2 bikes with 18-speed gears. The bike shop also sells 1 blue helmet and 1 yellow helmet. Use a possibility diagram to find the probability of getting an 18-speed bicycle and a blue helmet if one bike and one helmet are randomly selected from the shop.

6. Evelyn randomly draws a number card from one of the three cards on the right. After replacing the first drawn card, she randomly draws another card. The product of the two numbers is recorded.

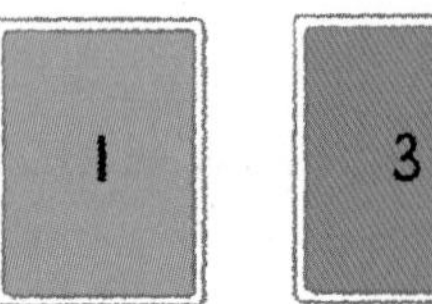

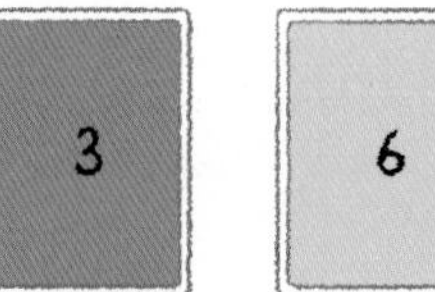

a Draw a possibility diagram to represent all possible outcomes.

b Using your answer in a, find the probability of forming a number greater than 10 but less than 30.

7 Ana and Devin watch television together for 2 hours. Ana selects a channel for the first hour, and Devin selects a channel for the second hour. Ana's remote control randomly selects from Channels A, B, and C. Devin's remote control randomly selects from Channels C, D, and E.

a Draw a possibility diagram to represent all possible outcomes for the channels they watch on television for 2 hours.

b Using your answer in a, what is the probability of watching the same channel for both hours?

8 A color disc is randomly drawn from a bag that contains the following discs.

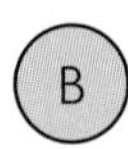

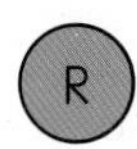

After a disc is drawn, a fair coin is tossed. Use a possibility diagram to find the probability of drawing a red disc and landing heads up.

9. Tiana tosses a fair coin three times. Use a tree diagram to find the probability of getting the same result in all three tosses.

10. Ms. Smith wants to make pancakes. She has 3 types of flour: cornmeal flour, whole wheat flour, and white flour. She also has 2 cartons of milk: whole milk and low fat milk. However, all the types of flour and milk are not labeled, so she randomly guesses which types of flour and milk to use for her pancakes. Assume that each type of flour and each type of milk is equally likely to be chosen.

   a Draw a tree diagram to represent all possible outcomes.

   b Using your answer in a, find the probability that Ms. Smith will use cornmeal flour and low fat milk for her pancakes.

Name: ______________________ Date: ______________

Independent Events

Learning Objectives:

- Identify independent events.
- Use the multiplication rule and the addition rule of probability to solve problems involving independent events.

New Vocabulary
independent events
multiplication rule of probability
addition rule of probability

THINK

Three people play a game that involves tossing two coins. The rules are:

- Player A wins if the results are 2 heads.
- Player B wins if the results are 2 tails.
- Player C wins if the 2 coins do not land on the same side.

Use a tree diagram to show the outcomes and find the probability of each person winning the game. Explain whether the game is fair.

ENGAGE

Ethan has two bags of red and green gummy bears. He randomly chooses a bear from each bag. Draw a diagram to represent all the possible outcomes. What is the probability of picking two bears of the same color? Explain.

LEARN Solve problems with independent events

1 Suppose you have a spinner with two equal sections and three color cards as shown.

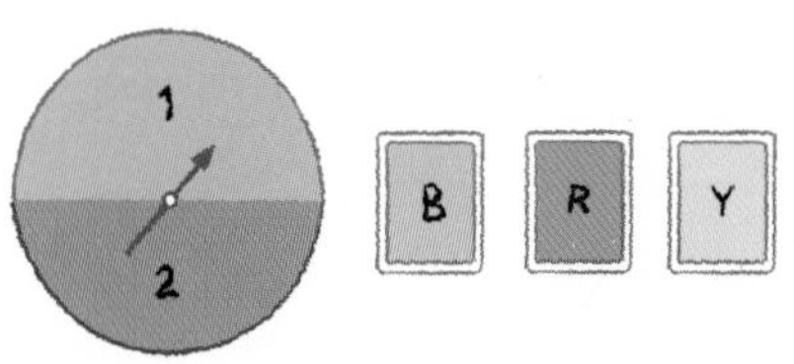

The event of spinning a 2 and the event of drawing a red card are independent events. Two events are independent if the occurrence of one event does not affect the probability of the occurrence of the other event. The outcome of the spinner will not affect the probability of drawing any of the color cards.

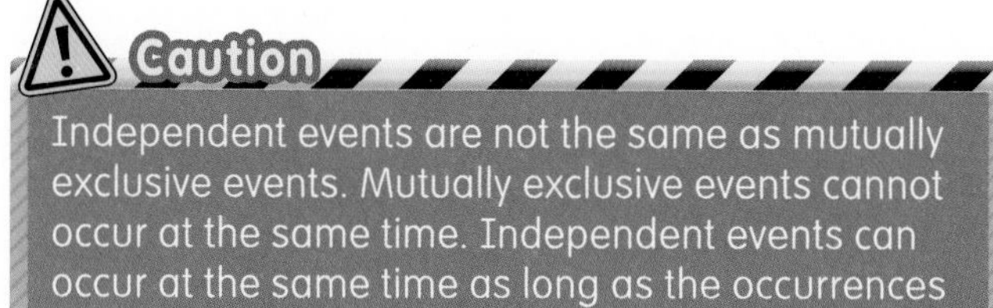

2 Consider the situation in 1. The tree diagram below represents the independent events that make up the compound event, and their corresponding probabilities.

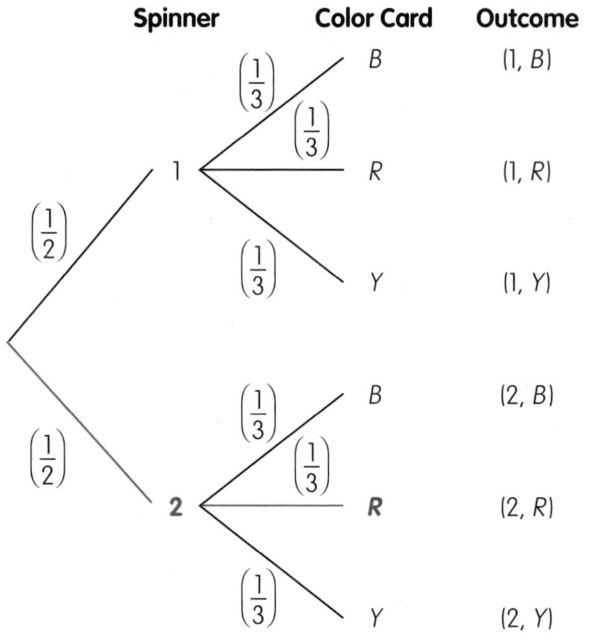

Spinner	Color Card	Outcome
1 $\left(\frac{1}{2}\right)$	B $\left(\frac{1}{3}\right)$	(1, *B*)
	R $\left(\frac{1}{3}\right)$	(1, *R*)
	Y $\left(\frac{1}{3}\right)$	(1, *Y*)
2 $\left(\frac{1}{2}\right)$	B $\left(\frac{1}{3}\right)$	(2, *B*)
	R $\left(\frac{1}{3}\right)$	(2, *R*)
	Y $\left(\frac{1}{3}\right)$	(2, *Y*)

B represents blue
R represents red
Y represents yellow

Since the spinner has two equal sections, the probability of getting any one of the two numbers is $\frac{1}{2}$. Since there is a fair chance of drawing any one of the three cards, the probability of drawing either a blue, red, or yellow card is $\frac{1}{3}$. The probabilities are labeled on the branches of the tree diagram.

From the tree diagram, you can see that there is a total of 6 equally likely outcomes. The probability of spinning a 2 and drawing a red card is: $P(2, R) = \frac{1}{6}$.

You can also use the multiplication rule of probability to find the probability of spinning a 2 and drawing a red card.

$P(2, R) = \mathbf{P(2) \cdot P(R)}$

$= \frac{1}{2} \cdot \frac{1}{3}$ Multiply P(2) and P(*R*).

$= \frac{1}{6}$ Simplify.

In general, for two independent events *A* and *B*, the multiplication rule of probability states that:
$P(A \text{ and } B) = P(A) \cdot P(B)$

3. Suppose the blue card is replaced by a red card as shown.

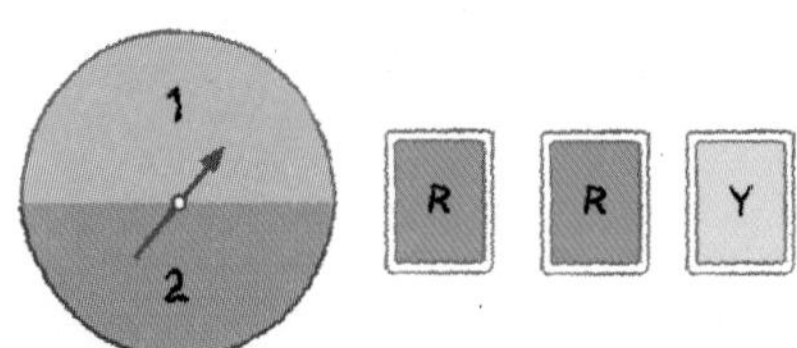

The possible outcomes will be:

Spinner		Color Card		Outcome
$\left(\frac{1}{2}\right)$	1	$\left(\frac{1}{3}\right)$	*R*	(1, *R*)
		$\left(\frac{1}{3}\right)$	*R*	(1, *R*)
		$\left(\frac{1}{3}\right)$	*Y*	(1, *Y*)
$\left(\frac{1}{2}\right)$	**2**	$\left(\frac{1}{3}\right)$	***R***	(2, *R*)
		$\left(\frac{1}{3}\right)$	***R***	(2, *R*)
		$\left(\frac{1}{3}\right)$	*Y*	(2, *Y*)

R represents red
Y represents yellow

There is a total of 6 outcomes. To find the probability of spinning a 2 and drawing a red card, you can see that 2 out of 6 outcomes are favorable. So, the probability is:

$$P(2, R) = \frac{2}{6}$$
$$= \frac{1}{3}$$

The tree diagram on page 339 can be simplified by combining the identical outcomes, (1, *R*) and (2, *R*), as shown below.

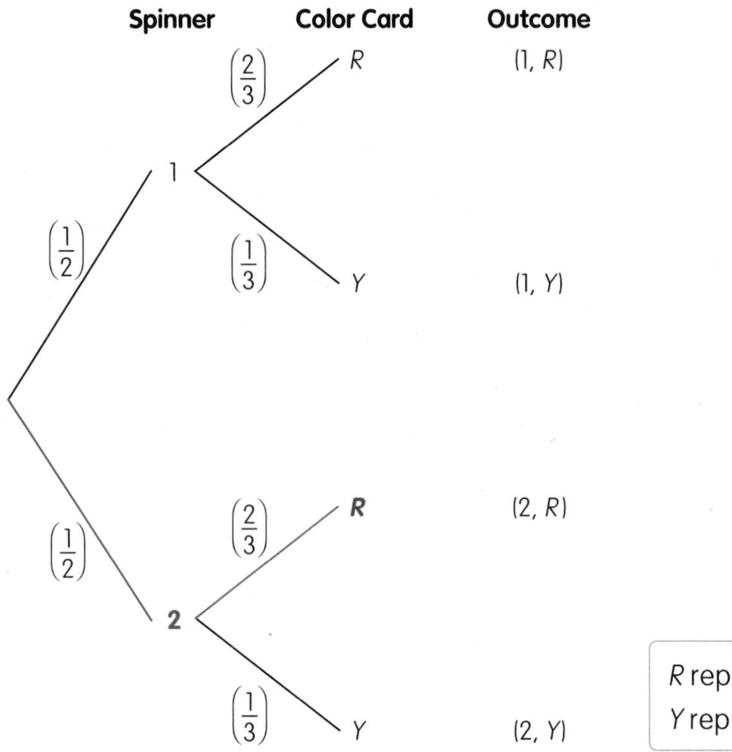

R represents red
Y represents yellow

The probability of drawing a red card is now greater than in the last situation where drawing a card of each color was equally likely. The simple event of drawing a color card has become a biased one since the probability of drawing a red card is not the same as the probability of drawing a yellow card.

Using the multiplication rule, find the probability of spinning a 2 and drawing a red card:

$P(2, R) = \mathbf{P(2) \cdot P(\mathit{R})}$

$= \mathbf{\frac{1}{2} \cdot \frac{2}{3}}$ Multiply P(2) and P(*R*).

$= \frac{1}{3}$ Simplify.

Compare the situations in 2 and 3. Which situation has a uniform probability model? Which situation has a nonuniform probability model? Explain.

4 A box contains 8 green balls and 4 red balls. A ball is randomly drawn from the box and the color of the ball is noted. The ball is then put back into the box and a second ball is randomly drawn. The color of the second ball is also noted.

a Find the probability of first drawing a green ball followed by a red ball.

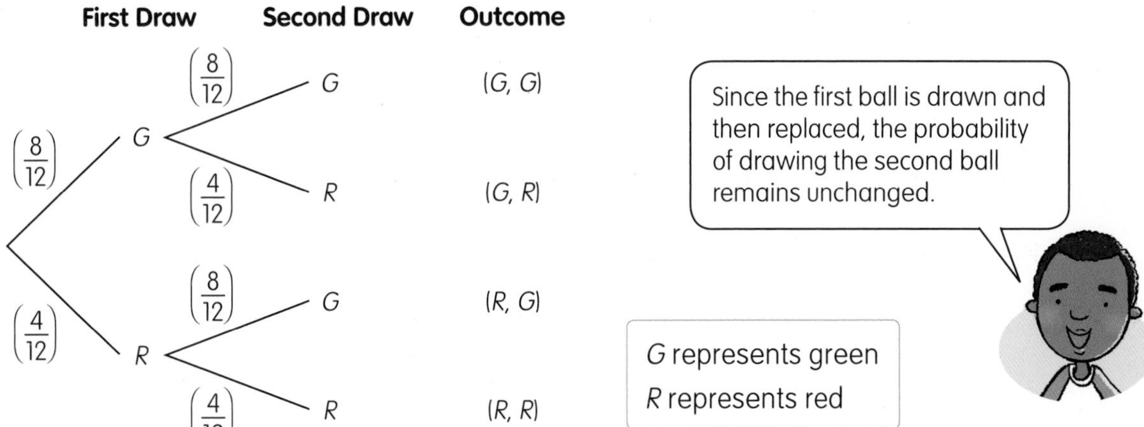

Since the first ball is drawn and then replaced, the probability of drawing the second ball remains unchanged.

$$\begin{aligned} P(G, R) &= P(G) \cdot P(R) \\ &= \frac{8}{12} \cdot \frac{4}{12} \\ &= \frac{2}{9} \end{aligned}$$

The probability of first drawing a green ball followed by a red ball is $\frac{2}{9}$.

b Find the probability of first drawing a red ball followed by a green ball.

$$\begin{aligned} P(R, G) &= P(R) \cdot P(G) \\ &= \frac{4}{12} \cdot \frac{8}{12} \\ &= \frac{2}{9} \end{aligned}$$

The probability of first drawing a red ball followed by a green ball is $\frac{2}{9}$.

c Find the probability of drawing two green balls.

$$\begin{aligned} P(G, G) &= P(G) \cdot P(G) \\ &= \frac{8}{12} \cdot \frac{8}{12} \\ &= \frac{4}{9} \end{aligned}$$

The probability of drawing two green balls is $\frac{4}{9}$.

d Find the probability of drawing two balls of the same color.

There are two favorable outcomes, (*G*, *G*) and (*R*, *R*), and they are mutually exclusive.

$$\begin{aligned} P(G, G) &= P(G) \cdot P(G) \\ &= \frac{8}{12} \cdot \frac{8}{12} \\ &= \frac{4}{9} \end{aligned}$$

$$\begin{aligned} P(R, R) &= P(R) \cdot P(R) \\ &= \frac{4}{12} \cdot \frac{4}{12} \\ &= \frac{1}{9} \end{aligned}$$

To find the probability of (*G*, *G*) or (*R*, *R*), find the sum of their probabilities.
Using the addition rule of probability,

$$\begin{aligned} P(\text{same color}) &= P(G, G) + P(R, R) \\ &= \frac{4}{9} + \frac{1}{9} \\ &= \frac{5}{9} \end{aligned}$$

The probability of drawing two balls of the same color is $\frac{5}{9}$.

> In general, for two mutually exclusive events *A* and *B*, the addition rule of probability states that:
> $$P(A \text{ or } B) = P(A) + P(B)$$

Activity **Comparing experimental and theoretical values of probability using computer simulations**

Work in groups.

① Use a spreadsheet software to simulate the tossing of two fair six-sided number dice, and to generate data to investigate how frequently the outcome of doubles (1 and 1, 2 and 2, ..., 6 and 6) occurs. Label your spreadsheet as shown.

	A	B	C	D	E	F
1	**Number Die A**	**Number Die B**	**Difference**			
2						
3						
4						
5						

② To generate a random integer between 1 and 6 in cell A2, enter the formula =INT(RAND()*6+1) to simulate rolling a number die. A random number from 1 to 6 should appear in the cell.

	A	B	C	D	E	F
1	**Number Die A**	**Number Die B**	**Difference**			
2	=INT(RAND()*6+1)					
3						
4						
5						

3. To model 100 rolls, select cells A2 to A101 and choose Fill Down from the Edit menu.

4. Repeat 2 and 3 for cells B2 to B101.

	A	B	C	D	E	F
1	Number Die A	Number Die B	Difference			
2	4	3				
3	6	4				
4	4	5				
5	1	1				

5. In cell C2, enter the formula =A2–B2. Select cells C2 to C101 and choose Fill Down from the Edit menu. If the numbers in columns A and B are the same, their difference will be 0. A difference of 0 indicates a doubles outcome.

6. To find out how many times the data show doubles occurring, enter the formula =COUNTIF(C2:C101,0) in cell D1.

	A	B	C	D	E	F
1	Number Die A	Number Die B	Difference	=COUNTIF(C2:C101,0)		
2	4	3	1			
3	6	4	2			
4	4	5	-1			
5	1	1	0			

7. Find the experimental probability of two number dice showing the same number by dividing the number you get in cell D1 by the total, 100 rolls.

8. Find the theoretical probability of rolling doubles with two fair number dice. Compare this theoretical probability with the experimental probability you obtained in the spreadsheet simulation. Are these two values the same? Explain.

When you conduct a greater number of simulations, such as 100 instead of 20, the experimental probability will be more likely to be closer to the theoretical probability.

TRY Practice solving problems with independent events

Solve.

1. A game is played with a fair coin and a fair six-sided number die. To win the game, you need to randomly obtain heads on a fair coin and a 3 on a fair number die.

   a Complete the tree diagram.

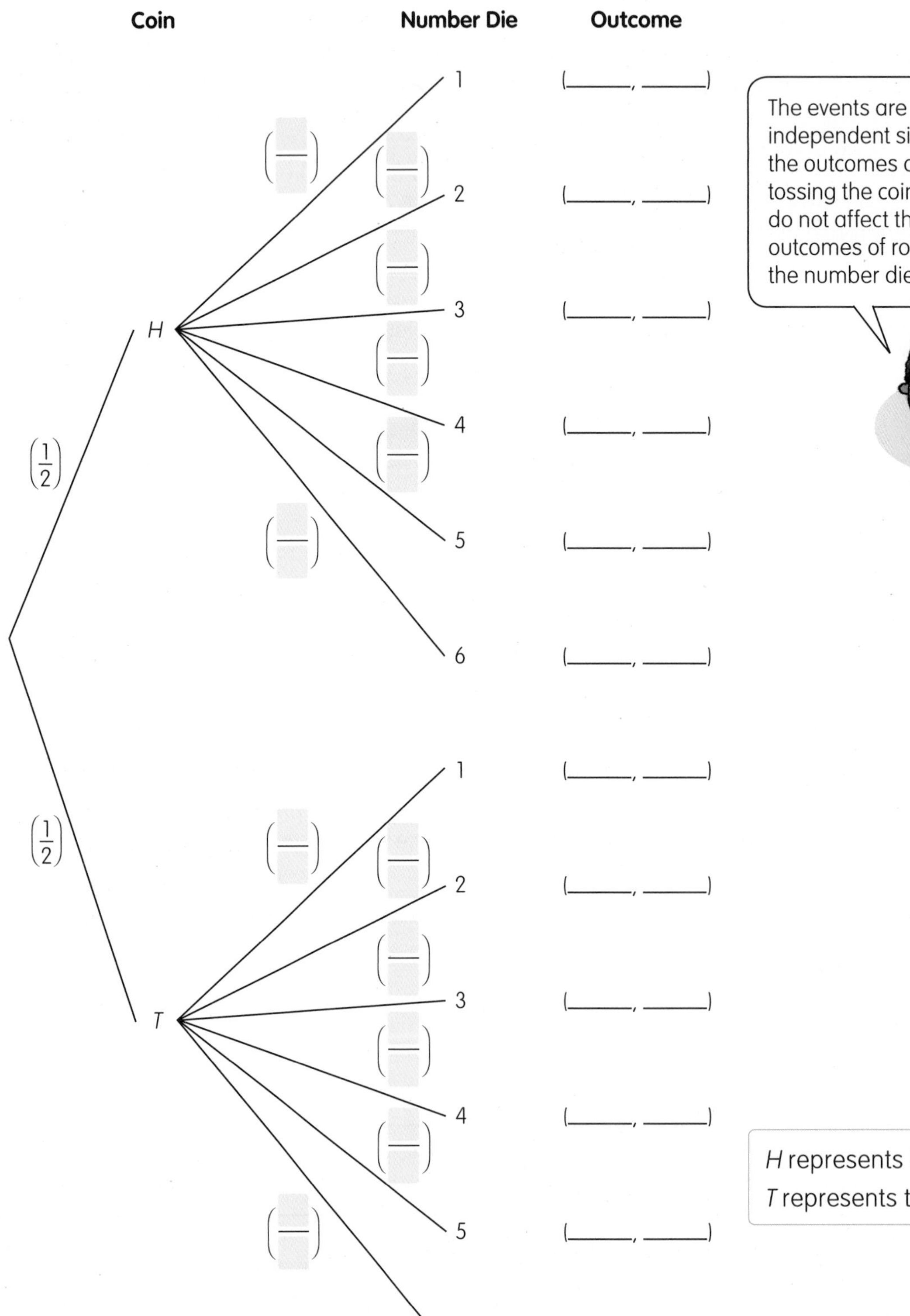

The events are independent since the outcomes of tossing the coin do not affect the outcomes of rolling the number die.

H represents heads
T represents tails

b Find the probability of winning the game in one try.

P(winning the game) = P(H, 3)
= P(H) · P(3)

= ______ · ______

= ______

2 A game is played with a bag of 6 color tokens and a bag of 6 letter tiles. The 6 tokens consist of 2 green tokens, 1 yellow token, and 3 red tokens. The 6 letter tiles consist of 4 tiles of letter A and 2 tiles of letter B. To win the game, you need to get a yellow token and a tile of letter B from each bag.

a Complete the tree diagram.

Token		Letter Tile		Outcome
$\left(\frac{2}{6}\right)$	G	$\left(\frac{4}{6}\right)$	A	(______, ______)
		$\left(\frac{\square}{\square}\right)$	B	(______, ______)
$\left(\frac{\square}{\square}\right)$	Y	$\left(\frac{\square}{\square}\right)$	A	(______, ______)
		$\left(\frac{\square}{\square}\right)$	B	(______, ______)
$\left(\frac{\square}{\square}\right)$	R	$\left(\frac{\square}{\square}\right)$	A	(______, ______)
		$\left(\frac{\square}{\square}\right)$	B	(______, ______)

G represents green
Y represents yellow
R represents red
A represents letter A
B represents letter B

b Find the probability of winning the game in one try.

P(winning the game) = P(Y, B)
= P(Y) · P(B)

= ______ · ______

= ______

The probability of winning the game in one try is ______.

3 In a bag, there are 9 blue balls and 1 orange ball. Two balls are randomly drawn, one at a time with replacement.

a Complete the tree diagram.

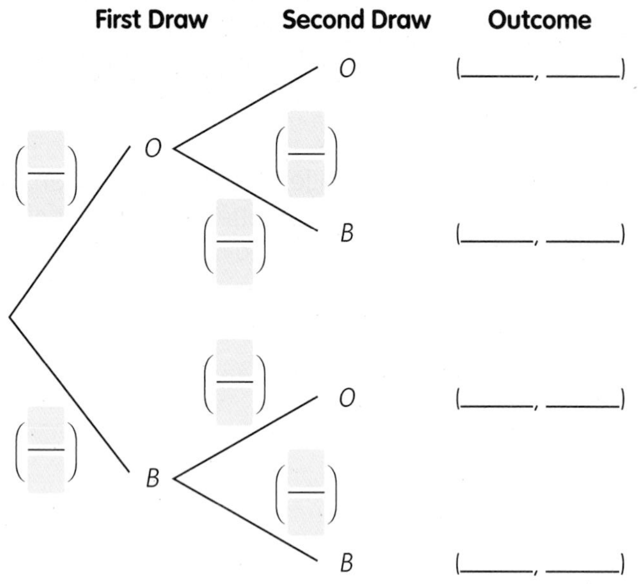

O represents orange
B represents blue

b Find the probability of drawing two blue balls.

c Find the probability of drawing an orange ball followed by a blue ball.

d Find the probability of drawing an orange ball both times.

4 Alex is taking two tests. The probability of him passing each test is 0.8.

a Find the probability of Alex failing each test.

Let P represent pass and F represent fail.
$P(F) = 1 - P(P)$

$= 1 - \_\_\_\_$

$= \_\_\_\_$

The probability of Alex failing each test is ____.

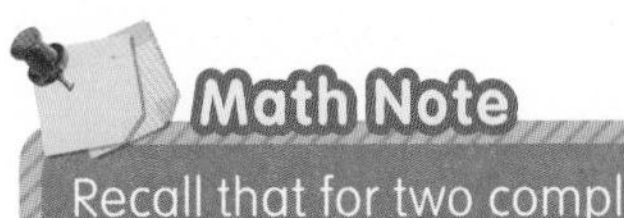

Math Note
Recall that for two complementary events, the sum of their probabilities is 1.

b Complete the tree diagram.

First Test		Second Test	Outcome
	(____)	P	(____, ____)
(0.8) P			
	(____)	F	(____, ____)
	(____)	P	(____, ____)
(____) F			
	(____)	F	(____, ____)

c Find the probability of Alex passing both tests.

$P(P, P) = P(P) \cdot P(P)$

$= \_\_\_\_ \cdot \_\_\_\_$

$= \_\_\_\_$

The probability of Alex passing both tests is ____.

d Find the probability of Alex passing exactly one of the tests.

$P(P, F) \text{ or } P(F, P) = P(P, F) + P(F, P)$
$= P(P) \cdot P(F) + P(F) \cdot P(P)$

$= \_\_\_\_ \cdot \_\_\_\_ + \_\_\_\_ \cdot \_\_\_\_$

$= \_\_\_\_$

The probability of Alex passing exactly one of the tests is ____.

Alex either passes the first test or the second test.

5 On weekends, Carla either jogs (J) or plays tennis (T) each day, but never both. The probability of her playing tennis is 0.75.

a Find the probability of Carla jogging on both days.

Since J and T are complementary,
$P(J) = 1 - P(T)$

$= 1 -$ ______

$=$ ______

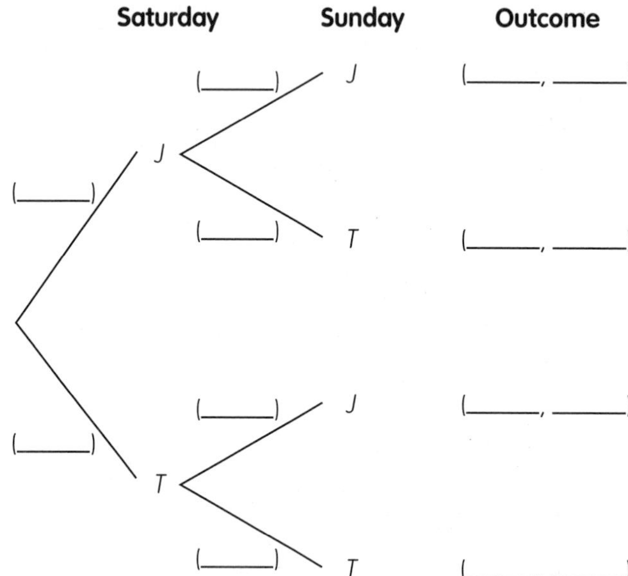

J represents jog
T represents tennis

$P(J, J) = P(J) \cdot P(J)$

$=$ ______ $\cdot$ ______

$=$ ______

The probability of Carla jogging on both days is ______.

b Find the probability of Carla jogging on exactly one of the days.

Name: ____________________ Date: ____________

INDEPENDENT PRACTICE

Draw a tree diagram to represent each situation.

1. Tossing a fair coin followed by drawing a marble from a bag of 3 marbles: 1 yellow, 1 green, and 1 blue.

2. Drawing two balls randomly with replacement from a bag with 1 green ball and 1 purple ball.

3. Drawing a ball randomly from a bag containing 1 red ball and 1 blue ball, followed by tossing a fair six-sided number die.

4. Tossing a fair coin twice.

5. Reading or playing on each day of a weekend.

6. Being on time or late for school for two consecutive days.

Solve.

7. Emma is playing a game that uses the spinner shown on the right and a fair coin. An outcome of 3 on the spinner and heads on the coin wins the game.

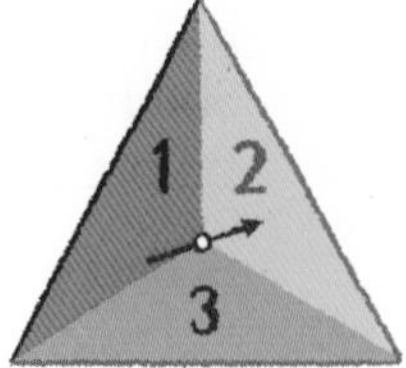

   a Draw a tree diagram to represent all possible outcomes and the corresponding probabilities.

   b Find the probability of winning the game in one try.

   c Find the probability of losing the game in one try.

8 There are 2 blue balls and 4 yellow balls in a bag. A ball is randomly drawn from the bag, and it is replaced before a second ball is randomly drawn.

a Draw a tree diagram to represent all possible outcomes.

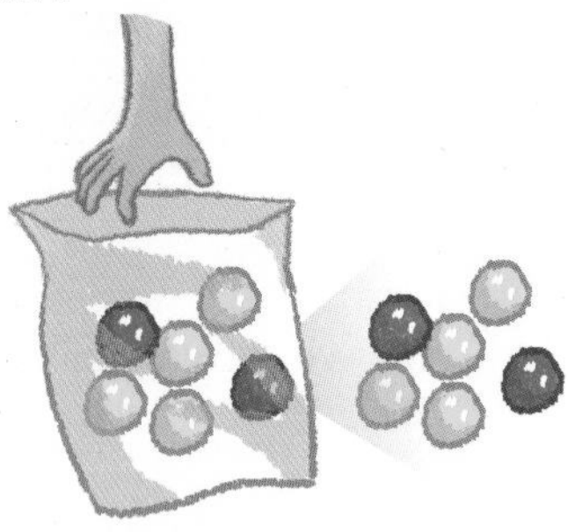

b Find the probability that a yellow ball is drawn first, followed by another yellow ball.

c Find the probability that a yellow ball is drawn after a blue ball is drawn first.

9 Rachel has 3 blue pencils and 2 green pencils in her pencil case. She randomly selects a pencil from her pencil case, and replaces it before she randomly selects again.

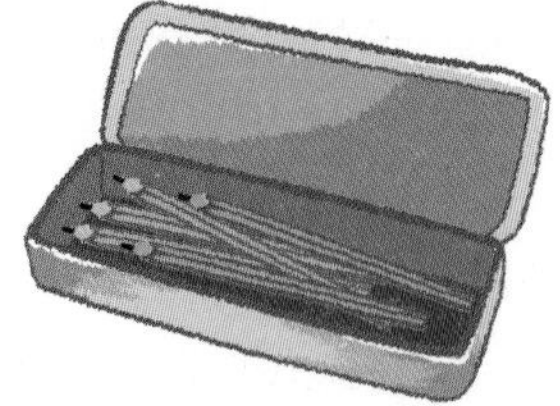

a Draw a tree diagram to represent all possible outcomes and the corresponding probabilities.

b Find the probability that Rachel selects 2 blue pencils.

c Find the probability that she selects 2 green pencils.

d Find the probability that she selects 2 pencils of the same color.

10 Dae has 4 fiction books, 6 textbooks, and 1 dictionary on his bookshelf. He randomly selects two books with replacement.

a Draw a tree diagram to represent all possible outcomes and the corresponding probabilities.

b Find the probability that Dae selects a fiction book twice.

c Find the probability that he first selects a textbook, and then a dictionary.

d Find the probability that he first selects a fiction book, and then a textbook.

11 Hunter tosses a fair six-sided number die twice. What is the probability of tossing an even number on the first toss and a prime number on the second toss?

12 The probability that Laila wakes up before 8 A.M. when she does not set her alarm clock is $\frac{2}{5}$. On any two consecutive days that Laila does not set her alarm clock, what is the probability of her waking up before 8 A.M. for at least one of the days?

13 The surface of the globe on the right is painted 30% yellow, 10% green, and the rest blue. Dylan spins the globe and randomly points to a spot on the globe twice. The color he points to each time is recorded.

a What is the probability that he points to the same color twice?

b What is the probability that he points to yellow at least once?

14 The probabilities of a dart landing on different rings of a dartboard are 4%, 12%, 20%, 28%, and 36% as shown. Jaden throws two darts at the dartboard.

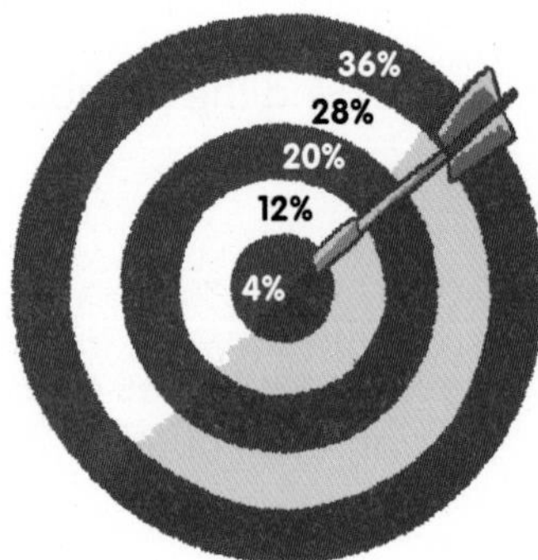

a What is the probability of the two darts landing on the same ring?

b What is the probability of the two darts landing on different rings of the same color?

Name: ______________________ Date: ____________

Dependent Events

Learning Objectives:

- Identify dependent events.
- Use the rules of probability to solve problems with dependent events.

New Vocabulary
dependent events

There are 3 red balls and 5 blue balls in a bag. Suppose you randomly pick two balls, one after another without replacement. What is the probability of getting two balls of a different color? Represent the events using a tree diagram and calculate the probability.

ENGAGE

Suppose there are 2 apples and 2 oranges in a bag. You randomly pick two pieces of fruit, one at a time without replacing the first piece of fruit. Explain how you would find the probability of picking two of the same fruit.

LEARN Solve problems with dependent events

1. There are a total of 5 cards in a pile. 3 are yellow and 2 are red. Suppose you draw two cards randomly, one after another, from the pile without replacing the first drawn card. After the first card is drawn, there are only 4 cards left in the pile.

   Since there is a change in the sample space for the second draw, the probability of drawing a card of each color changes after the first draw. When the occurrence of one event causes the probability of another event to change, the two events are said to be dependent.

   Let Y represent yellow and R represent red.

   First Draw

   $P(Y) = \frac{3}{5}$

   $P(R) = \frac{2}{5}$

   Since the events are dependent, the number of possible outcomes for the second event is reduced by 1 after the first event occurs.

   Second Draw

   $P(Y \text{ after } Y) = \frac{2}{4}$ There are 2 yellow cards left after 1 yellow card is drawn.

   $P(R \text{ after } Y) = \frac{2}{4}$ There are 2 red cards left after 1 yellow card is drawn.

   $P(Y \text{ after } R) = \frac{3}{4}$ There are 3 yellow cards left after 1 red card is drawn.

   $P(R \text{ after } R) = \frac{1}{4}$ There is 1 red card left after 1 red card is drawn.

2 You can represent the dependent events with a tree diagram.

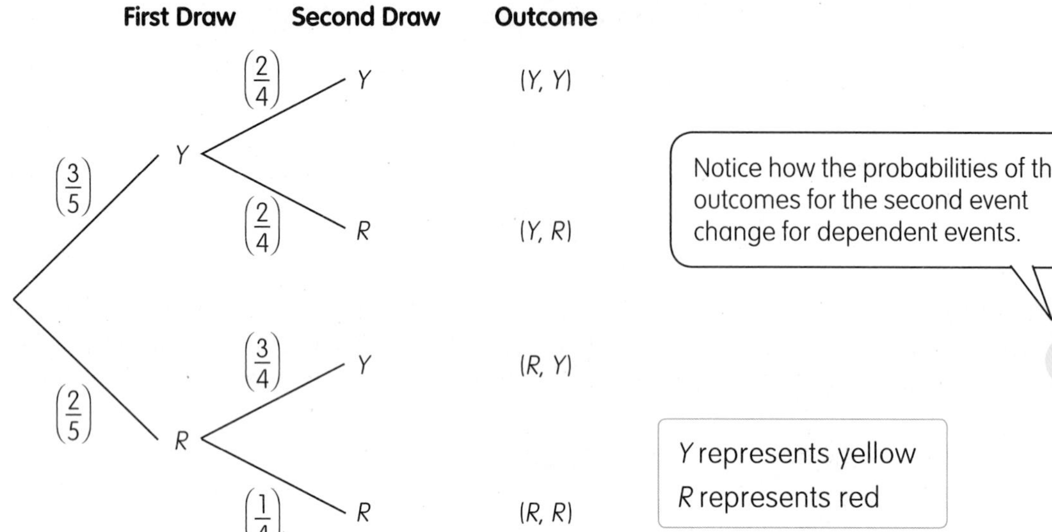

Notice how the probabilities of the outcomes for the second event change for dependent events.

3 Consider the 5-card scenario again. To find the probability of drawing 2 red cards, one after another without replacement, multiply the probability of drawing a red card in the first draw with the probability of drawing a red card in the second draw.

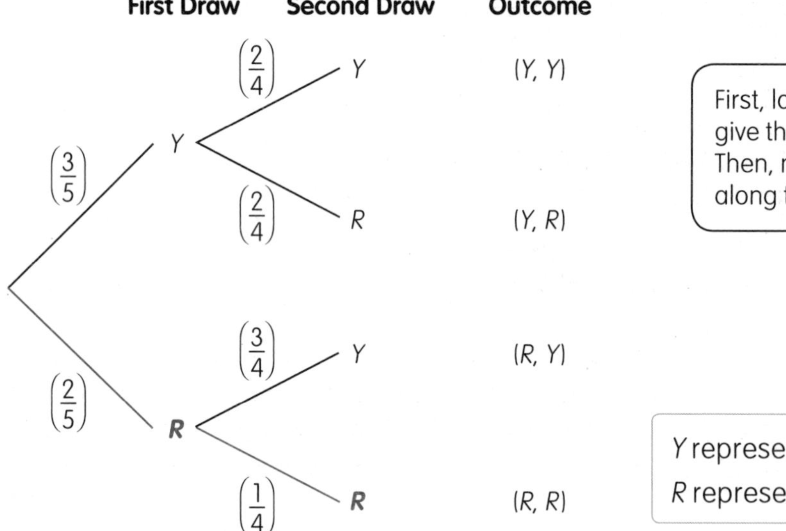

First, locate the branches that will give the favorable outcome (*R*, *R*). Then, multiply the probabilities along the branches.

Y represents yellow
R represents red

$P(R, R) = P(R) \cdot P(R \text{ after } R)$
$= \mathbf{\frac{2}{5}} \cdot \mathbf{\frac{1}{4}}$
$= \frac{1}{10}$

For this situation, you cannot simply count the outcomes to find the probability since the events do not have a uniform probability model.

In general, for two dependent events A and B, the multiplication rule of probability states that:
$P(A \text{ and } B) = P(A) \cdot P(B \text{ after } A)$

4 Luis randomly chooses to go to school by bus or by bicycle, but not both. The tree diagram below shows that his choice of transportation depends on the weather. The probability that it rains on a particular day is denoted by a. Assume that rainy and sunny days are mutually exclusive events.

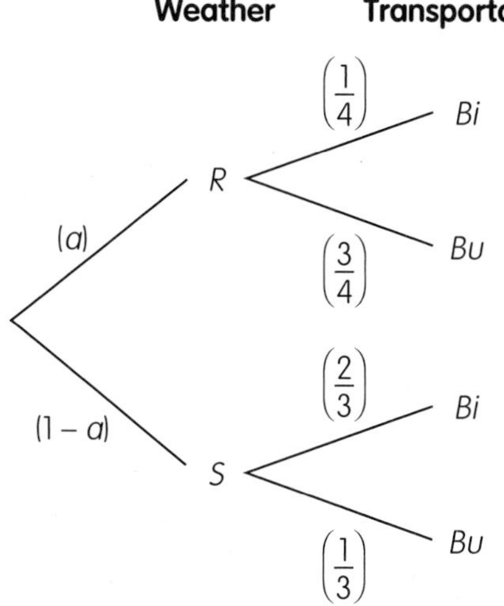

The probabilities of all branches from a node have a sum of 1.

R represents rainy day
S represents sunny day
Bi represents bicycle
Bu represents bus

a If the probability that it rains is $\frac{1}{2}$, find the probability that Luis will take a bus to school.

Find the probability that Luis takes the bus on a rainy day, and the probability that he takes the bus on a sunny day.

$P(R) = \frac{1}{2}$

$P(S) = 1 - \frac{1}{2}$ Events R and S are complementary.
$= \frac{1}{2}$

$P(Bu) = \frac{1}{2} \cdot \frac{3}{4} + \frac{1}{2} \cdot \frac{1}{3}$ Evaluate $P(R, Bu) + P(S, Bu)$.
$= \frac{13}{24}$

If the probability that it rains is $\frac{1}{2}$, the probability that Luis will take a bus to school is $\frac{13}{24}$.

b If the probability that it rains is $\frac{5}{8}$, find the probability that Luis will ride a bicycle to school.

$P(R) = \frac{5}{8}$

$P(S) = 1 - \frac{5}{8}$ Events R and S are complementary.

$= \frac{3}{8}$

$P(Bi) = \frac{5}{8} \cdot \frac{1}{4} + \frac{3}{8} \cdot \frac{2}{3}$ Evaluate $P(R, Bi) + P(S, Bi)$.

$= \frac{13}{32}$

Find the probability that Luis rides a bicycle on a rainy day, and the probability that he rides a bicycle on a sunny day.

If the probability that it rains is $\frac{5}{8}$, the probability that Luis will ride a bicycle is $\frac{13}{32}$.

TRY Practice solving problems with dependent events

Solve.

1. A deck of cards with the letters D, E, E, D are placed face down on a table. Two cards are turned over at random to show the letters.

a Find the probability of each possible outcome in the second draw.

Let D represent the letter D and E represent the letter E.

First Draw

$P(D) = \frac{2}{4}$

$P(E) = \frac{2}{4}$

Second Draw

$P(D \text{ after } D) = \frac{\square}{\square}$ There is ______ letter D card left after 1 letter D card is drawn.

$P(E \text{ after } D) = \frac{\square}{\square}$ There are ______ letter E cards left after 1 letter D card is drawn.

$P(D \text{ after } E) = \frac{\square}{\square}$ There are ______ letter D cards left after 1 letter E card is drawn.

$P(E \text{ after } E) = \frac{\square}{\square}$ There is ______ letter E card left after 1 letter E card is drawn.

b Complete the tree diagram.

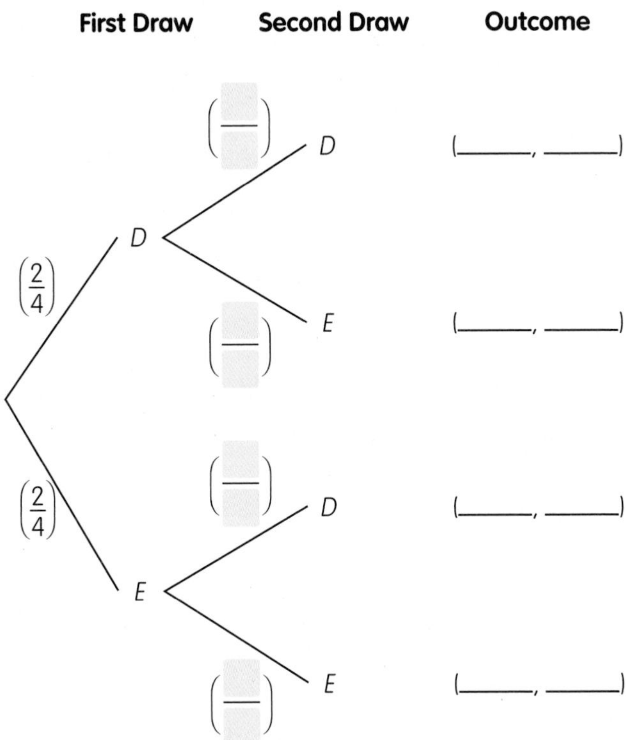

c Find the probability of picking a card with the letter E twice.

d Find the probability of picking a card with the letter D followed by a card with the letter E.

2 The tree diagram below shows how passing a test depends on whether a student studies (S) or does not study (NS) for the test. The probability that a student studies for the test is denoted by p. Assume that S and NS are mutually exclusive events.

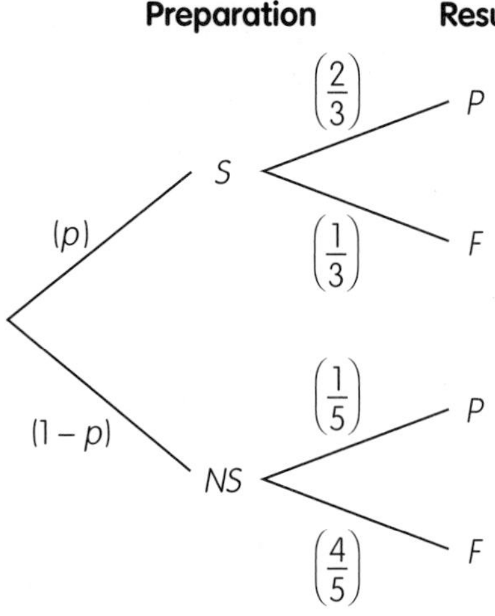

S represents study
NS represents does not study
P represents pass
F represents fail

a If the probability of studying is 0.4, find the probability that a student passes the test.

b If the probability of studying is 0.75, find the probability that a student fails the test.

LET'S EXPLORE

1 There are 2 blue balls and 1 red ball in a box. Suppose you pick a ball randomly from the box, one at a time without replacement.

Let B be the event of picking a blue ball.

$$P(B, B) = \frac{\square}{3} \cdot \frac{\square}{2}$$

2 There are 3 blue balls and 1 red ball in a box. Suppose you pick a ball randomly from the box, one at a time without replacement.

Let B be the event of picking a blue ball.

$$P(B, B, B) = \frac{\square}{\square} \cdot \frac{\square}{\square} \cdot \frac{\square}{\square}$$

3 There are 4 blue balls and 1 red ball in a box. Suppose you pick a ball randomly from the box, one at a time without replacement. Using your observations in 1 and 2, find the probability of first picking a blue ball, followed by 3 blue balls.

Name: ______________________ Date: ______________

INDEPENDENT PRACTICE

Determine whether each pair of events is dependent or independent.

1. Drawing 2 red balls randomly, one at a time without replacement, from a bag of 6 balls

2. Tossing a fair coin twice

3. Reaching school late or on time for two consecutive days

4. Flooding of roads during rainy or sunny days

Draw a tree diagram for each situation.

5. 2 balls are drawn at random, one at a time without replacement, from a bag of 3 green balls and 18 red balls.

6. The probability of rain on a particular day is 0.3. If it rains, the probability that Mia goes shopping is 0.75. If it does not rain, the probability that she goes jogging is 0.72. Assume that shopping and jogging are mutually exclusive and complementary, and that rain and no rain are complementary.

Solve.

7 Emma has a box of 13 colored pens: 3 blue, 4 red, and the rest black. What is the probability of drawing two blue pens randomly, one at a time without replacement?

8 A box contains 8 dimes, 15 quarters, and 27 nickels. A student randomly draws two coins, one at a time without replacement, from the bag. Find the probability that 2 quarters are drawn.

9 There are 9 green, 2 yellow, and 5 blue cards in a deck. Players A and B each randomly draws a card from the deck. Player A draws a card first before Player B. Find the probability that both players draw the same color cards.

10 The probability of Alex going to a library or a park depends on whether the weather is sunny or rainy. The probability of rain on a particular day is denoted by a. Assume that going to the library and going to the park are mutually exclusive and complementary.

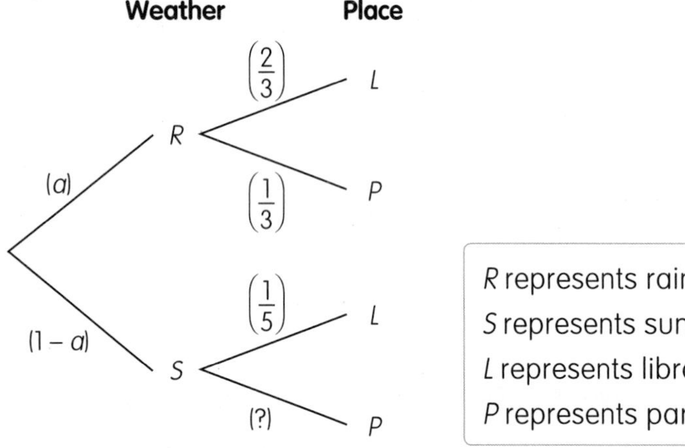

a If $a = 0.3$, find the probability that Alex goes to the park on any day.

b If $a = 0.75$, find the probability that he goes to the library on any day.

11 There are 15 apples in a fruit basket. 6 of them are red apples and the rest are green apples. Two apples are randomly picked, one at a time without replacement.

a Draw a tree diagram to represent all possible outcomes and the corresponding probabilities.

b Find the probability of picking a green apple and then a red apple.

c Find the probability of picking two green apples.

d Find the probability of picking two red apples.

12 There are 8 people in a room: 3 of them have red hair, 2 have blonde hair, and the rest have dark hair. Two people are randomly selected to leave the room, one after another, and they do not re-enter the room.

a Draw a tree diagram to represent all possible outcomes and the corresponding probabilities.

b What is the probability of a person with dark hair leaving the room first?

c What is the probability of a person with red hair leaving the room, followed by a person with blonde hair?

d What is the probability of two people with the same hair color leaving the room?

13 There are traffic lights at two intersections along a stretch of road. Having a red or a green pedestrian light at the first intersection is equally likely. If the pedestrian light is red at the first intersection, having a red pedestrian light at the second intersection is twice as likely as a green pedestrian light. Otherwise, having a red or a green pedestrian light at the second intersection is equally likely. What is the probability of having a red pedestrian light at the first intersection and a green pedestrian light at the second intersection? Draw a tree diagram to show all possible outcomes.

14 To get to work, Mr. Martin needs to take a train and then a bus. The probability that the train breaks down is 0.1. When the train breaks down, the probability that the bus will be overcrowded is 0.7. When the train is operating normally, the probability that the bus will be overcrowded is 0.2. What is the probability that the bus will not be overcrowded? Draw a tree diagram to show all possible outcomes.

Mathematical Habit 6 Use precise mathematical language

1. Use an example to explain the difference between possible outcomes and different outcomes.

Mathematical Habit 3 Construct viable arguments

2. A fair six-sided number die labeled 1 to 6 is rolled once. Issac thinks that the probability of getting a number that is either odd or prime is equal to the sum of the probability of getting an odd number and the probability of getting a prime number. Is he correct? Explain.

Problem Solving with Heuristics

1. **Mathematical Habit 1** **Persevere in solving problems**

   If there are 12 green and 6 red apples, find the probability of randomly choosing three apples of the same color in a row, without replacement. Show your work.

2. **Mathematical Habit 1** **Persevere in solving problems**

   Pedro has five $1 bills, ten $10 bills, and three $20 bills in his wallet. He picks three bills randomly in a row, without replacement. What is the probability of him picking three of the same type of bills? Show your work.

PUT ON YOUR THINKING CAP!

3 **Mathematical Habit 4** **Use mathematical models**

A pencil case contains 2 red pens, 1 green pen, and 1 blue pen. Sofia randomly picks 3 pens one at a time, without replacement.

a Find the probability of Sofia picking the same colored pen twice consecutively.

b Find the probability of Sofia picking the same colored pen three times consecutively.

4 **Mathematical Habit 1** **Persevere in solving problems**

Diego plans to visit Australia for a vacation, either alone or with a friend. Whether he goes alone or with a friend is equally likely. If he travels with a friend, there is a 40% chance of him joining a guided tour. If he travels alone, there is an 80% chance of him joining a guided tour.

a What is the probability of Diego traveling with a companion and not joining a guided tour?

b What is the probability of Diego joining a guided tour?

CHAPTER WRAP-UP

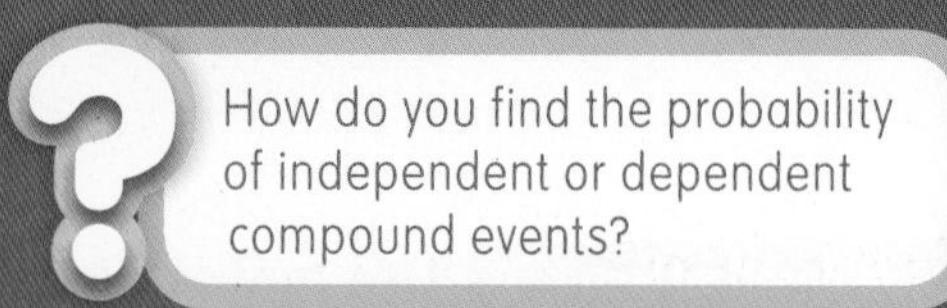

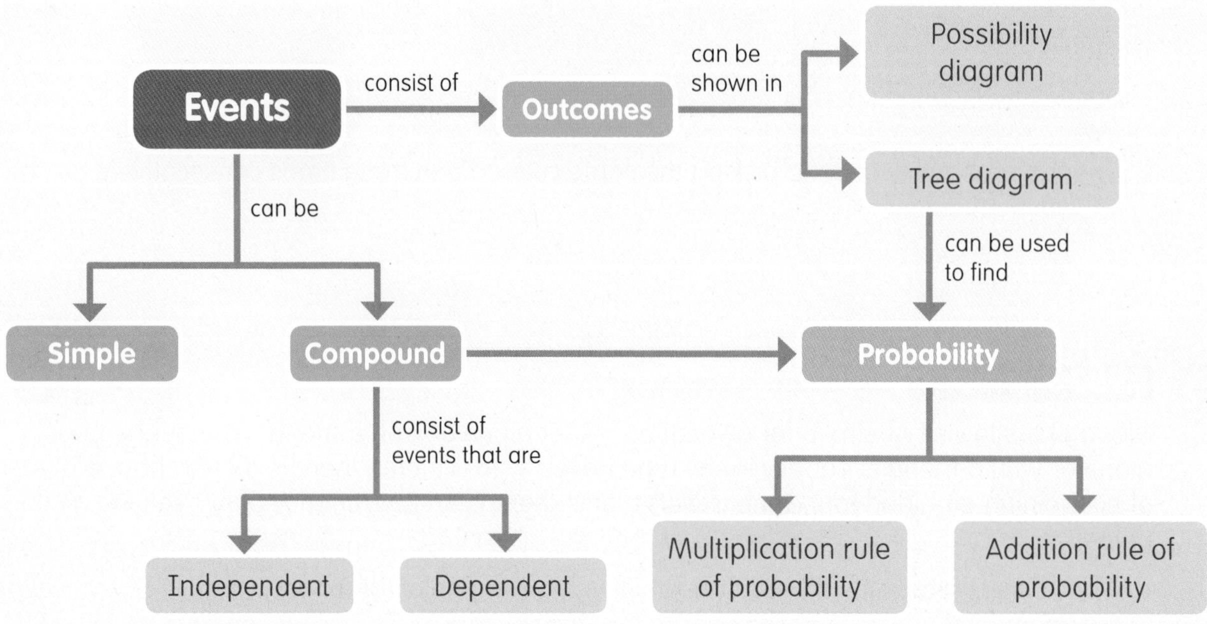

KEY CONCEPTS

- Compound events are events that are made up of two or more simple events.
- Possible outcomes of compound events can be displayed in possibility diagrams, such as organized lists, two-way grids, tables with ordered pairs, or tree diagrams.
- Simple events that make up compound events can be dependent or independent.
- When two events A and B are independent, the multiplication rule of probability states: $P(A \text{ and } B) = P(A) \cdot P(B)$.
- When two events A and B are dependent, the multiplication rule of probability states: $P(A \text{ and } B) = P(A) \cdot P(B \text{ after } A)$.
- For two mutually exclusive events A and B, the addition rule of probability states: $P(A \text{ or } B) = P(A) + P(B)$.

Name: ______________________ Date: ______________

State whether each event is a simple or compound event.

1. Drawing 2 yellow marbles randomly in a row from a bag of yellow and green marbles

2. Drawing 1 red pebble and 1 yellow pebble randomly in a row from a bag of red and yellow pebbles

3. Tossing a coin once

Draw the possibility diagram and state the number of possible outcomes for each compound event.

4. From three cards labeled A, B, and C, draw two cards randomly, one at a time with replacement

5. From a pencil case with 1 red pen and 2 blue pens, select two pens randomly, one at a time without replacement

6. Toss a fair four-sided number die, labeled 1 to 4, and a coin

Draw a tree diagram to represent each situation.

7 Spinning a spinner divided into four equal areas labeled 1 to 4, and tossing a coin

8 Picking two green apples randomly from a basket of red and green apples

Solve.

9 A fair four-sided number die is marked 1, 2, 2, and 3. A spinner, equally divided into three sectors, is marked 3, 4, and 7. Luke tosses the number die and spins the spinner.

a Use a possibility diagram to find the probability that the sum of the two resulting numbers is greater than 5.

b Use a possibility diagram to find the probability that the product of the two resulting numbers is odd.

10 A juggler is giving a performance by juggling a red ball, a yellow ball, and a green ball. All three balls have an equal chance of dropping. If one ball drops, the juggler will stop and pick up the ball and resume juggling. If another ball drops again, the juggler will stop the performance.

a Draw a tree diagram to represent all possible outcomes and the corresponding probabilities.

b Find the probability of dropping the same colored ball twice.

c Find the probability of dropping one green ball and one yellow ball.

11 In a running event, there is a half marathon category and a full marathon category. 60 people participated in the half marathon and 80 participated in the full marathon. Half of the people who participated in the half marathon warm up before the run, while three-quarters of the people who participated in the full marathon warm up. Assume that warming up and not warming up are mutually exclusive and complementary.

a A participant is randomly picked. Draw a tree diagram to represent all possible outcomes and the corresponding probabilities.

b What is the probability of randomly picking a person who participated in the full marathon and warms up before running?

c What is the probability of randomly picking a participant of the running event who does not warm up before running?

12 A bag contains 2 pumpkin muffins and 3 bran muffins. Samuel takes two muffins, one after another, without replacement.

a Draw a tree diagram to represent all possible outcomes and the corresponding probabilities.

b Find the probability of Samuel randomly getting two of the same type of muffins.

c Find the probability of Samuel randomly getting at least one pumpkin muffin.

13 Out of 100 raffle tickets, 4 are marked with a prize. Gabriel randomly selects two tickets from the box.

a Draw a tree diagram to represent all possible outcomes and the corresponding probabilities.

b What is the probability that Gabriel does not win any prizes?

c What is the probability that Gabriel gets exactly one of the prizes?

14 Bag A contains 25 tomatoes, 4 of which are rotten. Bag B contains 15 tomatoes, 6 of which are rotten. Jack randomly selects a tomato from Bag A followed by another random selection from Bag B.

a Draw a tree diagram to represent all possible outcomes and the corresponding probabilities.

b What is the probability that both tomatoes are rotten?

c What is the probability that exactly one tomato is rotten?

d What is the probability that at least one tomato is not rotten?

15 Zachary can choose to cycle, take a bus, or take a taxi to school. The probability of Zachary waking up late is 0.3. If he does not wake up late, the probability that he cycles is 0.5, takes a bus is 0.4, and takes a taxi is 0.1. If he wakes up late, the probability that he cycles is 0.05, takes a bus is 0.2, and takes a taxi is 0.75.

a Draw a tree diagram to represent all possible outcomes and the corresponding probabilities.

b Find the probability of Zachary waking up late and cycling to school.

c Find the probability of Zachary not waking up late and taking a taxi to school.

d Find the probability of Zachary taking a bus to school.

Assessment Prep

Answer each question.

16 The probability of Sara waking up after 8 A.M. on a weekend day is p. Assume that the events of Sara waking up after 8 A.M. and by 8 A.M. are mutually exclusive and complementary. If $p = 0.3$, find the probability that she will wake up by 8 A.M. on two consecutive weekend days.

(A) 0.09

(B) 0.3

(C) 0.49

(D) 0.7

17 State whether the following pair of events consists of independent events or dependent events.

From a pencil case, two colored pencils are randomly drawn, one at a time without replacement. Write your answer and your work or explanation in the space below.

This question has two parts.

18 A box contains 16 color cards: 5 red, 4 blue, and 7 green. Two cards are picked at random from the box, one after another without replacement. The tree diagram shows all possible outcomes and the corresponding probabilities.

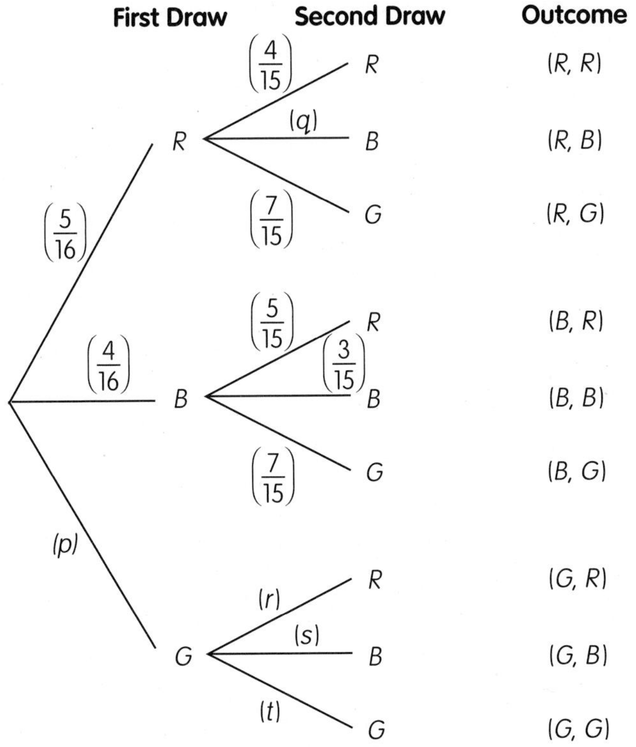

First Draw	Second Draw	Outcome
R $\left(\frac{5}{16}\right)$	R $\left(\frac{4}{15}\right)$	(R, R)
	B (q)	(R, B)
	G $\left(\frac{7}{15}\right)$	(R, G)
B $\left(\frac{4}{16}\right)$	R $\left(\frac{5}{15}\right)$	(B, R)
	B $\left(\frac{3}{15}\right)$	(B, B)
	G $\left(\frac{7}{15}\right)$	(B, G)
G (p)	R (r)	(G, R)
	B (s)	(G, B)
	G (t)	(G, G)

Part A

Find the values of p, q, r, s, and t. Write your answer and your work or explanation in the space below.

Part B

Find the probability that both cards are different colors. Write your answer and your work or explanation in the space below.

This question has two parts.

19 The tree diagram shows the probability of how Pedro spends his day gaming or cycling, depending on the weather. The probability of rain is denoted by a. Assume that gaming and cycling are mutually exclusive.

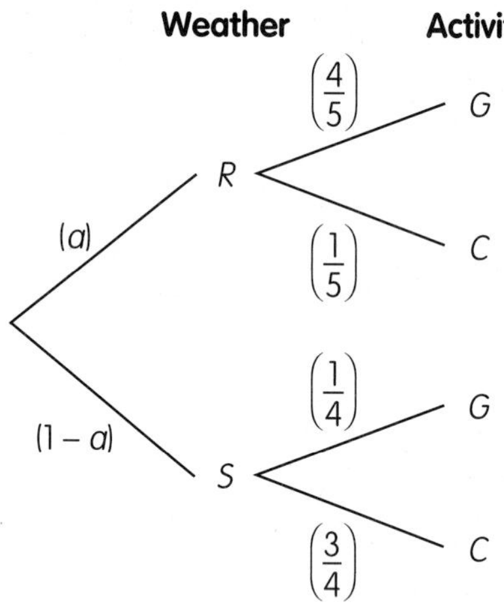

R represents rainy
S represents sunny
G represents gaming
C represents cycling

Part A

If $a = 0.4$, find the probability that Pedro will spend his day gaming. Write your answer and your work or explanation in the space below.

Part B

If $a = 0.75$, find the probability that Pedro will spend his day cycling. Write your answer and your work or explanation in the space below.

Name: ______________________ Date: ______________

A Fishing Trip

1. Grace and Lauren are fishing in a pond. There are 30 largemouth bass and 20 bluegill fish in the pond. Suppose the girls take turns to each catch a fish, without replacement.

   a Draw a tree diagram to represent all possible outcomes and the corresponding probabilities. Then, find the probability of both girls catching the same type of fish.

   b Are the events of Grace catching a fish and Lauren catching a fish independent? Justify your reasoning.

c Suppose Grace catches a fish first and she releases the fish back into the pond. Are the two events independent now? Justify your reasoning.

d Suppose the girls catch three fish, one at a time without replacement. Draw a tree diagram to represent all possible outcomes and the corresponding probabilities. Then, find the probability of the girls catching three largemouth bass.

2 Suppose Grace and Lauren play a game to determine who will take home their catch of the day. A card is randomly drawn from each of the following two decks of cards.

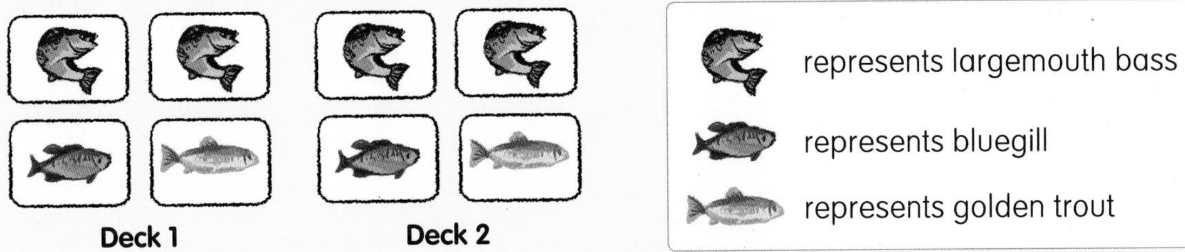

Grace wins if both cards show the same fish. Lauren wins if both cards show different fish. Is this game fair? Justify your reasoning using a tree diagram

3 Following the same rules of the game in 2, do you agree that the probability of picking two "largemouth bass" is equal to the probability of picking a "bluegill" and a "golden trout" since both events represent half of each deck of cards? Justify your reasoning.

Rubric

Point(s)	Level	My Performance
7–8	4	• Most of my answers are correct. • I showed complete understanding of the concepts. • I used effective and efficient strategies to solve the problems. • I explained my answers and mathematical thinking clearly and completely.
5–6.5	3	• Some of my answers are correct. • I showed adequate understanding of the concepts. • I used effective strategies to solve the problems. • I explained my answers and mathematical thinking clearly.
3–4.5	2	• A few of my answers are correct. • I showed some understanding of the concepts. • I used some effective strategies to solve the problems. • I explained some of my answers and mathematical thinking clearly.
0–2.5	1	• A few of my answers are correct. • I showed little understanding of the concepts. • I used limited effective strategies to solve the problems. • I did not explain my answers and mathematical thinking clearly.

Teacher's Comments

Glossary

A

- **addition rule of probability**
  For two mutually exclusive events *A* and *B*, the addition rule of probability states that P(*A* or *B*) = P(*A*) + P(*B*).

- **adjacent angles**
  Two angles that share a common vertex and side, but have no common interior points.
  Example:

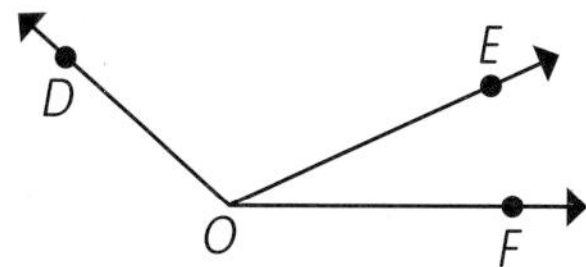

$\angle DOE$ and $\angle EOF$ are adjacent angles.

- **alternate exterior angles**
  The pairs of angles on opposite sides of the transversal for two lines, but outside the two lines.
  Example:

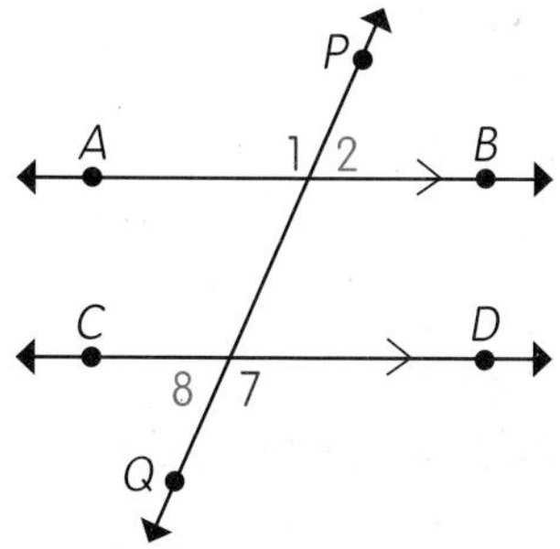

$\angle 1$ and $\angle 7$ are alternate exterior angles;
$\angle 2$ and $\angle 8$ are alternate exterior angles

- **alternate interior angles**
  The pairs of angles on opposite sides of the transversal for two lines, but inside the two lines.
  Example:

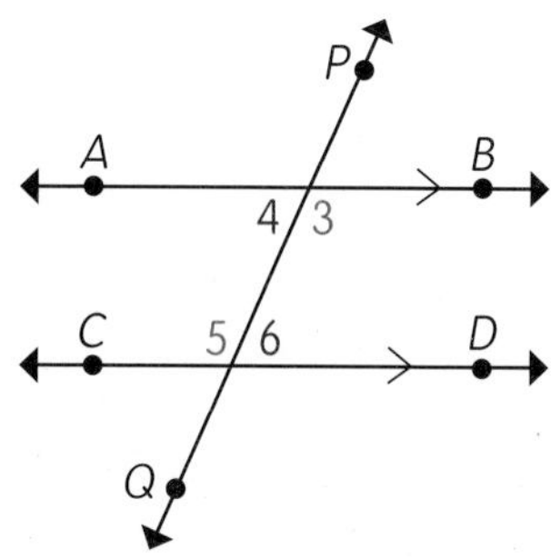

$\angle 3$ and $\angle 5$ are alternate interior angles;
$\angle 4$ and $\angle 6$ are alternate interior angles.

- **arc**
  A portion of a circle.
  Example:

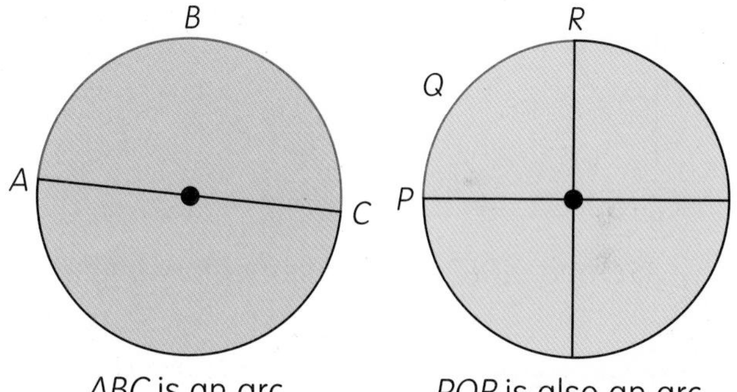

ABC is an arc. *PQR* is also an arc.

B

- **biased**
  A sample space in which one or more outcomes are favored.

- **biased sample**
  A sample in which members are not randomly selected.

C

- **center (of a circle)**
  A point within a circle that is the same distance from all points on the circle.

- **circumference**
  The distance around a circle.

- **complement**
  The complement of an event *E* consists of all the outcomes in the sample space that are not in event *E*.
  Example: When trying to roll a 6 on a die (event *E*), rolling a 1, 2, 3, 4, or 5 is the complement of event *E*.

- **complementary angles**
  Two angles whose angle measures total 90°.
  Example:

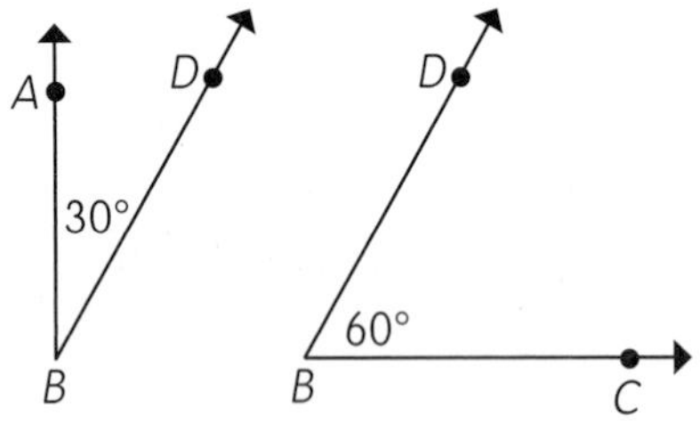

$\angle ABC$ and $\angle DEF$ are complementary angles.

- **complementary events**
  See *complement.*

- **compound event**
  Two or more events occurring together or one after another.

- **congruent angles**
  Two or more angles that have the same angle measure.

- **corresponding angles**
  The pairs of angles on the same side of the transversal for two lines and on the same side of the given lines.
  Example:

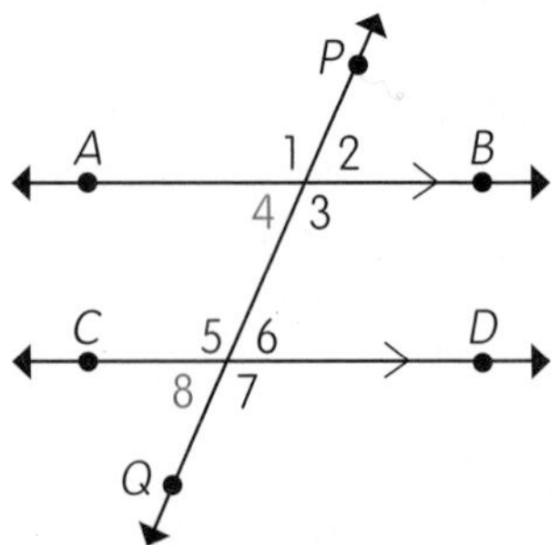

$\angle 1$ and $\angle 5$ are corresponding angles; $\angle 4$ and $\angle 8$ are corresponding angles.

- **cross section**
  A figure formed by the intersection of a solid figure and a plane.
  Example:

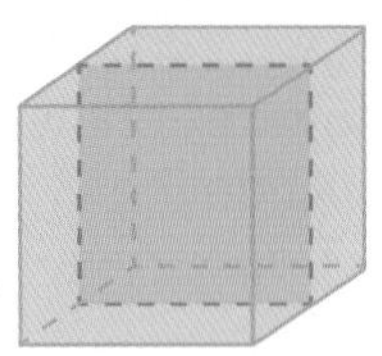

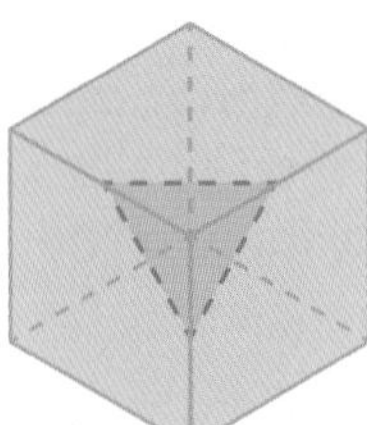

Two possible cross sections of a cube are a square and a triangle.

D

- **dependent events**
  Two or more events in which the occurrence of one event causes the probability of the other event(s) to change.

- **diameter (of a circle)**
  A line segment that connects two points on a circle and passes through its center; also the length of this segment.

E

- **event**
  A collection of outcomes from an activity.

- **experiment (probability)**
  An activity or a trial that has a well-defined set of possible outcomes, such as flipping a coin or rolling a number die.

- **experimental probability**
  Probability based on data collected or observations made in an experiment.

- **exterior angles (of a polygon)**
  The angle formed by one side of a polygon and the extension of an adjacent side.
  Example:

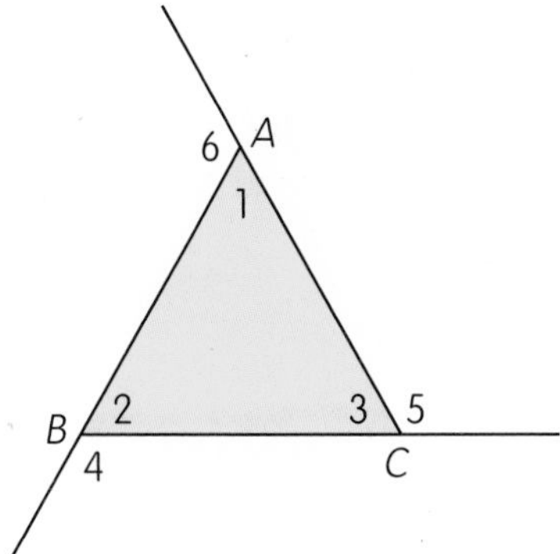

$\angle 4$, $\angle 5$, and $\angle 6$ are exterior angles.

F

- **fair**
  An experiment in which the probability of each outcome is the same.

I

- **included angle**
  The angle in a triangle formed by two given sides.

- **included side**
  The side in a triangle that is common to two given angles in the triangle.

- **independent events**
  Two or more events in which the occurrence of one event does not affect the probability of the other event(s).

- **inference**
  A conclusion about a population, made by projecting the results of a representative sample onto the whole population.

- **interior angles (of a polygon)**
  The angles formed by two adjacent sides of a polygon.
  Example:

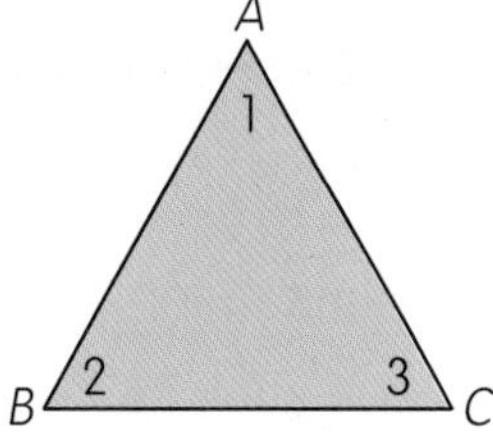

In triangle ABC, $\angle 1$, $\angle 2$, and $\angle 3$ are its interior angles.

M

- **multiplication rule of probability**
  For two independent events A and B, the multiplication rule of probability states that $P(A \text{ and } B) = P(A) \cdot P(B)$.
  For two dependent events A and B, the multiplication rule of probability states that $P(A \text{ and } B) = P(A) \cdot P(B \text{ after } A)$.

- **mutually exclusive (events)**
  Two events that cannot happen at the same time.

N

- **nonuniform probability model**
  A probability model in which the outcomes do not necessarily have equal probabilities.

O

- **observed frequency**
  The number of observations of a data value in an experiment.

- **outcome**
  All the possible results of an activity or experiment.

P

- **plane**
  A flat surface that extends infinitely in two dimensions.

- **population**
  All the members or objects about which you want information.

- **possibility diagram**
  A diagram, such as a two-way grid or table, that provides a list of all the possible outcomes of a simple or compound event.
  Example:

	R	*B*	*G*
H	(*R*, *H*)	(*B*, *H*)	(*G*, *H*)
T	(*R*, *T*)	(*B*, *T*)	(*G*, *T*)

  There are 6 possible outcomes.

- **probability**
  A description of how likely an event is to occur.

- **probability distribution**
  A table or a graphical display presenting all the outcomes of the sample space and their probabilities.

- **probability model**
  A model that represents a sample space of outcomes, events, and the probabilities of these outcomes and events.
  Example:

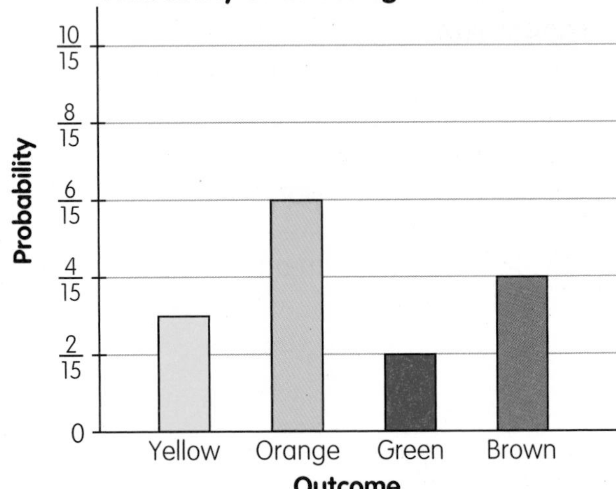

Q

- **quadrant (of a circle)**
  A quarter of a circle.

R

- **radii**
  Plural of *radius*. See *radius* (*r*).

- **radius (*r*)**
  A line segment connecting the center and a point on the circle; also the length of this segment.

- **random sample**
  A set of data randomly selected from a population so that every member of the population has an equal chance of being selected.

- **relative frequency**
  The ratio of the observed frequency of a data value to the total number of observations in a chance process.

S

- **sample**
  A set of data taken from a population.

- **sample size**
  The number of members in a sample.

- **sample space**
  The collection of all possible outcomes from an activity or experiment.
  Example: If you roll a number die, the sample space is {1, 2, 3, 4, 5, 6}.

- **scale**
  A comparison of a length in a scale drawing to the corresponding length in the actual object.
  Example: 1 foot = 12 inches

- **scale factor**
  The ratio of a length in a scale drawing to the corresponding length in the actual figure.

- **semicircle**
  A half of a circle.

- **simple event**
  An event that has one set of outcomes.

- **simple random sampling**
  A sampling method in which every member of a population has an equal chance of being selected.

- **stratified random sampling**
  A sampling method in which the population is divided into nonoverlapping groups from which members are randomly selected.

- **supplementary angles**
  Two angles whose angle measures total 180°.
  Example:

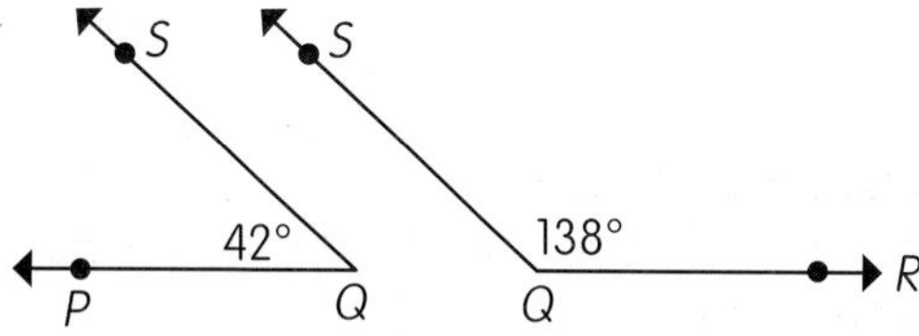

$\angle PQR$ and $\angle STU$ are supplementary angles.

- **systematic random sampling**
  A sampling method in which the first member is randomly selected, and subsequent members are selected at regular intervals.

T

- **theoretical probability**
  The ratio of the number of favorable outcomes to the total number of possible outcomes in an experiment.

- **transversal**
  A line that intersects two or more (usually parallel) lines.
  Example:

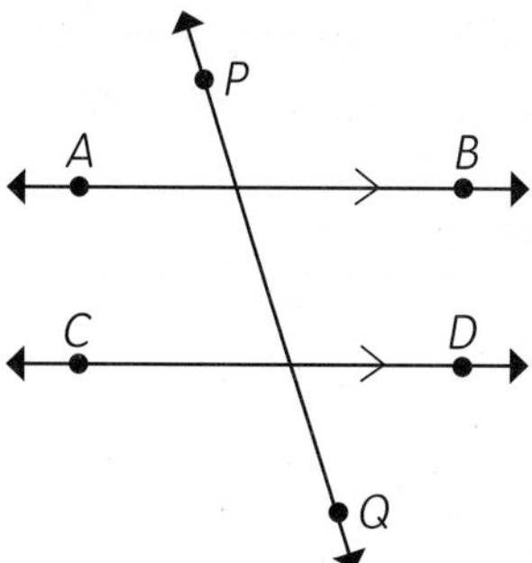

$\overleftrightarrow{PQ}$ is a transversal.

- **tree diagram**
  A type of possibility diagram (listing a sample space) that may also include the corresponding probabilities along the branches.

  Example:

First Toss	Second Toss	Outcome
H	*H*	(*H*, *H*)
	T	(*H*, *T*)
T	*H*	(*T*, *H*)
	T	(*T*, *T*)

  H represents heads
  T represents tails

  There are 4 possible outcomes.

U

- **unbiased sample**
  Also known as *random sample*.

- **uniform probability model**
  A probability model in which all the outcomes have an equal probability of occurring.

V

- **Venn diagram**
  A diagram that uses circles to represent relationships for simple events.
  Example:

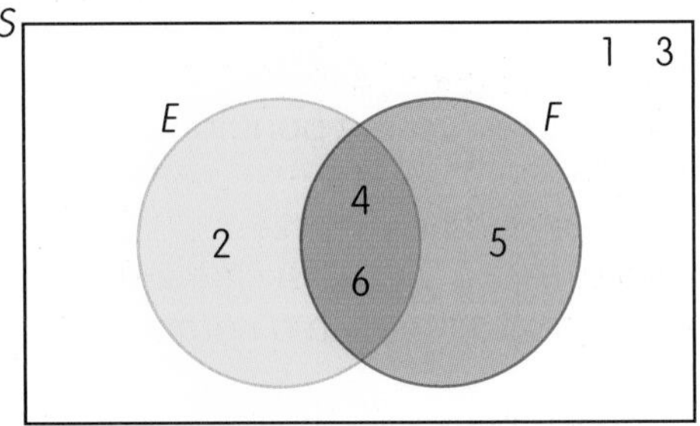

- **vertical angles**
  When two lines intersect at a point, they form four angles. The nonadjacent angles are vertical angles.
  Example:

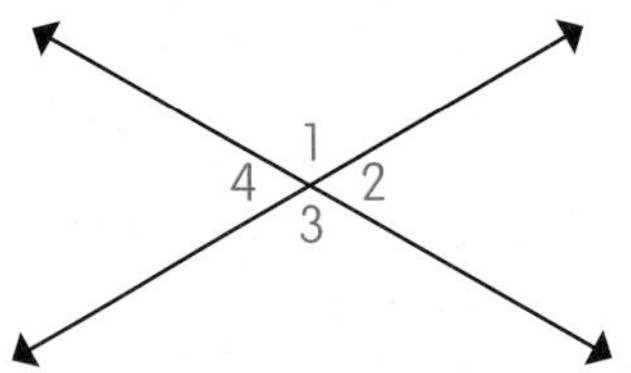

  $\angle 1$ and $\angle 3$ are vertical angles;
  $\angle 2$ and $\angle 4$ are also vertical angles.

Index

Pages in **boldface** type shows where a term is introduced.

D

Photo Credits

xiimm: © zlajo/123rf.com, xiimr: © zlajo/123rf.com, 1: © klikk/iStock.com, 59: Created by Fwstudio - Freepik.com, 71b: © James Griffiths/Dreamstime.com, 74mr: © ivector/Shutter Stock, 74b: © Luciano Mortula/Dreamstime.com, 75:© ardiwebs/Shutter Stock, 91bl: © zlajo/123rf.com, 91br: © zlajo/123rf.com, 111: Created by Fwstudio - Freepik.com, 119b: © Przemyslaw Koch/123rf.com, 119br: © Klavdiia Pyinskaia/123rf.com, 121: © Stefano Guidi/Shutter Stock, 142mr: © joxxxxjo/iStock.com, 145b: © Tasosk/Dreamstime.com, 159br: © MCE, 160tr: © MCE, 189: Created by Fwstudio - Freepik.com, 205l: © wiml/123rf.com, 205l: © kateleigh/123rf.com. 205l: © Leonid Tit/123rf.com, 205b: © iriana88w/123rf.com, 205bl: © gorra/Shutter Stock, 235mr: Currency and Coins Photos Courtesy of United States Mint, Bureau of Engraving and Houghton Mifflin Harcourt, 244tr: Currency and Coins Photos Courtesy of United States Mint, Bureau of Engraving and Houghton Mifflin Harcourt,291: Created by Fwstudio - Freepik.com, 293b: © vvoennyy/123rf.com, 310b: © Vectorpocket / Freepik, 311: © pkazmierczak/iStock.com, 315mm: Currency and Coins Photos Courtesy of United States Mint, Bureau of Engraving and Houghton Mifflin Harcourt, 319mr: Currency and Coins Photos Courtesy of United States Mint, Bureau of Engraving and Houghton Mifflin Harcourt, 363: Created by Fwstudio - Freepik.com, 364b: © simonbradfield/iStock.com, 365b: © simonbradfield/iStock.com, 375b: © LiuNian/iStock.com, 375bl: © AdShooter/iStock.com

Published by Marshall Cavendish Education
Times Centre, 1 New Industrial Road, Singapore 536196
Customer Service Hotline: (65) 6213 9688
US Office Tel: (1-914) 332 8888 | Fax: (1-914) 332 8882
E-mail: cs@mceducation.com
Website: www.mceducation.com

Distributed by
Houghton Mifflin Harcourt
125 High Street
Boston, MA 02110
Tel: 617-351-5000
Website: www.hmhco.com/programs/math-in-focus

First published 2020

ISBN 978-0-358-10192-5

Printed in Singapore

2 3 4 5 6 7 8 1401 25 24 23 22 21 20
4500799763 B C D E F

The cover image shows a Eurasian lynx.
This medium-sized wild cat can be found in the thick forests of Siberia, and in remote, mountainous parts of Europe and Asia. Eurasian lynxes have dark spots on their fur, long, black tufts at the tips of their ears, and they have excellent hearing. They are nocturnal hunters that approach their unsuspecting prey very quietly from out of the darkness. Although their numbers had previously dropped due to hunting, they are now increasing once again.